ARABIC CHRISTIAN THEOLOGY

ARABIC CHRISTIAN THEOLOGY

A Contemporary Global Evangelical Perspective

Dr. Andrea Zaki Stephanous, General Editor

ZONDERVAN

Arabic Christian Theology
Copyright © 2019 by Coptic Evangelical Organization for Social Services

ISBN 978–0-310–32026-5 (hardcover)

Requests for information should be addressed to:
Zondervan, *3900 Sparks Dr. SE, Grand Rapids, Michigan 49546*

Art direction: Tammy Johnson
Cover design: Studio Gearbox
Cover art: Shutterstock
Interior design: Matthew VanZomeren

Printed in the United States of America

19 20 21 22 23 /LSC/ 10 9 8 7 6 5 4 3 2 1

CONTENTS

Foreword 9

1. Arab Christians and the Old Testament 11
   Magdi Sadiq Gendi

2. The Concept of the Covenant in Evangelical Thought
   and Its Impact on the Middle East and North Africa:
   A Historical, Biblical, Theological, and Ethical Study 41
   Riad Aziz Kassis

3. Jesus and Judaism: His Identity and Relationship to Judaism 89
   Ghassan Khalaf

4. Religion and Politics: Ancient Prophecies and Contemporary Policies 211
   Makram Naguib

5. The Christian Woman 297
   Mary Mikhael

6. The Cross and the Power Issue: A Middle Eastern View 374
   Youssef Samir

7. Culture and Identity 423
   Andrea Zaki Stephanous

Scripture Index 469
Subject Index 481

FOREWORD

HOW WONDERFUL TO witness the birth of this great project in its current shape! This project—or dream—often occupied our minds as we lived with the dearth of indigenous Arabic Christian literature. We dreamt of being able to produce literature from our context and relevant to our culture. Then we undertook the research and worked until the project was done. And here it is in your hands, dear reader, one of many pioneering steps by which we seek to encourage theological thinking from our contemporary reality that will speak to us here and now.

This book includes seven articles from outstanding Arab theologians and writers who come from several countries and various ideological and theological backgrounds. We must here affirm our respect for diversity within unity, and therefore the opinions and theological views presented in this book reflect primarily the opinions of each author. The reader will also notice differences in their academic approaches and literary styles, all of which are further expressions of creative diversity.

We thank the committee that supervised the book in its various stages of production. We especially wish to express our deep thanks and appreciation to Dr. George Sabra for his heroic efforts and valuable feedback.

This book is the product of a partnership between Dar Al Thaqafa and Langham Literature, demonstrating Langham's commitment to supporting projects aimed at enriching Arabic and international Christian literature.

Langham Literature offers services in various areas, most notably Christian publishing.

Dar Al Thaqafa

Chapter One

ARAB CHRISTIANS AND THE OLD TESTAMENT

Magdi Sadiq Gendi

Rev. Dr. Magdi S. Gendi serves as Regional Director for the Middle East for the Overseas Council International (OCI). He was formerly professor of Old Testament at the Evangelical Theological Seminary in Cairo (ETSC). He holds a PhD from Luther Seminary, Minnesota, USA; an MTh from the University of Stellenbosch, South Africa; a BTh from ETSC; and a BSc from Assiut University.

⌇

SINCE THE ESTABLISHMENT of modern Israel as a religious state in the heart of the Middle East in 1948, there have been major changes not only in the composition of the nations of the region but also in their thought processes and religious ideas. One of the greatest changes, from my perspective, is how the adherents of each religion have come to view other religions. The escalating reciprocal violence that flows from the presence of a Jewish nation in a region with a Muslim majority has led to attempts to try to understand each other's religious background. So we find Arab Muslims and Christians alike beginning to read the Old Testament in an attempt to understand the reasons for the violence, expulsions, and killings the modern state of Israel inflicts on Arab Palestinians, both Christian and Muslim.

Some violent incidents in the Old Testament, combined with a wrong understanding of the principles for interpreting religious texts and mistaken assumptions about the other side and their beliefs, has led some Arab Christians to believe that the Old Testament is full of violence and that the God of the Old Testament endorses murder

11

and violence for the sake of his chosen people. This misinterpretation has resulted in deliberate neglect and marginalization of the Old Testament. Many Christians in Arab countries neither read nor preach from the Old Testament. They justify their refusal to do so by describing the God of the Old Testament as a God of bloodshed, murder, violence, and discrimination against all nations except the chosen nation of Israel.

The danger in their position lies not only in their misunderstanding of religious texts and wrong approach to the interpretation of God's Word, but also in their allowing social and political changes to overshadow his Word. Thus the unchanging text becomes subject to changing events, giving it a secondary status while establishing the transient as the primary window through which we read religious texts.

Old Testament Israel is now associated with the modern state of Israel. The people of modern Israel (though of many ethnicities and nationalities) are seen as the continuation of God's chosen people in the Old Testament. The establishment of modern Israel on Palestinian land is seen as the fulfillment of God's promises to his people. Thus it has become accepted that the violence practiced by the modern nation of Israel is an expression of its understanding of itself and its theological and religious understanding of God and what it means for his will to be done on earth.

A superficial reading of the Bible may suggest that the God presented in the New Testament is radically different from the God of the Old Testament. In the New Testament, God is shown as loving all people and as giving up his Son to make peace between himself and humankind and among people. Meanwhile the Old Testament contains stories about violence and death, and there God declares his love for one particular people rather than for all peoples. It is not surprising that the majority of Christians prefer reading the New Testament!

There is nothing new about the idea of separating the Old Testament from the New. As early as the second century AD, a heretic by the name of Marcion taught that the God of the Old Testament is not the God of the New Testament and that it is necessary to separate the New Testament, with its God of love, forgiveness, and peace, from the Old Testament with its God of violence and destruction. The early church took a stand against this heresy. But the idea has continued to appeal to theologians and thinkers right up to the present. Rudolf Bultmann, for example, claimed that the Old Testament is a Jewish book and is thus irrelevant for Christians. He insisted that the way God is depicted in the Old Testament is different from the way he is depicted in the New Testament, and therefore there is no need for Christians to read the Old Testament. In other words, to put it more precisely, Bultmann did not consider the Old Testament to be God's revelation to Christians as it was to ancient Israel. For Bultmann, the history of Israel was a history of failure of the rule of God and his people. Scholars from various schools of theology have completely rejected this idea.

What then is the image of God presented in the Old Testament? Is he really a God of bloodshed? Is he a racist, choosing one nation for himself and favoring them over the rest of the world? Can God be both loving and a killer at the same time? Does the presentation of God change in the New Testament from what it was in the Old Testament? Or is the God of the New Testament a different God from the one in the Old Testament? Did God's being change though he is the unchanging eternal one? How can God be one when he deals with people and manifests himself so differently in the Old Testament and in the New Testament?

UNDERLYING ASSUMPTIONS AND PRINCIPLES OF INVESTIGATION

God Is the Central Character in the Old Testament

Given the long expanse of time over which the Old Testament was written and the variety of authors and circumstances in the different periods during which the writing and compilation took place, it is not surprising that there are different images and representations of the character of God. For example, God is the creator, but he also sends a flood that destroys his creation. God is the one who rescues his people from Egypt, but he destroys most of them in the desert. God is the one who chooses a special people for himself, and yet he sends them into exile. We also find an image of a loving God who yet orders Israel to destroy some cities and expel people from their land in order to give the promised land to his people, whom he then sends into captivity. No wonder we find that the way God is described by various Old Testament authors can seem quite contradictory.

The Old Testament Presents a Relationship rather than a Systematic Theology

It is important to recognize that the Old Testament does not present a systematic theology or definition of who God is; rather, it presents a description of God as he is known and experienced by his people Israel in a living relationship. Therefore, the representation of God by the different authors of Scripture is not drawn from their own imagination but is rooted in real experience. Although God is greater than any other being or any human experience, the biblical texts do present us with particular representations of his divine presence. Thus the writers of the Old Testament do not invent or create the image of God; rather, they present an experiential description of this divine supreme presence in terms of its relationship with humanity in the context of faith.

Faith, then, is what connects history with theology, and the Old Testament scriptures are a record of the relationship between historical events and the development of faith and theological concepts. We see God as the new and active subject in every event, and we see him as the one already present before the everlasting event. So the biblical text presents a description of what is new and what was known before. God is the active power recognized in historical events in the context of the faith community. The Old Testament itself is a document of faith, representing the character of God through Israel's knowledge of and faith in him through various circumstances.

Consequently, the biblical narrative can be seen as a report or testimony to the divine revelation experienced in specific historical events. The story is the revelation, and so is the history. In other words, the history of Israel is part of this revelation, and the writers of the Old Testament are not merely external witnesses to this history, but have become, along with the biblical books, a part of this history of salvific revelation.

We must also recognize the divine role in inspiring this holy writing, for the writers of the Old Testament were not merely historians; they were also theologians as they were inspired by the Holy Spirit to record the history of God's relationship with the human race.

The Old Testament Needs to be Read with an Understanding of Its Context

Understanding the background, also known as the context, is one of the most important principles in interpreting the Bible. The context of every verse includes the following elements:

The Textual Context

The textual context is the relationship between the text and the surrounding text (for example, the chapter or book in which it is found) and the remote text (for example, the group of books of which this book forms part, or even the entire Old Testament or New Testament).

The Historical Context

The historical context is the religious, social, political, and cultural background to the text.

The Literary Context

The literary context of a text is its form or genre. Every literary genre, whether a story, history, poem, sermon, or prophecy, has its own principles of interpretation. For example, when we are reading a poetic text and come across the statement that "the trees will clap their hands," we recognize that this is poetry, not history or biology. The opposite is also true. So, for example, when the people of Israel cross the Red Sea, we cannot say that this is simply a metaphor, for it is presented as a historical event. In the same way, we need to approach the interpretation of biblical narratives differently from the way we approach prophetic texts that are intentionally written in specific poetic forms.

Different principles apply to the interpretation of each type of literary genre. Although there are certain foundational principles, we must also abide by the rules of interpretation that apply to each genre and avoid treating all texts as if they were written in the same genre.

The Context of the Whole Bible

We must not interpret any representation of God, or any biblical text, without reference to the whole picture of God presented in the entire Bible with both its Old and New Testaments. The written Word of God in both the Old and New Testaments is "useful for teaching, rebuking, correcting and training in righteousness, so that the servant of God may be thoroughly equipped for every good work" (2 Tim 3:16–17).

How then does the Old Testament, with its various sections, present God and his actions in the history of the people of faith? Some think that God is distant and detached from any event in human history and consider everything that happens in history a natural consequence of human action. But we must realize that God works through people and human reasoning, and therefore when one of the biblical authors describes a historical event, he regards God as the real doer and main subject of the event.

The Old Testament Has Different Parts

The Jews divided the Old Testament into three main sections: the Torah, the Prophets, and the Writings. We will be looking at the different representations of God in each of these sections.

The Old Testament begins with the five books of Moses, called the Torah, which represent the core of Jewish Scripture. The Torah sets the standard for the faith and life of the people of Israel; it is their living constitution. The Torah is followed by the Prophets, that is, books that confirm and explain the Torah. These books contain calls for justice and calls to repent and return to the teachings of the Torah. The Writings follow, representing Israel's response to God or to each other. Sometimes the response is in the form of praise, songs, and lamentations, as in the book of Psalms; at other times it takes the form of wise instruction as in the Wisdom books.

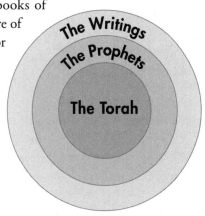

SECTIONS OF THE OLD TESTAMENT

Genesis 1–11 Introduces Many Old Testament Themes

The book of Genesis (the first book in the Torah) is considered an introduction to the constitution of the nation, and Genesis 1–11 is considered an introduction to the person of God and his divine nature. God is presented as the sole creator; there are no other gods. In the remainder of the book, we see the development of the bond between God the creator and his chosen people that connects them in a very special relationship. God's command to the first humans to be fruitful and fill the earth is eventually fulfilled through the twelve tribes who form the core of the nation of Israel. As the story goes on, God is presented as the righteous judge and redeemer, attributes that continue to be spoken of throughout the Bible. God the creator is also the one who acts in righteousness to redeem his people from slavery and injustice, and release them to freedom.

The many depictions of violence, murder, and revenge in the Old Testament are all negative characteristics that cannot be part of the Divine Being. But we can recognize that the execution of justice may, at first glance, appear to be an act of injustice or violence. When God executes justice, some may see it as injustice.

Concepts like covenant and law in the Torah present a true picture of God. In Deuteronomy we see a mixed image of a loving and a jealous God, a loving God who cares and a jealous God who avenges. The prophetic books continue to confirm God's oneness and his relationship with his chosen people, in which he demands submission and obedience to his commands. But we also start noticing the appearance of the idea of God being the God of all people, which supports and further clarifies the image of God as the righteous creator and redeemer. The Psalms and the Wisdom books represent Israel's response to God. In them we find descriptions of God and his sovereignty and power, and his wisdom from which humanity draws its wisdom. This part of the Old Testament places God in the center as the King and Lord of all creation who executes justice and loves his creation. He is present everywhere at all times and is intimately connected with his creation.

In Genesis 1–11 we observe the tension and struggle between life and death, between order and chaos, between an orderly creation and destruction. Amidst this polarity we see God as sovereign over creation, deciding the destiny of this universe. At the center of these events is God the righteous creator and redeemer.

God the creator cares for his creation and enters into a relationship with it. This relationship is distorted by human disobedience, which affects the whole creation and separates it from God. The sole exception is Noah, who has remained obedient and faithful to God in spite of all that is going on around him. He finds grace in God's eyes, and God the just executes justice, saving Noah while the rest of humanity is destroyed. This is when that third image, God the redeemer, comes into play as God enters an eternal covenant with Noah, promising never to destroy all humanity or creation again. These three characteristics of God—his creatorship, justice, and redemption—continue to intertwine until the end of the Old Testament. They represent the foundation upon which the divine–human relationship rests and through which God enters human history.

In the prophetic books God speaks as the founder and creator of Israel and as the judge who judges it through other nations. However, the prophets also speak of hope in the new Israel (Isa 44:6), a new political development that involves the rebuilding and reinhabiting of the land by the community of faith. In the Psalms and Wisdom books, we clearly see the psalmist asking the Creator to bless his creation (Ps 104:27–30). Several other texts throughout the Old Testament describe this relationship between God and creation, making Genesis 1–11 not only an introduction to some of the characteristics of God, but also a general framework for understanding God's relationship with humanity. This similarity between the different parts of the biblical text reflects the perspective of the people of Israel (the Old Testament texts were compiled in their final form during their era) including their conviction that Yahweh is the only God, the Creator and Lord of all creation and peoples. This Creator is described using human terms, or what humanity has to say about God.

You may have noticed that I have avoided talking about an essential characteristic of God, namely his love, though it is considered a critical axis connecting the divine revelation in the Old Testament with the New. The reason is that I do not see love as one of the divine characteristics but rather as the core of the divine being—God is love. Thus when God wanted to reveal himself to humans, his love was incarnated in Jesus, who is the completion and perfection of divine revelation.

The Old Testament Texts Are the Product of a Particular Culture

Finally, we need to recognize that the Old Testament texts are a product of a particular culture and civilization and that this has certain implications. First, although they are produced in a particular culture, the biblical texts remain relevant to our time and current circumstances. Second, we need to understand that religion and culture cannot be separated, for every religion was born within a certain culture and civilization. Religion is never born in a vacuum and never matures in an instant of time. To understand a religion, it is thus important to learn about the culture in which it originated. For example, we are disturbed when we read about violence done to the elderly, children, and even animals by the people of God at God's command:

> When the trumpets sounded, the army shouted, and at the sound of the trumpet, when the army gave a loud shout, the wall collapsed; so everyone charged straight in, and they took the city. They devoted the city to the LORD and destroyed with the sword every living thing in it—men and women, young and old, cattle, sheep and donkeys. (Josh 6:20–21)

We also read about the destruction of the city of Ai (Josh 8), and this and other examples seem to show the God of Israel and the people of Israel enjoying bloodshed. But we need to understand that people in those days believed that the true god was the one who gave his people victory and that when a nation was defeated, its god or gods were also defeated. Study of the history of religion shows that this understanding was widespread throughout the ancient Near East. The victory of a people is the victory of their god(s), and the defeat of a people is the defeat of their god(s).

This is why it is essential that we do not read these texts from the perspective of twenty-first-century ethics but acknowledge the prevailing perspective or world view of that ancient time. I will, however, deal with the idea of destruction from an ethical perspective in what follows.

GOD AND THE GODS

We have seen that Genesis 1–11 constitutes an introduction to the representation of God that continues throughout the Old Testament. God is presented as sovereign and in control of events from the beginning of creation until the restoration of his relationship with humanity in Genesis 10–11. Up to this point, there is no reference to any other gods.

This one God in Genesis 1–11 is referred to both by the general name, Elohim (Heb. *'ĕlōhîm*) or El (Heb. *'ēl*), and by the special name, Yahweh (Heb. *yĕhwāh*).[1] God's character is complex. While he is the creator who cares for his creation, he is also the great power that destroys creation. Yet we must note that it was humanity's actions and evil behavior that caused the change in God's dealing with creation. He is the unchanging element in all that happens.

Genesis 12 marks the start of a new phase in the development of the theology of Israel. In Genesis 11, Abraham's appearance opens the door to the establishment of a specific people among many other peoples. Genesis 12 is considered a new beginning because here we see God, the main actor, choosing not to deal with the entire human race but with a specific person, Abraham. Abraham's call to a covenant relationship with God and his willingness to respond to that call serve to introduce key theological issues dealt with throughout the Old Testament, namely the land (central to the historical books), the covenant (central to Israel's history and Scriptures), and God's chosen people (a concept that shapes the political ideology in the Torah and the Prophets).

God's appearance to Abraham in Genesis 12 and the remarkable promise he makes mark the beginning of a story, leaving the reader intrigued to find out what these events may lead to. God asks Abraham to leave his father's house and go to a place he does not know, and there God promises him a son. This promise must be fulfilled in the future, which invites readers to engage directly with the biblical narrative.

These developments introduce a new twist in God's dealing with this specific family. Though God's dwelling place is in heaven, he is with Abraham wherever he goes, for God is not confined by place. God is not the god of a specific city or region like the gods of the

---

[1] El is a masculine, singular Hebrew noun and is used to refer to "god," any god. It was recently discovered that El is also the name of one of the Ugaritic gods. But in the Old Testament Elohim, the masculine plural form of El, is used only to refer to Yahweh.

surrounding nations. Moreover, Abraham entered a direct relationship with God without any priestly mediation or religious practices. Even when Abraham went to new places like Egypt, established in its worship of Pharaoh and other gods, the God of Abraham was still sovereign. The God of Abraham is presented as a universal God who is not restricted by time or place. The reader sees the connection between the God of Abraham and the creator of the universe, "Yahweh Elohim," who is present in all these events and to all generations.

We also see God defining himself in terms of his relationship with human beings. In Genesis 28:13 and in many other biblical texts we hear God saying, "I am the LORD, the God of your father Abraham and the God of Isaac." God, the giver of life, was prepared to bind himself to a specific family and its descendants. So when God revealed himself to Moses, he said, "I am the God of your father, the God of Abraham, the God of Isaac and the God of Jacob." The God who spoke with Abraham is the same God who spoke to the subsequent generations all the way down to Moses.

As we trace the story of the generations that succeeded Abraham, we see two main threads emerge: the promise of a son (Gen 15:1–6) and the promise of land (Gen 15:7–21). In Genesis 15:7 the two promises are connected by the clarification that these two gifts come from God, who is the source of all gifts and the source of every hope. He will give the land to Abraham and will also give him descendants to settle in it.

He is the only God and there are no other gods beside him. He is the creator of the universe and everything in it, and he gave us an orderly creation. At the same time he is the restorer of order from chaos, as in the story of Noah. As the creator and the righteous one he will not allow chaos to rule over his creation but will intervene to restore order to everything distorted by humans. He did this not only in the days of Noah and Abraham but even when his people went down to Egypt. There they encountered many belief systems and many gods, but the Lord God (Yahweh Elohim) displayed his power over the gods of the Egyptians to make his people Israel acknowledge that there is only one God. The gods of the Egyptians could not stand before him. When Pharaoh asked Moses mockingly, "Who is the LORD, that I should obey him and let Israel go? I do not know the LORD and I will not let Israel go" (Exod 5:2), he was asking "Who is this god whom you claim is more powerful than I am?" This question is later echoed in the song of Aaron, Miriam, and the people:

> Who among the gods
>   is like you, LORD?
> Who is like you—
>   majestic in holiness,
> awesome in glory,
>   working wonders? . . .
> The LORD reigns
>   for ever and ever. (Exod 15:11, 18)

19

Thus Pharaoh's question was answered by the people of Israel after they had experienced God's redeeming work on their behalf. Their historical experience shaped their personal understanding of God, and these events are written in the Scriptures as a record of the faith of the people of Israel.

This shows that the Old Testament was written as a statement of the faith of the people of God, not merely as a record of Jewish history. It is the story of the faith of God's people throughout history. It is the story of God working in history through the people of faith.

It is now time to move on to looking at how the Old Testament writers represented God in the Torah, the Prophets, and the Writings.

GOD THE CREATOR

God the Creator in the Torah

When we speak about God the creator we need to pay attention to the language used to describe creation, the relationship between the Creator and creation, and the divine presence in creation.

The Language Used to Describe Creation

Many different words and metaphors are used to describe the act of creation, but in every case God is the subject of the verb. He is the one who acts, regardless of the verb employed: creates (Gen 1:27; Isa 43:1); makes (Gen 1:26); works out everything (Prov 16:4); builds (Amos 9:6); owns (Gen 14:19; see also Gen 12:1; Deut 32:18; Pss 90:2; 93:1; Isa 51:13).

In the hundreds of passages that refer to creation, God is always the only agent, for the act of creating is uniquely divine: "In the beginning God created the heavens and the earth" (Gen 1:1; Pss 33; 104). Some scholars point out that the act of creating is not something that happened only in the past, but is an ongoing process as God gives life to each creature.

Moreover, God's work in creation is not limited to creating the physical world but extends also to actions such as transforming chaos and restoring order to families, cities, and nations (see Gen 10–11, where the focus is on people). It involves establishing laws and regulations for society (Gen 9:1–7). All this is rooted in the story of creation (Gen 1:28; 2:16, 17). A passage like Exodus 15:1–21 echoes expressions used in the creation story as it describes the transformation from a state of chaos under an oppressive power to a safe and ordered community in the promised land.

Creation is not solely a matter of the past, for God the creator's role is not limited to Genesis 1 and 2. The verb used in Psalm 104:30 is the same one used in the creation narrative in Genesis 1 and 2, but in this psalm it refers to an ongoing act of creation.

Creation is not just an event when the earth was established; rather, it is a divine work in progress that protects and sustains God's creation. This means that God is in an ongoing relationship with his creation, creating every new day (Isa 4:19; 38:6; 41:20; 42:9; Jer 31:22). The language of the Prophet Isaiah in 42:14 and 49:19–21 is a testimony to both an original and an ongoing creation.

The Relationship Between the Creator and His Creation

From its very inception, the entire creation belonged to God, or in other words, it has a relationship with God. This relationship is mutual, for God also has a relationship with his creation. Although God has complete sovereignty over his creation, he also desires a close, personal connection with it. When God created human beings in his image, he entered into a covenant relationship with them. This covenant imposes obligation on both parties, for both have a responsibility in the covenant. Thus everything said about God is said in the light of this relationship.[2]

Walter Eichrodt focuses on accountability and responsibility in the context of this mutual relationship between God and the people of Israel established through the covenant.[3] But we must note that the covenant is not the foundation of the relationship, for God already spoke of Israel as his people before he made the covenant with them at Sinai. For example, God commanded Moses to say to Pharaoh, "Let my people go, so that they may hold a festival to me in the wilderness" (Exod 5:1). Thus the covenant in Sinai was not the basis for the relationship between God and Israel; rather, it was a formalization of the relationship. The relationship was present before the covenant was established. The same is true of the covenants with Noah, Abraham, and David. All these covenants start with a divine promise, divine election, divine deliverance, and a response of faith and worship. The promise or covenant is the framework in which the already existing relationship grows. T. Fretheim summarizes this relationship in these words:

> Israel's God is a relational God who has created a world in which interrelatedness is basic to the nature of reality; this God establishes relationships of varying sorts with all creatures, including a special relationship to the people of Israel.[4]

The Divine Presence in Creation

The God who created the universe is not far from it. Yes, he transcends it, but he is also in control of everything in it. He is immanent. God is indeed present and active in the world. He did not create the world and then withdraw from it, but he created it

[2] Walter Brueggemann, *Theology of the Old Testament: Testimony, Dispute, Advocacy* (Minneapolis: Fortress, 1997), 297.

[3] Walter Eichrodt, *Theology of the Old Testament*, 2 vols. (London: SCM, 1976), 1:36–69.

[4] Terence Fretheim, *God and World in the Old Testament: A Relational Theology of Creation* (Nashville: Abingdon, 2005), 16.

and entered into a relationship with it; and as long as the world exists, this relationship exists. For God is present in every event and active in every circumstance. Psalm 33:5 assures us of this truth: "The earth is full of his unfailing love." Everything that God does, whether executing justice or accomplishing salvation, is full of love. "The LORD is good to all; he has compassion on all he has made" (Ps 145:9).

Although the works of God focus on Israel, Genesis 1–11 and other passages show that God's relationship with the entire world is similar to his relationship with the people of Israel and with the church. God elects, judges, saves, establishes a covenant, restores, and blesses. God was active in his relationship with the world even before Israel came into being (Gen 20:3–7; Amos 9:7). And God has not stopped his work as creator and savior. Jonah, for example, tried to run from the presence of God (Jonah 1:3), yet he acknowledged God as the Creator (1:9). Moreover, although God left the temple (Ezek 10:1–22), this did not mean the absence of God (Ezek 11:6; 22). God is present in every place and time.

God, the Creator and Maker

Genesis 1:1–2:4 uses two main verbs to describe the act of creation: "create" (7 times) and "make" (11 times). Those verbs are used interchangeably, as in Genesis 1, where in verse 26 God says, "Let us make mankind," and the very next verse reads, "So God created mankind in his own image, in the image of God he created them."

In the Old Testament, the verb "to create" refers either to making something out of nothing or to the ongoing process of creating. Sometimes it is used to refer to the act of re-creation or transforming something already present (Ps 51:10; 102:18; Isa 41:20; 65:18). Scholars agree that God is always the subject when the verb refers to the process of creation or causing change, in the absence of explicit mention of any other actor.

The word "make" is also used in places like Isaiah (17:7; 27:11; 57:16). God is represented as being like a potter who forms the first human (Gen 2:19) from the dust of the earth and breathes into this new being the breath of life.[5]

God is also depicted as being like a surgeon when he takes out Adam's rib and uses it to form a woman, Eve (Gen 2:1–22). He is also shown making clothes from animal skins. These and many other examples throughout the Old Testament show God interacting with his creation. He does not withdraw into transcendence, but is intimately involved with what he has made.

Once again we should note that in Genesis 1–11 God interacts with his creation even before the existence of Israel, the nation through whom he eventually reestablishes a relationship with his creation. Genesis 1–11 depicts God as immanent and actively

---

[5] See also Job 33:6; Pss 103:14; 139:15; Isa 45:9; 64:8; Jer 18:1–6.

engaged with his creation, not as a being who resides in heaven and relates only to the people of Israel. Similar imagery continues throughout the Old Testament, demonstrating that God did not deal only with Israel but also with all nations. In the prophetic books, we see God dealing with other nations in a way similar to the way he deals with Israel. If we return to the rest of the book of Genesis (chs. 12–50), we see God entering the land of Egypt and even Pharaoh's palace (12:10–12). We see that he is known by Melchizedek (Gen 14:18–20) and that he cares for Hagar and Ishmael (Gen 16:8–21). We see him destroying Sodom and Gomorrah (Gen 18:16–19:29), and we see him acting in the life of Abimelek the Canaanite (Gen 20) and in the life of the Pharaoh of Egypt in the story of Joseph (Gen 37–50).

The theology of creation extends into the book of Exodus to further clarify the meaning of God giving life, protecting it, and blessing it (Exod 1:7; 12; 20), for in the act of redeeming Israel, God also redeemed his original purpose for creation. This purpose is displayed in the song of Miriam, Aaron, and Moses that all the people sang after they escaped Pharaoh's army and safely crossed the Red Sea (Exod 15). This song is rich with the language and terminology of creation theology, for God's acts as creator cannot be separated from his acts as redeemer and liberator. The purpose of the exodus was not just to liberate Israel from slavery; it was also for the sake of the whole creation (Exod 9:16). Thus, although the story of the exodus focuses on the deliverance of Israel, its ultimate purpose is to have God glorified in all creation (Exod 8:22; 9:14). The exodus was for the benefit of all creation, and Israel was a representative of the whole earth. God's Lordship over heaven and earth is powerfully displayed in the narrative, and his victory is not only over Pharaoh and the sea but over all the forces of evil and chaos (Exod 15:18).

After the liberation of the people of Israel, God once again proclaims that the whole earth is his and calls Israel to be a holy nation and a kingdom of priests (Exod 19:4–6). In effect, God calls Israel to act on his behalf by carrying out this priestly role among the nations in a way similar to that of a priest leading in worship. Such a priest both bears witness to God's redeeming work (Exod 18:8–12) and serves as an example by his obedience to God's law.[6] Therein lies a message to all creation. The salvation of Israel was not God's ultimate goal; his goal was for other nations also to come to know this redemption.

God the Creator in the Prophetic Books

The doctrine of creation is also present in the prophetic books. Although the message of the prophets centered on the call to repent and the offer of hope for the future, the theology and terminology of creation permeates these books. Consider Isaiah 40-55,

---

[6] See also Isa 41:21–29; 43:10–13; 44:6–8; 45:5–6, 14, 18–21; 46:9; 47:8–10.

which deals with the new creation and its creator. In those chapters, the verb "create" is used sixteen times; the verb "make" is used twenty-four times; and the verb "shape" is used fifteen times. Other verbs like "fashion," "stretch out," and "establish" are also used several times. It is worth noting that in this section of Isaiah 55–66, references to God's creation of foreign nations (Isa 56:1–8; 60:10–16; 66:18–20) are followed by a vision of a new heaven and a new earth (Isa 65:17; 66:22).

Israel's Identity and Its Relation to Creation

Isaiah wrote to the people of Israel when they were in exile suffering an identity crisis pertaining not only to their religious, political, and social identity but also to their human identity. The disasters they had experienced had caused them to lose confidence in themselves as human beings (Isa 41:14; 42:18–19; 43:18) and in their future (Isa 41:10, 13–14; 43:1, 5; 44:2, 8; 54:4). They despaired of life and lost the desire to live (40:29–31; 54:6). As Thomas W. Mann says, "How do you convince people who think of themselves as worms that they are, instead, still the beloved people of God? . . . How do you persuade people who think of themselves as 'nobodies' that they are 'somebodies'?"[7] Some might suggest that God could raise up another people to replace this nation. But from the perspective of Isaiah, God's messenger, who they actually are, is radically different from who they think they are. This is what God has to say about his people: "You are precious and honored in my sight, and . . . I love you" (Isa 43:4). The same message is repeated in Isaiah 44:1–2; 46:3–4; 51:16; and 54:8, 11. It is a direct statement from God to a despairing people that they are still his people and he loves them despite all that has happened.

Isaiah uses the language of creation theology to remind the people that it was God who created Israel and called them to be his chosen nation. This specific terminology of creation is not used with regard to any other people. We hear it when Isaiah speaks of the one who "created you, Jacob, he who formed you, Israel" (Isa 43:1; see also 43:7, 15, 21; 44:1; 45:9, 11; 51:13).

In addition to the language of creation, Isaiah also uses the language of giving birth (Isa 42:14; 46:3–4; 49:19–21; 66:6–13). God, who created and gave birth to his people, will remain faithful to his covenant and will save them in due time (Isa 46:3–4). God will not forget his people (Isa 44:2; 49:14–15). This language gives comfort and hope to a people who have despaired of God and of themselves. When hopeless people hear God saying, "you are precious . . . in my sight" (Isa 43:4; 49:5), they hear a clear proclamation of their value as human beings and their place and role in the world.

We need to remember that at that time the people of Israel were in exile in the heart of an empire that worshiped many gods. That too accounts for Isaiah's emphasis that there is no other god but Yahweh.

---

[7] Thomas W. Mann as quoted in Fretheim, *God and World*, 182.

Yahweh, the God of Israel, is not a tribal or regional god, nor is he one who enters into competition with other gods. Yahweh is the only creator, and all other gods are false gods (Isa 40:12, 22, 26, 28; 54:5). Yahweh is the Lord of creation (Isa 45:11–12). Even when Isaiah compares the exodus from Babylon to the exodus from Egypt, he describes God the creator as doing something new, and through which he is impacting the whole creation (Isa 40:27–31; 44:22–28; 45:11–17; 50:1–3; 51:12–16; 54:4–10).

God the Creator in the Writings

In looking at the Writings, I will limit myself to examples from the Psalms. As has been said, creation theology is expressed in various ways in all the books of the Old Testament, whether in Genesis or Isaiah or Job or the Psalms (Pss 8; 19; 104). All affirm that Yahweh, the God of Israel, is the creator of heaven and earth. So the commandment "You shall not make for yourself an image in the form of anything in heaven above or on the earth beneath or in the waters below" (Exod 20:4) reflects the ancient belief in three realms of creation, which are also referenced in the Psalms (Pss 24:2; 104:15; 148:4).

The faith that heaven and earth are dependent on God (Yahweh) the creator (Ps 8:6) originates from Israel's understanding that all life is dependent on the God who saved them and established a covenant with them. The doctrine of creation is, then, a confirmation of Israel's faith in the sovereignty of God and in creation's dependence upon him. Israel's confession that God made the earth means that it is his and that he is its Lord:

> The earth is the LORD's, and everything in it,
>   the world, and all who live in it. (Ps 24:1)

> The heavens are yours, and yours also the earth;
>   you founded the world and all that is in it. (Ps 89:11)

> The sea is his, for he made it,
>   and his hands formed the dry land. (Ps 95:5)

These texts also affirm the lordship and sovereignty of Yahweh, the God of Israel, over all creation. He is the only one worthy of worship and reverence because creation declares his glory and majesty (Pss 95; 104:24; Prov 3:19–20). By his word God made the universe out of nothing and set its order and boundaries. He designed creation to fulfill his purposes and remains engaged with it through laws he established to regulate and maintain life (Job 38:33; Ps 104:9; Jer 5:24; 31:35–36). This is why when God (Yahweh) completed his creation and inspected it to be sure that it was working to fulfill the purpose for which it was created, he declared it "very good" (Gen 1:31), for his glory fills the heaven and the earth (Exod 19:1–4).

God did not create the earth to be in chaos and ruin. He created the earth to be a dwelling for human beings (Isa 45:18). His plan is for creation to be in relationship with its creator through the covenant. Creation is the framework in which the relationship between God and humanity exists, giving humanity its worth (Ps 73:23–26). Humans are created in God's image (Ps 8:5).

The creation story is always linked to redemption because God's power and wisdom are manifested in his redemption of his people, as mentioned in Isaiah 40–55, but here there is also a new beginning (Isa 51:9–11). The redeeming Creator who makes things new (Ps 27:16–20; Isa 43:1) guarantees that everything will be made new.

This is God, the God of Israel, the Creator, who made creation to be in a vital relationship with him through the covenant. This theological framework has undergirded Israel's faith throughout its history, giving this people hope regardless of their circumstances.

GOD THE RIGHTEOUS JUDGE

Though humans are created in God's image, they are still finite, for God placed certain limitations on the first humans, saying: "You are free to eat from any tree in the garden; but you must not eat from the tree of the knowledge of good and evil, for when you eat from it you will certainly die" (Gen 2:16–17). This commandment means that humans are not absolutely free and should not cross the boundaries set for them by God. In giving it, God appears as a judge who gives humans the freedom to choose, and bases his judgment on their choice.

The sin of Adam and his descendants was not a trivial matter to God, and his judgment of it was not painless or uncomplicated. When God issued the command, he also revealed the penalty of disobedience. But when Adam and Eve sinned, God intervened so that sin would not have the final say. His intervention was not only for the sake of humanity but also because of the consequence their sin would have for the entire created order. God's intervention was intended to protect and preserve the cosmic order he created.

In Genesis 3:14–19, we see God intervening and confining the impact of sin in the life of the first human beings. Then in Genesis 6:5–6, he reveals the holistic effects of sin when his wrath and judgment fall on humans. But Noah found favor in God's eyes amidst destruction and ruin, and at the end of the flood story God promises never to destroy the earth or humans again. Thus destruction will never again have a cosmic or global impact.

God's promise in Genesis 8–9 does not mean that God will not intervene with condemnation again or will not judge again. In Genesis 12–50 God appears clearly as a righteous judge, whether in relation to those with whom he deals in a special way (Abraham, Isaac, and Jacob) or with other nations (Gen 15:16, 18–21) and with individuals like Abimelek (Gen 20:3–7). Here we must note that anger is not a divine attribute, and that judgment is not a consequence of God's anger; rather, it is a natural consequence of human choices, and at the same time it represents God's reaction and his response to the threatened creation. God's intervention and judgment are intended not only to punish the trespasser but also to protect the entire creation from the threat posed by the trespass. That is why God, the righteous judge, has this to say about himself:

> The LORD, the LORD, the compassionate and gracious God, slow to anger, abounding in love and faithfulness, maintaining love to thousands, and forgiving wickedness, rebellion and sin. Yet he does not leave the guilty unpunished; he punishes the children and their children for the sin of the parents to the third and fourth generation. (Exod 34:6–7)

The book of Exodus demonstrates that the ongoing process of creation was threatened. In Exodus 1:7 we are told that "the Israelites were exceedingly fruitful; they multiplied greatly, increased in numbers and became so numerous that the land was filled with them." This was a fulfillment of God's promises in Genesis, both in the creation narrative and in the promise to Abraham (Gen 15:5; 28:14). But this promise was threatened by the powerful Egyptian Empire. Egypt's Pharaoh represented the power of death that is opposed to the power of life.

Consequently, God's power was directed not only against the Egyptians but against any force that threatened creation. Thus although the plagues were directed against the Egyptian gods, we should also note the use of the phrase "all the earth" in Exodus 8:22 (see also Exod 9:14, 29; 19:5). All the earth belongs to God, the God of Israel, and the purpose of the plagues was to teach Pharaoh that there is none like God in all the earth (9:14), and for the name of God to be exalted in all the earth (9:16).

While liberating the people of Israel was one of the goals of the exodus, it was not the primary goal. Their liberation was intended to affect the whole creation. The goal was far larger than simply liberating a people from distress and hardship. It was to demonstrate the nature and power of God to the whole earth. Even the crossing of the Red Sea on dry land recalls the original creation, for in the exodus we see the process of re-creation, and a restoration of the original plan of creation.

When we think about the plagues that came on the Egyptians, we find ourselves asking questions: What were the Egyptians guilty of? Why did they have to endure all these plagues? Why didn't God target his plagues to Pharaoh alone? Why did the Egyptians have to suffer because Pharaoh sinned? These and other questions imply that the God of the Old Testament is a brutal God who longs for revenge. But there are some other points we need to acknowledge when thinking about the plagues:

- The people of God suffered greatly as slaves of the Egyptians, and no one defended them. The Egyptians needed to know what it was like to suffer.

- The people of God had lost their identity and their property, and their very existence was threatened. The Egyptians needed to experience the same thing.
- The people of God had lost their children at the hand of the Egyptians, and the Egyptians needed to know what this felt like (Exod.11:5; 12:29).
- The people of Israel had cried out in their pain and suffering (Exod 3:7, 9) and the Egyptians needed to experience similar pain (Exod 11:6; 17:30).
- Pharaoh was like a god to the Egyptians, and so God intervened to show them and all the earth who the true God is.

The plagues, then, were not simply God's punishment of the Egyptians but a means for God to reveal himself to his creation, thereby enhancing his relationship with that creation.

Judgment and punishment under any circumstance can be both negative and positive, and God's judgment of sinners (Ps 94:2) brings both good and bad news. It involves delivering the righteous from their suffering (Pss 76:9; 82:8) and it means punishing sinners (Ps 26:1). The judgment of God is always linked to human sin (Jer 5:12–17; 6:13–15), and is a natural consequence of human sin.

Yet, we must remember that God is not like human judges, for Jonah says this of him: "I knew that you are a gracious and compassionate God, slow to anger and abounding in love, a God who relents from sending calamity" (Jonah 4:2). God is not distant or neutral like a judge in a human court. God is connected to all the parties involved in the case. Thus when he takes his judgment seat, God is also sitting beside the one accused. For the accused is God's creation and has a relationship with God. Thus God is both the judge and the defense attorney for his creation.

We tend of think of God's judging human sin as if the parties in the courtroom are God and human beings. But the truth is, God is the judge and creation is the accused. By "creation" I mean not just the cosmos and the earth, not just the people of God, but the entire human race. And because all creation is interrelated and our human lives are interconnected, there is no separation between the righteous and the unrighteous when it comes to historical events. Both groups experience divine judgment. We see this in the punishment of Sodom and Gomorrah. But the judgment of God can also be for the people of God alone, as we see in Amos: "You only have I chosen of all the families of the earth; therefore I will punish you for all your sins" (Amos 3:2).

In the Old Testament we see God using emperors and kings from the Assyrian and Babylonian nations to execute his judgment on his people (Isa 10:5; 13:5; Jer 50:25). God even refers to Nebuchadnezzar, the king of Babylon (who was not Jewish), as his servant, the one he has chosen to carry out his punishment (Jer 25:9; 27:6; 43:10). God is actively engaged in his creation, even when he works through people other than chosen people. God the creator uses the political powers of the day to further his purposes for creation (Jer 27:5–6; 50:44).

In saying this, I am not implying God wants political leaders and armies to invade other nations or occupy their lands. God simply uses patterns of interaction that are already in place to demonstrate that he is active in current events. Some say that God encourages so-called holy wars, but God does not encourage people to start a holy war against another people. God is the creator God, who is actively involved in human history, and when he intervenes in the life and history of Israel, he does so for the sake of the whole world and not just for the sake of Israel.

The means God uses to carry out his righteous judgments may seem strange to us. Consider the following passages:

> I will smash them one against the other, parents and children alike, declares the LORD. I will allow no pity or mercy or compassion to keep me from destroying them. (Jer 13:14)

> After that, declares the LORD, I will give Zedekiah king of Judah, his officials and the people in this city who survive the plague, sword and famine, into the hands of Nebuchadnezzar king of Babylon and to their enemies who want to kill them. He will put them to the sword; he will show them no mercy or pity or compassion. (Jer 21:7)

> If, however, any nation or kingdom will not serve Nebuchadnezzar king of Babylon or bow its neck under his yoke, I will punish that nation with the sword, famine and plague, declares the LORD, until I destroy it by his hand. (Jer 27:8)

These verses state that God will use Nebuchadnezzar to punish Israel without mercy or compassion. But note that while God is the principal actor, he shares this role with Nebuchadnezzar. Jeremiah recognizes that God uses the forces available to discipline his people, his nation, and other nations.

From the beginning of creation, God established a system in which all human actions, whether good or bad, have consequences, and he made it clear that the consequences would match the actions. This is what theological scholars refer to as the law of natural consequence. The natural consequences of good actions are what theologians call blessings, and the natural consequences of evil actions are punishment or judgment. The words "guilt" or "evil" may be used to refer either to a sinful action or to the consequence of that action. (This point is clearest in more literal translations like the KJV. See Gen 19:15; Jer 6:19; 11:11, 23; 18:8, 11; Hos 8:7; 10:13.)

Ezekiel too says,

> The king will mourn,
>   the prince will be clothed with despair,
>   and the hands of the people of the land will tremble.
> I will deal with them according to their conduct,
>   and by their own standards I will judge them.
> Then they will know that I am the LORD. (Ezek 7:27)

As history moves on, Babylon gets to drink from the same cup from which Israel drank, as Jeremiah prophesied: "Repay her for her deeds; do to her as she has done. For she has defied the LORD, the Holy One of Israel" (Jer 50:29).

God sometimes handed his people over to another nation or to their enemies (Ps 81:11–12; Isa 34:2; 43:28; 47:6; 64:6–7; Jer 29:21). This does not mean that God failed in his dealings with them; what was happening to them was a natural consequence of their choices, as God makes plain in Ezekiel 22:31: "So I will pour out my wrath on them and consume them with my fiery anger, bringing down on their own heads all they have done, declares the Sovereign LORD." God allows humans to face the natural consequences of their actions, and yet in the midst of these consequences God always wants to start afresh. He may need to break up the soil in order to cultivate a new crop.

God's Judgment on Other Nations

The Old Testament includes judgments pronounced by the prophets on nations other than Israel (Exod 25–32; Isa 13–23; Jer 46–51; Amos 1–2; Nah; and Obad). These judgments generally focus on social injustice, especially during war, even when their battles were against Israel (Pss 2:5, 12; 56:7; 79:5–7; 110:5; Isa 10:12; 25; Jer 10:25; 50:25; 51:45; Ezek 25:14, 17; 36:1–7; Amos 1; 2; Zech 1:14–15). God's judgment on these people is still valid, although they are outside the framework of the covenant (in other words, they are not in a covenant relationship with God). Even though they have not been given the detailed ethical codes associated with the covenant, the concept of injustice still stands as an ethical standard by which God judges these peoples. Thus in Jeremiah 46:8, 15, 17, 25, we read that all evil and pride draw God's judgment (Jer 48:26, 29, 30, 35, 42; 50:24–27, 31–32; 51:6,11, 25, 26, 56). Thus the judgment of God is not on Israel alone but on all nations, for each nation is completely responsible for its own behavior and ethics, and must bear the natural consequences of its actions. No matter how much a nation may try to justify or excuse its wrongdoing, it must pay the price for what it has done.

God's judgment on nations other than Israel reveals that God's purposes are for all creation. Israel and other nations must acknowledge God and live by ethical codes or laws. The people of Israel could not say that God was unjust to punish them. Likewise, other nations cannot say that God is unjust because he did not punish them. God is completely just with his chosen people and with all the peoples of the earth. He is present in all the events of the universe and all peoples can experience God's presence in their midst, whether or not they recognize and acknowledge him. God is active in the lives of all peoples to fulfill his purposes for his creation.

When God called Jeremiah, he called him to be "a prophet to the nations," not just to one people, and gave him a role greater than merely a ministry of words: "I appoint you over nations and kingdoms to uproot and tear down, to destroy and overthrow, to build and to plant" (Jer 1:5,10). Repeatedly Jeremiah goes on to proclaim that the purpose of God's intervention in the life of nations is not just their deliverance and redemption but also the restoration of his creation. Thus he proclaims:

> At that time they will call Jerusalem The Throne of the LORD, and all nations will gather in Jerusalem to honor the name of the LORD. No longer will they follow the stubbornness of their evil hearts. (Jer 3:17; see also Jer 12:14–16; 16:19–21; 18:7–10)

The Prophet Amos has a similar message:

> Are not you Israelites
>   the same to me as the Cushites?"
>   declares the LORD.
> Did I not bring Israel up from Egypt,
>   the Philistines from Caphtor
>   and the Arameans from Kir?
> Surely the eyes of the Sovereign LORD
>   are on the sinful kingdom. (Amos 9:7–8)

God here does his saving work on behalf of the Palestinian and Aramean nations, just as he did for his people Israel (see also Isa 45:14, 22–23; 56:3–8; 66:18–19, 23; Zech 8:22, 23).

The God spoken of by the prophets is not a tribal God, interested only in the people of Israel. God is the creator of all humanity and he works for and cares for all peoples and nations (Jer 25:31; 32:27; 45:5). God cares for those nations in themselves, not just because of their relationship with Israel. At the same time, God works with and through the people of Israel for the sake of all other nations. All peoples are God's children, his creation, and God works with Israel for the sake of other nations.

God and War

From the second century until today, some Christians have viewed the Old Testament as filled with violence and killing. The heretic Marcion, for example, believed that the God of the Old Testament is the God of murder and bloodshed, while the God of the New Testament is the God of love, forgiveness, and reconciliation. This view is still found in many Christian and non-Christian circles today.

I have already acknowledged that there are some violent biblical texts. Some of this violence flows from a divine command (e.g. God's telling Israel to destroy a particular group). At other times God himself acts violently against specific people as he did at Sodom and Gomorrah, when confronting the Egyptians, and even with the people of Israel as we mentioned above. The other form of violence is that practiced by Israelites as they take violent revenge on persons or peoples (e.g. Exod 15:30; Josh 6; 8; 11; 24:12; Pss 3:7; 24:8; 137:9; Isa 42:13; Zeph 3:17).

In what follows I am not going to explain these verses away or justify the use of violence in any shape or form, especially when the violence is directed against innocent people, women, and children. Nor can I deny the presence of these texts and the huge misunderstandings around them over long centuries. I will simply try to show how Bible scholars have seen these texts from an ethical perspective and how we can understand them in the twenty-first century.

Here, then, are some general principles that can help us understand these texts:

First, we must understand these problem passages in light of the entire Bible, with both its Old and New Testaments, and what theologians refer to as progressive revelation. God reaches out to humans in a way they can understand in their time. When we look at the world in which these passages were written, we need to remember that these people did not separate the sacred from the secular. Religion and belief systems were foundational to their understanding of everyday life. Thus we must try to understand the language of violence in light of these peoples' understanding of war, revenge, and victory. The thought was that the true God was the one who brought victory to his people. However, divine revelation did not stop at orders to kill or to destroy, but progressed to the command "do not kill" in the Ten Commandments, followed by a command to "love your neighbor as yourself" (Lev 19:18). As God's revelation continued, it gradually progressed until it took the form of Jesus' teaching, "Love your enemies" (Matt 5:44). There are also numerous biblical references to God being merciful, compassionate, and slow to anger (Exod 34:6, 7; Num 14:8; Deut 4:31; 7:7; 9:7; Pss 86:5; 108:4; 145:8–9; Hos 11:4, 9; Joel 2:13; Amos 9:7).

Second, historical records, both ancient and modern, are never free of the ideology of the writers who recorded their understanding of events. This is true even of Israel's history. Thus when God expelled the Canaanites, Hittites, Amorites, Perizzites, Jebusites, and other peoples, this expulsion was recorded in a way that justified the entrance of the people of Israel into the promised land. Moses had warned Israel against making covenants with the original inhabitants of these lands or worshiping their gods (Deut 7:1–6, 25); thus it was necessary to have a complete separation between the people of God and these nations upon Israel's entry into the land. But at the same time, there is something called natural law, which we talked about earlier as the law of natural consequences. The nations that were driven out were not holy people and their ethics were substandard, and thus the Lord drove them out and gave their land to Israel. We find evidence of this in Moses' warning to the people:

> Do not say to yourself, "The LORD has brought me here to take possession of this land because of my righteousness." No, it is on account of the wickedness of these nations that the LORD is going to drive them out before you. It is not because of your righteousness or your integrity that you are going in to take possession of their land; but on account of the wickedness of these nations, the LORD your God will drive them out before you,

to accomplish what he swore to your fathers, to Abraham, Isaac and Jacob. Understand, then, that it is not because of your righteousness that the LORD your God is giving you this good land to possess, for you are a stiff-necked people. (Deut 9:4–6)

Third, the Lord also warned the people of Israel before they entered the promised land:

If you ever forget the LORD your God and follow other gods and worship and bow down to them, I testify against you today that you will surely be destroyed. Like the nations the LORD destroyed before you, so you will be destroyed for not obeying the LORD your God. (Deut 8:19–20)

That is exactly what happened when the people settled in the promised land and forgot the Lord God and worshiped other gods. God sent the Assyrians and Babylonians to take them out of the promised land into captivity. So just as God punished the original people of the land, so he used other people to punish his chosen people. God is a righteous judge over his people and all other peoples.

Fourth, Israel's history, beginning with Abraham (or Abram as he was named then) did not begin with violence. In Genesis 12–50 we see the forefathers negotiating with the original inhabitants of the land. And though the promise to Abraham included giving him the land of Canaan in the future (Gen 15:18–19), the language of violence and war has no place in the history of the patriarchs except in Genesis 14. Such language only starts to appear in the book of Exodus with the people leaving the land of Egypt ready for war (Exod 13:17) and Moses, Miriam, and Aaron singing, "The Lord is a warrior; the Lord is his name" (Exod 15:3). In the course of their wandering in the wilderness, they did encounter hostility and war (Num 10:9; 14:45; 20:18; 21:1, 23, 33; 31:4–7) and began to regard all of Israel's enemies as God's enemies (Judg 5:31).

Fifth, the expression "God is a warrior" was not used to frighten other nations or to incite attacks on other peoples but to express Israel's understanding of God's liberating and saving power. It was used after Israel's celebration of its salvation and freedom from its oppressors, for it was an experienced reality. Thus these words offer hope to the oppressed, prisoners, and the persecuted, reminding them that God can relieve them of oppression and liberate them.

Sixth, the words were not an excuse to kill, terrorize, or seize other peoples' lands. God listens to those who are oppressed and victimized when they cry out to him. At the same time, the fact that God is a warrior is a warning to oppressors, tyrants, and those who practice injustice, for God will intervene to vindicate the oppressed and bring justice among the peoples. Therefore, if oppressors do not repent of their oppression and injustice, they will see God intervene in a mighty way (Pss 24; 46; 72; 89; 104).

Seventh, God is just with all peoples, including the people of Israel, which explains the messages of prophets like Isaiah, Jeremiah, and Micah against false prophets who were popular with the people of Israel. The false prophets told the people what they wanted to hear; during times of war they proclaimed peace where there was no peace. The enemies of God, then, were not foreigners but were among the chosen people of God (Isa 1:24, 25; 10:5–14). The justice of God takes on an eschatological shape in passages like the following:

> In that day,
> the LORD will punish with his sword—
>   his fierce, great and powerful sword—
> Leviathan the gliding serpent,
>   Leviathan the coiling serpent;
> he will slay the monster of the sea. (Isa 27:1)

Eighth, God does not describe himself as a warrior. Rather, these were words the people of Israel used to express their understanding of God's dominion and sovereignty over all peoples and nations. He is the one who saves, redeems, and maintains justice for all peoples, including Israel. Only God can change individuals and peoples. Without him there is no hope for peace to reign or for humanity and creation to be restored to its original condition and the purpose for which God created it.

God uses his dominion, sovereignty, and power to bring about peace. From the beginning the purpose of creation was to acknowledge his divine presence, relate to him, and glorify him, all while living in peace. This is why God is committed to restoring peace to his creation, no matter the cost. In the midst of war, God sends a message of peace:

> For to us a child is born,
>   to us a son is given,
>   and the government will be on his shoulders.
> And he will be called
>   Wonderful Counselor, Mighty God,
>   Everlasting Father, Prince of Peace. (Isa 9:6)

Creation awaits, in the midst of war, the God of peace. For in a time of war, what is needed is a Prince of Peace. But Isaiah's words remind us that peace does not come through treaties; it requires a fundamental change in the thinking of the enemy. This is confirmed by the Prophet Micah:

> He will judge between many peoples
>   and will settle disputes for strong nations far and wide.
> They will beat their swords into plowshares
>   and their spears into pruning hooks.
> Nation will not take up sword against nation,
>   nor will they train for war anymore.
> Everyone will sit under their own vine
>   and under their own fig tree,

and no one will make them afraid,
>   for the LORD Almighty has spoken. (Mic 4:3–4)

This is the beginning of a new era where peace reigns (see also Joel 3:9–10). The Lord is a warrior, but not a warrior who kills, steals, and occupies. Rather, he is a warrior who brings peace, vindicates the oppressed, and releases captives—which is exactly what Jesus Christ has done.

GOD THE REDEEMER

Is it possible for the God who created this wonderful universe, who is present in it and in relationship with it, to also be God the redeemer? The answer to this question is that the concept of God as creator is inseparable from the idea of God the righteous judge and redeemer, for God cannot be judge and redeemer if he were not also the creator. The relationship between God and his creation necessitates that he is also the righteous judge and redeemer.

From creation's perspective (that of human beings), the divine presence is linked to the extent to which God relates to his creation. If the Old Testament gives us the history of redemption, then it must also present God's people and their understanding of this God, who is the creator, righteous judge, and redeemer. Because he is perfect and all-encompassing, he cannot be the creator without being the righteous judge, and he cannot be the righteous judge without being the redeemer. For God to be a creator, he must have a relationship with his creation, and in order for him to be a righteous judge, there must be a specific issue or case to preside over; and to be a redeemer, there must be those who need redemption. Thus one can say that humanity (the human race) forms the other half of the picture about God.

Yes, God is self-existent, perfect, and all-encompassing in his attributes, but it is humans who recognize and understand his divine presence and divine attributes. Thus, in order for us to fully understand human existence, we must grasp that the creature is simultaneously under judgment and redeemed. This is the perspective from which the Old Testament was recorded. Humanity in general (through a particular people) is the center and focus of God's care—they are the great divine project.

God is known to humans because he wanted to be known by them. God created the earth to be filled with humans whom he created in his own image. In other words, God created the world because he wanted to create human beings and because he wanted his image and likeness to fill the whole world. Thus, creation depends on God the creator, but at the same time the image of God (from a human's perspective) is shaped and defined by his work of God of creation.

Humans have a dual nature. The first man (Adam) was created from "the dust of the earth [*hā' ădāmāh*]," but God breathed the breath of life (spirit) into him. In other words, God gave human beings his spirit, the spirit of life. Humans are part of creation. In Genesis 2, we are told that creation was not complete until God created humans to work this earth. God then gave them dominion over the earth. With this dual nature, humans have become the mirror that reflects this divine presence, and thus it is only fitting that the human race be filled with praise to its creator.

But we must also note that from the outset, God set boundaries for his creatures and warned them that they would be judged if they transgressed those boundaries. When humans did indeed cross these boundaries, there was a price that someone had to pay. Put simply, for God to be a redeemer he must be a righteous judge, and for him to be a righteous judge he must be a creator. God the righteous judge opens the door to God the redeemer, who rescues and redeems. He saved Noah from the flood and restored the creation once again to its original purpose.

In this new beginning, the relationship between Creator and creation is restored, though it now takes formal shape in which God the creator makes a covenant with his creation, establishing certain rules. God will not break his covenant with humans and will not destroy them all again. He established an eternal covenant with them and their descendants (Gen 9:8–17). Noah responded with worship and sacrifices, showing that the continuation of this mutual relationship depends on both parties: God and human beings. This is the God who has revealed his name to us, and this is the history of God's relationship with human beings, in which God invites us to participate. This is the God who cares for his creation, which is the secret of the continuation of human existence. The God who is in a covenant relationship with humans is not silent or passive; rather, he acts on behalf of the human race and the entire creation. All this is summarized in St. Augustine's famous words, "You have made us for yourself, and our hearts are restless, until they can find rest in you."

The story of God in the Old Testament is the story humans tell about God. This story is presented through human experiences and in human language as this is the only way in which human beings can grasp anything of this universal and infinite God.

The concept of God as a redeemer is linked to the concept of the next of kin or the kinsman redeemer who, according to the family system in Israel, had to intervene to save relatives in a time of adversity or hardship (Lev 25:25–34, 48–52; Jer 32:7–8). This is why the Lord was referred to as Israel's redeemer when he intervened and rescued his people from adversity in the land of Egypt (Exod 6:6; 15:13). Additionally, it helps explain why the people of Israel presented an offering on behalf of their firstborn (Exod 13:11–15).

Although redemption and salvation are interrelated, they each have a distinct meaning. "Salvation" means liberation or rescue from slavery, prison, or debt, while "redemption" means paying the price needed to accomplish salvation. Thus salvation is the more inclusive term, while redemption refers to a particular act. The cost of redemption can vary widely—at its extreme we see the redeemer offering himself as a price to achieve the desired salvation of his people.

God the Redeemer in the Torah

We will now look at the image of God the redeemer in the Torah, but not in the Writings, although they are full of expressions and images that refer to this role (see Job 5:20; 6:23; Pss 19:14; 25:22; 26:11; 31:5; 33:28; 44:26; 49:7–8, 15; 69:19; 78:35; 103:4; 107:2; 119:134; Prov 23:11).

The fact that humans were created in God's image does not negate their finiteness. Therefore, humans have the capacity to fail in the duties and responsibilities assigned to them, which has negative consequences for the whole creation, for sin is destructive. Genesis 3–6 shows that humans used their freedom to damage their relationship with God. We see this in statements like this one: "The LORD saw how great the wickedness of the human race had become on the earth, and that every inclination of the thoughts of the human heart was only evil all the time" (Gen 6:5). The rest of the chapter shows that humans' evil had filled the earth (Gen 6:11–13) and corrupted the entire creation. God had to intervene so that sin would not have the final say.

Though the word "sin" is not used in Genesis 3, it is found in Genesis 4:7, where God says, "If you do what is right, will you not be accepted? But if you do not do what is right, sin is crouching at your door; it desires to have you, but you must rule over it." As we read the rest of the story we see the effect of sin not only on the divine-human relationship, but on all creation. The relationship between Adam and Eve was affected, and so was their relationship with God, which is why they tried to hide from him (Gen 3:10).

Despite this, God clothed them, making them garments of skin (Gen 3:21). It is important to note that God did not abandon them. He sought them out while they were still afraid and looked for them while they were ashamed, and this is what led them to confess their sin. We must also note the direct relationship between the cause and effect of sin, and how all aspects of life were affected by their sin. Yet, God remained in relationship with creation, which gives human beings hope for a future despite their expulsion from Eden. God covered and clothed Adam and Eve, but their sin resulted in death appearing in human life. We hear the Lord's words in Genesis 3:19: "By the sweat of your brow you will eat your food until you return to the ground, since from it you were taken; for dust you are and to dust you will return."

I do not think God originally created human beings to live forever—if he had done so, there would have been no reason for the Tree of Life to exist. Death is a part of the divine creation, and the Tree of Life was a way to ensure the continuity of life. But when humans sinned, God separated them from the Tree of Life and humans were faced with the stark reality of mortality (Gen 3:22).

We also see God's presence in the story of Cain and Abel. Although at that time there was no written prohibition of murder, this was a natural law embedded in creation. Human sin continues in Genesis 6, leading to the flood as a natural consequence. There is an extent to which this flood represents a reversal of the act of creation. Thus some scholars see Genesis 9:1–9 as the new act of creation or re-creation, where at the end of the story God establishes a covenant never to destroy the earth again. God promised salvation and accomplished it for both human and animal life, after which God established a covenant with humans. Thus God chose to be faithful to his creation even before Israel came into existence.

We see God's faithfulness in the remainder of the book of Genesis in his dealings with Abraham when he asks him to offer his son Isaac, and with Hagar as he delivers her from death in the wilderness (Gen 16:7–14; 21:15–21). In the latter example, we see God dealing with those whom we would consider outside the circle of faith (Gen 21:20), excluded from the people of God. Furthermore, God delivers Abimelek and his family from the consequences of sin (Gen 20:17–18). We also see how God was prepared to deliver Sodom and Gomorrah (Gen 18:16–19:29). In the story of Joseph we see God as the redeemer and savior, working behind the scenes on behalf of Joseph, the Egyptians, and the whole earth (Gen 41:57).

The image of God the redeemer is most evident in the exodus narrative. What God did with Israel in the exodus was for the benefit of all creation (Exod 9:16), as is shown in the song of Miriam and Aaron in Genesis 15. God the creator is the same as the God who redeemed Israel for the sake of the whole earth (Exod 8:22; 9:14, 16). So when God declares Israel to be a holy nation and a royal priesthood, he is actually assigning them their role on God's earth (Exod 19:5–6). In Israel's crossing the sea on dry land, we see a powerful symbol of God's re-creating and restoring creation to the purpose for which it was created. This redemption was intended to bring life and blessing to the whole creation. God's redemptive work continued as he led the people in the wilderness, giving them manna and water in a desert land, and was completed when he gave them his law. Obedience to the law became necessary if they were to live at peace with God.

Obedience to the law is a response to God's redemptive work, and not simply obedience for its own sake (Deut 24:18–22), and the redemption of Israel affected the entire creation and the whole earth (Deut 4:6).

God the Redeemer in the Prophets

I will limit my discussion of how the prophets refer to God the redeemer to Isaiah 40–55, for this section of Isaiah deals extensively with the topics of creation, new creation, redemption, and the hope of a better future for a people living in captivity (Isa 40:27; 49:14). It is important to note that Isaiah 56–66 also speaks of those who are not from the chosen people of God (Isa 56:1–8; 60:10–16; 66:18–22). We also note the use of terms like "new heavens" and "new earth" (Isa 65:17; 66:22), as the book of Isaiah opens and closes with visions of the new creation (Isa 2; 11; 65–66).

The second section of Isaiah starts with a message of comfort: "Comfort, comfort my people, says your God" (Isa 40:1; see also 12; 19; 49:13; 51:3; 52:9; 54:11; 57:18; 61:21; 66:13). God speaks to comfort a people who are enduring hardship, a people who had lost hope not only in their future but even in themselves. So the voice of God comes to them saying, "you are precious and honored in my sight, and . . . I love you" (Isa 43:4).

God reminds his people that he is their creator (Isa 43:7), and that he created them for his glory (Isa 42:14; 46:3–4; 49:19–21; 66:6–13). God, who created them, is the one who will redeem and save them (40:29–31; 44:21; 46:3–4). The issue of the salvation of the people and what God will do in the future is always connected to the language of creation. That is why we read in Isaiah 40:28, "The Lord is the everlasting God, the Creator of the ends of the earth. He will not grow tired or weary" (see also Isa 42:5; 44:2–3; 48:16).

We must also note God's commitment not only to Israel but also to the whole creation (Isa 54:9–10; Jer 31:35–37). Because God is the creator, he is the only one who can save. The Songs of the Suffering Servant provide the best statement of how he bore human sin (Isa 43:24–25; 53:5–6, 8, 11–12). These poems include all nations and peoples (42:1, 4; 49:1–6; 53:11–12). The one who issues the call is the God of the whole earth (45:5) and the Suffering Servant is the light of all the nations (49:6; 52:10). Thus, God's salvation of Israel (43:3) extends to include all nations (Isa 45:22, 23; 49:6; 51:5–6, 8; 52:10).

In chapters 40–55, Isaiah recalls the first exodus to present the message of the second exodus. This exodus will be even greater than the first one, and its effects will extend to all creation. The second exodus is more universal and inclusive and surpasses the first one. That is why the Lord tells his people to "forget the former things; do not dwell on the past. See, I am doing a new thing!" (Isa 43:18–19; see also 41:22–23; 42:9; 46:8–11; 48:3, 6; Jer 16:14–16).

The first exodus will not be the only redemptive work of God. God is already preparing something greater, a new and more inclusive exodus that will affect all creation:

> For your Maker is your husband—
> the Lord Almighty is his name—
> the Holy One of Israel is your Redeemer;
> he is called the God of all the earth . . . .
> Yet my unfailing love for you will not be shaken
> nor my covenant of peace be removed,"
> says the Lord, who has compassion on you. (Isa 54:5–10)

REFERENCES

Anderson, Bernhard W. *Contours of Old Testament Theology*. Minneapolis: Fortress, 1999.

Barton, John. *Understanding Old Testament Ethics: Approaches and Explorations*. Louisville: Westminster John Knox, 2003.

Bashta, Andraos and Adel Khory. *God in Christianity and Islam*. Harrisa, Lebanon: Pauline Library, 2003.

Brown, William P., ed. *Character and Scripture: Moral Formation, Community, and Biblical Interpretation*. Grand Rapids: Eerdmans, 2002.

Brueggemann, Walter. *Theology of the Old Testament: Testimony, Dispute, Advocacy*. Minneapolis: Fortress, 1997.

Craigie, Peter C. *The Problem of War in the Old Testament*. Grand Rapids: Eerdmans, 1978.

Eichrodt, Walter. *Theology of Old Testament*. London: SCM, 1976.

Fretheim, Terence F. *God and World in the Old Testament: A Relational Theology of Creation*. Nashville: Abingdon, 2005.

Kaiser, Walter. *Toward Old Testament Ethics*. Grand Rapids: Zondervan. 1993.

Kassis, Riad. *Why Don't We Read the Book that Jesus Read? Towards a Better Understanding of the Old Testament*. Cairo: Dar Al Thaqafa, 2007.

Khory, Adel Theodore. *Who is God? The Answer of Major Religions*. Gonya, Lebanon: Pauline Library, 2003.

Mills, Mary E. *Images of God in the Old Testament*. Collegeville, Minnesota: Liturgical Press, 1998.

Patrick, Dale. *The Rendering of God in the Old Testament*. Philadelphia: Fortress, 1981.

Shalhat, Victor. *The Issue of God in History: From the Bible to the Current Religious Phenomenon*. Beirut: Dar Al-Mashraq, 1997.

Youngblood, Ronald. *The Heart of the Old Testament*. Grand Rapids: Baker, 1998.

Chapter Two

THE CONCEPT OF THE COVENANT IN EVANGELICAL THOUGHT AND ITS IMPACT ON THE MIDDLE EAST AND NORTH AFRICA

A HISTORICAL, BIBLICAL, THEOLOGICAL, AND ETHICAL STUDY

Riad Aziz Kassis

Dr. Riad Aziz Kassis, a Syrian-Lebanese theologian, author, and scholar is international director of the International Council for Evangelical Theological Education (ICETE) and director of Langham Scholars Ministry (Langham Partnership). Ordained in the National Evangelical Church in Beirut, he has pastored the Christian Alliance National Evangelical Church of Damascus, and the National Presbyterian Church in Amar, Syria. He lectures in Old Testament Studies at the Arab Baptist Theological Seminary and the Near East School of Theology and is former executive director of the Johann Ludwig Schneller Institute, Lebanon, which engages in social outreach and religious education. Dr. Kassis holds a Master's degree in Old Testament studies from Regent College, Canada, and a PhD in Philosophy (Old Testament) from Nottingham University, UK. His publications include *The Book of Proverbs and Arabic Proverbial Works*, *The Land in the Bible*, and numerous articles.

THE CHRISTIAN FAITH is rooted in the Bible. If you were to ask a Christian, "What does the Bible consist of?" you would probably be told that it is divided into two parts, the Old Testament and the New Testament, terms that could be more literally translated as the Old Covenant and the New Covenant.[1] Thus it is not surprising that covenant theology is one of the most important features of Reformed theology. In fact, Reformed theology is often summed up as the theology of the covenant. Many students of biblical theology and the theology of the Old Testament believe that the concept of covenant is the thread linking all the books of the Old Testament and extending to the books of the New Testament.[2] The renowned Old Testament theologian Walter Brueggemann states that the main subject of the Bible is covenantal history, and that the main purpose of our reading and study of the Bible is to be committed participants in this covenantal history.[3]

Yet why is the word "testament" or "covenant" used to refer to the main two sections of the Bible? Why does the concept of the covenant have such great theological significance? What is its religious and historical background? What is meant by "the theology of the covenant"? Do the concepts of the covenant and covenantal theology affect our personal life and our church life? Or are they just issues that theologians discuss in their ivory towers? How does a correct understanding of the concept of the covenant affect our daily life and our role as citizens in the Middle East and North Africa? In this chapter I will be attempting to answer questions like these.

The chapter falls into four sections. The first shows the importance of studying the concept of the covenant and the way it affects our lives. It also presents some key issues that are affected by how clearly we understand this concept.

The second section is a theological study of the concept of the covenant from a biblical perspective. It includes a definition of the covenant and discusses its formulation, forms, and historical background within the culture of the ancient Near East. This section studies the covenants that God made with the patriarchs and the prophets in the Old Testament. It also sheds light on the concept of the new covenant proclaimed by Jeremiah and other prophets and the applications of this new covenant in the teachings of the Lord Jesus Christ and the writers of the New Testament.

Section three deals with the relationship between the covenant and the law of

---

[1] In academic circles, the books of the Old Testament are often referred to as the "Hebrew Bible." However, here I have chosen to use the term "Old Testament" because I am writing as an Arab Christian interpreting the Old Testament from a Christian perspective, which implies that there are both an Old and a New Testament.

[2] See, for example, W. Eichrodt, *Theology of the Old Testament*, trans. J. A. Baker, 2 vols. (Philadelphia: Westminster, 1951), vol.

1; N. T. Wright, *The Climax of the Covenant: Christ and the Law in Pauline Theology* (Edinburgh: T&T Clark, 1991); M. Horton, *God of Promise: Introducing Covenant Theology* (Grand Rapids: Baker, 2006).

[3] W. Brueggemann, *The Bible Makes Sense* (Louisville: Westminster John Knox, 2001), 13.

Moses, and its effects on our social and economic life. This relationship is presented through a discussion of the role of the law in the Old Testament in general and the Ten Commandments in particular.

Section four examines the covenant link to the land of Palestine and the way this affects the Palestinian issue. It discusses two main schools of thought that reflect two different theological systems: the Reformed school (tracing back to the Protestant Reformation) and Dispensationalism (which divides the history of God's dealings with human beings into eras called dispensations). I also touch on some of the views of the church fathers and contemporary theologians on this important subject.

THE IMPORTANCE OF THE CONCEPT OF THE COVENANT

Some people may think that covenant theology is a purely academic matter that does not affect our daily life. But nothing could be further from the truth. A good grasp of the concept of the covenant will have a profound, direct, and positive impact on life and reality in the Middle East and North Africa. In what follows, I will explain what I mean by this statement.

First, the Old Testament describes God as the maker and preserver of the covenant (Exod 34:10; 1 Kgs 8:23). The essence of this covenant—as we will see in detail later in this chapter—is the relationship between God and human beings, a relationship that has huge implications for how we conduct ourselves. This relationship cannot be properly understood without a sound grasp of what a covenant is and how this particular covenant feeds into our day-to-day behavior. The commandments and laws found in the Bible, which are essential elements governing human behavior and the social, economic, and moral relationships among people, were given within the framework of the covenant. Thus a correct application of the Old Testament commandments and laws depends on a sound understanding of the concept of the covenant, and should not be implemented without such proper understanding.

Second, human beings seek salvation from the power of sin and from judgment. Some wonder whether God grants this salvation on the basis of someone's good works and piety or whether the grace of God is poured out on believers without any merit on their part. Determining whether salvation is based on our good works or on God's grace has consequences for the life to come and for our conduct in this present life, as well as affecting our thinking about who God is, his attitude toward us, and what he requires from us.

The terms "covenant of law" and "covenant of grace" are often used by those who believe that the first relates to God's dealings in the Old Testament and the second to his dealings in the New Testament. Thus some conclude that in the Old Testament salvation was based on whether someone observed and upheld the law, whereas in the New Testament salvation is by grace alone. I have even heard a famous international preacher declare, "The Old Testament told people: 'Do this in order to live'; whereas the New Testament says: 'Live and do this.' The Old Testament is the covenant of the law, but the New Testament is the covenant of grace."

A better understanding of the concept of the covenant helps us to develop a better understanding of the relationship between salvation, grace, works, and God's dealings in the two Testaments. Thus it contributes to increasing our understanding and correcting our beliefs about salvation and the twin issues of justification and sanctification.

Third, the covenant does not only deal with the relationship between God and human beings but also with the relationship between God the creator and the physical creation. Therefore, the covenant that started with the first human beings in Eden is a covenant that has an impact on our current attitude to the creation that God committed into their care. Thus the covenant has implications for our attitude to environmental issues in general.

Fourth, our understanding of the concept of the covenant affects our understanding of the identity of God's people. For example, if we believe that the covenant God made with Israel continues unchanged today, then the identity of the people of God in our day is determined by ethnicity. However, if we believe that the form and content of the covenant have changed, then the identity of the people of God is not necessarily based on ethnicity. [4]

Fifth, the concept of the covenant in the Bible, especially in the Old Testament, is related to the land of Palestine. God promised Abraham and his descendants that the land of Canaan would be their everlasting possession. This promise was repeated to Moses, David, and other prophets and kings. Thus questions now arise: "Is the covenant God made regarding the land of Palestine still valid today?" "Does this covenant give the state of Israel the right to own the land of Palestine?" "Is this the only interpretation of the promise of the land as an everlasting inheritance?" This is a very important issue with serious consequences, both politically and morally. We need only read certain religious books or watch television programs that deal with this issue to see the overwhelming support given to the state of Israel without any consideration of the tragedy of the Palestinian people. All this is due to the belief that the covenant

---

[4] There is a difference between the ancient Hebrew people we read about in the Old Testament and the modern state of Israel. It is useful when Arab translations of the Old Testament and all writings related to the Old Testament make this distinction. We should also distinguish between the "Palestinians" mentioned in the Old Testament and the Arab Palestinians of today who live in the occupied territory. In English, these groups are distinguished by referring to modern inhabitants of the region as "Israelis" and the ancient people as the "Israelites," and by speaking of "Philistines" and "Palestinians." See my discussion of this matter in R. Kassis, "Christian Zionism: Evaluation and Critique" (Th.M. thesis, Regent College, 1993), 142n69.

God made with Israel as an ethnic group is still valid today.[5] Here are some examples that illustrate what I have just said:[6]

> Destruction awaits those who believe that God has finished with his chosen people. . . . Evangelicals have to carefully choose with whom they will stand. (David Brickner)

> Anyone who disputes Israel's right to the land of Canaan is actually rejecting God and his holy covenant with the Patriarchs. (Basilea Schlink)

> An Arab is not only an evil and a malicious liar; he is evil, dishonest, and malicious by nature! (Ramon Bennett)

A correct interpretation of the covenant, especially the promise regarding the land of Palestine, helps to clarify our thinking on this important issue in the Middle East and North Africa, and facilitates a just solution to the Palestinian question.

Sixth, our concept of the covenant does not affect only the political and moral aspects of the Palestinian question, especially the problem of the land, but goes beyond these to affect our faith and religious conduct. For example, it also has implications for our understanding of salvation and the practice of evangelism. If we believe that God's covenant with Israel is still valid, does this mean that there are two parallel covenants, one for Jews and another for non-Jews? If there are two parallel covenants, does this mean that there is no need to preach the good news of Jesus Christ to Jews, since there is an alternative route to salvation for them based on God's covenant with them?

Finally, the issue of the relationship between the Old and New Testaments is controversial in academic circles and there seems to be a lack of knowledge about it at the local church level. A correct understanding of the development of the idea of the covenant in the books of the Old Testament and the New Testament will help us identify the relationship between the old covenant and the new covenant and identify the points of continuity or discontinuity between them.

A BIBLICAL AND THEOLOGICAL STUDY OF THE COVENANT

We will now consider the concept of the covenant from a biblical perspective. I will start by defining the meaning of the covenant, its formulas, shapes, and historical

---

[5] See, for example, the following book by an American politician that provides a political and historical overview of the support that the state of Israel receives from evangelicals on the extreme right in the United States of America: D. Brog, *Standing with Israel: Why Christians Support The Jewish State* (Lake Mary, FL: Charisma House, 2006).

[6] These quotations are merely a few of the many sayings that Stephen Sizer refers to and refutes in his book *Christian Zionists: On the Way to Armageddon* (Beirut: The Arab Team of the Islamic-Christian Dialogue, 2005). Also published as *Christian Zionism: Road-map to Armageddon?* (Leicester: IVP, 2004). See http://www.sizers.org.

background in the context of the ancient Near East. This section explores the covenants God made with the patriarchs and prophets of the Old Testament. It sheds light on the concept of the new covenant that was proclaimed by Jeremiah and other prophets, and the applications of this new covenant in the teachings of Christ our Lord and the writers of the New Testament. This section lays the biblical and theological foundation for the rest of this chapter.

Defining the Term "Covenant"

A covenant can be defined as an agreement between two parties in which one or both of them promises either to carry out certain duties and obligations or to refrain from certain actions. The word "covenant" occurs some 287 times in the Old Testament. It is often accompanied by the verb "cut," perhaps in reference to the fact that the making of a covenant was accompanied by sacrifices. There are also other words and phrases which imply a covenant, such as "sworn agreement" or "oath" (Gen 26:28; Deut 9:5), "covenant of love" or "unfailing love," and "covenant of peace" (Deut 7:12; Num 25:12; Isa 54:10).

However, it is important to be aware that any study of the meaning of the covenant must not be restricted to the verses mentioned above but must also pay particular attention to the "covenant formula." This formula appears for the first time in Exodus 6:7, "I will take you as my own people, and I will be your God" (see also Lev 26:12; Deut 26:17–19; 29:12–13; 2 Sam 7:24; Jer 7:23; 11:4; 24:7; 30:22; 31:1; 32:38; Ezek 11:20; 14:11; 36:28; 37:23, 27; Zech 8:8). It expresses the intimate relationship between God and his people.

There are also other expressions that are similar to the covenant formula (see, for example, Exod 19:4–6; Pss 33:12; 95:7; 100:3; Hos 1:9; Zech 2:11). Sometimes the formula is abbreviated, with only one of its two parts being used. For example, "I will be your God" or similar words are found in Genesis 17:7; Exodus 29:45; Leviticus 11:45; 22:33; 25:38; 26:45; and Ezekiel 34:24. Similarly, sentences like "I will take you for my people" are found in Deuteronomy 4:20; 7:6; 14:2; 27:9; 28:9; 1 Samuel 12:22; 2 Kings 11:17; and Jeremiah 13:11.[7]

Covenants and Treaties in the Ancient Near East

The large number of international covenants/treaties discovered in the ancient Near East attests to their important role in the political and social life of the people of the time. These treaties were originally oral agreements, but as soon as writing developed they appeared in written form. Some of the most important covenants/treaties discovered

---

[7] For a detailed academic study of the covenant formula in the Old Testament and the early Jewish and Christian traditions, see K. Baltzer, *The Covenant Formulary in Old Testament, Jewish, and Early Christian Writings* (Oxford: Blackwell, 1971).

are those of the Hittites (1400–1200 BC) and the Assyrians (eighth and seventh centuries BC).

The oldest written treaty found was made between Ramses II of Egypt (1279–1212 BC) and the Hittite king Hattusili III (1275–1250 BC). It was a treaty between two parties of similar power and influence. But this was not always the case, for treaties and covenants were often made between a weaker party and a stronger one. The covenants God made in the Old Testament—as we will see below—are covenants of the second kind, for God the Almighty enters into a covenant with a weak party, whether an individual or a community.

The covenants mentioned in Deuteronomy and Joshua 24 are similar to the covenants/treaties of the ancient Near East in their form. It is also possible that the covenant with Abraham resembles the "covenant of grant" that was known in the ancient Near East (see the discoveries at Ugarit/Ras Shamra).[8]

The covenants/treaties of the ancient Near East had six main elements:

- An introduction that specified the parties to the treaty and their relationship to each other (Deut 1:1–6).
- A historical preamble setting out the circumstances that led to the making of the treaty (Deut 1:7–4:49).
- General stipulations regarding loyalty (Deut 5–11).
- Details of the responsibilities and duties of each party.
- A list of the names of those witnessing the treaty, who were generally gods (Deut 32; 30:19; 32:1).
- Blessings for those who obey the conditions of the covenant or treaty and curses on those who do not (Deut 27–28).[9]

Clearly the Old Testament is the child of its cultural, social, and religious environment. However, there are also some differences between the content of the ancient Near Eastern treaties and the covenants of the Old Testament.

Covenants in the Bible

The books of the Old Testament deal with two main kinds of covenants: covenants God made with individuals or communities, and covenants people made with each other or covenants between the ancient Hebrew people and their neighbors. Examples of covenants between individuals include those made between Abraham and Abimelech (Gen 21:22–32), Jacob and Laban (Gen 31:43–54), David and Jonathan (1 Sam 18:1–4; 20:8, 16; 23:18), and Nebuchadnezzar and Zedekiah (Ezek 17:12–19). Examples of

[8] T. J. Hegg, "The Covenant of Grant and the Abrahamic Covenant," *Theological Society Papers* (Portland, 1982).

[9] Some ancient treaties also include a requirement that official records of the treaty be periodically reread.

covenants between the ancient Hebrews and their neighbors include those made with the Gibeonites (Josh 9), the Arameans (1 Kgs 15:19), and the Assyrians (Hos 12:1). Here, however, we will study the covenants God made with individuals or the community.

Covenant with Noah

Some scholars suggest that the first covenant God made was the covenant of creation that is implicit in his commands to Adam and Eve in the garden of Eden (Gen 1–2).[10] However, the first explicit reference to a covenant occurs in God's words to Noah before the flood: "But I will establish my covenant with you, and you will enter the ark—you and your sons and your wife and your sons' wives with you" (Gen 6:18; see also 9:8–11). God's command to Adam and Eve to "be fruitful and increase in number; fill the earth and subdue it" (Gen 1:26–28) is similar to the covenant with Noah (Gen 9:1–7), but this similarity is insufficient to consider God's command to Adam and Eve a covenant.

There are three important things to note about God's covenant with Noah. First, this covenant comes within the context of God's blessing of Noah and includes the command that all human beings should respect their neighbors:

> And for your lifeblood I will surely demand an accounting. I will demand an accounting from every animal. And from each human being, too, I will demand an accounting for the life of another human being.
>
> > Whoever sheds human blood,
> > > by humans shall their blood be shed;
> > for in the image of God
> > > has God made mankind.
>
> As for you, be fruitful and increase in number. (Gen 9:5–7)

Throughout history, teachers of the Torah have considered these laws given to Noah as the general framework for order, security, and peace in society. This formula that holds individuals accountable for the life of their neighbors is what is needed in our societies in the Middle East and North Africa if we desire peace and harmony.

Second, God did not make that covenant with Noah and his household only, but with all living creatures. This is clear evidence that the whole earth with all that is on it is included in God's covenant. Therefore, we are all invited to care for all of God's creation. We Christians in the Middle East and North Africa need to work hard to preserve the environment, especially as we see the serious harm done to it each day![11]

Third, the covenant with Noah reveals God's love and care for humanity. He saved

---

[10] M. Horton, *God of Promise: Introducing Covenant Theology* (Grand Rapids: Baker, 2006), 40–43.

[11] A Rocha Lebanon, which is related to A Rocha International, is a practical model of a Christian approach to caring for the environment. For more information regarding this society and its activities, visit www.arocha.org and http://en.arocha.org/lebanon/index.html

Noah's family and promised never again to send such a flood. We also see his judgment and condemnation, since he is the holy and just God who condemns and judges sin. Thus in our lives and in the teaching in our churches we must present both the God of love, kindness, and grace and the holy, just, and judging God. Both aspects of God's nature need to be kept in balance if we are to understand God's dealings with human beings.

Covenant with Abraham

The covenant that is more important and defined than that with Noah is the covenant God made with the patriarch Abram. When we first hear of it, this covenant takes the form of a promise:

Go from your country, your people and your father's household to the land I will show you.

> I will make you into a great nation,
>   and I will bless you;
> I will make your name great,
>   and you will be a blessing.
> I will bless those who bless you,
>   and whoever curses you I will curse;
> and all peoples on earth
>   will be blessed through you." (Gen 12:1–3)

Later, however, the promise of the land is repeated in the context of a covenant ceremony (Gen 15:18), and Abram's name is changed to Abraham in one of the passages that confirm this covenant (Gen 17:1–8). The covenant with Abraham is repeated many times in the book of Genesis, and new elements are added to it.

The elements of the covenant with Abraham are as follows:

- a promise of posterity;
- a promise of blessing for Abraham and his descendants;
- a promise to glorify the name of Abraham;
- a promise to bless those whom Abraham blesses and to curse those he curses;
- a promise of land;
- a promise of blessing the nations;
- a promise of royal descendants.

As we read this list, some important questions come to mind: Were those promises fulfilled? If the answer is yes, how and when did that happen? If not, why not? Will they be fulfilled in the near or far future? Is the covenant with Abraham conditional or unconditional? I will answer these questions, and then go on to explore the issue of the promise of land in the fifth section of this chapter.

Promise of Posterity

The promise of posterity was repeated to Abraham many times in the book of Genesis (Gen 13:16; 15:5; 22:1, 17; 26:4; 28:3; 35:11–12; 48:4). It began to be fulfilled literally and historically after he left Egypt (Deut 10:22) as Isaiah the prophet reminds us when he quotes the Lord's words:

> Look to Abraham, your father,
>   and to Sarah, who gave you birth.
> When I called him he was only one man,
>   and I blessed him and made him many. (Isa 51:2; cf. Hos 1:10)

The obvious interpretation of this promise is that the number of Abraham's natural descendants will increase. However, the writers of the New Testament interpret the promise of posterity in three different ways:

- With reference to Abraham's physical descendants. In Mary's song of praise she says that God remembered his mercies as he spoke to Abraham and his descendants (Luke 1:55). The writer to the Hebrews refers to the physical offspring of Abraham through his son Isaac (Heb 11:18; see also, John 8:33, 37; Acts 7:5–6; Rom 11:1; 2 Cor 11:22). This understanding reflects the emphasis in the Old Testament.
- With reference to all who believe in Christ, regardless of their physical descent. The apostle Paul describes Abraham as the father of all who believe in Christ (Rom 4:13–18; see also Rom 9:6). Thus what determines whether people are descendants of Abraham is their belief in Christ, not any physical or racial consideration (Matt 3:8–9; Gal 3:7). Paul concludes his letter to the Galatians with the following confident affirmation:

  > So in Christ Jesus you are all children of God through faith, for all of you who were baptized into Christ have clothed yourselves with Christ. There is neither Jew nor Gentile, neither slave nor free, nor is there male and female, for you are all one in Christ Jesus. If you belong to Christ, then you are Abraham's seed, and heirs according to the promise. (Gal 3:26–29)

- With reference to Christ himself, as in the following quotation from the apostle Paul:

  > The promises were spoken to Abraham and to his seed. Scripture does not say "and to seeds," meaning many people, but "and to your seed," meaning one person, who is Christ. (Gal 3:16)

The apostle Peter also preached that the blessing that the descendants of Abraham would bring to all nations became a tangible reality in Jesus Christ (Acts 3:25–26).

We may sometimes be puzzled by the way the New Testament writers interpreted the Old Testament promises and linked them to the new era that began with Jesus Christ. However, there is no doubt that their understanding of the term "Abraham's descendants"—especially the second and third interpretations—opens the door to a new understanding of the identity of the people of God in Christian thought. Membership in this group is no longer restricted to those who are physically descended from Abraham but includes all who believe in Jesus Christ.[12]

We must also take note of the possibility of people who were not physical descendants of Abraham merging into the people of God. The Old Testament records cases where this happened (think of Ruth the Moabite, Rahab the Canaanite, and Naaman the Syrian [Ruth; Josh 2:9–11; 2 Kgs 5]). Jonah called a heathen people to repentance (Jonah), Job does not seem to have been of Jewish descent (Job),[13] and the Suffering Servant in Isaiah proclaims salvation to the whole earth (Isa 49:6). Speaking to those who returned from exile in Babylon, the Prophet Isaiah said that foreigners would have a share and portion with the people of God (Isa 56:3–7; see also Isa 2:1–5; Mic 4:1–5; Zech 2:10–13). Thus it is important to note that Matthew's genealogy of Jesus Christ (Matt 1:1–17) makes no mention of the most famous women in the history of Israel: Sarah, Rebekah, Rachel, and Leah. Instead, he mentions four women from heathen backgrounds who had no physical relationship to Abraham and his descendants—the Canaanites Tamar and Rahab, Ruth the Moabitess, and Bathsheba the Hittite. It is as if Matthew was setting out to show that it is God who decides who joins his people, and that the decision is not based on race or ethnic background.

Promise of Blessing to Abraham and His Descendants

There are three elements to the blessing that Abraham was promised: increased offspring, security for those offspring, and their role in bringing blessing to all nations. Looking at God's dealings with Abraham, Isaac, and Jacob in the book of Genesis, we note that this blessing was not merely spiritual but also included physical possessions (Gen 24:35–36; 26:12, 24; 35:11–48; 12:3–4). When the apostle Paul refers to this promise of blessing, he affirms that all believers, regardless of their ethnic affiliation, share in it (Gal 3:9). As for the content of this blessing, according to Paul it is the gift of the Holy Spirit:

> He redeemed us in order that the blessing given to Abraham might come to the Gentiles through Christ Jesus, so that by faith we might receive the promise of the Spirit. (Gal 3:14)

---

[12] For more on this subject, see R. N. Longenecker, *Biblical Exegesis in the Apostolic Period* (Grand Rapids: Eerdmans, 1975); P. Enns, *Inspiration and Incarnation: Evangelicals and the Problem of the Old Testament* (Grand Rapids: Baker, 2005), 113–65.

[13] The question of whether the books of Jonah and Job are historical does not affect their message that God cares for all the peoples of the world.

Promise to Glorify the Name of Abraham

The promise to glorify Abraham's name was specific to Abraham himself. It was fulfilled through the good reputation and fame he has enjoyed through the centuries. He has a prominent place in the Jewish, Christian, and Islamic traditions and is known as the father of believers and the friend of God.

Promise to Bless Those Who Bless Abraham and Curse Those Who Curse Him

One of the words translated "curse" is derived from a Hebrew verb that can mean "reduce." It refers to being humiliated and despised. Thus, anyone who does not appreciate Abraham and the depth of his faith and obedience to God will not enjoy the benefits of God's pleasure, and whoever honors Abraham and considers him an example of faith and obedience will enjoy them.

Promise of Blessing to the Nations

It is important to see this promise of blessing to the nations in its context in the book of Genesis.[14] The first eleven chapters of that book deal with the creation of the world and its inhabitants and the emergence of human sin, which led to God sending the flood. After the flood, the peoples of the earth continue to sin and face a dismal future, especially after the incident at the tower of Babel. By the time readers reach the time of Abraham, they are wondering about the future of all the peoples who have been mentioned so far. Has God stopped dealing with the nations? What is the next phase of God's plan to save them? It is in that context that we hear the promise that the nations will be blessed through Abraham. Though God has chosen Abraham and his descendants, he still has a deep interest in other nations. His promise to bless them reveals that his purpose in choosing and calling Abraham was universal in its scope, and was directed to all humanity.[15] The promise of blessing the nations is repeated when God confirms his covenant with Abraham with Isaac, Abraham's son (Gen 26:2–5).

No doubt, the people of Israel interpreted God's choosing of them in narrow ethnic terms, which was contrary to God's purpose. They believed that being chosen meant they were better than the other peoples of the earth, and accepted God's choice as giving them privilege rather than responsibility. However, God had clearly stated the purpose of his choice and the importance of the responsibility that accompanied it (Deut 7:6–8; see also Exod 19:4–6; Deut 10:14, 15). As Dr. Salim Sahyouni, Chairman of the Council of the National Evangelical Synod of Syria and Lebanon, said: [16]

---

[14] The Hebrew wording here is somewhat complex and requires much technical study. However, the essential meaning of the promise does not change: the Gentiles will receive God's blessing and Abraham and his descendants will be the means of conveying this blessing to all the nations of the earth.

[15] Farid Khuri, "The Old Testament and Its God and the New Testament and Its God" (Damascus: Christian Alliance National Evangelical Church, n.d.), 7–9.

[16] Chairman's address at the 67th Annual Meeting of the National Evangelical Synod of Syria and Lebanon, Friday July 7, 2006, Rabia, Lebanon, p. 2.

The covenant is a privilege God grants to the people of God. Yet, a privilege is always accompanied by a responsibility. We cannot separate the privilege from the responsibility and continue to enjoy God's presence in our midst and experience his blessings and goodness. The Lord told this to the Old Testament community through Isaiah:

> "If you are willing and obedient,
>   you will eat the good things of the land;
> but if you resist and rebel,
>   you will be devoured by the sword.
>   For the mouth of the Lord has spoken." (Isa 1:19–20)

The Old Testament contains many references to God's concern for the nations and his desire that his chosen people be a means of guiding other peoples to him.[17] Thus slaves were able to join the covenant that God made with his people (Isa 56:3–7; see also Deut 23:1–7). And at the inauguration of the temple, Solomon, the son of David, prayed that God would accept the prayer of foreigners (1 Kgs 8:39–43).

Israel's mission in the past should not be compared to the mission of the Christian church, which is to "go into all the world and preach the gospel to all creation" (Mark 16:15). Israel was not told to go to neighboring peoples in the Near East and tell them about God and his attributes, his love, and his requirements. Israel's call was to live according to God's law so as to be a means of drawing the surrounding peoples to God. The prophet Zechariah enunciated this clearly in the postexilic period around the end of the sixth century BC:

> The inhabitants of one city will go to another and say, "Let us go at once to entreat the LORD and seek the LORD Almighty. I myself am going." And many peoples and powerful nations will come to Jerusalem to seek the LORD Almighty and to entreat him.
>
> This is what the LORD Almighty says: "In those days ten people from all languages and nations will take firm hold of one Jew by the hem of his robe and say, 'Let us go with you, because we have heard that God is with you.'" (Zech 8:21–23)

The apostle Paul interprets the promise of blessing to the nations as being fulfilled in Jesus Christ and says that this blessing is for everyone who believes in Christ (Gal 3:8, 9, 14). As for the apostle John, he views the promise from an eschatological perspective:

> After this I looked, and there before me was a great multitude that no one could count, from every nation, tribe, people and language, standing before the throne and before the Lamb. They were wearing white robes and were holding palm branches in their hands. (Rev 7:9)

---

[17] Walter C. Kaiser Jr., *Mission in the Old Testament: Israel as a Light to the Nations* (Grand Rapids: Baker, 2000).

The promise to bless the nations thus reveals that the loving God is interested in the salvation of all humanity, and that his choice of Abraham and his descendants was not for their sakes alone. At the heart of the promise was the intention that they would be the means of conveying God's blessing to all nations. The Old Testament is full of examples of their failure to do this.

Promise of royal descendants

Some scholars argue that the promise that kings would be among Abraham's descendants was a later addition to the covenant with Abraham to give legal status to kingship in Israel. However, I see no reason why this promise should not have been part of the original covenant. Old Testament scholars sometimes reject such things on the same basis that they reject any miraculous elements such as prophecies and their fulfillment. For them, the Old Testament is just a human record.

This promise was made for the first time in Genesis 17:6. Abraham must have been astonished by it, just as he was astonished by the promise of a great number of descendants, especially as he grew very old and remained childless. Yet God is faithful and just to fulfill all his promises. The books of Samuel, Kings, and Chronicles tell us about the rise of the monarchy in Israel, the reign of David, and the renewal of the covenant with Abraham. We will look into this in more detail when discussing the covenant with David.

Covenant at Sinai

This covenant at Sinai is sometimes referred to as the covenant with Moses, the main character associated with it.[18] In proclaiming this covenant, God made it clear that it was not a completely new covenant but a continuance, extension, and confirmation of the covenant with Abraham (Exod 6:2–8; see also Deut 29:12, 13; Exod 2:24; 3:15–16).[19]

Covenant with David

The covenant with David is mentioned in 2 Samuel 7:8–16[20] and is summarized by the writer of Psalm 89:3–4, which quotes God as saying:

> I have made a covenant with my chosen one,
>> I have sworn to David my servant,
> "I will establish your line forever
>> and make your throne firm through all generations."

---

[18] Although all the other covenants are identified by the names of the individuals with whom they were made (e.g., Noah, Abraham, David), I prefer to name the covenant at Sinai for the place where it was given, since it was not so much a covenant with Moses as a covenant with the whole nation.

[19] For a comparison of the Sinai covenant with the other covenants, see works such as O. P. Robertson, *The Christ of the Covenants* (Phillipsburg, NJ: P&R, 1980), 186–99.

[20] The word "covenant" is not used in 2 Samuel 7, but elsewhere in the Old Testament God's promise to David is referred to as a covenant. For a detailed study of this, see D. G. Firth, "Speech Acts and Covenant in 2 Samuel 1–17," in *The God of Covenant: Biblical, Theological and Contemporary Perspectives*, ed. J. A. Grant and A. I. Wilson (Leicester: IVP, 2005), 79–99.

This covenant is similar to those associated with royal gifts, in which a king offered privileges to a loyal subject.[21] Such gift covenants were common in the ancient Near East. There are five main elements to the covenant with David:[22]

- A promise of royal descendants
- A promise of security through God being the Father of all David's royal descendants
- David's concern for the worship of God, even though his son Solomon would be the one to build the temple
- God's choice of the city of Jerusalem as the place with which his name would be associated
- A promise of the continuity, consistency, and eternity of the covenant.

Just as the covenant at Sinai was related to the covenant with Abraham that preceded it, so the covenant with David was related to the covenant at Sinai. Both include explicit references to the exodus from Egypt. In addition, they are similar in referring to (1) God giving the people the land, (2) God's presence with his people, giving them security and safety, and (3) God's concern to provide the necessary leadership for the people. At the same time, the covenant with David is different from the covenant at Sinai in that it includes a promise of royal descendants.

Reading the history of Israel prompts us to ask how the covenant with David was fulfilled, for there was no monarchy in Israel during the exile that lasted from 587 to 515 BC or in the postexilic period. The only way in which this covenant can be said to have been fulfilled is in the context of the New Testament, where Jesus Christ is presented as the son of David according to the flesh (Rom 1:3) and as the anointed King in whom the covenant with David is fully and completely fulfilled. When giving Jesus' genealogy, Matthew thus stresses that Christ is from the line of Judah (Gen 49:8–12) and a descendant of King David (Isa 11:1).

Though the kings of Israel generally failed to uphold the covenant relationship with God and act according to the standards of the law of Moses, the covenant with David did not lapse and God did not retreat from it; it was fulfilled in a more perfect and glorious way in Jesus Christ.

The New Covenant

In discussing the new covenant here, we are not referring to the New Testament but to the new covenant spoken of in the Old Testament. Although the exact words "new covenant" are used only once in the Old Testament (Jer 31:31), there are also scattered

---

[21] H. N. Richardson, "The Last Words of David: Some Notes on II Samuel 23:1–7," *JBL* 90 (1971): 257–66.

[22] W. Van Germeren, *The Progress of Redemption: The Story of* *Salvation from Creation to New Jerusalem* (Grand Rapids: Zondervan, 1988), 231–39.

references to this new covenant or some of its elements in books like Isaiah (54:9–10; 59:21), Ezekiel (11:19, 20; 36:26–28; 37:12–14), Hosea (1:10–11; 2:14–23), and Malachi (3:17). The problem we face is to understand which elements of this covenant lead to it being called a "new covenant." In other words, what is new in this covenant?

The table below offers a comparison of the new covenant with the earlier covenants.

It is clear that the new covenant is not completely new; it is a renewed covenant. It is a continuation of the covenant with Noah and with Abraham and the covenant at Sinai,[23] with further development of the aspect of personal knowledge of God. Knowledge of God is necessary in order to respond to God's love; consequently, it is one of the important bases for an intimate relationship between God and an individual or community.

The Old Testament notes that this new covenant would not be fulfilled in the life of the people of Israel as a whole; it would be fulfilled only in the small group referred to as "the faithful remnant" (see Isa 10:22, 23; 11:11; 37:31; Hag 1:12, 14; Zech 8:11, 12).[24] While the prophet Isaiah announced the return of this faithful remnant from

COMMON ELEMENTS BETWEEN THE NEW COVENANT AND OTHER COVENANTS
The relationship between God and his people.
The perpetuity of the covenant (Jer 32:40; 50:5; Ezek 3:26).
The promise of peace and spiritual and temporal blessings (Ezek 34:25–31; Deut 28:1–14).
The possibility of the forgiveness of sins (Jer 31:34; Ezek 16:63; Exod 34:6–10; Num 14:17–20).
The universality of the covenant; namely, the possibility that other nations may enjoy the blessings of the covenant (Isa 55:3–5; 56:3–8; Deut 23:1, 3).
The spirituality of the covenant; namely, the possibility of its presence in an individual's heart and soul (Jer 31:33; Deut 11:18; 30:6, 14; 10:16).[25]

DIFFERENCES BETWEEN THE NEW COVENANT AND OTHER COVENANTS
The possibility of personal knowledge of God (Jer 31:34). In all the other covenants, mediators such as the patriarchs, prophets, and priests conveyed this knowledge.
A more intimate and closer relationship between God and his people.

[23] For more on the close relationship among these covenants, see C. J. H. Wright, "God's Mission Through God's People," in *The God of Covenant: Biblical, Theological and Contemporary Perspectives*, ed. J. A. Grant and A. L. Wilson (Leicester: IVP, 2005), 76–78.

[24] For a detailed study of the remnant, see G. F. Hasel, *The Remnant: The History and Theology of the Remnant Idea from Genesis to Isaiah* (Berrien Springs, MI: Andrews University Press, 1972);

B. Peckham, *History and Prophecy: The Development of Late Judean Literary Traditions* (New York: Doubleday, 1993).

[25] G. Gibbs emphasizes the importance of the role of the Holy Spirit in the New Testament. See G. Gibbs "What Is New about the New Covenant in Two Pauline Epistles" (ThM thesis, Dallas Theological Seminary, May 2001).

exile, Matthew links the return from exile and the incarnation of Christ to show that in Christ this remnant finds true hope (Matt 1:17).

The New Testament writers indicate that this new covenant was completely fulfilled by the incarnation, life, death, resurrection, and ascension of Jesus Christ.[26] That is a point I will return to after a brief paragraph on the concept of the covenant in the period between the two Testaments.

The writings of the intertestamental period reveal that the people were looking forward to a time in which the Holy Spirit would work effectively in human hearts (Jub. 1:21–25; 1 Macc 4:46; 14:41). No doubt this is one of the elements included in the new covenant to which Jeremiah referred. However, we also find that the members of the Qumran community believed that they were the community of the new, everlasting covenant. The term "covenant" occurs more than a hundred times in their writings.

The New Covenant in the New Testament

The term "new covenant" occurs at least six times in the New Testament (1 Cor 11:25; 2 Cor 3:6; Heb 8:8, 13; 9:15; 12:24) and is used by the Lord Jesus Christ himself:

> In the same way, after the supper he took the cup, saying, "This cup is the new covenant in my blood, which is poured out for you." (Luke 22:20)

The apostle Paul uses the same term when speaking about the tradition regarding the purpose of the Last Supper or Eucharist (1 Cor 11:23–25). Mark records that Jesus said, "This is my blood of the covenant, which is poured out for many" (Mark 14:24). Thus he establishes a link between this meal and the Passover event (see Exod 24:8; Heb 9:20). Matthew records Jesus as saying much the same thing, but adds the words "for the forgiveness of sins": "This is my blood of the covenant, which is poured out for many for the forgiveness of sins" (Matt 26:28), thus linking what was said with Jeremiah 31:34.[27]

Here I will not deal with all the deep meanings implicit in the Eucharist. What I want to focus on is the way this sacrament relates to the concept of peace. What Christ our Lord did at that Supper fulfilled the words of the prophet Ezekiel: "I the LORD have spoken. I will make a covenant of peace with them" (Ezek 34:24–25; see also Ezek 37:26; Isa 54:10). Christ made a covenant of peace with his people when he faced the cross, suffering, and death.

The Christian church from the second to the fourth century affirmed the close link between the Eucharist and peace. It emphasized the importance of preaching about brothers and sisters achieving peace among themselves in accordance with the

---

[26] In *The Covenant Never Revoked: Biblical Reflections on Christian-Jewish Dialogue* (New York: Paulist Press, 1991), N. Lohfink argues that this new covenant was fulfilled after the exile and did not start with the coming of Jesus Christ.

[27] Not all the Greek manuscripts include the word "new" in their renderings of Mark 14:24 and Matthew 26:28.

commandment of Christ (Matt 5:23, 24). The liturgy called on those who held a grudge against someone to correct their attitude and included a holy kiss of peace and worshipers exchanging the greeting, "May the peace of Christ be with you."[28]

The church in the Middle East and North Africa urgently needs to return to the concept of the covenant of peace and to apply it practically in daily affairs. We do this when we accept one another and work together to build our societies, even if we do not agree in all our beliefs. The covenant of peace is fulfilled when we do not promote division and fragmentation but instead seek to resolve conflicts, starting with our own personal and social relationships. It is very important to learn from history that war brings only tragedy and destruction and that there is no substitute for a just peace.

Our mission as Christians of the Middle East and North Africa is not only to stop violence and wars but also to make our world and environment a place in which peace settles. We need to grasp that the peace that Christ fulfilled by making a covenant of peace with his people was not restricted to our personal peace with God but goes beyond that to peace with our brothers and sisters, all human beings, and even peace with the whole creation.

In the writings of the apostle Paul we see the concept of the new covenant mentioned in Jeremiah 31:31–34 appearing in many forms. Just as the new covenant is written on the tablets of the heart, so the Spirit of God lives in the hearts of the believers (2 Cor 3:2–3). Paul contrasts this new covenant with the old covenant, the covenant at Sinai, that was written on stone tablets and insists that the new covenant is far superior to the old (2 Cor 3:3, 14–15). He describes himself and the believers working with him in the church at Corinth as "ministers of a new covenant" (2 Cor 3:6).

The new covenant is dealt with at more length in the letter to the Hebrews, where in chapter 8:8–12 the writer includes the longest Old Testament quotation found in the New Testament, namely Jeremiah 31:31–34. The table below shows how the writer to the Hebrews compares the two covenants in order to show that the new covenant is superior to the covenant made at Sinai:[29]

In the person of Jesus Christ and through his redemption, all the covenants of the Old Testament were fulfilled. The covenant with Abraham was fulfilled when Christ became the promised "descendant." Through Christ, the promise of the blessing of the nations has been fulfilled. He also fulfilled the covenant at Sinai by fully obeying the law of the Lord and his commandments. Finally, he also fulfilled the covenant with David, for Christ is the promised Messiah and the King who will reign forever.[30]

---

[28] W. M. Swartley, *Covenant of Peace: The Missing Peace in New Testament Theology and Ethics* (Grand Rapids: Eerdmans, 2006), 185–88.

[29] W. A. Elwell, ed., *Baker Encyclopedia of the Bible*, 2 vols. (Grand Rapids: Baker, 1988), 1:537–38.

[30] For new research on the messianic concept of Jesus Christ and his relationship with Israel, see N. T. Wright, *Jesus and the Victory of God* (Minneapolis: Fortress, 1996), 477–539.

CHARACTERISTICS OF THE NEW COVENANT	HEBREWS
Better priesthood, with no need to change high priests every time the incumbent dies since the Great Priest lives forever.	7:23–25
Better priesthood in terms of the system of sacrifices, for there is no need for the high priest to offer sacrifices for his and his people's sins.	7:27; 9:25–28; 10:12
A sufficient, perfect, and final sacrifice, in contrast to the animal sacrifices that are of limited effectiveness.	9:11–14; 10:1–10
Better promises.	8:6
Complete.	8:7; 13:20
A direct relationship with God.	9:6–9, 14
Guarantees and assurances.	7:20–22
The promise of the Holy Spirit in an individual and a community.	6:4

Conditional or Unconditional?

If the loving, almighty God is the stronger party and the initiator of the covenants with the weaker party, is it possible for him to invalidate his covenant and withdraw his promise? If he says that a covenant is everlasting, does this not indicate that it is fixed and permanent, and consequently unconditional?

Some think that the covenants with Noah, Abraham, and David were unconditional, but that the covenant at Sinai was conditional. Others regard the covenant with Abraham as the essential covenant and see all the other covenants as merely extensions and branches of this covenant. If this view is correct, it follows that since the covenant with Abraham is unconditional, all other covenants that sprang from it or are related to it are also unconditional.

It is now time to examine the evidence for ourselves. We begin by noting that we can clearly distinguish two kinds of covenants in the books of the Old Testament. First, there are covenants made solely on God's initiative, in which he did not set any requirements or conditions for the individuals or communities to meet. Examples of this type of covenant include the covenant with Noah (Gen 9:9) and the covenant with David (2 Sam 7; 23:5; Ps 89:3; see also Jer 33:20; Hos 2:18). Second, there are covenants God initiates in which he does set requirements or conditions for the individual or community to meet.[31] Examples of these covenants include the covenant with Abraham and the covenant at Sinai. However, this classification seems to complicate things, for how can the covenant with Abraham be both everlasting and conditional? What are

---

[31] Some Old Testament scholars call the first kind of covenants "promissory" and the second "obligatory" or "administrative."

the conditions in the covenant with Abraham? How can we consider the covenant with David everlasting? How can we interpret the perpetuity of the covenant with David?

At first glance, the covenant with Abraham appears to be linked to the condition of circumcision (Gen 17:9–14). However, careful reading of the passage and of the sequence of events in the history of Abraham and his descendants shows that failure to meet the condition of circumcision does not invalidate the covenant. Individuals and groups who were not circumcised were excluded from the covenant, yet the covenant persisted with the community as a whole.

We have to read Genesis 17 both in its immediate context and in the context of the whole of Genesis. Chapter 17 begins with God saying: "I am God Almighty; walk before me faithfully and be blameless. Then I will make my covenant between me and you and will greatly increase your numbers" (Gen 17:1–2). When God renewed his covenant with Abraham after he showed his obedience to God by offering his son as a sacrifice, God said to him, "and through your offspring all nations on earth will be blessed, because you have obeyed me" (Gen 22:18). Note the close relationship between Abraham's behavior and his obedience to the will of God and the establishment of the covenant and its continuity.

The relationship established between God and Abraham meant that God expected a practical response of obedience from Abraham and also from his descendants. As a natural result of God's initiation of the covenant and the obedient response of Abraham and his descendants, God fulfills what he had promised (Gen 18:19). When confirming the covenant with Isaac, the son of Abraham, God concludes with the words, "because Abraham obeyed me and did everything I required of him, keeping my commands, my decrees and my instructions" (Gen 26:5).

The conditional language is both clearer and more prevalent in the covenant at Sinai than it is in the covenant with Abraham:

> Then Moses went up to God, and the LORD called to him from the mountain and said, "This is what you are to say to the descendants of Jacob and what you are to tell the people of Israel: 'You yourselves have seen what I did to Egypt, and how I carried you on eagles' wings and brought you to myself. Now if you obey me fully and keep my covenant, then out of all nations you will be my treasured possession. Although the whole earth is mine, you will be for me a kingdom of priests and a holy nation.' These are the words you are to speak to the Israelites." (Exod 19:3–6)

In addition to this, one of the essential differences between the covenant with Abraham and the covenant at Sinai is that with the former there are no direct pledges from Abraham and his descendants to observe the covenant; whereas the latter includes promises from the people to accept this covenant and observe its stipulations (Exod 24:3–8). Also, the Sinai covenant, like the covenants/treaties of the ancient Near East, includes a list of the blessings for obedience (Deut 28:1–14) and curses for disobedience (Deut 28:15–68).

The Sinai covenant was confirmed, renewed, and accepted by the people on at least five separate occasions. Each time, the people pledged anew to observe the conditions of the covenant. The first time was on the plains of Moab before entering the land of Canaan (Deut 5:2–3; 8:18; 29:1). The second was in Shechem, where a covenant renewal ceremony was held after the people entered Canaan (Josh 24:24–27). The third time was in the days of King Jehoiada (2 Kgs 11:17). The fourth time was in the days of King Josiah, after the discovery of a version of the book of the law in the temple (2 Kgs 23:3). The last occasion was after the return from exile in the days of Nehemiah (Neh 8:1–12).

The covenant with David is characterized not only by the absence of conditional language but also by three other important points. First, there is the repetition of "forever" three times in four successive verses (2 Sam 7:13–16). Second, there use of a Hebrew word that refers to the perpetuity of the covenant, but which it is almost impossible to translate precisely into any other language, *khesed*.[32] In English Bibles it is translated "love" or "steadfast love" (ESV). It is used to refer to the constant, stable love of God shown to David and his royal descendants (2 Sam 14–16). The third point to note is that the perpetuity of this covenant is tied to the duration of the creation (Ps 89:28–36).

Although the covenant with David is an eternal one that God will never renege on, this does not mean that David and his royal descendants can do whatever they want. In fact, God repeatedly told David and other kings to walk in righteousness and justice and to defend the poor (see, for example, Ps 72). David and his successor kings would sin and God would punish every sin and evil; yet his grace and love (steadfast love) would continue unchanged.

The eternal nature of the covenant with David led some Old Testament prophets to refer to it when they wanted to encourage Israel (Isa 8:23–9:6; 11:1–9; Amos 9:11; Mic 5:2–5; Jer 1:24–27; 23:5–6; 30:8–9; 33:14–26). However, when they wanted to convey a message of judgment, they turned to the Sinai covenant.

It is also worth mentioning that the apostle Paul does not refer to the covenant with David in his writings but does refer to the covenant with Abraham and the covenant at Sinai. As the apostle to the Gentiles, he spoke positively of the covenant with Abraham since it referred to God's blessing extending to the nations and the Gentiles. He spoke somewhat more negatively of the covenant of Sinai, saying that those who clung to it were still under the slavery of the law (Gal 4:21–31).

---

[32] For a survey of the way this word is used in the Old Testament, see Appendix 2 in R. P. Nettelhorst, *Does God Have a Long Nose?*, self-published, November 2015, http://www.theology.edu/longnose.htm. See also N. Glueck, *Hesed in the Bible*, ed. E. L. Epstein, trans. A. Gottschalk (Cincinnati: Hebrew Union College, 1967/New York: Ktav, 1975); K. D. Sakenfeld, *The Meaning of Hesed in the Hebrew Bible: A New Inquiry* (Missoula: Scholars, 1978).

To conclude, when we speak about covenants, we tend to think of contracts, legal agreements, and transactions. But this approach warps the biblical concept of a covenant. So we will next turn our attention to the relation between the covenant and the law, and the effect this has on our relationships and our economic, social, and human life. For now, suffice it to say that the covenant in the Bible is not a transaction between a buyer and a seller; it is an expression of the intimate relationship that God desires to have with human beings, motivated by his grace, love, and compassion. Thus it is only natural that God desires a positive response, and that human beings should be pleased to respond positively to God's love and grace.

When we speak about God's "conditions" in his covenants with human beings, we have to understand this in a relational framework.[33] Our being in a right relationship with God leads automatically to a change in our behavior. The covenant expresses the new relationship with God and our acceptance of this relationship with gratitude for God's mercy and grace. The new behavior springs from this acceptance. Brueggemann put it like this: "We are invited to live in a faithful response to this faithful covenant partner."[34]

THE COVENANT AND THE LAW

We cannot speak about the covenant without also talking about the law,[35] for the law is directly related to the covenant since they complement each other. As Dr. Van Wijk-Bos says, "The covenant without torah [the Law] is meaningless and torah without covenant is hopeless."[36]

The Old Testament law has been compared to a compass, a mirror, and a thermometer.[37] A compass points us in the right direction when we lose our way, and so does the law. A mirror reveals the reality of our appearance to us and indicates what we need to change, and so does the law. A thermometer takes our temperature and in the same way our obedience to God's laws indicates the depth of our love and obedience to God.

In what follows I deal with the relationship between the covenant and the law, and how this affects our personal, social, and economic life.

Ancient Near Eastern Laws and Old Testament Law

When talking about the law in Israel, we must not ignore the fact that Israel was not the only group to have laws; laws were common in the ancient Near East. The most

---

[33] For a wider study of the concept of personal responsibility and the relationship emerging from the covenant, see O. P. Robertson, "Current Reformed Thinking on the Nature of the Divine Covenants," *WTJ* 40 (1977): 63–76.

[34] Brueggemann, *The Bible Makes Sense*, 6.

[35] The word "law" was used in this section to refer to the divine commandments in the Old Testament, though I restrict my comments after that to the Ten Commandments that form an essential part in the law of the Old Testament.

[36] J. W. H. Van Wijk-Bos, *Making Wise the Simple: The Torah in Christian Faith and Practice* (Grand Rapids: Eerdmans, 2005), 19.

[37] S. Briscoe, *The Ten Commandments* (Wheaton: Harold Shaw, 1993), xix–xx.

important of these ancient codes of laws that we know of were the Code of Hammurabi (eighteenth century BC), the Codex of Lipit-Ishtar (first half of the second millennium BC), the Code of Ur-Nammu (nineteenth century BC), and the Assyrian laws (fifteenth century BC).

The most important collections of laws in the Old Testament are the Covenant Code (Exod 21–23), the Holiness Code (Lev 19–26), and the Deuteronomic Code (Deut 12–26).

Comparison of the laws of the ancient Near East and the Old Testament law reveals many similarities. For example, except for a few details, there is great similarity between Exodus 21:28–32 and the regulations of the Code of Hammurabi 250–251 regarding what to do if a stray bull causes harm. What does this mean? Does it indicate that the Old Testament is simply the product of the civilizations and laws of the ancient Near East?

As was said when speaking of the resemblance between ancient Near Eastern covenants and Old Testament covenants, especially in the book of Deuteronomy, the Old Testament is the child of its cultural environment. In that environment, laws were widespread and obviously Israel shared many laws with the peoples of the area. At the same time, there are certain unique elements in Old Testament laws:

- *Their form.* Ancient Near Eastern laws were punitive and were formulated along the lines of "if you do X, your punishment will be Y." We see that formula in many Old Testament laws; however, what we also see but do not find elsewhere is something being forbidden without mention of a specific punishment, as in the Ten Commandments. This is significant, for it indicates that the Old Testament law did not only set out to establish legal limits and prescribe punishments. It also shows the positive side of the law and encourages right conduct. In other words, it sets out to do what educationalists call reinforcing positive behavior.
- *Their content.* The Old Testament laws reflect a concern for individual well-being and for social justice that is absent in other law codes. For example, the punishments prescribed under Assyrian law could include amputation. A man's lips could be cut off if he forced another man's wife to kiss him. However, the Old Testament law does not mention this type of punishment. Moreover, the Code of Hammurabi discriminates between social classes, punishing those from the lower classes more severely than members of the nobility who commit the same offense.[38]

---

[38] See G. E. Mendenhall, *Law and Covenant in Israel and the Ancient Near East* (Pittsburgh: The Biblical Colloquium, 1955); D. R. Henry, "A Comparison of the Mosaic Law and the Code of Hammurabi" (B.Div. thesis, Northwestern Theological Seminary, June 1957).

- *Their concerns.* Ancient Near Eastern laws were not concerned to promote community life; their sole goal was to protect the community. The Old Testament law, however, includes laws that are intended to bring people closer to each other and enhance their social participation (Exod 23:14–17). There are many such laws in the book of Deuteronomy.
- *Their source.* Hammurabi attributes his code to the sun god Shamash, but when we read it, it clearly comes from the king. The Old Testament law, however, is characterized by its direct attribution to the one God (Jehovah) who is the source of the law. The role of priests and prophets is restricted to teaching the law and encouraging the people to live by it.

The Ten Commandments

The Ten Commandments are found in many places in the Old Testament, the most important of which are Exodus 20:1–17; 34:10–28; and Deuteronomy 5:1–21.[39] The text reads as follows:

And God spoke all these words:

"I am the Lord your God, who brought you out of Egypt, out of the land of slavery. You shall have no other gods before me.

You shall not make for yourself an image in the form of anything in heaven above or on the earth beneath or in the waters below. You shall not bow down to them or worship them; for I, the Lord your God, am a jealous God, punishing the children for the sin of the parents to the third and fourth generation of those who hate me, but showing love to a thousand generations of those who love me and keep my commandments.

You shall not misuse the name of the Lord your God, for the Lord will not hold anyone guiltless who misuses his name.

Remember the Sabbath day by keeping it holy. Six days you shall labor and do all your work, but the seventh day is a sabbath to the Lord your God. On it you shall not do any work, neither you, nor your son or daughter, nor your male or female servant, nor your animals, nor any foreigner residing in your towns. For in six days the Lord made the heavens and the earth, the sea, and all that is in them, but he rested on the seventh day. Therefore the Lord blessed the Sabbath day and made it holy.

Honor your father and your mother, so that you may live long in the land the Lord your God is giving you.

---

[39] For contemporary studies on the Ten Commandments see, for example, W. P. Brown, ed., *The Ten Commandments: The Reciprocity of Faithfulness*, Library of Theological Ethics (Louisville: Westminster John Knox, 2004), 171–317; R. Shelly, *Written in Stone: Ethics for the Heart* (West Monroe: Howard, 1994).

You shall not murder.

You shall not commit adultery.

You shall not steal.

You shall not give false testimony against your neighbor.

You shall not covet your neighbor's house. You shall not covet your neighbor's wife, or his male or female servant, his ox or donkey, or anything that belongs to your neighbor." (Exod 20:1–17)

The Order and Number of the Ten Commandments

Some who study the Ten Commandments may be surprised to discover variations in their order and number. For example, the tenth commandment, which talks about coveting, is sometimes divided into two as in Deuteronomy 5:21, so that the ninth commandment is "You shall not covet your neighbor's wife," and the tenth commandment is "You shall not set your desire on your neighbor's house or land, his male or female servant, his ox or donkey, or anything that belongs to your neighbor." The following table shows how the Ten Commandments are ordered in the Jewish and Christian traditions.[40]

The Ten Commandments in the Context of the Covenant

The covenant precedes the commandments and provides the framework for interpreting them. Thus we must emphasize that God's grace precedes his commandments, rather than vice versa. In other words, after God had entered into a loving covenant with the people of Israel, and as a result of that covenant, he showed his love by saving them from slavery in Egypt. The commandments came after they had been freed and were not a requirement or a condition for being freed. Thus, keeping the commandments was not the reason Israel was delivered from the burden of slavery. Salvation and deliverance came by the grace of God.

This point is important for our own spiritual life. First, it means that experiencing the grace of God precedes the experience of obeying him. We often seem to believe that a sinner has to read the Bible and reform his life by repentance and good works before he can experience peace and joy. However, any such belief is contrary to the gospel, which states that God accepts sinners and welcomes them as they are. Salvation, peace, and joy are not achieved by our own efforts but by the love of God expressed in the life, death, resurrection, and ascension of Jesus Christ.

Second, correct understanding of the relation of the commandments to the covenant shapes the pattern of our lives. If we are to live in true obedience to God, we have to be

---

[40] Brown, ed., *The Ten Commandments*, 319; W. Harrelson, *The Ten Commandments and Human Rights* (Philadelphia: Fortress, 1980), 45–48.

VERSES	NUMBERING OF COMMANDMENTS IN JEWISH TRADITIONS	NUMBERING OF COMMANDMENTS IN REFORMED AND ORTHODOX TRADITIONS	NUMBERING OF COMMANDMENTS IN CATHOLIC, LUTHERAN AND EPISCOPALIAN TRADITIONS
Exod 20:2; Deut 5:6	First	Introduction to the commandments	First
Exod 20:3; Deut 5:7	Second	First	First
Exod 20:4–6; Deut 5:8–10	Second	Second	First
Exod 20:7; Deut 5:11	Third	Third	Second
Exod 20:8–11; Deut 5:12–15	Fourth	Fourth	Third
Exod 20:12; Deut 5:16	Fifth	Fifth	Fourth
Exod 20:13; Deut 5:17	Sixth	Sixth	Fifth
Exod 20:14; Deut 5:18	Seventh	Seventh	Sixth
Exod 20:15; Deut 5:19	Eighth	Eighth	Seventh
Exod 20:16; Deut 5:20	Ninth	Ninth	Eighth
Exod 20:17; Deut 5:21	Tenth	Tenth	Ninth and tenth

convinced that our obedience to him is a response to his grace and love, not an attempt to earn his grace and love (see Rom 5:8; Eph 2:4–10).

The Ten Commandments Reflect God's Character

The Old Testament law reflects the relationship between God's character and what he wants from an individual or a community. The introductory sentence to the Holiness Code in Leviticus 19–26 advises people to be sanctified and holy in both their religious and their community life: "Consecrate yourselves and be holy, because I am the LORD your God. Keep my decrees and follow them. I am the LORD, who makes you holy" (Lev 20:7–8).

God describes himself in the following terms:

The LORD your God is God of gods and Lord of lords, the great God, mighty and awesome, who shows no partiality and accepts no bribes. He defends the cause of the fatherless and the widow, and loves the foreigner residing among you, giving them food and clothing. (Deut 10:17–18)

In keeping with this, he commands human beings to "love those who are foreigners, for you yourselves were foreigners in Egypt" (Deut 10:19; see also 16:11, 14; 24:19–21; 27:19). The fact that the commandments reflect the character of God means that our obedience to these commandments helps form God's image in us.

The Ten Commandments Are a Gift of God

John Calvin preached and wrote beautifully about the Ten Commandments.[41] He divided the law into three parts: the moral law, the civil law, and the ritual law. He considered that the ritual law was ended by the coming of Christ, and that the civil law was related to a definite social, political, and economic system—except for some general principles that could be applied in any society. He regarded the Ten Commandments as part of the moral law, which is applicable in any time and place.

Adherents of classical Dispensationalism, which is widespread in conservative and fundamentalist evangelical circles, reject these divisions and argue that the Old Testament law still applies to ethnic Jews, but not to the New Testament church. F. G. Zaspel, for example, distinguishes between what he calls the law of God, the law of Moses, and the law of Christ, and argues that Christians are required to obey only the law of Christ.[42]

Some in Reformed evangelical circles also take an extreme position and advocate theonomy,[43] that is, they argue the need to continue to observe both the moral and civil laws.[44]

Calvin did not think that the purpose of the commandments was restricted to informing us of the will of God and its application; rather, he saw the commandments as God's gift to us and our acceptance of them as an expression of our gratitude to God. The commandments are a gift that helps us to grow morally and ethically.

Thinking of the commandments as a gift has two corollaries. First, it shows that the commandments are an expression of God's love for us, for the loving God has given

---

[41] See John Calvin, *Sermons on the Ten Commandments*, trans. B. W. Farley (Grand Rapids: Baker, 2000). See also his concept of how to interpret and apply them as set out in J. P. Burgess, "Reformed Explication of the Ten Commandments," in *The Ten Commandments: The Reciprocity of Faithfulness*, ed. William P. Brown (Louisville: Westminster John Knox, 2004), 78–99.

[42] F. G. Zaspel, "The Continuing Relevance of Divine Law," lecture, the Eastern Regional Evangelical Theological Society, 3 April 1992. For more on the relationship of the law to Christians in the new covenant from the perspective of classical Dispensationalism, see, for example, J. Barentsen, "The Law and Gospel Debate: A Contribution from a Structural Analysis of Romans and Galatians"

(ThM thesis, Grace Theological Seminary, May 1985); G. Gibbs "What is New about the New Covenant in Two Pauline Epistles" (S.T.M. thesis, Dallas Theological Seminary, May 2001).

[43] An English word of Greek origin meaning "the Law of God."

[44] G. L. Bahnsen, *Theonomy in Christian Ethics* (Nutley, NJ: Craig, 1977); W. S. Barker and W. R. Godfrey, eds., *Theonomy: A Reformed Critique* (Grand Rapids: Zondervan, 1990). See also the discussion of the Old Testament law and its application for Christians in W. G. Strickland, ed., *Five Views on Law and Gospel* (Grand Rapids: Zondervan, 1996); D. P. Fuller, *Gospel and Law: Contrast or Continuum? The Hermeneutics of Dispensationalism and Covenant Theology* (Grand Rapids: Eerdmans, 1980).

us this gift. God chose to be in a covenant with his people; he offered them the gift of the commandments as an inseparable part of this covenant.

Second, our obedience to the commandments must spring from our response to this loving and gracious God. This eliminates any idea of the commandments being burdensome. Marty Stevens brings out the link between the Ten Commandments and human responsibility by using two German words, *Gabe* and *Ausgabe*. The first means "present" or gift, and the prefix "*aus-*" means "from" or "out of." Our responsibility springs from or out of the gift!

Stevens undertook detailed research into the Ten Commandments in the Old Testament and in Jewish rabbinical writings. His conclusion was as follows:

> God has acted in all of history to create, redeem, empower, and command. The response? The obedience of trust, learned from ancestors in the faith through Scripture. Christians trust that the God who chose and rescued the particular historical community of Israel is the God seen and known in Jesus the Christ of Nazareth. This God bestows good gifts on the human community (Gabe) and commands the proper employment of those gifts for the benefit of all people (Ausgabe).[45]

The Ten Commandments Are a Source of Joy and Pleasure

We sometimes speak as if we believe that the commandments are unsettling and depressing and that those who obey them are miserable. But that reflects a very strange understanding of God's purpose in giving them. In reality, those who obey the commandments experience profound joy and pleasure and appreciate the value and importance of the commandments. The God who gave the commandments is the loving Creator who cares about our happiness.[46] Note, for example, the psalmist's attitude toward the commandments or the law:

> I rejoice in following your statutes
> > as one rejoices in great riches.
> I meditate on your precepts
> > and consider your ways.
> I delight in your decrees;
> > I will not neglect your word. (Ps 119:14–16; see also 119:35, 44–48, 97–105)

The Ten Commandments are an important way for believers and nonbelievers to express their gratitude to God, which is a cause of joy and gladness.[47] Our thankfulness

---

[45] M. Stevens, "The Obedience of Trust: Recovering the Law as Gift," in Brown, *The Ten Commandments*, 144–145.

[46] Playing with words, R. Mehl titled his book *The Ten(der) Commandments: Reflections on the Father's Love* (Sisters, OR: Multnomah, 1998). The title reinforces his point that the God who gave these commandments is loving and tender in his dealings with human beings.

[47] C. W. Christian, *Covenant and Commandment: A Study of the Ten Commandments in the Context of Grace* (Macon, GA: Smyth & Heelys, 2004), 60.

to God finds positive expression in our social relationships. Thus, it is quite clear that the person who does good to others enjoys happiness.

The Ten Commandments Are a Source of Freedom

We sometimes resent the commandments, feeling that they are curbing our freedom and imposing a heavy burden. We feel free and joyous when we find an opportunity to evade them. We are like the young men who enjoy running traffic lights and boast about doing so, as if they were heroes.

But the commandments are not arbitrary restrictions on our freedom; rather, they give us true freedom. Confronted by them, we discover that we are sinners, perishing without the grace and mercy of God. It is when the Holy Spirit convicts us of sin that we find the true freedom that Christ spoke of:

> To the Jews who had believed him, Jesus said, "If you hold to my teaching, you are really my disciples. Then you will know the truth, and the truth will set you free."
>
> They answered him, "We are Abraham's descendants and have never been slaves of anyone. How can you say that we shall be set free?"
>
> Jesus replied, "Very truly I tell you, everyone who sins is a slave to sin. Now a slave has no permanent place in the family, but a son belongs to it forever. So if the Son sets you free, you will be free indeed." (John 8:31–36)

Note the close relationship between abiding in Christ's words (his commandments) and experiencing freedom. The apostle James similarly links freedom and the law (Jas 2:8, 12–13).[48]

The Social Dimension of the Ten Commandments

I enjoy watching the opening ceremony of the FIFA World Cup and the match that follows. But imagine what soccer would be like if there were no rules and every team played just as they wished. The existence of rules enables the players to play seriously and fairly and the audience to enjoy the game. The same applies to God's commandments; they establish boundaries so that we can enjoy our life; they do not deprive us of our freedom, instead they fulfill it.

Although the Ten Commandments use a singular pronoun, they are not addressed only to individuals. The singular is appropriate because it forces each of us to take them seriously, as if they are directed to us personally, yet we cannot ignore the fact that each person's application of these commandments has a positive social dimension.

Reformed thought also believes that we should not look at the Ten Commandments

---

[48] For more information on the relationship between the law and freedom, see D. R. Turin, "The Place of Law in the Life of the Believer: A Reconstructionist Perspective" (paper presented at the Northwest Meeting of the Evangelical Theological Society, 18 March 1989); J. R. Caines, "Perfect Freedom: The New Testament Believer and the Old Testament Law" (D.Min. thesis; St. Louis Covenant Theological Seminary, 1987).

from a narrowly personal perspective but should extrapolate from the principles in them to expand their application to the church and to civil society as a whole. For example, the principle of obedience in the command to honor our parents can be applied to our relations with all ecclesiastic and civil authorities that conform to the will of God. Obeying them is an expression of our acknowledgment of God's authority.[49]

There is much talk these days about democracy and how to apply it in Arab communities. I do not claim that the Ten Commandments address all aspects of democratic life; however, I affirm that the Ten Commandments include the seeds of democratic principles which, if applied, could contribute to establishing the basis for democracy.[50]

Dr. Walter Harrelson, professor of Old Testament at Vanderbilt University, thinks that the United Nations' Universal Declaration of Human Rights includes sublime principles for preserving human rights. If we add to them the moral heritage found in the Ten Commandments, we are supporting human rights and presenting a contemporary formulation of the Ten Commandments:[51]

1. Do not have more than single absolute allegiance.
2. Do not give ultimate loyalty to any earthly reality.
3. Do not use the power of religion to harm others.
4. Do not treat with contempt the times set aside for rest.
5. Do not treat with contempt any member of one's family.
6. Do not do violence against fellow human beings.
7. Do not violate the commitment of sexual love.
8. Do not claim the life or goods of others.
9. Do not damage others through misuse of human speech.
10. Do not lust after the life or goods of others.

The Ten Commandments: Principles or Rules?

Do the Ten Commandments deal with specific cases only, or do they contain principles that can be applied in different circumstances? The answer may be found by looking at some academic studies which show that the Ten Commandments mentioned in the book of Exodus are explained and set out in more detail in the book of Deuteronomy:[52]

Looking at the Ten Commandments in the book of Deuteronomy confirms that the commandments contain principles that can be applied in multiple circumstances and various places.

---

[49] For other examples of extending the commandments in Reformed thought, see J. P. Burgess, "Reformed Explication of the Ten Commandments," in Brown, *The Ten Commandments*, 94, 97–98.

[50] L. Ska, "Biblical Law and the Origins of Democracy," in Brown, *The Ten Commandments*, 146–58; W. Harrelson, *Ten Commandments and Human Rights* (Philadelphia: Fortress, 1980).

[51] Harrelson, *Ten Commandments*, 192, 193.

[52] S. A. Kaufman, "The Structure of the Deuteronomic Law", *Maarav* 1 (1978–1979), 105–58; Walter Kaiser, Jr. *Toward Old Testament Ethics* (Grand Rapids: Zondervan, 1983), 127–37.

COMMANDMENT	CORRESPONDING PASSAGE IN DEUTERONOMY
First	Chapters 5–11
First and Second	12:1–31
Third	13:1–14:27
Fourth	14:28–16:17
Fifth	16:18–18:22
Sixth	19:1–22:8
Seventh	22:9–23:18
Eighth	23:19–24:7
Ninth	24:8–25:4
Tenth	25:5–16

Practical Applications of the Commandments Today

I want to conclude this section on the Ten Commandments by offering some practical principles we can draw from them. The Ten Commandments are still important even in our contemporary society,[53] since the principles they uphold affect all aspects of life, including our personal, family, technological, social, church, and national life. In an age where many people, even Christians, stray from spiritual and moral values, we need to understand the importance of the law of God and its application in our Arab lands if there is to be a better present and a more glorious future for us and for our children, communities, and countries.

THE COVENANT AND THE PALESTINIAN QUESTION

It is now time to discuss the relationship between the covenant and ownership of the land of Palestine.[54] Our understanding of this topic affects how we respond to one of the main political, social, and economic issues in the Arab world. The way we interpret God's covenant has a direct effect on the issue of the land of Palestine. Why? How does our theology of the covenant affect the political and social reality of the Middle East and North Africa?

---

[53] Habib Saad, *The Ten Commandments in Modern Time* (Cairo: Christian Nile Press, n.d.).

[54] See also the following sources that deal with Palestinian issues from an evangelical Christian perspective: C. Chapman, *Whose Promised Land? The Continuing Crisis over Israel and Palestine* (Grand Rapids: Baker, 2002); Riad Kassis, *The Land in the Bible* (Damascus: Alif Baa' al-Adeeb, 1990); Makram Naguib, *An Arab Interpretation of the Second Coming of Christ: Zionist Claims for the End Times* (Cairo: Dar Al Thaqafa, 2002); Ikram Lamei, *The Zionist Penetration of Christianity* (Cairo: Dar El Shorouk, 1991); Ikram Lamei, *Is There a Relationship Between the Conversion of the Jews and the Second Coming of Christ?* (Cairo: Dar Al Thaqafa, 1990); Zachariah Nasr Allah, *The Second Coming of Christ between the Zionisist Claims and the Religious Truths* (Cairo: Dar El Kalema, 2002); Manfred W. Kohl, "Towards a Theology of Land: A Christian Answer to the Israeli–Arab Conflict," in *The Land Cries Out: Theology of the Land in the Israeli—Palestinian Context*, ed. Salim J. Munayer and Lisa Loden (Eugene, OR: Cascade, 2011), 265–81.

THE COMMANDMENT	THE PRINCIPLES
I am the LORD your God, who brought you out of Egypt, out of the land of slavery. You shall have no other gods before me. (Exod 20:2–3)	Gratitude for the grace of God. Worship of the one Creator God. Consecration of our life to God.
You shall not make for yourself an image in the form of anything in heaven above or on the earth beneath or in the waters below. You shall not bow down to them or worship them; for I, the LORD your God, am a jealous God, punishing the children for the sin of the parents to the third and fourth generation of those who hate me, but showing love to a thousand generations of those who love me and keep my commandments. (Exod 20:4–6)	Believing in the glorious almighty God. Worshiping God in the right way. Believing in the unlimited God. Acknowledging that God cannot be modified as we wish.
You shall not misuse the name of the LORD your God, for the LORD will not hold anyone guiltless who misuses his name. (Exod 20:7)	Honoring God, his name, and values in all aspects of life. Avoiding swearing by God. Honoring the name of God. Refraining from practical and intellectual atheism.
Remember the Sabbath day by keeping it holy. Six days you shall labor and do all your work, but the seventh day is a sabbath to the LORD your God. On it you shall not do any work, neither you, nor your son or daughter, nor your male or female servant, nor your animals, nor any foreigner residing in your towns. For in six days the LORD made the heavens and the earth, the sea, and all that is in them, but he rested on the seventh day. Therefore the LORD blessed the Sabbath day and made it holy. (Exod 20:8–11)[55]	Believing in God the Creator. Trusting the gracious God. Taking rest for the renewal of life. Rest and worship are to go together. Behaving as if all we have is God's. Taking care of what God gives us.
Honor your father and your mother, so that you may live long in the land the LORD your God is giving you. (Exod 20:12)	Offering care and respect to parents. Respecting authorities. The priority of the family.

---

[55] For a valuable study of the commandment regarding the Sabbath from Jewish and Christian perspectives, see A. J. Heschel, "A Place in Time," in Brown, *The Ten Commandments*, 214–22; K. Greene-McCreight, "Restless Until We Rest in God: The Fourth Commandment as Test Case in Christian 'Plain Sense' Interpretation," in Brown, *The Ten Commandments*, 223–36.

THE COMMANDMENT cont.	THE PRINCIPLES cont.
You shall not murder. (Exod 20:13)	Saying No to revenge. Saying No to violence. Saying Yes to peace. Saying Yes to the human life. Saying Yes to protecting human beings.
You shall not commit adultery. (Exod 20:14)	Maintaining purity and fidelity. Caring for one's life partner. Using sex rightly. Preserving and protecting the family.
You shall not steal. (Exod 20:15)	Respecting the property of others. Caring for the needs of others. Saying No to kidnapping.[56]
You shall not give false testimony against your neighbor. (Exod 20:16)	Keeping good relationships with the neighborhood. Refraining from gossip. Honesty and faithfulness. Preserving justice. Keeping away from redundancy.
You shall not covet your neighbor's house. You shall not covet your neighbor's wife, or his male or female servant, his ox or donkey, or anything that belongs to your neighbor. (Exod 20:17)	Avoiding envy and greed. Caring for the property of others. Maintaining good social relationships with others. Treasuring contentment.

I will begin by looking at the concept of the land in the Old Testament, and comparing it with the same concept in the New Testament. I will refer to two main evangelical schools of thought that reflect two different theological systems.[57] They are the Reformed school (which can be traced back to the Protestant Reformation) and the Dispensationalist school (which divides the history of God's dealing with human beings into time periods or dispensations).[58] I will also discuss the views of the church fathers and contemporary theologians.

---

[56] Jewish traditions note that the meaning of the commandment "Do not steal" is "Do not kidnap"; i.e., do not kidnap a person, since coveting includes stealing and not just the thought of coveting. See D. J. Zucker, *The Torah: An Introduction for Christians and Jews* (New York: Paulist Press, 2005), 103.

[57] For a comprehensive review of these two traditions, see R. T. Mangum, "A Future for Israel in Covenant Theology: The Untold Story," lecture, the Evangelical Theological Society, Nashville, TN,

16 November 2000, 15–18 (see esp. 14n60).

[58] For further comparison of those two schools see works such as W. R. Willis and J. R. Master, eds., *Issues in Dispensationalism* (Chicago: Moody, 1994); C. Ryrie, *Dispensationalism* (Chicago: Moody, 1995); J. H. Gerstener, *Wrongly Dividing the Word of Truth: A Critique of Dispensationalism* (Brentwood: Wogemuth & Hyatt, 1991); K. A. Mathison, *Dispensationalism: Rightly Dividing the People of God?* (Phillipsburg: Presbyterian & Reformed, 1955).

The Land and the Covenant in the Old Testament

The land occupies a prominent place in the Old Testament.[59] Many Old Testament researchers consider it central to understanding the Old Testament as a whole.[60] As noted earlier, both the covenant with Abraham and the Sinai covenant include the promise of land. So we need to look at what the Old Testament has to say about this promise.

The Promise of the Land

God promised the land to the patriarch Abraham at the same time as promising that he would have a son in his old age (Gen 12; 13; 15; 17). The promise of land was repeated to Isaac (Gen 26:3) and Jacob (Gen 28:4, 13). Before his death in Egypt, Joseph reminded his brothers of it (Gen 50:24). After liberating the people from slavery in Egypt, Moses led them to the promised land, where they would remain until the Assyrian exile in 722 BC and the Babylonian exile in 587 BC.

The Land as the Gift of God

There was no way that the people of Israel could claim that the land was theirs or that they deserved to have it given to them. The Old Testament asserts that the land belongs to God: "To the LORD your God belong the heavens, even the highest heavens, the earth and everything in it." (Deut 10:14). The people of Israel had no inherent right to it: "the land must not be sold permanently, because the land is mine and you reside in my land as foreigners and strangers" (Lev 25:23). However, though the land belongs to God, in his love and grace he promised to give it to Abraham and his descendants. Yet this promise does not mean that there are no conditions attached to the enjoyment of this gift.

If you are puzzled about how a gift can come with conditions, an example may clarify things: Suppose that my wife and I were to give our daughter an expensive car as a present for her twentieth birthday. We would talk to her about it like this: "We bought you this car because we love you. Since we do not want you to be hurt, we advise you to drive carefully; if you don't, we will have to take it back." The car is our present to our daughter; the condition is for her safety. As long as she drives carefully, she can keep the car; however, if she does not do so, we will take the car away from her. Is this not similar to what God said to the people of Israel through Moses?

> After you have had children and grandchildren and have lived in the land a long time—if you then become corrupt and make any kind of idol, doing evil in the eyes of the LORD your God and arousing his anger, I call the heavens and the earth as witnesses against

---

[59] For a historical, academic study of the land of Palestine in Jewish, Christian, and Islamic thought, see M. Sharon, ed., *The Holy Land in History and Thought* (Leiden: Brill, 1988).

[60] See, for example, W. D. Davies, *The Gospel and the Land* (Berkeley: University of California Press, 1974); W. Brueggemann, *The Land* (Philadelphia: Fortress, 1977).

you this day that you will quickly perish from the land that you are crossing the Jordan to possess. You will not live there long but will certainly be destroyed. The LORD will scatter you among the peoples, and only a few of you will survive among the nations to which the LORD will drive you. (Deut 4:25–27)

The people's rebellion against God during their journey from Egypt delayed their arrival in the land. Only those who believed were allowed to enter the land (Num 14:28–30). Not even Moses was allowed to enter it, for he too had disobeyed God (Deut 4:21).

Calvin, the great reformer, noted that the covenant does not only put God under an obligation; it also imposes an obligation on human beings. Although the covenant is unconditional on God's part, it is conditional for human beings. If they do not observe the conditions of the covenant, they lose the blessings of the covenant.[61]

The Old Testament prophets, one after another, warned that Israel was doing evil and not practicing mercy, justice, and righteousness and that thus they would not continue to enjoy the blessing of the land (see, for example, Hos 4:1–3; 9:1–3; Zech 8–14). The result was the Assyrian exile in 722 BC and the Babylonian exile in 587 BC.

However, we have to realize that the message of the prophets was not only a message of condemnation but also one of hope. At the core of this hope were God's covenants that expressed his love and grace. Even if we were to take back the car from our daughter, this would not affect our love for her. In the same way, God can take the land back due to the rebellion of his people and their departure from his holy law; however, he will not abrogate his everlasting covenant. God is faithful to his covenants in spite of our faithlessness and disobedience. How great and deep is the grace of God!

Note that God's justice also extends to foreigners, for they too are able to share in the land. Ezekiel wrote,

You are to distribute this land among yourselves according to the tribes of Israel. You are to allot it as an inheritance for yourselves and for the foreigners residing among you and who have children. You are to consider them as native-born Israelites; along with you they are to be allotted an inheritance among the tribes of Israel. In whatever tribe a foreigner resides, there you are to give them their inheritance," declares the Sovereign LORD. (Ezek 47:21–23)

By God's grace and under the leadership of Ezra, Nehemiah, and Zerubbabel, the people of Israel were able to return to the land of Canaan. Yet, as before, this return had to be accompanied by the return of their minds, hearts, and wills to God. The people longed for rest and security after the tragedies of the exile. Did they get it? How?

---

[61] P. A. Lillback, *The Binding of God: Calvin's Role in the Development of Covenant Theology* (Grand Rapids: Baker, 2001), 169–75.

The Land and the Concept of Rest

When we speak about the land, we must not ignore the concept of rest that is associated with ownership of the land. Israel's ownership of the land was not the main aim per se; what was more important was the rest and security they would enjoy in the land. We can see this in Moses' words as he told the people what awaited them in the land,

> You will cross the Jordan and settle in the land the LORD your God is giving you as an inheritance, and he will give you rest from all your enemies around you so that you will live in safety. (Deut 12:10)

After their arrival in the land, we are told:

> So the LORD gave Israel all the land he had sworn to give their ancestors, and they took possession of it and settled there. The LORD gave them rest on every side, just as he had sworn to their ancestors. Not one of their enemies withstood them; the LORD gave all their enemies into their hands. (Josh 21:43–44)

As we study the history of Israel, we see that this expected rest was not enjoyed, as it should have been, even after the return from exile. We see this in the words of the returned exiles:

> See, we are slaves today, slaves in the land you gave our ancestors so they could eat its fruit and the other good things it produces. (Neh 9:36)

It may only have been during the Maccabean era (142–65 BC) that the people were able to enjoy some rest. Did God's promises of rest evaporate? Is there hope of enjoying this rest in the future? When will that happen?

The Land and the Covenant in the New Testament

Given the importance of the covenant in the Old Testament, it is strange that the New Testament is almost silent on this matter. I will first discuss what the books of the New Testament do say about this issue of the land, and then I will deal with the reason for this silence.

The Lord Jesus Christ referred to the land when he said: "Blessed are the meek, for they will inherit the earth" (Matt 5:5). He was quoting Psalm 37:11: "The meek will inherit the land and enjoy peace and prosperity." The writer of that psalm was referring to the meek among the people of Israel; however, Jesus Christ speaks about all who believe in him inheriting the kingdom of God.

Earlier I mentioned that the apostle Paul expanded the concept of Abraham's descendants to include all who believe in Jesus Christ. Here I want to look more closely at his words:

The promises were spoken to Abraham and to his seed. Scripture does not say "and to seeds," meaning many people, but "and to your seed," meaning one person, who is Christ." (Gal 3:16)

The verse Paul quotes comes from the same passage in Genesis as the promises related to the land (Gen 13:15; 17:8; 24:7). Paul repeatedly affirms that those who are in Christ are the heirs to the promises of Abraham (Gal 3:29). But what do they inherit? The apostle Paul answers that the heirs of the promises, who are also heirs of the land promised to Abraham and his descendants, will inherit not only the land but also the whole earth! He regards the promise to Abraham as being extended to all and as now embracing the whole world:

It was not through the law that Abraham and his offspring received the promise that he would be heir of the world, but through the righteousness that comes by faith. (Rom 4:13)

Paul and Peter use this concept of inheritance to signify that believers will inherit the kingdom of God, which is wider and more universal than any specific land in a specific geographical area (Acts 20:32; 1 Cor 9:6; Gal 5:21; 1 Pet 1:4).[62]

When the apostle Paul quotes the Old Testament commandment to obey parents ("Honor your father and your mother, so that you may live long in the land the LORD your God is giving you" [Exod 20:12]), he quotes it as follows:

"Honor your father and mother"—which is the first commandment with a promise—"so that it may go well with you and that you may enjoy long life on the earth." (Eph 6:2–3)

He does not mention the words, "in the land that the Lord God is giving you." By deleting them, he extends the promise in this commandment to the whole earth, and does not restrict its application to the land of Canaan, as in Deuteronomy. The promise of blessing related to the land that belonged to Israel in the past has now been applied to all the people of the world. Thus we see a broadening of the concept of the land in the New Testament.

We may ask why the New Testament does not have more to say about the land of Palestine. Some may think it is because the Old Testament is material and the New Testament is spiritual, thus implying that there is no continuity between the two Testaments.[63] There are two points I want to make in response to this: First, we cannot call the Old Testament "material" and the New Testament "spiritual"; both deal with material and spiritual matters. Second, there is continuity regarding the covenant and the land between the Old and the New Testaments. This continuity has to be understood along the lines mentioned above, both regarding the ongoing nature of the covenant

---

[62] C. Chapman, "God's Covenant—God's Land," in *The God of Covenant: Biblical, Theological and Contemporary Perspectives*, ed. J. A. Grant and A. I. Wilson (Leicester: IVP, 2005), 223.

[63] For more on Calvin's attitude to the constancy of the covenants and their close linkage, see Lillback, *The Binding of God*, 146–50.

and the extension of the concept of the land and its universality. I should stress that the concept of the expansion and universality of the land extends to include God's promise to all believers of a new material land in which righteousness dwells (2 Pet 3:13; Rev 21:1). The "old" Jerusalem that was the center of attention for Israel in the context of the old covenant becomes the "new" Jerusalem in the context of the new covenant (Heb 12:22; Rev 21:2). Its inhabitants are not necessarily physical descendants of Abraham but include all the peoples of the world (Rev 3:12; 21:24). They are the members of the church, the bride of Christ and the inhabitants of Jerusalem, the adorned bride (2 Cor 11:2; Rev 21:2, 9; 22:17).

The Covenant in Reformed Thinking

Reformed theology distinguishes between three kinds of covenants:[64]

- *The covenant of redemption* is an everlasting covenant among the persons of the Trinity by which God chose his people in the Son who is the mediator to bring them to salvation through the work of the Holy Spirit.
- *The covenant of creation or the covenant of works* is the covenant God made with Adam before the fall, by which Adam shares the moral attributes of God by obeying his commandments and acts as an analogy to God his creator.
- *The covenant of grace* is a covenant God made with fallen humanity because of his love and grace. The basis of this covenant is Jesus Christ's complete fulfillment of the covenant of works and his worthiness to justify sinners.

The various covenants mentioned in the Old Testament are simply facets of the one covenant of grace that pervades biblical history and embraces the one people of God in both the Old and New Testaments. Thus, the Christian church is an extension of the people of God in the Old Testament and inherits all the promises, either in a spiritual or material sense, or both.

The Covenant in Classical Dispensationalism

The theological perspective of classical Dispensationalism is as follows:[65]

---

[64] M. Horton, *God of Promise: Introducing Covenant Theology* (Grand Rapids: Baker, 2006), 77–110.

[65] The variant of classical Dispensationalism known as "progressive Dispensationalism" emerged in the early nineties and was restricted mainly to academic circles. It has not achieved broad recognition in churches. For a comparison of the concept of the covenant in those two schools of Dispensationalism, see T. T. Maalouf, "An Appraisal of the New Covenant in Progressive Dispensationalism" (ThM thesis; Dallas Theological Seminary, 1993). See also the following book, which deals with the three main issues on which they differ, namely the method of interpretation, fulfillment of the covenants, and the church and Israel: H. W. Bateman IV, *Three Central Issues in Contemporary Dispensationalism: A Comparison of Traditional and Progressive Views* (Grand Rapids: Kregel, 1999).

- The coming of Christ and his rejection by the Jewish people.
  Dispensationalists hold that God's "watch" has been stopped as regards
  his promises and dealings with the chosen people, and that the Christian
  church is a parenthetical phase. After the end of the age of the church,
  God's watch will restart and he will completely fulfill all the promises and
  covenants made to and with the Jewish people.
- All the covenants, including the promise of the land, will be fulfilled
  literally for the people of Israel—partially in the near future (the return of
  the Jews to the land of Palestine), and wholly in the unknown future (the
  period of the millennial kingdom after the second coming of Christ).

According to this school of thought, the covenants mentioned in the Old Testament,
including the new covenant spoken of by the Prophet Jeremiah, are special and exclusive
covenants for the Jewish people,[66] and there is no scope for applying them in a spiritual
form to the Christian church. Israel is Israel, and the church is the church, and there
is no mixing between them.[67] This is considered the essential disagreement between
classical Dispensationalism and Reformed theology.[68]

Colin Chapman summarizes how these theological ideas take shape in the reality
of the Middle East and North Africa:[69]

- On the basis of the promise to Abraham, the Jews have a divine right to
  the land of Palestine.
- The return of the Jews to Palestine that began in the nineteenth century is
  the fulfillment of prophecies.
- The rise of the state of Israel has special theological importance since it
  heralds the coming of Christ.
- Christians must both support and defend the state of Israel.

In brief, Reformed theology argues that the ancient promises to and covenants with
the people of Israel were fulfilled in Jesus Christ and the church he established. There
are no grounds for the Jewish people seeking fulfillment of those promises today. Thus,
the promise of the land of Palestine has to be interpreted either spiritually or in terms of
the new earth that believers will inherit after the second coming of Christ. By contrast,
Dispensationalism posits that the promises and covenants made to the people of Israel

---

[66] There is, of course, great difficulty in determining who
exactly is a Jew. See, for example, C. E. Hayes, *Gentile Impurities
and Jewish Identities: Intermarriage and Conversion from the Bible
to the Talmud* (Oxford: Oxford University Press, 2002).

[67] R. D. McCune, "The Church and the Abrahamic Covenant"
(ThM thesis, Grace Theological Seminary, May 1966); C. A.

Blaising and D. L. Bock, eds., *Dispensationalism, Israel, and the
Church: The Search for Definition* (Grand Rapids: Zondervan, 1992).

[68] R. Saucy, "The Crucial Issue Between Dispensational and
Non-Dispensational Systems," *CTR* 1 (1986): 150–56.

[69] Chapman, "God's Covenant—God's Land," 236.

in the past will be fulfilled literally for the people of Israel today and in the future. Thus Dispensationalists believe that the promise of the land of Palestine has begun to be fulfilled and will continue one way or another until the end of the world.[70]

Other Theological Views

Besides the Reformed and Dispensational options outlined above, there are other theological opinions that deal more broadly with the relationship between the covenant and the giving of land to Israel in the present and with the position of the Jewish people in the present and the future.

In some branches of the Reformed school, such as the Dutch Reformed school, the idea has emerged that since the church is the heir of the Old Testament covenants, God has completely rejected the Jews.[71]

Other theologians like Karl Barth and Markus Barth believe in the existence of one covenant of grace in the Old and the New Testaments and one chosen people. However, they define this chosen people as consisting of both the church and Israel. Israel resists this choice, whereas the church accepts it. In the Barths' opinion, the mission of the church is not to preach to Jewish people but to engage in loving dialogue with them. They believe, however, that even though the church offers loving dialogue, the Jews will not truly believe in Christ until after his second coming. According to them, the rise of the state of Israel in our time is an expression of God's faithfulness to his people.

A somewhat similar solution to the relationship between Christ and Israel is presented by John Gager, who frames it in terms of two parallel covenants. Gager believes that Christ is the fulfillment of God's promises for the Gentiles, but not for the Jews. Consequently, there is one way for the Gentiles and another way for the Jews.[72] However, some evangelical and Catholic theologians believe that there are two parallel covenants, one for the Jews and another for the Christian church.[73]

The German theologian Norbert Lohfink argues that we cannot speak about two separate or parallel covenants, but only about one covenant and a double way for salvation.[74] Bruce Ware concludes his research into Israel and the church and the two peoples of God by saying that ethnic Israel participates with the church in one new covenant; however, each remains separate in their identities as two different peoples of

---

[70] The main tenets of classical Dispensationalism include (1) a very literal system of interpretation; (2) belief that the Jews are the chosen people; (3) belief that the return of the Jews and their possession of the land of Palestine represents the fulfilment of the promise and the prophecies; (4) belief that Jerusalem is the everlasting capital of Israel; (5) expectation that the temple in Jerusalem will be rebuilt; (6) belief that the battle of Armageddon is imminent.

[71] This belief is called Replacement Theology or Supersessionism. It holds that the church completely replaced Israel in God's

plan and that there is now no relationship between God and Israel.

[72] Holwerda, *Jesus & Israel: One Covenant or Two* (Grand Rapids: Eerdmans, 1995), 10–26.

[73] See the proceedings of the theological conference about the attitude of the Apostle Paul toward Judaism in the fall of 1989: D. Migliore, ed., *The Church and Israel: Romans 9–11*, supplementary iss. 1, *Princeton Seminary Bulletin* (1990).

[74] N. Lohfink, *The Covenant Never Revoked*, 45–51.

God. He affirms that ethnic Israel will keep enjoying the elements of the political and geographical promise of God, and that they will be restored as a nation to the land of Palestine.[75]

It is worth mentioning that within Dispensationalism there are different opinions regarding the application of "the new covenant." Some believe that it applies to Israel alone; others say that there is a new covenant for the church and another for Israel. A third party says that there is one covenant now that will be manifested later. These different opinions are not linked to any particular era; they have been present ever since the rise of Dispensationalism.[76]

The apostle Paul was able to combine his belief that the covenants of the Old Testament were fulfilled in Jesus Christ and the church with his belief that the ethnic people of Israel are condemned for not receiving Christ (Rom 11:12, 25; 1 Thess 2:14–16) and that there is a spiritual present and future for them.[77] However, I cannot find any theological reason for the continuation of ethnic Israel as "the people of God" or any evidence of their receiving any promises related to a specific geographical land or any political advantages at the expense of the Palestinian people or any other people. The apostle Paul writes:

> I ask then: Did God reject his people? By no means! I am an Israelite myself, a descendant of Abraham, from the tribe of Benjamin. God did not reject his people, whom he foreknew . . . .
>
> As far as the gospel is concerned, they are enemies for your sake; but as far as election is concerned, they are loved on account of the patriarchs, for God's gifts and his call are irrevocable. Just as you who were at one time disobedient to God have now received mercy as a result of their disobedience, so they too have now become disobedient in order that they too may now receive mercy as a result of God's mercy to you. For God has bound everyone over to disobedience so that he may have mercy on them all.
>
> Oh, the depth of the riches of the wisdom and knowledge of God!
>> How unsearchable his judgments,
>> and his paths beyond tracing out!"
> "Who has known the mind of the Lord?
>> Or who has been his counselor?" (Rom 11:1–2, 28–34)

In chapters 9–11 of his letter to the Romans, the apostle Paul deals with the issue of the unbelief of Israel and makes two main points. The first is that there is no room for ethnic superiority in the Christian faith (9:30–31; 11:18, 21, 25, 30–31). The second is

---

[75] B. A. Ware, "The New Covenant and the People(s) of God," in *Dispensationalism, Israel, and the Church: The Search for Definition*, ed. C. A. Blaising and D. L. Bock (Grand Rapids: Zondervan, 1992), 96–97.

[76] Bateman IV, *Three Central Issues*, 34.

[77] Chapman, "God's Covenant," 243–44; Holwerda, *Jesus & Israel*, 147–76.

that God's "rejection" of Israel is neither final (ch. 9), nor random (ch. 10), nor absolute (ch. 11). Here we have to distinguish between the choice of a nation for salvation and the choice of individuals within that nation for salvation. For this reason, the apostle Paul says,

> It is not as though God's word had failed. For not all who are descended from Israel are Israel. Nor because they are his descendants are they all Abraham's children. On the contrary, "It is through Isaac that your offspring will be reckoned." In other words, it is not the children by physical descent who are God's children, but it is the children of the promise who are regarded as Abraham's offspring. (Rom 9:6–8)

Paul insists that there is a distinction within ethnic Israel, and he thus uses the word "Israel" with two different meanings in Romans 9:6. On the one hand it refers to the physical descendants of Abraham and on the other it refers to the faithful remnant existing within the physical descendants of Abraham. Thus we have what can be described as "Israel as a nation" and "the chosen Israel within this nation."[78] To clarify this idea, Paul points out that although Ishmael was a physical descendant of Abraham (Gen 15:3; 16:15; 21:13), he was not among his spiritual descendants (Gen 17:19; 21:21), although Isaac was (Rom 9:7–9). In the same way, we can compare Jacob and Esau (Gen 25:23; Mal 1:2–4; Rom 9:10–13).[79]

The Old Testament contains many references to the people of God as an ethnic people (Exod 6:7; Deut 7:6) and to the "true Israel"—the people of God who are characterized by obedience and faith (Exod 19:6; Lev 26:3–12). The first group is characterized by physical circumcision; the second is characterized by spiritual circumcision (Deut 10:16; 30:6).[80]

The apostle Paul assures his readers that God has been faithful to his promises to and covenants with his ethnic people through his faithfulness to the faithful and godly remnant within the nation (Rom 9:26–29; 1 Kgs 19:17ff.). What the nation as a whole failed to achieve due to its lack of faith and its disobedience to God was fulfilled by this faithful remnant through faith accompanied by good works.

Yet the apostle Paul notes that God did not reject his people absolutely; the door of salvation is open to every Jew who believes in Christ our Lord. Faith is the way to become a member of this godly remnant. To clarify this idea, Paul uses the image of an olive tree (Rom 11:16–24). An olive tree has one root, and believing Jews and Gentiles are grafted onto that root by God's mercy. Thus Gentile believers cannot boast to Jewish believers about their status (Rom 11:18–22). Nonbelieving Jews can also be grafted onto this root when they believe in Jesus Christ (Rom 11:23).

---

[78] R. T. Beckwith, "The Unity and Diversity of God's Covenant," *TynBul* 38 (1987): 93–118; L. A. DeCaro, *Israel Today: Fulfillment of Prophecy?* (Philadelphia: P&R, 1974), 116–17.

[79] H. N. Ridderbos, *Paul: An Outline of his Theology* (Grand Rapids: Eerdmans, 1975), 343.

[80] B. K. Waltke, "A Response," in *Dispensationalism*, ed. Blaising and Bock, 349.

The apostle Paul speaks about the salvation of the Jews when he writes: "and in this way all Israel will be saved" (Rom 11:26a). This verse can be interpreted in many ways.[81] Proponents of Dispensationalism take it as referring exclusively to a wide-scale, unprecedented conversion of the Jews to Christianity in the end times. Most of them believe that the return of the Jews to the land of Palestine is preparation for this mass conversion. Though some followers of the Reformed school do not exclude the possibility of this conversion, they believe it is not necessarily to be on an unprecedented scale. However, they see no relationship between the return to the land of Palestine and the second coming of Christ.

I, on the other hand, would think that this verse does not describe a future state but a present reality. The Greek word translated "and in this way" or "and so" is an assertion that does not refer to the future but to the means or the way in which something happens.[82] In other words, what Paul is intending to say is that in this age both Jews and Gentiles are saved in the same way—by the grace of God through believing in Jesus Christ.[83]

Some would argue that the words, "the deliverer will come from Zion; he will turn godlessness away from Jacob" (Rom 11:26b) must refer to a future time, but that position is not necessarily correct. In this verse the apostle Paul is quoting Isaiah 59:20–21; 27:9 (cf. Rom 11:27 with Jer 31:34) to show that repentance is a necessity for enjoying the blessings of the covenant and that this can only be accomplished by receiving the Savior who comes from Zion, the city of King David.

In closing this brief discussion of Romans 9–11, I would like to stress the following two points: First, God has only one people in the Old and the New Testaments. This people has continuity based on the only way of salvation that God has declared. God does not distinguish between peoples or show favoritism for one ethnicity. All who believe in Christ and act righteously are acceptable to him and enter into a covenant with him. Second, there is a real possibility that the Jews will be converted to Christ, but this conversion is not related to a return to the land of Palestine. The visions based on end-time theories are just the dreams of some who enjoy cinematic thrills and excitement and prefer to escape to the future rather than confront present reality and fulfill the requirements of righteousness. Such people would do better to work in cinema production or to wake from their deep sleep and listen to the words of the Lord through the Prophet Amos:

> I hate, I despise your religious festivals;
>   your assemblies are a stench to me.

---

[81] Kassis, "Christian Zionism," 88, 119.

[82] C. E. B. Cranfield, *The Epistle to the Romans*, vol. 2 of *The Epistle to the Romans* (Edinburgh: T&T Clark, 1979), 576.

[83] A. Hoekema, *The Bible and the Future* (Grand Rapids: Eerdmans, 1974), 145.

> Even though you bring me burnt offerings and grain offerings,
> > I will not accept them.
> Though you bring choice fellowship offerings,
> > I will have no regard for them.
> Away with the noise of your songs!
> > I will not listen to the music of your harps.
> But let justice roll on like a river,
> > Righteousness like a never-failing stream! (Amos 5:21–24)

What Is the Solution to the Arab-Israeli Conflict?

The Arab-Israeli conflict over the land of Palestine (and the other occupied territories) is an issue that requires much study and analysis. I am not suggesting political theories and answers to this thorny problem. However, this chapter will not be complete without offering some help in understanding this conflict, if not in solving it.

First, I must again insist that the migration of ethnic Jews to the land of Palestine in the twentieth century did not fulfill the covenants of the Old Testament and that it has no theological value or significance. The theologian and Old Testament scholar Christopher Wright agrees: "Jewish Palestine is nowhere referred to with any theological significance in the New Testament."[84]

Of course, there are human considerations and historical and emotional relationships involved in this issue. But to restrict discussion of the land of Palestine to the Bible and to use this as a reason for its occupation is to involve the Bible in a contemporary political issue with which it has nothing to do. It is more appropriate to resolve this conflict peacefully on the basis of negotiations led by the international community (a tactic that is used elsewhere in the world but that is ignored when it comes to the issue of the land of Palestine). We cannot resolve this issue by quoting verses culled from various parts of the Old Testament to support the claims of Zionism.

Second, Christians in the Middle East and North Africa, especially evangelical Christians, must make a positive contribution to resolving this conflict in peaceful ways. Their contribution should include at least the following:

1. *Assisting Palestinians* who are economically, educationally, and socially disadvantaged through civil associations and churches, especially in the fields of health, education, and professional training.

2. *Affirming the importance of justice and respect for human rights.* According to Bishop George Khodr, Eastern Christians must be committed to "fight Zionism as an ethnic theory and practice. Zionism is not only contrary to human rights but also to equal human dignity . . . , but you are committed to God's justice and to the rights of

---

[84] C. J. H. Wright, *An Eye for an Eye: The Place of Old Testament Ethics Today* (Downers Grove, IL: InterVarsity, 1983), 92.

the Palestinian people. You, Eastern Christians, reject Zionism theologically and do not see it as rooted in the Old Testament."[85] Chawkat Moucarry stresses that justice must be accompanied by peace, since God is the God of both peace and justice. This means that the international community has to stop applying a double standard when it comes to enforcing the resolutions of international bodies. Moucarry shows that the United Nations resolutions were rapidly applied in the conflicts between Iraq and Kuwait, Indonesia and East Timor, and Serbia and Kosovo. However, it seems that Israel is the only state that ignores these resolutions and pays no penalty for flouting them.[86]

3. *Helping the Christian church to take a just stand on the Arab-Israeli conflict.* Informed readers may be astonished as they watch and read the mass media in many Western countries and see how many evangelical groups support and are allied to the state of Israel.[87] Sometimes those groups are referred to as "Zionist Christians," but I cannot bring myself to link the word "Christian" with the word "Zionist." Therefore, I prefer to refer to them as "groups supporting Zionism in the name of Christianity," which is what the Middle East Council of Churches calls them.[88]

During the Israeli aggression against Lebanon in the summer of 2006, I wrote several articles in English that were published online and in print.[89] Some of them were translated into French, Chinese, German, and Finnish. I received hundreds of positive responses; most of them expressing gratitude for hearing an Arab evangelical viewpoint regarding the reality of the Middle East that was not known to them. Others, most of them fundamentalist conservative evangelicals, were furious about what I had said and to my astonishment supported the continuation of the war against Lebanon.

Yet, to be fair, I must admit that there are many evangelicals—individuals, institutions, and churches—both in the United States and Europe who do understand the reality of the Middle East and North Africa and its issues, especially the Palestinian issue. Between 1971 and 1979, the statement known as the La Grange Declaration Against Christian Zionism was signed by five thousand American church leaders. The statement upheld the importance and necessity of considering human rights, justice, and

[85] Bishop George Khedr, "The Old Testament and Zionism," *An-Nahār* (Beirut), 11 April 1992.

[86] C. Moucarry, *The Prophet & the Messiah: An Arab Christian's Perspective on Islam and Christianity* (Downers Grove, IL: InterVarsity, 2001), 280.

[87] For a historical study of the emergence of these groups and their theological beliefs see, for example, Kassis, "Christian Zionism," 5–60.

[88] Nasr Allah Zachariah, *The Second Coming of Christ: Between Zionist Claims and Religious Truths* (Cairo: Dar Elkalema, 2003), 225–27.

[89] Riad Kassis, "The Sorrow of Survival," *EthicsDaily.com*, 21 August 2006, www.ethicsdaily.com/the-sorrow-of-survival-cms-7786; Kassis, "Hate Cannot Drive Out Hate," *EthicsDaily.com*, 17 August 2006, http://www.ethicsdaily.com/hate-cannot-drive-out-hate-cms-7775; Kassis, "Civilized Discrimination!," *Alsharq* (blog), 13 August 2006., http://www.alsharq.de/2006/mashreq/libanon/civilized-discrimination/; Kassis, "Turning Water into Blood," *EthicsDaily.com*, 5 August 2006, http://www.ethicsdaily.com/turning-water-into-blood-cms-7715; Kassis, "A 'Prayer' to Condoleezza Rice: After the Water Turns to Blood at Qana, How Long?," *Christianity Today* (online), 2 August 2006, http://www.christianitytoday.com/ct/2006/augustweb-only/131–32.0.html; Kassis, "The Silent Human Conscience: What Should I Tell My Daughter When Bombs Fall and the Great Nations Say Nothing?," *Christianity Today* (online), 24 July 2006. http://www.christianitytoday.com/ct/2006/130/12.0.html.

peace for the Arab Palestinian people.[90] In 1987, in a private interview Dr. John Stott, the famous evangelical writer and theologian said, "After considerable study, I have concluded that Zionism and especially Christian Zionism are biblically untenable."[91]

One of the older evangelical churches in the United States, the PC(USA) has taken practical, positive steps regarding Palestine and the Palestinian issue by calling on its members to boycott companies or investment agencies that work in Israel.[92] This was not the only church to take such a positive stand on the Palestinian issue. Other traditional evangelical churches in the United States that have openly supported peace and the rights of the Palestinian people include the Lutheran Church—Missouri Synod, the Reformed Church in America, the United Church of Christ, the Mennonite Church USA, the Evangelical Lutheran Church in America, the United Methodist Church, and the Episcopal Church. There are also a growing number of university professors, researchers, and evangelical theologians in the United States and Europe who support this trend through their writings and lectures. Their numbers include Ann E. Helmke, Arthur Preisinger, L. Michael Spath, Donald E. Wagner, Stephen Sizer, Colin Chapman, Bishop Kenneth Cragg, P. Walker, and Gary M. Burge.

Some Palestinian Christian thinkers have also written about their personal experiences and attitudes, calling for an end to the occupation and supporting peace.[93] Naim Ateek presents many important ideas and practical suggestions, based on his experience of the lived reality of Palestine. If applied, these ideas would contribute to solving the conflict and achieving a comprehensive peace based on justice and respect for human rights. Dr. Ateek is also the founder and president of the Saleel Center, which supports serious dialogue and aims at achieving a just and comprehensive resolution of the Palestinian issue.[94]

4. *Distinguishing between anti-Semitism and the concept of election and covenant.* Christians who reject the use of the Old Testament to support the occupation of land of Palestine do not have to go to the opposite extreme and embrace anti-Semitism. We must not confuse Judaism as a religion and the need of the Jews for salvation through Christ, as Christianity teaches, with Zionism with its expansionist ambitions, political greed, and immoral practices. We need to recognize that there is a vast difference between Judaism, a Semitic religion that is based on the Old Testament and other

---

[90] To review this statement, see wakeupfromyourslumber.com/the-la-grange-declaration-against-christian-zionism/

[91] D. E. Wagner, *Anxious for Armageddon: A Call to Partnership for Middle Eastern and Western Christians* (Scottdale: Herald, 1995), 80.

[92] See pcusa.org/worldwide/israelpalestine/resources.htm#sheets, the website of the Evangelical Presbyterian Church in the United States, which provides valuable resources. See also the following Internet sites for articles and studies of the Palestinian issue from a Christian perspective and information about civil organizations that work for achieving peace in the Middle East

and North Africa: http://www.sizers.org; http://www.paxchristiusa.org; http://www.paxchristi.net; http://www.fosna.org; and http//www.christianzionism.org.

[93] See, for example, Riah Abu El-Assal, *Caught in Between: The Story of an Arab Palestinian Christian Israeli* (London: SPCK, 1999); E. Chacour, *Blood Brothers* (Eastbourne: Kingsway, 1984); Audeh Rantisi, *Blessed Are the Peacemakers: The Story of a Palestinian Christian* (Guildford: Eagle, 1990).

[94] Naim Ateek, *Justice, and Only Justice: A Palestinian Theology of Liberation* (Maryknoll, NY: Orbis, 1999), 163–87.

Jewish writings, and Zionism, which is a racist, colonial ideology that uses religion to motivate its followers and achieve its political ends.[95]

It is worth noting that there are even some Jewish groups that firmly reject Zionism and its ideologies and practices. They include Neturei Karta,[96] Satmar, and Gush Shalom. There are also many Jewish thinkers and researchers who are critical of aggressive Zionist practices against the Palestinian people. Such people include Amos Benny Morris and Marc Ellis.

CONCLUSION

I wish to conclude by pointing to other benefits that come with understanding the concept of the covenant and applying what we know in our daily lives.

A correct understanding of God's covenant motivates us to live a life of righteousness, holiness, and godliness. When we realize that we are justified by the grace of God, which we do not deserve, and that God justifies us because of the covenant of grace he made with us, we will respond to this grace by living a life of obedience and holiness. Our goal is not to earn our justification, for we can never do that; rather we will long to walk in holiness. Here is where we come to understand the relation between justification and sanctification, for in practical experience we cannot separate the two. True believers who have experienced justification must continue to walk in the faith in order to remain sanctified. No believer who has experienced God's justification can claim that as long as they are in a covenant with God, they can live as they please. Those who enter into a covenant with God have to fulfill the conditions of the covenant in order to receive the blessings of the covenant.

God, who in his grace took the initiative to make a covenant with us, is the one who can enable us by his power, Spirit, and grace to continue in the life of sanctification in this covenant. Thus the apostle Paul can say that he is "confident of this, that he who began a good work in you will carry it on to completion until the day of Christ Jesus" (Phil 1: 6), and that "it is God who works in you to will and to act in order to fulfill his good purpose" (Phil 2:13).

Our grasp of the covenant is reflected in at least three aspects of our life with others. The first relates to the covenants that we make, whether covenants of friendship or business agreements. The second relates to the covenants that link us to the community of faith, the church. The third relates to married couples and the covenant of marriage. Our understanding and experience of the covenant with God motivates us to be committed to faithfulness and honesty in our covenants with others. This has a positive impact on our family, professional, social, and national lives.

---

[95] K. Cragg, *The Arab Christian: A History in the Middle East* (Louisville: Westminster John Knox, 1991), 243.

[96] For valuable information on this movement, see its official site www.nkusa.org.

Finally, the concept of the covenant gives believers assurance of the love of God and of the stability of this love. Such assurance yields an incomparable sense of security. When we have the conviction that God who enters into covenant with people is the same God who bestows life and whom we can trust, this gives our lives a purpose and a significance that makes life worth living. Our faith that God is both the maker of the promises and their preserver gives us hope and optimism for the future, in spite of all we see around us that prompts frustration and despair. The God who enters into a covenant with us is a loving God who intervenes in history for his people and who will also secure the end of history for their benefit. His covenant has not ended; it is constant until we experience fully and completely the new creation—the new heavens and the new earth.

The main purpose of the book of the Revelation was to encourage and comfort a community of faith that was enduring persecution and sufferings. It is striking that when the writer talks about hope, he refers to the covenant formula:

> Then I saw "a new heaven and a new earth", for the first heaven and the first earth had passed away, and there was no longer any sea. I saw the Holy City, the new Jerusalem, coming down out of heaven from God, prepared as a bride beautifully dressed for her husband. And I heard a loud voice from the throne saying, "Look! God's dwelling place is now among the people, and he will dwell with them. They will be his people, and God himself will be with them and be their God. 'He will wipe every tear from their eyes. There will be no more death' or mourning or crying or pain, for the old order of things has passed away."
>
> He who was seated on the throne said, "I am making everything new!" Then he said, "Write this down, for these words are trustworthy and true." (Rev 21:1–5)

How much we in the Middle East and North Africa, surrounded by suffering, oppression, and danger, need to cling to the promises of God that will be completely fulfilled and to wait in hope for the time when God will make everything new!

We may think that by entering into a covenant with God and being faithful in our commitment to him, we will be saved from grief and suffering. However, the truth is that through our covenant with God we will face grief and suffering, but will also be able to overcome them. After entering a covenant with God, Abraham suffered grief and pain when God asked him to offer his only son as a sacrifice, the son who was the son of the promise and the fulfillment of God's covenant with him. Eliezer Berkovits expresses the feelings Abraham must have had at that time by putting the following words on the lips of Abraham as he spoke to God:

> Almighty God! What you are asking of me is terrible. I do not understand you. You contradict yourself. But I have known you, my God. You have loved me and I love you. My God, You are breaking your word to me. What is one to think of you! Yet I trust you. I trust you.[97]

---

[97] E. Berkovits, *With God in Hell: Judaism in The Ghettos and Death Camps* (New York: Sanhedrin, 1979), 124.

Chapter Three

JESUS AND JUDAISM

HIS IDENTITY AND RELATIONSHIP TO JUDAISM

Ghassan Khalaf

Dr. Ghassan Khalaf was born in Kafr Shima, Lebanon. A former president of the Arab Baptist Theological Seminary in Lebanon, he has served several terms as President of the Convention of Baptist Evangelical Churches in Lebanon and has pastored the Hadath Baptist Church in Beirut. Dr. Khalaf holds a PhD from the Evangelical Theological Faculty in Leuven, Belgium, and has studied theology, Greek, and the Arabic translation of the Bible. He has authored several books including *A Greek–Arabic New Testament Concordance*, *Lebanon in the Bible*, *The Syntactic Meanings of the Adnominal Genitive in the Pauline Corpus*, *Jesus and Judaism*, and *The Art of Preaching*. He has also overseen the translation into Arabic of *The Lion Handbook to the Bible* and has served as translator and editor on several New Testament translation projects from Greek into Arabic. He was the chief Arabic translation editor for publications put out by the Middle East Council of Churches. His areas of specialization are New Testament, ethics, hermeneutics, and Greek.

PREFACE

TWO EVENTS RELATED to the Jews shook the world in the twentieth century. The first was the genocidal treatment of the Jews by the Nazis in Germany, which ended in 1945. The second was the displacement of the Palestinian people and the establishment of the state of Israel on their land by Zionists in 1948. The first event occurred in central Europe, whereas the second took place in the heart of the Arab Middle East. The first event generated great sympathy for the Jews in the West due to the oppression they endured. The second event generated overwhelming hatred of Zionists in Arab peoples, and sometimes a hatred of all Jews due to their oppression of the Palestinians. Those feelings of sympathy and hatred are still present today, and have been transferred in one way or another to Jesus Christ since he was of Jewish background.

Western Christians—because of their love for Jesus Christ and sympathy for the Jews—began to focus on and stress his Jewish background. There have been many expressions of regret about past failures to fully acknowledge his Jewishness. Meanwhile Judaism, which had long denied Jesus' Jewish identity, has begun to show growing openness to accepting him as a Jew and as a historical Jewish teacher.

Meanwhile, some Christians from the Arab Middle East—because of their love for Jesus Christ and hatred for the Jews—have rejected his Jewish background and instead seek to associate him with Canaanite-Phoenician or Syrian culture.

This study seeks to shed light on this disagreement about Jesus Christ and his relationship to Judaism, to consider the implications of these two views, and to put things in the right perspective. It also examines the ebb and flow of the relationship between Judaism and Christianity as regards Jesus Christ, and the effects of this relationship. In the face of the call to separate Jesus from his Jewish identity, this study affirms the validity of the biblical and historical evidence concerning his cultural and racial identity.

This study also includes a full treatment of the concept of the messianic Jesus, since his messianic status is based on the titles he used for himself or titles the church ascribed to him. From these titles, we can deduce his understanding of his identity, calling, and mission as the Savior of Israel and of the whole world.

We will examine the reasons Jesus of Nazareth often took a stand against the religious establishment of his age, represented by religious sects and the Jewish authorities. We will also consider why the Jews for their part rejected the teachings of Jesus and his claim to be the Christ, the Son of God, and the Son of Man.

This study seeks to shed more light on the nature of the relationship between Jesus and Moses, the church and the synagogue, Christianity and Judaism. There is still a gap in the minds of most Christians and non-Christians as regards the relationship between Israel and the church. Is the church a splinter sect of Judaism? Are the people of Israel part of the church? Do they form one people existing in continuity from the Old Testament to the New Testament, or is there no relationship between them? Are they two parallel peoples that do not meet? Will the rise of the Christian church, which Jesus began and the small group of Jews around him spread from Jerusalem to the ends of the earth, eventually make the Jews so jealous that most of them return to Christ? Did Jesus abrogate Israel to replace it with his church?

Amid ambiguity and confusion and questions that require gentle answers, I hope I have succeeded in putting up some signposts that may help us arrive at an objective and constructive attitude, "For we cannot do anything against the truth, but only for the truth" (2 Cor 13:8).

I do not know when the theological debate about Christianity and Judaism, specifically about the personality and messianic role of Jesus and the relationship between the church and Israel, will start in the Middle East. This debate has begun in the West, but it will not happen in the East without dialogue and tension. The aim of this chapter is to raise the awareness of Christians and encourage discussion, research, and a Christ-like response to these issues.

Ghassan Khalaf
Beit Mery, Lebanon
8 March 2007

PROGRESS IN ACKNOWLEDGING THE JEWISHNESS OF JESUS

The Jewishness of Jesus, or his ethnic connection to the Jewish people, is generally accepted. Nobody seriously questions it. Yet Christians have ignored his heritage, leading to tensions with Judaism that have persisted for generations. Meanwhile the Jews have denied Jesus' Jewishness. The Talmud questions his origins by suggesting that his father was a Gentile. But in the modern era both parties have moved toward greater acceptance of the Jewishness of Jesus. We will look to at least three of the reasons for this change.

Guilt about the Holocaust on the Part of Westerners and the Church

The Holocaust, that is, Hitler and his Nazi party's attempt to exterminate all Jews, marked a turning point for Western peoples and Christian churches in their attitudes toward Jews. Evidence of the Nazi's atrocities against defeated peoples, and especially against the Jewish people in Germany and in occupied countries in Europe such as Poland, Holland, and France, led to growing sympathy for the Jews throughout Europe and in America.

Among those blamed for what had happened was Martin Luther, the first Protestant Reformer. He had harshly criticized Jews and attributed every problem to them, thus contributing to the atmosphere of hatred for Jews among the German people that led to the rise of Nazi anti-Semitism.[1] Blame was also heaped on the Catholic Church, led by Pope Pius XII, for not having spoken out against the extermination, as it should have. Lutheran Protestants, the largest denomination in Germany, blamed themselves for not opposing Hitler and preventing his rise to power. They attributed this to the pacifistic political theology of Lutheranism. By contrast, Calvinism has an activist political theology, represented by the attitudes of the theologian Karl Barth.[2]

---

[1] James Carroll, *Constantine's Sword, the Church, and the Jews* (Boston: Mariner, 2001), 426–28.

[2] Helmut Thielicke, *Theological Ethics, II. Politics* (London: Adam and Charles Black, 1969), 565.

The change in attitude toward the Jews led to a new interest in the identity of Jesus as a Jew. Some European churches insisted on reasserting his Jewish identity, claiming that ignoring this had led to the growth of the anti-Semitism and hostility to the Jews that had resulted in the Holocaust in Nazi Germany.[3]

Ignorance of Jesus' Jewish origins had led to a complete separation of Jesus from his religious background. The general public considered Jesus a Christian, not a Jew. Perhaps the best evidence of this is something that was noted in the 1930s during Hitler's rule in Germany. Some shops selling pictures and statues of Jesus of Nazareth displayed a sign that read, "Entry forbidden to Jews." Neither those who put up such signs nor visitors to the shops realized that the one represented in those pictures was of Jewish origin. For Christians and Germans, Jesus' Jewish origins were beyond their imagining.[4] In reaction to the complete separation between Jesus "the Christian" and Jesus "the Jew," Karl Barth, the most famous theologian of that era, made his claim that "Jesus Christ would not be what he is were he not the Christ . . . who is the Jew Jesus."[5]

Growing Dialogue between Christians and Jews

The teaching of the apostle Paul in the early years of the spread of Christianity resulted in the church becoming independent of Judaism. Paul proclaimed the uselessness of circumcision (Gal 5:15) and taught that there was no need to observe the law of Moses to gain God's approval (Rom 3:20, 28). He maintained that the only way to be righteous before God was through faith in Jesus Christ and belief in general (Rom 1:17).

The gap between the church and the synagogue continued to widen after the destruction of Jerusalem by the Romans in AD 70 and reached a point of no return after the Romans stifled the revolt led by Bar Kokhba (a name that means "Son of the Star" in Aramaic) in AD 132. The Christians responded to these events by quoting the words of Hebrews 8:13: "By calling this covenant 'new,' he has made the first one obsolete; and what is obsolete and outdated will soon disappear." They also quoted Hebrews 13:10: "We have an altar from which those who minister at the tabernacle have no right to eat." The Jews, for their part, began to include curses directed at Christians in their liturgy. While Christians were not explicitly named, they were clearly the targets of the cursing of the heretics, which every Jew was expected to join in to prove their loyalty.[6]

The fall of Jerusalem and the failure of the Bar Kokhba revolt increased Christians' confidence in the truth of their message and its superiority to Judaism. Church patriarchs began to issue statements to the effect that the church and Christianity had

---

[3] Bernard Reitsma, "The Jewishness of Jesus: Relevant or Essential?" *NETR* 26 (2005): 60.

[4] Oskar Skarsaune, *In the Shadow of the Temple* (Downers Grove, IL: InterVarsity, 2002), 135.

[5] Karl Barth, *Dogmatics in Outline*, trans. G. T. Thomson (London: SCM, 1949), 72.

[6] Philip S. Alexander, "The Parting of the Ways: from the Perspective of Rabbinic Judaism," in *Jews and Christians: The Parting of the Ways*, ed. James D. G. Dunn (Grand Rapids: Eerdmans, 1999), 7–10.

replaced the synagogue and Judaism, as we can see in the Epistle of Barnabas and in the writings of Justin Martyr.

The rupture between Christianity and Judaism was complete. Thereafter, interaction between the two faiths fluctuated; sometimes relations were peaceful, at other times they were harsh and violent. Jews suffered much at the hands of Christians. For example, some endured evangelism by force and were compelled to be baptized. They suffered social pressure for being different and were the targets of religious fanatics because they were accused of having crucified Jesus. They were accused of poisoning wells, and every pandemic was attributed to them as if it were a blow struck by God because of their presence. Consequently, Jews were often massacred in various parts of Europe.[7] Most of the suffering they endured in the Middle Ages was at the hands of church tribunals.

Christians, on the other hand, endured far less suffering at the hands of the Jews, for the Jews were always a minority in Christian countries. The Jewish assault on Christians focused on refuting the evidence pointing to Jesus of Nazareth as the promised Messiah and on distorting his teachings and ethics. The most vicious harm the Jews did to Christians was when they pointed out weak points in Christian strongholds in Europe to Muslim attackers, enabling Muslims to capture these castles. Moreover, the Jews in Spain were part of a conspiracy to bring back the Arabs (Moors) to Spain after they had been driven out in the late fifteenth century.[8] Such events increased Christians' suspicion of Jews. Let us also not forget that during the wars between Turkey and Europe the Jews "taught the Turks the secret of the manufacture of gunpowder and cannon,"[9] another fact that increased hatred of the Jews in Europe.

The breach in the relationship between Christianity and Judaism in the religious arena continued throughout three centuries: from the seventeenth century to the nineteenth century. On the social level, relationships were hostile and distant and so Jewish migration to Islamic countries and to Eastern Europe increased. Wherever they stayed, the Jews lived in what were called "ghettos," depriving them of contact with the rest of the population. They were also prohibited from owning land.

Over time, relations began to improve, and gradually Jews came to be woven into the social fabric of Europe—particularly in England, France, Holland, Germany, and Italy—due to their financial and economic expertise, their craftsmanship, art, and scholarship, and through intermarriage. The same thing happened with the Jews who migrated to America, where they found the best environment in which to escape religious persecution.

Good intentions between the two religions began to appear around the middle of the nineteenth century. Christian churches, especially Protestant churches, began to

[7] Carroll, *Constantine's Sword*, 277.

[8] James Parkes, *The Conflict of the Church and Synagogue* (Philadelphia: Jewish Publication Society of America, 1961), 368.

[9] Solomon Grayzel, *A History of the Jews* (Philadelphia: Jewish Publication Society of America, 1968), 462.

send missionaries to the Jews in Europe and America in order to draw them to the Christian faith—this time by convincing them rather than by forcing them to convert, as had happened in the Middle Ages. These churches insisted that their evangelism was motivated by love of the Jewish people and the conviction that eschatological promises of salvation were made to the Jews, as explained by the apostle Paul in Romans 11. Missionaries from Anglican and Presbyterian churches came from England and America, and worked among the Jews settling in Jerusalem and Palestine in the mid-1800s. These two church groups, and others, also worked among the Jews in Europe and America.

Christians' attempts to evangelize the Jews were not well received by the Jews, who accused them of arrogance for considering Christianity superior to other religions. This reaction made the Protestant missionaries reconsider their methods of evangelizing Jews and become more sensitive in dealing with them. The result was meetings, dialogue, and exchanging of experiences between the two groups, which paved the way for more mutually positive attitudes.

As for the Jews, rabbis and teachers of the Jewish law began to study the New Testament and the teachings of Jesus and Paul more seriously. They undertook apologetic studies in order to preserve the Jewish tradition. One such apologist was Isaac Leeser from Philadelphia, USA, who wrote prolifically in the mid-nineteenth century. He and others like him hoped to preserve Judaism in America by strengthening the faith of the Jews in their tradition on the one hand and earning the respect of Christians on the other.[10]

Harris Weinstock, a liberal Jewish thinker, helped Jewish-Christian relations make great strides. In 1900 he challenged the Central Conference for American Rabbis to include a subject called "the life and teachings of Jesus" in the curricula of Jewish religious schools in America. Weinstock wanted to affirm that Jesus was a distinguished Jewish rabbi. He published a book entitled *Jesus the Jew* in which he shared his views regarding the complementary nature of the two religions—insisting that neither could have survived without the other. He claimed that by abolishing the ritual aspects of Judaism and affirming its ethical aspects, Paul spread the ethics of Judaism all over the world—something which the inward-looking Jews had failed to do. In his opinion, Christianity would not have arisen without Judaism, and the Jewish mission would not have spread to the whole world as quickly without Christianity.[11] Weinstock's views were like a pebble dropped in the stagnant lake of Jewish thought, causing ripples that are still expanding.

In 1930 the famous Jewish scientist Claude J. G. Montefiore published a book in which he compared the teachings of Jewish rabbis and the teaching in the gospels. He concluded that there is nothing in the teaching and sayings of Jesus that is not

---

[10] George L. Berlin, *Defending the Faith* (Albany: SUNY, 1989), 73.   [11] Ibid.

paralleled in rabbinic literature. However, he did note Jesus' incomparable ethical and humanitarian intensity and his total personal involvement with what he taught.[12]

Shortly afterwards, the world fell into the global struggle that became World War II, which lasted from 1939 until 1945. This protracted war held the world's attention and distracted it from intellectual and theological communication. Thus attempts at rapprochement between religions were frozen. But the war did not distract the Nazis, who, before and during the war, inflicted extreme persecution and perpetrated genocide against the Jews in Germany and in the countries occupied by Nazi Germany.

The first positive change in the attitude of the Christian church toward Judaism after the Second World War and the Holocaust took the form of an article produced by the World Council of Churches (including Orthodox and Protestant churches) at its first meeting in 1948. This document acknowledged the extermination of six million Jews and the church's failure to do its utmost to resist anti-Semitism. It also acknowledged that churches in the past had helped to foment hostility to the Jews, regarding them as the prime enemies of Jesus Christ.[13]

The most outstanding evidence of the new openness of Christianity to Judaism occurred as a result of the Second Vatican Council, which Pope John XXIII summoned in 1962. In 1965 this council issued a statement dealing with the relationship of the Catholic Church to Judaism.[14] It can be summarized as follows:

- The people of the New Covenant are linked to the offspring of Abraham by a shared spiritual bond and a common heritage and so should seek to foster mutual respect, together with theological study and fraternal dialogue.
- The church accepts that the Old Testament revelation came through the Jewish people.
- The olive branches representing the Gentiles draws sustenance from the well-cultivated olive tree into which they were grafted.
- The church remembers that Paul said that Christ was from the Jews according to the flesh, and that the apostles who were the pillars of the church were Jewish.
- The Jews are still dear to God because of the promises he made to the patriarchs, since God does not repent of his gifts.
- The crucifixion of Jesus by a few Jews cannot be laid to the charge of all the Jews in his day or in later ages until today. Moreover, we should not regard the Jews as being cursed by God.
- The church condemns all persecution of anyone by anyone and opposes all forms of anti-Semitism at any time and by anyone.

[12] Skarsaune, *In the Shadow of the Temple*, 139, 140.

[13] Frymer-Kensky et al., eds., *Christianity in Jewish Terms* (Boulder: Westview, 2000), 40.

[14] Pope Paul VI, *Nostra Aetate: Declaration on the Relation of the Church to Non-Christian Religions* (Vatican: The Holy See, 28 October 1965).

This statement marked a turning point in Christian–Jewish relations owing to the importance of the Catholic Church and its global status on the one hand and to the painful history between Catholics and the Jews on the other. Anyone who reviews the relationship between the two religions on the Internet will be surprised by the large number of statements coming from the Vatican and its circles after the statement of the Second Vatican Council, and also by the statements that followed from various Protestant churches that included the main points mentioned in the statement of the Second Vatican Council and supported its implications.

However, the positive atmosphere between Christianity and Judaism in these circles should not lead us to think that everything is going well between the people of these religions. Since the mid-1900s there has been a growing movement in America, Russia, and Israel encouraging Jews to accept Jesus Christ. The movement is called Jews for Jesus and its adherents are referred to as messianic Jews. To counter this movement and limit its reach, a rabbinic court in Massachusetts issued a decree in the early 1970s stating that any Jew who becomes a Christian is a traitor to their people and has no right to marry a Jewish woman, join a synagogue, or to be buried in a Jewish cemetery.[15]

Israel Shahak, a contemporary Jew living in Israel, describes the negative attitude Jews have toward Christians, an attitude that continues up to the present:

> Judaism is imbued with a very deep hatred towards Christianity, combined with ignorance about it. This attitude was clearly aggravated by the Christian persecutions of Jews; but it is largely independent of them . . . .
>
> [This] hatred and malicious slander against Jesus . . . is based on inaccurate and even slanderous reports in the Talmud and post-Talmudic literature—which is what Jews believed until the nineteenth century and many, especially in Israel, still believe . . . .
>
> The most popular accounts . . . are even worse, for . . . they accuse him of witchcraft. . . . The very name "Jesus" was for Jews a symbol of all that is abominable, and this popular tradition still persists. . . . The Gospels were equally detested, and they were not allowed to be quoted (let alone taught) even in modern Israeli Jewish schools . . . .
>
> For theological reasons, mostly rooted in ignorance, Christianity as a religion is classed by rabbinical teaching as idolatry. This is based on a crude interpretation of the Christian doctrines on the Trinity and the Incarnation. All the Christian emblems and pictorial representations are regarded as "idols"—even by those Jews who literally worship scrolls, stones, or personal belongings of "Holy Men."[16]

On the theological level, the most prominent result of the rapprochement between the two religions was the emergence of what is called "the third quest for the historical

---

[15] Ruth A. Tucker, *Not Ashamed: The Story of Jews for Jesus* (Multnomah: Sisters, 1999), 95.

[16] Israel Shahak, *Jewish Religion, Jewish History: The Weight of Three Thousand Years* (London: Pluto, 1997). Available online at whale.to/b/shahak_q.html.

Jesus," which focused on the importance of understanding Jesus through his Jewish background.[17] The positive Christian attitude embodied in this quest eventually drew a positive response from some Jews, as is evident in the publication of the book *Christianity in Jewish Terms,* which states that its aim is to promote better understanding between the two religions.[18]

Secular Philosophies That Affirm Human Equality

The French Revolution in 1789 deeply affected European thinking regarding democratic principles of government based on liberty, equality, and fraternity. Where the Catholic Church had failed to spread these principles, which are in line with the gospel, humanistic philosophers succeeded, and the result was faster human development in many fields.

The new calls for democracy and equality had a positive impact on the lives of Jews in Europe. Philosophical calls for the separation of church and state began to pervade European society, enabling Jews to enjoy more stability and become integrated in the environments in which they lived. However, the European community was not yet ready to accept revolutionary ideas related to democratic governance and the equality of all. European kings and the nobility were especially opposed to these ideas, which represented a threat to them and their hereditary position.

But belief in the equal rights and duties of all members of human communities, seeing all people as free and deserving of honor because of their shared humanity, and the rejection of discrimination on the basis of their skin color, race, and culture—all these new affirmations—pushed back the darkness that had hung over humanity for centuries. Nazi philosophy tried to turn back the clock by classifying human races vertically, with Arians at the top of the ladder of progress and Semitic peoples at the bottom. The result was suffering and tragedy. But European society and the American society that emerged from it cured themselves and corrected their path. The result was the firm establishment of democratic principles and the rejection of any form of monopoly power or absolute rule that leads to oppression and rule over people's consciences.

After the middle of the twentieth century it was no longer acceptable to categorize people in comparative ways, describing some as flawed, odd, inferior, or backward and others as superior or more progressive. Hostility to Semitic peoples and disparagement of other cultures shrank and was replaced by mutual respect among human ethnicities and religions, in spite of their differences. Liturgies no longer pronounced curses on those of other religions and accusations of blasphemy were no longer hurled.

In this atmosphere of relief from racial tension and growing amity, it became easier for both Christians and Jews to accept the Jewishness of Jesus and think of him as a

---

[17] Skarsaune, *In the Shadow of the Temple,* 138, 139.   [18] Frymer-Kensky et al., eds., *Christianity in Jewish Terms.*

Jew. Thus in Christian circles there was no longer resistance to talking about the Jewish background of Jesus, and Jewish thinkers were willing to accept Jesus of Nazareth as one of theirs.

ATTEMPTS TO SEPARATE JESUS FROM HIS JEWISH BACKGROUND

What has been said so far relates to the situation in the West. But while Europe had been the scene of conflict between Christians and Jews at both the religious and social levels for more than a thousand years, Eastern Christians and Jews in the Fertile Crescent and the Nile Valley lived under the rule of Islam. There were no tensions between them and the Jews were not persecuted by Christians, as happened in the Christian West. Rather, the relationship between Christians and Jews in the East was generally sympathetic, for both lived in the shadow of Islam, sometimes under fair rule and at other times subject to the fluctuating moods of despotic rulers.

As sympathy for the Jews began to rise in the West after the Holocaust, a new problem emerged in the heart of the Middle East—the establishment of the state of Israel in 1948 and the displacement of the Palestinian people. The Palestinian people are composed of both Muslims and Christians, and both tasted the anguish of displacement, loss of land and property, and denial of the possibility of returning home. Their suffering stirred up hatred of Jews in both Christians and Muslims, especially after the Israeli military takeover of Jerusalem with its Christian and Islamic holy sites in 1967.

Christians in the Fertile Crescent and in the Nile Valley sympathized with the rights of the Palestinian Muslims and Christians. They resisted the Jews' claims to own the land of Palestine on the basis of Old Testament texts. In public statements, Eastern Christianity has condemned all acts of injustice toward the Palestinian people by Israel. Moreover, it has stressed that any solution to the problem of the Middle East must be based on justice, since peace without justice is surrender. Of course, the churches and the countries in the region have also condemned the acts that can be classified as terrorism, such as explosions targeting civilians and the destructive bombing of villages, whether by Palestinians or Israelis.

In this context, one in which there is growing hatred of Jews, it is natural that the Jewishness of Jesus is regarded as a sensitive issue. Thus Arab Christian scholars largely ignore Jesus' Jewish origins and do not mention his cultural background. Sermons in Christian churches in the Middle East avoid any mention of the word "Israel" or the Jewish people, lest the hearers or Muslims listening through the media misunderstand what is being said. The reason for avoiding these terms is the fear of linking what is said about the children of Israel in the Old Testament—the last book of which dates back to the fourth century BC—with the Israeli reality on the ground in the twenty-first century. Although the "children of Israel" and "Israel" are mentioned forty-three times in the Qur'an, and the words "Jew" or "Jewish" occur nine times, the whole issue remains a sensitive one for Christians living in an Arab environment.

Patriotism and a desire to support the Palestinian people against the injustices inflicted upon them by Zionist occupation has led some Arab Christians to go too far, to the point where they reject anything remotely related to Judaism on either the humanitarian or the religious level. They do not distinguish between Judaism and Zionism, and so consider all Jews Zionists and reject the Old Testament, the Jewish Torah, as Zionist propaganda. They build a wall between the Old Testament and the New Testament. They forget, or try to forget, that all Eastern Christian churches consider the Old Testament a legacy that has been passed on to us because Jesus Christ replaced Judaism with his church when he completed and fulfilled in himself all the elements of Judaism as a nation, a system of worship, and a law. He transcended Judaism and taught the highest levels of spirituality and ethics, which have spread around the world.

While discussion of the Jewishness of Jesus flourished in the West, such talk was largely ignored by Christians in the Middle East. Some intellectuals and Christian clergy even reacted strongly against it, and began to claim that Jesus was of Lebanese or Syrian origin, stressing his Phoenician-Canaanite-Aramaic background. It was as if the Jewishness of Jesus was a defiling "leprosy" from which they wished to save him.

Muslims, however, tend to take the Jewishness of "Isa" or Jesus and his Jewish heritage for granted, as it is mentioned in the Qur'an.

It is now time to look at the most important attempts by thinkers, writers, and researchers to separate Jesus from his Jewish background.

Claim That Jesus Was of Syrian-Syriac-Aramean Origin

In 1941–1942 Antoun Saadeh, founder of the Syrian Social Nationalist Party, wrote a number of articles in response to the poet Rashid Salim ah-Khuri, "the village poet," who attacked both Christianity and Islam, claiming that they restricted social progress. These articles were later published in a book entitled *Islam in Its Two Missions: Christianity and Islam.* The articles set out to demonstrate the spiritual benefits found in these two religions, which, if applied, might contribute to progress. Saadeh did, however, urge the two religions to separate matters of religion from political matters.

In this book, Saadeh did not refer to Judaism negatively. In fact, he talked about all religions with respect, but he did separate Jesus from his Jewish origin. Although he did not elaborate on the subject, his brief statement is significant:

> Jesus was not Jewish and he had no "Jewish fathers." . . . Jesus was Syrian, who used to address people in Aramaic. He refused to be called "Son of David," as the Jews wished. In reply, he said: "How can they say that the Christ is David's son? For David himself says in the book of Psalms, 'The Lord said to my Lord, sit at my right hand, till I make

thy enemies a stool for thy feet.' David thus calls him Lord, so how is he his son?" (Luke 20:41). By saying this, Jesus rejected all attempts to regard him as a Jew related to David, in accordance with Jewish tradition. It is not right to say that the Messiah was a Jew. He is the son of the Syrian environment.[19]

Analysis of this quotation shows that Saadeh gives several reasons for separating Jesus from his Jewish origin:

- Christ's virgin birth and divine origin. The evidence for this is Saadeh's use of quotation marks around the words "Jewish fathers" in the quotation above. The gospels themselves affirm that Joseph was not Jesus' father, but merely his guardian and teacher. But what about Mary, Jesus' mother? Was she not a Jew?

- Jesus spoke Aramaic. Saadeh denies the Jewishness of Jesus on the basis that he spoke Aramaic, an Eastern Syriac language. But it is well-known that the Jews switched from speaking Hebrew to speaking Aramaic during their exile in Babylon. Babylonian conquests led to Aramaic becoming the common language of the entire Fertile Crescent, including Palestine, until it was displaced by the spread and dominance of Arabic. So it was natural for Jesus to speak in Aramaic, like everyone else in the region. Is it valid to call Jesus a Syrian and deny his Jewish origin just because he spoke a Syriac language? Would Saadeh consider everyone who speaks Arabic an Arab?

- Jesus' own words in his argument about the title "Son of David," when he said "David thus calls him Lord, so how is he his son?" Saadeh suggests that Jesus was refusing to do what the Jews wanted and identify himself as a descendant of David.[20] But was that what Jesus was doing in this exchange? Or was he trying to teach that his association with David transcends human genealogy because he is divine? It is possible that Jesus wanted to say that he is not just a son of David's line but is David's Lord, and that thus his message transcends the call for restoring the earthly kingdom of David since Christ's kingdom is heavenly and spiritual. Moreover, if Matthew and Luke had wanted to show Jesus denying his descent from David, why would they both trace his genealogy back to David at the start of their gospels (Matt 1:1, 6, 17; Luke 3:31)?

- As "the son of the Syrian environment," Jesus could not be a Jew. It seems that Saadeh wants to separate Jesus from his Jewish identity both by denying that he was from David's line and by asserting his cultural ties to Syria. Saadeh

---

[19] أنطون سعادة، الإسلام في رسالتيه: المسيحية والمحمدية؛ English translation [hereafter, ET]: Antoun Saadeh, *Islam in Its Two Missions: Christianity and Islam*, 3rd ed. (Beirut, 1958), 18–19. طبعة 3 (بيروت، 1958)، 18–19.

[20] Ibid., 113.

argues that "Syria was a highly civilized country with civil legislation. Then the Jews came and borrowed religious doctrines from the Syrians—the idea of a God who sees but is never seen, the omniscient Creator of heaven and earth—and they made him the source of legislation."[21]

- No one denies the effect of culture and geography on the content of the Jewish Torah and thus on Jewish thinking and culture. The environmental and cultural impact of the Canaanites, the Arameans, and the Sumerian-Akkadians on the Jewish people and their religion and culture is evident in the use of the name "El" (Heb. *'ēl*) for God, in the story of creation, in the story of Adam and Eve, in the story of the flood, in the law, and in the engineering structure of the temple. Echoes of Sumerian, Babylonian, and Ugaritic epics and the cults of Baal and Ashtoreth from the Phoenician city of Tyre are often noted in the Old Testament. Sometimes prophets and writers borrowed things from their environment that suited their faith, and at other times they condemned and banned things that contradicted their beliefs. There is no harm in the Jews borrowing from those around them and being affected by them. This is a natural effect of history and geographic proximity.

Saadeh interprets "Syria" as embracing the whole Fertile Crescent, including Iraq, Syria, Lebanon, Palestine, and Jordan. In that sense, were the Jews not also Syrian? How can he say that "the Jews came and borrowed religious doctrine from the Syrians"? Did the Jews come to this "Syria" from outside or were they already living there? No one questions the fact that Abraham, the forefather of the Jewish race, came from the city of Ur in southern Iraq, followed the Euphrates River to Haran north of Aleppo, then traveled down the Orontes River, passing the Bekaa Valley and Damascus, and then followed the Yarmouk River (the Jordan) to Beersheba in the Negev. This was the route followed by trade caravans and armies in ancient days. The Jews were inhabitants of this "greater Syria"; they migrated from one place to another within its geographical bounds and were influenced by their Syrian environment, except for a period of three centuries that they spent in Egypt.[22]

The Torah does not hesitate to admit that the Jewish patriarchs (Abraham, Isaac, and Jacob) came from nomadic Aramean tribes that traveled from one place to another in the Fertile Crescent. When Abraham wanted to find a wife for his son Isaac, he told his servant to "go to my country and my own relatives and get a wife for my son Isaac" (Gen 24:4). The servant then went to Mesopotamia (the land between the Tigris and

[21] Ibid., 65.
[22] 113 ,(1959 ،بيروت: دار الثقافة) فيليب حتي، لبنان في التاريخ; ET: Philip Hitti, *Lebanon in History* (Beirut: House of Culture, 1959), 113.

Euphrates Rivers) to the town of Nahor (24:10), where he found Rebekah, who was the "daughter of Bethuel the Aramean from Paddan-aram" (Gen 25:20). In Deuteronomy 26:5 the Jewish people are commanded to say, "My father was a wandering Aramean, and he went down into Egypt with a few people and lived there and became a great nation, powerful and numerous." The prophet Ezekiel rebuked the Jews for abandoning the worship of the Lord, and being idolatrous and worshipping Baal, like their neighbors. Thus he told them, "'Like mother, like daughter.' You are a true daughter of your mother. . . . Your mother was a Hittite and your father an Amorite" (Ezek 16:44–45). In the time of Abraham and for a thousand years after him the Amorite tribes were scattered throughout the lands of the Fertile Crescent, while the Hittite tribes were located to the west of them.[23]

Thus the obvious question is this: Why should we reject Jesus' Jewish origins and affirm his "Syrian" origin when the Jewish people were themselves an integral part of the "Syrian" peoples, among whom their ancestors lived? It is even possible to say that the Jewish patriarchs transcended their neighbors religiously, so that their spirituality was exalted, and great prophets arose among them, and from them came the Lord Jesus Christ.

Claim that Jesus' identity was Galilean-Phoenician-Lebanese

The prophet Isaiah wrote:

> In the past he humbled the land of Zebulun and the land of Naphtali, but in the future he will honor Galilee of the nations, by the Way of the Sea, beyond the Jordan—
>
> > The people walking in darkness
> >   have seen a great light
> > on those living in the land of deep darkness
> >   a light has dawned. (Isa 9:1–2)

These words were applied to Jesus who lived in Capernaum by the Sea of Galilee in the territory of Zebulun and Naphtali (Matt 4:12–17). Some people suggest that Jesus was deeply influenced by the intellectual and religious openness that characterized the people living in "Galilee of the nations" and rejected the closed-mindedness of the Jews in Jerusalem who were obsessed with their status as "the chosen people." The following are some of those presenting this view.

---

[23] See entries for "Amorite" and "Hittite" in various Bible dictionaries.

Philosopher Kamal Youssef al-Hajj

In 1974 Dr. Kamal Youssef al-Hajj, professor of philosophy at the Lebanese University in Beirut, published a 910-page book entitled *The Concise Philosophy of Lebanon*. In the chapter of this book that deals with Christ (pp. 163–197), al-Hajj does not deny Jesus' Jewish origins but says that he was influenced by the Phoenician culture he encountered on his frequent visits to Lebanon.[24] According to al-Hajj the Jews rejected Jesus for three ideological reasons: the mystery of the Trinity, the mystery of the incarnation, and the mystery of redemption. He says that the message of Jesus has no value if it does not fulfill these three goals or mysteries, and that the Jews strongly resisted it because it contradicted their intellectual biases.[25]

Kamal al-Hajj uses these three mysteries to link Jesus with Canaanite-Phoenician thought, claiming that these ideas were present there in mythological form. He argues that the Trinity was foreshadowed by the Phoenician trinity of El, Tammuz, and Olam, who were associated with the Phoenician city of Gebal. Similarly, a trinity appears at the beginning of the Enuma Elish in the form of Abzu, Tiamat, and Mummu.[26] The incarnation and the redemption are represented in the story of the Gebali deity Tammuz/Adonis, who was killed by a wild boar during a hunt in the Lebanese forests near Afqa, the source of the Abraham River. The goddess Ishtar/Venus mourned him and raised him from death.[27] Kamal al-Hajj argues that

> the Canaanite-Phoenician heritage included these three mysteries, even if in mythical form. A myth was then the only way to express man's nearness to heaven. . . . What we regard as myths, the Canaanite-Phoenicians regarded as representations of universal truth, which was transformed by the coming of Christ. We err when we underestimate myths. When studied carefully as understood by the Canaanite-Phoenicians, all the mysteries of Christianity—the Trinity, incarnation, and redemption—can be seen in those myths.[28]

Kamal al-Hajj was a committed Christian and does not deviate from the Christian doctrines of the Trinity, incarnation, and redemption. Here is what he says about the Trinity:

> All the works done by God were done through his perfect universal love. For God is love. He is one who loves and is loved; and he is the love that connects both. The one who loves is God the Father; the one loved is the Son, and love is the Holy Spirit. This is the mystery of the Trinity.[29]

[24] كمال يوسف الحاجّ, معالم الفكر الإنساني: موجز الفلسفة اللبنانيّة (بيروت: مطابع الكريم الحديثة, 1974), 195; ET: Kamāl Youssef al-Hajj, *Milestones of The Intellect of Mankind: An Outline of Lebanese Philosophy* (Beirut: Kreim Lebanon, 1974), 195.

[25] Ibid., 170.

[26] أنيس فريحة, ملاحم وأساطير من الأدب الساميّ (بيروت: دار النهار, 1967), 89; ET: Anis Freiha, *Epics and Legends of Semitic Literature* (Beirut: Dār an-Nahār, 1967), 89.

[27] الحاج, موجز الفلسفة اللبنانية (182), Op; ET: Al-Hajj, *Milestones of the Intellect of Mankind*.

[28] Ibid., 196.

[29] Ibid., 178.

On the topic of the incarnation and redemption, he says:

Who can do this supreme task? A mediator who is himself both the creator and a creature, a mediator who is both God and man . . . so that the recompense is infinite, thus offering the divine justice what is needed to atone for all our sins. . . . Here we are referring to two actions: a descending action by which the heavenly essence takes on an earthly representation, and an ascending action by which what is earthly transcends its earthly existence to take on some kind of divine essence. This is the mystery of the incarnation, which is at the core of the mystery of the Holy Trinity. This is sacred theology.[30]

Kamal al-Hajj argued that the mindset in southern Lebanon in the area of Tyre and Sidon was more accepting of the mysteries that Jesus Christ came to proclaim and fulfill because myths had paved the way for his coming. He finds lessons and principles in Jesus' meeting with a Canaanite woman in southern Lebanon. These lessons include the demolition of the walls between Jews and Canaanites and the love that has to prevail among all nations.[31]

Christian theologians have long attempted to interpret the Canaanite myths to which Kamal al-Hajj refers as intellectual preparation that God allowed so that in later times people would accept the theological truths and the work of redemption that was manifested in Jesus Christ and accomplished through him.

Historian Youssef Hourany

Youssef Hourany has studied the ancient intellectual history of the region located between the Mediterranean Sea, Egypt, the desert, Iran, and Turkey. In 1992 he published a book entitled *Lebanon in the Value of Its History (Phoenician Era)*. Chapter nine of this book deals with "the humanity of God and the divinity of man." In this chapter he sets out to show that El was the god worshiped in this region and that he had an organized priesthood to whom Abraham gave a tithe. He describes El as a high, gracious, and universal god whose throne was in Lebanon and who spent most of this time there. Hourany maintains that in the letter to the Hebrews the apostle Paul understood the status of Melchizedek, the priest of El, and thus associated him with the priesthood of Christ.

Comparing El and Yahweh (Heb. *yĕhwāh*), the God of the Hebrews, Hourany describes El as the universal God of the whole earth, whereas Yahweh is a national, domestic, local God. He asserts that there is a similar contrast between El and Baal in Canaanite theological thinking. He goes on to claim that endowing Baal with human attributes and titles that merge his powers with those of human powers is an essential element in Canaanite and Phoenician thought, expressing the closeness of divinity to humans and

---

[30] Ibid., 179.　　　　　　　　　[31] Ibid., 184–91.

humans' ambitions to divinity.[32] Hourany concludes by saying that "the god 'El' in his peace, balance and dignity, is not a super-god, but a model human . . . a human god."[33]

All that Hourany says in chapter 9 sets the scene for chapter 10, where he deals with what he refers to as Christianity prior to Christ. He sets out to show that the Christian idea of incarnation and redemption

> was nothing but the Canaanite and Phoenician idea of the hero, the divine human or the human god, . . . the great son of god who dies in order to renew life and rises from the dead and ascends to heaven so as to be the Baal of the new age.[34]

Hourany also argues that Canaanite thought could accommodate the unity of God in three persons since the two religious approaches are intellectually similar:

> This concept is by no means very distant from the realistic approach of the mind searching for the cause and the causative through the effects, which believes in a holy vital trinity that provides for the birth of a third being after the coupling of two previous beings.[35]

Hourany thinks that Jesus was raised in this type of theological atmosphere:

> The idea of overturning Jewish traditions and religious customs would not have brewed in his mind if he had not met with social philosophies and human traditions different from those he had known in the society of his childhood, for intellectual dialogue alone is what calls forth renewal. This intellectual dialogue would not be possible for Jesus in a land other than Lebanon, which was nearby and free from the power of Jewish beliefs. In Lebanon, there was a custom of sacrificing sons, and there, God was willing to have human sons, and people were willing to have divine human beings.[36]

Hourany concludes that Jesus and Christianity inherited the Phoenician civilization and generalized it to all humanity. He says:

> If we want to show accord between Christ and Lebanon, we will find that it started in the life of Jesus and spread with Christianity. It was from the ancient Lebanese civilization that Christianity inherited its universality and its mystery of redemption, its priesthood, hymns, customs, beatification of men, feasts, and relationships around the Mediterranean Sea.[37]

Youssef Hourany's intellectual attitudes do not go far beyond those of Kamal Youssef al-Hajj, but he broadens and rationalizes his ideas. In so doing, however, he

---

[32] يوسف الحوراني, لبنان في قيم تاريخه: العهد الفينيقي (بيروت, 206–7 ,(1972), دار المشرق; Youseff al-Hourany, *Lebanon in the Values of Its History: The Phoenician Era* (Beirut: Dār al-Machreq, 1972), 206–7.

[33] Ibid., 210.

[34] Ibid., 223.

[35] Ibid., 224.

[36] Ibid., 230.

[37] Ibid., 244.

exaggerates to such an extent that Christianity is stripped of all novelty and reduced to nothing more than a Canaanite myth in new clothes. He argues that the ideas of incarnation, redemption, and resurrection simply reflect Phoenician ideas that took root and flourished in Jesus and his early followers. In so doing, he blithely ignores the historical facts on which Christianity is based. Christianity without a historical reality is just an illusion. The statement that we repeat in the Nicene Creed, "He was crucified for us under Pontius Pilate," affirms the historicity of the Christian faith, which is foundational to it.

Father Botros Daw

Father Botros Daw is famous for his five-volume history of the Maronites, published under the title *The Religious, Political, and Cultural History of the Maronites*. In 1980 he published a sixth volume entitled *Lebanon in the Life of Christ*, in which he dealt with the relationship of Jesus to Lebanon.

Father Daw starts by talking about Galilee as a natural extension of the mountains of Lebanon, deriving its fertility from its relation to Lebanon.[38] He then refers to the settlement of Canaanite-Phoenicians in Galilee after Joshua entered the land of Palestine.[39] In the eighth century BC, the Jews were affected culturally and religiously by the Canaanites and intermarried with them. Thus Galilee was ethnically mixed, with a Jewish minority.[40] This situation continued until the days of the Maccabees and the time of Christ and explains Isaiah's reference to the region as "Galilee of the Gentiles."[41]

After stating that Phoenician-Lebanese influence extended to Jews in all parts of Palestine, Father Daw adds:

> Thus Christ grew up in an environment that was both Jewish and Lebanese. He was a Lebanese and a Jew at the same time; and his Lebanese identity was not less than his Jewish one, especially in its intellectual and cultural aspects. Therefore, Galilee is the cradle of Christianity. In Jewish and Lebanese Galilee, Christ grew up and worked as an adult, conducted most of his mission . . . and performed his miracles. From Galilee he chose his disciples, walked on the Sea of Galilee, and calmed its storms. The life of Galilee and Lebanon is reflected in the teachings of the Savior, his symbols, parables and style. . . .
>
> Christianity is radically related to Lebanon because of the person of its founder who lived in a Lebanese environment and because Phoenician beliefs prepared the minds and hearts of people intellectually and psychologically to accept Christianity, its beliefs, and its theology. . . . The books of the Old Testament that were bred in Lebanese culture

---

[38] الأب بطرس ضو, لبنان في حياة المسيح, تاريخ الموارنة الدينيّ والسياسيّ و الحضاريّ: الجزء 6 (لبنان: دار النهار الناشر, 1980), 77; ET: Father Botros Daw, *Lebanon in the Life of Christ*, vol. 6, *The Religious, Political, and Cultural History of the Maronites* (Lebanon: Dār an-Nahār an-Nāsher, 1980), 77.

[39] Ibid., 79.
[40] Ibid., 80–82.
[41] Ibid., 83.

were the introduction to the New Testament. Thus there is an eternal inextricable link between Lebanon, Christ, and Christianity.[42]

Father Daw, a historian, also argued that Christ was even baptized in Lebanese water, since the Hasbani River, the major tributary of the River Jordan, flows from Mount Hermon in Lebanon:

> Thus the bond between Christ and Lebanon was somehow consecrated when the waters of Lebanon in the River Jordan touched his divine body. One of the results of this bond between Christ and the Lebanese waters was that the heavens were opened to the sons of men and the Holy Spirit of God came upon him in bodily form like a dove, a dove of purity, meekness, love, and peace for humankind.[43]

Father Daw maintains that the first Lebanese to confess that Jesus was the Son of God and follow him was Nathanael, who came from Cana in Galilee (John 2:21).[44] He argues that Cana (Qana) was located near Tyre in South Lebanon, and was not the city by that name near Nazareth. He says that it was in Cana near Tyre that Jesus miraculously turned water into wine at a wedding (John 2).[45]

> In Qana, Lebanon, Christ showed his glory and divine power when he performed his first miracle, thus his disciples believed in him and he initiated his universal global message.[46]

Father Daw notes that Jesus spoke the Aramaic language, which he regards as the language of Lebanon, and that the Jews adopted Aramaic in Babylon during the exile and brought it back with them to Palestine.[47] He also asserts that Jesus was deeply affected by Phoenician-Lebanese culture—a point that is not supported either by the texts of the gospels or by Jesus' teaching.

Father Daw has much more to say about Christ and Lebanon, but what has been mentioned here should be enough to give a fair sample of his views and those of other Lebanese scholars.

Father Youssef Yammine

In 1999, Dr. Youssef Yammine, a Maronite priest, published a 732-page book entitled *Christ was Born in Lebanon and Not in Judea*. In the introduction to this book, he states:

> This study sets out to prove that Christ was born in Lebanon . . . that the incarnation took place in Lebanon. . . . Jesus Christ, his mother the Virgin Mary and his father Joseph

---

[42] Ibid., 85–86.
[43] Ibid., 116.
[44] Ibid., 139.
[45] For arguments refuting the claim that Cana of Galilee lies near (Tyre, see the item "Cana" pp. 176–82 in the reference: غسان خلف, لبنان

في الكتاب المقدس (بيروت: دار منهل الحياة, 1985 ;ET: Ghassan Khalaf, *Lebanon in the Bible* (Beirut: Source of Life Publishing House, 1985).
الأب بطرس ضو, لبنان في حياة المسيح (لبنان: الناشر المؤلف, 46,
156 ,(1980 ; ET: Daw, *Lebanon in the Life of Christ*.
[47] Ibid., 199–203.

the carpenter and all his relatives were not of Jewish descent and consequently were not from the line of David. . . . They were Lebanese from the Lebanese town of Qana.[48]

In another book, *Cana of Galilee in Lebanon*,[49] published in 1994, Father Yammine sets out to prove that the town of Qana in Southern Lebanon is the same as the Cana in Galilee mentioned in John 2:1–11, where Jesus and his mother Mary attended a wedding at which he turned water into wine and his disciples believed in him. Yammine argues that Jesus manifested his glory (divinity) in Lebanon where he performed this miracle, and that his church was established in Lebanon because that was where he did his first miracles and where his disciples believed in him.[50]

Father Yammine also tries to prove (pp. 69–180) that Jesus was Lebanese because he was born in Bethlehem. According to him, the Bethlehem in which Jesus was born was a village in the northern foothills of Mount Carmel, near Haifa, in the area inhabited by the tribe of Zebulun (Josh 19:15), not the Bethlehem in the south near Jerusalem in the land of Judea.[51] In making this claim, he relies on Micah's prophecy about Christ:

> But you, Bethlehem Ephrathah,
>> though you are small among the clans of Judah,
> out of you will come for me
>> one who will be ruler over Israel,
> whose origins are from of old,
>> from ancient times. (Mic 5:2)

On the basis of two references in Genesis 35:19 and Genesis 48:7, he suggests that Ephrath is Bethlehem, but not the town by that name that lay within the tribal territory of Benjamin close to Jerusalem, but rather a town in the north, near Mount Carmel. Father Yammine ignores the point that the text of Micah's prophecy placed Bethlehem Ephrathah in the area of the tribe of Judah. Nor does he not take into account the words of 1 Samuel 17:12, "Now David was the son of an Ephrathite named Jesse, who was from Bethlehem in Judah," where the text clearly relates Ephrathah to Bethlehem and the land of Judea. He also ignores the point that the Bethlehem in the territory of Zebulun, which existed in the time of Joshua, had long since vanished by the time of Jesus' birth.

By the end of his chapter, Father Yammine concludes that Jesus was born in Phoenician Lebanon, since the Phoenician borders extended to Mount Carmel in the south. He then argues that since Jesus was born in Phoenician Lebanon, he cannot be a Jew.

---

[48] الأب يوسف يمين, المسيح ولد في لبنان لا في اليهودية (إهدن, لبنان: منشورات إيلبنانيون, 1999), 40–44; ET: Father Youseff Yammine, *Christ Was Born in Lebanon and Not in Judea* (Ehden, Lebanon: Publications of 'Iilebnāniūn 1999) 40–44.

[49] الأب يوسف يمين, قانا الجليل في لبنان (إهدن, لبنان: منشورات إيل, 1994); ET: Father Youseff Yammine, *Cana of Galilee in Lebanon* (Ehden, Lebanon: Publications of 'Iil 1994).

[50] Ibid., 78–80.

[51] We may also ask whether by saying that Jesus was born in Bethlehem in Zebulun Father Yammine contradicts his earlier assertion that Jesus was born in Qana, near Tyre.

Father Yammine also tries (pp. 181–253) to prove that Jesus was not a physical descendant of David. He bases his argument on the two different records of the lineage of Jesus in Matthew chapter 1 and Luke chapter 3, and on Jesus' reference to the phrase, "The LORD says to my lord: 'Sit at my right hand until I make your enemies a footstool for your feet'" (Ps 110:1). After quoting these words, Jesus says, "David himself calls him 'Lord.' How then can he be his son?" (Mark 12:37). Father Yammine attributes the idea that Jesus was descended from David to the Jewish Christians who wrote the New Testament and expresses astonishment that there are still Christians today who believe that Jesus was of the lineage of David, in spite of the scientific proof and objective historical criticism showing that the link between Jesus and David was a construct of Jewish Christian imagination.[52]

Father Yammine also argues that Jesus was not a Jew[53] because he told some Jews, "You belong to your father, the devil" (John 8:44). Father Yammine regards this saying as conclusive proof that Jesus was not a Jew. However, he does not bother to investigate whom Jesus was talking to, nor whether they claimed to believe in him (John 8:30–31), nor whether they represented a certain group of Jews like the teachers of the law and the Pharisees (John 8:48), who were the people John usually referred to as "Jews." (Compare the account of this event in the Gospel of John and in the other gospels). The Gospel of John includes historical paradoxes that reflect the prevailing relationship to Jews in the Christian community in which John lived at the time of writing his gospel.[54]

Father Yammine goes on to assert that Jesus was a Canaanite,[55] basing his arguments on two things. The first is the similarity between Jesus and the Phoenician-Canaanite god, Baal or Adonis, who was worshiped as dying and then rising again.[56] This comparison is striking given that in reviewing Matthew 12:22–24 Father Yammine relates "Beelzebul," a term referring to the prince of demons, to Adonis the Canaanite Baal. How can he then say that Jesus is similar to Baal![57]

Second, he argues that the writer of the letter to the Hebrews links Jesus' status as a high priest with the priesthood of the Canaanite Melchizedek, not with the priesthood of the Jewish Aaron. Thus Father Yammine concludes that Jesus interpreted his own mission in terms of being a priest after the order of Melchizedek, the Canaanite king and priest, and did not see himself as one of the Jewish people. What Father Yammine ignores is that the writer to the Hebrews differentiates between the "mission" of Jesus as a priest after the order of the Canaanite Melchizedek and his physical Jewish "lineage."

---

[52] الأب يوسف يمين, المسيح ولد في لبنان لا في اليهودية),
207, 223, 226; ET: Yammine, *Christ Was Born in Lebanon and Not in Judea*, 207, 223, 226.

[53] Ibid., 277–85.

[54] Bruce Chilton, *The Anchor Bible Dictionary* [hereafter, *ABD*], vol. 6 (New York: Doubleday, 1992), 847.

[55] الأب يوسف يمين, المسيح ولد في لبنان لا في اليهودية, 98–286;
ET: Yammine, *Christ Was Born in Lebanon and Not in Judea*, 286–98.

[56] Ibid., 314.

[57] Ibid., 286.

He also ignores other references to Jesus in the Letter to the Hebrews: "For surely it is not angels he helps, but Abraham's descendants. For this reason he had to be made like them" (Heb 2:16, 17). He also ignores the words "for it is clear that our Lord descended from Judah" (Heb 7:14).

Father Yammine insists that since Jesus came from Galilee of the nations, he was not a Jew, because a person is born of the land and its people, and is the child of the land's history and geography.[58]

> In this Galilee environment, Jesus Christ was born and lived. It was a progressive, open environment that had a global element. In this environment that was fully prepared for the idea of "universality humanity," . . . Christ was the faithful son of Galilee, the real and only "son of El."[59]

Father Yammine suggests that the ancestors of Jesus and his parents Joseph and Mary were from Qana near Tyre in southern Lebanon and were obliged to go to Nazareth in Galilee two or three centuries before Jesus was born. There the Maccabees forced them to be circumcised to become Jews. Thus Jesus was born in a Jewish environment. All this was done in order to fulfill an ancient prophecy.[60] But if Father Yammine wants to separate Jesus from his Jewish background and thinks that the Jews forced Jesus' ancestors to become Jewish, why does he work so hard to link an old forgotten prophecy, by a Jewish prophet, to Jesus?

Father Yammine did nothing different from what earlier authors had done in denying Jesus' Jewish descent and separating him from Jewish culture. However, he did it at length, writing a book of over 700 pages, in which he included a large number of arguments. Yet he offers researchers little actual evidence; consequently, his work remained a breathless search for ways to link Jesus to Lebanon, with or without evidence!

Bishop George Khedr

Some highly educated scholars have addressed the tendency to strip Jesus of his Jewish background and relate him to Canaanite or Syrian cultures. One of the most famous of those scholars was Bishop George Khedr. In some valuable articles on this subject in the newspaper *Alnahar,* he summed up the issues well.

Bishop Khedr has this to say concerning the racial and cultural background of Jesus:

> I cannot understand how a believer denies the Old Testament according to the rules of modern interpretation. Such hostility to the Torah has non-theological motives, and so this is not the place to debate it. Nor do I understand why the glorification of a

---

[58] Ibid., 382.
[59] Ibid., 147.
[60] Ibid., 387, 390. It seems that Father Yammine is referring to Moses, who said, "The LORD your God will raise up for you a prophet like me from among you, from your fellow Israelites. You must listen to him" (Deut 18:15).

Canaanite or Sumerian heritage has to be erected on the rubble of the Hebrew heritage, if we truly value learning. . . .

Because of our faith in the divinity of the Savior, that is what we focus on, and so we are less concerned about researching his earthly identity. Besides emphasizing his descent from Abraham, and the confirmation of "laymen" that the Lord was linked to Canaan or Lebanon, the important thing is his Sonship to the Father. If nothing else convinces them of his kinship to the Israelite prophets, nothing will convince me of his kinship to El and all the ethnic mixture around El.[61]

In response to those who deny the resurrection of Christ, relating it to the myth of Adonis' resurrection, Bishop Khedr says:

You start from Christ, and after that I do not mind whether you like to say that the myth of Adonis' resurrection foreshadows the death and resurrection of the Savior or not, or whether you believe that Adonis' mythical death and resurrection actually occurred.

You start from the Lord; then you can go wherever you want. Everything else is just history of religions, a history in which myths are all equal, and every one of us adopts the story he wants. We do not mind admiring the story of Adonis, though it is not real. However, the reality of the crucifixion and what follows is the subject of your faith, if you are among the believers in Christ.[62]

Bishop Khedr also affirms Jesus' kinship to Abraham and to David, and his cultural kinship to Judaism:

The physical kinship of Jesus of Nazareth to Abraham is obvious for Matthew and Luke, and his kinship to David is clear for Paul. As to his descent from Adam, when read carefully, Luke explains that Christ is the apex of all humanity. . . .

We have no reason to make Jesus Syrian. To do so goes against the New Testament's insistence that Jesus came from the lineage of David. We should not distort history by projecting current struggles onto the past. The most important thing to note, however, is that Jesus of Nazareth was clearly understood when he quoted the Old Testament, and his frequent visits to the Jewish synagogues on the Sabbath, and when reading of the prophets in the synagogue of Nazareth. That shows that the Lord read Hebrew easily, the language that was used only by the rabbis; but his mother tongue was Aramaic, in which he preached in the synagogue of Nazareth about the text of Isaiah. . . .

All these words tell us about the humanity of Christ. This is history, and we are not embarrassed to say that Jesus of Nazareth came in his humanity as foreseen by the prophets, nor that he may have been familiar with Hebrew thinking after the writing of

[61] 18, المطران جورج خضر/مقالة أحد النسبة (بيروت, جريدة النهار); ET: Bishop George Khedr, "The Sunday كانون الأول/ديسمبر (1999)‎ of Descent," *An-Nahār Newspaper* (Beirut), 18 December 1999.

[62] Ibid. There seems to be an important connection between the

date of Father Yammine's 1999 book *Christ was Born in Lebanon* and the article by Bishop Khedr, which appeared about fifty days later in the same year.

the Torah. There is evidence that he was aware of the current schools of interpretation in his country, though nothing proves that he was indebted to the teaching of the monks who lived in Qumran.[63]

Those "monks who lived in Qumran" mentioned by Bishop Khedr were the Essenes, who lived near the caves when the Dead Sea Scrolls were found. After discovering the manuscripts they left and noticing a few expressions that were similar to those used by the apostles and the gospel writers, researchers quickly concluded that Jesus, like John the Baptist, must have been an Essene.

The lack of information about the early life of Jesus and what happened to him in the years between twelve and thirty have prompted some scholars to develop various theories to close this gap. For example, the writer Mikhail Naimy was curious about where Jesus spent these years and was not convinced that he spent them working as a carpenter with his father Joseph, as the gospel implies. He thought that Jesus hid the secret of his whereabouts for all those years even from his closest friends, except perhaps John the Baptist. Naimy's search for where Jesus might have gone sometimes led him to Persia and at other times to India, guided by Luke's story of the Magi. But he was hesitant to take any definite position because he could not see anything in Jesus' preaching that would serve as a link to Krishna, the Buddha, or Confucius. When Naimy read about the Essenes of Qumran, he thought Jesus may have lived with them during that gap in his life, in complete secrecy.[64]

Bishop George Khedr had this response to those who argued that Jesus lived at Qumran or traveled to India:

> Jesus of Nazareth was not affected in any way by Hindu or Buddhist thought. It is a myth to say that the Lord traveled to India. This idea first arose in the nineteenth century in the mind of an English writer, but it is baseless. The most convincing argument against it is that you cannot find even one Hindu concept in the Gospels. However, this does not mean that human beings do not sometimes think along the same lines. As to the question some people raise, "Where did Christ live before the age of thirty?" the answer is simple: he worked as a carpenter in Nazareth, for Jewish traditions did not allow him to preach before that age.[65]

Where others had sowed confusion, Bishop George Khedr puts things in perspective. Many are eager to weigh in with their opinions on Christ, Christianity, the Old Testament, the relationship between the church and Israel, and other important subjects,

---

[63] المطران جورج خضر، مقالة أجداد المسيح (بيروت، جريدة النهار، 13؛ ET: Bishop George Khedr, "The Ancestors of Christ," *Al-Nahār* (Beirut), 13 December 2003.

[64] Naima devoted a chapter to this hypothesis in his book: من

وحي المسيح (بيروت: كؤسسة نوفل, 1974)؛ ET: *Inspired by Christ* (Beirut: Kassh Nōfal, 1974).

[65] المطران جورج خضر، مقالة أجداد المسيح؛ ET: Bishop George Khedr, "The Ancestors of Christ."

but few bother to engage in serious academic study before engaging with these subjects. But when Bishop Khedr joined the discussion, the bread was given to the baker.

Conclusion

We have now looked at the most important intellectual and cultural ideas that are afloat in the Middle East when it comes to attempting to separate Jesus from his Jewish roots. The views presented are representative of all the opinions held, and there is no need to explore them in more detail. They included affirmations of the Syrian or Lebanese origins of Jesus, his Galilean-Aramaic cultural background, and the influence of Canaanite-Phoenician religion on his teaching. Not all of the writers cited sought to deny every aspect of Jesus' Jewish origins, but all of them, without exception, wanted to strip him of his Jewish cultural and religious background.

We concluded the section with the refutation of these ideas by Bishop George Khedr. At this point, no more needs to be said on this topic.

JESUS' ETHNIC IDENTITY IN THE NEW TESTAMENT

It is now time to turn to the New Testament to learn more about the early Christian testimony regarding Jesus' ethnic identity. There is no doubt that different schools of theological thought are represented in the New Testament. The best example of this is the clear differentiation between the supporters of James in Jerusalem and Paul in his mission among ethnic Gentiles. Some try to trace the separation of Jesus from his Jewish identity to the writings of the apostle Paul, who, they believe, was free of the influence of "Jewish Christianity." Thus it is important to carry out a comprehensive survey of early Christian writings about this issue in order to determine the truth of the matter.

Jesus' Ethnicity in the Synoptic Gospels

The Synoptic Gospels (Matthew, Mark, and Luke) have a compatible and integrated line of thought and so can be studied together as we investigate Jesus' ethnic identity.

The genealogies in Matthew 1 and Luke 3 agree that Jesus is a descendant of Abraham, Isaac, Jacob, and David. Although some argue that the differences in the names in some parts of the genealogies cast doubt on Jesus' relationship to the Jews, the differences are not sufficient to ignore the diligence shown by both Matthew and Luke in compiling Jesus' genealogy. Both reach the same conclusion that Jesus is a descendant of David and that his ancestry can be traced back to Abraham. Seen in this light, the differences in the genealogies are a positive sign.

In the birth narratives, Matthew states that when the Magi inquired about the newborn Jesus they referred to him as "king of the Jews" (Matt 2:2). In Luke, this title and his descent from David are implicit in the words of the angel Gabriel announcing his birth:

> He will be great and will be called the Son of the Most High. The Lord God will give him the throne of his father David, and he will reign over Jacob's descendants forever; his kingdom will never end. (Luke 1:32–33)

Jesus' birth occurred at the time of a census ordered by the Roman emperor Caesar Augustus, and Luke records that

> Joseph also went up from the town of Nazareth in Galilee to Judea, to Bethlehem the town of David, because he belonged to the house and line of David. (Luke 2:4)

Luke states that Jesus was circumcised as a Jew on the eighth day, and that since he was the firstborn his parents took him to Jerusalem to offer him to the Lord, in accordance with the law of Moses (Luke 2:21–23). There, old Simeon took the baby up in his arms and said,

> Sovereign Lord, as you have promised,
>   you may now dismiss your servant in peace.
> For my eyes have seen your salvation,
>   which you have prepared in the sight of all nations:
> a light for revelation to the Gentiles,
>   and the glory of your people Israel. (Luke 2:29–32)

The three gospels also all mention the following incident:

> While Jesus was teaching in the temple courts, he asked, "Why do the teachers of the law say that the Messiah is the son of David? David himself, speaking by the Holy Spirit, declared:
>
> > "The Lord said to my Lord:
> >   'Sit at my right hand
> > until I put your enemies
> >   under your feet.'"
>
> David himself calls him 'Lord.' How then can he be his son?" (Mark 12:35–37; cf. Luke 20:41–44; Matt 22:41–46)

At first glance, it may seem that Jesus, who was aware of his messianic role, was denying that the Messiah comes from the line of David. However, a more careful reading shows that Jesus was making the point that the status of the Messiah is far greater than that of David, for David called him Lord. Jesus was not denying that as a human being he was from the line of David.

We also have to consider the context in which this argument with the teachers of the law occurred. These were a group of scholars. So Jesus poses a theological riddle to show the shallowness of their knowledge of the Torah and its interpretation. We are told that no one could answer him (Matt 22:46) and that the crowd standing around heard him "with delight" (Mark 12:37).

Clearly neither Matthew nor Luke interpreted Jesus' words as a denial of his kinship to David according to the flesh, for both of them had earlier recorded Jesus' genealogy, which confirms his descent from David.

Jesus' Ethnicity in the Writings of John

Jesus' ethnic identity is established at the start of the Gospel of John in this famous verse:

> He came to that which was his own, but his own did not receive him. Yet to all who did receive him, to those who believed in his name, he gave the right to become children of God. (John 1:11–12)

It is clear from this sentence that Jesus' people, "his own," were the Jewish people. They did not accept him, but non-Jews who did accept him became children of God.

The Samaritan woman at the well clearly identified Jesus as a Jew, saying, "You are a Jew and I am a Samaritan woman. How can you ask me for a drink?" (John 4:9). During his talk with her, Jesus said: "You Samaritans worship what you do not know; we worship what we do know, for salvation is from the Jews" (John 4:22). In this conversation, Jesus was referring to himself as being the Messiah and the Savior who had come to fulfill the prophecies and embody the Jewish heritage of salvation from Abraham until Jesus himself (compare John 5:39 with the context of John 4:22–26).

There is also evidence that Jesus was well known in his community, as is clear from the following incident:

> At this the Jews there began to grumble about him because he said, "I am the bread that came down from heaven." They said, "Is this not Jesus, the son of Joseph, whose father and mother we know? How can he now say, 'I came down from heaven'?" (John 6:41–42)

The book of Revelation testifies that Jesus is "the Lion of the tribe of Judah, the Root of David" (Rev 5:5), and John quotes Jesus as saying: "I, Jesus, . . . am the Root and the Offspring of David" (Rev 22:16).

The book of Revelation also contains a symbolic image of a woman clothed with the sun, with the moon under her feet and a crown of twelve stars on her head, who is about to give birth to a male child who will rule all the nations with an iron scepter. That image is a clear reference to the Jewish nation from which came Jesus Christ the savior–king (Rev 12:1–5).

The image of the Lamb standing on Mount Zion together with 144,000 from Jewish tribes points to Jesus Christ as the head of the religion that followed him wherever he went (Rev 14:1–6; cf. 7:1–8).

Jesus' Ethnicity in Acts

In the book of Acts, Peter refers to Jesus' Jewish identity in his sermon on the day of Pentecost, which was addressed to the people of Jerusalem and summoned them to repentance and faith in Jesus as the promised Messiah. In that sermon, Peter said that God promised David that his offspring would include a king who would sit on his throne. This was achieved through the resurrection of Christ who is sitting at the right hand of the Father (Acts 2:24–36).

There is also evidence of the Jewishness of Jesus in Peter's second sermon, which he preached after healing the lame man at the gate of the temple. In that sermon he said, "The God of Abraham, Isaac and Jacob, the God of our fathers, has glorified his servant Jesus" (Acts 3:13). Then Peter referred his hearers to Moses' prophecy: "'The Lord your God will raise up for you a prophet like me from among your own people'" (Acts 3:22). Peter applied this prophecy to Jesus. He also quoted the promise to Abraham, that through his offspring all the nations of the world would be blessed (Acts 3:25), and referred to Jesus as the one coming from the lineage of Abraham to bless everyone by turning them from their wicked ways (Acts 3:26).

Acts also records the apostle Paul speaking of the Jewishness of Jesus in the first sermon in which he spoke about the history of the Jewish people. Speaking in Pisidian Antioch, he said, "He made David their king. . . . From this man's descendants God has brought to Israel the Savior Jesus" (Acts 13:22–23).

Jesus' Ethnicity in the Letters of the Apostle Paul

Paul also mentions Jesus' ethnic identity in his letters. At the beginning of his letter to the Romans, he contrasts Jesus' humanity and divinity and speaks of Jesus in these terms:

> who as to his earthly life was a descendant of David, and who through the Spirit of holiness was appointed the Son of God in power by his resurrection from the dead. (Rom 1:3–4)

In a similar comparison that confirms the Jewishness of Jesus, Paul speaks of

> those of my own race, the people of Israel. Theirs is the adoption to sonship; theirs the divine glory, the covenants, the receiving of the law, the temple worship and the promises. Theirs are the patriarchs, and from them is traced the human ancestry of the Messiah, who is God over all, forever praised. (Rom 9:3–5)

Speaking of Jesus as the Savior of both Jews and Gentiles, Paul again mentions Jesus' ethnic identity:

For I tell you that Christ has become a servant of the Jews on behalf of God's truth, so that the promises made to the patriarchs might be confirmed and, moreover, that the Gentiles might glorify God for his mercy. As it is written:

> "Therefore I will praise you among the Gentiles;
> I will sing the praises of your name."

Again, it says,

> "Rejoice, you Gentiles, with his people."

And again,

> "Praise the Lord, all you Gentiles;
> let all the peoples extol him."

And again, Isaiah says,

> "The Root of Jesse will spring up,
> one who will arise to rule over the nations;
> in him the Gentiles will hope." (Rom 15:8–12)

In the second letter to the Corinthians, Paul's reference to seeing Christ from a human perspective has raised some controversy. The actual wording of the text is as follows:

> And he died for all, that those who live should no longer live for themselves but for him who died for them and was raised again.
> So from now on we regard no one from a worldly point of view. Though we once regarded Christ in this way, we do so no longer. Therefore, if anyone is in Christ, the new creation has come: The old has gone, the new is here! (2 Cor 5:15–17)

This letter was written at a time when there was a crisis in the apostle Paul's relationship to the church in Corinth. In his absence, some people whom he calls "super-apostles" had come to the church (2 Cor 11:5; 12:11). These men were probably not any of the twelve apostles but were people who boasted about their privileges and talents (2 Cor 11:18–23). Paul wanted to warn the people in Corinth against those apostles, "who take pride in what is seen rather than in what is in the heart" (2 Cor 5:12). In other words, these people were boasting about worldly things such as their relatives and lineage, whereas Paul wanted to be humble and focus solely on the love of Christ (2 Cor 5:14). He saw himself as having died with Christ to all worldly boasting (2 Cor 5:15). He did not want Christians to value people for merely human attributes. He makes an absolute statement that even if we knew "Christ from a worldly point of view" (that is, in terms of knowing his ancestry and origins and even in terms of the honor Jews accorded to the Messiah) we no longer think of him in these terms (2 Cor 5:16). Since

117

Christ's death and resurrection, those who are in Christ are a new creation. They have no relation to the things that were once important, for everything has become new (2 Cor 5:17). Chapter 3 of Paul's letter to the Philippians clearly illustrates what he means when he talks of judging people from a worldly point of view.

In his letter to the Galatians, Paul refers to God's promise to Abraham that in his offspring all nations would be blessed. He identifies Jesus Christ as the descendant of Abraham through whom this promise is fulfilled, so that the blessing given to Abraham can now come to the Gentiles (Gal 3:14–16).

It is also worth noting Paul's exhortation to Timothy:

> Remember Jesus Christ, raised from the dead, descended from David. This is my gospel. (2 Tim 2:8)

Here Paul again links the resurrection of Christ and his descent from David. Here the link may even be stronger than the similar link in Romans 1:3–4, for the phrase "descended from David" may refer to either Jesus' genealogy or his royal status. Both meanings may well be present, for they are complementary.

Jesus' Ethnicity in the Letter to the Hebrews

The writer to the Hebrews has this to say about Jesus Christ:

> For surely it is not angels he helps, but Abraham's descendants. For this reason he had to be made like them, fully human in every way, in order that he might become a merciful and faithful high priest in service to God, and that he might make atonement for the sins of the people. (Heb 2:16–17)

The writer of this letter is addressing his words exclusively to Jews, which is why he speaks of "Abraham's descendants" rather than "Adam's descendants." He is saying that Jesus helps Abraham's descendants because they are his "brothers," and he has to be like them in everything.

The letter to the Hebrews is characterized by its emphasis that the priesthood of Jesus is associated with the priesthood of Melchizedek rather than that of Aaron. Some have used this point to separate Jesus from his Jewish origins and relate him to the Canaanites. However, the writer of Hebrews insists on Jesus' Jewish origins, for he says, "it is clear that our Lord descended from Judah, and in regard to that tribe Moses said nothing about priests" (Heb 7:14).

Conclusion

The New Testament authors are in agreement that Jesus was a Jew. None of them denies it—not even those like Paul and Luke who were more liberated from Jewish traditions.

Jesus himself is also never recorded as having said anything to indicate that he was not a Jew. The lack of clear reference to Jesus' ethnic identity in the letters of James and Jude is not because his ethnicity was disputed but because it was assumed to be axiomatic.

JESUS' CULTURAL IDENTITY

The New Testament makes it clear that Jesus was ethnically Jewish, but what about his cultural identity? Was it also Jewish?

This question arises because ethnic identity and cultural identity are not always aligned. They do align if, for example, someone is born of Armenian parents in Armenia, grows up and is educated there, speaking the Armenian language, and grows old and dies in that country. However, a person's ethnic and cultural identity may not be in full alignment if they have been exposed to other cultures through study or emigration. And there are cases in which there is no correlation between someone's ethnicity and their cultural identity, as when a person with a certain ethnicity is separated from his or her parents and other relatives while an infant and is raised as an orphan in a foreign cultural environment. Such a person's cultural identity becomes completely separated from their ethnic origin.

What then of Jesus' cultural identity? Did his ethnic and cultural identities match? Was his Jewish identity affected by other cultures and civilizations? Or was he completely separated from his Jewish cultural origins?

Answering this question requires an extensive study of aspects of Jesus' cultural identity.

Jesus' Upbringing and Home Life

Jesus was born in a Jewish family and his parents cared for him in his infancy. Mary breastfed him and Joseph took care of him. They did for him what every Jewish family does for its children. They took him to Jerusalem to be circumcised on the eighth day, and gave him a Jewish name, "Jesus" (Luke 2:21), meaning "Joshua," after the leader who followed Moses. Both Joseph and Mary had Jewish names. Joseph was the name of Jacob's beloved son, and Mary was the name of Moses' sister. At that time the meaning of a name was an important indication of parents' expectations for their child.

Jesus grew up in his Jewish family, nurtured emotionally and intellectually on the stories of the Torah and inherited religious traditions. When he became a boy, the lanes and meadows of Nazareth were his playground. The boys of Nazareth and his relatives and neighbors were his companions. Every year he went with his family to attend the Passover in Jerusalem and to worship in the temple. Thus the religion and social culture of his parents were deeply embedded in his consciousness. Luke says,

"The child grew and became strong; he was filled with wisdom, and the grace of God was on him" (Luke 2:40).

Jesus' Religious Upbringing

At some point between the ages of five and seven, a Jewish boy would be sent to the synagogue to learn how to read and write and to study the text of the Torah, the interpretations of those texts by Jewish rabbis, and the regulations governing religious practices. The course of study lasted seven years, during which time a Jewish boy became familiar with the teachings of his religion, and was ready to practice and apply them. There is evidence that Jesus was an intelligent pupil, for he was only twelve when he was found "in the temple courts, sitting among the teachers, listening to them and asking them questions. Everyone who heard him was amazed at his understanding and his answers" (Luke 2:46–47). This incident shows that by that age he had completed the religious education given to boys at that time.[66]

When Jesus started his public mission at the age of thirty, he visited the Jewish synagogue in Nazareth and was given the book of Isaiah to read. He read out a prophecy concerning himself (Luke 4:16–21). The book of Isaiah was written in Hebrew, and the reason Jesus was able to read it was because he had studied that language as a boy in the synagogue. The uneducated could not read Hebrew because it had died out in daily use in Palestine and had been replaced by Aramaic after the return from the exile.

Jesus' Language

The Aramaic language spread throughout the Fertile Crescent, from Iraq to Palestine, during the days of the Babylonian Empire. It replaced Hebrew during and after the exile, many centuries before the birth of Jesus. The Old Testament offers evidence that the Jewish people returning from the exile did not know their mother tongue, Hebrew. That was why Ezra needed translators to stand beside him when he was teaching the law (Neh 8:1–8).

When Jesus was born, the first words he heard were in Aramaic, and as he grew he began to use the language of his birth. There is evidence that this was the language he used in daily life in the gospels (in Mark's Gospel alone we note words like, "Boanerges"—3:17; "Talitha"—5:41; "Corban"—7:11; "Ephphatha"—7:34; "Abba"—14:36; "Eloi, Eloi, lema sabachthani?"—15:34).

Aramaic was also the language used by the teachers of the law in interpreting the texts of the Torah and the books of the Old Testament. Thus it was not a cultural addition to Hebrew; it was the formal, religious, public language of the Jews at the time of

---

[66] See chapter 1 of William Barclay, *Educational Ideals in the Ancient World* (Grand Rapids: Baker, 1974).

Jesus. Aramaic was so closely identified with the Jews that it was even called Hebrew (see John 19:20; Acts 21:40; 22:2). There are indeed similarities between the two languages, for both are part of the Semitic family of languages that includes Phoenician, Assyrian, Arabic, and Abyssinian.[67]

Did Jesus speak Greek as well as Aramaic? Scholars do not have a conclusive answer, but they are likely to assume that he did, for Greek was widespread as a second language throughout the lands that had once been conquered by Alexander the Great.

Jesus' Use of the Old Testament

One evidence of Jesus' cultural identity is his deep knowledge of the books of the Old Testament, which were the ultimate heritage of the Jewish people and the foundation of their religious thinking. The Old Testament was central to Jesus' teaching and was the subject of his dialogue with the religious leaders, teachers of the law, and Pharisees. Jesus did not quote any poet, writer, philosopher, or scholar of his age. All that he had memorized was the Torah and the stories and models of the Old Testament. In his teachings, talks, and dialogues with the Jews and with his disciples, Jesus quoted directly or indirectly from about 144 texts from 24 books of the Old Testament.[68] Comparison of the volume of quotations recorded in the first three gospels and the number of Old Testament books from which he quoted with the space allocated to his teachings in the same three gospels is evidence of the significant place of the Old Testament in his thinking and teaching.

While reading the Old Testament, Jesus was aware that it spoke about him and the mission he came to accomplish. This was very clear on the day he read from the book of Isaiah in the synagogue at Nazareth, and then said, "Today this scripture is fulfilled in your hearing" (see Luke 4:16–21).

Jesus also said, "You study the Scriptures diligently because you think that in them you have eternal life. These are the very Scriptures that testify about me" (John 5:39).

Jesus' Teaching

The cultural identity of teachers is exposed through the content, examples, and applications they present in their teaching. Similarly for Jesus, his cultural identity appears through his teaching, as a review of the topics he addressed will show.

Jesus' teaching revolved around the law of Moses and the interpretation of its provisions. For example, he taught about the permanence of the law (Matt 5:17–20) and spoke about murder, adultery, swearing, revenge, love of neighbors and enemies (Matt 5:21–48), and keeping the Sabbath in the right way (Matt 12:1–14).

---

[67] الأب سامي حلاق، مجتمع يسوع: تقاليده وعاداته (بيروت، دار المشرق، 1999)، 127–28; ET: Father Sāmi Halāq, *The Society of Jesus: His Traditions and Customs* (Beirut: Dār al-Machreq, 1999), 127–28.

[68] R. T. France, *Jesus and the Old Testament* (Grand Rapids: Baker, 1980), 259–63.

The prayer Jesus taught his disciples included a view of God as a father, hallowing the name of God, and the desire for the coming of God's kingdom so that his will would be done on earth as it is in heaven. Jesus excelled on these topics (Matt 6:9–13).

He also taught about doing good works and applying the law and addressed topics such as giving, prayer, fasting, not treasuring money, and not condemning others (Matt 6:1–7:5). He also talked about eating without washing one's hands (Matt 15:1–20), marriage and divorce (Matt 19:1–12), and loving God and loving others as ourselves as a summary of the law (Matt 22:34–39).

In his parables Jesus taught about the love of a father who waits for his lost son (Luke 15); forgiving others just as God forgives us (the wicked slave [Matt 18]); regarding anyone in need as our neighbor, regardless of their ethnicity or religion (the Good Samaritan [Luke 10]); persistence in prayer (the unjust judge [Luke 18]); being ready to meet the Lord (the ten virgins [Matt 25]); confession of sins prior to gaining forgiveness (the Pharisees and the tax collector [Luke 18]); the priority of being rich toward God over earthly riches (the rich fool [Luke 12]); and humility (not taking the front seat [Luke 14]).

In addressing all these topics, and in his teaching about "the kingdom of God" that was the basic foundation of his message, Jesus stayed within the limits of the Jewish theological context of his time. We do not hear any echoes of religious or philosophical ideas or teachings outside the framework of the Torah and the Jewish apocalyptic literature that was prevalent in the period between the Old and New Testaments. All of this indicates that Jesus' cultural identity was purely Jewish.

Conclusion

To determine someone's cultural identity we need to know about their home life, schooling and religious education, the language they speak, and the subjects they think about and on which their future depends. These are the issues we looked at in order to learn more about Jesus' cultural identity. In regard to all these issues, it is clear beyond doubt that Jesus was purely Jewish in his cultural identity, although it is also true that in some areas of his teaching he went far beyond the narrow Jewish view in order to explain the law. He also addressed ideas and principles that can be generalized to apply to all humanity.

JESUS' TITLES AND THEIR IMPLICATIONS FOR HIS IDENTITY AND MISSION

A survey of the main titles Jesus himself used and of how the early church extended the use of these titles shows that they were all from the Old Testament. Jesus did not choose a title outside the Jewish religious context presented in the books of the Law, the

Prophets, and the Writings; that is to say, the entire biblical heritage at that time (Luke 24:44). If we want to be more specific, we can say that Jesus found himself in the books of Psalms, Isaiah, and Daniel more than in any other books of the Old Testament. We know this from his declarations about himself. However, the church found references to Jesus all over the Old Testament and thus could claim that "all the prophets testify about him" (Acts 10:43). This confirms that his identity is a product of his heritage.

What follows is a presentation of the main titles Jesus used for himself and those ascribed to him, analyzing the origin of each title, its meaning, and the message Jesus wanted to convey through it.

First Title: Messiah or Christ

The first foundation on which Christianity stands is the truth of the claim that Jesus of Nazareth is the promised Messiah. This fact shines out from the first sermon Peter preached to the Jews in Jerusalem on the day of Pentecost, when he said, "Therefore let all Israel be assured of this: God has made this Jesus, whom you crucified, both Lord and Messiah" (Acts 2:36).

The central question about the identity of Jesus is the question that he himself asked his disciples, "'But what about you?' he asked. 'Who do you say I am?' Peter answered, 'You are the Messiah'" (Mark 8:29). He then urged his disciples not to reveal his identity to anyone.

When the high priest questioned Jesus before handing him over to Pilate, the Roman governor, he asked him,

"Are you the Messiah, the Son of the Blessed One?"

"I am," said Jesus. "And you will see the Son of Man sitting at the right hand of the Mighty One and coming on the clouds of heaven." (Mark 14:61–62)

Before we discuss the relationship of Jesus of Nazareth to the Christ or Messiah from a theological perspective, there are a few points of language to clarify.

"Jesus"—the personal name of the Savior—is derived from the Hebrew name "Joshua," which is itself a compound formed from the words "Yahweh" and the Hebrew verb that means "save." The meaning of the name is spelled out in Matthew 1:21, "You are to give him the name Jesus, because he will save his people from their sins."

The word "Christ," which is used as a title for Jesus, derives from the Greek word *christos* that was used to translate the Hebrew word *mashiah*, meaning "the Anointed." This usage in turn derives from the Old Testament practice of anointing kings and priests with oil when they were appointed to office. These men were then referred to as "the Lord's anointed," meaning that they had been set apart for that particular office by the Lord himself.

Anointing involved pouring oil or fat or aromatic perfume on the head of the one who was to be a king (2 Sam 5:3) or a priest (Exod 28:41) at the time of his inauguration. The anointing of prophets is not mentioned in the Old Testament, except when the Lord commanded Elijah to anoint Elisha to take his place (1 Kgs 19:16) and when God issued the warning, "Do not touch my anointed ones; do my prophets no harm" (1 Chr 16:22; Ps 105:15).

There are many examples of a king being referred to as "the anointed one." For example, Psalm 2:2 refers to the Lord's "anointed," and 2:6 makes it clear that he is a king who has been "installed . . . on Zion, my holy mountain." This was said about David on the day of his crowning, and the following verse reads,

I will proclaim the LORD's decree:

> He said to me, "You are my son;
> today I have become your father." (Ps 2:7)[69]

Peter referred to Jesus as anointed in the sermon he preached at Cornelius' house:

God anointed Jesus of Nazareth with the Holy Spirit and power, and . . . he went around doing good and healing all who were under the power of the devil, because God was with him." (Acts 10:38)

In the history of Israel the title "anointed one" was used of both kings and priests. With the passing of time, however, the royal use came to dominate the priestly use, especially after the kingship was established in Israel. This explains the meaning of *mashiah* in Daniel: "From the time the word goes out to restore and rebuild Jerusalem until the Anointed One, the ruler, comes" (Dan 9:25). The word "Messiah" (John 1:41), which means "anointed one," is frequently used to refer to this figure mentioned in the book of Daniel and in Jewish literature of the intertestamental period.[70]

The Old Testament prophets linked the promised Savior to the royal line of David. In other words, the king coming to save the people and the Gentiles would be a descendant of David. This belief was sustained by God's promise to King David that he would raise up a king from his offspring and that his house and his kingdom would endure forever (2 Sam 7:16, 26, 29). Isaiah stated that a shoot would arise "from the stump of Jesse"

---

[69] For additional references to the king being "God's anointed," see 1 Sam 2:10; 12:3; 26:23; 2 Sam 19:21–22; 22:51; 23:1; 2 Chr 6:42; Ps 132:10.

[70] Arabic speakers prefer to use the word *Massieh* (Christ) instead of "Messiah," and the word *Masihani* instead of "messianic," when we translate directly from Hebrew to Arabic. Since these are related languages, there is no need to translate from Hebrew to Arabic through Greek, which may lead to losing meaning and destroying the roots of words. Arabic scholars have also attempted to clarify the theological terms related to Christology. It has been suggested

that in Arabic we should use the word *Masihania*, "exploring the person and teachings of Christ," for "Christology," using *Masihani* for "Christological," and using *Mashieh* for "Messiah" which means "the promised Christ whom the Old Testament prophesied would come to establish God's kingdom"; also, using *Mashihi* for "messianic," and *Mashihia* for "Messianism," namely the doctrine of the coming of Christ. See مسرد الألفاظ اللغويّة اللاهوتيّة (ET: The Glossary of Theological Language) in the beginning of the Jesuit translation of the New Testament (بيروت: دار المشرق, طبعة عام 2000; ET: Beirut: Dar Al Mashreq, 2000).

(David's father), and that the Spirit of the Lord would rest on him so that he would judge with justice and slay the wicked. Peace will prevail in his age so the wolf will live with the lamb, and the earth will be full of the knowledge of the Lord. This king will "stand as a banner for the peoples; the nations will rally to him, and his resting place will be glorious" (see Isa 11:1–10)

Isaiah identified this coming king as a descendant of David, saying,

> For to us a child is born,
>   to us a son is given,
>   and the government will be on his shoulders.
> And he will be called
>   Wonderful Counselor, Mighty God,
>   Everlasting Father, Prince of Peace.
> Of the greatness of his government and peace
>   there will be no end.
> He will reign on David's throne
>   and over his kingdom,
> establishing and upholding it
>   with justice and righteousness
>   from that time on and forever. (Isa 9:6–7)

Hosea prophesied that the Israelites would live many days without king or prince or sacrifice, but that afterwards they will

> seek the LORD their God and David their king. They will come . . . to the LORD and to his blessings in the last days. (Hos 3:4–5)

Micah states that a ruler over Israel would come from Bethlehem in the land of Judah, the clan from which David came. This ruler's

> origins are from of old,
>   from ancient times . . . .
> He will stand and shepherd his flock
>   in the strength of the LORD, . . .
> for then his greatness
>   will reach to the ends of the earth.
> And he will be our peace. (Mic 5:4–5)

A similar prophecy rang out from Zechariah, who composed a beautiful poem:

> Rejoice greatly, Daughter Zion!
>   Shout, Daughter Jerusalem!
> See, your king comes to you,
>   righteous and victorious,

lowly and riding on a donkey,
> on a colt, the foal of a donkey.
I will take away the chariots from Ephraim
> and the warhorses from Jerusalem,
> and the battle bow will be broken.
He will proclaim peace to the nations.
> His rule will extend from sea to sea
> and from the River to the ends of the earth. (Zech 9:9–10)

All these passages from the Old Testament indicate that the coming anointed king would be David's offspring and associate the Messiah with royal status rather than with a priestly or prophetic role. They also emphasize that the Christ is a future royal figure, in whose age peace will prevail on earth. For all these reasons, Jesus was reluctant to use the title "Messiah," for it had royal and political implications that could be misunderstood.

There are many references to the coming Messiah at the start of the Gospel of Luke. For example, "Today in the town of David a Savior has been born to you; he is the Messiah, the Lord" (Luke 2:11). Luke tells of the revelation to Simeon by the Holy Spirit "that he would not die before he had seen the Lord's Messiah" (Luke 2:26). Luke also records the prophecy of Zechariah: "He has raised up a horn of salvation for us in the house of his servant David" (Luke 1:69). All these indicate the ripening expectation among the Jews that the Messiah, the promised Savior, would soon come to bring "salvation from our enemies and from the hand of all who hate us" (Luke 1:71).

This increasing expectation is also evident in the literature of the intertestamental period, that is, writings dating from the three hundred years between 250 BC and AD 50. Many of these books are known as the Pseudepigrapha because their authors adopted names other than their real names, naming themselves after Enoch, Solomon, Ezra, and the like, just as today writers use aliases to hide their real names.

The Pseudepigrapha reveal the emotions of the Jewish people who were waiting for salvation from the rule of ethnic Gentiles. They longed to be able to worship the Lord freely, unencumbered by the pressures of foreign traditions and customs. The Jews, who observed the provisions of the law of Moses, were very sensitive to any tradition alien to their heritage. One of the pseudepigraphic psalms, attributed to Solomon but actually dating back to one hundred years before the birth of Jesus Christ, clearly shows the longing of that age for the coming of the savior–king to save the people and restore their dignity.

> See, O Lord, and raise up for them their king, the son of David,
> > at the time which you chose, O God, to rule over Israel your servant.
> And gird him with strength to shatter in pieces unrighteous rulers,
> > to purify Jerusalem from nations that trample her down in destruction,

in wisdom of righteousness, to drive out sinners from the inheritance . . .
>   and to reprove sinners with the thought of their hearts.
And he shall gather a holy people whom he shall lead in righteousness,
>   and he shall judge the tribes of the people
>   that has been sanctified by the Lord his God.
And he shall not allow injustice to lodge in their midst any longer,
>   Nor shall there dwell with them any person who knows evil;
>   for he shall know them, that all are their God's sons. . . .
He shall be a righteous king, taught by God, over them,
And there shall be no injustice in his days in their midst,
>   for all shall be holy, and their king the anointed of the Lord. . . .
For he shall strike the earth with the word of his mouth forever. . . .
And he shall not weaken in his days, relying on his God;
>   For God has made him strong in the holy spirit,
>   And wise in the counsel of understanding, with strength and
>   righteousness. . . .
This is the majesty of the king of Israel, which God knew,
>   To raise him up over the house of Israel to discipline it.
His word will be more refined than costly gold, the finest.
>   In the congregations he will discerningly judge the tribes
>   of a sanctified people. . . .
Happy are those who shall live in those days,
>   to see the good things of Israel
>   that God shall accomplish in the congregation of the tribes.
May God hasten his pity upon Israel;
>   May he deliver us from the uncleanness of profane enemies.
The Lord himself is our king forever and ever.
>   (Psalms of Solomon 17:23–46)[71]

This psalm with its many messianic references is an example of the literature of the period between the two Testaments. Similar references are found in the pseudepigraphic book of Enoch, which is quoted in the Letter of Jude in the New Testament. The book of Enoch speaks of "the Son of Man" who appears before "the Lord of Spirits" and is "the Light of the Nations" and "the hope of those who grieve in their hearts." The kings of the earth will fall before this righteous one and will not be raised up, because "they denied the Lord of spirits and his Messiah" (1 En. 48:2, 4, 8, 10).[72]

The book also speaks of "the Righteous One," another messianic title, saying:

---

[71] Kenneth Atkinson, trans., *Psalms of Solomon*, in *A New English Translation of the Septuagint: and the Other Greek Translations Traditionally Included under That Title*, ed. Albert Pietersma and Benjamin G. Wright (Oxford: Oxford University Press, 2009).

[72] All quotations from 1 Enoch are taken from H. F. D. Sparks, ed., *The Apocryphal Old Testament* (Oxford: Clarendon, 1984).

> When the community of the righteous appears, and the sinners are judged for their sins, . . . and when the Righteous One appears before the chosen righteous whose works are weighed by the Lord of spirits, . . . where will be the dwelling of the sinners? . . . It would have been better for them if they had not been born! (1 En. 38:1–2)

The writer of Enoch also used the title "the Chosen One" for the Messiah (note that in Luke 9:35 God says, "This is my Son, whom I have chosen; listen to him"):

> On that day the Chosen One will sit on the throne of glory and will choose their works and their resting-places will be without number; and their spirits within them will grow strong when they see my Chosen One and those who appeal to my holy and glorious name. On that day, I will cause my Chosen One to dwell among them, and I will transform heaven and make it an eternal blessing and light. (1 En. 45:3, 4)

The Old Testament, the Apocrypha, and the pseudepigrapha all proclaim that the arrival of the age of the Messiah will be accompanied by great signs, some on earth and others in the heavens. It will begin with judgment (Isa 13:6–8). The wicked will try to hide from his face (1 En. 102:1–3), and the whole course of nature will be disrupted (As. Mos. 10:4–6). People will kill each other and parents will even turn on their children (1 En. 100:1–2). Divisions will increase even among the Jews (T. Jud. 22:1–2). There will be horror, distress, wars, earthquakes, and fires (2 Bar. 70:2–8), and destruction will fill the whole earth (Isa 24:14–23).

After that time of judgment, the age of the Messiah will be characterized by peace, righteousness, and justice (Isa 9:2–7; 11:1–5). Jerusalem will be saved from its enemies (Isa 52:1–12), the glory of the Lord will be manifested there (Bar 4:21–25), and many Gentile kings will come with presents to the God of heaven (Tob 13:10–14). Peace will prevail among the nations, allowing the weapons of war to be turned into agricultural implements. "Nation will not take up sword against nation, nor will they train for war anymore" (see Isa 2:2–4).

Because of all that was said in the Scriptures and the pseudepigrapha about the promised Messiah, the nature of his kingship, and the phenomena that would accompany his coming, there was a growing longing for and expectation of his arrival in the years leading up to the birth of Jesus. But these expectations did not end with his birth and the prophetic utterances of Simeon, Anna, and Zechariah. Even thirty years later, when John the Baptist appeared calling for repentance because the kingdom of God was near, some Jewish leaders sent a delegation to ask him if he was the Messiah (John 1:20). It seems that the spirit of expectation was intense and persistent so that whenever someone appeared declaring a message from God, questions were raised about whether he might be the promised Messiah. While some people seem to have expected the return of Elijah and Jeremiah (Matt 16:14) on the basis of texts like Malachi 4:5 or other traditions, the expectation that the Messiah would come was the most prominent.

When John the Baptist testified that Jesus was the Son of God and the Lamb of God (John 1:34, 36), Andrew heard what John said and followed Jesus. And when Andrew met Peter, his brother, he said to him: "We have found the Messiah" (John 1:40, 41).

Jesus never said publicly that he was the Messiah, because at that time the messianic hope of the Jews was related to a political role. The Messiah they longed for would be a military king descended from David who would free the nation from the yoke of Roman imperialism and restore the ancient glory of Jerusalem. They never imagined that the Messiah's mission would include a humble entry to Jerusalem on a donkey, accompanied by waving palm branches and children's cheers (Zech 9:9–10); they never imagined that this would be followed by denial, beating, torture, and death (Isa 53). As for Jesus, the revelation of his sovereign rule was postponed until the time determined by God (Acts 1:6–7). Thus he told Pilate, "My kingdom is not of this world. If it were, my servants would fight to prevent my arrest by the Jewish leaders. But now my kingdom is from another place" (John 18:36). John says that after Jesus fed the crowd of 5,000 people, they wanted to declare him king. But Jesus "withdrew again to a mountain by himself" (John 6:15). The evidence points to the conclusion that Jesus sought a universal, spiritual kingdom in which God would rule over the hearts of all, whereas the Jews were looking forward to a national kingdom, limited to the Jews alone and under God's rule.

Jesus and his disciples lived everyday lives among the people, as dictated by the needs of the mission that determined his works and teachings. He did not refer to his messianic identity but left his disciples to discover it themselves. Almost three years passed before he posed a specific question to his disciples about who they thought he might be. When he did, Peter answered him, "You are the Messiah" (Mark 8:29), "God's Messiah" (Luke 9:20), or "You are the Messiah, the Son of the living God"(Matt 16:16). It is generally agreed by scholars that the answer given in Mark is the closest to Peter's original wording, and that Luke and Matthew have expanded it slightly to help their readers understand the meaning of the word "Messiah." As we know, each apostle was writing for his own audience. But the authors of all the gospels concur that the word used was "Messiah," which confirms that this word was central to the declaration. Jesus' reaction to Peter's declaration was to praise him (Matt 16:17), but he also strongly warned them not to tell anyone about his identity.

The second important occasion on which Jesus declared his messiahship was while standing before the high priest, the chief priests, and the teachers of the Jewish law during his trial (Mark 14:53). There, Jesus publicly declared his identity while surrounded by his enemies, not his friends. The high priest asked him a direct question: "Are you the Messiah?" And Jesus answered directly and clearly, "I am." This occasion was unusual since those present with the high priest were the highest religious authorities in the Jewish nation. The question also was unusual, since it was related to the royal messianic figure promised by the prophets, who, it was hoped, would be "the one who was going to redeem Israel" (Luke 24:21).[73] Jesus' answer was unusual too, since he did not confine himself to the simple assertion that he was indeed the Christ but continued: "And you will see the Son of Man sitting at the right hand of the Mighty One and coming on the clouds of heaven" (see Mark 14:61–62). With these words, Jesus associated himself with the Messiah and indicated that he was "the Son of Man," the one who was given eternal power and an everlasting kingdom (Dan 7:13–14). No wonder that the high priest tore his clothes in rage! He could not imagine that the Son of Man, the one who was expected to be the King of kings and Lord of lords, would stand before him in chains. So "they all condemned him as worthy of death" (Mark 14:64). But, as was foretold, "The stone the builders rejected has become the cornerstone" (Ps 118:22; 1 Pet 2:7).

From that time on, the title of Messiah or Christ was associated with Jesus, until today he is known as "Jesus Christ." Thus there is a need to explain that "Christ" is not a surname but a title and to point out its messianic and royal overtones. That need is still present, especially among the Jews, just as it was in the time of Paul, who testified to the Jews that the Jesus of whom he spoke was the promised Christ (Acts 18:5).

This extended explanation of the messianic nature of Jesus has served to prove the point that this is the first foundation on which Christianity stands.

Second Title: Son of God

Jesus used the Aramaic word "abba," meaning "father,"[74] in the darkest time of his struggle in the garden of Gethsemane as he anticipated the horror of crucifixion (Mark 14:36). His crying out of this word must have deeply affected those who heard him, and so they repeated it and passed it on until Mark recorded it in his gospel in its original Aramaic form. Paul used it twice (Rom 8:15; Gal 4:6). Whether this word does actually reflect a very intimate relationship between a son and a father as Joachim Jeremias says,[75] or is simply an ordinary phrase, as James Barr argues[76] —and both of them are great scholars—its main implication is clear; Jesus knew that God was his Father in a unique way.

Jesus so often referred to God as his Father that there was no need for those who wrote the gospels to use the Aramaic word each time it occurred. Here are some examples: "Didn't you know I had to be in my Father's house?" (Luke 2:49); "All things have been committed to me by my Father" (Matt 11:27; Luke 10:22); "This was not revealed to you by flesh and blood, but by my Father in heaven" (Matt 16:17); "Stop turning

---

[73] The king in Israel was called "the Lord's anointed" and was considered to be the heart and life of the nation, "our very life breath" (Lam 4:20).

[74] According to Bishop George Khedr, *Abba* is the Aramaic word that children use for their father. It has been transferred to Arabic, as shown in this article, بيروت: جريدة النهار "الميلاد وما إليه"; ET: Kheder, "Christmas, etc.," *Beirut an-Nahār*.

[75] Joachim Jeremias, *The Prayers of Jesus* (London: SCM, 1976), 65.

[76] James Barr, "Abba Isn't Daddy," *JTS* 39 (1988): 28–47.

my Father's house into a market!" (John 2:16); "until that day when I drink it new with you in my Father's kingdom" (Matt 26:29); "My Father, if it is possible, may this cup be taken from me" (Matt 26:39, 42); "I am going to send you what my Father has promised" (Luke 24:49); "I am ascending to my Father and your Father" (John 20:17).[77]

Jesus' own use of the Aramaic word "abba" is sometimes recorded not in Aramaic but in Greek. This is what we think Matthew did in quoting from Mark. Where Mark 14:36 records that Jesus used the word "abba" in the garden of Gethsemane, Matthew 26:39 has the Greek expression, "My Father." We can compare this with Jesus' use of "Father" on intimate occasions such as in his intercessory prayer (John 17:1, 5, 21, 24) and in times of suffering, as when he cried out on the cross: "Father, into your hands I commit my spirit" (Luke 23:46).

Jesus' frequent references to his sonship to the Father, as established by the references cited above, crystallized the fact that he was the Son of God in the minds of the disciples. This belief was confirmed by their hearing the Father's voice that came from heaven at the baptism of Jesus: "You are my Son, whom I love; with you I am well pleased" (Mark 1:11; Luke 3:22; Matt 3:17); and again on the day of the transfiguration: "This is my Son, whom I have chosen; listen to him" (Luke 9:35; see Mark 1:11; Matt 17:5). All three Synoptic Gospels recount these two incidents.

It is true that Jesus did not use the exact title "Son of God" to refer to himself, explicitly saying, "I am the Son of God." However, the way he addressed God as his heavenly Father left no doubt about the matter. And he left it to his disciples and those around him to discover his true identity. There were some who did this: Nathanael said, "you are the Son of God" (John 1:49); those possessed by demons asked, "What do you want with us, Son of God?" (Matt 8:29); and Peter said, "You are the Messiah, the Son of the living God" (Matt 16:16). There is also the confession of the Roman officer at the cross when Jesus died, "Surely this man was the Son of God!" (Mark 15:39).

It is true that Jesus sometimes used the generic word "Son" to indicate that he was the Son of God. He does this once in the Synoptic Gospels, saying,

> All things have been committed to me by my Father. No one knows who the Son is except the Father, and no one knows who the Father is except the Son and those to whom the Son chooses to reveal him. (Luke 10:22; Matt 11:27)

He does it three times in the Gospel of John: "So if the Son sets you free, you will be free indeed" (John 8:36), "I will do whatever you ask in my name, so that the Father may be glorified in the Son" (John 14:13), and "Father, . . . glorify your Son, that your

---

[77] The expression "my father" is used directly by Jesus four times in Luke, 14 times in Matthew, and 25 times in John. It is mentioned in Mark only once, indirectly (Mark 8:38).

Son may glorify you" (John 17:1). But his use of the word "Son" is insignificant compared to the number of times and the range of occasions on which he used the word "Father" or the expression "My Father."

The use of the title "Son of God" for Jesus was confirmed by his resurrection, as is clear from the words of the apostle Paul,

> regarding his Son, who as to his earthly life was a descendant of David, and who through the Spirit of holiness was appointed the Son of God in power by his resurrection from the dead: Jesus Christ our Lord. (Rom 1:3–4)

Paul also links the sonship of Jesus with the resurrection in the sermon recorded by Luke in the book of Acts:

> What God promised our ancestors he has fulfilled for us, their children, by raising up Jesus. As it is written in the second Psalm:
>
> "You are my son;
>> today I have become your father." (Acts 13:32–33)

We can also establish a link between the two verses that have just been quoted and these verses:

> But those who are considered worthy of taking part in the age to come and in the resurrection from the dead will neither marry nor be given in marriage, and they can no longer die; for they are like the angels. They are God's children, since they are children of the resurrection. (Luke 20:35–36)

The supreme declaration of Jesus' sonship is found in the prologue to the Gospel of John:

> The Word became flesh and made his dwelling among us. We have seen his glory, the glory of the one and only Son, who came from the Father, full of grace and truth. . . . No one has ever seen God, but the one and only Son, who is himself God and is in closest relationship with the Father, has made him known. (John 1:14, 18)

John used the Greek word *monogenēs* to say that Jesus is the only unique and incomparable Son of God. The fact of his being the only Son of God who is equal to and one with the Father in essence is clear from the opening line of John's Gospel:

> In the beginning was the Word, and the Word was with God, and the Word was God. (John 1:1)

John formed the phrase in a way that indicates that the Word shared the essence of God himself. That is why the New English Bible translates these words as "and what God was, the Word was."

Jesus himself explained the meaning of his claim to be the Son of God when the Jews accused him of healing on the Sabbath:

> So, because Jesus was doing these things on the Sabbath, the Jewish leaders began to persecute him. In his defense Jesus said to them, "My Father is always at his work to this very day, and I too am working" (John 5:16–17)

John commented on these words as follows:

> For this reason they tried all the more to kill him; not only was he breaking the Sabbath, but he was even calling God his own Father, making himself equal with God. (John 5:18)

John's explanation of Jesus' sonship is clear here: the Son is equal to his Father in nature. Just as a human son is equal to his father in his human nature, so the divine Son is equal to his Father in his divine nature. By the same logic, the offspring of a human is human, but the offspring of God is divine.

The early church used John's words "born of God" (1 John 5:18) as it created eloquent confessions of faith, setting out the nature of Jesus' sonship in all its sublimity and stressing the equality or unity in essence between the Father and the Son. The most widely used of these confessions is the Nicene-Constantinopolitan Creed, which was adopted at Nicaea in AD 325 and amended in Constantinople in AD 381. It says in part:

> We believe in one God, the Father Almighty, Maker of heaven and earth, and of all things visible and invisible;
> And in one Lord Jesus Christ, the Son of God, the Only-begotten, Begotten of the Father before all ages, Light of Light, Very God of Very God, Begotten, not made; of one essence with the Father, by whom all things were made.

The title "Son of God" was used of Jesus more than any other title, except the title "Christ," which became part of the common form of his name "Jesus Christ." Peter's confession in the Gospel of Matthew has echoed throughout time: "You are the Messiah, the Son of the living God" (Matt 16:16). That this was the belief of the church was confirmed by the preaching of Saul of Tarsus, later the apostle Paul, who "began to preach in the synagogues that Jesus is the Son of God . . . [and] the Messiah" (see Acts 9:20–22). The apostle John says that those who believe that Jesus is the Son of God overcome the world (1 John 5:5) and speaks of his Master as "Jesus Christ, the Father's Son" (2 John 3).

Third Title: Son of Man

Jesus frequently referred to himself as the Son of Man, and his disciples or those who wrote the gospels used this title when speaking of him. But it is found only in the gospels, and nowhere else in the rest of the New Testament except once in the book of Acts, where Luke quotes the dying Stephen as saying, "I see heaven open and the Son of Man standing at the right hand of God" (Acts 7:56). Similar wording is used, but not as a title, in Hebrews 2:6. Revelation 1:13 and 14:14 refer to seeing someone "like a son of man."

Jesus generally avoided referring to himself as the Son of God and the Christ, but he did not hesitate to use the title "Son of Man." It was clearly the title he preferred. So it is strange that this title that Jesus himself used fell out of use, whereas the titles he avoided are the ones by which he has been known throughout history.

So we have to ask why Jesus would prefer to use the title Son of Man rather than any of the other options? What did this title imply? Was there any danger for Jesus in using this title?

To answer these questions we have to learn more about the meaning of this title and the implications of using it in the contexts where we find it.

First Meaning: A Human Being

Ninety-three times in the book of Ezekiel, beginning at Ezekiel 2:1, the prophet is addressed as "son of man," or literally in the Hebrew, "son of Adam." Here the meaning is clearly "human being," and the Lord is stressing that Ezekiel is a mere man.

This interpretation of the phrase is supported by the words of the psalmist:

> When I look at your heavens, the work of your fingers,
> the moon and the stars, which you have set in place,
> what is man that you are mindful of him,
> and the son of man that you care for him?
> Yet you have made him a little lower than the heavenly beings
> and crowned him with glory and honor.
> You have given him dominion over the works of your hands;
> You have put all things under his feet. (Ps 8:3–6 ESV)

This whole psalm speaks about "man" as just a human being. But the writer to the Hebrews also sees a messianic dimension in this psalm (Heb 2:5–9).

We can also judge the meaning of this phrase from the fact that David used the plural form "O men" to refer to people in general (Ps 4:2 ESV), as did Jesus when he said, "all sins will be forgiven the children of man" (Mark 3:28 ESV).

Second Meaning: The Sovereign King

In the book of Daniel, "son of man" has a different meaning. The expression is found in an Aramaic passage:

> I saw in the night visions,
> and behold, with the clouds of heaven
> there came one like a son of man,
> and he came to the Ancient of Days
> and was presented before him.

> And to him was given dominion
>> and glory and a kingdom,
> that all peoples, nations, and languages
>> should serve him;
> his dominion is an everlasting dominion,
>> which shall not pass away,
> and his kingdom one
>> that shall not be destroyed. (Dan 7:13–14 ESV)

Here the "son of man" is someone far greater than a mere man. The context shows that he has the right to stand before God, to have power and kingship, to receive the worship of all nations and to reign forever. This is more than just a man. He is a someone with authority!

Which of these two meanings of the expression "son of man" did Jesus have in mind when he referred to himself as the Son of Man? Was he indicating his humanity or his lordship and messianic role? To answer that question, we have to dig deeper.

Interpretation of the "Son of Man" in Daniel

To whom does the phrase "the son of man" in Daniel 7 refer? The answer is, "the saints of the Most High." This much is clear from the rest of chapter 7. The "son of man" appears after Daniel has seen four great beasts (a lion, a bear, a leopard, and a fourth beast with iron teeth). These beasts represent four sequential kingdoms, the last of which inherited the previous kingdoms and controlled their territory. This kingdom will persecute the "saints of the Most High," meaning Daniel's people, the Jews. Then God, "the Ancient of Days," will intervene and strip this oppressive kingdom of its authority and transfer its greatness and power to "the saints of the Most High." There is a parallelism within the chapter, with the vision of "the son of man" coming after the vision of the four beasts at the start of the chapter, and the reference to "the saints of the Most High" coming after the interpretation of the four beasts at the end of the chapter. Thus it appears that "the son of man" is equivalent to "the saints of the Most High" (cf. Dan 7:13, 14, 26–27).

While we cannot ignore this interpretation, Christian scholars do question why the first reference to the "son of man" is in the singular, referring to an individual, whereas "the saints of the Most High" is a plural expression. Who is this person who gathers in himself all "the saints of the Most High"? Our questions regarding the title "son of man" increase!

The Title "Son of Man" in the Intertestamental Period

We have to turn to the pseudepigrapha if we are to know what the people of Jesus' day understood in regard to the Son of Man mentioned in Daniel. What we find is that the title "Son of Man" is often used in the book of 1 Enoch. For example, the writer describes the Son of Man as being with the Ancient of Days, whose hair is white as wool and as having a face as beautiful as that of an angel. When Enoch asked one of the angels who this man was, he was told:

> This is the Son of Man who has righteousness, and with whom righteousness dwells; he will reveal all the treasures of that which is secret, for the Lord of spirits has chosen him, and through uprightness his lot has surpassed all before the Lord of Spirits for ever. And this Son of Man whom you have seen will . . . cast down the kings from their thrones and from their kingdoms, for they do not exalt him . . . and do not acknowledge whence their kingdom was given to them. (1 En. 46:1–6)

He goes on to say that the Son of Man was given his name before creation, and that he was named in the presence of the Ancient of Days before the creation of the sun and stars. He is a staff to the righteous, helping them not to stumble and fall. He is "the hope of those who grieve." He preserves the righteousness because "they have hated . . . this world of iniquity, and all its works and its ways." The powerful kings who relied on "the work of their hands" will not be able to save themselves "on the day of their distress." Thus the Lord of spirits will deliver them to his chosen ones and they will "burn before the righteous, and sink before the holy, and no trace will be found of them." No one will help them because "they denied the Lord of spirits and his Christ" (1 En. 48:2–10).

The book of Enoch goes on to say that when sinners see the Son of Man sitting on his glorious throne, they will be filled with terror. Kings and princes will glorify him as he has dominion over all. He was hidden from the very beginning, but was in the presence of God the Most High who manifested him to the chosen ones. All the kings and the great will fall on their faces before the Son of Man, worshipping him and pleading for mercy. However, the Lord of spirits will deliver them to angels to be punished because they persecuted his children and chosen ones. Meanwhile the righteous and the chosen ones will be saved, and the Lord of spirits will be above them all and they will live with the Son of Man, clothed with robes of glory (1 En. 62:5–16).

The writer of the book of Enoch ends his section on the Son of Man by describing him sitting on the throne of judgment, having been assigned the task of erasing the sinners who misled the world from the earth. Once that is done, there will be no corruption, for the Son of Man will be manifest and will sit "on the throne of his glory . . . and the word of that Son of Man will be strong before the Lord of spirits" (1 En. 69:26–29).

A review of all that is said about the Son of Man in the above passages shows how the writer of 1 Enoch interpreted and built on what was said about the Son of Man in Daniel 7:13–14. Some of what is said in 1 Enoch is echoed in passages like Matthew 25:31; John 5:27; 2 Thessalonians 1:7–8; and Revelation 1:14. Thus the passages from Daniel and the book of 1 Enoch together help to clarify the popular understanding of the Son of Man who would be manifested in the last days.

Use of "Son of Man" in the New Testament

Matthew, Mark, and Luke all record Jesus using the title "Son of Man" when referring to himself. They also use this title to refer to him. We will now look at the various contexts in which it is used.

When healing a paralyzed man, Jesus used the title "Son of Man" in the context of his authority to forgive sins: "But I want you to know that the Son of Man has authority on earth to forgive sins" (Mark 2:10). We can judge the importance of this claim from the reaction of the teachers of the law who said, "He's blaspheming! Who can forgive sins but God alone?" (Mark 2:7).

There is also an indication that the title "Son of Man" was used in the context of the authority to legislate, for Mark wrote: "The Sabbath was made for man, not man for the Sabbath. So the Son of Man is Lord even of the Sabbath" (Mark 2:27–28). The "so" in the last sentence means "for this reason" and was either said by Jesus or is a comment from Mark (cf. Mark 7:19). Jesus here changes the concept of the Sabbath and makes it a blessing rather than a prison.

In some contexts we also find the title "Son of Man" being used interchangeably with references to Jesus' being the Messiah, suggesting that the titles "Son of Man" and "Messiah" are seen as synonymous.

> Jesus . . . asked his disciples, "Who do people say the Son of Man is?" . . .
> "But what about you?" he asked. "Who do you say I am?"
> Simon Peter answered, "You are the Messiah." (Matt 16:13–16; Mark 8:27–29)

Jesus promptly warned them not to make his identity public, and then "began to teach them that the Son of Man must suffer many things and be rejected" (Mark 8:30–31; Luke 9:21, 22). In this incident, not only do the two titles "Son of Man" and "Messiah" unite in the person of Jesus, but also the notion of suffering is linked with glory—the Son of Man is simultaneously the Glorious One and the Suffering Savior.

We see the same link in the following passage from the Gospel of Mark:

> "If anyone is ashamed of me and my words in this adulterous and sinful generation, the Son of Man will be ashamed of them when he comes in his Father's glory with the holy angels."
> And he said to them, "Truly I tell you, some who are standing here will not taste death before they see that the kingdom of God has come with power."
> After six days Jesus took Peter, James and John with him and led them up a high mountain, where they were all alone. There he was transfigured before them. His clothes became dazzling white, whiter than anyone in the world could bleach them. And there appeared before them Elijah and Moses, who were talking with Jesus.
> Peter said to Jesus, "Rabbi, it is good for us to be here. Let us put up three shelters—one

for you, one for Moses and one for Elijah." (He did not know what to say, they were so frightened.)

Then a cloud appeared and covered them, and a voice came from the cloud: "This is my Son, whom I love. Listen to him!"

Suddenly, when they looked around, they no longer saw anyone with them except Jesus.

As they were coming down the mountain, Jesus gave them orders not to tell anyone what they had seen until the Son of Man had risen from the dead. They kept the matter to themselves, discussing what "rising from the dead" meant. And they asked him, "Why do the teachers of the law say that Elijah must come first?"

Jesus replied, "To be sure, Elijah does come first, and restores all things. Why then is it written that the Son of Man must suffer much and be rejected?" (Mark 8:38; 9:1–12)

The title "Son of Man" is mentioned in the context of suffering three times in the three prophesies Jesus made about his death to his disciples before going to the cross. The first prophecy occurred just after Peter had declared that Jesus was the Messiah:

He then began to teach them that the Son of Man must suffer many things and be rejected by the elders, the chief priests and the teachers of the law, and that he must be killed and after three days rise again (Mark 8:31; Matt 16:21; Luke 9:22)

The second prophecy came after Jesus came down from the Mount of Transfiguration and healed a child:

They left that place and passed through Galilee. Jesus did not want anyone to know where they were, because he was teaching his disciples. He said to them, "The Son of Man is going to be delivered into the hands of men. They will kill him, and after three days he will rise." (Mark 9:30–31; Matt 17:22–32; Luke 9:44)

Jesus gave the third prophecy about his suffering and death when he was in Judea before arriving at Jericho on his way to Jerusalem:

They were on their way up to Jerusalem, with Jesus leading the way, and the disciples were astonished, while those who followed were afraid. Again he took the Twelve aside and told them what was going to happen to him. "We are going up to Jerusalem," he said, "and the Son of Man will be delivered over to the chief priests and the teachers of the law. They will condemn him to death and will hand him over to the Gentiles, who will mock him and spit on him, flog him and kill him. Three days later he will rise." (Mark 10:32–34; Matt 20:17–19; Luke 18:31–33)

These three prophecies affirm the link between the title "Son of Man" and suffering, and show that the glorious Son of Man mentioned in Daniel as having eternal authority has to go through the valley of tears before being exalted to the throne following the resurrection.

The title "Son of Man" is also used in the eschatological context of Christ's coming to reign on earth at the end of time. The descriptions of his coming include references to Daniel's vision of the Son of Man coming on the clouds:

> In my vision at night I looked, and there before me was one like a son of man, coming with the clouds of heaven. He approached the Ancient of Days and was led into his presence. (Dan 7:13)

Add to this the reign and authority given to the son of man by the Ancient of Days, so that all the nations will worship him and he will reign over them forever.

Students of the apocalyptic literature that was widely read in the late Old Testament period and in the intertestamental period will notice that in those writings great events such as God's judgment or the coming of the Messiah are accompanied by global phenomena that are described with rhetorical exaggeration to indicate their seriousness. This is clearly seen in the following description of the coming of the Son of Man given by Jesus and recorded in the three Synoptic Gospels:

> The sun will be darkened,
>   and the moon will not give its light;
> the stars will fall from the sky,
>   and the heavenly bodies will be shaken.
>
> Then will appear the sign of the Son of Man in heaven. And then all the peoples of the earth will mourn when they see the Son of Man coming on the clouds of heaven, with power and great glory. And he will send his angels with a loud trumpet call, and they will gather his elect from the four winds, from one end of the heavens to the other. (Matthew 24:29–31; Mark 13:24–27; Luke 21:25–27)

The title "Son of Man" was also used in the context of having the authority to judge and to question people about what they had done during their lives on earth. This usage is linked to the glory of the Son of Man mentioned in Daniel. It is in this context that Jesus said;

> If anyone is ashamed of me and my words in this adulterous and sinful generation, the Son of Man will be ashamed of them when he comes in his Father's glory with the holy angels. (Mark 8:38)

The point is made even more clearly in Matthew 25:31–33:

> When the Son of Man comes in his glory, and all the angels with him, he will sit on his glorious throne. All the nations will be gathered before him, and he will separate the people one from another as a shepherd separates the sheep from the goats. He will put the sheep on his right and the goats on his left.

There is also mention of the Son of Man's judgment on Israel; that is, his asking the tribes of Israel about their attitude to him.

> Jesus said to them: "Truly I tell you, at the renewal of all things, when the Son of Man sits on his glorious throne, you who have followed me will also sit on twelve thrones, judging the twelve tribes of Israel." (Matt 19:28)

In the Gospel of John, we see the title "Son of Man" used in the context of having the authority to judge:

> For as the Father has life in himself, so he has granted the Son also to have life in himself. And he has given him authority to judge because he is the Son of Man. Do not be amazed at this, for a time is coming when all who are in their graves will hear his voice and come out—those who have done what is good will rise to live, and those who have done what is evil will rise to be condemned. (John 5:26–29)

The title "Son of Man" is also used in relation to the highest possible position at the right hand of God. Using the title in this context indicates that the Son of Man assumes the highest power in the universe. This is in complete accord with what was said in the book of Daniel about the Son of Man:

> There before me was one like a son of man, coming with the clouds of heaven. He approached the Ancient of Days and was led into his presence. He was given authority, glory and sovereign power; all nations and peoples of every language worshiped him. (Dan 7:13–14)

Jesus referred to this status when he stood before the high priest who asked him:

> "Are you the Messiah, the Son of the Blessed One?"
>
> "I am," said Jesus. "And you will see the Son of Man sitting at the right hand of the Mighty One and coming on the clouds of heaven." (Mark 14:61–62)

We should pay attention to the fact that Jesus, at this most critical moment in his earthly life, declared that he was both the Messiah and the Son of Man, uniting in himself the two titles. That was why the high priest tore his clothes and accused him of blasphemy. He could not believe that the person standing before him on trial was the "Lord of glory" (1 Cor 2:8).

The church's understanding of the linkage of Jesus and the Son of Man was deepened by the words of Stephen, the first martyr, as he lay dying, "I see heaven open and the Son of Man standing at the right hand of God" (Acts 7:56).

In his description of Jesus at the start of the book of Revelation, John remembers the image of someone "like a son of man" in Daniel 7 and redraws it in the light of Jesus' postresurrection glory, offering a wonderful symbolic metaphor for Jesus' person, work, and status:

I turned around to see the voice that was speaking to me. And when I turned I saw seven golden lampstands, and among the lampstands was someone like a son of man, dressed in a robe reaching down to his feet and with a golden sash around his chest. The hair on his head was white like wool, as white as snow, and his eyes were like blazing fire. His feet were like bronze glowing in a furnace, and his voice was like the sound of rushing waters. In his right hand he held seven stars, and coming out of his mouth was a sharp, double-edged sword. His face was like the sun shining in all its brilliance.

When I saw him, I fell at his feet as though dead. Then he placed his right hand on me and said: "Do not be afraid. I am the First and the Last. I am the Living One; I was dead, and now look, I am alive for ever and ever! And I hold the keys of death and Hades." (Rev 1:12–18)

All the above evidences combine to indicate that Jesus used the title "Son of Man" in the sense described in the book of Daniel, affirming the fact that he was indeed the coming king and fully aware of the implications of his claim. No doubt, he preferred to use the title "Son of Man" rather than "Messiah" because the latter had connotations of political and earthly power. The title "Son of Man" had no political connotations, but did have eschatological overtones referring to the rule of God at the end of time through the person he had chosen, the one closest to him, the Son of Man. God will give him an eternal reign and all nations will worship him.

In conclusion, I reject the opinion that Jesus used the title "Son of Man" to refer to himself as just a human being, instead of using the first-person pronoun "I" or the third person pronoun "he."[78] Rather, Jesus chose to use the title "Son of Man" in his daily conversation about himself in various ways in order to establish the idea that he was the Son of Man in the minds of his hearers.

However, there are some who argue that Jesus was not referring to himself when he used the title "Son of Man," but to someone else, the royal eschatological figure who would be coming to rule the world under God's authority. These people base their belief on sayings of Jesus such as, "I tell you, whoever publicly acknowledges me before others, the Son of Man will also acknowledge before the angels of God" (Luke 12:8), and "If anyone is ashamed of me and my words in this adulterous and sinful generation, the Son of Man will be ashamed of them when he comes in his Father's glory with the holy angels" (Mark 8:38). On this basis, they separate Jesus from "the Son of Man," saying that Jesus did not consider himself the Son of Man, but that after the resurrection his followers linked him to the Son of Man, as can be seen in the gospels.[79] However, Jesus'

---

[78] Geza Vermes, professor of Jewish studies in Oxford University, expressed this opinion in an article entitled: "استعمال بار ناشا في الآرامية اليهودية"; ET: "The Use of *Bar Nasha* in Jewish Aramaic." It was first published in an appendix to Matthew Black's *An Aramaic Approach to the Gospels and Acts*, 3rd ed. (Oxford: Oxford University Press, 1967).

[79] One of the most prominent proponents of this view was A. J. B. Higgins, who wrote several articles and books on this subject, one of which is *Jesus and the Son of Man* (Philadelphia: Lutterworth, 1964).

frequent use of the title "Son of Man," and the variety of contexts in which this title was used of Jesus, as well as Jesus' own declarations that he was the Son of Man—the last of which was before the high priest–undermine the claim of those who believe otherwise.

It remains to be said that the title "Son of Man" was widely misunderstood because it stands in contrast to the title "Son of God." Since the title "Son of God" refers to Jesus' divinity, it was natural to assume that the title "Son of Man" refers to his humanity. Thus, the meaning of the title "Son of Man" as it relates to his global eschatological reign and dominion over history began to fade over time, to be replaced by the meaning that Jesus was just a human being. I pray that this misperception has been corrected by the evidence I have just presented and that the Son of Man will be manifested to us as he is in the New Testament.

The best conclusion to this section of the chapter is the question posed to the blind man who was told by Jesus to wash in the pool of Siloam. After healing him, Jesus asked, "Do you believe in the Son of Man?" (John 9:35).

Fourth Title: Servant of the Lord

After analyzing the titles "Messiah," "Son of God," and "Son of Man," which Jesus used for himself or that were used by the church when speaking of him, we come to the fourth title, "Servant of the Lord." This title is the last one, completing all the titles that reveal Jesus' messiahship and his mission of salvation, with all that it required.

Before linking this title to Jesus Christ, we have to make an objective analysis of the places in which it is found in the Old Testament, especially in Isaiah. We do so because the identity of the servant of the Lord is controversial. Does he represent the people of Israel, the faithful remnant, Isaiah himself, one of the prophets, or the promised Christ? Did the life of Jesus fulfill what was said about this servant? After analyzing the texts, we will see which of these interpretations most agrees with all the implications of the identity of the suffering servant and his mission.

But before we can do that, we need to examine the etymology of the term "servant of the Lord" and its usage in the Old Testament.

The Word "Servant"

The expression "servant of the Lord" in Arabic parallels the expression "servant of Yahweh" in Hebrew (Isa 42:19). In both cases, this "servant" is a bond-slave who does not serve for wages but because he is owned by his master. A slave has no will of his own; there is only the will of his master, and a slave carries out the master's will.

The Greek word *doulos* means a bond-servant. This meaning of the word is clear in the parable recorded in Luke 17:7–10:

> Suppose one of you has a servant plowing or looking after the sheep. Will he say to the servant when he comes in from the field, "Come along now and sit down to eat"?

Won't he rather say, "Prepare my supper, get yourself ready and wait on me while I eat and drink; after that you may eat and drink"? Will he thank the servant because he did what he was told to do? So you also, when you have done everything you were told to do, should say, "We are unworthy servants; we have only done our duty."

The word "servant" or slave was also used metaphorically of the steward who managed the affairs of the house or the field on behalf of the householder and under his supervision. This was paid work. It was in this sense that Eliezer of Damascus was a servant in Abraham's household (Gen 15:2). We see a similar relationship in Genesis 24:2: "He said to the senior servant in his household, the one in charge of all that he had, 'Put your hand under my thigh.'" Jesus was speaking of the job of a steward when he said:

> Who then is the faithful and wise manager, whom the master puts in charge of his servants to give them their food allowance at the proper time? It will be good for that servant whom the master finds doing so when he returns. (Luke 12:42–43)

Since the Hebrew word "servant" is the same word used to refer to a slave or a boy (Gen 22:3; 37:2; 1 Sam 17:33), the Septuagint translated it with the Greek word *pais*, meaning boy or young man, in places where the word "servant" was used in Hebrew in Isaiah 42:1; 44:1, 21; 49:6; 52:13; whereas in Isaiah 49:3, 5, the word *doulos* was used as a translation of the word "servant" in Hebrew. There is evidence of this usage in the New Testament also, in the story of the healing of the centurion's servant: "Say the word, and my servant will be healed" (Luke 7:1–10).

From the trove of Greek religious terminology in the Septuagint, Luke borrowed the word *pais* (boy, servant) from the book of Isaiah to use in the book of Acts, using it when referring to Jesus in Acts 3:13, 26 and 4:27, 30, and to David in Acts 4:25. The older Arab translations also use the word "boy" in these places. However, the new Catholic translation uses the word "servant" to match the Hebrew text in the book of Isaiah, which makes it easier to show that Jesus is the servant of the Lord.

The Servant of the Lord in the Old Testament

Being a servant of the Lord, serving God faithfully and doing his will, is an incomparable honor. Thus a title of humility becomes a title of honor. Such is the difference between serving unjust people and serving the just and righteous God. This lofty meaning of the word "servant" was present in the Old Testament as a title for Abraham, who was known as the friend of God: "For he remembered his holy promise given to his servant Abraham" (Ps 105:42). It was also used for Moses the lawgiver: "the people feared the LORD and put their trust in him and in Moses his servant" (Exod 14:31; see also "Moses the servant of the LORD" [Deut 34:5]). It was used as a title for Joshua: "Joshua son of Nun, the servant of the LORD" (Josh 24:29), and for King David: "Go and tell my servant David, 'This is what the LORD says: Are you the one to build me a house to dwell in?'" (2 Sam 7:5, 8). It was also used of the prophet Elijah, "The LORD has done what he announced through his servant Elijah" (2 Kgs 10:10), the patient Job, "my servant Job" (Job 1:8; 2:3; 42:7–8), and for Isaiah and the other prophets, "Just as my servant Isaiah has gone stripped and barefoot" (Isa 20:3); "Surely the Sovereign LORD does nothing without revealing his plan to his servants the prophets" (Amos 3:7).

The writer of Isaiah was familiar with the concept of being a servant of the Lord and its honorable heritage, and so he used this title in Isaiah 40–55 to describe the person we will now be studying.

The Servant of the Lord in Isaiah

In Isaiah 40–55 the word "servant" (singular) occurs nineteen times in the form meaning "the servant that belongs to the Lord." Thus this section of Isaiah is often known as "The Book of the Servant of the Lord." All the chapters from 40–55 are in poetic form, with no prose at all. The four poems in this section that deal extensively with the servant and are considered messianic are known as the Servant Songs or the Songs of the Suffering Servant. They do not share this name with other poems that are not considered messianic.

What follows is a comprehensive presentation of these poetic passages, including the four Servant Songs, with a brief explanatory comment on the identity and nature of the servant of the Lord. As always, we have to read the whole context in which these passages occur in order to get the full picture of this important subject. These verses may be described as the holy of holies when it comes to understanding Jesus' messianic role.

First Passage

> But you, Israel, my servant,
>> Jacob, whom I have chosen,
>> you descendants of Abraham my friend,
> I took you from the ends of the earth,
>> from its farthest corners I called you.
> I said, "You are my servant";
>> I have chosen you and have not rejected you.
> So do not fear, for I am with you;
>> do not be dismayed, for I am your God.
> I will strengthen you and help you;
>> I will uphold you with my righteous right hand.
> "All who rage against you
>> will surely be ashamed and disgraced;
> those who oppose you
>> will be as nothing and perish.
> Though you search for your enemies,
>> you will not find them.

> Those who wage war against you
>> will be as nothing at all.
> For I am the LORD your God
>> who takes hold of your right hand
> and says to you, Do not fear;
>> I will help you." (Isa 41:8–13)

The passage is God's message to the Israelite people who were in exile in Babylon. It encourages them to respond to the call and return to their land. They are addressed using the names "Israel" and "Jacob," a reference to the grandsons of Abraham, a point that is driven home by the reference to them as "you descendants of Abraham my friend." The word "servant" occurs twice in this passage to indicate that the people of Israel are specially designated as having the role of being God's servant. Here the singular form of the word "servant" clearly refers to the entire nation.

Second Passage

> "Here is my servant, whom I uphold,
>> my chosen one in whom I delight;
> I will put my Spirit on him,
>> and he will bring justice to the nations.
> He will not shout or cry out,
>> or raise his voice in the streets.
> a bruised reed he will not break,
>> and a smoldering wick he will not snuff out.
> In faithfulness he will bring forth justice;
>> he will not falter or be discouraged
> till he establishes justice on earth.
>> In his teaching the islands will put their hope."
> This is what God the LORD says—
> the Creator of the heavens, who stretches them out,
>> who spreads out the earth with all that springs from it,
>> who gives breath to its people,
>> and life to those who walk on it:
> "I, the LORD, have called you in righteousness;
>> I will take hold of your hand.
> I will keep you and will make you
>> to be a covenant for the people
>> and a light for the Gentiles." (Isa 42:1–6)

In this passage the servant is called "my servant" and described as "my chosen one in whom I delight," and God promises to "put my Spirit on him." Three times the text links the servant and the role of delivering truth and light to the rest of the nations.

Now to the question: Does the word "servant" here refer to the people of Israel? Or does it refer to an individual? A number of the descriptions of what the servant does use singular verbs; for example, "He will not shout or cry out, or raise his voice in the streets." However, the conclusive statement that confirms that servant here is an individual is this: "I . . . will make you to be a covenant for the people and a light for the Gentiles." If "servant" was being used to refer to the people of Israel, how could the people of Israel be a covenant for the people of Israel? Thus, here the servant must be an individual. This was the opinion of the early church, for Matthew considers Isaiah 42:1–4 a prophecy referring to Jesus Christ (Matt 12:17–21).

Scholars refer to this passage as the first of the Servant Songs, since it speaks of a unique servant. The other three songs are found in Isaiah 49:1–7; 50:4–9; and 52:13–53:12.

Third Passage

"Hear, you deaf;
    look, you blind, and see!
Who is blind but my servant,
    and deaf like the messenger I send?
Who is blind like the one in covenant with me,
    blind like the servant of the LORD?
You have seen many things, but you pay no attention;
    your ears are open, but you do not listen."
It pleased the LORD
    for the sake of his righteousness
    to make his law great and glorious.
But this is a people plundered and looted,
    all of them trapped in pits
    or hidden away in prisons.
They have become plunder,
    with no one to rescue them;
they have been made loot,
    with no one to say, "Send them back."
Which of you will listen to this
    or pay close attention in time to come?
Who handed Jacob over to become loot,
    and Israel to the plunderers?
Was it not the LORD,
    against whom we have sinned?
For they would not follow his ways;
    they did not obey his law. (Isa 42:18–24)

In this passage God argues with his people. We may ask how he can call on the deaf to hear and the blind to see. But what is happening here is that God is mocking those who were supposed to see, namely his own people, those whom he gave the title "the servant of the Lord." It seems that the people of Israel claimed that they desired righteousness and honored the law, but they were not prepared to walk in the way of the Lord or obey his law. There was thus no need for Israel to search for those who had punished them and sent them into exile, for the one who had done this was the Lord against whom they had sinned.

This passage deals with the nation of Israel that had sinned against the Lord even though it was called to be his servant. We need to remember the difference between "the servant of the Lord" as a people here and "the servant of the Lord" as an individual when we come to Isaiah 53, where the servant suffers not because of his own sins but because of the sins of his people (53:8) and in order to redeem the Gentiles (Isa 52:15).

Fourth Passage

> "You are my witnesses," declares the LORD,
>> "and my servant whom I have chosen,
> so that you may know and believe me
>> and understand that I am he.
> Before me no god was formed,
>> nor will there be one after me.
> I, even I, am the LORD,
>> and apart from me there is no savior.
> I have revealed and saved and proclaimed—
>> I, and not some foreign god among you.
> You are my witnesses," declares the LORD, "that I am God." (Isa 43:10–12)

Here God tells his people, "you are my witnesses" and again refers to them as his "servant" (singular). He wants them to witness to him and to his faithfulness, as befits a good servant of God.

Fifth Passage

> Yet you have not called on me, Jacob,
>> you have not wearied yourselves for me, Israel.
> You have not brought me sheep for burnt offerings,
>> nor honored me with your sacrifices.
> I have not burdened you with grain offerings
>> nor wearied you with demands for incense.
> You have not bought any fragrant calamus for me,
>> or lavished on me the fat of your sacrifices.
> But you have burdened me with your sins
>> and wearied me with your offenses.
> I, even I, am he who blots out
>> your transgressions, for my own sake,
>> and remembers your sins no more.

> Review the past for me,
>> let us argue the matter together;
>> state the case for your innocence.
> Your first father sinned;
>> those I sent to teach you rebelled against me.
> So I disgraced the dignitaries of your temple;
>> I consigned Jacob to destruction
>> and Israel to scorn.
> But now listen, Jacob, my servant,
>> Israel, whom I have chosen.
> This is what the LORD says—
>> he who made you, who formed you in the womb,
>> and who will help you:
> Do not be afraid, Jacob, my servant,
>> Jeshurun, whom I have chosen.
> For I will pour water on the thirsty land,
>> and streams on the dry ground;
> I will pour out my Spirit on your offspring,
>> and my blessing on your descendants. (Isa 43:22–44:3)

In this passage God admonishes his people and judges them. He says to them, in effect, "You did not worship me properly; instead, you burdened me with your sins. So I will condemn you and send you into exile to be humiliated." But then he adds, "but I will forgive you." God does this for his own sake, and promises them a coming blessing.

Here the text again reminds us that the people sinned against the Lord, even though they are, as a whole, called "the servant of the Lord," and that the Lord punished them for their sins.

Sixth Passage

> "Remember these things, Jacob,
>> for you, Israel, are my servant.
> I have made you, you are my servant;
>> Israel, I will not forget you.
> I have swept away your offenses like a cloud,
>> your sins like the morning mist.
> Return to me,
>> for I have redeemed you."
> Sing for joy, you heavens, for the LORD has done this;
>> shout aloud, you earth beneath.
> Burst into song, you mountains,
>> you forests and all your trees,
> for the LORD has redeemed Jacob,
>> he displays his glory in Israel. (Isa 44:21–23)

This passage repeats what has been said before, as the Lord says, "Remember, Israel, . . . you are my servant. . . . Return to me, for I have redeemed you." He reminds his people that they went astray from him and that they have to return to him because he has redeemed them.

Seventh Passage

> This is what the LORD says—
> > your Redeemer, who formed you in the womb:
> I am the LORD,
> > the Maker of all things,
> > who stretches out the heavens,
> > who spreads out the earth by myself,
> who foils the signs of false prophets
> > and makes fools of diviners,
> who overthrows the learning of the wise
> > and turns it into nonsense,
> who carries out the words of his servants
> > and fulfills the predictions of his messengers,
> who says of Jerusalem, "It shall be inhabited,"
> > of the towns of Judah, "They shall be rebuilt,"
> > and of their ruins, "I will restore them,"
> who says to the watery deep, "Be dry,
> > and I will dry up your streams,"
> who says of Cyrus, "He is my shepherd
> > and will accomplish all that I please;
> he will say of Jerusalem, 'Let it be rebuilt,'
> > and of the temple, 'Let its foundations be laid.'" (Isa 44:24–28)

It is clear from the context that here the prophet uses the word translated "servants" to refer to himself. He is saying that God has a servant who prophesies that Jerusalem will be rebuilt. God also has other messengers, other prophets whom he sends, and all of them too prophesy about the return of the people from exile and the rebuilding of Jerusalem and its temple. There is indeed an argument for giving the title "servant" to Isaiah, for elsewhere in the book we read, "Then the LORD said, "Just as my servant Isaiah has gone stripped and barefoot for three years" (Isa 20:3).

Eighth Passage

> This is what the LORD says to his anointed,
> > to Cyrus, whose right hand I take hold of
> to subdue nations before him
> > and to strip kings of their armor,
> to open doors before him
> > so that gates will not be shut:

> I will go before you
> > and will level the mountains;
> I will break down gates of bronze
> > and cut through bars of iron.
> I will give you hidden treasures,
> > riches stored in secret places,
> so that you may know that I am the LORD,
> > the God of Israel, who summons you by name.
> For the sake of Jacob my servant, of
> > Israel my chosen,
> I summon you by name
> > and bestow on you a title of honor,
> > though you do not acknowledge me. (Isa 45:1–4)

Cyrus, king of Persia, is here referred to as the Lord's "anointed." In other words, he is a king whom God has raised up to serve him and accomplish his purposes—though Cyrus did not even know the God of Israel. God raises Cyrus to help the people of Israel return to their land. Here the word "my servant" is again used to refer to the people of Israel.

Ninth Passage

> Leave Babylon,
> > flee from the Babylonians!
> Announce this with shouts of joy
> > and proclaim it.
> Send it out to the ends of the earth;
> > say, "The LORD has redeemed his servant Jacob." (Isa 48:20)

The text here also refers to the departure of the people of Israel from Babylon and their return to their land. The sentence "the LORD has redeemed his servant Jacob" indicates that God will save his people from the exile.

Tenth Passage

> Listen to me, you islands;
> > hear this, you distant nations:
> Before I was born the LORD called me;
> > from my mother's womb he has spoken my name.
> He made my mouth like a sharpened sword,
> > in the shadow of his hand he hid me;
> he made me into a polished arrow
> > and concealed me in his quiver.
> He said to me, "You are my servant,
> > Israel, in whom I will display my splendor."

But I said, "I have labored in vain;
>I have spent my strength for nothing at all.
Yet what is due me is in the LORD's hand,
>and my reward is with my God."
And now the LORD says—
>he who formed me in the womb to be his servant
to bring Jacob back to him
>and gather Israel to himself,
for I am honored in the eyes of the LORD
>and my God has been my strength—
he says:
"It is too small a thing for you to be my servant
>to restore the tribes of Jacob
>and bring back those of Israel I have kept.
I will also make you a light for the Gentiles,
>that my salvation may reach to the ends of the earth."
This is what the LORD says—
>the Redeemer and Holy One of Israel—
to him who was despised and abhorred by the nation,
>to the servant of rulers:
"Kings will see you and stand up,
>princes will see and bow down,
because of the LORD, who is faithful,
>the Holy One of Israel, who has chosen you." (Isa 49:1–7)

Here too we have to answer an important question related to the identity of the servant: Is the servant the people of Israel or an individual? The statement "You are my servant, Israel, in whom I will display my splendor" leads some people to insist that here the "servant" refers to Israel as a people. However, it is difficult to sustain this position in light of the clear indication that God raises up the servant in order to make Israel return to him.

But in calling the servant "Israel," the passage indicates that he represents the people of Israel. Thus the servant has to be someone who bears in himself the essence of the nation. He wants to save it, and so he suffers and sacrifices himself for it. But his only return for this is hatred; however, he will be the one to turn the nation back to God.

God honors him by saying, in effect, "It is not enough for you to save only your own people; I will make you a light for the Gentiles to bear my salvation to the ends of the earth." The early church understood this saying as referring to Jesus, as mentioned by Paul and Barnabas in Acts 13:47.

Scholars call this passage the second Servant Song, for it is one in the group of songs which indicate that the servant is an individual. The other three songs are found in Isaiah 42:1–7; 50:4–9; 52:13–53:12.

Eleventh Passage

The Sovereign Lord has given me a well-instructed tongue,
    to know the word that sustains the weary.
He wakens me morning by morning,
    wakens my ear to listen like one being instructed.
The Sovereign Lord has opened my ears;
    I have not been rebellious,
    I have not turned away.
I offered my back to those who beat me,
    my cheeks to those who pulled out my beard;
I did not hide my face
    from mocking and spitting.
Because the Sovereign Lord helps me,
    I will not be disgraced.
Therefore have I set my face like flint,
    and I know I will not be put to shame.
He who vindicates me is near.
    Who then will bring charges against me?
    Let us face each other!
Who is my accuser?
    Let him confront me!
It is the Sovereign Lord who helps me.
    Who will condemn me?
They will all wear out like a garment;
    the moths will eat them up.
Who among you fears the Lord
    and obeys the word of his servant?
Let the one who walks in the dark,
    who has no light,
trust in the name of the Lord
    and rely on their God." (Isa 50:4–10)

The above passage is known as the Third Servant Song. It is one in a group of songs that speak about the servant as an individual. This song expresses sadness about the servant's suffering: "I offered my back to those who beat me, my cheeks to those who pulled out my beard; I did not hide my face from mocking and spitting" (Isa 50:6). Some scholars suggest that the servant here is the writer himself, whether Isaiah or the author of this section of the book of Isaiah. However, it seems more likely that these words reflect the situation of the same person referred to in the previous passage (Isa 49:1–7) and in the one that follows (Isa 52:13–53:12), namely, the servant who suffers for his people.

Twelfth Passage

See, my servant will act wisely;
 he will be raised and lifted up and highly exalted.
Just as there were many who were appalled at him—
 his appearance was so disfigured beyond that of any human being
 and his form marred beyond human likeness—
so he will sprinkle many nations,
 and kings will shut their mouths because of him.
For what they were not told, they will see,
 and what they have not heard, they will understand.
Who has believed our message
 and to whom has the arm of the LORD been revealed?
He grew up before him like a tender shoot,
 and like a root out of dry ground.
He had no beauty or majesty to attract us to him,
 nothing in his appearance that we should desire him.
He was despised and rejected by mankind,
 a man of suffering, and familiar with pain.
Like one from whom people hide their faces
 he was despised, and we held him in low esteem.
Surely he took up our pain
 and bore our suffering,
yet we considered him punished by God,
 stricken by him, and afflicted.
But he was pierced for our transgressions,
 he was crushed for our iniquities;
the punishment that brought us peace was on him,
 and by his wounds we are healed.
We all, like sheep, have gone astray,
 each of us has turned to our own way;
and the LORD has laid on him
 the iniquity of us all.
He was oppressed and afflicted,
 yet he did not open his mouth;
he was led like a lamb to the slaughter,
 and as a sheep before its shearers is silent,
 so he did not open his mouth.
By oppression and judgment he was taken away.
 Yet who of his generation protested?
For he was cut off from the land of the living
 for the transgression of my people he was punished.

He was assigned a grave with the wicked,
    and with the rich in his death,
though he had done no violence,
    nor was any deceit in his mouth.
Yet it was the LORD's will to crush him and cause him to suffer,
    and though the LORD makes his life an offering for sin,
he will see his offspring and prolong his days,
    and the will of the LORD will prosper in his hand.
After he has suffered,
    he will see the light of life and be satisfied
by his knowledge my righteous servant will justify many,
    and he will bear their iniquities.
Therefore I will give him a portion among the great,
    and he will divide the spoils with the strong,
because he poured out his life unto death,
    and was numbered with the transgressors.
For he bore the sin of many,
    and made intercession for the transgressors. (Isa 52:13–53:12)

This is the last, climactic passage speaking about the servant. It is the last time the servant is mentioned in Isaiah. It is climactic because it speaks about the bitter suffering of the servant and his subsequent glorification.

What is said in this song about the servant of the Lord fits with what was said about him in the first song (Isa 42:1–7) and the third song (Isa 49:1–7)—he will be the source of salvation for his people and for all the nations of the world.

It is clear that the servant in this text is not simply the nation of Israel, although some see him in this way. But how can the servant both be Israel and bear the sins of all Israel? Moreover, if the reference is to an entire people, what does the following statement mean: "He was assigned a grave with the wicked, and with the rich in his death" (Isa 53:9)?

Others think that the "we" in this song refers to the Gentiles, who see the servant Israel suffering as a people not because of their own sins but for the sins of the Gentiles and for their salvation. Those who hold this view quote this passage:

Surely he took up our pain and bore our suffering, yet we considered him punished by God, stricken by him, and afflicted. But he was pierced for our transgressions, he was crushed for our iniquities. (Isa 53:4, 5)

However, this interpretation is implausible, for Isaiah 40–55 frequently states that Israel is suffering because of its own sins, not for the sins of others (Isa 40:2; 42:24–25; 43:24–28; 44:22; 50:1). Thus we can insist that this passage clearly reveals that the servant of the Lord is suffering for the sins of Israel, not that Israel is suffering for the sins of the Gentiles. The Gentile nations cannot consider Israel "stricken by God" since they do not know God. However, Israel considers the servant stricken by God (because of his own sins, for why else should he be stricken?). But God did not strike him because of his sins, but because of the sins of Israel and the other nations; he was "pierced for our transgressions, he was crushed for our iniquities" (Isa 53:4–5).

There are some who argue that the servant in this passage is the writer of the book of Isaiah. This is a natural question when hearing this passage. Like the Ethiopian eunuch who was in charge of the treasury of Candace, we ask, "Who is the prophet talking about, himself or someone else?" (Acts 8:34). In response to the eunuch's question, Philip began with this very passage of Scripture and told him the good news about Jesus. Thus the early church considered this passage about the servant of the Lord to be a prophecy about Jesus Christ. Those who have tried to argue otherwise lack evidence to support their opinion.

The Identity of the Servant of the Lord in Isaiah

The above analysis clearly shows that the phrase "servant of the Lord" is used in Isaiah 40–55 with three different referents: the people of Israel, Isaiah the prophet, and the individual suffering servant. We will now look at each of these in more detail.

- *The servant represents the people of Israel* (Isa 41:8–13; 42:18–24; 43:10–12; 43:22–44:3; 44:21–23; 45:1–4; 48:20). There are various permutations of this view, with some seeing the servant as representing the whole people of Israel, some arguing that he represents the pious remnant who suffered at the hands of and with their people, and some claiming that the reference is to a group of prophets or priests who represent the people and suffer for their sake.
- *The servant is the prophet Isaiah* (Isa 44:24–28). Because the text does not mention the name Isaiah, some argue that the reference is to whoever wrote this passage, or to a particular prophet who called for a return to their land, or even to a group of prophets, for translated literally the text is "carries out the words of his servant [singular] and fulfills the predictions of his messengers [plural]."
- *The servant is an individual suffering servant of the Lord* (Isa 42:1–7; 49:1–7; 50:4–10; 52:13–53:12). The four servant songs all clearly refer to a person who represents the whole nation. But who is this individual? Some say Hezekiah, Jehoiachin, Isaiah, Jeremiah, Ezekiel, or Zerubbabel. Others argue that this suffering person referred to as both "the servant of the Lord" and as "Israel" must be someone who represents the essence of the nation and exemplifies it. Who else can this person be but the heir of David's throne, Israel's king and promised Messiah, as stated in the closing paragraphs of Isaiah 40–55:

Give ear and come to me;
    listen, that you may live.
I will make an everlasting covenant with you,
    my faithful love promised to David.
See, I have made him a witness to the peoples,
    a ruler and commander of the peoples.
Surely you will summon nations you know not,
    and nations you do not know will come running to you,
because of the LORD your God,
    the Holy One of Israel,
for he has endowed you with splendor. (Isa 55:3–5)

On this basis that the "servant" is a king from David's line and a ruler of the peoples, the early church took this as an eschatological messianic fact and identified the suffering servant of the Lord with Jesus Christ, the Savior of the people of Israel and of all the nations of the world.

Jesus and the Title "Servant of the Lord"

The title "servant of the Lord" is different from the other titles Jesus used to identify himself. It refers to him specifically as the laboring servant whose sacrificial service culminates in death on the cross. But Jesus never directly claimed this title, just as he did not claim the title "Son of God." Instead, he carried out the work that goes with this title. All his life he lived out what is implied by the description of the suffering servant of the Lord in Isaiah 40–55. The title Jesus did not use in words was his because of his humble service. He was the servant of the Lord par excellence.

When Jesus read the Old Testament, did he actually see himself in the figure of suffering servant of the Lord? There can be no doubt that he did. The picture of the servant who suffers for the sins of all humanity, both his own people and the Gentiles, laid out the path to the cross.

The three main titles by which Jesus is known are the Son of God, the Messiah or Christ, and the Son of Man. All these titles indicate his divinity, uniqueness, greatness, and authority. However, the title "Servant of the Lord" indicates his humility, his suffering, and his redeeming death for the salvation of all. Without this title, the picture of Jesus as the suffering Savior is incomplete.

But do we have any other evidence that Jesus saw that his suffering was prophesied in the Old Testament? Yes, for it seems that the Servant Songs, especially in Isaiah 53, were the natural framework for the hints he gave about his suffering. He was probably referring to them when he said it is "written that the Son of Man must suffer much and be rejected" (Mark 9:12).

The reference to rejection is clear in the second Servant Song:

This is what the LORD says—
>
> the Redeemer and Holy One of Israel—

to him who was despised and abhorred by the nation,
>
> to the servant of rulers:

"Kings will see you and stand up,
>
> princes will see and bow down,

because of the LORD, who is faithful,
>
> the Holy One of Israel, who has chosen you." (Isa 49:7)

Another reference to suffering is found here:

He was despised and rejected by mankind,
>
> a man of suffering, and familiar with pain.

Like one from whom people hide their faces
>
> he was despised, and we held him in low esteem. (Isa 53:3)

Jesus made reference to this rejection, linking himself with the servant in Isaiah, by saying: "I tell you that this must be fulfilled in me. Yes, what is written about me is reaching its fulfillment" (Luke 22:37). These words are preceded by a direct quotation from the fourth Servant Song in Isaiah, where it says: "because he poured out his life unto death, and was numbered with the transgressors" (Isa 53:12).

Jesus also made a third reference to the servant songs of Isaiah:

Jesus took the Twelve aside and told them, "We are going up to Jerusalem, and everything that is written by the prophets about the Son of Man will be fulfilled. He will be delivered over to the Gentiles. They will mock him, insult him and spit on him; they will flog him and kill him. On the third day he will rise again." (Luke 18:31–33)

The details of the suffering Jesus would undergo are mentioned in the Servant Songs. The third song says:

I offered my back to those who beat me,
>
> my cheeks to those who pulled out my beard;

I did not hide my face
>
> from mocking and spitting. (Isa 50:6)

In the fourth song we read,

By oppression and judgment he was taken away.
>
> Yet who of his generation protested?

For he was cut off from the land of the living
>
> for the transgression of my people he was punished. (Isa 53:8)

The fourth indication that Jesus linked his atoning death with the servant of the Lord is found in the words, "This is my blood of the covenant, which is poured out for many" (Mark 14:24; Matt 26:28). Jesus said these words on an intimate occasion, during the Last Supper with his disciples, when he said that his time had come. We can link this saying to the fourth Servant Song by looking at the similarity of the sentences:

> But he was pierced for our transgressions,
>> he was crushed for our iniquities. . . .
> We all, like sheep, have gone astray,
>> each of us has turned to our own way;
> and the LORD has laid on him
>> the iniquity of us all. . . .
> For he was cut off from the land of the living
>> for the transgression of my people he was punished. . . .
> By his knowledge my righteous servant will justify many,
>> and he will bear their iniquities. . . .
> For he bore the sin of many,
>> and made intercession for the transgressors. (Isa 53:5, 6, 8, 11, 12)

Clearly Jesus alluded to the servant of the Lord, but did he ever use this title for himself? The closest he comes to doing so is in his allusion to Isaiah 53 when he was speaking to his disciples about greatness and service:

> You know that those who are regarded as rulers of the Gentiles lord it over them, and their high officials exercise authority over them. Not so with you. Instead, whoever wants to become great among you must be your servant, and whoever wants to be first must be slave of all. For even the Son of Man did not come to be served, but to serve, and to give his life as a ransom for many. (Mark 10:42–45)

In this passage he uses the Greek verb "serve," the noun form of which means "servant." In a parallel passage in the course of which he also speaks of himself as the Son of Man, he says: "But I am among you as one who serves" (Luke 22:27).

The final phrase in the earlier quotation, "and to give his life as a ransom for many," is the conclusion and climax of Isaiah 53:

> because he poured out his life unto death,
>> and was numbered with the transgressors.
> For he bore the sin of many,
>> and made intercession for the transgressors. (Isa 53:12)

It is abundantly clear that Jesus saw himself in the account of the servant's nature and his suffering in the Servant Songs in Isaiah. He did not explicitly say that he was the servant of the Lord, but he lived out the character of the servant in all respects until he reached his goal and was raised on the cross, giving himself to redeem his people Israel and all the nations of the world. This was the main mission of the servant of the Lord.

The Early Church and the Servant of the Lord

The book of Acts shows that from its earliest days, the church identified Jesus with the servant of the Lord. The two are united in the prophecy and its fulfillment. We see this in Peter's sermon and in the prayer of the disciples.

The first sign of the attribution of the title "the servant of the Lord" to Jesus in Acts occurs after the healing of the paralyzed man at the gate of the temple. When the people were astonished at what happened, Peter said to them,

> The God of Abraham, Isaac and Jacob, the God of our fathers, has glorified his servant Jesus. You handed him over to be killed, and you disowned him before Pilate, though he had decided to let him go. You disowned the Holy and Righteous One and asked that a murderer be released to you. . . .
>
> And you are heirs of the prophets and of the covenant God made with your fathers. He said to Abraham, "Through your offspring all peoples on earth will be blessed." When God raised up his servant, he sent him first to you to bless you by turning each of you from your wicked ways. (Acts 3:13–14, 25–26)

Here the word translated "servant" is one that means "slave" or "boy" in Greek (see also Luke 7:2). The translators of the Septuagint used the same Greek word to translate the Hebrew word "servant" in Isaiah 42:1; 44:1, 21; 49:6; and 52:13.

In this passage in Acts, Jesus is also spoken of as the "Righteous One," an expression that echoes Isaiah 53:11, where it says, "by his knowledge my righteous servant will justify many, and he will bear their iniquities."

The second and last reference to Jesus as the servant of the Lord in Acts is found in the prayer of the persecuted church:

> Sovereign Lord, . . . You spoke by the Holy Spirit through the mouth of your servant, our father David:
>
> > "Why do the nations rage? . . .
> > The kings of the earth rise up
> >   and the rulers band together
> > against the Lord
> >   and against his anointed one."
>
> Indeed Herod and Pontius Pilate met together with the Gentiles and the people of Israel in this city to conspire against your holy servant Jesus, whom you anointed. . . . Now, Lord, consider their threats and enable your servants to speak your word with great boldness. Stretch out your hand to heal and perform signs and wonders through the name of your holy servant Jesus. (Acts 4:24–30)

The Greek word for "boy" or "servant" occurs three times in this prayer. It is used as a title for David, whom God called "my servant" (2 Sam 7:5, 8), and then it is used twice as a title for Jesus: "your holy servant Jesus."

So far we have only been looking at the use of the word "servant" and relating it to "the servant of the Lord" in Isaiah. But there are many other places in the New Testament where the concept of the suffering servant is associated with Jesus and his suffering (leaving aside those verses in which Jesus himself made this association):

- In the Gospel of Matthew, Jesus is linked to the servant of the Lord in 8:16–17 (referring to Isa 53:4) and again in 12:15–21 (referring to Isa 42:1–3).
- In the book of Acts, there is the exchange between the Ethiopian eunuch and Philip. When the eunuch asked who the prophet was talking about in Isaiah 53, Philip began to tell him the good news about Jesus, beginning "with that very passage of scripture" (Acts 8:32–35). It is also said that in their preaching, Paul and Barnabas associated Jesus with the role of the servant as a "light for the Gentiles" (Acts 13:47; quoting Isa 49:6).
- In his letter, Peter uses four expressions derived from Isaiah 53:5, 6, 9, 12, linking Jesus to the servant of the Lord (1 Pet 2:21–24).

These obvious signs that the early church saw Jesus as the servant of the Lord in Isaiah 40–55 indicate that it was an article of faith that the prophecies of Isaiah about the servant of the Lord were fulfilled in Jesus Christ.[80]

It is clear to those who study "the servant of the Lord" in Isaiah and the relationship of the figure to Jesus of Nazareth that Jesus understood himself as being that servant and that he lived and died in that understanding. This was also the way the early church understood him, as revealed in the gospels, the book of Acts, the letters of Paul, and the rest of the New Testament. This is decisive evidence that in his person and his mission Jesus embodied Jewish thinking about the salvation he came to accomplish, not the ideas of any neighboring culture.

Conclusion regarding All Four Titles

This brief study of Jesus' four main titles—the Messiah/Christ, the Son of God, the Son of Man, and the Servant of the Lord—has shown that the first title indicates his royal status in Israel, the second reveals his origin and deity, the third reveals his global sovereignty over all nations, while the fourth title indicates his humanity, suffering, and death to redeem all humanity.

---

[80] Christopher North's study of the suffering servant is still an incomparable scholarly reference. After presenting all the Jewish and Christian interpretations of the suffering servant, he moves on in the second part of his book to a critical analysis of Isaiah 40–55. He concludes that there is general agreement that the picture of the servant finds its final fulfillment in Christ. Christopher R. North, *The Suffering Servant in Deutero-Isaiah* (London: Oxford University Press, 1948).

The meanings associated with these four titles cover all aspects of who Jesus is. The first three titles relate to aspects of his glory, whereas the fourth one relates to his humility, pain, and death on the cross (Phil 2:8). If we use only the first three titles, we are not doing him justice. However, the fourth title, "the servant of the Lord," fully expresses Jesus' identity and mission.

In the two Testaments, Jesus has many other titles that we have not considered here, including Prince of Peace, the Good Shepherd, Immanuel, the Savior of the world, the Prophet, the Word, the King, the Lord, the Son of David, the Faithful one, the Image of God, the Great High Priest, the Mediator, the Intercessor, the Lamb of God, the Way and the Truth, the Resurrection and the Life, the Cornerstone, the Light of the World, and so on. However, all these titles can be subsumed under the four main titles we have studied.

Finally, these four titles indicate that Jesus was intimately connected to his Jewish heritage, which permeates the books of the Old Testament. The titles Jesus used for himself, or those used of him by others, all emanate from concepts rooted in the Old Testament that Jesus developed and fulfilled in himself. This indicates the authenticity of his Jewish identity revealed in the teachings of the prophets. By reformulating and generalizing the religious background from which he sprang, Jesus became the Savior of the world.

JESUS' RELATIONSHIP TO JUDAISM IN HIS TIME

Now that we have proved Jesus' Jewish identity and his Jewish cultural background throughout his upbringing and education, it is time to investigate his relationship to the Judaism of his time, and to describe the areas of agreement and of tension in this relationship until his death on the cross. Here we have to deal with another question: Jesus may have been born a Jew and raised as a Jew, but did he remain a Jew? If the answer is yes, why did the Jews crucify him? If the answer is no, why does the church insist on and emphasize his Jewishness? There is no simple answer to these questions; we need to engage in considerable study before formulating our reply. So what follows is a presentation of the various phases of Jesus' relationship to the Judaism of his era as it was manifested in his family, his people, the Jewish teachers and chief priests, and on the public and official levels.

First Phase: Jesus in the Bosom of Judaism—from Birth to Age Thirty

The first period we will study covers Jesus' childhood and the years in which he was growing up, studying the Torah in the local synagogue school in Nazareth, and working with his father Joseph in a carpenter's shop.

The writers of the four gospels tell us very little about this part of Jesus' life. All we know about it comes from one incident that happened when Jesus was about twelve years old. This was the occasion when Jesus was lost in the crowded alleys of Jerusalem during the feast.

> After three days they found him in the temple courts, sitting among the teachers, listening to them and asking them questions. Everyone who heard him was amazed at his understanding and his answers. (Luke 2:46–47)

This early incident in the life of Jesus reveals his early study of the Torah and his ability to ask and answer questions about it within the limits of his knowledge at that time. We can conclude from this incident that Jesus had similar discussions with his peers in the later years of his life until the age of thirty, when he started his public mission.

During that time, Jesus lived within the traditional Jewish education system, without leaving or defying it. Thus it is valid to say that Jesus in this phase was living in the bosom of Judaism.

Second Phase: Jesus and Judaism—Teaching in Synagogues

To judge from the account given in the Gospel of Mark—the historical basis on which both Matthew and Luke built—the second phase of Jesus' life can be described as one in which he lived and taught the Jewish faith. In other words, what he said and what he did was in agreement with Judaism. That is why he was called on to teach in Jewish synagogues and did his miracles there.

In Mark's Gospel, this phase starts in 1:21, where for the first time we see Jesus entering a synagogue in Capernaum and teaching there. Mark goes on to tell us that Jesus spoke to his disciples about the necessity of going to nearby villages to preach, and continues, "So he traveled throughout Galilee, preaching in their synagogues and driving out demons" (Mark 1:39). This is evidence that Jesus was widely received as a teacher in Jewish synagogues.

This stage was not without tensions between Jesus and the Pharisees who dominated the synagogues. Mark mentions that on one occasion when Jesus entered a synagogue on a Sabbath (the Jewish day of worship and rest) there was a man with a shriveled hand, and Jesus was closely watched to see whether he would heal the man on the Sabbath. When he did so, the Pharisees and the Herodians began to plot how they might kill him (Mark 3:1–6).

Jesus began to teach and preach everywhere. He did not restrict himself to teaching in the synagogues, for heaven was God's throne and the earth was his footstool. His reputation preceded him in all the cities and villages of Galilee. Thus the whole town gathered at the door of Simon's home to be healed from various diseases (Mark 1:29–34). We also see Jesus going to the hills, where "people still came to him from everywhere" (Mark 1:45). He taught in houses (Mark 2:1; 3:19), beside the Sea of

Galilee (Mark 1:16; 3:7; 4:1; 5:21), in markets (Mark 6:56), and in the home of a ruler of a synagogue (Mark 5:39).

This phase ends with Jesus entering the synagogue of Nazareth, his hometown (Mark 6:1–6). When he began to teach there, the people were amazed at his wisdom and inquired about the source of his power to work miracles. Since he was from their town and they knew him very well, they were surprised and asked each other quietly, "Isn't this the carpenter?" (Mark 6:3). But they did not believe what he was saying, and so he left them and went to other nearby villages.

After this incident, Mark no longer shows us Jesus entering synagogues to teach. Jesus was no longer in agreement with Judaism, and the rift between him and official Judaism began to widen.

Third Phase: Jesus in Confrontation with Judaism—a Series of Clashes

This next stage of Jesus' relationship with Judaism begins with some scribes—teachers of the law—coming from Jerusalem to meet Jesus. The earlier tension between Jesus and the Pharisees had continued to increase, and so a delegation of scholars was sent from Jerusalem—the center of the Jewish religion—in response to a request from the Pharisees in Galilee (Mark 7:1). This delegation and a group of Pharisees met with Jesus. At some point during this meeting, some of Jesus' disciples ate without washing their hands. This aroused the ire of the teachers of the law, who considered it a violation of the law and a rebellion against the traditions of the elders and rabbis (Mark 7:2–3).

Jesus used the opportunity to speak about the importance of distinguishing between God's instructions and people's explanations of these instructions. In Jesus' day, traditions had a very important place in Judaism and the teachers of the law were skilled in conferring an aura of holiness on the inherited explanations of the law. They shackled people with futile procedures, rituals, and customs that burdened them with needless duties. Jesus rebuked the authorities for this, using a quotation from Isaiah:

> "'These people honor me with their lips,
>   but their hearts are far from me.
> They worship me in vain;
>   their teachings are merely human rules.'
>
> You have let go of the commands of God and are holding on to human traditions."
> And he continued, "You have a fine way of setting aside the commands of God in order to observe your own traditions!" (Mark 7:6–9)

On this same occasion, Jesus talked to the crowd and offered them the ultimate principle for distinguishing what is pure and what is impure:

Nothing outside a person can defile them by going into them. Rather, it is what comes out of a person that defiles them. (Mark 7:14–15)

It is on this basis, Mark records, that Christians consider all kinds of food pure (Mark 7:19).

There was thus a serious confrontation between Jesus and Judaism. His public rejection of the traditions of elders was the beginning of his clash with official Judaism. How could he pour new wine into old wineskins? It would burst the skins (Mark 2:22). Thus Jesus continued on his course, regardless of the cost.

Later, Jesus rejected a request by the Pharisees to show them a miracle from heaven. The text says that Jesus "sighed deeply and said, 'Why does this generation ask for a sign?'" (Mark 8:11–12). Then he began to warn his disciples, saying, "Be careful. . . . Watch out for the yeast of the Pharisees and that of Herod" (Mark 8:15), by which he meant their teachings that opposed his.

It was in this atmosphere of tension that Jesus began to prophesy about his death (Mark 8:31; 9:31) and became more careful about announcing where he would go next, as indicated by the words, "They left that place and passed through Galilee. Jesus did not want anyone to know where they were" (Mark 9:30).

Jesus then set out with his disciples to go to Jerusalem. As they approached the eastern border of Judea at the Jordan, he was confronted by a group of Pharisees who asked him a question about divorce, hoping to trip him up (Mark 10:1–12). If he said anything that could be interpreted as opposing Moses and his law, they would file a complaint against him and send him to trial.

Jesus' response was honest and direct, as he accused them of being "hard-hearted." He pointed them to God's command about marriage when he created Adam and Eve, long before the law was given to Moses: "That is why a man leaves his father and mother and is united to his wife, and they become one flesh" (Gen 2:24). He concluded, "Therefore what God has joined together, let no one separate" (Mark 10:9).

Mark uses this incident to show how the Pharisees were hounding Jesus.

As Jesus and his disciples continued on to Jericho on route to Jerusalem, the disciples were confused and afraid. How can fearful people feel calm? The only way to do so is to deny the coming danger. Black clouds were gathering on the horizon of the relationship between Jesus and official Judaism. Jesus realized what was going to happen, and in these difficult days he chose to tell his disciples the truth about what he felt and what was going to happen to him:

"We are going up to Jerusalem," he said, "and the Son of Man will be delivered over to the chief priests and the teachers of the law. They will condemn him to death and will hand him over to the Gentiles, who will mock him and spit on him, flog him and kill him. Three days later he will rise." (Mark 10:33–34)

These words confirm the reality of the confrontation and tension between official Judaism and Jesus. What would the future bring?

Fourth Phase: Jesus Is Rejected by Official Judaism—the Last Week and the Cross

The fourth phase begins with Jesus entering Jerusalem and ends with his crucifixion. Mark records enough of the happenings during this period to give us a clear picture of the crisis. Jesus began to escalate the tone of his teachings and attitudes, while the teachers of the law and Pharisees were plotting to kill him.

Jesus entered Jerusalem from Bethany, riding on a donkey in fulfillment of the prophecy of Zechariah (Zech 9:9), and so the people shouted:

> Hosanna!
> Blessed is he who comes in the name of the Lord!
> Blessed is the coming kingdom of our father David! (see Mark 11:7–10)

One can imagine the reaction of official Judaism, represented by the chief priests and teachers of the law, to this celebration of Jesus which turned into a public festival and because of which "the whole city was stirred" (Matt 21:10).

The next day, Jesus and his disciples were on their way from Bethany to Jerusalem. It was probably the beginning of April, which was not the season for figs. Suddenly Jesus pronounced a curse on a fig tree on which he had not found fruit, saying: "May no one ever eat fruit from you again" (Mark 11:12–14). Till today, a dispute continues about the symbolic relationship between the fig tree and the Jewish nation![81] If there was some relationship between them in the mind of Jesus, this would be his strongest statement yet about the futility of Judaism, or at least of the Jewish religious leaders at that time. Do his words as he wept over Jerusalem, "They will dash you to the ground . . . because you did not recognize the time of God's coming to you" (Luke 19:44) echo the statement, "because it was not the season for figs" (Mark 11:13)?

Things now began to move quickly and dramatically. The temple of God in Jerusalem had become a market, full of the tables of moneychangers and the benches of those selling doves for sacrifices. When Jesus entered the temple,

> [He] began driving out those who were buying and selling there. He overturned the tables of the money changers and the benches of those selling doves, and would not allow anyone to carry merchandise through the temple courts. And as he taught them, he said, "Is it not written: 'My house will be called a house of prayer for all nations'? But you have made it 'a den of robbers.'"

---

[81] See العهد الجديد: قراءة رعائية (بيروت, جمعية الكتاب المقدس, 2004), 90n; ET: The New Testament: A Pastoral Reading (Beirut: Bible Society, 2004). Robert H. Gundry, *Matthew* (Grand Rapids: Eerdmans, 1982), 416.

> The chief priests and the teachers of the law heard this and began looking for a way to kill him, for they feared him, because the whole crowd was amazed at his teaching. (Mark 11:15–18)

Jesus' clearing the temple of those who abused it and exploited it—some of whom may have been associates of the priests—was the climax of his challenge to the Jewish religious authorities. They could have excused anything else, but not this. Jesus had defied them in their own house, the center that was under their direct control. It was becoming clear that Jesus wanted religious reform to extend even to the religious capital and the temple. Through reforming the head, the whole body would be reformed. At this point, the chief priests and teachers of the law in Jerusalem decided to put an end to what Jesus was doing. Tolerating him would be suicide for them. Thus they decided to get rid of him and "began looking for a way to kill him" (Mark 11:18).

The Jewish leaders did not forget what Jesus had done in the temple. Mark says that they came to Jesus the next day and asked him directly, "Who gave you authority to do this?" They asked this particular question because they were the authority when it came to what happened in the temple. But Jesus knew how to deal with them, and so he replied with a question: "John's baptism—was it from heaven, or of human origin? Tell me!" And when they recognized that they would be in a crisis if they gave either answer, they replied: "We don't know." To which Jesus replied: "Neither will I tell you by what authority I am doing these things" (Mark 11:28–33).

Jesus did not stop at that point, but went on to tell a parable about an owner of a vineyard who rented it to some farmers and went away on a journey:

> At harvest time he sent a servant . . . to collect from [the tenants] some of the fruit of the vineyard. But they seized him, beat him and sent him away empty-handed. Then he sent another servant to them; they struck this man on the head and treated him shamefully. He sent still another, and that one they killed. He sent many others; some of them they beat, others they killed.
>
> He had one left to send, a son, whom he loved. He sent him last of all, saying, "They will respect my son."
>
> But the tenants said to one another, "This is the heir. Come, let's kill him, and the inheritance will be ours." So they took him and killed him, and threw him out of the vineyard." (Mark 12:2–8)

Then Jesus asked a rhetorical question, "What then will the owner of the vineyard do?" He answered his own question: "He will come and kill those tenants and give the vineyard to others."

The chief priests and teachers of the law understood what Jesus was saying in this parable—he was talking about them. They remembered what their fathers had done to the prophets whom God had sent to them. This parable exposed their intentions toward Jesus. Thus they became furious and wanted to arrest him, but they hid their anger for fear of the crowd's reaction.

The situation between Jesus and the Jewish religious authorities had reached the point of no return. For their part, they were glad that Judas was prepared to betray Jesus and promised him silver if he helped them to arrest him (Mark 14:11). For his part, Jesus told his disciples on the night of his arrest that one of them would betray him and added, "the Son of Man will go just as it is written about him" (see Mark 14:18, 21).

The sun rose on Friday of that week, and before it reached its zenith, those who were passing the place called Calvary outside Jerusalem would have seen three crosses surrounded by Roman guards. On the middle cross a person named Jesus was hanging. The reason for his crucifixion was stated on a notice posted above his head, "The King of the Jews" (Mark 15:26).

Fifth Phase: Jesus' Triumph—"The Stone Rejected by the Builders Becomes the Cornerstone"

The final phase of Jesus' relationship with Judaism starts with the dawn of Sunday. On that day, the risen Jesus appeared to his disciples. This stage has continued without ending due to the day of Pentecost, the day on which the Holy Spirit came on Jesus' followers in Jerusalem.

Anyone reviewing the early stage of the church's history can see that the same religious authorities, the same official Judaism that hounded and persecuted Jesus until it killed him, continued to work actively to get rid of his followers. Opposition to him did not disappear after the religious leaders had incited the authorities to kill him. His enemies bribed the guards at his tomb to deny the news of his resurrection and told them to say that Jesus' disciples came and stole the body while they were asleep (Matt 28:11–13).

Then they went on to persecute the early church. After Peter's sermon on the day of Pentecost, the church's rapid growth, the spread of the good news of Jesus among the inhabitants of Jerusalem, and the tumult accompanying the healing of the crippled man at the temple gate, the teachers of the law and the captain of the temple guard arrested Peter and John as they were talking to the people and put them in jail (Acts 4:1–3). The next day, they brought them to be tried by the religious authorities in Jerusalem— the same leaders who had judged Jesus and had him crucified. This trial was attended not only by the chief priests, the teachers of the law, and the elders, but also by Annas (the former high priest), Caiaphas (the current high priest), and the other members of the high priest's family. "They had Peter and John brought before them and began to question them: 'By what power or what name did you do this?'" (Acts 4:7). In his response, Peter told them that Jesus is

> the stone you builders rejected,
> which has become the cornerstone. (Acts 4:11)

Supporters of official Judaism put great pressure on the early church. To prevent the new movement from continuing to spread, they threatened Jesus' followers and commanded them not to preach in his name (Acts 4:18). When the Christians disobeyed this command, they were again arrested and put in jail (Acts 5:17–18). But the apostles were miraculously released from the jail and continued to preach about Jesus Christ all over Jerusalem. The high priest and his associates had them arrested yet again and wanted to execute them. But a Pharisee named Gamaliel, a teacher of the law who was honored by all the people, intervened and recommended that they be released. Thus, the apostles were merely flogged and threatened (Acts 5:17–40).

The early Christian community continued to face pressures and persecution. For example, some people complained about Stephen and accused him of contradicting the teachings of Moses. He was obliged to defend himself before the Sanhedrin, and his trial ended with his being stoned to death. Saul watched this and approved of it (Acts 7:54–8:1).

Saul then launched a wave of severe persecution of the church. He began to go from house to house, dragging men and women off to prison. This led to the scattering of the Christians, who continued to preach the word wherever they went in Judea and Samaria (Acts 8:1–3). Not content with wreaking havoc in Jerusalem,

[Saul] went to the high priest and asked him for letters to the synagogues in Damascus, so that if he found any there who belonged to the Way, . . . he might take them as prisoners to Jerusalem. (Acts 9:1–2)

Saul/Paul later wrote about this, saying,

You have heard of my previous way of life in Judaism, how intensely I persecuted the church of God and tried to destroy it. (Gal 1:13)

Saul's persecution of Christians ended with his conversion when a light shone on him as he was on his way to Damascus (Acts 9:3–5). However, persecution continued under King Herod. He cut off James' head, and when he saw that this pleased the Jews, he arrested Peter, who, except for God's intervention, would have met the same fate (Acts 12:1–10).

The final case of persecution of the church in Jerusalem mentioned in Acts took place when the whole city was aroused against Paul. A mob dragged him out of the temple intending to beat him to death, but he was saved by the commander of the Roman troops stationed near the temple (Acts 21:27–32).

As the church grew and extended to the Gentile world, so did the persecution the Jews inflicted to those who followed Jesus. Eventually, most of those who belonged to the church were Gentiles who had chosen to follow Christ. With this change in the balance of power, the tension between Jews and Christians eased. Unfortunately, the church that faced persecution by the Jews in its early history began to persecute the Jews in the Middle Ages, inflicting on them, through the Inquisition courts, twice as much suffering as the Christians had faced.

Conclusion

What became of the relationship between Jesus and Judaism? Did Jesus leave some link between himself and Judaism when he said, "the kingdom of God will be taken away from you and given to a people who will produce its fruit" (Matt 21:43), or did he sever all ties? What did official Judaism do? Did it retreat after crucifying Jesus? Did it stop persecuting the followers of Jesus? Did it leave room for reconciliation by accepting Gamaliel's advice?

> Leave these men alone! Let them go! For if their purpose or activity is of human origin, it will fail. But if it is from God, you will not be able to stop these men; you will only find yourselves fighting against God. (Acts 5:38, 39)

Our study leads us to conclude that at the heart of the problem between Jesus and official Judaism was the identity and teaching of Jesus. Jesus himself was the problem, and his statement that he was the Messiah and the Son of Man was the point of no return when they passed judgment on him (Mark 14:61–62). As to his teachings, official Judaism could not accept that Jesus was going to move Judaism away from literal adherence to the law to the freedom found in obeying the spirit of the law—a change that would produce greater righteousness than rigid adherence to the letter of the law (Matt 5:20, 21, 27, 31, 33, 38, 43).

The well-known scholar C. F. D. Moule says that the main basis of the charge against Jesus by official Judaism was his claim to have a direct relationship with God. Jesus was greater than the ability of Judaism to comprehend; thus the link with Judaism was severed, for he transcended it.[82]

REASONS FOR JUDAISM'S REJECTION OF JESUS OF NAZARETH

We have looked at the relationship between Jesus and official Judaism from its calm beginnings until the stage of total rejection, which reached its climax in Jesus' crucifixion. We have seen his constant challenge to the Jewish religious authorities, whether in explaining the Torah or in his claim to be the Christ and the Son of Man. We have also seen the prejudice of the Jewish religious authorities against Jesus and their rejection of his teachings, which they considered a danger to the nation (John 11:45–50).

---

[82] C. F. D. Moule, "Jesus, Judaism, and Paul," in *Tradition and Interpretation in the New Testament*, ed. G. F. Hawthorne and O. Betz (Grand Rapids: Eerdmans, 1987), 43.

We must, however, also present the reasons why the Jewish authorities rejected Jesus' messianic role and questioned the validity of the early church's claim that he is the Son of God and the legal heir of all that is in Judaism. While it is true that I am writing as a follower of Jesus, and that the gospels and the rest of the New Testament were written by Christians, I will strive for maximum objectivity as I present this information and examine the historical sources, whether Christian or otherwise.

The reasons for Judaism's rejection of Jesus were many and various. Some of them were related to his interpretation of the law and his rejection of traditions that were based on literal interpretations and the commentaries of elders and teachers of the law. Some may have thought that he focused too much on people's hearts rather than their actions, or maybe the problem lay in his claim to be the Messiah, the Lord of the Sabbath, and the legal heir of Judaism, as was evident in his statement that the temple was his father's house. The writers of the gospels also reveal some of the accusations the Jews leveled against Jesus in their debates with him. What follows is a presentation of some of these reasons.

Jesus' Birthplace

There are no prophecies saying that the Messiah would come from Nazareth. Thus there were many arguments about Jesus' origins, the town from which he came, and places mentioned in the Old Testament in association with the Messiah. We see evidence of this in the arguments recorded in John 7:40–52. There, some people were saying that Jesus was a prophet while others said he was the Messiah. The objection to the latter claim was that Jesus was from Nazareth, whereas the Messiah would come from Bethlehem, the town of David. Nicodemus is told to search the books and see that no prophet would come from Galilee.

This objection persisted and is the reason why the gospel writers stress that Jesus was born in Bethlehem (Luke 2:1–7; Matt 2:1) even though he was raised in Nazareth (Luke 4:16). Nevertheless, this Jewish objection played a role in raising doubts about Jesus being the promised Messiah.

Jesus' Claim of His Ability to Forgive Sins

When Jesus said, "Your sins are forgiven," the immediate response of the teachers of the law was "This is blasphemy. Who can forgive sins but God alone?" (see Mark 2:7). This was one of the first objections to Jesus' claims.

Jesus' Refusal to Be Restricted by Inherited Traditions

The teachers of the law and the Pharisees were shocked when they saw Jesus eating and drinking with tax collectors and sinners (Mark 2:16). They were also shocked to see his disciples eating without washing their hands (Mark 7:2). Jesus rebuked these religious teachers for their habits and their teachings, which were full of hypocrisy (Matt 23). How then could they not reject him?

Jesus' Transcendence of the Commandments That Distinguished between Clean and Unclean Food

Jesus taught that people are defiled by what comes out of their mouths, not what goes into them. This teaching indicated that all foods were clean (Mark 7:15, 18–19). By saying this, Jesus was challenging the clear text of the law regarding clean and unclean animals (Lev 11). This was a serious matter for the Jews, who regarded the law as holy.

Jesus' Forbidding Divorce and Adding to the Teaching of Moses

When the Pharisees asked Jesus about divorce and said that Moses permitted them to divorce their wives, Jesus took them back to Genesis, where it says that a man and his wife become one flesh and said that what God has joined together we should not separate. He accused them of being hard-hearted, which is why Moses permitted divorce (Mark 10:2–9). They regarded such teaching as being in defiance of the law of Moses.

The most significant objection is mentioned in Matthew 5:21–48, where Jesus said that the law of Moses said this, but I say that. Such words angered the Jews.

Jesus' Failure to Observe the Sabbath Laws

When Jesus allowed his disciples to pick some heads of grain on the Sabbath and eat them, the Pharisees accused them of doing something that was forbidden on the Sabbath (Mark 2:24). The Pharisees and the Herodians plotted to kill Jesus after he healed a man with a shriveled hand on the Sabbath (Mark 3:1–6). The Jews' view was that Jesus did not respect the Sabbath but, as he put it, insisted on doing good on the Sabbath. They suggested that he should do his good works on any other day except the Sabbath. But he defied them and continued doing good and healing people on the Sabbath, greatly angering his Jewish opponents (Luke 13:10–17).

Jesus' Claim to Use the Power of God in Casting Out Demons

Because Jesus drove out demons and trained his disciples to do the same (Mark 3:11, 15; 6:7), the teachers of the law who came from Jerusalem accused him of being possessed by Beelzebub[83] and claimed that he drove out demons using the power of the prince of demons (Mark 3:22, 30). They clearly did not think Jesus' power came from God, and thus it followed that those who opposed him were serving God. Such an accusation could have led to his being assassinated by a zealot.

---

[83] A sarcastic name for Satan that means "the lord of the flies."

Jesus Exercising Authority in the Temple Without Permission

Jesus' expulsion of the traders from the temple, telling them, "Get these out of here! Stop turning my Father's house into a market!" (John 2:16), was viewed as suspicious because it was seen as rebellion against the Jewish religious authorities. They plotted to kill him because they were afraid of him (Mark 11:18).

Jesus' Claim to Be the Messiah

When the high priest charged Jesus under oath, asking him: "Tell us if you are the Messiah, the Son of God" (Matt 26:63), Jesus declared that he was indeed God's Son. The high priest then tore his clothes and said, "He has spoken blasphemy." The chief priests did not accept Jesus' claim to be Messiah because he did not display the power they expected of the Messiah. He gave no sign that he was going to free the country from Roman rule and establish Jewish law as the constitution for the country. How could they accept someone who had been arrested as the Messiah, their sovereign king? Thus they rejected him.

Jesus' Dying on the Cross Was Considered a Curse

Jesus' death on a cross was a shock for any Jew who knew the law, for according to the law, anyone who was hanged was cursed by God (Deut 21:22–23). Paul refers to this when he speaks of Jesus redeeming us from the curse of the law by becoming cursed himself (Gal 3:13). Jews were so disgusted by the manner of Jesus' death that they could not even entertain the idea that he might be innocent or that he could possibly be the messianic savior.

Jesus' Claim That the Messiah Had to Suffer

Christians interpret Isaiah 53 as a prophecy about Jesus, the suffering servant of the Lord. The Jews reject this interpretation because they take the servant songs in Isaiah 42–53 as referring to the people of Israel, and consider the servant of the Lord a metaphor for Israel. The servant's suffering was associated with the suffering the Jewish people endured during their exile to Babylon. Later Jewish interpreters also associate it with the torture and persecution that the Jews endured in the Inquisition in the Middle Ages and in the Holocaust in modern times.

The Jews rejected the idea of a suffering Messiah, for they believed he would be a powerful king who would come to deliver them. They expected him to save them from the power and authority of Rome, not to suffer at Roman hands. How could they accept that a man who was humiliated, rejected, and crucified was the sovereign king who would come to rule and reign?

Jesus' Claim That God Is His Father

The Jews hated Jesus speaking of himself as the Son of God. The first reason for this was the link between this title and the coming messianic king (compare Ps 2 with Peter's declaration in Matt 16:16, and the question of the high priest in Mark 14:61). The second was that they deemed that a son shares his father's nature. The Gospel of John makes their objection clear when it says:

> For this reason they tried all the more to kill him; not only was he breaking the Sabbath, but he was even calling God his own Father, making himself equal with God. (John 5:18)

Finally, the Jews considered themselves—as a people—the "Son of God" (see Exod 4:22, "Israel is my firstborn son"; and Isa 63:16; 64:8; Jer 3:4, 16, "you are our Father"). That is why they told Jesus, "The only Father we have is God himself" (John 8:41). Jesus' claim that God is his Father, restricting the title "Son of God" to himself only, put him in direct conflict with them.

The Christian Claim That Jesus Alone Is the Savior

The Jews rejected the Christian claim that salvation is only for those who accept Jesus as Savior (Acts 4:12). They considered themselves God's chosen people (Ps 105:6; Isa 43:10, 20; 45:4) who had been appointed stewards of the law, which they must obey for their own good (Deut 5:33). They believed that salvation is in God, and it is to him alone that all should look for salvation (Isa 43:11; 46:22).

Christians' Acceptance of Gentiles as Full Partners Who Believed in Christ

We are told that Jesus commended a Roman officer by saying, "Truly I tell you, I have not found anyone in Israel with such great faith" (Matt 8:10). John tells us that Jesus was glad when he heard that some Greeks[84] wanted to meet him (John 12:20–24). And Luke mentions Peter's words: "The promise is for you and your children and for all who are far off—for all whom the Lord our God will call" (Acts 2:39). Peter also tells the Jews,

> And you are heirs of the prophets and of the covenant God made with your fathers. He said to Abraham, "Through your offspring all peoples on earth will be blessed." When God raised up his servant, he sent him first to you to bless you by turning each of you from your wicked ways. (Acts 3:25–26)

---

[84] It is clear from the word "Hellenes" (Gr. *hellēnes*) that these were Greeks who believed in God but had not converted to Judaism. It is likely that the Ethiopian eunuch was in the same category (Acts 8:27).

These incidents and the decision of the Council of Jerusalem regarding accepting Gentiles (Acts 15:17) angered the Jews in Jerusalem, who felt that Christians were now treating Gentiles as their equals. So when Paul visited Jerusalem and went to the temple, the Jews accused him of bringing Greeks into the temple with him and tried to kill him (Acts 21:27–32). They vigorously resisted the admission of Gentiles into their spiritual heritage. This matter was put beyond doubt by their response to Paul's words that Christ had brought salvation for the Gentiles too: "Rid the earth of him. He's not fit to live" (Acts 22:22). For the Jews, the idea of Gentiles being their equals was contrary to the law and unthinkable.

Christians' Belief in the Necessity of Atonement for Forgiveness of Sins

The writer of the Letter to the Hebrews, who was previously a Jew, says,

> In fact, the law requires that nearly everything be cleansed with blood, and without the shedding of blood there is no forgiveness. (Heb 9:22)

He goes on to say that Jesus offered himself as a sacrifice in order to bear our sins (Heb 9:28) and to cleanse our consciences (Heb 9:14).

Things were difficult for the Jews after the destruction of Jerusalem and the temple by the Romans in AD 70. There was no longer any altar on which to offer animal sacrifices for the forgiveness of sins, which strengthened the Christians' argument that God had provided a remedy for sin through the atoning sacrifice of Jesus Christ his Son. There was thus no longer any need for anyone to go to the temple; no need even for a temple in which sacrifices were offered for the forgiveness of sins.

However, the Jews thought that God had provided them with an alternative means for the forgiveness of sins through prayer and faithful repentance, with no need for blood atonement. They had lived without a temple, altar, or sacrifice on the many occasions when they had been scattered in various countries far from the temple, as had happened during the exile when the temple was also destroyed. Solomon had mentioned this in his prayer at the dedication of the first temple:

> When they sin against you—for there is no one who does not sin—and you become angry with them and give them over to their enemies, who take them captive to their own lands, far away or near; and if they have a change of heart in the land where they are held captive, and repent and plead with you in the land of their captors and say, "We have sinned, we have done wrong, we have acted wickedly"; and if they turn back to you with all their heart and soul in the land of their enemies who took them captive, and pray to you toward the land you gave their ancestors, toward the city you have chosen and the temple I have built for your Name; then from heaven, your dwelling place, hear their prayer and their plea, and uphold their cause. And forgive your people, who have sinned against you. (1 Kgs 8:46–50)

Psalm 19:7–10 well expresses the thoughts of the Jews in exile:

> The law of the LORD is perfect,
>> refreshing the soul.
> The statutes of the LORD are trustworthy,
>> making wise the simple.
> The precepts of the LORD are right,
>> giving joy to the heart. . . .
> The decrees of the LORD are firm,
>> and all of them are righteous.
> They are more precious than gold,
>> than much pure gold; they are sweeter than honey.

They thought that the law was enough and that there was no need for blood sacrifice.

Christians' Interpretation of the Texts of the Torah Was Partial and Not Objective

The heated debate between Jews and Christians continued from the first century until the middle of the second one,[85] and increased with the passing of time and the swelling numbers of Christian writings. The Jews recorded their objection to the Christians' claim that the virgin birth of Jesus fulfilled the prophecy of Isaiah 7:14. This objection was mentioned by Justin Martyr in his *Dialogue with Trypho*.[86] The Jewish Trypho insisted that the reference to a virgin who gives birth was incorrect according to the Hebrew text of the book of Isaiah. The exact word used there refers to a girl or a young woman who may have been married, perhaps to King Hezekiah in whose days the prophecy was fulfilled when the Assyrians invaded Judea.[87]

Justin based his counterargument on the text of the Septuagint translation, which used the word *parthenos* in Greek, which means "virgin." Jewish scholars had translated the Hebrew word as "virgin" in the Septuagint about two centuries prior to the birth of Jesus of Nazareth, which means that they had understood it in this way. For in those days a girl or an unmarried woman was a virgin.

The Jews responded that if the original writer had wanted to use the word meaning specifically "virgin," he would have chosen to use a well-known Hebrew word with that meaning (used in Gen 24:16; Exod 22:16; Job 31:1). Jewish scholars concluded that Christians used the Septuagint translation because it suited their purposes, and that is

---

[85] Historians consider AD 135 the year in which Christianity broke from Judaism once and for all. The occasion was the complete destruction of the temple by the Romans after the Bar Kochba revolt. After that date, each religion went its own way.

[86] Martin Hengel, "The Septuagint as a Collection of Writings Claimed by Christians" in *Jews and Christians: The Parting of the Ways*, ed. James D. G. Dunn (Grand Rapids: Eerdmans, 1999), 50.

[87] See the notes on Isaiah 7 in Adele Berlin, Marc Zvi Brettler, Michael A. Fishbane, eds., *The Jewish Study Bible: Tanakh Translation* (Oxford: Oxford University Press, 2004), 798–99.

why the Jews later rejected it, saying the day the seventy scholars translated the Torah into Greek for king Ptolemy "was as bad for Israel as the day they made the golden calf." Other Jewish scholars taught that darkness covered the world for three days when the Torah was written in Greek in the days of Ptolemy.[88]

Trypho makes a number of other points concerning his rejection of the Christians' interpretation of the Torah, but we mention only this one as an example of the debates that raged in those days.

Various Additional Reasons

With the passing of time, arguments and counterarguments mounted on both sides. The reasons for Judaism's rejection of Jesus as Christians understood him became well established. Jewish scholars doubted the virgin birth and that Jesus was from the lineage of David. They fought his teachings, believing they would lead to the end of the Torah and the Jewish law. They rejected his atoning death, claiming that blood is not necessary for the forgiveness of sins and that even if it were necessary, God would not want a human sacrifice. Jewish scholars challenged Christians to find even one prophecy in the Old Testament referring to the resurrection of the Messiah. They resisted any Christian claims that the Messiah was divine or the Son of God, as Christians call him. Rather, they saw him as a leader arising from among the people: "a prophet like me from among you" (Deut 18:15).[89]

The Jews believed that when the Messiah returned, he would restore them to their land if they were in exile and enable them to conquer their enemies. Thus if Jesus Christ was the promised Messiah, he would have saved them from Roman rule. However, the opposite occurred: Within a generation of Jesus' coming, the Romans destroyed Jerusalem and scattered its inhabitants. Another great disaster fell on the Jewish people after the Bar Kochba revolt in AD 132–135, which the Romans crushed with great severity. The Jews were scattered from Palestine to the ends of the earth. How could Jesus of Nazareth be the promised Messiah while they were suffering such humiliation?

The rabbis resisted the worship of Jesus as practiced by Christians and considered it worship of a human being, whereas worship is for God alone. They also rejected the Christian doctrine of the Holy Trinity, considering this development an ethnic influence. They insisted that God is one: "Hear, O Israel: The Lord our God, the Lord is one" (Deut 6:4).[90]

---

[88] Martin Hengel, *The Septuagint as Christian Scripture: Its Prehistory and the Problem of Its Canon,* trans. Mark E. Biddle (Grand Rapids: Baker, 2004), 43–45.

[89] It is not surprising that Jewish and Muslim scholars are in agreement regarding the grounds for rejecting Jesus' deity and Christian doctrines like the Trinity, for Jews lived in the Arabian Peninsula from the beginning of the fifth until the seventh century

and spread their reasons to the population there for rejecting Jesus and Christianity.

[90] For a comprehensive look at the reasons why rabbis rejected Jesus as the Messiah, his teachings, and Christian beliefs regarding him, see the multivolume work by Michael L. Brown, *Answering Jewish Objections to Jesus,* 4 vols. (Grand Rapids: Baker, 2000–2006).

Jewish scholars did not accept the doctrines of original sin or the fall, and strongly resisted attempts to make them Christians so that they might be saved. They were confident that they had been saved and did not need salvation from any other source (Jer 31:34–37). The following is a brief summary of the content of the Torah, as Jewish rabbis understand it, that explains the way of salvation through the law:

- God created a perfect world full of justice. He made human beings in his own image, equal to God in terms of strength of will.
- Human beings sinned because of pride and were cast out of the perfect world and left to die. God gave humankind the Torah to purify us from sin.
- Those who humbly learn from the Torah may repent and freely accept God's will. Those who do so will be restored to Eden/Paradise and eternal life.[91]

Conclusion

Official Judaism, determinedly and for reasons it finds logical, rejected Jesus of Nazareth, his teachings, his claims, and the claims of his church and followers once and for all, since it considered them contrary to the Torah and its interpreters. This rejection coincided with the beginning of Christianity and took shape over the following few centuries, the period to which we have limited our study. However, it seems the Jewish rejection of Jesus and Christianity continues to the present time, for there are no signs to the contrary. There are only small buds suggesting the possibility of eventual rapprochement and understanding.

UNANSWERED QUESTIONS

We have now looked at the reasons Jews rejected Jesus and Christianity and have seen that this rejection was due to the challenge Jesus posed by his claims about himself and his teachings and actions, which threatened the very existence of Judaism. However, there are still some hard questions to be asked. These questions include the following: Was Jesus' challenge directed to official Judaism, represented by the nation's religious leaders whom he saw as misleading the people, or was he attacking Judaism in its teaching, theology, and way of life? How did the attitudes of Jews and Christians to each other develop after the crucifixion and the destruction of Jerusalem? Did their attitudes tend to be negative or positive? Is it possible

---

[91] Jacob Neusner, *Judaism in the Beginning of Christianity* (Philadelphia: Fortress, 1984), 188.

to describe the relationship between the church and Judaism at that time as weak, or was it completely nonexistent?

Was the relationship to Judaism the same among Jewish Christians as among Gentile Christians? Was there an intellectual difference and struggle between James, the pillar of the church of Jerusalem, and the Jewish Christians on one side and Paul the apostle to the Gentiles and the Hellenistic Roman Christians on the other? What settled matters between them in the end? I hope the next section will bring some answers to these and similar questions.

THE ATTITUDE OF JESUS AND THE EARLY CHURCH TO JUDAISM

The death of Jesus on a cross, a humiliating Roman tool of execution, instigated by the Jews who shouted "Crucify him!" was the climax of the conflict between Jesus and the leaders of Judaism in his time. This conflict extended to the relationship between Judaism and Jesus' early followers, who accused the Jews, especially the Jewish religious authorities, of killing Jesus.[92]

Jesus' attitude to the Jews was expressed most eloquently in the parable predicting his death: The owner of the vineyard (God) will come and kill those tenants (the Jewish leaders) and give the vineyard to other tenants (Christ's apostles), who will give him his share of the crop at harvest time.

> Therefore I tell you that the kingdom of God will be taken away from you [Jews] and given to a people [the church] who will produce its fruit. (Matt 21:43; see Matt 21:41; Mark 12:9)

The conclusion to this parable clearly shows that the Jewish religious leaders wanted to kill Jesus and destroy the church. They tried to do this by crucifying Jesus and persecuting his followers. Jesus, for his part, made a public declaration (recorded by his followers and the church who agreed with him) that God would condemn the Jewish nation and strip it of the privilege of serving the kingdom of God, that is, the privilege of spreading the good news of Abraham's blessing to the Gentiles through Jesus Christ and manifesting God's will through Jesus to all humanity.

Jesus confirmed his attitude to Judaism, as represented by its leaders, with sayings such as, "Look, your house [the temple] is left to you desolate [God will desert it]" (Luke 13:35; Matt 23:38), while telling his followers to "go and make disciples of all nations" (Matt 28:19).

---

[92] See Acts 2:23, "and you, with the help of wicked men, put him to death by nailing him to the cross"; Acts 3:13–15, 17, "I know that you acted in ignorance, as did your leaders"; Acts 4:8–10, "Rulers and elders of the people! . . . Jesus Christ of Nazareth, whom you crucified"; Acts 5:30, "whom you killed"; Acts 6:15; 7:1, 52, "The righteous one. And now you have betrayed and murdered him."

The Methodology for Unifying the Christian View of Judaism

How should we set about obtaining a comprehensive description of the attitude of Jesus and his church to Judaism? It seems that the place to start is with a systematic examination of the attitude of Jesus and his apostles and the early church in the first century as a whole. We need to adopt this approach, for it is impossible to separate the teachings of Jesus from the teachings of the early church. Jesus' sayings and teachings were spread as the writings of the apostles were circulated among the early church communities. So the teachings of Jesus recorded in the gospels became the prevailing concepts in the early Christianity that confronted Judaism,[93] and all the New Testament was influenced by it. For this reason, I will consider that Jesus and his disciples and those who wrote the New Testament all agree on matters related to their attitude toward Judaism.

The Core Passage That Reveals Jesus' Relationship to Judaism

Matthew 5:17–20 is considered decisive in determining the relationship between Jesus and Judaism. Whenever there was conflict about this subject, this passage was always at the center. It reads:

> Do not think that I have come to abolish the Law or the Prophets; I have not come to abolish them but to fulfill them. For truly I tell you, until heaven and earth disappear, not the smallest letter, not the least stroke of a pen, will by any means disappear from the Law until everything is accomplished. Therefore anyone who sets aside one of the least of these commands and teaches others accordingly will be called least in the kingdom of heaven, but whoever practices and teaches these commands will be called great in the kingdom of heaven. For I tell you that unless your righteousness surpasses that of the Pharisees and the teachers of the law, you will certainly not enter the kingdom of heaven. (Matt 5:17–20)

Here is a list of possible interpretations of Jesus' words, "I have come to fulfill them," in this passage: (1) deepening the law; (2) adding commandments to the law; (3) replacing the old law with a more sublime one; (4) replacing the law with the spirit of love; (5) proving the correctness and validity of the law; (6) showing the importance of perfect application of the law's requirements; (7) strengthening people to preserve

[93] In regard to the parable of the tenants, compare Mark 12:8, 9 ("So they took him and killed him, and threw him out of the vineyard. What then will the owner of the vineyard do? He will come and kill those tenants and give the vineyard to others") with Matthew 21:39–41 (which says that the tenants "took him and threw him out of the vineyard and killed him"). This is exactly what happened to Jesus. He walked to Calvary from Jerusalem and died on the cross outside the city (as mentioned in Heb 13:12). Whereas Mark says that the owner will "come and kill those tenants," Matthew, writing after the destruction of Jerusalem in AD 70, says that he "will bring those wretches to a wretched end." Thus he was able to describe the death of the tenants this way. We see a similar contrast in regard to the parable of the banquet. In Luke it says, "not one of those who were invited will get a taste of my banquet" (Luke 14:24), whereas Matthew 22:7 says, "The king was enraged. He sent his army and destroyed those murderers and burned their city." Matthew was very aware of the destruction of Jerusalem as he recorded his memories of Jesus in his gospel.

the commandments of the law; and (8) fulfilling the prophetic content of the law and the prophets.[94]

An objective approach to understanding this passage has to consider its context. This passage occurs in the Sermon on the Mount, after the Beatitudes and before the antithetical sayings ("it was said to you, . . . but I tell you") in chapter 5. It seems as if this passage is an introduction, meant to absorb some of the shock the audience would have experienced when they heard what was to follow. What then is the importance of this introduction? And why was there an anticipation of shock?

This introduction was necessary because those who heard the sermon were Jews who respected the law and respected Moses who gave them the law. In the antithetical sayings, Jesus puts himself in opposition to Moses and even speaks as one superior to Moses.

Thus the question: Is it possible, through what has been said earlier in this passage and the declarations that follow, to clearly discern Jesus' attitude to Judaism?

A critical analytical view of this passage and what follows indicates that we can give a positive answer to this question. For it is clear from the beginning of the passage, especially at verse 17, that Jesus did not want to abolish the law or to destroy the teachings of the prophets of Israel.[95] However, he wanted to complete and fulfill them. The text of the antithetical sayings in chapter 5 reveals what Jesus meant by saying that he did not come to abolish the law but to fulfill it.

- In saying, "I have come to fulfill the law," Jesus wanted to reveal the deep spiritual meaning of the law. Thus, he taught "do not be angry" rather than "do not commit murder" (see Matt 5:22) and "do not look lustfully" rather than "do not commit adultery" (see Matt 5:27).
- In saying, "I have come to fulfill the law," Jesus meant that he wanted to correct the provisions of the law. This is clear in his objection to the statement, "Anyone who divorces his wife [the tacit meaning being, "for any reason"] must give her a certificate of divorce." He said instead that there should be no reason for divorce except adultery (Matt 5:32). When Jesus was questioned about this matter in Matthew 19:3–9, he corrected the provisions of the law by citing other suitable texts in the law.
- In saying, "I have come to fulfill the law," Jesus meant that he would add commandments to the law in order to raise it to a higher ethical standard. He forbade swearing, asking instead for complete honesty (Matt 5:34, 37),

---

[94] John Nolland, *The Gospel of Matthew*, NIGTC (Grand Rapids: Eerdmans, 2005), 218.

[95] The Law and the Prophets are the most important parts of the Jewish Torah. They are followed by the Psalms and the books of proverbs and history (Luke 24:44).

and rejected the commandment "eye for eye and tooth for tooth" literally and practically. He offered a loftier law for quenching violence by not responding to abuse with abuse (Matt 5:38–39). He even countered the law's command to "love your neighbor" with the command to "love your enemies and pray for those who persecute you" (Matt 5:44–45).

Jesus wanted to show the difference between a poor teacher and a great teacher. In his opinion, a great teacher (including himself) is one who applies the law he teaches. He contrasts such a teacher with the teachers of the law and the Pharisees who taught the law without applying what they had taught (Matt 23:3).

Analysis of the passage shows that Jesus stressed the importance of motives and intentions, that is, the deep spiritual meaning of the commandments of the law, rather than the literal text that condemns persons only after they have committed an offense. This made his moral and behavioral requirements higher than those practiced and required by the traditional teachers of the law. As he said,

> unless your righteousness surpasses that of the Pharisees and the teachers of the law, you will certainly not enter the kingdom of heaven. (Matt 5:20)

The Relationship between Christianity and Judaism

Having looked at Matthew 5, we can now discuss the attitude of Jesus and the church to Judaism. All who have theorized about this begin in one way or another with that chapter. What follows is a description of the attitude of Jesus and the early church to Judaism as represented in its law and the interpretations of the law compiled by the leading rabbis. We are not wrong if we describe the real situation of the Jewish view of the law by saying that the law of Moses represented Judaism as a religion, an identity, and a nation. Thus any modifications or violation of the law was considered extreme rebellion and required total rejection and denial.

Embrace: Christianity as a Jewish Denomination

Some hold that Jesus and the early church accepted Judaism as it was, lived within its law, and wanted to continue to do so. They believed in the possibility of its development from within. Those who hold this view do not think that Jesus revolted against Judaism, for he was himself a Jew. He lived according to Jewish tenets and was subject to its law. He was circumcised, observed the Sabbath, and attended synagogues. His crucifixion is attributed solely to the envy of the religious leaders. This interpretation of events is supported by Mark 15:10 and Matthew 27:18.

Supporters of this view also point out that the early church gathered in the temple for worship in Solomon's Colonnade (Acts 5:12) and that Peter and John went to the temple for the afternoon prayer (Acts 3:1). Three years after Paul's dramatic conversion on his way to Damascus, he returned to Jerusalem, and we are told that he prayed at the temple and had a vision there (Acts 22:17).

Many years later, we hear that the elders of the church in Jerusalem that was led by James talked with Paul about the law:

> You see, brother, how many thousands of Jews have believed, and all of them are zealous for the law. They have been informed that you teach all the Jews who live among the Gentiles to turn away from Moses, telling them not to circumcise their children or live according to our customs . . . so do what we tell you. There are four men with us who have made a vow. Take these men, join in their purification rites and pay their expenses, so that they can have their heads shaved. Then everyone will know there is no truth in these reports about you, but that you yourself are living in obedience to the law. . . .
>
> The next day Paul took the men and purified himself along with them. Then he went to the temple to give notice of the date when the days of purification would end and the offering would be made for each of them. (Acts 21:20–26)

All the above evidence shows that Jesus and the early church lived, worshiped God, served him, and presented their message within the context of Judaism, not outside it, and continued to do so for many years. Does such behavior indicate their intention to make a sudden break between the old and the new, bringing division between the two parties?

Walter Kaiser says that even if Jesus and his followers used language that contained striking terms such as "new covenant" (Heb 8) and "new wine" (Matt 9:16–17), they meant "renewed things," not completely new things, for Jesus did not bring new things, he only renewed the old ones.[96]

Those who see Jesus and the early church as just an extension, with some development, of traditional Jewish teachings point to the words of Jesus in Matthew 5:17, "Do not think that I have come to abolish the Law or the Prophets; I have not come to abolish them but to fulfill them." Yet their approach eliminates all other options for interpreting Matthew 5. What do we make of the fact that we see Jesus adding to the commandments of the law and presenting teachings that transcend the law?

Supporters of this opinion rely on the historical criticism of Reimarus, Strauss, Harnack, and others,[97] and expressed by Karl Jaspers as follows:

> Jesus put forward no new system of morality but purified the biblical ethos and took it seriously as if it were already fulfilled in God's Kingdom. He lived it without regard for the consequences in the world, for the world was soon to perish.[98]

---

[96] Stanley N. Gundry and Louis Goldberg, eds., *How Jewish is Christianity? Two Views on the Messianic Movement* (Grand Rapids: Zondervan, 2003), 54.

[97] G. Theissen and A. Merz, *The Historical Jesus: A Comprehen-* *sive Guide* (Minneapolis: Fortress, 1998), 350.

[98] Karl Jaspers, *Socrates, Buddha, Confucius, Jesus*, vol. 1 of *The Great Philosophers*, trans. E. B. Ashton (New York: Harcourt, Brace & World, 1962), 65.

In response to the question, "What was Jesus like?" Karl Jaspers gives his view:

It is easy to say what Jesus was not. He was not a philosopher who reflects methodically and systematically orders his ideas. He was not a social reformer who makes plans; for he left the world as it was, it was about to end in any case. He was not a political leader aiming to overthrow one state and found another. . . . He founded no cult, for like the early Christians he participated in the Jewish cult; he did not baptize and he established no organization, no congregation, no church.[99]

G. Kittel, E. P. Sanders, and C. G. Montefiore all agree that in his interpretation of the Torah, and even in his verbal objection to its commandments in Matthew 5, Jesus did not deviate from rabbinic exegesis. He taught the content of the Torah and did not deviate from it.[100]

The above opinions represent the overall thinking of those who believe that the attitude of Jesus and the early church toward Judaism was consistent with its law, rituals, and rabbinic teaching. Neither he nor the early church thought about separating from Judaism; rather, they intended to remain in Judaism as a group or a sect like the Pharisees and the Sadducees.

However, it is an exaggeration to say that Jesus "did not baptize and he established no organization, no congregation, no church." What, then, is the meaning of his saying, "Do not be afraid, little flock, for your Father has been pleased to give you the kingdom" (Luke 12:32), and why did he choose twelve disciples, one of whom was a treasurer, which indicates what we can at least call a budding organization?

Reformation: Correction of Deviations of Judaism from the Law

There are others who see the attitude of Jesus and the early church to Judaism as a reforming one. The aim, as they see it, was to transform Judaism, correcting its deviation from the text of its law and making it a more transcendent religion on the ethical and religious levels by abolishing the system of animal sacrifice. Thus it would become a universal religion, extending Abraham's blessing to all the nations.

They add that the rumors spread against Jesus and the early church expressed Judaism's fear of the statements and actions of Jesus and his followers. The Jews believed that Jesus and his disciples were misleading the people (Matt 27:63; John 7:12; 2 Cor 6:8) since their teachings were different from those of the Jewish law. In this context, we can understand the desire of some of the Jews from the Synagogue of the Freedmen to launch an attack on Stephen:

We have heard Stephen speak words of blasphemy against Moses and against God. . . . This fellow never stops speaking against this holy place and against the law. For we have

---

[99] Ibid., 75.

[100] Theissen and Merz, *The Historical Jesus*, 351.

heard him say that Jesus of Nazareth will destroy this place and change the customs Moses handed down to us. (Acts 6:11–14)

But why, if we accept the argument that Jesus stayed within the Jewish framework and the law of Moses in his teaching, was there any need for him to say this:

No one sews a patch of unshrunk cloth on an old garment. Otherwise, the new piece will pull away from the old, making the tear worse. And no one pours new wine into old wineskins. Otherwise, the wine will burst the skins, and both the wine and the wineskins will be ruined. No, they pour new wine into new wineskins. (Mark 2:21–22)

The "new" indicates that what Jesus was teaching went beyond the old law and the traditional teachings of the elders and teachers of the law.

As an extension of this idea, F. C. Baur considered that Jesus' ethical teaching was "pure morality" and that the Sermon on the Mount contains "the absolute significance of the moral idea." As to the antithetical sayings in the Sermon on the Mount ("It was said, . . . but I tell you), Jesus contrasted his teachings with the teachings of Moses. In his teaching

the inner is opposed to the outer, the conviction to the action, the spirit to the letter. . . . 'although [Jesus] himself still observed as many of the old traditional forms as possible, and thus put new wine in the old skins, he did so with the definite awareness that the new content would soon enough break the old form.' This happened later in the form of Paul's universalism.[101]

It could be said that the reformation Jesus called for in Judaism was similar to the reformation Martin Luther called for in sixteenth-century Catholicism. Jesus did not resist or reject the fundamentals of the Jewish faith, namely believing in God and the Torah; what he did resist were doctrinal and behavioral deviations and the dominance of human traditions. This was what Martin Luther did. He did not reject the correct foundations of the Catholic faith, but resisted what Jesus rejected in Judaism. Jesus rejected the deviations in Judaism, thus he was crucified and expelled from the faith. Similarly, Luther resisted the deviations of the Catholic Church in his time, and thus he was expelled from the church.

Radical Separation: Separating Christianity from Judaism

Still others argue for a radical separation of Christianity and Judaism on the basis of the attitude of the writer of the Letter to the Hebrews and his view of the relationship between the old and the new covenants and the superiority of Jesus to all the Jewish symbols. For example, the writer of Hebrews says that Jesus deserved more honor than Moses:

---

[101] Ibid., 350.

Jesus has been found worthy of greater honor than Moses, just as the builder of a house has greater honor than the house itself. (Heb 3:3)

Where Moses was a faithful servant in God's house, Jesus is the Son in that house (Heb 3:5–6). Moreover, compared to Aaron and Levi, Jesus is a priest forever in the order of Melchizedek (Heb 5:6).[102]

If perfection could have been attained through the Levitical priesthood—and indeed the law given to the people established that priesthood—why was there still need for another priest to come, one in the order of Melchizedek, not in the order of Aaron? (Heb 7:11)

Thus, Jesus as a high priest

does not need to offer sacrifices day after day, first for his own sins, and then for the sins of the people. He sacrificed for their sins once for all when he offered himself. For the law appoints as high priests men in all their weakness; but the oath, which came after the law, appointed the Son, who has been made perfect forever. (Heb 7:27–28)

Regarding the law and its relationship to the priesthood, the writer to the Hebrews says, "For when the priesthood is changed, the law must be changed also" (Heb 7:12). And since Jesus is a priest forever in the order of Melchizedek, and not on the basis of the Levitical laws regarding descent, it follows that

the former regulation is set aside because it was weak and useless (for the law made nothing perfect), and a better hope is introduced, by which we draw near to God. (Heb 7:18–19)

The writer to the Hebrews carries on to explain the failure of the law and repeated sacrifices to make perfect those who draw near to God, since the law "is only a shadow of the good things that are coming" (Heb 10:1). The law with its sacrifices is just a shadow, but the reality is that "we have been made holy through the sacrifice of the body of Jesus Christ once for all" (Heb 10:10).

Those words refer to both the law and the Old Testament since the law is the core of the Old Testament. The writer to the Hebrews says, "For if there had been nothing wrong with that first covenant, no place would have been sought for another." Thus he seeks to show that the law has flaws, and that God wants to make a new covenant with the people of Israel. He explains what this covenant is and then adds:

By calling this covenant "new," he has made the first one obsolete; and what is obsolete and outdated will soon disappear. (Heb 8:13)

---

[102] "The Lord has sworn / and will not change his mind: // You are a priest forever, / in the order of Melchizedek" (Ps 110:4).

Concerning the Jewish temple in Jerusalem, which was the glory of Israel and the place where sacrifices were offered, the writer to the Hebrews says,

> If he were on earth, he would not be a priest, for there are already priests who offer the gifts prescribed by the law. They serve at a sanctuary that is a copy and shadow of what is in heaven. (Heb 8:4–5)

The temple in Jerusalem, according to the writer, is merely a pale shadow of the real temple which is in heaven (Heb 8:5). This heavenly temple is the greatest and most perfect, for it is not man-made (Heb 9:11). The earthly temple and its sacrifices are merely "copies of the heavenly things" and "only a copy of the true one" (Heb 9:23–24). Therefore, the writer expects the end of the temple (Heb 9:8), saying that these external regulations apply only until the time a new order is instituted (Heb 9:10). Since this new order has come, Jesus is now the high priest of the house of God (Heb 6:20). The writer also affirms that Christians "have an altar from which those who minister at the tabernacle have no right to eat" (Heb 13:10). In saying this, he separated Christianity from Judaism.

A quick review of the content of the letter to the Hebrews shows the following: (1) Jesus the Son is greater than Moses the servant. (2) Unlike Aaron, Jesus is a priest forever in the order of Melchizedek, therefore his kingdom will not end. (3) Since the kingdom has changed, the law has been changed and abolished because it was inadequate. It did not make anybody perfect. Jesus offers a better way to approach God. (4) Though the sacrifices offered according to the law did not make anybody perfect, the sacrifice of Jesus sanctifies us. (5) The new covenant was instituted on the cross, and the old one "is obsolete and outdated" and so "will soon disappear" (Heb 8:13). (6) The earthly Jewish temple is about to end and is just a shadow of the real heavenly temple in which Jesus serves as a high priest. (7) There is no relationship between the Christian altar and the Jewish altar.

The Letter to the Hebrews makes a strong case for the separation of Christianity and Judaism. However, it is not only this letter that deals with this subject in the New Testament. The book of Revelation includes even stronger statements about the Jews. For example, John records the words of the Lord Jesus Christ, who died and came to life again, about the Jews who were slandering the church of Smyrna, saying that they are not Jews but "a synagogue of Satan" (Rev 2:9). He repeats this phrase in Revelation 3:9. Referring to the place of worship of the Jews as "the synagogue of Satan" is an accusation targeting not just individuals but the whole system of Judaism. Moreover, the writer of the Revelation describes "the great city" where our Lord was crucified, namely Jerusalem, as "figuratively called Sodom and Egypt" (Rev 11:8). Both names represent places on which the wrath of God rests and his judgment falls.

Even Paul, though he was known for his love of his people and even wished that he might be "cut off from Christ for the sake of my people, those of my own race" (Rom 9:3), weighs in against the Jews. Speaking about them in his letter to the Thessalonians, he says,

> For you, brothers and sisters, became imitators of God's churches in Judea . . . You suffered from your own people the same things those churches suffered from the Jews who killed the Lord Jesus and the prophets and also drove us out. They displease God and are hostile to everyone in their effort to keep us from speaking to the Gentiles so that they may be saved. In this way they always heap up their sins to the limit. The wrath of God has come upon them at last. (1 Thess 2:14–16)

On another occasion, Paul and Barnabas preached in a Jewish synagogue in Pisidian Antioch. The Jews asked them to speak again on the next Sabbath:

> On the next Sabbath almost the whole city gathered to hear the word of the Lord. When the Jews saw the crowds [including many Gentiles], they were filled with jealousy. They began to contradict what Paul was saying and heaped abuse on him.
>
> Then Paul and Barnabas answered them boldly: "We had to speak the word of God to you first. Since you reject it and do not consider yourselves worthy of eternal life, we now turn to the Gentiles." (Acts 13:44–46)

Words such as these reveal the early church's attitude to Jews.

Paul also spoke out against anyone who tried to insist that Gentile believers should be subject to the Jewish law. He says that such people should be "under God's curse!" (Gal 1:9). In the same letter, Paul records a confrontation he had with the apostle Peter in Antioch, saying: "You are a Jew, yet you live like a Gentile and not like a Jew. How is it, then, that you force Gentiles to follow Jewish customs?" (Gal 2:14). He insisted that people are not justified by doing the works of the law, but through believing in Jesus Christ (Gal 2:16), "for if righteousness could be gained through the law, Christ died for nothing" (Gal 2:21). When he asks, "Why, then, was the law given at all?" he answers, "It was added because of transgressions" until Jesus had come (Gal 3:19–22). Thus, the covenant of the law, and the Jewish worship system based on it, was just a temporary stage between the time of Abraham and the coming of Jesus Christ.

> The law was our guardian until Christ came that we might be justified by faith. Now that this faith has come, we are no longer under a guardian. (Gal 3:24–25)

Paul ends his letter to the Galatians by equating circumcision (practiced by Jews as prescribed in the law) and uncircumcision (the state of the Gentiles):

> For in Christ Jesus neither circumcision nor uncircumcision has any value. The only thing that counts is faith expressing itself through love. (Gal 5:6; see 6:15)

These voices in the New Testament, as well as Paul's resistance to attempts to make the gospel Jewish, led to attempts to completely separate Christianity from Judaism. Some took this so far as to suggest that the God of the Old Testament was not the Father of Jesus Christ, and that Jesus was sent by another God for the salvation of humanity.

The group who wanted to completely separate Jesus from the Old Testament is represented by Marcion,[103] who was a contemporary of church fathers like Tertullian, Irenaeus, and Justin Martyr. Marcion thought that churches were not adhering to Paul's teachings that oppose the Jewish law. He saw that some churches had adopted the morals, customs, and traditions of the Old Testament, and that some Christian teachers considered Christianity a continuity of Judaism.[104] He regarded this as a regression to Judaism, and so rejected these ideas as contradictory to the teaching of Paul. However, instead of correcting and reforming matters, he went to the extreme of rejecting the very basis of Christianity in the Old Testament.

Marcion claimed that Paul was the only genuine apostle and thus he relied only on Paul's letters in formulating Christian beliefs. He accepted only the Gospel of Luke as a genuine account of the life of Jesus, since it was void of Jewish influence, but only after he had omitted the first three chapters because they contradicted his opinion. In AD 185 Irenaeus referred to this mutilation of the Gospel of Luke by Marcion as circumcision of the Gospel.

Marcion wanted to separate Jesus from the God of the Old Testament, and thus he contented himself with one gospel (Luke) and with the writings of one apostle, Paul. Marcion's thinking revolved around two focal points: the contrast between the gospel and the law, and the contrast between the God of love who sent Jesus in the New Testament and the God of justice in the Old Testament.[105]

Marcion's views are still found among Christians from time to time.[106] Such views try to loosen the link between the two Testaments, and between Judaism and Christianity. There have, for example, been calls for making the Old Testament a separate book, no longer linked to the New Testament in one Holy Bible.

Dispensationalism: Different Destinies for Israel and the Church

Dispensationalists hold that God has separate and unique arrangements or dispensations for Israel and the church, or for the godly of the Old Testament and the saints

---

[103] Marcion was born in AD 80 or 90 in the region of Pontus in what is now Northern Turkey. He called for the complete separation of Christianity from Judaism and the rejection of the Old Testament. However, the church in Rome condemned his teaching as it undermined the basis of faith in Christ. Marcion was excommunicated, but continued to spread his ideas, which became popular all over the Roman Empire. He still had followers in Syria in the fifth century AD.

[104] See Barnabas and 1 Clement as examples of this tendency.

[105] J. J. Clabeaux, "Marcion," *ABD* 4:514–16.

[106] Mikhail Naimy, a Lebanese writer, wrote, "The God of Moses was the God of the Jews only. He was a jealous, malicious tyrant and very cruel . . . whereas the God of Jesus is not 'the Lord of the hosts,' he is a 'Father' before everything, the Father of all people, . . . the Lord of mercy, . . . the Lord of Love". See Naimy's, من وحي المسيح (بيروت: مؤسسة نوفل (1974)، 98–97; ET: *Inspired by Christ* (Beirut:, Novell Foundation, 1974).

of the New Testament. They regard the church as the sixth of the seven dispensations through which God relates to humankind over the whole course of human history, from its beginning until its end. These are the Dispensation of Innocence (before the entry of sin), the Dispensation of Conscience (living according to a fallen conscience), the Dispensation of Human Government (an organized society under some form of government), the Dispensation of Promise (God's promises to Abraham and his family), the Dispensation of Law (the law of Moses), the Dispensation of Grace (the stage of the church), and the Dispensation of the Millennial Kingdom (the reign of Christ on earth for a thousand years).[107]

On this view the church is a temporary interlude or parenthesis that exists because of the Jews' rejection of Jesus as their promised Messiah. Jesus came with the message of the kingdom of which he was king. When the Jews rejected their king and crucified him, the kingdom of God temporarily ceased to progress on earth. Because of this rejection, the door of salvation was opened to non-Jews and the age of the church began. At the end of the age of the church, when the full number of Gentiles receives salvation, the church will be raptured to heaven, where it will stay in spiritual glory. Then Jesus Christ will return to the earth to reign over it as the Messiah, King of Israel on his throne in the earthly Jerusalem for a thousand years, thus achieving "the kingdom of heaven."

According to this view, the church is merely a temporary interlude. God's works and promises belong primarily to Abraham and his physical descendants, because

as far as election is concerned, they are loved on account of the patriarchs [Abraham, Isaac and Jacob], for God's gifts and his call are irrevocable. (Rom 11:28–29)

Supporters of this view reject the idea that Israel is an interlude in the history of humanity, although only two of the dispensations concern Israel while the other four belong to the Gentiles and the church, and the seventh and last one is common. However, for dispensationalists Israel is not a forerunner of the church, nor is Israel a dawn that will grow to become complete morning in Jesus until it reaches full day in the church. According to them, the biblical view is that the Jewish nation, not the church, is the be-all and end-all of God's plan for humanity.

Dispensationalism maintains that God has two peoples, the Jewish nation and the church, each of which has a separate plan and destiny. The Jewish nation is theocratic (a divine king; a chosen people; and a promised land), whereas the church is spiritual (born in the day of Pentecost; Christ is its head; its people are mixed, but consist mainly of Gentiles; and its scope is the whole world). Each group has a different destiny. The

---

[107] See حليم إبراهيم أرسناوي, صدى النبوات, طبعة ثانية (بيروت, 1981), 16–25; ET: Halīm Ibrāhīm Orsenaoa, *The Echo of Prophecies*, 2nd ed. (Beirut, 1981), 16–25.

ultimate destiny of the Jewish nation is a paradise on earth, a kingdom where peace and righteousness prevail under the reign of Christ. The ultimate destiny of the church, which is the spiritual body of Christ, is in heaven after the rapture.[108]

Elements of this view appeared in the form of scattered statements by the church fathers and began to take shape in the writings of Pierre Poiret, Johnathan Edwards, and Isaac Watts in the eighteenth century. However, the person who systematized and spread this teaching in the nineteenth century was John Darby (1800–1882). It spread through Britain and Europe and was promoted in the United States by the publication of the Scofield Reference Bible. L.S. Chafer deepened and generalized it through the seminary he established in Dallas, Texas.[109]

In the 1980s, some, including professors at Dallas Seminary, began to express doubts about some aspects of dispensationalism. They recognized that some of the ideas promoted were not biblically defensible. For example,

- They reject the notion that the church is merely a parenthesis in God's plan and instead assert that it is an introduction to the kingdom of God.
- They reject the idea that God has two separate purposes, one for Israel and one for the church, and insisted that God has one purpose: to establish his kingdom in which Israel and the church will share.
- They reject the distinction between the people of Israel and the church as regards their eternal state, saying that both will share the state of glory during and after the Millennium, because they are one people.[110]

We should be careful to avoid thinking that Jesus has two brides, for he has one bride, one "wife," the bride of the Lamb, the church. This church includes the Old Testament people of God because it has inherited them. Thus the church has experienced linear historical expansion, as it now includes both Jews and Gentiles in one body, as well as broad geographical expansion. This church in all its length and breadth is one church.

Separating the faith of Israel from the faith of the Gentiles ultimately leads to two peoples and two brides, who are in competition. But Jesus does not have two brides; Israel and the church are not competitors, and they are no longer two peoples. Both Jews and Christians combine to form the one body of Christ, the church. As Paul says:

> So in Christ Jesus you are all children of God through faith. . . . There is neither Jew nor Gentile, . . . for you are all one in Christ Jesus. (Gal 3:26–28)

---

[108] Wayne Grudem, *Systematic Theology* (Grand Rapids: Zondervan, 1994), 859, 860; George E. Ladd, *The Last Things* (Grand Rapids: Eerdmans, 1978), 9.

[109] C. C. Ryrie, "Dispensationalism," in *Evangelical Dictionary of Theology*, ed. Walter A. Elwell (Basingstoke: Marshall-Pickering,

1985), 322.

[110] Grudem, *Systematic Theology*, 860. For more on this topic, see Craig A. Blaising and Darrell L. Bock, eds., *Dispensationalism, Israel, and The Church: The Search for Definition* (Grand Rapids: Zondervan, 1992).

This is the scene represented by the vision of "the Holy City, the new Jerusalem, coming down out of heaven from God" as the bride of the Lamb (Rev. 21:2).

Fulfillment: Jesus Christ and the Church Complete and Inherit Israel

The final view to be presented sees Jesus and the church as the completion of Judaism. In other words, Jesus and the church are the fulfillment for which Judaism paved the way through its law and system of worship and the prophecies of its prophets about the promised Christ, the Savior of the world (Luke 2:30–32).

This view is different from the views mentioned earlier. It is not like the traditional view that keeps Jesus and the church in the shadow of Judaism. It goes beyond the second view, which aims at changing Judaism by reforming its deviation from the law so as to make it loftier in its ethics and cultic practices by abolishing the system of animal sacrifice. However, those who support the fulfillment perspective do not go as far in separating Judaism and Christianity as the third radical view, which completely separated Judaism from Christianity and the God of the Old Testament from the God of the New Testament. Neither does this view resemble that of the dispensationalists, who consider Israel and the church two different parts of God's work of salvation—each having its own nature and destiny. The fulfillment perspective sees Jesus as an embodiment of Judaism in his person and life. He lived as an Israelite and in his person he replaced the temple, the priesthood, the sacrificial system, and the law. He also replaced the Jewish nation with the church, which includes all races including the Jews. This view does not separate the past from the present, nor does it destroy the basis on which Christianity was built. It incorporates aspects of the Jewish law and carries them forward in a new, continuous, and progressive way. It considers Jesus and his followers the godly remnant that God raised up to continue his plan. We can describe this view as transferring the heritage from Moses to Jesus and from Judaism to the church.

The best way to understand this view, which is rooted in many parts of the New Testament, is by studying it through the imagery used to express it.

Foundation and the building

The image of Judaism as a foundation implies that the old is not destroyed but is used as a base to build on. This interpretation is supported by Jesus' words: "Do not think that I have come to abolish the Law or the Prophets; I have not come to abolish them but to fulfill them." (Matt 5:17). It is also clear in the words of the writer to the Hebrews and the apostle Paul. The writer to the Hebrews, however, describes the law as being weak and useless (Heb 7:18). Though he stresses his rejection of the law as a way of salvation, Paul confirms that "the law is holy, and the commandment is holy, righteous, and good" (Rom 7:12).

This relationship is also shown by the use of the same names in the two Testaments, though with new implications. Paul refers to his people as "Israel," but speaks of the church as "the Israel of God" (Gal 6:16). Instead of speaking of "the kingdom of Israel" (Josh 1:4; 1 Sam 15:28; 24:20), Jesus spoke of "the kingdom of God" to indicate God's reign over human hearts.[111] There is also a noticeable comparison between "the kingdom of Israel" and "the kingdom of God" at the start of the book of Acts (Acts 1:3, 6).[112]

Tree and the branches

This image of a tree with branches indicates that there is continuity rather than separation between Judaism and Christianity. The apostle Paul uses this image when he speaks about the olive tree. He says that its root is Judaism and that the Gentile Christians are branches that have been grafted into it. Branches that were cut off in the past will be grafted back into the tree if they believe. This image reveals the organic relationship between the Jewish root and the new people of God, the church, and shows the natural link between them (Rom 11:16–24).

Despite his strong words about the Jewish law and priesthood, the writer of Hebrews also points to the relationship, based on faith rather than on the law, between Old Testament believers and New Testament believers. He lists the names of men and women of faith and their accomplishments, from Abel to Samuel and the prophets. Then he concludes by saying,

> These were all commended for their faith, yet none of them received what had been promised, since God had planned something better for us so that only together with us would they be made perfect. (Heb 11:39–40)

He goes on to describe the Old Testament believers as "a cloud of witnesses" surrounding the New Testament believers who are now running the race. He appeals to them to fix their eyes on "the pioneer and perfecter of faith," Jesus, so that they will not grow weary and lose heart (Heb 12:1–3). In sketching this picture, the writer to the Hebrews indicates the continuity of the path and the common destiny of the faithful people of God in both testaments.

The book of Revelation includes another example. In a dramatic vision, John is shown the final goal of the plan of salvation that God accomplished through his Son Jesus Christ, presented as the Lamb (Rev 21:9–14). What John sees is the holy city, the heavenly Jerusalem, shining with the glory of God. It is surrounded by a high wall with gates and foundation stones. On the gates are written the names of the twelve

---

[111] In Matthew's Gospel, the expression is "kingdom of God," rather than "kingdom of Heaven" (ملكوت السماوات [*malakūt al-samawat*]). It is worth mentioning that "kingdom" ("ملكوت" [*malakūt*] and "مملكة" [*mamalakat*]) have the same meaning in Arabic, but Christians preferred to use the term "ملكوت الله" (*malakūt al-llah*) from Aramaic, to distinguish it from any other political or earthly kingdoms. The word "ملكوت" (*malakūt*) is also used four times in the Koran.

[112] As Jesus was teaching his disciples after his resurrection about "the kingdom of God," they asked him, "Lord, are you at this time going to restore the kingdom of Israel?" (Acts 1:3, 6). How did they understand the term "kingdom of God"? He answered them to the effect that they should preach him and then the kingdom of God would reach to the ends of the earth.

tribes of Israel (representing the people of the Old Testament). The foundation stones are inscribed with the names of Christ's twelve apostles (representing the people of the New Testament). This city is the place where God dwells with human beings. The text calls it "the bride, the wife of the Lamb," namely the church which is the bride of Christ (see 1 Cor 11:2; Eph 5:32). This city has no altar, since God and Christ are its altar (Rev 21:22). There is no more eloquent statement of the unity of the faithful ones of both Testaments and their common destiny than this acknowledgement that together they constitute the bride of Jesus (Rev 21:2, 9).

Pillar and base

Jesus embodied Judaism in his person. Thus, all that Judaism contained of the law, the priesthood, sacrifices, and the altar are found in him. The following points clarify this concept:

- *Jesus subsumes the law and declares a new law,* as is demonstrated in many places in the New Testament. The antithetical sayings in his Sermon on the Mount ("it was said . . . , but I tell you"), indicate that he has subsumed the old law and is giving a new law. Many of his sayings in the Gospel of John also refer to this. Jesus refers to himself as the bread coming down from heaven and says that whoever eats this bread will live forever. He links this bread to his words, which he says "are full of the Spirit and life" (John 6:51, 63). He teaches what the Father taught him (John 8:26–28), and speaks what the Father commanded him (John 12:49–50). And he offers a new commandment—love (John 13:34):

  > Anyone who does not love me will not obey my teaching. These words you hear are not my own; they belong to the Father who sent me." (John 14:24)

  Paul says, "Christ is the culmination of the law so that there may be righteousness for everyone who believes" (Rom 10:4). This is the most eloquent statement that Jesus subsumes the law and is himself its fulfillment.

  The writer to the Hebrews has this to say:

  > In the past God spoke to our ancestors through the prophets at many times and in various ways, but in these last days he has spoken to us by his Son, whom he appointed heir of all things, and through whom also he made the universe. (Heb 1:1–2)

  God spoke in the last days (through the incarnation) in his Son Jesus Christ (the manifestation of his will) and made him heir of everything (including the law). God declared his spiritual and moral demands in the law, written on two tablets of stone. However, Jesus was the manifestation of God's spiritual and moral demands embodied in a human life of flesh and blood (John 1:14–18).

If the commandment is a lamp and the law is a light, according to the book of Proverbs 6:23, then Jesus is the light of the world, and his new law leads to life (John 8:12).

- *Jesus embodies the priestly system and offers a new priesthood.* The Letter to the Hebrews is the first line of defense for this statement, for there Jesus is often referred to as a high priest.[113] He is presented as a high priest from the tribe of Judah, representing a radical change to the system of priesthood: "For it is clear that our Lord descended from Judah, and in regard to that tribe Moses said nothing about priests" (Heb 7:14), thus "there must also be a change of the law" (see Heb 7:12).

  One of the results of Jesus becoming a high priest is the breaking down of the barrier between the Levites as a line of priests and the other tribes. In the new Christian concept, all the people of God are priests (1 Pet 2:9; Rev 1:6) and Jesus is the only mediator and intercessor between people and God.[114]

- *Jesus embodies the sacrifices since he offered himself as a unique and final sacrifice.* John the Baptist was the son of a priest. He knew the sacrificial system and its value, and yet when he saw Jesus coming to him, he shouted out, "Look, the Lamb of God, who takes away the sin of the world!" (John 1:29). This testimony of John is highly significant. This was also the perspective from which Jesus understood himself and his call, declaring that

  > even the Son of Man did not come to be served, but to serve, and to give his life as a ransom for many. (Mark 10:45)

  The apostle Paul says that Jesus died for all humanity and that through him, God reconciled the world to himself, not counting our sins against us, so that we will be without blemish (2 Cor 5:14–21; Col 1:20–22). These words indicate that Jesus is the only perfect atoning sacrifice.

  The writer to the Hebrews also says that Jesus achieved eternal redemption by offering himself as a sacrifice, the blood of which is shed only one time: "We have been made holy through the sacrifice of the body of Jesus Christ once for all" (Heb 9:12, 26; 10:10).

  The book of Revelation also comments on this subject in a text in which the redeemed people address Jesus, saying,

  > "You are worthy . . . because you were slain, and with your blood you purchased

---

[113] Heb 2:17; 3:1; 4:14–15; 5:5, 10; 6:20; 7:17, 26; 8:1; 10:21.   [114] John 14:6; 1 Tim 2:5; Heb 7:25; 1 John 2:1.

for God persons from every tribe and language and people and nation. You have made them to be a kingdom and priests to serve our God, and they will reign on the earth." (Rev 5:9–10)

- *Jesus reduces the temple to his person and presents himself as a "place" to meet God.* The "tent of meeting" (the portable temple) where Israel gathered was not a place where the people met each other; rather, it was the place where God met with his people. A better name for it would be "the tent of God's meeting" or "the tent of God's meeting with his people." This is the concept that John presents when he says,

> The Word became flesh and made his dwelling among us. We have seen his glory, the glory of the one and only Son, who came from the Father, full of grace and truth. (John 1:14)

When Jesus died, the curtain of the temple was torn in two from top to bottom. The fact that Matthew, Mark, and Luke all record this incident indicates its symbolic importance (Matt 27:51; Mark 15:38; Luke 23:45). In the time of Jesus, the temple had two cloth curtains, an internal one that separated the holy of holies from the sanctuary and an external one that separated the outer court from the sanctuary where the priests served.[115] The external curtain was far finer and more beautiful than the inner one and could be seen from afar. Thus it seems that Mark was referring to the outer curtain when he describes what had happened at the time of Jesus' death:

> With a loud cry, Jesus breathed his last. The curtain of the temple was torn in two from top to bottom. And when the centurion, who stood there in front of Jesus, saw how he died, he said, "Surely this man was the Son of God!" (Mark 15:37–39)

The wording may indicate that the centurion who saw Jesus dying also saw the curtain tearing.[116] Which of the two curtains was torn, the internal or the external? The answer depends in part on whether the centurion saw the curtain from afar. R. T. France comments on this controversy:

> The tearing of the outer curtain would be more of a public event, but the symbolism of the violent opening of the Holy of Holies by the tearing of the inner curtain might be thought to be theologically more telling.[117]

Regardless of which curtain was torn, the theological significance cannot

---

[115] Josephus, *The Jewish War*, 5.5.4–5.
[116] See Robert H. Gundry, *Mark* (Grand Rapids: Eerdmans, 1993), 950.
[117] R. T. France, *The Gospel of Mark: A Commentary on the Greek Text*, NIGTC (Grand Rapids: Eerdmans, 2002), 656.

be less than the announcing of the ending of the old temple system and the establishing of Jesus, by his death, as a unique, perfect, and everlasting sacrifice.

The most eloquent image indicating that Jesus is the new eternal temple is found in John's description of the new Jerusalem: "I did not see a temple in the city, because the Lord God Almighty and the Lamb are its temple" (Rev 21:22).

Jesus told the Samaritan woman:

> A time is coming and has now come when true worshipers will worship the Father in the Spirit and in truth. God is spirit, and his worshippers must worship him in the Spirit and in truth. (John 4:20–24; see also John 4:10, 42)

With these words, Jesus set the new rule for universal worship, in which the temple will not be the center and place of worship, but rather Jesus, the gift of God and the Savior of the world.

Faithful Remnant

Jesus and his early followers represent the faithful remnant that holds the torch and continues in the way. This is clear in Romans 9–11, where Paul explains the delay of the Jews in accepting the message of Jesus. He says that the word of God and his promises regarding the salvation of the Jews did not fail and God did not reject his people, for "I am an Israelite myself." But not all who are descended from Israel are Israel. In other words, it is not the natural children who are God's children, but it is the children of the promise who are regarded as Abraham's offspring. When the people strayed at the time of King Ahab and fell into pagan worship, they killed God's prophets and destroyed his altars. But the Bible says that God had preserved seven thousand people who did not worship Baal (Rom 11:4, quoting 1 Kgs 19:18).

Earlier, Paul had quoted Isaiah:

> Though the number of the Israelites be like the sand by the sea,
>   only the remnant will be saved. (Rom 9:27, quoting Isa 10:22)

> Unless the Lord Almighty
>   had left us descendants,
> we would have become like Sodom,
>   we would have been like Gomorrah. (Rom 9:29, quoting Isa 1:9)

Paul's point is that he and the other Jews who believed that Jesus of Nazareth is the Christ form "the remnant" that will hold the banner of faith and continue on the path. As for the rest of the Jews, they have run into the stumbling stone and turned out to be a stubborn people who resist God's call.

The concept of the remnant is very important throughout Scripture, starting from Adam. Adam's fallen descendants incurred God's judgment. But at the time of judgment,

God raised a remnant, namely Noah and his house, to continue as his people. And when the offspring of Noah turned away from God, God raised another remnant, Abraham and the patriarchs, to continue the journey. When the tribes of Israel strayed and there was no hope in Saul the first king, God raised David to continue the journey. When the house of David fell to Nebuchadnezzar who took the Jews into exile in Babylon, God raised Ezra and Nehemiah and Zerubbabel to return to rebuild the temple and the wall and to restore the nation. At a time when the people of Israel were described as "the lost sheep of Israel" (Matt 10:6), God raised Jesus and his disciples to be "the remnant" that would carry the message of salvation to all the nations of the world. The apostle Paul says,

> What if he did this to make the riches of his glory known to the objects of his mercy, whom he prepared in advance for glory—even us, whom he also called, not only from the Jews but also from the Gentiles? (Rom 9:23–24)

Thus the concept of the remnant has deep theological meaning. It reveals the relationship between God's justice and his mercy on the one hand, and God's sovereignty and purpose and humanity's role in fulfilling, or hindering, God's purposes on the other. Abraham and his descendants are the best example of this. God's promise to Abraham was that through his descendants all the nations of the world would be blessed, and so Abraham became a nation. However, when the nation strayed, how would God punish it? If the descendants of Abraham were wiped out, how could the blessing of Abraham be extended to all the nations of the world? Raising up a remnant allows the straying people to be judged while leaving a faithful remnant to continue to fulfill God's purpose.

> And though a tenth remains in the land, it will again be laid waste. But as the terebinth and oak leave stumps when they are cut down, so the holy seed will be the stump in the land. (Isa 6:13)

And so things continue throughout history so that God's promises and covenants are not abrogated.

Jesus and his disciples were the faithful remnant of Israel, raised up to accomplish God's promises of salvation to Israel and to all nations, and are referred to as "saints" and "the people of the Most High" (Dan 7:27 and several times in the New Testament).[118]

Jesus' Dual Identity: An Individual and the Embodiment of Israel, the People of God

Jesus in his person represents Judaism and unifies it in himself and is united to it; then he releases it to accomplish God's purpose of extending the blessing of Abraham to all

---

[118] These titles are used of Christians more than forty times in Acts, the Letters, and Revelation. Here are a few of these instances: Acts 9:13; Rom 8:27; 1 Cor 14:33; 2 Cor 1:1; Eph 1:15; Phil 4:21; Col 1:4; 1 Tim 5:10; Heb 13:24; Rev 5:8.

nations. We see this when we look at the life of Jesus as told in the gospels, especially the Gospel of Matthew. It becomes clear as we compare the successive events in the history of Israel with the events of Jesus' life:

1. Israel as a nation is related to Abraham, and so is Jesus (Matt 1:1).
2. Jacob and his children go to Egypt to escape famine and return after the exodus. Joseph and Mary take Jesus to Egypt to escape from Herod, and he returns with them after the death of Herod (Matt 2).
3. The people of Israel escape Egypt by passing through the waters of the sea,[119] and Jesus is baptized by John in the water of the Jordan (Matt 3).
4. After crossing the sea, the people of Israel go into the wilderness of Sinai (a time of trial and testing) where they stay for forty years. After his baptism, Jesus goes into the wilderness to be tempted by Satan and stays there for forty days (Matt 4).
5. In the wilderness, Moses received the commandments of God on Mount Horeb. Jesus went up onto a mountain to present his teaching, the Sermon on the Mount, in which the antithetical sayings remind us of Horeb: "It was said to you . . . , but I tell you . . ." (Matt 5).
6. Jacob (Israel) had twelve sons, each of whom became the patriarch of one of the tribes that constituted the Israelite nation. Jesus chose twelve disciples to be apostles (Matt 10). It is clear that Jesus wanted his person and his disciples to be the counterpart to Jacob and his sons, so that we can look to him as a substitute for Jacob, or Jacob's heir. This argument is proven beyond any doubt by Jesus' words: "At the renewal of all things, when the Son of Man sits on his glorious throne, you who have followed me will also sit on twelve thrones, judging the twelve tribes of Israel" (Matt 19:28).
7. Acting to the advice of his father-in-law, Moses chose seventy judges to help him in hearing cases and problem-solving (Exod 18:13–27; 24:1; Num 11:16–17). Jesus too chose seventy disciples besides the twelve and sent them out to preach (Luke 10:1). Some scholars relate the seventy disciples to the seventy nations mentioned in the table of the nations in Genesis 10, suggesting that the mission of the twelve was to the Jews, whereas the mission of the seventy was to the Gentiles.[120]
8. Finally, after the destruction of Jerusalem in 586 BC, the people of Israel went into exile in Babylon and returned in the fifth century BC. They endured a hard and difficult experience that was followed by the joy of return. Their experience

---

[119] Paul likens Israel's passing through the Red Sea to baptism (1 Cor 10:1–2).

[120] Victor P. Hamilton, *The Book of Genesis,* NICOT (Grand Rapids: Eerdmans, 1990). See also I. Howard Marshal, *Commentary on Luke,* NIGTC (Grand Rapids: Eerdmans, 1978), 412–15.

was described in Ezekiel as being like death and resurrection (Ezek 37:1–14). Similarly, Jesus died and returned to life again.

This comparison between the history of Israel and the events of Jesus' life indicates that he represents Israel and substitutes for them. In the end, he will judge them. This comparison and its implications complete the picture of the servant of the Lord. This phrase in Isaiah refers to both the people of Israel and Israel as an individual. The servant both represents the people and redeems them, and his salvation extends to all the nations of the world (Isa 49; 53). Again, according to Daniel, the figure referred to as the Son of Man is both a single individual (Dan 7:13–14) and the people of the Most High (Dan 7:27). He is the new, true Israel, and anyone who rejects him loses the benefits of the covenant and the promise. Those who follow him carry on their faith in God through the new covenant that Jesus made by his death and resurrection. This is how Jesus saw himself, and how the church saw him.

Inheritance and Replacement

This image of an inheritance and replacement communicates the idea that the church replaced Israel, with the result that the Jews' inheritance has now been passed on to the Christian church. We can conclude that this is the case from what has been said about the parable of the owner who gave his vineyard to tenants and went on a journey (Matt 21:33–43). The conclusion of that parable was that the vineyard would be taken from Israel and given to another nation that would produce a harvest.

We can also trace this image in what the writers of the New Testament did with symbols. They attributed the characteristics of Israel in the Old Testament to the church in the New Testament, referring to the church as the bride, the vine, a holy nation, a kingdom of priests, and a chosen people paralleling the people of Israel and the kingdom of Israel.[121]

The change in the day of worship from Saturday to Sunday also marks an important change in the Christian view of the law of the Sabbath in Judaism. The replacement of Saturday by Sunday as the day of worship signals the replacement of Judaism by Christianity and the distinction between them. Sunday was adopted as the day of worship in Christianity because the resurrection of Jesus occurred on Sunday, and Jesus' repeated appearances were on Sundays. The day of Pentecost when the Holy Spirit came on the disciples was also a Sunday.[122] Changing the day of worship from Saturday to Sunday led to Christianity's departure from Judaism.

Similarly, Holy Communion replaced the Jewish Passover. The fact that Communion

---

[121] Compare Hos 2:16 and Eph 5:32; Ps 80:8 and John 15:1–2; Exod 19:6 and 1 Pet 2:9; Exod 19:6 and Rev 1:6; Isa 43:20 and 1 Pet 2:9; Josh 8:33 and Gal 6:16; 1 Sam 24:20 and Mark 1:15 and Rom 14:17.

[122] The Day of Pentecost comes on Sunday, fifty days (7 x 7 = 49) after the Jewish Passover, which occurs always on Saturday.

was celebrated every Sunday, unlike the Jewish Passover that was celebrated only once a year, marks it not only as a New Testament ritual but also buttresses the distinction between Christianity and Judaism.[123]

The apostolic church fathers and those who followed them supported the idea that the church replaces Israel. The Epistle of Barnabas states that God transferred the Jews' inheritance to Christians due to the faithlessness of Israel. Clement of Rome regards the church as the people of God, and Ignatius warns that those who live as Jews will not receive grace. Justin Martyr considers the church to be the true Israel. According to Irenaeus, God's promises to Israel are for the church. Tertullian calls on Israel to serve the church because the church came after Israel and Israel was a symbol of the church. Irenaeus saw Israel as a symbol of the church, which is the real and spiritual Israel.[124]

This understanding continues from Augustine until the present time. The one who best expressed the relationship between Israel and the church was George Ladd, New Testament professor and expert on the topic of Jesus and the kingdom. He affirms that when Jesus said to Peter, "you are Peter and on this rock I build my church," he was not speaking of restoring and rebuilding the nation of Israel. Rather, he was establishing a new nation that would replace Israel. He deliberately uses the word *ekklēsia* (translated "church") because in the Septuagint this was the Greek word used in many references to the people of God.[125]

The Point of Linkage and Communication

Jesus and his twelve disciples were the linking point between the people of the Old Testament and the people of the New Testament. Jesus was born into Judaism and grew up as a Jew, and he chose the twelve disciples to represent the twelve tribes of Israel. They were all Jews. But official Judaism rejected Jesus and crucified him. Jesus died and was resurrected. Then came the day of Pentecost, and the Holy Spirit filled the disciples and the followers of Jesus who were gathered in an upper room in Jerusalem. The disciples went out and preached to those who were feasting in Jerusalem and told them the good news about the resurrected Jesus and the necessity of believing in him in order to receive the Holy Spirit. Three thousand people believed and joined the community of Jesus.

The day of Pentecost was the formal starting point of the Christian church, and the beginning of its growth all over the world. Thus we can say that the church did not start from nothing; it started from the nucleus of the Jewish disciples of Jesus. From

---

[123] Hebrews 13:10, "We have an altar from which those who minister at the tabernacle have no right to eat," may refer also to the Lord's Supper.

[124] Ronald E. Diprose, *Israel in the Development of Christian Thought* (Rome: IBEI, 2000), 76–92.

[125] George Ladd, *A Theology of the New Testament* (Grand Rapids: Eerdmans, 1993), 107–9.

them it went to the Jews, beginning in Jerusalem and then to the Gentiles all over the world. The disciples of Jesus and his early followers were all Jewish and they became the church. This confirms the continuity between the people of the Old Testament and the people of the New Testament on the one hand, and confirms the starting of the church, on the other hand, as one new people consisting of Jews and non-Jews. Therefore, the church is not a second people of God that came after the first one, the people of Israel; rather, it is a continuation of the first people after the church had been born within it. It marked a new beginning.[126]

Does the church as a replacement of Israel do away with God's promise of salvation for the Jewish nation? Paul's answer is a decisive "no" (Rom 9–11). Paul's heart's desire and his prayer to God was that the Jewish people would be saved in Christ, who "is the culmination of the law so that there may be righteousness for everyone who believes" (Rom 10:4). Then he asks, "Did God reject his people?" and answers, "By no means!" He gives himself and other Jews who believed in Jesus as examples showing that God had not rejected his people.

Then he offers an illustration of two olive trees. One is a good olive tree—the Israel that knows God; the other is a wild olive tree—the Gentiles who do not know God. Some branches were cut from the good olive tree because they did not believe in Jesus Christ. Then some branches were cut from the wild olive tree because they believed in Jesus Christ and were grafted into the good olive tree.[127]

Paul's purpose in using this illustration is to show that a Gentile who believes in Jesus should not boast over a Jew who has not yet believed, for a Jew in his spiritual inheritance represents the good olive tree onto which the Gentile was grafted. Thus, the Jewish root is the one that holds the Gentiles' branches, not the opposite.

Paul points out that some Jews were cut from the good olive tree because of their disbelief, and a group of Gentiles grafted in because of their faith. If a Gentile falls from the faith, he will be cut from the olive tree. On the other hand, if a Jew turns from disbelief and believes, he will be grafted back into the olive tree since God is able to return a branch to its place. If God is able to graft a wild olive branch into a good olive tree, in spite of their different natures, then he is surely able to reattach a branch to the tree from which it was cut.

Paul concludes that Israel has experienced a partial hardening and that when the full number of Gentiles has embraced faith, then the Jewish people will again become open to the gospel. (Note the comparison between "the full number of the Gentiles" and "all Israel.") Then he continues,

---

[126] Millard J. Erickson, *Christian Theology*, 2nd ed. (Grand Rapids: Baker, 1998), 1058.

[127] Paul says that this is contrary to nature. Usually, branches are taken from a good tree to be grafted in a wild tree, so that the wild tree gives good fruit. However, Paul here goes beyond the natural case to reveal the purpose of this illustration.

> As far as the gospel is concerned, they [the Jews] are enemies for your sake; but as far as election is concerned, they are loved on account of the patriarchs, for God's gifts and his call are irrevocable. (Rom 11:28–29)

Paul is describing changes. At one time the Jews obeyed God; then they disobeyed him. At one time the Gentiles did not know God; then they obeyed him. If disobedience is characteristic of both parties, the mercy of God will also flow to both.

In this unique passage in Romans 9–11, we see God's purpose concerning the Jews who did not accept Jesus. God intends their salvation, which will happen in due time. On the basis of Paul's logic and his explanation of God's plan of salvation for both Jews and Gentiles, every Christian church should allocate a place in its creed to the return of the Jews to faith at the end of time. Neither Jesus nor Paul nor the Christian church has closed the door to God's people. All the time, the doors of the church stand open and its call is addressed to Jews and all the nations of the world.

Hans Küng, a Catholic theologian, puts it well:

> The fate of Jews and Gentiles, of Israel and the Church, is mysteriously interwoven. No one has any reason for pride; we all have grounds for hope. For all of these will come at the end a common eschatological salvation, in which rejection and election will be balanced out. The horizon of the new as of the old people of God is bounded, in the darkness of the present, by the bright hope which is common to both: the coming of salvation for the whole of mankind. The final aim of God's plan of salvation is not the salvation of the Gentiles nor the salvation of the Jews, but the salvation of all men, the salvation of the one and entire people of God composed of Gentiles and Jews . . . .
>
> We are a long way here from any hostility to the Jews, which would see them as a rejected people; for here, Paul is writing in all earnestness of Israel's election, which no failure has been able to reverse. And yet we must ask whether a Jew would be able to understand the Jew Paul; and here we must have no illusions. In order to understand the Jew Paul, a Jew would have to follow Paul: without ceasing to be a Jew, without being a deserter or renegade to a "different faith," but precisely in full loyalty to the God of Abraham and Isaac and Jacob, he would have, like Paul, to become a Christian, to confirm anew his faith in the one true God, who in the Jew Jesus of Nazareth acted, decisively and eschatologically, for the salvation of Israel and of the whole world. Then he would be able to understand how the new people of God is a continuation of the old people of God, despite the change of direction, an eschatological fulfillment, despite the new creation, of the ancient people of God.[128]

There are no more eloquent words with which to conclude this section on the relationship between Christianity and Judaism. But the debate continues, for only when completeness comes will what we know in part disappear (1 Cor 13:10).

---

[128] Hans Küng, *The Church* (New York: Doubleday, 1976), 196–97.

THE CHRISTIAN ATTITUDE TO THE JEWISH JESUS

In the first part of this chapter, we presented Western Christianity's attitude to the Judaism of Jesus and the Jews. It is characterized by growing support for Jews due to the West's sense of guilt following the Nazi Holocaust. However, support for the Jews has become so extreme in some Christian circles in Europe and America that any criticism of the actions of individual Jews or of the Jewish state, even in matters of conscience or ethics, is regarded as evidence of anti-Semitism.

We then considered the attitude of Eastern Christianity to the Judaism of Jesus and Judaism as a religion, and especially to the Zionist movement. It is characterized by a growing rejection of Judaism due to Israel's refusal to give the Palestinian people their lawful rights, its savagery in dealing with those who live in the region, and its failure to compensate those who were displaced.

It is almost as if the West and the East have exchanged roles. The Christian West persecuted the Jews for centuries, whereas in the East Muslims and Christians were tolerant of the Jews for centuries. Then what happened? Because of the Holocaust, the West suddenly changed from hating to loving the Jews, to the extent of identifying with them. And due to the expulsion of the Palestinians from their homes, the tolerant East began hating the Jews to the extent of completely rejecting them.

Both extremes are unacceptable. In spite of the conflict in the Middle East in the 1960s and the failure to establish a lasting peace based on justice, the inhabitants of the region and those who fight injustice must always maintain an objective perspective on ideas and on conflicting humanitarian, religious, and ethical issues. These elements are powerful because they are general, but this makes them a double-edged sword that may harm the one who wields them. This applies to Israelis too. To abolish radicalism, the church in the West has to love the Jews but not engage in a one-sided identification with them or with Judaism. We say "the church" because not all the West is the church. Meanwhile the church in the East has to love the Jews because they are fellow human beings. Again, we say "the church" because not all the East is part of the church. The church has to distinguish between Judaism and the injustices of Zionism, and resist all kinds of injustice whatever its source. That was what Jesus did.

In this regard, Bishop Khedr has this to say:

> The danger we face in this age is either to exaggerate our hatred for the Jews to the point where we also hate the whole Old Testament, or to exaggerate our support for the Jews until we lose sight of the uniqueness of the gospel. In both cases, the Jews are at the center.
>
> Some of those who have suffered injustice at the hands of Jews, like the Arabs, call for abandoning the Torah as they consider it the book of nationalistic Judaism. Others tend to sympathize with the Jews, whom they previously persecuted over centuries. However, to compensate for that persecution, theology tends to accept Judaism and its importance

in salvation. Both attitudes, however, contradict the uniqueness of the New Testament, for either hatred or great sympathy is fatal and contrary to the truth of the faith. . . .

There is a Jewish cause in which we do not share. We cannot be anti-Semitic, for we defend the freedom of the Jews everywhere, since we are sons of inviolable freedom. Enmity to Jews puts us in the realm of racism, which both Islam and Christianity reject and is not in accord with pure Arabism. There is a Jewish issue that we face with all free men, and we draw a distinction between Judaism and racism.[129]

The Attitude of Western Christianity: Supporting the Jewishness of Jesus and Judaism

There is a growing awareness and a strong sense of remorse among Westerners, and Western churches, about their behavior to the Jews over the centuries, which reached its apex in the Holocaust. This remorse is what causes the reaction against all that is anti-Semitic and spurs unconditional support of Jews and a desire to compensate them. This led to Western support of the establishment of the state of Israel, in spite of the injustices this entailed for Palestinians.

The American church historian Jaroslav Pelikan deals with this issue in his book *Jesus Through the Centuries: His Place in the History of Culture.* He welcomes the growing recognition that Jesus was a rabbi, a Jewish teacher, and hoped that it would have a positive effect on "the relation between the synagogue and the church, or between the people to whom Jesus belonged and the people who belong to Jesus." In the past, ignoring the Jewishness of Jesus resulted in a relationship between Christians and Jews that could be called "a red [bloody?] line" that runs through the history of culture on the religious, political, and ethical levels. Pelikan points to Marc Chagall's painting, *White Crucifixion,* in which the loincloth on the crucified Jesus is the prayer shawl of a devout rabbi. The image references Jesus' words to his disciples, "they will put you out of the synagogue; in fact, the time is coming when anyone who kills you will think they are offering a service to God" (John 16:2). Ironically, some of those who considered themselves Christians inverted this and thought that persecuting the Jews was a service to God!

Then Pelikan poses a profound but difficult question:

Would there have been such anti-Semitism, would there have been so many pogroms, would there have been an Auschwitz,[130] if every Christian church and every Christian home had focused its devotion on icons of Mary, not only as the Mother of God

---

[129] المطران جورج خضر "بانتظار العيد" (بيروت، صحيفة النهار (20 /12 /1987; ET: Bishop George Khedr, "Waiting for the Feast," *An-Nahār* (Beirut) newspaper, 20 December 1987.

[130] Auschwitz was the vast concentration camp in Poland in which thousands of Jews were killed by the Nazis during the Second World War. Its name has come to symbolize all extermination camps.

and Queen of Heaven but as the Jewish maiden and the new Miriam, and on icons of Christ not only as Pantocrator but as Rabbi Jeshua bar-Joseph, Rabbi Jesus of Nazareth, the Son of David, in the context of the history of a suffering Israel and a suffering humanity?[131]

Today, we can also ask whether the increased attention the Western church is now paying to the Jewishness of Jesus has led to the Palestinian calamity at the hands of Zionists.

While it is valid to argue that focusing on the Jewishness of Jesus is important if we are to avoid the curse of renewed anti-Semitism, it is also important to recognize the clear distinction between Christianity and Judaism that Jesus himself introduced by his teaching. Failure to draw this distinction leads Christians to identify with Jews to such an extent that some wear a necklace in which the cross lies in the center of the Star of David. Those wearing this necklace are often unaware of the theological implications of the fact that the symbol of Christianity is being set within the context of political Judaism and the state of Israel.

Some television preachers in America threaten God's judgment on politicians in Washington if they show any inclination to give Palestinians some of their legal rights in the ongoing conflict in the Middle East. There have been dialogues between some Christian churches and Jewish religious leaders in which statements have been signed agreeing that it is not necessary to preach to the Jews—do Christians who sign such statements think that the Jews do not need the crucified Messiah? Some Christian teachings now seem to make the church an extension of Judaism or a denomination within Judaism. Some even go so far as asking whether accepting the Jewishness of Jesus and accepting him as a Jew is essential for salvation.[132]

While belief in the Jewishness of Jesus is clearly not a condition for salvation, it is necessary for understanding salvation. In Acts 17, Luke gives an account of the sermon Paul preached to the citizens of Athens at the Areopagus. In this sermon, Paul did not mention anything about the Jewish background of Jesus but stressed that God had raised him from the dead and appointed him as judge. If the Jewishness of Jesus were necessary for salvation, Paul would not have left that out of his sermon.

However, it is also clear that when Paul and the other apostles were making disciples, they taught them about the Old Testament, for it provides the background and the basis for Christian teaching.

If belief in the Jewishness of Jesus were necessary for salvation, it would also be necessary to observe the Jewish law, practice circumcision, keep the Sabbath, make pilgrimages to the temple in Jerusalem, offer animal sacrifices, and so forth. However,

---

[131] Jaroslav Pelikan, *Jesus through the Centuries* (New Haven: Yale University Press, 1999), 19–20.

[132] Bernard Reitsma, "The Jewishness of Jesus: Relevant or Essential," *NETR* 26.1 (2005): 57.

in reality, Jesus, Paul, and the other apostles abolished all these practices and established a relationship with God that is based on faith and love and intellectual discernment through the guidance of the Holy Spirit when choosing what is best for human body, soul, and spirit and for healthy relationships. Christians interpreted all the Jewish customs in the Old Testament as symbols or foreshadowing of the light that shone in Christ. Thus the meaning of the Old Testament remained, but its forms and customs ended.[133]

If identification with Judaism and insisting on the Jewishness of Jesus and his Jewish background is so important as to be essential, why did Paul, who loved his people, say that as a Christian, he worships God in the spirit and does not rely on the flesh? Relying on the flesh for him meant boasting about his circumcision and the fact that he belonged to Israel, the tribe of Benjamin, and the Pharisees. He was known for his religious zeal and his strict observance of the law. Now, however, he dismisses all these privileges as worthless compared to knowledge of Christ (Phil 3:4–8).

When it comes to affirming the importance of knowing the Jewish background of Jesus in order to understand his call and mission, and the whole Christian faith built on the belief that Jesus is the Messiah promised in the Old Testament, and in order to understand the Son of Man, the suffering servant of the Lord who embodies Israel and the wisdom of the divine law, we can note the words of Karl Barth, the evangelical Swiss theologian who resisted the Nazi genocide of the Jews. He stated that Jesus of Nazareth, the promised Messiah, is the manifestation of God's identity and will, the one who "comes out of Israel, born of Mary the Virgin, and yet from above." He represents Israel, and is thus its fulfillment and consummation. Thus, the calling of Israel and its mission has to be understood as being manifested and fulfilled in Jesus Christ. For this reason, Israel and Jesus Christ are a foundation and a building, two indivisible parts, both in the past and throughout history and eternity. Israel is nothing without Jesus Christ; but without Israel, Jesus is not Jesus Christ. As the fulfillment of Israel, he is the one who sends the life and light given to it by God's grace to the Gentiles and all the nations of the world.[134]

In his book, *The Jesus I Never Knew*, Philip Yancey has this to say about the importance of understanding Jesus' Jewish background in order to understand his person and mission: "I can no more understand Jesus apart from his Jewishness than I can understand Gandhi apart from his Indianness."[135] This is true. We cannot understand anyone unless we know something about their environment and society and the age in which they live. On the same page, Yancey quotes the German Jewish thinker Martin

---

[133] المطران جورج خضر, من مقالة بعنوان جذور المسيح (بيروت, 13/ 12/ 1987, صحيفة النهار); ET: Bishop Georges Khedr from an article entitled "The Roots of Christ," *An-Nahār Newspaper* (Beirut), 13 December 1987.

[134] Karl Barth, *Dogmatics in Outline* (London: SCM, 1949), 72–81.

[135] Philip Yancey, *The Jesus I Never Knew* (Grand Rapids: Zondervan, 1995), 50.

Buber: "We Jews know [Jesus] in a way—in the impulses and emotions of his essential Jewishness—that remains inaccessible to the Gentiles subject to him." This too is true. However, we have to say, on the other hand, that both Jews and Gentiles who believe that Jesus is the crucified and risen Christ and that he is the Son of God, and who have become one in him, know Jesus—in the essence of his divinity and broad humanity—in a way that is not open to his fellow Jews!

Holistic Attitude of Historical Christianity to the Jewishness of Jesus and Judaism

There are Christians in the West who love the Jews because Jesus the Savior is descended from them racially and culturally. They turn this love into complete support for them, born out of the sense of guilt toward the Jew due to their persecution by the Nazis. There are Christians in the East who hate all Jews completely for what they have done to the land of Palestine and its people. But they had a problem because Jesus was a Jew. So they reject his Jewishness and assign him a different cultural and racial background, without regard to historical facts. Thus we have to deal with the following question: What is the objective historical attitude of Christianity to the Jewishness of Jesus and the followers of Judaism?

In answering this question, on the basis of the New Testament writings and later historical statements we can say that the Christian church in general has always respected the Jewishness of Jesus and has not denied it (ignoring the vagaries of some religious and civilian princes). The church respected Judaism, though it condemned the behavior of some Jews. We can thus say that the Christian church has respected the Jewishness of Jesus, but has not emphasized it. Christianity has always been aware of the sensitivity of the relationship between racial Judaism and the cultural Jewishness of Jesus. It has not separated them, but has emphasized mostly his cultural Jewishness. The reasons for doing this can be summarized as follows.

The Belief That Jesus Is the Incarnate Son of God

Jesus' early followers believed him to be the Son of God, the Lord of glory, the splendor of the glory of God, and the incarnate Word of God. These expressions of faith are all found in the New Testament, written in the first century AD. We also have the Nicene Creed, dating from the fourth century AD, which states:

> We believe . . . in one Lord Jesus Christ, the only begotten Son of God; begotten of his Father before all worlds, . . . who for us men and our salvation, came down from heaven. And was incarnate by the Holy Ghost of the Virgin Mary, and was made man.

This belief that Jesus is the eternal Son of God makes him someone who comes through Judaism to reach people of every era and area, rather than someone who "emerges" from Judaism. He is a divine being who enters humanity through Mary in the Jewish culture, a culture that was already replete with divine dealings and manifestations. He is the Messiah, who was nurtured by this culture as an infant, who studied it, comprehended it, embodied it, concentrated it, fulfilled it, and transcended its limitations so that the light of God would shine through him all over the world.

In conclusion, we can quote Bishop George Khedr: "Because of our faith in the divinity of the Savior, this is what we stress; the search for his earthly identity is less important in practice."[136]

The Belief That Jesus Is the Risen and Ascended Lord

Faith in Jesus' sonship and his coming from above are not the only reasons we do not focus our attention on his earthly identity. Another reason is his resurrection from the dead and ascension to heaven, where he sits at the right hand of God. Paul says that the Messiah, though Jewish in terms of his human ancestry, became "God over all, forever praised" (Rom 9:5). In the incarnation, Jesus became limited to time and space; in his resurrection and ascension he transcended time and space. In the incarnation, he came as a Jew; in the resurrection he departed as Lord of all humanity. The Son of God who descended in the incarnation to "the lower, earthly regions," is the one who was raised in resurrection: "He who descended is the very one who ascended higher than all the heavens, in order to fill the whole universe" (Eph 4:10).

Given that Jesus was glorified with the resurrection, becoming the firstborn of all who rise from death, and transcends history, it is difficult to limit him racially to Judaism, except on the historical level.

The Belief That the Church Is Essentially Nonracial, for
Jesus Is the Savior of Both Jews and Gentiles

The third reason that Jesus' Jewish identity is not stressed is the nonracial nature of the church. Jesus, the founder of the church, captured the essence of the message of the suffering servant of the Lord when he said,

> I have other sheep that are not of this sheep pen. I must bring them also. They too will listen to my voice, and there shall be one flock and one shepherd. (John 10:16)

Jesus suffered to save both Jews and Gentiles. Thus the apostle Paul insists that those who are baptized into Christ have put on Christ, and in him there is no difference between a Jew and a Gentile (Gal 3:27–28). It was because of this belief that Jesus transcended race and belief in the nonracial church that Luke did not halt Jesus' genealogy at Abraham but took it back all the way to Adam, the head of humanity. The

---

[136] المطران جورج خضر، مقالة أحد النسبة (بيروت، جريدة النهار؛ كانون الأول/18 ديسمبر 1999)‎. ET: Article by Bishop George Khedr "The Sunday of Descent" (Beirut: an-Nahār newspaper, 18 December 1999).

same belief led Matthew to mention two Gentiles, Rahab and Ruth, in the genealogy of Jesus (Matt 1:5).

There is no stronger expression of this truth than the words Paul used in the Letter to the Ephesians to describe the unity of the church formed of both Jews and Gentiles in Christ. Jesus is described as our peace, the one who united the two groups, eliminating enmity and reconciling them both through him into one whole, in the one body of the church, reconciling them to God through the cross. Thus, both groups have access to the Father by one Spirit, since the Gentiles have become fellow citizens with God's people and members of God's household. So this building rises to become a holy temple, with both Jews and Gentiles as living stones contributing to making a dwelling in which God lives by his Spirit. The mystery of Christ is the extension of God's salvation to the Gentiles. This mystery was hidden but it was manifested to the apostles of Christ and his prophets by the Holy Spirit. The content of this manifestation

> was not made known to people in other generations as it has now been revealed by the Spirit to God's holy apostles and prophets. This mystery is that through the gospel the Gentiles are heirs together with Israel, members together of one body, and sharers together in the promise in Christ Jesus. (Eph 3:5–6)

The words "together with" make it clear that the Gentiles are not just an extension but a complementary, indivisible part of the body of Christ that is the church.

After hearing these words about the nonracial and united nature of the church as the one people of God, why would the church want to emphasize Jesus' racial Jewishness? It is not acceptable for the church that calls for universality, to support partiality. God, who manifested himself in accordance with the advance of human history from tribalism to universal humanity, does not retreat to racism.

There are two sayings of the apostle Paul that establish the attitude of Christianity to the Jewishness of Jesus and his cultural and Jewish backgrounds. The first one is found in the following paragraph from the letter to the Romans:

> For I could wish that I myself were cursed and cut off from Christ for the sake of my people, those of my own race, the people of Israel. Theirs is the adoption to sonship; theirs the divine glory, the covenants, the receiving of the law, the temple worship and the promises. Theirs are the patriarchs, and from them is traced the human ancestry of the Messiah, who is God over all, forever praised! (Rom 9:3–5)

In these verses the apostle Paul acknowledges and praises the Jewish nation because Jesus came from it. Here we see the Jewishness of Jesus and his racial background. But what about his being "God over all [all peoples] forever praised"?

The second saying is found in 2 Corinthians, where Paul speaks about the desire of some to boast and praise themselves, an attitude that he rejects (compare 2 Cor 5:12

with 2:17–3:18, the contrast between the servants of the old covenant and those of the new covenant). Then he continues, still with regard to the desire to boast, to remind Christians that we died with Christ in order to live not for ourselves but for him (2 Cor 5:14–15). Then comes the main point:

> So from now on we regard no one from a worldly point of view. Though we once regarded Christ in this way, we do so no longer. Therefore, if anyone is in Christ, the new creation has come: The old has gone, the new is here! (2 Cor 5:16–17)

From the wider context of 2 Corinthians 3, it is clear that "the old" refers to "the Old Testament," which has become new in Christ. Thus, we no longer emphasize the Jewishness of Jesus that is related to the Old Testament and Israel according to the flesh; instead, we now emphasize the new Israel of God:

> Neither circumcision nor uncircumcision means anything; what counts is the new creation. Peace and mercy to all who follow this rule—to the Israel of God (Gal 6:15–16)

Paul also says:

> For it is we who are the circumcision, we who serve God by his Spirit, who boast in Christ Jesus, and who put no confidence in the flesh. (Phil 3:3)

In conclusion, we must stress and emphasize the religious and cultural background of Jesus rather than his ethnic background, although these are related. The cultural background of Jesus is essential and fixed; it forms the historical background for understanding him. By contrast, his ethnic identity was subsumed by the church, which includes both Jews and Gentiles, where there are no racial barriers because Jesus Christ the incarnated, crucified, risen, and ascended Lord, is its all in all.

Finally, we must not forget that the purpose and goal of the gospel is not for people who believe in Christ to become Jews but to become children of God. Jesus brings people into his kingdom from every ethnicity and culture in the world, perfecting, purifying, and reforming them all. So the point at issue is not whether Christians believe in the Jewishness of Jesus, because that is a fact. The more important issue is for Jews to believe in the "Christian" Jesus!

Chapter Four

RELIGION AND POLITICS

ANCIENT PROPHECIES AND CONTEMPORARY POLITICS

Makram Naguib

Dr. Makram Naguib was awarded a BTh in 1967, a Licentiate in Philosophy in 1982, and a PhD from San Francisco Theological Seminary in 1992. He is former pastor of Heliopolis Evangelical Church and the former chairman of the board of directors of the Evangelical Theological Seminary in Cairo, where he is also professor of expository preaching. He is a member of the General Evangelical Council of the Evangelical Fellowship and a member of the board of the Coptic Evangelical Association for Social Services (CEOSS). Dr. Naguib has written and translated more than forty books.

IT IS IMPORTANT to begin by defining the words "politics" and "politician." "Politics" has two meanings. The broader definition refers to the life of a city (*polis* in Greek), and the responsibilities of ordinary citizens (*politēs*). It embraces all aspects of life in human society and can be defined as the art of living together in a society.

In a narrower sense, "politics" refers to the science of government and the development and implementation of specific policies that politicians wish to promote through legislation. If we contemplate the life of Jesus Christ, it is clear that he never engaged in politics in the narrower sense of the word. He did not call political meetings, support political programs, or lead political opposition. However, he did come into the world to participate in the life of society, and he sent his disciples out into the world with the same purpose and mission. He also announced a new and different social system, namely the kingdom of God, which was seen as challenging old values and modes of conduct. Thus, in the broadest sense of the word, his revolutionary teachings had political implications.

In light of Christ's example, the mission of the church community has to address both the social and political aspects of life. Moreover, while the church as a whole cannot engage in party politics, individual Christians are free to use all available legal channels to participate in and interact with social and political issues.

But when the topic of religion and politics is raised these days, the debate is not about whether religion should influence opinions on political matters. Through long and protracted debate, which we cannot deal with here, that issue has largely been resolved. The issue that now dominates the discussion in many parts of the world, and especially in the Arab world, is the mixing of religion with politics and politics with religion by interpreting religious texts literally in order to achieve political goals.

On January 2, 2007, Salama Ahmed Salama wrote a column in *Al-Ahram* newspaper under the title "Religion and Politics 2006" in which he had this to say:

> The most dangerous phenomenon this year has been the religious dimension affecting international relations and the emergence of a sectarian dimension in regional conflicts. Many people expected that religion would decline with the rise of science and the spread of postmodernism, but instead the twenty-first century has witnessed an unexpected return to religion among new generations.
>
> Today the conflict is no longer between the religious and the irreligious, as it was in the twentieth century; it has become a confrontation between religion that recognizes the role of the intellect and freedom of thought and religion that is based on fanaticism and blind conformity. This shift is reflected to varying degrees in the Islamic world, especially in its relations to the West where some fanatical Islamic movements have adopted the violent, radical approach that culminated in the incidents of September 2001 in America and the explosions in London and Madrid.

The mixing of religion and politics is not new. It emerges from time to time, and is currently important because of the spread of religious movements around the world. Once again there are theories about the end of the world and the link between current events and the second coming of Christ, and there is debate about the Zionist Christian trends and currents that mix religion and politics in the Arab-Israeli conflict around the Palestinian issue.

In what follows, I will try to give an overview of this phenomenon and its effects, with a particular emphasis on how we should respond to it.

THE END OF HISTORY, ZIONISM, AND THE RETURN OF CHRIST

Whenever the world is undergoing shifts and changes, and whenever some great historical incident affects the course of world events or events in a significant part of the world, theories regarding the end of the world or the end of history emerge. Interest in the second coming of Christ increases. Libraries become filled with books explaining prophecies and the events that will accompany their fulfillment, all proclaiming that Christ's return is imminent. This pattern was seen at the time of the French Revolution and during the first and second world wars.

When the Soviet Union collapsed, Francis Fukuyama, an American political scientist, said that human government had reached its final form in the model of liberal democracy. Hegel, Marx, and Lenin made similar pronouncements in the past.[1] Daniel Bell, an American professor of sociology at Harvard University, declared the end of ideology.[2] Samuel P. Huntington proclaimed that what would follow would be a clash of civilizations and religions.[3]

Right-Wing Religious Groups

Following the Second Gulf War, Fayez Fares published a book entitled *The Gulf War and the End of the Age* in which he included the following excerpt from an article published in the British newspaper *The Times* on Saturday, 22 September 1990:

> Even though the Gulf area is thousands of miles away from America, some extreme right-wing religious sects and groups in America have—as usual—used the Gulf crisis as further evidence to bolster their theories that the end of the world is at hand. They say that the agreement between Russia and America marks the beginning of Russia's role in the Middle East. This would lead to war with Israel and pave the way for the battle of Armageddon and the end of the world.[4]

Talk about the end of the world and the second coming of Christ has heated up recently due to Israel's possession of nuclear weapons, the support given to it from all quarters, the attempts to Judaize Jerusalem by destroying the Al-Aqsa Mosque and rebuilding Solomon's Temple, the disruption of peace negotiations, Likud's coming to power supported by extreme right-wing groups, and so on. Thus, some people try to interpret the great truths of our Christian faith in light of contemporary, changeable political events.

At the same time, they form their views—as we will see later—on the basis of literal interpretations of biblical texts and prophecies without regard to their historical background or the spirit of the Bible as a whole. Because they define the signs and prophecies in light of contemporary historical events, they fall into error themselves and spread differences and divisions in the church of Christ—especially when they

---

[1] Mohamed Hassanein Heikal, *Egypt and the Twenty-First Century* (Cairo: Dar El Shorouk, 1994 [in Arabic]), 23.

[2] Daniel Bell, *The End of Ideology* (Cambridge, MA: Harvard University Press, 1962).

[3] Samuel P. Huntington, *The Clash of Civilizations and the Remaking of World Order* (New York: Simon & Schuster, 1996).

[4] Fayez Fares, *The Gulf War and the End of the World* (Cairo: Dar Al Thaqafa, 1991 [in Arabic]), 6.

sow confusion about the nature of divine revelation and of biblical texts and mix what is Jewish with what is Christian, religion with politics, and so on.

Even an American movie like *Independence Day* includes elements of these views, which appear to constitute the imaginative background to the story. That movie tells of an alien attack on earth and of the events that accompany the end of the world. At its close, the camera focuses on a Jewish man who has tried to save the earth and reconstruct it, and who then celebrates the world's Independence Day. In the final scene, we see him standing by the pyramids. This scene leaves more than one message with the audience. The first suggests that the Jews built the pyramids, a claim that contradicts history; the second contradicts the spirit of the Bible as it suggests that only Jews will remain on earth to reconstruct the millennial kingdom—as they believe it to be.

Zionist Trends and Radical Evangelicals

Zionism has been embraced by some radical evangelical denominations, sects, and organizations in the West, especially those that emerged from what is called dispensationalism, a school of thought that arose in the nineteenth century. This type of thinking emerged most clearly during the Reagan administration in the United States of America and fits well with the plans of the Zionist movement as first laid out at the conference in Basel, Switzerland, in 1897.

The nineteenth-century proponents of these views included the Irishman John Nelson Darby (1800–82), the founder of the Plymouth Brethren, who studied at Trinity College, Dublin. These views were supported by Cyrus I. Scofield, who published the Scofield Reference Bible in 1909. More recently, they were promoted by Hal Lindsey in books like *The Late Great Planet Earth* and *There's a New World Coming*.

The Rise of Religion and the Arab Defeat of 1967

Social and political changes in the United States in the 1960s resulted in the rise of the Christian right. Reda Helal comments:

> The civil rights movement and the war in Vietnam led to severe divisions in American society and among Christians. Liberals advocated direct action such as sit-ins and demonstrations, whereas conservatives preferred to emphasize the effect of religion on the individual conscience. Evangelicals rose up to confront social and political developments.[5]

It was natural for the political right-wing to position itself to oppose the social and political changes in the seventies. The rise of the Christian right was also linked to the rising currents of Zionist Christianity, especially after the Arab defeat of 1967, Israel's

---

[5] Reda Helal, *The Jewish Christ and the End of the World* (Cairo: Dar El Shorouk, 2000 [in Arabic]), 82–84.

victory, and its occupation of Jerusalem. Some considered these events a confirmation of Old Testament prophecies and a harbinger of the imminent return of Christ. Thus the Christian right-wing gradually swelled in the eighties and nineties until it became an effective voting force in elections for the presidency and the US congress.[6]

The leaders of this trend had considerable financial influence, especially in the media, and more specifically in American television. They included men like Pat Robertson, the son of Virginia senator A. Willis Robertson. Pat Robertson graduated from Yale Law School and went on to manage a television network with 1,300 employees. He founded the 700 Club and ran for president in 1988. Other leaders included Jimmy Swaggart, Jim Bakker, Oral Roberts, and Jerry Falwell (founder of the organization known as the Moral Majority), Kenneth Copeland, Richard De Haan, Rex Humbard, Dale Crawley, James Robison (whom President Reagan invited to offer the opening prayer at the Republican National Convention in 1984), and John Walvoord. Other leaders include Ralph Reed, director of the organization known as the Christian Coalition of America, which was founded by Pat Robertson. Robertson was succeeded as president of the Christian Coalition by Don Hodel, who had served in the Reagan cabinet. This coalition was influential in congressional elections in 1994 and 1996.[7]

Some Protestant denominations in Egypt and the Arab world have adopted similar interpretations of Scripture, the only difference being that here they are driven by literal interpretations of prophecy rather than by political motives. But whatever the motives of those propagating these ideas, their continuous repetition in the literature of these evangelical groups and denominations has led some authors and thinkers to mistakenly link the Zionist movement to the Protestant Reformation that began in Europe in the fifteenth century. That Reformation was fueled by the religious, intellectual, scientific, and political changes associated with the Renaissance, and was completed in the sixteenth century. Attempts to link the Reformation with Zionism run counter to the basic principles of the Reformers. Nevertheless, the claim that there is such a link has led to a deep suspicion of all things Protestant, for many in the Arab world believe that all Protestants accept and promote these ideas.

The Problem of Overgeneralization

In the Middle East, many who write about groups espousing Zionist ideas refer to them generally as "evangelical" or "Protestant." They do not distinguish between different denominations or acknowledge that groups like the Presbyterian churches in the West

---

[6] Ibid., 13.

[7] For more details, see Grace Halsell, *Prophecy and Politics: The Secret Alliance Between Israel and the U.S. Christian Right* (Chicago: Lawrence Hill, 1989; Arabic translation by Muhammad al-Sammak [Cairo: Dar El Shorouk, 1989]), esp. 19–37. The same book was translated in Homs, Syria, by Abd El Hady Abla, under the title *Biblical Thought and Nuclear War: Evangelical Missionaries on the Way of Atomic Resurrection*. It was reprinted for the third time in 1988.

and in the Near East completely disagree with Zionist thinking and strive to counteract it. But it is difficult to counter the effect of books and articles with titles like "Evangelical Fundamentalism" or "Christian Zionism." Readers are deeply affected by what they read, even though it is based on irresponsible generalization. The writers of such books draw on the terminology used in Western publications and they (and some Western writers) use terms loosely, without much grasp of their implications and history. Thus both writers and readers fall into the trap of generalization.

A Call for Discernment

Some writers have begun to distinguish between evangelicals who advocate Zionism and Presbyterians and other Christians who reject it. For example, the Lebanese writer Muhammad al-Sammak has written:

> The most important basis for evangelical opposition in America is the National Council of Churches of Christ, which includes the Presbyterian Church together with other churches and about forty million Protestant Americans. . . . There are also other periodicals such as Sojourners (based in Washington), The Other Side (based in Philadelphia), and the Reformed Journal (issued in Michigan). These periodicals are persistent in their criticism of zealously literal interpretation and Zionist tendency within evangelical churches and present their ideas clearly and consistently. The leaders of these churches meet the American president and his administration and write to them, issuing statements and holding seminars to inform public opinion, while supporting Arab issues. In 1995, 40% of the American people rejected the fundamentalist position.[8]

In the Middle East in general and in Egypt specifically, all Christian Orthodox, Catholic, and Presbyterian churches together or separately have played an important role in clarifying theological and biblical thinking, both at international conferences and forums and among local groups. They have addressed organizations such as the World Council of Churches, the Middle East Council of Churches, the National Middle Eastern Presbyterian Caucus in America (Rev. Fuad Bahnan), the General Assembly of the Presbyterian Church in America (Rev. Dr. Victor Makari), and the Sabeel Ecumenical Liberation Theology Center (Rev. Dr. Naim Stifan Ateek). Their work is also evident in the books and publications referred to in this chapter. Such work is particularly important at a time when Israeli arrogance has reached such heights that it again threatens to bring destructive violence among the peoples of the region. Consequently, we are all called to refute these allegations and support Arab rights.

An important book that helps in making this differentiation and avoiding the problem

---

[8] Muhammad al-Sammak, *Evangelical Fundamentalism* (Malta: Islamic World Studies Center, 1991 [in Arabic]), 165, 167.

of generalization and conflation is *A City on a Mountain* by Tarek Mitri.[9] Mitri distinguishes between civil religion, church religion, revival movements, and new religious groups. He also differentiates between Protestant groups, for Protestants are not one homogenous unit, nor are all conservative evangelicals necessarily fundamentalists or Zionists. Finally, he deals at length with the difference between evangelicalism and Zionist Christianity and agrees that there is no essential link between them.[10]

In a lecture on this book, Dr. George Sabra agreed with Tarek Mitri's conclusion. In his presentation, he examined trends and the four main theological groupings that have formed within the Protestant world: the classical, the liberal, the fundamentalist, and the missionary. He identified the different attitudes of each group in regard to the three elements shaping Zionist Christian thought, namely biblical roots, eschatological expectations, and individual literal interpretation of the Bible. He warned of the danger of overthrowing the historical centrality of Christ and exchanging it for the centrality of eschatological events.

In 1996 the French thinker Roger Garaudy published a book that was translated into English and Arabic. The English title was *The Founding Myths of Modern Israel*.[11] This book caused an uproar in France and led to Garaudy (age 83) being put on trial in November 1996. He had few supporters except Abbé Pierre, whose great popularity did not prevent him from standing against the mainstream.

Millenarianism

The spread of Zionist thinking was facilitated by the millenarian[12] assumption that every thousand years some important event transforms the course of human history and that all history will come to an end after a specific period of a thousand years.

> Myths concerning the end of history at the end of the first millennium (the end of the tenth century AD) were widespread throughout Europe. They resulted in the devastation of whole cities and vast areas of land as people left their work and professions and devoted themselves solely either to worship or to frenetic enjoyment of life's pleasures—all the more so because a comet appeared in the sky at that time and a myth spread that a comet would be one of the signs of the destruction of the world and the coming of doomsday.
>
> The Jewish idea of the millennium penetrated both Christian and Muslim beliefs. One of the most famous to talk about the end of history in the second millennium was a French physician and fortune-teller of Jewish origin, called Nostradamus—although

---

[9] Tarek Mitri, *A City on a Mountain* (Beirut: Dar El Nahar, 2004 [in Arabic]).

[10] The Middle East Council of Churches, *What Is Western Fundamentalist Christian Zionism?* (Cyprus: Limassol, 1988).

[11] Roger (Ragaa) Garaudy, *The Founding Myths of Modern Israel* (Newport Beach, CA: Institute for Historical Review, 2000). Published in Arabic by Dar El Ghad El Arabi, Cairo, 1996.

[12] For more on this subject, see the chapter with this title in Faheem Aziz, *The Theological Thought of Paul* (Cairo: Dar Al Thaqafa, 1977 [in Arabic]).

he claimed that the resurrection would not happen with the end of the present history of civilization. He expected another civilization to start in the first century of the third millennium, and only when that civilization ended would history itself end and doomsday come.[13]

The historian and sociologist Ibn Khaldun demonstrated the fallacy of millenarian thinking. While acknowledging that there are repetitive cycles in the history of civilizations, he denied that these cycles bear any relation to a set number of years.

In 1996, John Leslie, a British professor of philosophy and cosmology, published a controversial book entitled *The End of the World: The Science and Ethics of Human Extinction*.[14] Drawing on the work of Brandon Carter, a philosopher and scientist who put forward what is known as the Doomsday argument, Leslie argues that the world may well end by the close of the twenty-first century as a result of the risks threatening the environment, and consequently human beings. These risks include chemical and germ warfare, nuclear explosions, cosmic and volcanic eruptions, the impact of a comet, terrorism, risks related to the use of computers and software by organized crime, contaminated fertilizers, the spread of fatal viruses, the possible reemergence of a severe ice age, the expansion of the ozone hole, and global climate change.

THEOLOGICAL CONCEPTS

If we are to correct our course and address the risk posed by generalizations and the mixing of religion with politics and old prophecies with contemporary policies, we need to pay attention to theological concepts such as eschatology, God's kingdom, and the people of God, and we need to be aware of how our thinking on these matters affects our attitude to the state of Israel. In addition, we need to pay attention to interpretative principles and how they apply to prophetic and apocalyptic texts.

Eschatology

In broad terms, the word "eschatology" refers to prophecies and events related to the coming of the Messiah, his mission, and the fulfillment of the kingdom of God either in the present or in the future. More specifically, the word refers to future events associated with the end times. Thus the study of eschatology involves studying what the Bible teaches about the events of the last days.

In what follows, we will focus on two broad schools of thought, the first of which is dispensationalism. For those who hold to this view,

---

[13] Samy Khashaba, *Intellectual Terms* (Cairo: Academic Library, 1994 [in Arabic]), 262.

[14] John Leslie, *The End of the World: The Science and Ethics of Human Extinction* (New York: Psychology Press, 1996).

the inspiration of the whole Bible leads to the conclusion that the whole Bible is of equal theological value. The many prophecies of the Bible are like the pieces of a jig-saw puzzle which only need to be fitted together to give us a grand mosaic of God's redemptive purposes for the present and the future.[15]

An alternative approach is to interpret prophecies and biblical texts in light of the progressive nature of divine revelation in the Bible, relying on the familiar principles of the historical-grammatical method of interpretation.[16] This is the approach advocated by the Presbyterian church.

But before we discuss eschatology, we have to address the nature of divine revelation and determine what principles apply when it comes to the interpretation of eschatological passages in the Bible.

The Nature of Divine Revelation

Revelation is God's revealing of himself to us. There is a vast gulf between finite human beings and God the infinite creator, between rebellious self-centered people drowning in their sin and separated from God, and God the righteous judge. How can that gap be bridged? This was Job's lament: "If only I knew where to find him; if only I could go to his dwelling!" (Job 23:3).

God is absolute and far greater than our thoughts or understanding:

"For my thoughts are not your thoughts, neither are your ways my ways," declares the LORD. "As the heavens are higher than the earth, so are my ways higher than your ways and my thoughts than your thoughts." (Isa 55:8–9)

Zophar the Naamathite had this to say:

Can you fathom the mysteries of God? Can you probe the limits of the Almighty? They are higher than the heavens above—what can you do? They are deeper than the depths below—what can you know? Their measure is longer than the earth and wider than the sea. (Job 11:7–9)

It was thus necessary for God to reveal himself, intervening in the events of history as the Redeemer and Savior of humankind. In so doing, he also revealed the depths of human sin and of our suffering and need. The fullness of this divine revelation comes in one person, Jesus Christ, who came to reconcile human beings with God.

God's intervention in all of Old Testament history, including his covenant with Abraham, the exodus from Egypt, the giving of the law on Mount Sinai, the exile, and all the various manifestations of God to his people lead to this crux:

---

[15] George Eldon Ladd, *The Last Things: An Eschatology for Laymen* (Grand Rapids: Eerdmans, 1978), 7–9.

[16] Ibid. See also John Stott, *Focus on Christ* (Eastbourne, UK: Kingsway, 1985), 18–27.

> In the past God spoke to our ancestors through the prophets at many times and in various ways, but in these last days he has spoken to us by his Son, whom he appointed heir of all things, and through whom also he made the universe. The Son is the radiance of God's glory and the exact representation of his being, sustaining all things by his powerful word. After he had provided purification for sins, he sat down at the right hand of the Majesty in heaven. (Heb 1:1–3)

In this rich and wonderful paragraph, we see revelation in action, purpose, frame, time, quality, and content.[17]

The *action* is present in the word "spoke." God spoke in the past through his word, and he has also spoken to us in Christ. If we do not talk to each other, we remain strangers. If we talk, we get to know each other. This was the case between human beings and God. God was unknown, a stranger to us, but because he spoke we have come to know him and see him. In the past he did this in words; but in the last days he has spoken in a person, his Son Jesus Christ.

As for the *purpose*, we see it in the second action God took: "God was reconciling the world to himself in Christ" (2 Cor 5:19; see also John 1:14–18; Matt 11:25–30). In Jesus Christ we see someone who lives in a way that is fully responsive and obedient to God. Thus the eyes of faith see in Jesus the God who came as Redeemer and as the one who shows us what we should be.

Concerning the *frame*, we note that the revelation was in Christ Jesus. In previous revelations, God appeared in his glory, majesty, perfection, and purity. When Jesus came, he manifested God in his life, ministry, and teachings. In biblical terms, Jesus also manifested himself as the new Israel, the servant of God who represented both the individual (Isa 53) and the people (Isa 54). As the Son of Man he represented both together (Dan 7:13–14, 15–27). As Christ revealed the full response of a human being to God, he did so not only as an individual but also as a representative of his people. The people, that is, the people of God, the church, are an important part of the revelation. The only way we can fully respond to God and understand ourselves and our identity and ministry is within the framework of the people of God. Each individual has a unique personality, but the only place we can fully live and have a role among the people of God is as members of the body of Christ.

Regarding the *time*, God spoke to the ancestors in the past, "but in these last days he has spoken to us by his Son." We have thus been living in the last days ever since Christ came and introduced the New Testament era.

In terms of the *quality* and *content* of the revelation, the plural pronoun "us" refers to the people of God all around the world from every class, culture, and race.

---

[17] Aziz, *Interpretation* (Cairo: Dar Al Thaqafa, 1986 [in Arabic]), 175–82.

So, God's revelation in Christ is as follows:

- Final, since it is in the last days.
- Universal, since it is for the whole world.
- Historical, since it is related to specific events in the salvation history recorded in the two Testaments in the Bible, and is also at the center of the history of the whole world.
- Dynamic, living, and effective, for it has a deep effect on our whole being. It is a revelation that creates a crisis as we are confronted by God and have to recognize our attitude to him.
- Unified, progressive, and manifold. What do we mean by this? First, that "God spoke to our ancestors through the prophets at many times and in various ways"—including visions, dreams, prophecies, teachings, events, stories, psalms, and proverbs. Finally, he has spoken to us in Christ through his life, teachings, and mission. Many civilizations, languages, and other variables were involved in this revelation, which means that it was diverse. However, within this diversity, there has always been one clash, one story—God's revelation of himself as Redeemer, and the human response to this divine initiative. This is the thread that binds all this diversity together.

God's revelation of himself was progressive throughout the stages of salvation history. It culminated in the full divine revelation in the person of Jesus Christ, in whom and through whom revelation was complete. Christ's greatness is evident in relation to the universe. He is the creator, "through whom also he made the universe"; he is the protector and preserver, "sustaining all things by his powerful word"; and God has appointed him "heir of all things." We also see his greatness in relation to God the Father: He is the blessed Son, the owner of the glorious name that is superior to that of angels (Heb 1:4). He has a unique nature, as he "is the radiance of God's glory and the exact representation of his being," words that indicate his unique equality with God. This was a key verse in the theological battles that raged about the nature of Christ in the fourth and fifth centuries and has been used to refute various heresies.[18]

God's divine initiative was manifested in his gracious revelation of himself. God came to us with love and redemption through Jesus Christ, who is full of grace, truth, gentleness, and righteousness. In him we see God's nature and his attitude toward us. We grow in our Christian understanding when the Holy Spirit enlightens our minds so that we continually know God's glory that was manifested in Christ. All that we

---

[18] Riad Kassis, *The Land in the Bible* (Damascus: Alif Baa' al-Adeeb Press, 1991), 17.

know about God has come through Christ, and all that we have received from God we have received in Christ.

This is the truth of divine revelation and its progressive nature. Father George Kanawaty makes the same point in his book, *Christianity and Arab Civilization*.[19] In discussing the inspiration of the Bible in the opening chapter of that book, he cites the same paragraph from Hebrews 1 cited above, and says,

> One of the main features of this inspiration is its gradual manifestation throughout history. It did not come all at once; it coincided with the circumstances and needs of humanity. There is a correlation between the various stages of inspiration which, according to Christianity, are all directed toward the coming of Christ, prophesying about it and referring to it under the cover of various symbols and actions. . . . Christ is the end and goal of salvation history, and the one to whom it is directed. Christ came with the new covenant, and the old covenants merely pointed to him. Christ makes it possible for Christians to enter this covenant as they are the heirs of Abraham through faith. As for the law, it was only given as a guarantee of the covenant, as a teacher that leads to Christ in whom all the promises are fulfilled.[20]

Development of Eschatology

It is now time to apply what we have learned about progressive revelation to eschatology, or in other words, to what the Bible teaches regarding the events of the last days. This will give us a better understanding of the concept of the second coming of Christ and the millennial kingdom.

We will study the development of this concept in the Old Testament, the message of the prophets, the teaching of Christ, and the writings of the apostle Paul.

Eschatology in the Old Testament

The Old Testament deals with the people of Israel, the descendants of Abraham, the man whom God called and with whom he established a covenant whereby Abraham's descendants would be God's chosen people (Gen 12:1–7). This covenant is referred to as the Abrahamic covenant, referring to the promise God made to Abraham when he called him from Ur in the south of Iraq to go to the land of Canaan.

This promise is repeated several times in Genesis (Gen 13:14—17; 15:1–21; 17:1–22; 22:15–18). It states first that Abraham's descendants will become a great nation, as numberless as the stars in the sky and the sand on the seashore. Secondly, it speaks of the promised land (Gen 15:18). Thirdly, it states that these descendants will be a blessing to all the nations of the earth.

---

[19] George Kanawaty, *Christianity and Arab Civilization* (n. p.), 19.   [20] Ibid.

The Abrahamic covenant was followed by the Mosaic covenant at Sinai (Exod 19; 20), and finally by the Davidic covenant in which God promised to establish an eternal kingdom for David's descendants (2 Sam 7). Thus Israel was formed as a nation with leaders, judges, kings, priests, and a temple.

The Old Testament is mainly the story of this nation and its attitude toward God's promise; its wars with other nations; its times of revival and of rebellion and delusion; its times of unity and rest and of division; and its times of victories and of military, political, and spiritual defeat. Ultimately, the nation went into exile—the Northern Kingdom led off by Assyria in 722 BC and the Southern Kingdom by Babylon in 586 BC. The exile lasted some seventy years. Then during the days of the Persian Empire, Cyrus allowed the people to return to their land under the leadership of Ezra and Nehemiah. Thereafter God spoke to them through the prophets Haggai, Zechariah, and Malachi.

Eschatology and the message of the prophets

The prophets prophesied during the time of the kings and the exile. They emphasized the attitude of the people toward God's promise, denouncing Israel's rebellion and announcing the judgment that was coming on them, as well as speaking about the rebellion of the nations that attacked Israel and God's coming judgment on those nations too. The prophets also proclaimed God's mercy and held out the hope of future salvation through the coming Messiah, who would set the people free, forgive their sins, and achieve all that was promised.

Because the nation was enduring harsh treatment and was threatened on all sides, the prophets' words about future hope and salvation went to the opposite extreme. They spoke in terms of military, political and spiritual salvation, an earthly kingdom, and a theocratic state in which the Messiah would rule the earth. They emphasized the idea that the Messiah would be a king more than the idea that he would be "the Son of Man" or "the Servant of the Lord."

The reason for their fixation on kingship was their understanding of God's promise. They interpreted salvation and hope in national terms relating to the Jewish people. They also focused on the idea that they were God's chosen people.

Throughout history, the combination of nationalism and a belief in being a chosen people has often had negative consequences. The Jews thought that God existed for their benefit alone. This racist assumption of their supremacy over all other nations continues to motivate contemporary Zionism.

The prophets tried to expand the people's thinking about God and his promises. They understood that God is for all nations and the Lord of the whole earth, and so they tried to shift the people's vision of the hope and salvation offered by the coming Messiah toward a more comprehensive vision, rather than one rooted solely in nationalism (Amos 9:7; Isa 2:2–5, 25–27, 40–66; Mal 1:11; Jonah 3:10; 4:2, 10–11). The prophets also called for renewal of the covenant (Jer 31:31–34; Ezek 36:26–28).

Eschatology and the Teaching of Jesus

When Christ came, he declared that the Law and the Prophets and the whole of the Old Testament were holy; however, their holiness and greatness lay in their relationship to the great events that God was doing in his day. Moreover, Christ declared that the Old Testament with its history, laws, and prophecies was fulfilled in him and in his ministry and message. He is the center of history and the fulfillment of the Law and the Prophets, the one who could say, "Do not think that I have come to abolish the Law or the Prophets; I have not come to abolish them but to fulfill them" (Matt 5:17).

If the Old Testament was looking forward to the kingdom of God, Jesus came to manifest this kingdom in his person: "'The time has come,' he said. 'The kingdom of God has come near. Repent and believe the good news!'" (Mark 1:15). In Luke's Gospel, he announces that "the kingdom of God has come upon you" (Luke 11:20). The Old Testament presented pictures of what the longed-for Messiah would be like; in Christ all those pictures came to completion. He was the servant of the Lord of whom Isaiah spoke (Isa 61:1–3; Matt 9:11; Luke 4:16–21) and the son of man mentioned in Daniel (Dan 7:13; Mark 14:62).

Jesus interpreted the Old Testament eschatologically, that is, in light of what is to come. In his first coming, he partially fulfilled its vision of his person and mission, and the full vision will be completed at his second coming (Matt 24:42; Luke 11:25–27; John 14:3). Christ revealed that the events of the end of the age include the entire story of salvation throughout history, from his first coming until his second coming.

In his response to Peter's confession of him as the Messiah, Christ declared that he would build his own church (Matt 16:18). The Messiah rules over the saints of the Most High (Dan 7:13–14, 18–27), who constitute the new Israel. This is apparent even in Christ's choice of twelve disciples (a reference to the twelve tribes of Israel) and in his speaking of them as his "little flock" to whom the Lord is pleased to give the kingdom (Luke 12:32). This designation recalls the Old Testament statements about the faithful remnant who would take the message of life to the whole world—the task that God had given to Israel but Israel had not fulfilled. This failure was the reason Jesus told the Jews that the kingdom of God would be taken from them and given to another nation (Matt 21:43), which is the church.

Christ gave his disciples instructions for a new type of living when he told them that "unless your righteousness surpasses that of the Pharisees and the teachers of the law, you will certainly not enter the kingdom of heaven" (Matt 5:20). He unveiled to them the mysteries of the kingdom of God (Matt 11:25; Luke 10:21) and then gave them a new mission to preach the kingdom of heaven (Luke 10:1–24). Finally, he gave them his name, so that whoever received them received him, and whoever rejected them rejected him (Mark 9:41; Matt 10:40–41).

In all this, we see Christ giving material form to the eschatological concepts in the Old Testament and transforming them through his person and ministry and in his formation of his church—the new community that replaced the old one. All this will come to completion at the second coming of Christ.[21]

Eschatology in the thought of the apostle Paul

The message and teachings of the apostle Paul are strongly related to evangelism, life in Christ, and his belief in the imminent return of Christ. Time is short. The lost have to turn to Christ, and believers have to live godly lives as befits the saints of the Lord.

Yet despite his firm belief in the second coming of Christ and his stress on its importance in regard to living a life of service and readiness, Paul gives no indication whatsoever of a specific time when this will happen. On the contrary, he affirms that the coming of Christ will be sudden, saying that "for you know very well that the day of the Lord will come like a thief in the night" (1 Thess 5:2) and insisting that he knows nothing about the exact time of his coming.

What, then, did the apostle Paul mean when he talked about Christ's imminent return? The answer is in the same chapter as the verse referred to above: "But you, brothers and sisters, are not in darkness so that his day should surprise you like a thief" (1 Thess 5:4). His point is that since believers have received the light that came into the world and have become the children of this light, the coming of the Lord should be a key concern: "You are all children of the light and children of the day. We do not belong to the night or to the darkness. So then, let us not be like others, who are asleep, but let us be awake and sober" (1 Thess 5:5–6). He affirms the same truth in his letter to the Romans: "The night is nearly over; and the day is almost here. So let us put aside the deeds of darkness and put on the armor of light" (Rom 13:12).

The apostle thus relates what has happened to what is going to happen: the light that has shone to the daylight that is about to dawn. The past, the present, and the future are all included in God's one plan of salvation. Those who bear the stamp of the Spirit and have experienced salvation live out and await the coming glory. Thus the experience of the present bears with it the expectation of the future, and the expectation of the future confirms the experience of the present.[22]

The apostle also taught that expectation of Christ's second coming does not reduce the importance of life in the present. In fact, he rebuked those who used the prospect of the Lord's return as an excuse for disorderly conduct:

> In the name of the Lord Jesus Christ, we command you, brothers and sisters, to keep away from every believer who is idle and disruptive and does not live according to the

---

[21] Aziz, *Theological Thought* (n. p.), 405–8.   [22] Ladd, *The Last Things*, 27–28.

teaching you received from us. For you yourselves know how you ought to follow our example. We were not idle when we were with you. (2 Thess 3:6–7)

He also affirmed the value of time, saying,

Be very careful then, how you live—not as unwise but as wise, making the most of every opportunity, because the days are evil. Therefore do not be foolish, but understand what the Lord's will is. (Eph 5:15–17; Col 4:5)

He instructed believers to "do good to all people" (Gal 6:10) and submit to the authorities (Rom 13:1–8). The reason he gives for positive Christian conduct is the imminent return of Christ (Rom 13:11–14). Thus the expectation of Christ's return is a positive thing. The passage of time and the long delay in Christ's coming should not make the church or a believer lose the depth, power, and meaning of living a life of expectation while awaiting his return.

The apostle Paul also confirmed the principle that the Old Testament has to be interpreted in light of the New Testament and the person and message of Christ. His interpretation of the Old Testament was Christocentric, based on the centrality of Christ alone:

He made known to us the mystery of his will according to his good pleasure, which he purposed in Christ, to be put into effect when the times reach their fulfillment—to bring unity to all things in heaven and on earth under Christ. (Eph 1:9–10)

God has one purpose that he has been fulfilling throughout history, and this purpose is foreshadowed in the historical events relating to the fall of Adam (Rom 5:12–21; 1 Cor 15:45–50; 1 Tim 2:13–14) and in the faithfulness and faith of Abraham (Gal 3:19). Ultimately, this solemn purpose was manifested in the coming of Christ and his life, mission, death, resurrection, ascension, assumption of his seat at the right hand of the Father, the outpouring of the Holy Spirit, and the establishing of the church, and will be manifested in Christ's second coming to judge the living and the dead. Here we see evidence of progression in the fulfillment of the purpose and covenant of God.

It is worth noting that the apostle Paul expressed his understanding of the history of Israel in the Old Testament by using the word translated "type" or "pattern" in Romans 5:14. He sees the history of Israel in the Old Testament as a type or pattern for the history of the church, which is the new Israel.

For I do not want you to be ignorant of the fact, brothers and sisters, that our ancestors were all under the cloud and that they all passed through the sea. They were all baptized into Moses in the cloud and in the sea. They all ate the same spiritual food and drank the same spiritual drink; for they drank from the spiritual rock that accompanied them, and that rock was Christ. Nevertheless, God was not pleased with most of them; their bodies were scattered in the wilderness.

Now these things occurred as examples to keep us from setting our hearts on evil things as they did. Do not be idolaters, as some of them were; as it is written: "The people sat down to eat and drink and got up to indulge in revelry." We should not commit sexual immorality, as some of them did—and in one day twenty-three thousand of them died. We should not test Christ, as some of them did—and were killed by snakes. And do not grumble, as some of them did—and were killed by the destroying angel.

These things happened to them as examples and were written down as warnings for us, on whom the culmination of the ages has come. (1 Cor 10:1–11)

In writing to the Ephesians, Paul refers to Christ as "our peace." Through his flesh he made two groups one by tearing down the wall of hostility that separated them. All this was done "according to his eternal purpose that he accomplished in Christ Jesus our Lord" (Eph 2:14–3:11).

Despite the stance of Jesus and Paul, issues relating to the kingdom of God and the people of God are still hotly debated today. At the root of the matter is the insistence by some that all biblical inspiration is on the same theological plane. They reject the idea of progressive revelation, and with it the idea of the progressive fulfillment of the covenant, that is, the covenant of salvation, in history. Dispensationalists argue that the Bible contains two different stories (the story of Israel in the Old Testament and the story of the church in the New Testament), two kingdoms (the kingdom of God and the kingdom of heaven), two peoples and two plans of God (a plan for Israel and a different plan for the church), and two different destinies for Israel and the church. Christ's theocratic earthly reign is for Israel, the people of God with whom he will reign literally on earth, while spiritual rule from heaven will be for the church when it is taken there.[23]

But are there really two kingdoms, two peoples, and two different plans and destinies? Or do we have one plan, one covenant that has been progressing and moving forward within the framework of the kingdom of God and the people of God? What is the concept of the kingdom? Who are the people of God?

The Kingdom of God

Early in the Gospel of Mark we are told,

> After John was put in prison, Jesus went into Galilee, proclaiming the good news of God. "The time has come," he said. "The kingdom of God has come near. Repent and believe the good news!" (Mark 1:14–15)

As we know, the life and ministry of Jesus focused on the kingdom of God. Jesus

---

[23] Aziz, *The Kingdom of God* (Cairo: Dar Al Thaqafa, 1988), 9–67, 211.

did not give a specific definition for this term, which suggests that it was well known to his audience. It refers to God's authority and reign.

In the Old Testament, "the kingdom of God" was understood with reference to God's supreme authority as the creator and savior. However, the reign of God as savior did not achieve its intended purpose in the Old Testament and thus a future hope was an authentic and persistent part of the faith of the Old Testament people of God. In the New Testament, however, Jesus declares that the kingdom has arrived with his coming to earth.

While Mark and Luke refer to the "kingdom of God," Matthew prefers to use the expression "kingdom of heaven," for he was addressing Jews who treated the name of God as holy. Thus he speaks of the "kingdom of heaven" thirty-two times and only uses the phrase "kingdom of God" six times. John refers to the "kingdom of heaven" only in the dialogue between Christ and Nicodemus (John 3:3–5).

The New Testament evidence shows that Jesus used these two expressions interchangeably, which indicates that they are synonyms. There is no truth to the idea that the "kingdom of God" is for Gentiles and begins with the incarnation of Christ whereas the "kingdom of heaven" is only for Jews.

The Bible generally and the New Testament in particular also speak of "the kingdom of darkness" or the kingdom of the devil, which is doomed to end. It is contrasted with the eternal kingdom of God or the kingdom of heaven. So the kingdom of God, which is also the kingdom of heaven, is a spiritual kingdom, not a physical kingdom. Christ made this clear when he said,

> My kingdom is not of this world. If it were, my servants would fight to prevent my arrest by the Jewish leaders. But now my kingdom is from another place. (John 18:36)

The spiritual nature of the kingdom is also evident in the temptations that Jesus faced and in his declaration of his mission and the nature of his work.

> Jesus, full of the Holy Spirit, left the Jordan and was led by the Spirit into the wilderness, where for forty days he was tempted by the devil. He ate nothing during those days, and at the end of them he was hungry.
>
> The devil said to him, "If you are the Son of God, tell this stone to become bread."
>
> Jesus answered, "It is written: 'Man shall not live on bread alone.'"
>
> The devil led him up to a high place and showed him in an instant all the kingdoms of the world. And he said to him, "I will give you all their authority and splendor; it has been given to me, and I can give it to anyone I want to. If you worship me, it will all be yours."
>
> Jesus answered, "It is written: 'Worship the Lord your God and serve him only.'"
>
> The devil led him to Jerusalem and had him stand on the highest point of the temple. "If you are the Son of God," he said, "throw yourself down from here. For it is written:

"'He will command his angels concerning you to guard you carefully; they will lift you up in their hands, so that you will not strike your foot against a stone.'"

Jesus answered, "It is said: 'Do not put the Lord your God to the test.'"

When the devil had finished all this tempting, he left him until an opportune time. (Luke 4:1–13)

Jesus' own understanding of his mission and the nature of his work were spelled out in the incident in Nazareth where he quoted Isaiah 61:1–3:

Jesus returned to Galilee in the power of the Spirit, and news about him spread through the whole countryside. He was teaching in their synagogues, and everyone praised him.

He went to Nazareth, where he had been brought up, and on the Sabbath day he went into the synagogue, as was his custom. He stood up to read, and the scroll of the prophet Isaiah was handed to him. Unrolling it, he found the place where it is written:

"The Spirit of the Lord is on me, because he has anointed me to proclaim good news to the poor. He has sent me to proclaim freedom for the prisoners and recovery of sight for the blind, to set the oppressed free, to proclaim the year of the Lord's favor."

Then he rolled up the scroll, gave it back to the attendant and sat down. The eyes of everyone in the synagogue were fastened on him. He began by saying to them, "Today this scripture is fulfilled in your hearing."

All spoke well of him and were amazed at the gracious words that came from his lips. "Isn't this Joseph's son?" they asked.

Jesus said to them, "Surely you will quote this proverb to me: 'Physician, heal yourself!' And you will tell me, 'Do here in your hometown what we have heard that you did in Capernaum.'"

"Truly I tell you," he continued, "no prophet is accepted in his hometown. I assure you that there were many widows in Israel in Elijah's time, when the sky was shut for three and a half years and there was a severe famine throughout the land. Yet Elijah was not sent to any of them, but to a widow in Zarephath in the region of Sidon. And there were many in Israel with leprosy in the time of Elisha the prophet, yet not one of them was cleansed—only Naaman the Syrian."

All the people in the synagogue were furious when they heard this. They got up, drove him out of the town, and took him to the brow of the hill on which the town was built, in order to throw him off the cliff. But he walked right through the crowd and went on his way. (Luke 4:14–30)

The spiritual nature of the kingdom is also evident in the apostle Paul's words: "The kingdom of God is not a matter of eating and drinking, but of righteousness, peace, and joy in the Holy Spirit" (Rom 14:17).

The kingdom of God is an eternal kingdom; therefore, it is both present and future. It is present because it has come in Christ (Matt 11:11; 12:28; 13:1–52; Mark 4; Luke 16:16; 17:21), and it is future because it will be fully manifested at the second coming of Christ in power and glory (Matt 6:9–13; Luke 11:2–4).

The kingdom of God is also a comprehensive kingdom that includes all peoples, both Jews and Gentiles: "People will come from east and west and north and south, and will take their places at the feast in the kingdom of God" (Luke 13:29).[24]

Jesus also told the Jews that because of their disobedience "the kingdom of God will be taken away from you and given to a people who will produce its fruits" (Matt 21:43). This new "people" or nation is the church that he established as a new community that replaced the old one. Thus the church has become the mediator of the kingdom in the world, the heir of the kingdom, and the scope of its effectiveness, as Jesus is the King of the church.

The People of God

A king has a kingdom and a people. So we will move on from the concept of the one kingdom to the concept of the one people, as summarized by Paul in his wonderful words in Romans:

> A person is not a Jew who is one only outwardly, nor is circumcision merely outward and physical. No, a person is a Jew who is one inwardly; and circumcision is circumcision of the heart, by the Spirit, not by the written code. Such a person's praise is not from other people, but from God. (Rom 2:28–29)

Paul does not associate spiritual circumcision with a specific race or with natural superiority but with the Lord Jesus:

> Watch out for those dogs, those evildoers, those mutilators of the flesh. For it is we who are the circumcision, we who serve God by his Spirit, who boast in Christ Jesus, and who put no confidence in the flesh. (Phil 3:2–3)

He speaks of physical circumcision as mutilation in order to stress its uselessness for spiritual life, and so indicates his rejection of Jewish practices as the way to become a Christian. He gives a new definition of what constitutes a true Jew, a member of the people of God that transcend the limits of race, ancestral descent, and customs: "There is neither Jew nor Gentile, neither slave nor free, nor is there male and female, for you are all one in Christ Jesus" (Gal 3:28). His reason for saying this becomes clear in the next verse: "If you belong to Christ, then you are Abraham's seed, and heirs according to the promise" (Gal 3:29; see also Rom 4; Col 3:11).

Paul also quoted Isaiah 28:16, saying,

> See, I lay in Zion a stone that causes people to stumble
> and a rock that makes them fall,

---

[24] Aziz, *Theological Thought*, 305–27.

and the one who believes in him will never be put to shame. (Rom 9:33)

He prefaced these words with quotations from Hosea:

> I will call them "my people" who are not my people;
>> and I will call her "my loved one" who is not my loved one

and,

> In the very place where it was said to them,
>> "You are not my people,"
>> there they will be called "children of the living God." (Rom 9:25–26)

In order to confirm this fact, Paul wondered:

> Is God the God of Jews only? Is he not the God of Gentiles too? Yes, of Gentiles too, since there is only one God, who will justify the circumcised by faith and the uncircumcised through that same faith. (Rom 3:29–30; see also 1 Tim 2:4–6; Rom 2:6–11; 3:9)

Here Paul is alluding to the holy covenant that God gave to the church, mentioned in Jeremiah 31:31–34 and in Ezekiel 11:19 and 36:26. He explicitly mentions this covenant in 1 Corinthians 11:25:

> In the same way, after supper he took the cup, saying, "This cup is the new covenant in my blood; do this, whenever you drink it, in remembrance of me."

This covenant was not dependent on the law since it would be written on believers' hearts. The law thus becomes internalized in all people. This is the new covenant to which the old covenant pointed, the one God made by the blood of Jesus. It is a renewal of the covenant with Abraham, as Paul says:

> What I mean is this: The law, introduced 430 years later, does not set aside the covenant previously established by God and thus do away with the promise. (Gal 3:17)

From all the above we see that the church, which is composed of Jews and Gentiles, is the true people of God, the one that has inherited the promises and advantages that were given to old Israel. We should also note Paul's words:

> What agreement is there between the temple of God and idols? For we are the temple of the living God. As God has said:
>> "I will live with them and walk among them, and I will be their God, and they will be my people." (2 Cor 6:16)

The church is the heir of the promise and the glory of God is in its midst:

Through whom we have gained access by faith into this grace in which we now stand. And we boast in the hope of the glory of God. (Rom 5:2)

The creation itself will be liberated from its bondage to decay and brought into the freedom and glory of the children of God. (Rom 8:21)

Now if the ministry that brought death, which was engraved in letters on stone, came with glory, so that the Israelites could not look steadily at the face of Moses because of its glory, transitory though it was, will not the ministry of the Spirit be even more glorious? (2 Cor 3:7–8)

There are three other important questions we will try to answer in what follows.

First Question: What about "Israel According to the Flesh"?

We find the answer to this question in chapters 9 to 11 of Paul's letter to the Romans. In these chapters the apostle dealt with the nature of Israel, Israel in the present, and the hope of Israel. His views may be summarized as follows:

- Not all Jews rejected Christ; some did believe in him. Their belief is linked to the idea of the faithful remnant based on God's promise, God's righteousness, and God's grace, not on human righteousness. Paul gives two examples of this: Isaac, who is the son of the promise rather than Ishmael; and Jacob, who, in contrast to Esau, was chosen before birth (9:10–13). He confirms this truth in his admonition in 9:14–21.
- Paul then goes on to talk about the remnant, quoting from Hosea in Romans 9:25–26 and from Isaiah in Romans 9:27–29. He applies this in the present to Jews and Gentiles, showing that God's purpose is to include the Gentiles (Rom 9:22–25) and confirming that the wall between the two groups has been removed.
- Then comes the question; what was the main sin of Israel? Paul's answer is that they tried to reach God independently through the works of the law, in contrast to the Gentiles who received the grace of God and his work by faith alone (9:30–10:21). The true Israel, then, is the Israel of the promise and faith, not Israel according to the flesh.
- Does this mean that God has rejected his people? The apostle insists that he has not done so (11:1). But, he adds, all that has happened is in accordance with God's purpose so that the Gentiles would be included in the kingdom and the Jews would become jealous. Thus the Gentiles would become the means of salvation for the Jews since the Jews had failed to become the means of salvation for the Gentiles (11:1–14). So the hardening of the Jews opened

the door for the Gentiles, and the inclusion of the Gentiles made the Jews jealous to return to the Lord.

- The apostle also addresses the Gentiles, advising them not to boast since they are like a wild olive that has been grafted by grace into the original olive tree. Thus the Gentiles have become partners in the original olive tree, enjoying its richness. If some original branches were broken off, that was because of their unbelief. The Gentiles stand fast only through faith, so "do not be arrogant, but tremble" (11:14–24).

- Ultimately, the full number of the Gentiles will come in and all Israel will be saved, for the will of God is salvation for all, and the church of God, the new Israel by grace through faith in Christ, is composed of both Jews and Gentiles. This is the mystery that Paul announces in Ephesians 3:1–11. Thus the consistent purpose of God is "that he may have mercy on them all" (11:25–32). The love of God is still calling all.

Paul concludes with a wonderful hymn that expresses his fascination with God's richness, wisdom, and knowledge:

> Oh, the depth of the riches of the wisdom and knowledge of God!
> How unsearchable his judgments,
> and his paths beyond tracing out!
> "Who has known the mind of the Lord?
> Or who has been his counselor?"
> "Who has ever given to God,
> that God should repay them?"
> For from him and through him and for him are all things.
> To him be the glory forever! Amen. (Rom 11:33–36)

Here the apostle, as usual, links teaching to praise and theology to worship (in other words, he unites theology and doxology). When he saw God's love and mercy that pursues all people, Jews and Gentiles, he could not help but praise God.

The poet Francis Thompson knew what it was to experience the siege of God's love and mercy. He wrote about it in these words:

> I fled Him, down the nights and down the days;
> I fled Him, down the arches of the years;
> I fled Him, down the labyrinthine ways
> Of my own mind; and in the mist of tears
> I hid from Him, . . .
> From those strong Feet that followed, followed after.
> But with unhurrying chase,

> And unperturbed pace,
> Deliberate speed, majestic instancy,
> They beat—and a Voice beat
> More instant than the Feet—
> "All things betray thee, who betrayest Me."[25]

The story of God's pursuing love and mercy has not yet ended.

The Truth of the Unity of the People of God

On the basis of all that has been said above, we must insist on the unity of the people of God in the two Testaments. There is no place for the dispensationalist view that there are two covenants—one the work of Christ with the church through his blood, and the other a covenant with Israel that will be fulfilled in the future. There is no place for saying there will be a great renewal of the covenant with Moses, that the work of Christ and the church is a hiatus that will end with the rapture, and that thereafter God will fulfill his promise to his people, the Jews. In this view, the age of the church is presented as a through train that God prepared after he had failed in his original purpose for the Jews, the slow train. The through train started with the crucifixion of Christ and the beginning of the age of the church. At that point, the "slow train" stopped to allow the through train, the train of the church, to proceed. When the through train completes its journey by reaching its final destination with the rapture of the church, God will return to restart the original slow train and fulfill his purpose by establishing his earthly kingdom for a thousand years.

There are no grounds for this interpretation since the people of God are one people in whom all the promises have been fulfilled through the one covenant of redemption that has been fulfilled progressively in Christ and in his people from the beginning till the end (Rom 9:6–8; Gal 3:27–29; Eph 2:11–22; Heb 10:11–23).

The way of salvation is the same for all people (Rom 10:12–13), and the people of God share one destiny (Heb 12:25–29). The unshakeable kingdom of God and the kingdom of heaven are the same for all people (Heb 12:28)—it is a spiritual kingdom, one people, one covenant, one plan, one destiny, and one church.

Second Question: Are Contemporary Jews God's Chosen People and Is All Palestine the Historical Homeland of the Jews?

Perhaps we can formulate this question differently: Is Israel—which is now a military entity—the same Israel that was mentioned in the Bible? Who is the true Israel, the people of God who continue to exist in the present? This is a theological question; however, in our time it has taken on nontheological dimensions and has become the

---

[25] Francis Thompson, "The Hound of Heaven."

center of attention and a matter of considerable urgency. What has made it so is that many people, especially in the West, say that "Israel is the homeland of God's chosen people. They spent centuries in exile but have now returned to their homeland. The modern state of Israel is a direct extension of the Old Testament nation."

Such thinking promotes political trends that favor Zionism. Thus it is necessary to ask questions about the identity of Israel. Though we are not politicians, our answer will naturally reflect our direct interest in clarifying our political stance.

There are three important points we need to focus on: the history of Israel, the history of the religious idea, and the theological issue—what should our attitude be as Christians? Thus, the answer to the question will also have three aspects: historical, religious, and theological.

The History of Israel

The twelve tribes entered Canaan—which was the first pillar of Israel—around 1240 BC. However, they did not become united as a state until after the establishment of the monarchy in about 1020 BC, with Saul as Israel's first king, followed by David, and then Solomon. In their days, the kingdom reached its maximum regional expansion and its maximum political and military strength. After the death of Solomon in about 922 BC, the kingdom was divided into two parts, known as the Northern Kingdom (Israel) and the Southern Kingdom (Judah). The Northern Kingdom existed for about two centuries, until in 722 BC the Assyrians captured Samaria, its capital, and took its inhabitants into exile.

The small Southern Kingdom had limited political autonomy. From 734 BC on, it was a vassal of the Assyrian Empire. When Babylon replaced Assyria as a superpower at the end of the seventh century, the Southern Kingdom came under Babylonian rule, remaining independent only in name. When the kingdom rebelled against Babylon, Jerusalem was destroyed in 586 BC and its inhabitants were deported to Babylon. They remained in exile until Cyrus the Persian conquered Babylon in 539 BC and gave permission for the Jews to return to Judah in 538 BC. Those Jews who returned formed a Jewish community in Judah. Politically, they remained a province of the Persian Empire.

Alexander the Great destroyed the Persian Empire in 331 BC. After his early death, his empire was divided into four kingdoms. Egypt came under the rule of the Ptolemies and Syria fell under the Seleucids. Until 198 BC, Palestine was ruled first by Egypt and then by Syria. Roughly a century later (143–63 BC), the Jews succeeded in regaining their political independence under the Maccabees, whose kingdom eventually reached the size it had been during the reign of Solomon. In AD 63, Palestine came under Roman rule, where it remained until AD 70, when the Jews rebelled and the Romans destroyed Jerusalem, ending the Jews' existence as an organized political community in Palestine.

Clearly, Israel only enjoyed independence for a short period during the time of David and Solomon. Thereafter Judah was reduced to a small province and only enjoyed true political independence in the days of the Maccabees. These historical facts refute the idea that all Palestine is the historical homeland of the Jews.

The History of the Idea

In the Old Testament God chose the Jews to be his own people in a special way. This idea is incorporated in the New Testament and was supported by Christ himself. It is a key thread in the Old Testament. However, there were developments in regard to the content associated with this idea. Here we do not have the time and space to deal with these developments in detail, so we will simply focus on the general outline.

In the early days, the people of God took shape as a moral and political entity and lived within clear boundaries. Hence David's complaint when he was obliged to live outside the land and away from his people:

> Now let my lord the king listen to his servant's words. If the Lord has incited you against me, then may he accept an offering. If, however, people have done it, may they be cursed before the Lord! They have driven me today from my share in the Lord's inheritance and have said, "Go, serve other gods." (1 Sam 26:19)

It was this territorial element that made the exiles feel that it was impossible for them to worship God, and so they asked,

> How can we sing the songs of the Lord
> while in a foreign land? (Ps 137:4)

They believed that by being among the people of Israel, they were members of the people of God. There was thus a close relationship between religion and the state.

However, this close relationship gradually became more flexible, as is evident in the book of Jeremiah. He prophesied between 627 BC and 586 BC and addressed the religious weakness and spiritual bankruptcy of Judah and Jerusalem generally and in the temple specifically. Instead of seeing the temple as representing God's presence among them, the people regarded it as the dwelling place of the God who would defend them. The temple was a source of comfort and security rather than a reminder to avoid moral and ethical wrongdoing. Since they assumed that God was automatically in their midst, there was little concern for true obedience to him. People brought the prescribed sacrifices and then did as they pleased. Thus the temple became a den of thieves from which people drew a false sense of security while behaving sinfully. It became a hindrance rather than a help to true religion.

Thus we find Jeremiah saying,

> Do not trust in deceptive words and say, "This is the temple of the Lord, the temple of the Lord, the temple of the Lord!" If you really change your ways and your actions

and deal with each other justly, if you do not oppress the foreigner, the fatherless or the widow and do not shed innocent blood in this place, and if you do not follow other gods to your own harm, then I will let you live in this place, in the land I gave your ancestors for ever and ever. But look, you are trusting in deceptive words that are worthless.

Will you steal and murder, commit adultery and perjury, burn incense to Baal and follow other gods you have not known, and then come and stand before me in this house, which bears my Name, and say, "We are safe"—safe to do all these detestable things? Has this house, which bears my Name, become a den of robbers to you? But I have been watching! declares the LORD. (Jer 7:4–11)

Despite Jeremiah's warnings, attitudes in Jerusalem did not change, leading to the prophecy in which he spoke of a basket of good figs and a basket of bad figs (Jer 24:1–8). The bad figs represented the inhabitants of Jerusalem, whereas the good figs represented the people who had been taken into exile in Babylon in 597 BC. The latter group represented the hope for the future.

The crucial point to note is that the true religion, or the hope of restoring it, lay with the exiles. The prophet clearly declared that God would be with the exiles if they sought him with all their hearts:

This is what the LORD, the God of Israel, says: "Like these good figs, I regard as good the exiles from Judah, whom I sent away from this place to the land of the Babylonians." (Jer 24:5)

God is thus not tied to any specific place but is present and can be worshipped in any place where people seek him sincerely and do not merely maintain appearances or utter empty words.

The prophet Ezekiel (593–571 BC) makes much the same point as Jeremiah. Ezekiel was one of the exiles in Babylon, and he addressed his message to the Jews there and in Jerusalem. He told the exiles to abandon the idea that God dwelt only in Jerusalem, since God is everywhere. He affirmed this in his visions in which he saw God leaving the temple and Jerusalem (Ezek 10:15; 11:22) and being present in Babylon (Ezek 1). Ezekiel insisted that God can be worshipped anywhere.

When Cyrus the Babylonian allowed the Jews to return to Judah in 538 BC, some returned, while the rest—perhaps the majority—stayed in Babylon. From then on, Babylon was an important center of Jewish religious life. Nehemiah is a shining example of the godly Jews in Babylon. This great reformer twice traveled to Jerusalem to introduce reforms that saved Judaism from being lost in other religions and cultures (444–432 BC). He was one of those who had the honor of sustaining Judaism. Yet Nehemiah was not based in Palestine but in Babylon (then a part of the Persian Empire) where he held a high position.

Alexandria, too, was an important Jewish center where tens of thousands of Jews lived in the centuries before Christ. The Alexandrian Jews preserved their emotional and psychological ties to Palestine, even though most of them had never lived there and did not know the Hebrew language. It was they who in about 250 BC translated the Old Testament from Hebrew into Greek. From this and other evidence we know that the Jews in Alexandria had a strong religious life. Judaism had clearly freed itself from geographic or regional ties and national borders. Of course, the Jews still had strong emotional ties to their homeland, as was natural. However, it was not central to their religious life.

For a third example besides Babylon and Alexandria, we can think of the apostle Paul, in whose days thousands of Jews lived in Syria, Central Asia, and Greece. During his missionary journeys, the apostle Paul almost always began by preaching in a local synagogue (Acts 13:14; 14:1; 17:1).

All these examples show us that long before the time of Christ, Judaism had ceased to be associated with a people as a political unit at a specific place. More Jews lived outside Palestine than inside it, and the tie that linked them was religious rather than political. The connection between religion and the state had been dissolved, and Israel (as the people of God) had ceased to be a national community living in a specific country. Instead, it had become a community of believers who had spread to many countries, cultures, and languages.

There was another important development that was confined to Palestine itself. Earlier ages had witnessed Israel's coming into existence as a nation and as the people of God. However, the national element began to fade after the exile with the rise of the distinction between the nation and the religious community. This became particularly clear during the Maccabean revolt and the period of independence that followed. All the Jews were united in revolting against Syrian occupation and they gained their religious freedom in 162 BC. At this point the group known as the Hasidim (a pious, orthodox group) refused to continue the war as they were not fighting for political freedom. They identified themselves as a religious rather than a political community. The remainder of the Jews continued to fight until they gained political freedom and set up a state. Then, nationalistic Jews started to persecute and kill pious Jews.

There are clear differences between the modern state of Israel and the state that existed in the past. Then, the nation considered itself to be the people of God and regarded its enemies as enemies of the people of God. Now, the nation includes religious communities and groups opposed to religion. "The people of God" are now the believing community within the nation, while the rest of the nation is hostile to the people of God. We see an example of this attitude in Psalm 139:19–22, which speaks about the enemies of the people of God who are within the nation.

The previous paragraphs contain a rough outline of the religious development of Israel. In the beginning there was a people (or nation) that lived in a specific land and were known as the people of God. After the exile, the ties between these three elements were broken. Only some Jews lived in Palestine; a far greater number lived outside Palestine. Thus, the people of God became a religious community that had no relation to any land or nation. With the destruction of Jerusalem and the temple in AD 70, the regular life of the Jews in Palestine came to an end. Yet Judaism remained since it had freed itself from attachment to a specific land or nation. Judaism had taken flight and become a religion without a country.

The Theological Issue

A crucial question now arises: Where do we find the extension and continuation of the Old Testament people of God? There have long been Jewish communities throughout the world. The important element in these communities is not that they are located in Palestine or that their members are Jewish by birth: rather, it is that they adhere to the Jewish faith. However, this is not the end point of our thinking as Christians. God chose Israel as his own special people in order to prepare for the coming of Christ. Christ declared plainly that God wants to share his love with the whole world. Now, it has become possible for every human being—through believing in Christ—to be one of the people of God. This is what we refer to as the true unity of the people of God.

The truth that we must recognize is that Christ did not dismiss the people of the Old Testament in order to establish a new people. We cannot say that the church is a substitute for the people of Israel, as if the people of the Old Testament were simply replaced by a different people. Rather, Christ destroyed the wall that separated the people of God from the rest of the world. The Old Testament people of God (the believing Jewish community) remained connected to God, and all the nations of the world are now called to share in this connection through believing in Jesus Christ. Thus the Jews have to receive Christ, who proclaimed that he came to fulfill the Old Testament and declare its real purpose. To become a real believer, a Jew has to receive Christ as the Messiah. Some Jews received Christ, but others have not yet done so. We can say that the Jews who have received Christ, together with all other believers in Christ all over the world, represent the extension and continuation of the people of God.

In the Bible God states how one can become a member of his people. Before Christ, this was through receiving and obeying the prophetic message of the Old Testament; now, it is through believing in Christ who is the full revelation of God. On this basis, Jews who have not received or confessed Christ are not part of the community of the people of God, whereas people from other countries and nations are part of that community.

This means that from the days of Moses, the people of God have been one people, manifested first in Israel, then in the community of believing Jews, and then in all those who receive and believe in Christ. Thus we find, from a purely theological point of view, that the Christian church, which is the community of believers all over the world, is in continuity with the people of God of the Old Testament. This is quite obvious in the New Testament. Jesus himself made it clear that mere descent from Abraham is not enough to make someone a member of the people of God; what matters is faith and obedience:

> Do not think you can say to yourselves, "We have Abraham as our father." I tell you that out of these stones God can raise up children for Abraham. (Matt 3:9)

In his first letter, the apostle Peter quotes words addressed to the ancient Israelites, "you will be for me a kingdom of priests and a holy nation" (Exod 19:6) and applies them to the church, implying that the church shares the same attributes:

> But you are a chosen people, a royal priesthood, a holy nation, God's special possession, that you may declare the praises of him who called you out of darkness into his wonderful light. (1 Pet 2:9)

Thus the answer to the question "Who are the people of God?" is that they are the people who share the covenant of God. At first, this was limited to those who were included in the Mosaic covenant, but in Christ the covenant has been widened to include the whole world. This means that the church—both biblically and theologically—is the direct continuation and extension of the people of God in the Old Testament.

Third Question: What Should Be Our Attitude to the Modern State of Israel?

On the basis of what has been said so far, we can assert some important truths.

1. God's promise to and covenant with Abraham was fulfilled worldwide in at least three phases: In the days of Joshua,

   > The LORD gave Israel all the land he had sworn to give their ancestors, and they took possession of it and settled there. The LORD gave them rest on every side, just as he had sworn to their ancestors. Not one of their enemies withstood them; the LORD gave all their enemies into their hands. Not one of all the LORD's good promises to Israel failed; every one was fulfilled. (Josh 21:43–45)

   Then in the days of Solomon,

   > Solomon ruled over all the kingdoms from the Euphrates River to the land of the Philistines, as far as the border of Egypt. These countries brought tribute and were Solomon's subjects all his life. (1 Kgs 4:21)

   Then after the Babylonian exile in the fifth century BC, Nehemiah acknowledged,

   > You are the LORD God, who chose Abram and brought him out of Ur of the Chaldeans and named him Abraham. You found his heart faithful to you, and you made a covenant with him to give to his descendants the land of the

Canaanites, Hittites, Amorites, Perizzites, Jebusites and Girgashites. You have kept your promise because you are righteous. (Neh 9:7–8)

Thus the prophecy in regard to the land was completely fulfilled:

For he remembered his holy promise given to his servant Abraham. He brought out his people with rejoicing, his chosen ones with shouts of joy; he gave them the lands of the nations, and they fell heir to what others had toiled for. (Ps 105:42–45)

2. As regards the people, we know that the people of the Northern Kingdom that formed after the division of the kingdom of Solomon were scattered when they were taken into exile in Assyria in 722 BC. The Northern Kingdom ceased to exist. The Southern Kingdom was ended by the Babylonian exile in 586 BC, but in 538 BC Cyrus allowed the exiles to return. They completed the rebuilding of the temple in 516 BC and survived conquest by Alexander the Great (333 BC), the rule of the Seleucids, and persecution by Antiochus Ephiphanes. After the Maccabean revolt, the Jews enjoyed a period of independence lasting from 143 BC until they were taken over by the Romans in 63 BC. Jerusalem and the temple were destroyed in AD 70 in the aftermath of the first Jewish revolt against Rome. A second failed revolt led to a final crushing blow, with the Jews being scattered in the diaspora.

3. The New Testament stresses the important role that faith played in the covenant with Abraham and in the Old Testament prophecies and proclaims the fulfillment of the covenant and the prophecies in Christ the Messiah, as is clear both at the heart of the Old Testament (Jer 31:31–34) and the New Testament (Matt 5:17). The people of God—as we have seen—are the new Israel that includes people of both Jewish and Gentile descent (Gal 3:28; Rom 10:2).

4. The modern state of Israel is the product of the Zionist movement that was launched at a conference in Basel, Switzerland, in 1897. The goal of the movement was to promote Jewish colonization of Palestine, establish an organization linking all Jews around the world through local and international associations, and strengthen Jewish nationalism. Thus began the process of moving European Jews to Palestine, which was then a part of the Ottoman Empire. Theodor Herzl worked hard to get official recognition for the establishment of a Zionist entity in Palestine. He received some European recognition of Zionism because it offered a way of reducing the number of Jews in Europe. Thus it came about that Zionism would become a dominant force among Jews all around the world, while at the same time creating a base for Western colonialism at the core of the Arab world.[26]

---

[26] Ahmed Sedky El Dagani, "The Silent Contract between the Western Civilization and the Zionist Movement," *Al Ahram,* 16 November 1996. See also Dr. Mustafa Mahmoud, "The time approached," *Al Ahram*, 23 November 1996.

5. On the basis of the above, we affirm that there is no relation, whether close or distant, between the modern state of Israel and the "people of God" mentioned in the prophecies of the Old Testament. The prophecies of nationhood were fulfilled within the timeframe of the Old Testament, and in the New Testament their spiritual aspect has been fulfilled in Christ and the church, which is the new spiritual Israel that embraces all people, Jews and Gentiles, from all the nations of the earth. Those sects and groups who keep speaking of the association between the second coming of Christ and the modern state of Israel, the rebuilding of the temple, the battle of Armageddon, and the end of the world are out of line with biblical theology.

6. The Presbyterian church, along with other Christian churches in the East and the West, has worked hard to present the correct biblical and theological position at local and international conferences and forums. It has also published books that explain the content of the Word of God in a way that is accessible to any reader who wants to understand divine truth in all its fullness. However, it is important that pastors and preachers present this teaching to their people, young and old, so that they are not left prey to the other ideas that fill the ecclesiastical arena in regard to this important biblical and theological issue.

7. This issue has a very important national dimension for us as Egyptians and Arabs in our conflict with the state of Israel. We need to understand it if we are to refute the arguments that Israel uses to justify its seizure of Arab land, some of which it has occupied since the war of 1967. This is particularly important given that the region is passing through a difficult period, with rising extremism in Israel and the Likud party attempting to freeze the peace process and revise and rewrite the peace principles worked out in previous agreements. Therefore, all sects and groups that have accepted Zionist thinking—whether knowingly or unknowingly—must correct their attitude in the light of the plain and crystal-clear word of God on the one hand, and the depth of their identity and authentic nationalism on the other hand.[27]

PRINCIPLES OF INTERPRETATION

At this point it is important that we pause to consider hermeneutics, or principles of interpretation; for our study has shown, as Dr. Sabra said in his spoken commentary on the book of Tarek Mitri:

> The root of Zionist Christianity lies in a literal reading of the entire Bible and an approach to interpretation that sees it as an inspired book in which each verse or statement has its

---

[27] Aziz, *The Kingdom of God*, 253–258.

own unique authority, apart from the center and purpose of the book, which is God's revelation of himself in Jesus Christ.[28]

The most important principles of interpretation are outlined below.

First Principle

We should not interpret biblical texts or base our Christian faith on changeable and unstable political events.

Second Principle

The Old Testament must be interpreted in the light of the New Testament as a whole, for the Old Testament is Holy Scripture and the New Testament interprets that Scripture. We also have to interpret the Old Testament in the light of the person, work, and mission of Christ, for Jesus Christ and his redeeming work are the center of all that was written, as Scripture testifies. All the messianic concepts and images in the Old Testament were completely fulfilled in the person and mission of Jesus. For example:

a) The first image of a savior is a compound image such as the woman's offspring who would crush the serpent's head. This image is found in both Genesis 3:15 and Revelation 12:3–5 and is picked up in the image of a military ruler in Numbers.

> I see him, but not now;
>> I behold him, but not near.
> A star will come out of Jacob;
>> a scepter will rise out of Israel.
> He will crush the foreheads of Moab,
>> the skulls of all the people of Sheth.
> Edom will be conquered;
>> Seir, his enemy, will be conquered,
>> but Israel will grow strong.
> A ruler will come out of Jacob
> and destroy the survivors of the city. (Num 24:17–19)

There is also the image of a "prophet" (Deut 18:15, 18, 19).

b) The second image of a savior is of a king who is the son of David: The people embraced the idea of a coming military ruler, a golden age, the divine covenant, and a savior who would be a descendant of David (2 Sam 7:13, 16, 29). They

---

[28] The Middle East Council of Churches, *What Is Western Fundamentalist Christian Zionism?*

clung to this even after the division of the kingdom (Isa 9:7; 11:21) and the devastation of the seed of David (Jer 23:5; 30:9). Even in the time of the exile, in which the people's hope was broken, Ezekiel prophesied that the Lord's covenant with the house of David still stood:

> My servant David will be king over them, and they will all have one shepherd. They will follow my laws and be careful to keep my decrees. They will live in the land I gave to my servant Jacob, the land where your ancestors lived. They and their children and their children's children will live there forever, and David my servant will be their prince forever. I will make a covenant of peace with them; it will be an everlasting covenant. I will establish them and increase their numbers, and I will put my sanctuary among them forever. My dwelling place will be with them; I will be their God, and they will be my people. Then the nations will know that I the LORD make Israel holy, when my sanctuary is among them forever. (Ezek 37:24–28)

c) The third image of the Messiah is as the savior, who has existed from the days of old, and the eternal father. The prophets Micah and Isaiah prophesied of him:

> But you, Bethlehem Ephrathah,
>   though you are small among the clans of Judah,
> out of you will come for me
>   one who will be ruler over Israel,
> whose origins are from of old,
>   from ancient times. (Mic 5:2)

> For to us a child is born,
>   to us a son is given,
>   and the government will be on his shoulders.
> And he will be called
>   Wonderful Counselor, Mighty God,
>   Everlasting Father, Prince of Peace.
> Of the greatness of his government and peace
>   there will be no end.
> He will reign on David's throne
>   and over his kingdom,
> establishing and upholding it
>   with justice and righteousness
>   from that time on and forever.
> The zeal of the LORD Almighty
> will accomplish this. (Isa 9:6–7)

This same image is used of wisdom in the book of Proverbs (Prov 8:23–30) and of the one who spreads peace (Isa 11:1–9). He is God (Isa 9:6).

d) The fourth image of the savior is the "son of man." This image recurs repeatedly in the book of Ezekiel and twice in the book of Daniel. In Daniel 8:17 the expression simply means "son of Adam," as in Ezekiel, but in Daniel 7:13–14 the expression is more striking:

> In my vision at night I looked, and there before me was one like a son of man, coming with the clouds of heaven. He approached the Ancient of Days and was led into his presence. He was given authority, glory and sovereign power; all nations and peoples of every language worshipped him. His dominion is an everlasting dominion that will not pass away, and his kingdom is one that will never be destroyed.

e) The fifth image of the Messiah is the "servant of the Lord," a fascinating subject addressed mainly in the Songs of the Suffering Servant in the book of Isaiah. The most famous of these songs is found in Isaiah 52:13–53:12.[29]

All these images were fulfilled in the person and mission of Jesus. Thus this brief excursion into Christology confirms the principle that the Old Testament should be interpreted in light of the New Testament in general and specifically in light of the person and redeeming mission of Jesus Christ.[30]

Third Principle

We should not interpret clear and direct passages or texts by more obscure texts. In fact, the exact opposite is true. For example, we should not interpret what is said about the end times and the second coming of Christ in the two letters to Thessalonians in light of the book of Revelation; rather, we should interpret the book of Revelation in the light of what was said in Thessalonians.

The book of Revelation is very different from other apocalyptic writings that appeared in the intertestamental period, the time when the voice of prophecy was silent. It was, in general, a time of humiliation and persecution for the Jews. It was then that the apocalyptic style emerged as a way of encouraging the people by showing them the present and the future in a new light.

In the book of Revelation, John draws on images that had been used before, but he infuses them with very different meanings. For example, there is a great difference between Christian and Jewish apocalyptic books when it comes to the way they describe the Messiah whom the Jews were expecting to come and fulfill prophecies. John describes

---

[29] Ladd, *Last Things*, 9–18. [30] Aziz, *The Kingdom of God*, 253–58.

him as a slaughtered Lamb, even though he is also "the Lion of the tribe of Judah" (Rev 5:5). He rides out victorious in order to conquer, but the sword he wields comes from his mouth (Rev 19:15). He fights with his holy word, not with a physical sword that lacerates the bodies of his enemies. But he faces the same enemies: beasts that emerge from the land and from the sea, followed by the dragon. The world with its enmity to the people of God still exists, and the weapons of evil are still the same; what is different is that the camp of righteousness is no longer using the weapons of the world, as the Jews thought it would.[31] The apostle Paul makes the same point:

> For though we live in the world, we do not wage war as the world does. The weapons we fight with are not the weapons of the world. On the contrary, they have divine power to demolish strongholds. (2 Cor 10:3–4)

We have to be careful not to attach Jewish meanings to Christian expressions and not to interpret the message of the book of Revelation in the New Testament in terms of Jewish thought, for to do so is to distort the truth and stray into non-Christian mazes.

Fourth Principle

We should not take a word, or a statement, or a text, in isolation and build a whole doctrine on it without studying it in the light of the whole Bible. This principle includes the idea of simplicity and a preference for the natural meaning of a text. God is light, and he has spoken in order to be understood. This is the general meaning of "harmony," leading us to study the Bible with a discerning spirit, comparing spiritual things with spiritual things, for God has spoken without contradicting himself.[32]

For example, the phrase "the coming of Christ" does not always refer to his second coming. The Bible also uses it to refer to Christ's other comings, such as his return after his resurrection ("I will not leave you as orphans; I will come to you" [John 14:18]). Sometimes he uses the words "I am coming" to refer to his second coming, but he also uses them to refer to his coming with the power of the Holy Spirit and the victory of the church: "Truly I tell you, some who are standing here will not taste death before they see that the kingdom of God has come with power" (Mark 9:1).

The range of meaning of Christ's references to his "coming" becomes clearer when we look at his words in Matthew 24. There he does speak of his second coming, but does so against the background of his words at the end of the previous chapter:

> Jerusalem, Jerusalem, you who kill the prophets and stone those sent to you, how often I have longed to gather your children together, as a hen gathers her chicks under her wings, and you were not willing. Look, your house is left to you desolate. (Matt 23:37–38)

---

[31] John R. W. Stott, *Christian Counter-Culture* (Downers Grove, IL: InterVarsity, 1978), 24–25.

[32] Makram Naguib, *Creative and Contemporary Methods* (Cairo: Dar Al Thaqafa, 1996 [in Arabic]), 26–42.

The disciples were shocked by these words, and drew his attention to the magnificence of the temple buildings. But Jesus did not change what he had said:

"Do you see all these things?" he asked. "Truly I tell you, not one stone here will be left on another; every one will be thrown down." (Matt 24:1–2)

Thus what is being spoken of here is his coming to judge Jerusalem and destroy the temple.

In Matthew 24:15, Jesus says,

So when you see standing in the holy place 'the abomination that causes desolation,' spoken of through the prophet Daniel—let the reader understand.

This verse is referring to the prophecy in Daniel 11:31:

His armed forces will rise up to desecrate the temple fortress and will abolish the daily sacrifice. Then they will set up the abomination that causes desolation.

The sacrilege referred to here is linked to the four kingdoms mentioned in Daniel 2; 7; 8; and 11 (see comments above on the second principle of interpretation) and specifically to the acts of Antiochus Epiphanes, who was king of Syria, one of the kingdoms that emerged from the division of the empire of Alexander the Great. He is represented by the small horn in Daniel 8:9–11, 23–25 and is the subject of the discourse in Daniel 11:21–45. Antiochus built an altar to Zeus in the temple in Jerusalem and offered a pig on this altar, thus polluting the temple. Judah Maccabee liberated the temple and punished Antiochus Epiphanes and Syria, his kingdom. This event serves as an introduction to the coming of Christ in the flesh, which Daniel presents as the fifth kingdom, the kingdom of Christ, the last link in the chain of Daniel's prophecies.

In Matthew 24, Jesus was referring to this incident and saying that similar desecration would take place when Titus, a Roman general, destroyed the temple in AD 70.

Clearly Jesus was here talking about the judgment on Jerusalem and the destruction of the temple. Yet, his talk also touched on the subject of his second coming. Jesus wanted his coming to judge Jerusalem to be seen as a scaled-down version and confirmation of his second coming to judge the world.

The terms in which the destruction is described confirm that Matthew 24 is apocalyptic in nature; and so it uses images that are not meant to be taken literally. Similar images are often found in Jewish apocalyptic literature and in the Old Testament (e.g. Isa 34:4; Joel 2:31).[33]

---

[33] For more on this topic, see John L. Bray, *Matthew 24 Fulfilled* (Florida: John L. Bray Ministry, 1996).

Other references to Jesus' coming may also refer to his second coming, as in Jesus' words, "when the Son of Man comes in his glory, and all the angels with him, he will sit on his glorious throne" (Matt 25:31).

What has been said so far makes it clear that if a statement is taken without consideration of the spirit and context of the whole book and the historical circumstances in which it was written, we may fall into confusion and go astray, as many have indeed done.

There are a number of expressions that readers have to take pains to interpret accurately, with an awareness of the way they were used in the age in which they were written. These include "a thousand years" and "the first resurrection." We will consider these expressions in the pages that follow. At this point, it is enough to mention that the first resurrection is the spiritual resurrection of all who receive the Lord Jesus as their personal Savior and Lord. Paul refers to this in Ephesians:

> But because of his great love for us, God, who is rich in mercy, made us alive with Christ even when we were dead in transgressions—it is by grace you have been saved. And God raised us up with Christ and seated us with him in the heavenly realms in Christ Jesus. (Eph 2:4–6)

Thus, it is a spiritual resurrection. Similarly, the "second death" is a spiritual death that involves complete and eternal separation from God, as is affirmed in Revelation 2:11: "Whoever has ears, let them hear what the Spirit says to the churches. The one who is victorious will not be hurt at all by the second death."

Fifth Principle

The fifth principle we have to note is the difference in perspective between the Old Testament and the New Testament that flows from the fact that divine revelation is progressive and culminates in Christ, who is at the center of all that is written. This principle is not intended to drive a wedge between the two Testaments but to show that they see events from different perspectives. They are closely related, and one current flows in both of them, namely, the great redeeming work of God which was being prepared in the Old Testament and was completed in the New Testament.

The relationship between the two Testaments can be summarized in terms of confirmation, finalization, dependence, reaffirmation, and consummation. The New Testament confirms the truths of the Old Testament and then puts them in their final form. It depends on their existence and explains them, putting its stamp on the thought forms and truths of the Old Testament. Finally, it expresses the consummation of God's progressive revelation, namely, the consummation of the truths of the Old Testament in the New Testament, for every truth is built on another truth until the full revelation is manifest.

We can thus recognize the difference in the perspective of the two Testaments, especially in regard to the glorious work of redemption.[34] Throughout the Old Testament, redemption was not presented as completed in the present but as a hope for the future (Gen 49:10; Num 24:17–19; Isa 9:6–7; Jer 31:31–34; Ezek 20:33–44). None of these prophecies, or any others, state that eternal salvation has been accomplished. Salvation is anticipated as a future reality awaited by the saints and patriarchs of old (Heb 11:13–16).

In the New Testament, however, things are different. The saints experienced in their own lives and in the lives of others that this redemption had been accomplished. Thus, they speak of it using the perfect tense [indicating past action that continues in the present] rather than a future tense:

> That which was from the beginning, which we have heard, which we have seen with our eyes, which we have looked at and our hands have touched—this we proclaim concerning the Word of life. The life appeared; we have seen it and testify to it, and we proclaim to you the eternal life, which was with the Father and has appeared to us. We proclaim to you what we have seen and heard, so that you also may have fellowship with us. And our fellowship is with the Father and with his Son, Jesus Christ. We write this to make our joy complete. (1 John 1:1–4)

John's use of the perfect tense indicates that what they had touched and seen is effective in their lives. Salvation has been completed by the perfect work of Christ, and Christ is our living hope. It is true that the final completion of this work, the salvation of our bodies, will be in the future, for "this inheritance is kept in heaven for you, who through faith are shielded by God's power until the coming of the salvation that is ready to be revealed in the last time" (1 Pet 1:4–5), but it is not a separate step, it is complementary to the work that Jesus started for the world and in the world.

Also, the kind of salvation that was expected in the Old Testament is different from the salvation that occurred in the New Testament. Salvation in the Old Testament is spiritual, political, and military. The Messiah in the Old Testament is a spiritual, political, and military ruler who establishes a theocratic state. In the New Testament, however, salvation is spiritual, and the Messiah saves his people from their sins. It is true that this salvation encompasses the whole of life—spiritual, civil, military, social, and economic—yet crucially it is the saving of life and liberating it from captivity to sin, resurrecting it from the grave of sin, and indwelling it with the Holy Spirit and the Word of God. All these give us Christian standards and values that affect every aspect of our lives. Because this is a spiritual salvation, it is not gained by the sword, crooked diplomacy, double standards, or any earthly theocracy.

In the Old Testament, great importance was attached to obedience to the law and to the temple rituals as ways to salvation—even in the words of the covenant in Jeremiah

---

[34] Aziz, *Interpretation*, 355.

31:31–34. In the New Testament, the effectiveness of the righteousness gained by the works of the law has ended, for the law was only our guardian until Christ came:

> Before the coming of this faith, we were held in custody under the law, locked up until the faith that was to come would be revealed. So the law was our guardian until Christ came that we might be justified by faith. Now that this faith has come, we are no longer under a guardian.
>
> So in Christ Jesus you are all children of God through faith, for all of you who were baptized into Christ have clothed yourselves with Christ. There is neither Jew nor Gentile, neither slave nor free, nor is there male and female, for you are all one in Christ Jesus. If you belong to Christ, then you are Abraham's seed, and heirs according to the promise. (Gal 3:23–29)

The apostle Paul repeatedly stressed this principle, and so lighted the way for us by revealing the glorious purpose of God.

Some people think that the Old Testament is nationalistic and racist. They take certain texts to imply that salvation and glory would be for Israel first or only, and if there was any place for the other nations in God's plan of salvation it would only be through submitting wholly to the Jews. But this is mistaken. God promised Abraham from the beginning that all nations would be blessed through him and his descendants, and that promise is repeated in many texts, especially in the Psalms and Isaiah. And then the New Testament makes it clear that the promise is fulfilled through Jesus Christ, as the gospel of salvation is preached to all nations, so that in Christ "there is neither Jew nor Gentile, neither slave nor free, nor is there male and female, for you are all one in Christ Jesus" (Gal 3:28).

Sixth Principle

Apocalyptic texts must be interpreted in accordance with the rules governing the genre. In the Bible, there are apocalyptic passages in the books of the Old Testament prophets Ezekiel, Daniel, Isaiah, and Zechariah, as well as in Matthew 24, Mark 13, and from chapter 4 onward in the book of Revelation.

The Greek word *apokalypsis*, which is used in Revelation 1:1, means "revelation," or the uncovering or manifestation of what is hidden. The word indicates that what follows is obscure and that we have to apply ourselves if we are to appreciate it and unlock its symbolism. We will look at this kind of writing when we study the nature of apocalyptic texts.

It is important to recognize that apocalyptic writing is a genre focused on delivering a message rather than describing events.[35] Faheem Aziz confirms this point in his book on hermeneutics:

---

[35] Leon Morris, *Apocalyptic* (Grand Rapids: Eerdmans, 1972), 53.

When an apocalyptic writer describes a vision, he does not describe something that has literally happened to him and that he has seen; he adopts a new style of writing that the situation in which he has found himself requires.[36]

That is why it is dangerous to interpret apocalyptic writings literally.

Seventh Principle

It is important to pay attention to the correct approach to prophecies, or the prophetic texts in the Bible generally and in the Old Testament in particular. We will deal with this genre as we study the nature of prophetic texts.

PROPHETIC TEXTS

Understanding the role and message of the prophets helps us to come to a correct biblical and theological way of thinking. It protects us from confusing facts and making unwarranted generalizations; from confusing biblical texts with political documents, as is happening among Zionist evangelicals; and from generalizing when speaking about the evangelicals as if they constitute one solid block.

Who Were the Prophets?

Some people think of the prophets as social reformers and preachers who cared for the moral and ethical life of the people. They rebuked their contemporaries for their moral failings and exhorted them to live up to a higher standard. However, the prophets of the Old Testament were not social reformers—though their message was not devoid of a moral dimension. They were not merely moralizers. The righteousness they called for was what God had commanded; God's command set the standard for the life of righteousness and goodness the prophets called for.

There are others who regard the prophets as astute political observers who had the ability to read the signs of the times and predict what would happen in the future. Yet, the prophets of the Old Testament were not political counselors who advised and warned the people and kings on the basis of their own wisdom and intelligence.[37] Their message was not some kind of political analysis or abstract political prediction; rather, their interference in political matters was within the framework of the Word of God and his will for a particular king.

Many ordinary people think of a prophet as someone who predicts the future. This notion is encouraged by newspapers that publish astrologers' predictions for the

---

[36] Aziz, *Interpretation*, 355–56.

[37] Elizabeth Achtemeier, *Preaching from the Old Testament* (Louisville: John Knox, 1989), 109.

coming year. However, the prophets of the Old Testament dealt with the past and the present and tried to interpret history in the light of the events that were affecting their hearers. They also dealt with the future, yet, their message was never confined to the future. Moreover, talking about the future was neither their primary role nor even a major part of their work.

The bulk of what the prophets said was a message for the present that included admonition, rebuke, correction, and teaching that took into account the people's past and their attitude toward the covenant and the promises related to it. The prophets thus addressed the peoples' rebellion against or obedience to the covenant and called for repentance while reminding them of promised blessings.[38]

Prophets were "covenant enforcement mediators" and God's spokesmen.[39] Kaiser describes them as the "revolutionaries" of the Old Testament who called for revival, reformation, and turning back to the Word of God.[40] The key to both revival and reformation was repentance and establishing righteousness and justice for the Jews and for all nations.

The topic to which the prophets devoted the least attention was the future or the future hope, a fact that is related to their attitude toward the covenant and the God of the promise.[41] When they spoke about the future they were not just presenting an academic address or making deductions about what would happen; they were delivering a spiritual message, stressing that God is the Lord of history and that he directs it as he wishes in order to achieve the purpose for which he has shaped all the events of history. The people of God have to obey and live a life of holiness in order to benefit from the divine program that has a decisive effect on their lives as hearers of the word. Their motto should be the commandment, "You shall have no other gods before me" (Exod 20:3).

Thus the prophets' message was not intended to satisfy curiosity about the future; it was intended to be no more than a limited revelation of what the people at that time needed to know about what was going to happen.

Despite this deliberate limitation, there were some prophecies that contributed to what we call "progressive revelation," namely, the gradual revelation over time of an eschatological future. But eschatology in the Old Testament did not deal with the end of the world; it had to do with the changing path of the nation's history within the framework of its relationship with God. Thus in the Old Testament eschatology is related to the covenant and its renewal (Jer 31:31–34) and is fulfilled in the New

---

[38] Aziz, *Interpretation*, 392–428.

[39] Gordon Fee and Douglas Stuart, *How to Read the Bible for All Its Worth* (Grand Rapids: Zondervan, 2014), 190–93.

[40] Walter C. Kaiser, *The Old Testament in Contemporary Preach-*

ing (Grand Rapids: Baker, 1973), 93–95.

[41] Stephen H. Travis, *I Believe in the Second Coming of Jesus* (Grand Rapids: Eerdmans, 1987), 12–34.

Testament, in which God pours out his Spirit on all people and brings in his kingdom of righteousness and peace:

> And afterward,
>> I will pour out my Spirit on all people.
> Your sons and daughters will prophesy,
>> your old men will dream dreams,
>> your young men will see visions.
> Even on my servants, both men and women,
>> I will pour out my Spirit in those days. (Joel 2:28–29)

> He will judge between many peoples
>> and will settle disputes for strong nations far and wide.
> They will beat their swords into plowshares
>> and their spears into pruning hooks.
> Nation will not take up sword against nation,
>> nor will they train for war anymore.
> Everyone will sit under their own vine
>> and under their own fig tree,
> and no one will make them afraid,
>> for the LORD Almighty has spoken.
> All the nations may walk
>> in the name of their gods,
> but we will walk in the name of the LORD
>> our God for ever and ever. (Micah 4:3–5)

Interpreting Prophetic Texts

As we have seen, the prophets of the Old Testament were revolutionaries of a sort. They did not address their words primarily to the systems and organizations within their societies but to the individuals who established those systems, organizations, and societies. Their starting point was the Word of God, not political and social problems.

It is true that as revolutionaries the Old Testament prophets hated and rejected all kinds of injustice and oppression; however, they saw these as diseases, symptoms of deeper spiritual problems that required every person to interact with the revealed word of God. Thus they addressed their message to people of influence such as judges, politicians, merchants, and priests, the people who were capable of bringing about change in society.

Recognizing this makes it easier for us to apply their message in the new framework of the present. But how can theological interpretation bridge the gap between the ancient original context and contemporary hearers?

Inadequate Approaches to Prophetic Texts

In the Hebrew Bible, some of the books we call "historical books" are identified as prophetic books.[42] Thus books such as Joshua, Judges, 1 & 2 Samuel, and 1 & 2 Kings are sometimes referred to as the Former Prophets, while the other prophetic books (Isaiah, Jeremiah, Ezekiel, and the shorter books) constitute the Latter Prophets.

Walter Kaiser uses an example from the life and service of Elijah (as set out in 1 Kgs 17–2 Kgs 2) to clarify the problems that may face a scholar preaching on the life and ministry of Elijah. In doing this he draws on Harrop's book *Elijah Speaks Today: The Long Road into Naboth's Vineyard*,[43] which deals with various interpretations of 1 Kings 21, the tragic incident of Jezebel's murder of Naboth and Ahab's stealing of his vineyard. Harrop shows how interpreters are affected by their own background, with their doctrinal positions and beliefs drawing them into partiality and subjectivity and thus shaping the applications that they claim come straight from the text. Kaiser uses Harrop's work to illustrate four inadequate models for understanding prophetic texts.

Prophetic Typological Approach

It is natural for Bible scholars to identify symbols that serve as keys to the text. Persons, events, and systems in the Old Testament are seen as pointing to the complete truth, foreshadowing the reality. This is not the issue we are addressing here. Thus the inadequate approach might better be called the "contemporary typological approach." When those with this approach interpret the story of Naboth's vineyard, they tend to focus on excoriating contemporary Ahabs for exploiting minorities, workers, or the poor, taking their land and offering the proceeds of their exploitation to contemporary Jezebels who already live in luxury.

There is no question that this is a message that needs to be heard, but can it really be preached on the basis of this passage? Is this the central point in the biblical text? Is this the message that it highlights? Or are we merely taking the names of Ahab, Jezebel, and Naboth and looking for contemporary equivalents? This model is sometimes called reverse typology because present circumstances are seen as reflecting the past, and the biblical text is secondary.

The flaw in this model is that it focuses on describing the diseases of society, but without reference to divine revelation. Where is God at work redeeming history in the Bible when we are discussing economic and social circumstances?[44] The call for social change is legitimate and necessary; however, it has to be based on a firmer foundation than just applying biblical names to contemporary injustices.

---

[42] Walter C. Kaiser, *Toward an Exegetical Theology* (Grand Rapids: Baker, 1981), 185ff.

[43] Gerald G. Harrop, *Elijah Speaks Today: The Long Road into Naboth's Vineyard* (Nashville: Abingdon, 1975), 59–86.

[44] James Daane, *Preaching with Confidence* (Grand Rapids: Eerdmans, 1980), 4–6.

Prophetic Action Approach

The prophetic action approach draws on more than just a name or two and inhabits a space larger than the text as it identifies thoughts and systems in the past or in contemporary culture. Those who use this model will regard Ahab's seizure of Naboth's vineyard as a case of state and government interests trumping the interests of individuals and citizens, even though the text says that Ahab offered Naboth a fair exchange, saying,

> Let me have your vineyard to use for a vegetable garden, since it is close to my palace. In exchange I will give you a better vineyard or, if you prefer, I will pay you whatever it is worth. (1 Kgs 21:2)

They argue that the key problem is that the little man is being swamped by social and political systems, as happens in modern democratic societies.[45]

While this interpretation may be attractive, it still does not focus on the revealed, authoritative word of God in this text or on the message that this chapter sets out to communicate. True, it does acknowledge the theology of private property, as mentioned in the Ten Commandments, and the teaching that in the case of Israel there was no separation between real estate and its owners. Land was not a commodity to be bought and sold; the land had to remain with the owners to whom God had given it since God is the supreme and original owner of the land: "The land must not be sold permanently, because the land is mine and you reside in my land as foreigners and strangers" (Lev 25:23). The same point is made in the Psalms: "The earth is the LORD's, and everything in it, the world, and all who live in it" (Ps 24:1).

However, the prophetic action model goes off the rails when it links Ahab's personal desires with institutional systems such as socialism, big government, and the welfare state. Elijah condemned Ahab as an individual, not the system or the philosophy or the program by which he governed. Moreover, he wanted Ahab to repent and be changed in himself; he did not call for a change in the policies of the state.

Once again, those who adopt this model of interpretation do not dig deeply into the text. They impose their own ideas on the text so that it carries the message they want to proclaim. The biblical passage serves mainly as a backdrop for the interpreters' personal views, for which they then claim God's authority.

Prophetic Motto Approach

Those who adopt the prophetic motto approach to interpretation seize on only one text in an entire passage. For example, they pounce on 1 Kings 21:7:

> Jezebel his wife said, "Is this how you act as king over Israel? Get up and eat! Cheer up. I'll get you the vineyard of Naboth the Jezreelite."

---

[45] Harrop, *Elijah Speaks Today*, 67–68.

They then use this text as the basis for either denouncing or supporting women's liberation, citing numerous other Old and New Testaments texts, and veer into a discussion of submission in marriage as set out in Ephesians 5:22.

Those who adopt this approach seem to be unaware of the principles of interpretation referred to earlier. Excited by the idea of women's emancipation, they seize on stories in which women play a strong role and compare those women to Jezebel. They suggest practical applications in an attempt to increase the impact of the text and give the story a contemporary application. But did the writer of 1 Kings 21 intend to discuss the issue of women's emancipation when he wrote this passage? Do the main idea and the key elements in this passage indicate that this chapter has anything to do with that issue, or even refer to it? Moreover, why would the writer put the key statement for interpreting the whole passage on the lips of one of the participants in the story, especially given that the one through whom God actually speaks in the story is the prophet Elijah?

Those who adopt the motto approach have some prior message they want to communicate. They simply search for a suitable verse from the Bible, without regard for its biblical context. Such an approach is not biblical, for it does not deal with the biblical text as such.

Prophetic Parable Approach

Some choose to use the passage as if it were a parable. Rather than focusing on a particular person, situation, or statement, they deal with the whole passage. If preaching, such interpreters use the first part of the message to tell the story of Naboth and his vineyard all the way through to the murder of Naboth and Ahab's seizing of his land. Then suddenly they move on to talking about some contemporary incident that parallels the story of Ahab and Naboth and also ends in tragedy. What is happening here is what James A. Sanders calls "dynamic analogy."[46] It is an explicit comparison between the tensions and stresses in ancient Israel and similar tensions in our present society. This kind of comparison tries to show that every situation resembles another one.

But it this all there is to this story? Are there not other things we can learn from 1 Kings 21? What was the original writer's purpose, and what were the main principles he wanted to convey?

The prophetic parable approach is no more satisfactory than the previous three approaches. It eliminates the prophetic words of judgment and promise that we find in 1 Kings 21:17–29. Even though some scholars dismiss those verses as not being part of the original text, to ignore them is to violate the integrity of the text. We have to

---

[46] James A. Sanders, *Torah and Canon* (Philadelphia: Fortress, 1972), 16.

deal with the text in the form in which it currently exists. We have to insist that the full revelation includes the whole passage and declare the prophetic words of judgment and hope that are explicitly part of it.

A Better Approach to Prophetic Texts

The four inadequate models we have just looked at do shed light on what we need to know in order to be able to better interpret prophetic texts:

- The essence of the prophet's message
- The prophetic style
- Steps in and principles of interpretation and application.

The Essence of the Prophets' Message

The word "homiletics" is derived from two Greek words: *homo*, which means "the same," and *legō* which means "I say/speak."[47] Thus preaching is the art and science of conveying to hearers the same message that is in the biblical text. If we return to the text we are dealing with, 1 Kings 21, we will find one of the important principles for interpreting the prophets to contemporary hearers. The text offers two alternatives—blessing and judgment—and asks all who hear the prophetic words in all times to respond to them with honest repentance, regardless of whether they are individuals, a religious organization, or a community of believers who form the people of God. All are called to repent and seek the Lord or return to the Lord. This is the main message of the prophets, which Zechariah expressed as follows:

> Do not be like your ancestors, to whom the earlier prophets proclaimed: This is what the LORD Almighty says: "Turn from your evil ways and your evil practices." But they would not listen or pay attention to me, declares the LORD. Where are your ancestors now? And the prophets, do they live forever? But did not my words and my decrees, which I commanded my servants the prophets, overtake your ancestors?
>
> Then they repented and said, "The LORD Almighty has done to us what our ways and practices deserve, just as he determined to do." (Zech 1:4–6)

Every message of judgment or hope is always linked to a condition. Hope and blessing are for all who genuinely return to the Lord, and judgment is for all who do not listen to his voice and refuse to repent. We find the perfect formulation of this conditional principle in Jeremiah 18:7–10:

> If at any time I announce that a nation or kingdom is to be uprooted, torn down and destroyed, and if that nation I warned repents of its evil, then I will relent and not inflict on it the disaster I had planned. And if at another time I announce that a nation or

---

[47] Kaiser, *Exegetical Theology*, 193.

kingdom is to be built up and planted, and if it does evil in my sight and does not obey me, then I will reconsider the good I had intended to do for it.

This conditional formula is applied in many places. For example, we see it in the account of Jonah's preaching the message that the Lord had given him to the people of Nineveh and their response and repentance (Jonah 3).

What applies to peoples and nations also applies to individuals:

When Ahab heard these words, he tore his clothes, put on sackcloth and fasted. He lay in sackcloth and went around meekly.

Then the word of the LORD came to Elijah the Tishbite: Have you noticed how Ahab has humbled himself before me? Because he has humbled himself, I will not bring this disaster in his day, but I will bring it on his house in the days of his son. (1 Kgs 21:27–29)

When the repentance is temporary and without firm, honest roots, the blessing is lost, as happened with Ahab when he consulted the false prophets before consulting the Lord through the prophet Micaiah the son of Imlah, who confronted him with the truth. Ahab died in the war that followed (1 Kings 22).

This is the central message of the prophets. Amidst the evils of society, individuals, governments, and contemporary systems, there is a place for healing and hope—provided peoples and individuals return to the Lord and repent of their sins. This idea is given wonderful expression in 2 Chronicles 7:14:

If my people, who are called by my name, will humble themselves and pray and seek my face and turn from their wicked ways, then I will hear from heaven, and I will forgive their sin and will heal their land.

The specific declarations in Leviticus 26; Deuteronomy 28; and Haggai 1 clearly set out the message of all the prophets. Repentance is the way to experience the goodness of God. Social injustices will be corrected when those responsible for such situations are touched by the grace of God and experience it in their lives.

Effective presentation of any prophetic text to contemporary hearers has to be based on the essential message of the prophets, within the frame of the literary, linguistic, and theological structure of the text in the various parts of the prophetic books.

The Prophetic Style

The prophets received their messages in visions and dreams: "When there is a prophet among you, I, the LORD, reveal myself to them in visions, I speak to them in dreams" (Num 12:6). The false prophets, however, misused dreams: "I have heard what the prophets say who prophesy lies in my name. They say, 'I had a dream! I had a dream!'" (Jer 23:25). As for visions, the Old Testament uses two different words when referring to them. One of these words is used when God gives his word to a prophet, and the word itself, rather than something that is seen, is the subject of the vision (see Isa 1:1; 2:1; Amos 1:1; Mic 1:1). The second word translated "vision" means a vision of some physical object. Jeremiah, for example, saw a branch of an almond tree (Jer 1:11, 12) and Amos saw a group of visions (Amos 7:1, 7; 8:1). The vision itself is not the revelation; rather, it is the means that God uses to convey his message to his people.

The prophets also used parables (2 Sam 12:1–7; Isa 5:1–7; Ezek 16; 23) and symbolic actions (1 Kgs 11:29, 30; 2 Kgs 13:14; Ezek 4:1–3). These were not only a way to convey the message; they themselves were the message. The prophets also referred to current events in which God spoke to them with a message that had a great effect on the life of the people. Moreover, the Lord sometimes used the personal life of a prophet to give him a message for the people, as happened with Hosea (Hos 1; 2) and Amos (Amos 4:12; 8:1–3). At other times, God used things a prophet saw in his everyday life, as happened when Jeremiah saw a potter (Jer 18), Jonah sat under a plant (Jonah 4), and Moses saw a bush that was on fire (Exod 3:1–5).

Steps and Principles

I will now briefly mention some of these steps that apply when interpreting the prophets.[48]

Step 1. Apply the known rules of interpretation. These include paying attention to the language, history, and assumptions made. We also need to look for the main idea in a passage, and for parallel ideas in the rest of the book in which that passage occurs, and evaluate it in light of the whole word of God.

Step 2. Recognize that every prophecy forms part of a larger whole and that we need to grasp how all the parts link in order to interpret each part correctly. For example, when we read Zechariah 9:13, we may assume that the kingdom of God is to be established by military force:

> I will bend Judah as I bend my bow
> > and fill it with Ephraim.
> I will rouse your sons, Zion,
> > against your sons, Greece,
> > and make you like a warrior's sword

However, when we read other passages, we see that the imagery of war is used to bring out the point that the Messiah is a king, but a king of peace.

> Rejoice greatly, Daughter Zion!
> > Shout, Daughter Jerusalem!
> See, your king comes to you,
> > righteous and victorious,

---

[48] See also Aziz, *Interpretation*, 425–28.

> lowly and riding on a donkey,
>> on a colt, the foal of a donkey. (Zech 9:9)
> For to us a child is born,
>> to us a son is given,
>> and the government will be on his shoulders.
> And he will be called
>> Wonderful Counselor, Mighty God,
>> Everlasting Father, Prince of Peace. (Isa 9:6)

Step 3. Clarify the message of the text, and its original audience. What kind of prophecy is this? Is it intended to teach, exhort, encourage, promise, or denounce? Does it address the present or the future? Is it conditional or not? Has it happened historically or is it still to happen? Did it happen in the Old Testament or in the New Testament? Does the prophecy have a single fulfillment or multiple fulfillments? For example, the prophecy in Isaiah 7:14–16 was fulfilled with the birth of the child to whom Isaiah referred in his own day; yet the same prophecy was also fulfilled in Christ, in a different way. Similarly, the desolating sacrilege referred to in Daniel happened historically in the days of Antiochus Ephiphanes; yet it is also still to come (2 Thess 2:3–12). The prophecies of the destruction of Jerusalem were historically fulfilled, but they will also have another fulfillment in the events of the end of the world (Mark 13:7–27).

It is also important to consider the nature of the poetic writing of the prophecies, with its parallel thoughts, contrasts, similarities, short sentences, and imagery. There is a good example of this in Joel 3:18–20:

> In that day the mountains will drip new wine,
>> and the hills will flow with milk;
>> all the ravines of Judah will run with water.
> A fountain will flow out of the LORD's house
>> and will water the valley of acacias.
> But Egypt will be desolate,
>> Edom a desert waste,
> because of violence done to the people of Judah,
>> in whose land they shed innocent blood.
> Judah will be inhabited forever
>> and Jerusalem through all generations.

We also see poetry in what the prophet says about Babylon:

> She will never be inhabited
>> or lived in through all generations;
> there no nomads will pitch their tents,
>> there no shepherds will rest their flocks.

But desert creatures will lie there,
  jackals will fill her houses;
there the owls will dwell,
  and there the wild goats will leap about. (Isa 13:20–21)

In describing the coming era of peace, the prophet says,

The wolf will live with the lamb,
  the leopard will lie down with the goat,
the calf and the lion and the yearling together;
  and a little child will lead them.
The cow will feed with the bear,
  their young will lie down together,
  and the lion will eat straw like the ox.
The infant will play near the cobra's den,
  and the young child will put its hand into the viper's nest. (Isa 11:6–8)

Step 4. Focus on the historical interpretation of the prophecy, and recognize that the prophets were responding to situations in which people were individuals with their own needs. Thus we have to pay attention to the interaction between their belief in God and the social, political, and economic world in which they lived. Their historical context is a pointer to the intended spiritual or symbolic interpretation. Unfortunately, when interpreting a text such as Daniel 12:1–3, some supporters of the idea of a millennial kingdom focus on the metaphor rather than on what this passage would have meant to its original hearers, which would, in turn, guide us in interpreting it. They do this even though they interpret many other metaphorical passages literally.

Step 5. Remember the first two principles of interpretation: a) Do not interpret prophecies in the light of changing political events; b) interpret them in the light of the New Testament and the person and mission of Jesus Christ in whom and through whose ministry all the words of the Law and the Prophets were fulfilled.

Step 6. Build a bridge that not only links the original meaning of the prophecy with its fulfillment, but also links the meaning that the prophet intended, and which his audience understood, to the message for us today.

Step 7. Interpret prophecies within the historical context of the audience to whom they were addressed. The prophecies were in the first place God's message to them and were related to their circumstances. When it comes to the interpretation of prophecies that refer to the future, we need to apply them within the framework of the person and mission of the Lord Jesus and the New Testament church (see the diagram below). We also have to look at the parts that have multiple fulfillment, as was mentioned in the third principle of interpretation, and apply them not only within their historical context, or in the light of the first coming of Christ in the flesh, but also in the light of the far future that the New Testament links to the second coming of Christ, and in the light of texts that talk about the second coming in the New Testament, such as the two letters to the Thessalonians.

We can present these as three concentric circles, as shown in the following diagram:[49]

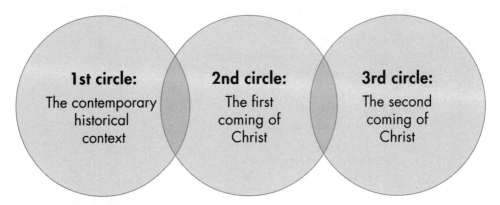

1st circle:
The contemporary historical context

2nd circle:
The first coming of Christ

3rd circle:
The second coming of Christ

We will illustrate this approach by presenting two prophecies from the Old Testament and the texts that refer to their fulfillment or application in the New Testament:

Practical Applications of Prophetic Texts

My earlier book, *Return to Awareness and Prophecies of Hope*,[50] includes a study of fifteen prophecies made by Ezekiel. Here, I will use the following two passages as examples of application.

First Application: This Kind of Religion (Ezek 11:14–21)

The word of the LORD came to me: "Son of man, the people of Jerusalem have said of your fellow exiles and all the other Israelites, 'They are far away from the LORD; this land was given to us as our possession.'

"Therefore say: 'This is what the Sovereign LORD says: Although I sent them far away among the nations and scattered them among the countries, yet for a little while I have been a sanctuary for them in the countries where they have gone.'

"Therefore say: 'This is what the Sovereign LORD says: I will gather you from the nations and bring you back from the countries where you have been scattered, and I will give you back the land of Israel again.'

"They will return to it and remove all its vile images and detestable idols. I will give them an undivided heart and put a new spirit in them; I will remove from them their heart of stone and give them a heart of flesh. Then they will follow my decrees and be

---

[49] Makram Naguib, *The Second Coming of Christ and the End of History* (Cairo: Dar Al Thaqafa, 1997 [in Arabic]), 66.

[50] Makram Naguib, *Return to Awareness and Prophecies of Hope* (Cairo: Dar Al Thaqafa, 2000 [in Arabic]), 19–21, 63–72.

THE OLD TESTAMENT PROPHECY	ITS NEW TESTAMENT FULFILLMENT

Isaiah 49:6
 	
It is too small a thing for you to be my servant
    to restore the tribes of Jacob
    and bring back those of Israel I have kept.
I will also make you a light for the Gentiles,
    that my salvation may reach to the ends of the earth.
	Acts 13:46–47
	
	Then Paul and Barnabas answered them boldly: "We had to speak the word of God to you first. Since you reject it and do not consider yourselves worthy of eternal life, we now turn to the Gentiles. For this is what the Lord has commanded us:
	
	'I have made you a light for the Gentiles,
	    that you may bring salvation to the ends of the earth.'"

Amos 9:11–12
 	
In that day
I will restore David's fallen shelter—
    I will repair its broken walls
    and restore its ruins—
    and will rebuild it as it used to be,
so that they may possess the remnant of Edom
    and all the nations that bear my name."
	Acts 15:14–17
	
	Simon has described to us how God first intervened to choose a people for his name from the Gentiles. The words of the prophets are in agreement with this, as it is written:
	
	"After this I will return
	    and rebuild David's fallen tent.
	Its ruins I will rebuild,
	    and I will restore it,
	that the rest of mankind may seek the Lord,
	    even all the Gentiles who bear my name."

careful to keep my laws. They will be my people, and I will be their God. But as for those whose hearts are devoted to their vile images and detestable idols, I will bring down on their own heads what they have done, declares the Sovereign LORD."

Structure

Chapter 11 of the book of Ezekiel speaks about judgment and hope. We can divide this chapter into three parts:

- *11:1–13* speaks about the evil leaders and how they harmed their people and nation since they did not carry out their responsibilities faithfully.
- *11:14–21* speaks about a message of hope for the people exiled in Babylon.
- *11:22–25* speaks about the removal of God's glory from Jerusalem.

Background

The background to this biblical text is the Babylonian exile, which occurred in three phases:

- In 606 BC in the time of Jehoiakim, king of Judah.
- In 597 BC in the time of Jehoiachin, king of Judah.
- In 586 BC in the days of Zedekiah, king of Judah. At that time Jerusalem and the temple were completely destroyed and burned. All that the Lord had spoken through his prophets was fulfilled (2 Chr 36:1–20).

Thus there was a time when some Jews were in exile while others were still living in Jerusalem. The latter group included the prophet Jeremiah, who delivered spiritual messages to the people and attempted to bring about revival. Meanwhile the prophet Ezekiel lived among the exiles in Babylon. Those who remained in Jerusalem tended to despise those in exile. They thought that the fact that they lived and worshipped in Jerusalem guaranteed them God's favor. After all, Zion was God's dwelling place and he was in a relationship to his land and people. By contrast, those in Babylon feared that they had no rights in the land nor any relationship with God.

Those who stayed in Jerusalem thought that God was not in Babylon since the temple was not in Babylon. They were proud of being in Jerusalem, proud of their Jewish nationality, and their life in Jerusalem. They even identified themselves with Jerusalem, saying: "Haven't our houses been recently rebuilt? This city is a pot, and we are the meat in it" (Ezek 11:3). However, the Lord himself defended his exiled people and made it clear that he himself would be a sanctuary for the remnant in Babylon:

> This is what the Sovereign LORD says: "Although I sent them far away among the nations and scattered them among the countries, yet for a little while I have been a sanctuary for them in the countries where they have gone." (Ezek 11:16)

Most interpreters take these words as indicating that the exile would be short, for the Lord himself was promising to restore his people, gather them from the nations and countries where they had been scattered, and give them the land of Israel.

As for those still living in Jerusalem in the land of Israel, the Lord said:

> But as for those whose hearts are devoted to their vile images and detestable idols, I will bring down on their own heads what they have done. (Ezek 11:21)

In discussing this text, I will focus on three main issues.

The Relationship between Religion and Life

There is a type of religion that is related to a place, a particular form, and a particular style of worship. The supporters of this kind of religion confine God to certain molds, imagining that he exists only in these molds and cannot move beyond them. This kind of religion is related to the past, to the long history of worship, to popular religiosity, to the practice of attending the temple, sheltering in the institutions and the buildings that have been established together with the systems and regulations that have been erected as empires.

I acknowledge the importance of religious institutions and administrative systems as frameworks for a spiritual message. I also know that buildings are a means for reaching out and that regulations are a way to maintain order. However, if these "tools" do not promote spiritual revival for individuals and the community within the local church, they have no value.

The group that stayed in Palestine took shelter in the land, the temple, and the forms of worship; however, they did not uphold the holiness of the Lord of the earth and did not know the ways of the Lord of the temple. Nor did they know the true meaning of worship. The problem was not in the temple, the land, or the worship; these are important and valuable for every believer. But what is most important is the essence of true worship and spiritual experience.

Another type of religion was found in the exiled group who had lost their land and their religious structures, yet did not lose the spiritual truth of the presence of God, who said, "I have been a sanctuary for them." They had a direct spiritual relationship with him. This group lost the link to the past and moved away from the old shelter in Jerusalem, but they became more flexible and open to new experiences, and more capable of understanding God's work with them in exile. They were open to a new experience of God, and the effects of change and conversion and purification began to appear among them. Thus God said:

> I will give them an undivided heart and put a new spirit in them; I will remove from them their heart of stone and give them a heart of flesh. (Ezek 11:19)

This exiled group realized that the essence of spiritual experience is a personal relationship with God. God looked at both groups, and saw these two kinds of religion. Then he showed Jeremiah a vision of two baskets of figs. The first basket was full of very good figs and represented the group that went to the exile. They were the ones who practiced humility, recognized their need, and surrendered to God. They confessed their sins and showed true repentance and experienced the winds of purification and renewal. The second basket was full of very bad figs that could not be eaten. It represented the group in Jerusalem who took shelter in the land and the temple and so did not respond to God. The word of the Lord came to show that the holy God could not accept that kind of religion.

God asks for a religion that starts from within and is not constrained by external appearances. He wants souls that can be affected by the Word of God's grace and the work of his Holy Spirit. He wants true worship, not traditional routines. He is pleased with practical religion that reforms our everyday behavior with our families, colleagues, and society. Life has to reflect true faith. Jesus praised the Samaritan who showed mercy to a needy man; he did not praise the Levite or the priest who ignored the love of their neighbor under the false cover of a hollow religion (Luke 10). The apostle John teaches us,

> This is how we know who the children of God are and who the children of the devil are: Anyone who does not do what is right is not God's child, nor is anyone who does not love their brother and sister. (1 John 3:10)

> If anyone has material possessions and sees a brother or sister in need but has no pity on them, how can the love of God be in that person? (1 John 3:17)

Do we have this kind of religion?

The Relationship between the Church and the Society

The Jews who stayed in Jerusalem believed that Babylon was a foreign land with no relationship to God since it was unclean. Thus, many of the exiles believed that they were without a homeland. In their grief they refused to sing to the Lord and withdrew into themselves. They abandoned their message and their testimony and lived waiting for the new earth and the new heaven. Psalm 137 tells us about their response when they were asked to sing:

> By the rivers of Babylon we sat and wept
>> when we remembered Zion.
> There on the poplars
>> we hung our harps,
> for there our captors asked us for songs,
>> our tormentors demanded songs of joy;
>> they said, "Sing us one of the songs of Zion!"
> How can we sing the songs of the LORD
>> while in a foreign land? (Ps 137:1–4)

Yet the Lord sent them a clear message through Jeremiah, saying:

> Build houses and settle down; plant gardens and eat what they produce. Marry and have sons and daughters; find wives for your sons and give your daughters in marriage, so that they too may have sons and daughters. Increase in number there; do not decrease. Also, seek the peace and prosperity of the city to which I have carried you into exile. Pray to the LORD for it, because if it prospers, you too will prosper. (Jer 29:5–7)

Ezekiel confirmed God's presence with them in the exile in Babylon (Ezek 11:16). Yes, "the earth is the LORD's, and everything in it, the world, and all who live in it" (Ps 24:1). God chose Israel to be a channel of blessing for other nations. Yet Israel refused to deal with any other nation, and dismissed non-Jews as "dogs." They forgot that the Lord had said that the whole earth was his: "Now if you obey me fully and keep my covenant, then out of all nations you will be my treasured possession. Although the whole earth is mine, . . ." (Exod 19:5). Perhaps they even thought that the Lord would deal only with the Jews. But where is it said that the Lord has confined himself in a certain land to deal with only one people?

Sometimes we too think like those exiled Jews. We think that we live in a strange land, and that this earth is not ours; thus, we withdraw and abandon our testimony due to a false pietism. The type of alienation that the heroes of faith adopted and lived by was related to their spiritual expectations and longing for the coming of the Messiah. Yet Christ completed the work for us, and when the apostle Paul speaks about our estrangement as Gentiles from the covenant people, he immediately adds that now in Christ we share the same access to God as the Jews:

> For through him we both have access to the Father by one Spirit.
> Consequently, you are no longer foreigners and strangers, but fellow citizens with God's people and also members of his household. (Eph 2:18–19)

When we pray "Your will be done," we make heaven start on earth, and acknowledge that our Lord is the God of the whole creation and all human beings with all their religions and races. So the earth is our homeland and we are called to witness with our life through positive attitudes and a sense of responsibility. We have to be a message of love, peace, and noble values, and must contribute effectively to the progress of our countries toward a better life.

The Relationship between Life, the Message, and the Gospel

The divine promise to restore the exiled Jewish people to their land and give them a new opportunity in their relationship with God (Ezek 11:17–20) is repeated in Ezekiel 36:24–28. Some claim that this prophecy has not yet been fulfilled. However, as evangelicals we believe that it was fulfilled historically in the time of King Cyrus and prophetically in Christ. Today, the church, the community of the Lord Jesus Christ that is called to witness to the world, has replaced the old Israel as the new spiritual Israel (Gal 6:16; 1 Pet 2:9, 10). God set aside Israel as a people and gave its privileges to another nation that bears the required fruit, which is the one church that is composed of the believers of both Jewish and Gentile origin.

The message of Ezekiel then bears what we may call a "gospel." It gives us the basis and the way to a transformed life (first issue) and offers us the way to change society (second issue).

There was a time when Ezekiel was close to despair:

> Now as I was prophesying, Pelatiah son of Benaiah died. Then I fell facedown and cried out in a loud voice, "Alas, Sovereign LORD! Will you completely destroy the remnant of Israel?" (Ezek 11:13)

267

Yet the words of this prophecy came to proclaim the gospel of hope amidst judgment, the message of grace and mercy in the midst of wrath. This hope and grace are for you and me, if we realize that the gospel opens for us the way to repentance and purification (Ezek 11:18, 19). Through honest repentance and a purified life, we can rejoice in these promises. However, if we do not repent but take shelter in the appearance of religion rather than its essence, the literal faith rather than its fruit, the voice of the Lord says to us:

> But as for those whose hearts are devoted to their vile images and detestable idols, I will bring down on their own heads what they have done. (Ezek 11:21)

The gospel calls for a new structure within us for accepting a heart of flesh from the hands of God, a heart that feels and responds to God, one heart for one purpose.

Second Application: Contemporary Crises and Confused Questions (Ezek 29:1–16)

In the tenth year, in the tenth month on the twelfth day, the word of the LORD came to me: "Son of man, set your face against Pharaoh king of Egypt and prophesy against him and against all Egypt. Speak to him and say: 'This is what the Sovereign LORD says:

> "I am against you, Pharaoh king of Egypt,
>   you great monster lying among your streams.
> You say, 'The Nile belongs to me;
>   I made it for myself.'
> But I will put hooks in your jaws
>   and make the fish of your streams stick to your scales.
> I will pull you out from among your streams,
>   with all the fish sticking to your scales.
> I will leave you in the desert,
>   you and all the fish of your streams.
> You will fall on the open field
>   and not be gathered or picked up.
> I will give you as food
>   to the beasts of the earth and the birds of the sky.

Then all who live in Egypt will know that I am the LORD.

"You have been a staff of reed for the people of Israel. When they grasped you with their hands, you splintered and you tore open their shoulders; when they leaned on you, you broke and their backs were wrenched.

"Therefore this is what the Sovereign LORD says: I will bring a sword against you and kill both man and beast. Egypt will become a desolate wasteland. Then they will know that I am the LORD.

"Because you said, 'The Nile is mine; I made it,' therefore I am against you and against your streams, and I will make the land of Egypt a ruin and a desolate waste from Migdol to Aswan, as far as the border of Cush. The foot of neither man nor beast will pass through it; no one will live there for forty years. I will make the land of Egypt desolate among devastated lands, and her cities will lie desolate forty years among ruined cities. And I will disperse the Egyptians among the nations and scatter them through the countries.

"Yet this is what the Sovereign LORD says: At the end of forty years I will gather the Egyptians from the nations where they were scattered. I will bring them back from captivity and return them to Upper Egypt, the land of their ancestry. There they will be a lowly kingdom. It will be the lowliest of kingdoms and will never again exalt itself above the other nations. I will make it so weak that it will never again rule over the nations. Egypt will no longer be a source of confidence for the people of Israel but will be a reminder of their sin in turning to her for help. Then they will know that I am the Sovereign LORD."

This part of the Word of God has a double benefit. First, it is a part of the Word of God and as such it is good and beneficial for our salvation and growth in Christ. Second, from here up to chapter 32, the book of Ezekiel deals with our precious country, Egypt. In the four chapters from Ezekiel 29 to 32, God shows his interest in a country and people other than Israel.

This prophecy dates back to about 587 BC, one year before Nebuchadnezzar besieged Jerusalem, captured it, and took its residents into exile in Babylon. We can deduce this date by comparing it to the date mentioned in Ezekiel 24:1.

At that time, Zedekiah was the king of Judah. He succeeded the righteous king Josiah, but was very different from his predecessor in his attitude toward God. The Word of God that came to Zedekiah through Ezekiel and Jeremiah commanded him to submit to the king of Babylon and not rebel against him. Zedekiah refused to listen and tried to rebel against Babylon. He even made an alliance with other enemies of Babylon. Zedekiah did not obey the Lord and would not listen to the message of the Lord or try to understand his will. He did not seek salvation in God; rather, he turned to Egypt and found in Pharaoh his refuge and support. At that time, Egypt was a superpower. However, the Egyptian army was defeated by the Babylonians at the famous battle of Carchemish, after which Babylon became the superpower to which all peoples had to submit. Zedekiah's attempted alliance with Egypt did not bring him the support he needed.

The prophecy we are looking at gives some details about what happened. God vowed to punish Egypt since it had not helped Judah, but he would also punish Babylon for flaunting its victories.

What message did Ezekiel want to convey through this text?

Structure

We can divide the story into the following parts:

- Introduction (29:1, 2)
- Two metaphors for the Pharaoh of Egypt (29:3–9)
  - Pharaoh the great dragon who embodies pride and arrogance and has no need of God
  - Pharaoh the staff of reed that will fail anyone who relies on it
- God's punishment for Egypt's failure to help Israel (29:10–16)

There are two approaches to explaining God's punishment of Egypt as depicted in 29:12:

> I will make the land of Egypt desolate among devastated lands, and her cities will lie desolate forty years among ruined cities. And I will disperse the Egyptians among the nations and scatter them through the countries.

Some argue that forty years elapsed between Nebuchadnezzar's battle with Egypt and Persia's battle with Egypt, at which time there was further destruction. Others argue that these verses are symbolic, and that this period was not limited but refers to a long period during which Egypt was ruined politically and economically. This destruction is manifested in the dispersion that happened to the people of Egypt, resulting in Egypt never again rising to the status of a superpower.

When discussing this prophecy, there are three important questions that I will address:

- Does this passage—and other passages that refer to Egypt—deal with historical matters or with the future? Some Christians think that the fulfillment of these prophecies lies in the future and try to interpret the Word of God literally and apply it to current events. They expect the River Nile to dry up, which will lead to massive famine and disaster. Israel will then prosper at the expense of Egypt, paving the way for the second coming of Christ and the establishment of his blessed millennial kingdom on earth. But this interpretation ignores the fact that this text is clearly and directly related to the past—specifically to an incident that happened in 587 BC when Egypt was a superpower. We should not take a biblical text that speaks about a specific historical reality and apply it to the present or the future. The way to benefit from this historical story is to learn a spiritual lesson. The drying up of the River Nile and other curses are events in the past.
- Will evil prevail in the world until the end? Will God allow evil to grow unchecked? Why does he let overwhelming evil prevail? When will God intervene to put an end to all this?

- Is there a relation between contemporary crises and the cross of our Lord Jesus Christ? Is there a message for minorities in this text that deals with a historical crisis? Is there something we can say to encourage a minority in contemporary crises?

I will address these questions in what follows.

Evil May Prevail Temporarily

This present world has been put under the sway of the devil, and so from time to time evil is dominant. In many historical periods, the people of God have suffered because of this, and we can still hear their cries. Think of Asaph pondering the success of the wicked in Psalm 73, or listen to Habakkuk:

> How long, LORD, must I call for help,
>   but you do not listen?
> Or cry out to you, "Violence!"
>   but you do not save?
> Why do you make me look at injustice?
>   Why do you tolerate wrongdoing?
> Destruction and violence are before me;
>   there is strife, and conflict abounds. (Hab 1:2, 3, see also 1:13)

We also find similar complaints in the writings of Isaiah, Jeremiah, Amos, Job, and others.

In Habakkuk 2:1–4, God answered his prophet and told him that a time is coming when he will intervene to put an end to the suffering of believers and punish the wicked for their wickedness and transgression. Believers, however, must wait with patience and hope for the Lord to act, for he is the judge of the whole earth who brings justice. Thus, he says:

> See, the enemy is puffed up;
>   his desires are not upright—
>   but the righteous person will live by his faithfulness. (Hab 2:4)

The time will come when God will intervene and settle the battle for the benefit of his people. In the meantime, we have to cling to the Lord.

Is there a relationship between this idea and the cross of Jesus? Yes, for in the cross we find all the answers for these confused questions. The cross was the pinnacle of injustice and the ultimate curse. Those who looked at Christ there might well have thought that evil had conquered goodness forever. But the resurrection converts the cross into the pinnacle of blessing. The cross proclaims the wisdom of God that converts a curse into blessing. The cross confirms that the reins of history are always in the hands of the Lord, and nothing can be out of his hands. We can "know that in all things God works for the good of those who love him, who have been called according to his purpose" (Rom 8:28). We do not always know how God does this, and we may not always realize all the details in this regard, but we believe that the Lord does all things for our benefit and for his glory. What a wonderful hope!

God's Sovereignty over All That Happens

We generally study history from a political perspective, but this approach is inadequate when it comes to seeing the work of God in history. History is God's before it is ours, for history reveals plainly how God intervenes in human life—both in the lives of individuals and kingdoms.

> The decision is announced by messengers, the holy ones declare the verdict, so that the living may know that the Most High is sovereign over all kingdoms on earth and gives them to anyone he wishes and sets over them the lowliest of people. (Dan 4:17)

God cuts off kings and appoints other kings. He controls events and directs the course of history. He leads kings and protects peoples and he is always over any circumstance. We cannot isolate religion from politics, for we cannot isolate God from history.

In the passage we are looking at, God leads Nebuchadnezzar and uses him to punish Judah, which had strayed from him and rebelled against him. He also leads Pharaoh to take the attitude that serves his divine purposes. God controls the superpowers of the world and moves them according to his will; he is the Lord of history who controls the destinies of individuals and peoples and holds the political cords in his hand. There is no point in relying on anything or anybody else. The message of God for Zedekiah was that Egypt was a weak staff that would break if anyone leaned on it. In spite of its greatness, Egypt could not protect him or support him and so he should not put his confidence in it. There is a curse on those who rely on human strength.

What about us? Don't we often rely on someone or something other than the Lord? Some of us put our confidence in things like our money, social position, health, and youth. Yet history and the Word of God confirm that these things are useless. The true shelter and the only fortress is the Lord alone, who gives and blesses all things when we accept them as gifts from his generous hand.

The Position of Minorities

In this passage, the people of God appear as a weak nation caught between competing superpowers. Was this the true cause of their defeat? Of course not; they were defeated and went into exile because they had not relied on the Lord and had not upheld his honor.

God is the king who reigns over the world and controls the superpowers; therefore, no one who belongs to him should feel weak or inferior. As believers we belong to the Lord of the whole earth, and God our father is responsible for us and cares for us. Why then should we fear? As some have said, "If you are alone and God's truth is on your side, you are a majority." Our confidence in God's care for us should not be shaken since he holds us and guides us in the crises of life. The voice of Christ assures us: "Do not be afraid, little flock, for your Father has been pleased to give you the kingdom" (Luke 12:32).

APOCALYPTIC TEXTS

There are many reasons why it is important to know something about apocalyptic literature. The first is that it is of great interest in the Arab world, where there is often confusion about the difference between apocalyptic and eschatology. Thus some build eschatological doctrines on apocalyptic texts that they interpret literally. A second reason is the great interest Bible scholars and theologians have shown in apocalyptic writings since the second half of the twentieth century. Some regard these texts as the basic source from which Christian theology emerged.[51] A third reason is that because of the interest in these texts, we have to be able to deal with them and understand them if we are to proclaim their real message.

The Meaning of the Word "Apocalyptic"

The Greek word *apokalypsis* in Revelation 1:1 means "disclosure" or "revelation." Thus, the books described as "apocalyptic" reveal what is hidden or concealed. The term "apocalyptic literature" is applied to a group of Jewish and Christian writings with certain specific features written in the two centuries prior to Christ and in the first century AD. The ideas and concepts in these writings are also referred to as apocalyptic. Thus, we may find that a book contains apocalyptic sections, although the book as a whole is not considered apocalyptic (although scholars sometimes disagree about the classification of specific texts).

Apocalyptic writing flourished in the intertestamental period, but we also find apocalyptic elements in the books of Old Testament prophets like Ezekiel, Daniel, Isaiah, and Zechariah. In the New Testament, such elements are also found in Matthew 24, Mark 13, and the book of the Revelation starting from chapter 4.

Why Did the Apocalyptic Style Emerge?

George Eldon Ladd offers three important reasons for the emergence of the apocalyptic style of writing.[52] These are widely accepted and are summarized as follows by Faheem Aziz:[53]

---

[51] Aziz, *Interpretation*, 391–412.
[52] Ladd, *Last Things*, 52–53. See also Ronald S. Wallace, *The Lord Is King: The Message of Daniel* (Downers Grove, IL: IVP,

1979), 24.
[53] Aziz, *Interpretation*, 353–54.

First, the emergence of the righteous remnant of the lost nation. "The righteous remnant" is a prophetic designation for the group mentioned in passages like Isaiah 26:2:

> Open the gates
>> that the righteous nation may enter,
>> the nation that keeps faith.

In Isaiah 37:4, we read:

> It may be that the LORD your God will hear the words of the field commander, whom his master, the king of Assyria, has sent to ridicule the living God, and that he will rebuke him for the words the LORD your God has heard. Therefore pray for the remnant that still survives.

Some groups, like the Hasideans or the Pharisees, took this title for themselves and considered themselves the "remnant" that worshipped God faithfully amidst a nation that had deviated from him and lost the true vision of the future.

The writings produced by such groups were a form of protest against the age and circumstances in which they lived. Similar writings were produced by the Christian community when they began to experience persecution.

Second, the reality of evil and suffering. In ancient times, there was a simple expectation that God would punish wrongdoers and the wicked and reward the righteous. However, Jewish experiences after the exile led to a rethinking of this belief. Although the Jews who had returned to Judah were by no means perfect, they were no longer attracted to the abominations of the past. They no longer worshipped idols but trusted in the law and stressed the importance of obeying it. Yet in spite of this, they were still subject to one nation after another, and enjoyed freedom for only a few years under the Maccabees.

They held to a higher moral standard than their neighbors, but they were not successful and did not enjoy peace and stability. They still endured pain and witnessed evil at work.

Third, the ceasing of prophecy. Prophets had led the nation for many centuries, pointing to the right way to serve God. But as their voices faded, no more prophets emerged. Some lamented, "the prophets have died." Something had to emerge to fill the void, and the place of the prophets was gradually filled by the apocalyptic writers. They spoke to the people by writing in a certain style and from a specific perspective. Although these writers were not of the same stature as the prophets, they too spoke to people's hearts and imagination. What they had to say was not easy, but their faith was strong and in a very difficult time they encouraged people to continue to cling to God right to the end. They manifested heroic faith, for they believed God and his promises regarding the righteous remnant.

This third point is the most significant of all. The apocalyptic writings are rooted in prophecy; they emerged to fill the void left by the disappearance of prophets. The writers were very different from the prophets, but they shared the same faith that had led the people of God in the past.

How Do We Interpret Apocalyptic Writing?

Leon Morris says:

> We should understand apocalyptic writing as a literary device, a way of getting the message across. It set forth the teachings of the author, but it did not give a description of something that actually happened.[54]

Gordon Fee reminds us:

> Apocalypses are literary works from the beginning. . . . [A]n apocalypse is a form of literature. It has a particular written structure and form.[55]

When apocalyptic writers describe a vision, they are not describing something that has happened to them or that they have seen; rather, they are using a style of writing that is necessitated by their circumstances. They are not telling us about their own unique encounter with God. They do not expect us to believe that stars literally fell from the sky and turned into bulls, nor that cows mating with these bulls literally gave birth to elephants, camels, and donkeys (1 En. 85:1–6; see also 89:1, 10). These details are simply their way of communicating their message in vivid, visionary terms.

The prophets, by contrast, wrote about real encounters with God and relayed the message they heard. This contrast between "hearing" and "seeing" is sometimes said to distinguish apocalyptic writers from prophets.[56]

Our basis for making this point about claims of literal truthfulness is that the majority of the apocalyptic books—except those in the Bible—were attributed to people who lived many centuries before the books were written. The book of Enoch, for example, is attributed to Enoch in the seventh generation after Adam. The book of Jubilees that deals with Jewish feasts and the priesthood is attributed to Moses. The names of at least twenty famous people are associated with apocryphal books, yet in none of these books is there any mention of the name of the real author.[57]

There are several possible reasons for the omission of the writers' own names. It may be that it was thought that the age of prophecy had ended and that the prophetic canon had closed, so that people were no longer ready to listen to a different, contemporary writer describing a vision. Thus, the writers of the apocalyptic books concealed their

---

[54] Morris, *Apocalyptic*, 55.
[55] Fee and Stuart, *How to Read the Bible*, 260.
[56] Aziz, *Interpretation*, 355–56.
[57] Morris, *Apocalyptic*, 54.

real names and identities and instead wrote under the name of some ancient hero. The visions would then be written in a manner suited to the person to whom the book was attributed.

Given that the apocalyptic books written in the two centuries before Christ and the century after his birth were attributed to people who lived long before then, we can say that the authors did not intend the visions they described to be taken literally but were using a literary device to convey a message.

By contrast, the two apocalyptic books in the Bible, Daniel and Revelation, are associated with contemporary figures, Daniel and the apostle John (Rev 1:4, 9; 22:8). In the case of John, it may be that the Christian church had realized that prophecy had returned and that there was thus no need to conceal the name of the writer.[58]

Features of Apocalyptic Writing

If apocalyptic writing was a literary style, what are the most important features of that style? We need to know this if we are to be able to understand it and interpret it correctly.

Symbolism

Symbolism is one of the most important features of apocalyptic writing. Apocalyptic texts are full of references to beasts, rivers, mountains, stars, angels, and religious figures. The writers freely borrow and reuse these symbols to express their ideas. While the meaning of the symbols may have been clear to contemporary readers, they often puzzle us today, but we should not forget that the original readers knew the key to these symbols and were able to interpret them.[59] It is also possible that the meaning of some of the symbolism was known in certain Jewish circles, but was not widely shared.[60]

We also need to remember that a symbol may have more than one meaning. The correct interpretation will depend both on the context and on when it was used, for the meaning of symbols is not static, but develops over time.

Among the important symbols in the apocalyptic books are numbers like 3, 4, 7, 10, and 12. The number 70 is often found in Jewish apocalyptic books, while the number 7 recurs in the book of the Revelation.

Revelations

As stated above, the very word "apocalypse" means "revelation," and the apocalyptic books are full of special revelations that purportedly came to the ancient heroes whose names are associated with the books. These revelations often come in the form of visions. The revelations do not relate to the era of the supposed author but to the era

---

[58] Aziz, *Interpretation*, 356–57.
[59] Ibid., 357.

[60] Isidore Singer, ed., *The Jewish Encyclopedia*, 12 vols. (New York: Funk & Wagnalls, 1925), 1:672.

of the unknown writer, that is, to the two centuries before Christ and the century in which he came.

The hero who supposedly receives the revelation may speak with an angel or he may be taken up to heaven to receive it. Most of the revelations focus on the end-time; or in other words, they deal with the end of the world and the start of the kingdom of God. The writers looked "forward to the time when God would bring a violent, radical *end* to history, an end that would mean the triumph of good and the final judgment of evil."[61]

The revelations to the hero of an apocalyptic book may also relate to heavenly mysteries or to natural or historical phenomena that cannot be known without revelation. They are specially revealed to the hero or to the group among whom he lives. The writers used this as an indirect way to present the Word of God.

Dualism

Apocalyptic writings are filled with dualism. Some even go so far as to say that "the Most High has made not one world but two" (2 Esd 7:50). They assert that although the present is full of pain and suffering, the future will be filled with joy and salvation. The writers contrast good and evil, good spirits and evil spirits, light and darkness, white and black, the people of God and the people of the devil, the present temporal evil age and the coming eternal age of blessing in which the will of God will be fully manifested. When God intervenes, he does not do so in order to reform this earth but to create a new earth and a new heaven.[62]

Some scholars attribute this dualism to the influence of Persian thought, but others argue that it is a development of ideas that were already present in the Old Testament (Isa 32:15–18; 65:17; 66:22).[63] Torrey says the apocalyptic writers "certainly assimilated from the beginning more or less foreign material but in its essential features it seems to have been truly Jewish in origin."[64]

This dualism resulted in a pessimistic view of the world as full of corruption and evil and impossible to put right. Jewish attempts to bring in God's rule through rebellion against their oppressors repeatedly failed, especially in AD 70 and AD 132. These failures bolstered the apocalyptic writers' contention that the world is beyond saving and that when God intervenes he will not reform this evil world but will create a new heavens and a new earth. They had complete confidence that God would win in the end and destroy this world. In their focus on the destruction of this world, they differ from the prophets who called for reform since the prophets believed that history could be redeemed. Apocalyptic writers deny that this is possible.

---

[61] Fee and Stuart, *How to Read the Bible*, 260.

[62] Morris, *Apocalyptic*, 49.

[63] G. E. Ladd, "Apocalyptic," in *Evangelical Dictionary of The-* *ology*, ed. Walter. A. Elwell (Grand Rapids: Baker, 1984), 62.

[64] Charles C. Torrey, "Apocalypse," *JE* 1:669–75. Available online: www.jewishencyclopedia.com/articles/1642-apocalypse.

Apocalyptic Writings and Prophecies

I have already drawn attention to some differences between apocalyptic writers and prophets. Now it is time to focus on the most important differences between them.

Orientation of the Message

It is generally believed that the prophets delivered a message from God to people in a specific place and time, dealing with urgent issues of the time, whereas apocalyptic writers were less interested in the details of their own time and more focused on a revelation regarding the future. Yet some of the prophets spoke about future events, and apocalyptic writings did convey a message to the people in their time. So what is the real difference between them? Aziz puts it this way:

> While the prophets place their emphasis on the word of God for their age and proclaim a message from God to his people for guidance and warning, the apocalyptic writers emphasize revealing and contemplating the future; this is the message they send to their contemporaries.[65]

View of History

The apocalyptic writers viewed history as a succession of ages and times in which God works to bring to fruition a plan or a purpose that will be completed outside history. For God is not the only one at work in history; the devil and evil forces oppose God's plan and his people. Thus historical events are the work of the devil and do not reveal God's plan. Instead, knowledge of God's purposes comes through apocalyptic writings that were kept hidden from ancient heroes such as Abraham and Moses until the age in which they were to be proclaimed. The will and plan of God for his people was hidden from view in the period between the last Old Testament prophets and the time of the apocalyptic writer.[66] History was corrupt and there was no way in which God's purposes could be fulfilled through it.

By contrast, the prophets saw God at work in historical events. In history God had made a covenant with his people because he had chosen them. In history, God had led them from one era to another and declared his will to them in specific and recorded historical events. The prophets looked at history as the setting or context for achieving the purposes of God in the near and distant future.

Thus, for the prophets, history was the history of redemption and salvation. Redemption happens in history through concrete historical events that people experienced and the prophets explained. History can be redeemed. It is not, as the apocalyptic writers insisted, so evil that it cannot be redeemed and must ultimately be destroyed by God.[67]

---

[65] Aziz, *Interpretation*, 359.
[66] Ibid., 360.

[67] Wallace, *The Lord Is King*, 25–26.

Apocalyptic Writings and Eschatological Thinking

The difference between the apocalyptic and prophetic views of history throws light on the difference between apocalyptic and eschatological ideas. Whereas the apocalyptic writers say that history is utterly corrupt and the purpose of God cannot be fulfilled through it, the prophets who speak about eschatological matters say that God works in history and redeems it.

In the New Testament, Jesus Christ is the first one to speak in eschatological terms. He is one who came within history in the fullness of time and he is directing and controlling the course of history and will complete what he has started. He is working with his Holy Spirit in history and within people to convict the world of sin, righteousness, and judgment; to lead people to God the Father; to perfect the saints; and to fulfill the mission of the church.

While it is true that both apocalyptic thinking and eschatology are future-oriented, the apocalyptic view sees the future as completely new, with no relation to the present, whereas, eschatological thinking sees that the future has already begun. We have been living in it since the incarnation and it will culminate in Christ's return in glory. Thus the future is an extension and completion of the present.[68]

It follows that the church relies on eschatology rather than on apocalyptic thinking. Eschatology cares about both the first and second comings of Christ, not just about the end of history. In the New Testament, we do not find extensive apocalyptic thinking; rather, there are a few scattered sayings that have an apocalyptic background and reflect the literary style of apocalyptic writing. But we do not find a revelation or disclosure of apocalyptic secrets. Instead, we find thoughts and teachings for the present that are presented in apocalyptic terms.[69]

Failure to recognize these facts leads some to approach apocalyptic portions of the Bible with the mindset of Jewish apocalyptic thinkers and a preoccupation with signs of the times. Such people also often take texts literally, ignoring their historical and literary background. This type of thinking was widespread in the nineteenth century and laid the foundations for many current eschatological doctrines.

We have to be careful not to impose Jewish ideas on Christian writing and not to interpret apocalyptic texts in the Bible in the same way as Jews do. To do so is to distort the truth and lose our way in non-Christian mazes, as happened with John Nelson Darby (1800–1882) and C. I. Scofield who popularized Darby's ideas in 1909. Some evangelical groups still support their ideas. These groups have emerged from the tradition of radical literal interpretation that mixes what is Jewish with what is Christian and the religious with the political.

---

[68] Aziz, *Interpretation*, 361–62.   [69] Ibid., 363.

Apocalyptic Texts in the Bible

Let us conclude our study of the difference between apocalyptic, prophetic, and escha-tological thinking by examining a few apocalyptic texts in the Bible.

The Book of Daniel

The book of Daniel opens with Daniel in exile with his people in Babylon. In chapters 2, 7, 8, and 11, it speaks of four empires (Babylonian, Medo-Persian, Greek, Roman), and the division of the Greek Empire into four parts after the death of Alexander the Great. After this division, Egypt was governed by the Ptolemies, and thus the king of the south referred to in Daniel 11:5 is Ptolemy Soter (322–305 BC). Meanwhile the Seleucids governed Syria and came into regular conflict with the Ptolemies. One of the Seleucids, Antiochus Epiphanes went to Palestine and defiled the Jewish temple in Jerusalem by slaughtering a pig on the altar. He persecuted the Jews severely for three-and-a-half years, until Judah Maccabee delivered and cleansed the temple (Dan 8:9–11, 23–25; 11:21–45).

The message of Daniel for his exiled nation was that the Babylonian Empire, which had taken them into captivity (Dan 8:19), would end and would be followed by three other empires. Yet during this time God would establish his kingdom in Christ, the Messiah who would embody the expectations of the godly. He is the hope for the future (Daniel 9:24–27). Thus the authority to decide the fate of peoples and individuals was not in the hand of men or governors; it is solely in the hand of the Almighty God:

> At that time Michael, the great prince who protects your people, will arise. There will be a time of distress such as has not happened from the beginning of nations until then. But at that time your people—everyone whose name is found written in the book—will be delivered. Multitudes who sleep in the dust of the earth will awake: some to everlasting life, others to shame and everlasting contempt. Those who are wise will shine like the brightness of the heavens, and those who lead many to righteousness, like the stars for ever and ever. (Dan 12:1–3)

This is the historical culmination of the message of the book, which is intended to encourage exiles and those being persecuted by the Syrian Antiochus Epiphanes, whose reign of terror is described in terms of years in Daniel 12:7 and in terms of days in Daniel 12:11–12. However, the whole of Daniel 11:36–12:4 refers to a fulfilled prophecy. In the long term, Antiochus Epiphanes represents the antichrist before the coming of Christ in the flesh and every antichrist until the second coming of Christ.

The relation between the book of Daniel and the Old Testament is like the relation between the book of Revelation and the New Testament. The book of Daniel can even be referred to as "the Revelation of the Old Testament." It contained a message of con-solation for godly people in the time between the exile and the incarnation. Similarly the book of Revelation is a message of consolation for godly people in the time between the destruction of Jerusalem and the return of the Lord Jesus (Titus 2:11–13; Rev 7:1; 22:17, 20).

Dispensationalists, however, do not recognize the apocalyptic nature of the book of Daniel and ignore the date and context in which it was written. So they meld its prophecies regarding the Syrian king with the events and prophecies of the New Testament era. Consequently, they assume that references to Syrian rule refer to the Roman Empire and deduce that the "small horn" (which represented Antiochus Epiphanes) represents the Roman Catholic Church.[70]

The result of this confusion is that they miss Daniel's encouraging message that the surrounding kingdoms that were persecuting the Jews, and especially the fourth kingdom, would be destroyed by God's intervention and that the fifth kingdom, the kingdom of Christ, would come when Christ comes in the flesh. Instead, dispensationalists argue that the kingdom of Christ will not come until after the annihilation of the Roman Catholic Church, which means that his kingdom has not yet come.

In interpreting the "times" mentioned in Daniel, dispensationalists claim that every day represents one year and thus that these texts predict the time of the annihilation of the Roman Catholic Church and the coming of Christ. However, this interpretation is delusory since it is not consistent with the nature of apocalyptic texts and ignores the text's historical context. It causes great problems by mixing apocalyptic Jewish writings with Christian eschatology.

Matthew 24

The background to Matthew 24, as is clear from the end of the previous chapter in Matthew's Gospel, is Christ talking about the judgment of Jerusalem and the destruction of the temple:

> Jerusalem, Jerusalem, you who kill the prophets and stone those sent to you, how often I have longed to gather your children together, as a hen gathers her chicks under her wings, and you were not willing. (Matt 23:37)

The disciples were shocked and asked Jesus to look at the architecture of the temple, thinking that he might perhaps modify what he had said. But he answered,

> Do you see all these things? . . . Truly I tell you, not one stone here will be left on another; every one will be thrown down. (Matt 24:2)

Christ then went on to talk about the desolating sacrilege:

> So when you see standing in the holy place "the abomination that causes desolation" spoken of through the prophet Daniel—let the reader understand—then let those who are in Judea flee to the mountains. (Matt 24:15–16)

---

[70] Ibid., 44–46.

In saying that, he was referring to the following passage from Daniel:

> His armed forces will rise up to desecrate the temple fortress and will abolish the daily sacrifice. Then they will set up the abomination that causes desolation. (Dan 11:31)

The words from Daniel refer to the last of the four kingdoms mentioned in Daniel 2, that is, the kingdom of Alexander the Great, which was divided into four subkingdoms after his death. The words refer specifically to the actions of Antiochus Epiphanes, who was king of Syria, one of the four subkingdoms. Antiochus is represented by the small horn mentioned in Daniel 8:9–11 and is the subject of Daniel 11:21–45. It was he who built an altar for Zeus in the temple and offered a pig on it, thus desecrating the temple. Eventually Judah Maccabee freed the temple and punished Antiochus Epiphanes and his kingdom, Syria. This event is seen as a prelude to the coming of the Messiah, whose kingdom Daniel refers to as a fifth kingdom that follows the other four.

When Jesus referred to these events in Matthew 24, he was saying that they would be repeated by the Romans, who also desecrated and destroyed the temple in AD 70.

The background to this chapter clearly speaks about the judgment on Jerusalem and the destruction of the temple. However, it also refers to the second coming of Christ. Jesus used his coming to judge Jerusalem as a miniature version of his final judgment and as confirmation that he would return to judge the world.

The reference to "the abomination that causes desolation" indicates that Matthew 24 is an apocalyptic text, and thus is not to be interpreted literally. The chapter also uses other familiar apocalyptic images from Jewish literature and the Old Testament (see, for example, Isa 34:4; Joel 2:31).[71]

The events mentioned in this chapter were all fulfilled when Jerusalem fell, which is why Jesus could say

> Truly I tell you, this generation will certainly not pass away until all these things have happened. (Matt 24:34)[72]

Mark 13

Some scholars see Mark 13 as an apocalyptic text and refer to it as "the Little Apocalypse." They say that Christians took an earlier apocalyptic vision and modified it to suit their purposes. This is Bultmann's position in *The History of the Synoptic Tradition*.

However, many scholars—including C. E. B. Cranfield in *The Gospel according to Mark*[73] and Joachim Jeremias in his *New Testament Theology*[74]—completely reject this

---

[71] Ibid.
[72] The historical and biblical background to Matthew 24 is discussed at length in Bray, *Matthew 24 Fulfilled*.
[73] C. E. B. Cranfield, *The Gospel according to St Mark: An Introduction and Commentary*, Cambridge Greek Testament Commentaries (Cambridge: Cambridge University Press, 1959).
[74] Joachim Jeremias, *New Testament Theology* (London: SCM, 1971).

opinion. While agreeing that the language and some of the images used in the chapter are apocalyptic, they insist that there are also real differences between the contents of this chapter and apocalyptic writing.

Cranfield points out that in the Jewish apocalyptic tradition what is said is addressed to the apocalyptic writer, who then reports what he saw and heard. However, in this chapter, Jesus' words are addressed to a group and take the form of a command; there is not the slightest suggestion of a vision revealing some secret teaching. What we have is an exhortation to faith and obedience, even when enduring trials. In fact, even the repeated command to be vigilant and faithful in following Jesus goes against the apocalyptic tendency to stress the impossibility of reform and the uselessness of toil.

Cranfield also points to the absence of other apocalyptic idioms and themes in Mark's Gospel as a whole and in this chapter specifically. Such themes include a holy war; the return of exiles; sensual, earthly salvation; judgment on the nations; the wonderful life hereafter; the last judgment; the overthrow of Satan; and the destruction of evil.

Moreover, there are elements in this chapter that are not only out of step with contemporary apocalyptic thinking but directly contradict it. Such elements include references to the harm that would fall on Israel with the prophesied events and the destruction of the temple. The differences are so great that some think that Mark 13 cannot be the work of an apocalyptic writer or a writer influenced by apocalyptic thinking.

Faheem Aziz confirms all this, saying,

> the Gospel writer wanted to discourage a preoccupation with apocalyptic thinking and looking for signs of the times and encourage true discipleship. Thus he started the chapter with a series of warnings intended to draw their minds away from apocalyptic thinking. Then he explained these warnings using some apocalyptic terminology, but he transforms this terminology by applying it in historical terms related to the present time and contemporary events. Thus he eliminated the apocalyptic element.[75]

The Book of Revelation

Those who assume that Mark 13 is an apocalyptic passage that bears the marks of Jewish apocalyptic writing tend to take a similar position in regard to the book of Revelation. Their reasons for doing so are as follow:[76]

- The very name "Revelation" suggests this link, for it is a Latin translation of the Greek word "apocalypse."

---

[75] Aziz, *Interpretation*, 364–65.

[76] Faheem Aziz, *Introduction to the New Testament* (Cairo: Dar Al Thaqafa, 1980 [in Arabic]), 646–48.

- The book is full of symbols and imagery that are similar to those in apocalyptic writings. There is mention of rivers, books, seals, trumpets, bowls, horses, numbers, beasts, and mountains, all of which are seen in a vision by a writer who is in an exalted spiritual state (4:1; 17:3; 21:10) and which are given to him by an angel (1:1; 22:8).
- Like apocalyptic writings, Revelation speaks about the events of the end times, and about the persecution and suffering inflicted on the people of God by a false prophet, the beast, the dragon, and all the forces of evil. Then God intervenes, bringing victory to his chosen ones and judgment on the evil powers.
- The book has a practical purpose and, like apocalyptic writings, is filled with spiritual and moral advice. It consoles the persecuted, encouraging them to cling to their faith in Christ until death (13:9, 10; 14:13; 16:15; 19:9; 20:6).

In spite of all these similarities with apocalyptic writings, a discerning scholar can see many differences between the book of Revelation and other apocalyptic writings:

- The writer claims repeatedly that the book is a "prophecy" (1:3; 22:7, 10, 18, 19). As we have seen, there is a considerable difference between vision and prophecy. The writer insists that the vision he conveys is the Word of God and the testimony of Jesus Christ (1:2).
- Though the book agrees with apocalyptic writings in its message that God will comfort his people and will judge evil and evildoers, its overall message is more like that of the prophets. It calls the people of God to repentance and emphasizes the importance of living a godly life. The messages to the seven churches clearly show that the writer does not gloss over the sins of Christians (2:5, 16, 21, 22; 3:3, 19).
- Like apocalyptic writings, the book of Revelation deals with the end of time, yet it has a different perspective to the other writings. The apocalyptic writers regarded history as corrupt beyond redemption and argued that God had no option but to destroy history in order to begin afresh. John does not share this apocalyptic pessimism. Despite the intense demonic attacks that characterize the end times, John, like the prophets, sees history as the locus of God's activity and his redeeming work by the death, resurrection, and victory of the Lamb. This great work is shared by believers who have conquered Satan "by the blood of the Lamb and with the word of their testimony" (12:11). Thus, salvation starts in history and there is no despair or pessimism regarding God's redemption of the history of the world.
- Whereas the apocalyptic writers used pseudonyms borrowed from the heroes

of the past, the author of Revelation simply states that his own name is John (1:1). He sees no need to borrow a name from the distant past and link it to the present in order to establish his credibility to readers who believed that the age of prophecy had passed. John felt free to use his own name because he believed that prophecy had returned to the church and that God had come again to his people with comforting words and with a call to repentance.

- The writer of the book of Revelation differs from the apocalyptic writers in that he does not present the story of the sweep of history to announce the preparations God has been making to sweep away history with its wickedness and corruption and to establish his new kingdom. John spoke to his age as the prophets did, that is, to announce the Word of God to his contemporaries. Only after doing that did he look forward to the fulfillment of God's purpose and his wrath. He can be said to embody "the prophetic tension between history and eschatology."[77]

Looking at John's symbolism, the beast represents the historical Rome as well as the eschatological antichrist to come. Thus his account of the persecution that fell on the churches of Asia Minor in the first century is more severe than the reality of the persecution that occurred, for he looked through it to the persecution that will fall on believers when the antichrist comes. Thus, John saw the future end foreshadowed in historical events, just as the prophets did. They talked to their contemporaries and at the same time pointed to the future "day of the Lord" (compare Isa 7:14 with Matt 1:23; Hos 11:1 with Matt 2:15; Jer 31:31–34 with Heb 8:8–12).

We can thus conclude that the book of Revelation is a prophetic book that was written in the style of apocalyptic writings in that it is full of images, symbols, and visions that serve to proclaim the reality of God's presence in the present and throughout history. The author focuses on the slaughtered Lamb, the historical event that has become the center of revelation. Thus, the book of Revelation calls for repentance and a return to the Word of God. Readers are exhorted to raise their eyes to heaven to see Jesus, who holds all power and authority in the church and in history.

John presents this message many times in the book of Revelation; however, each time he offers the same message in a new form or style. Since the book of Revelation is all about revealing the truth and reality behind the symbol—the author "made it known" (1:1)—the important thing is not the external form or style but the deep meaning and the message.

---

[77] Ladd, "Apocalyptic," 53.

The Message of the Book of Revelation

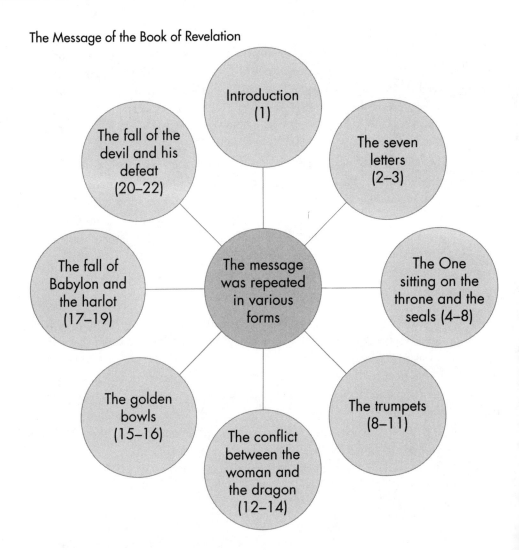

Practical Applications of Apocalyptic Texts
Return to Life; the Resurrection of a Nation

The hand of the LORD was on me, and he brought me out by the Spirit of the LORD and set me in the middle of a valley; it was full of bones. He led me back and forth among them, and I saw a great many bones . . . on the floor of the valley, bones that were very dry. He asked me, "Son of man, can these bones live?"

I said, "Sovereign LORD, you alone know."

Then he said to me, "Prophesy to these bones and say to them, 'Dry bones, hear the word of the LORD. This is what the Sovereign LORD says to these bones: I will make breath enter you, and you will come to life. I will attach tendons to you and make flesh come upon you and cover you with skin; I will put breath in you, and you will come to life. Then you will know that I am the LORD.'"

So I prophesied as I was commanded. And as I was prophesying, there was a noise, a rattling sound, and the bones came together, bone to bone. I looked, and tendons and flesh appeared on them and skin covered them, but there was no breath in them.

Then he said to me, "Prophesy to the breath; prophesy, son of man, and say to it, 'This is what the Sovereign LORD says: Come, breath, from the four winds and breathe into these slain, that they may live.'" So I prophesied as he commanded me, and breath entered them; they came to life and stood up on their feet—a vast army.

Then he said to me: "Son of man, these bones are the people of Israel. They say, 'Our bones are dried up and our hope is gone; we are cut off.' Therefore prophesy and say to them: 'This is what the Sovereign LORD says: My people, I am going to open your graves and bring you up from them; I will bring you back to the land of Israel. Then you, my people, will know that I am the LORD, when I open your graves and bring you up from them. I will put my Spirit in you and you will live, and I will settle you in your own land. Then you will know that I the LORD have spoken, and I have done it, declares the LORD.'" (Ezek 37:1–14)

These verses are among the most famous in the book of Ezekiel. They represent the first half of chapter 37 in that book. The second half of the chapter (vv. 15–28) contains the prophecy of the two sticks.

The opening verse makes it clear that what we have here is a record of a vision that Ezekiel saw:

The hand of the LORD was on me, and he brought me out by the Spirit of the LORD and set me in the middle of a valley; it was full of bones. (Ezek 37:1)

Similarly, near the start of the book we read:

The hand of the LORD was on me there, and he said to me, "Get up and go out to the plain, and there I will speak to you." So I got up and went out to the plain. And the glory of the LORD was standing there, like the glory I had seen by the Kebar River, and I fell facedown. (Ezek 3:22–23)

In the earlier passage Ezekiel proclaims judgment on the people of God; in the later one (ch. 37) he announces the return of life after death and proclaims the resurrection of the dry bones.

The vision of dry bones conveys two ideas, the first of which is the absence of awareness and the end of hope.

Have we not all found ourselves standing at the tomb of our hopes and dreams? Have we not all felt on occasion that our ship of ambition has sailed and foundered or been wrecked on cruel rocks? Your experience of this may be personal, in your family, or even in your community. Who has not cried out with Job, "where then is my hope—who can see any hope for me?" (Job 17:15, 16). This is a place we may often come to. Do we not feel many times that we are on the verge of losing all hope? Do we not face situations that push us to despair?

This was Ezekiel's experience when he saw what remained of his nation after some ten years of exile. The people were like dry bones spread across the desert. The survivors may even have seen such scenes of desolation as the Babylonians forced them to walk the long miles into exile in Babylon (Ezek 37:1, 2). To Ezekiel's eyes, the whole nation had become like dry bones and sealed tombs; there was no hope. The people thought that their life had been cut off, and there was no longer even a gleam of light. They were inert and as good as dead.

The difference between the living and the dead is awareness. Those who are dead or unconscious do not respond to any external influences. They cannot. But a lack of awareness is a great problem when it is found among the living. A nation or a community is either active and responding or is passive and unresponsive to present events and future needs.

Spiritual death in an individual or a community is marked by an absence of awareness and a lack of response to any influences. Those who are spiritually dead are confused. They see trivial things as important and important things as trivial. Their values are so confused that they focus on what is transient and ignore what is eternal. They can no longer judge reality aright and cannot distinguish the signs of the times and the spirit of the age. Thus they live with poverty and intellectual and spiritual loss.

This lack of awareness is present not only in individuals but also in communities like a church or a nation. A whole group may manifest a lack of awareness and an inertia that no longer responds to external stimuli. We see this pattern of behavior in church history, for there were times when the church lost its spiritual awareness and forgot its true status. At such times, it also lost its perspective on what was going on around it. Similarly, in the Old Testament we see the leader of the people, the king who represented God, committing murder and adultery and falling into a deep moral slumber. He was spiritually unaware and did not face up to the wrong he had done, nor did the people remind him of it, until the day when the prophet of God faced him, saying "you are that man" and awakened him from his spiritual sleep.

The frozen immobility of death also reflects poverty of thinking. A church that is dead gets confused in its teaching and loses the ability to distinguish between the cheap and the precious since it has lost its standard—the Word of God. Many churches that are in a spiritual coma are carried every which way by every wind of doctrine and are deceived by all kinds of false spirituality.

Spiritual death results in a loss of vision, moral corruption, an inability to take action, and a poverty of thought. Have we not seen this in our churches, our societies, and in the Arab world in which we live? We have long lived in a desert where we are unconscious and unaware.

When the Lord asked the prophet, "Son of man, can these bones live?" Ezekiel replied, "Sovereign Lord, you alone know" (Ezek 37:3). In other words, in human terms, it might be impossible, yet God can do anything; nothing is impossible for him. And God does do the impossible, turning the bones into a great army that serves the living God.

This is the gospel in Ezekiel. After showing us the painful reality, Ezekiel moves quickly to show us life emerging anew from the dead bones. It is a real miracle; God gives life to something that has died, for our God is the God of the impossible. He alone is capable of giving new birth to a nation that died and ceased to exist. Is not this miracle repeated every day when God raises sinners from the tombs of their sins? Does he not delight us every day with believers who wake from their sleep and begin to proclaim the gospel and evangelize the living for Christ? Therefore, God's call to the church is to return to life; for the missing spiritual pulse again to begin to beat; and to return to the glory of the church and to the proclamation of the good news of the gospel. Do we not all long for a new resurrection of this kind?

Ezekiel shows us this resurrection taking place in two phases:

- *First phase.* In the first phase (Ezek 37:4–8) the bones respond to the ministry and prophecy of the prophet. This is the beginning of the resurrection, when the bones join together but still lack spirit. The important factor in this phase is to offer the Word of God even to the dead. Ezekiel is commanded to "prophesy," that is, teach and preach, to the dead. Here we see the faith and sincerity of Ezekiel who saw the reality as it was, yet believed God's promise and obeyed God's voice in spite of that reality. He continued preaching faithfully until the miracle happened. His example teaches us to remain in our ministry until the time appointed by God comes, when he does the miracle and gives life to those to whom we minister. As the apostle Paul says, "Let us not become weary in doing good, for at the proper time we will reap a harvest if we do not give up" (Gal 6:9).
- *Second phase.* The first phase is to prophesy to the bones by proclaiming the Word of God; the second phase (Ezek 37:9, 10) is to prophesy to the spirit by prayer for the work of the Holy Spirit. Through confident faithfulness, persistence in the Word of God, and continual prayer, the Spirit of God works within us and gives us power for life and ministry. The one who breathed the breath of life into Adam (Gen 2:7) still has the power to bestow life by his word and raise the dead.

The Spirit of God changes reality, makes history, and restores life and awareness to those who are insensible and unaware. He writes his law on the heart so that his word dwells richly within and the mind is enlightened, life is renewed, ministry becomes fruitful, and values are set right as vision clears. How powerful is the Word of God when it is combined with prayer through which the Holy Spirit works and raises those dead in sin?

Have you lost awareness and become inert? Do you now want to return to life? Do you want the miracle to come true in you? Open yourself to the work of the Holy Spirit through studying the Word of God prayerfully and you will see that the Holy Spirit will restore your life and vitality.

The message of this chapter in Ezekiel offers hope and good news as it affirms the possibility of life from death for every human being. This is what happened through the work of Jesus Christ for us. Everyone who believes in him will pass from death to life—to the fullness of enlightened, growing, and fruitful life. Jesus spoke truly when he said, "I have come that they may have life, and have it to the full" (John 10:10).

This is the message of hope to every gathering and every church: Rise and awake from loss and death to a life of awareness, testimony, and fruitfulness.

It is a message of hope to the nation, and even to the whole world, which lives at the edge of the abyss in complete unconsciousness of its peril and without a true perspective and awareness of its responsibility. It is a gospel of hope that is found in Christ.

The Call for Unity

The word of the LORD came to me: "Son of man, take a stick of wood and write on it, 'Belonging to Judah and the Israelites associated with him.' Then take another stick of wood, and write on it, 'Belonging to Joseph (that is, to Ephraim) and all the Israelites associated with him.' Join them together into one stick so that they will become one in your hand.

"When your people ask you, 'Won't you tell us what you mean by this?' say to them, 'This is what the Sovereign LORD says: I am going to take the stick of Joseph—which is in Ephraim's hand—and of the Israelite tribes associated with him, and join it to Judah's stick. I will make them into a single stick of wood, and they will become one in my hand.' Hold before their eyes the sticks you have written on and say to them, 'This is what the Sovereign LORD says: I will take the Israelites out of the nations where they have gone. I will gather them from all around and bring them back into their own land. I will make them one nation in the land, on the mountains of Israel. There will be one king over all of them and they will never again be two nations or be divided into two kingdoms. They will no longer defile themselves with their idols and vile images or with any of their offenses, for I will save them from all their sinful backsliding, and I will cleanse them. They will be my people, and I will be their God.

'My servant David will be king over them, and they will all have one shepherd. They will follow my laws and be careful to keep my decrees. They will live in the land I gave to my servant Jacob, the land where your ancestors lived. They and their children and their children's children will live there forever, and David my servant will be their prince forever. I will make a covenant of peace with them; it will be an everlasting covenant. I will establish them and increase their numbers, and I will put my sanctuary among them forever. My dwelling place will be with them; I will be their God, and they will be my people. Then the nations will know that I the LORD make Israel holy, when my sanctuary is among them forever.'" (Ezek 37:15–28)

We have seen that chapter 37 of the prophecy of Ezekiel consists of a vision and a prophecy; the vision of the dry bones in verses 1–14 and the prophecy of the two sticks in verses 15–28. We have discussed the vision under the title "Return to life; resurrection of a nation," and now we turn to the prophecy.

There is a clear relationship between the vision and the prophecy. Once we grasp the main thrust of Ezekiel's thought, it is clear that the whole chapter has one message, a message that we can understand better when we study the context in which it was given. The people were deeply shocked by the fall of Jerusalem and their exile to Babylon. This shock shook their faith and filled them with despair and disappointment. That was why they were saying, "Our bones are dried up and our hope is gone; we are cut off" (Ezek 37:11). Similar feelings filled the hearts of Arab peoples after our defeat by Israel in the war of June 1967. We too felt that the nation had died. The question then was, "Can these bones return to life?" The answer was, "No, it's impossible."

It is to these broken people that the prophet brings a message that dry bones may indeed return to life and that the broken nation may be resurrected, for God can do that. He is the Lord Almighty; he is able to raise people from the dead and to bestow life since he is the source of life. The prophet then described some features of the age of the Messiah: a new leadership, a restored land, reconstructed cities, worship pleasing to God, a life that manifests the glory of God, and so on.

The vision and the prophecy both present the same message, with differences in style and emphasis. In recounting his vision, the prophet used the apocalyptic style, emphasizing that the Spirit of God will revive the nation and turn it from dry bones (a skeleton) into a great army that is effective for the Lord. In presenting the prophecy, the prophet used a symbolic style. Symbolism is a feature of apocalyptic style, as we have seen, just as symbols and the symbolic acts are part of the prophetic style. It is a style that Ezekiel used often (see, for example, Ezek 4; 5).

The teaching of the symbolic prophecy with the two sticks is that the old division between Judah and Israel, which had begun directly after the death of King Solomon, would end and all the people would be united in the new nation in one land and one kingdom under one king. We find a hint of this in Ezekiel 37:11,

Then he said to me: "Son of man, these bones are the people of Israel. They say, 'Our bones are dried up and our hope is gone; we are cut off.'"

Thus the main idea of the prophecy is the unity of the nation after its revival; the main idea of the vision is the nation's resurrection. In the prophecy, the resurrected nation is reunited. The key idea of unity as the hope of the nation is gradually introduced by the prophet through a symbolic act followed by an explanation.

- *Symbolic action.* In 37:15–20 Ezekiel took two sticks and then united them as one long stick to be held up before the eyes of the nation to express the idea of unity.
- *Explanation.* The explanation in 37:21–28 consists of two paragraphs full of promises. Each paragraph ends with the statement, "They will be my people." The first paragraph (37:21–23) speaks of the gathering of the people, their return to the land, their unity, and their purification. The second paragraph (37:24–27) speaks of obedience, eternal stability, and the covenant of peace, which includes a double blessing: "I will . . . increase their numbers, and I will put my sanctuary among them forever." Above all, the nations will know that Yahweh is the Lord (37:28). These promises with all that they include are a repetition of the prophecies in Ezekiel 34:11–31 and Ezekiel 36:22–30.

The idea of unity symbolized by two sticks goes back to Zechariah 11:7–14. Yet in Zechariah, the two sticks represent division, not unity, since God had decided to break his covenant with the tribes because of their sins (Zech 11:10, 14). In Ezekiel, however, the two sticks represent the reunification of the nation.

There is a constant, latent longing for unity in the Bible. We find this longing in all of what we call "the early prophecies" (Isa 11:13; Joel 3:18; Hos 1:11). This longing is still felt all over the world. Today, the world is entering what is called a "new era," with the end of the Cold War between the superpowers and the beginning of an age of cooperation and accord. The removal of the Berlin Wall that separated East and West Germany has reunited the people of Germany, and the adoption of a common European currency has unified Europe. All the borders between European countries are open and the world seems to be moving toward unity in a new global system of integration and cooperation. Such movements confirm that the Spirit of God is still working in the world today and directing events toward the stability in which peoples can develop and build their future. There is even a faint hope of eventual reunification of North and South Korea after a summit meeting between the presidents of those two countries.

But the Bible reminds us that the roots of human division lie deep. Since the first entrance of sin into human experience, from the days of Cain and the division of the first family until today, jealousy, insecurity, selfishness, and a lack of forgiveness continue to mar our lives. There is not only physical murder but also the murder of relationships within families. Church divisions also bring us deep sorrow, not to mention the denominational divisions rooted in the history of the church, and the divisions on the national level.

The voice of God on the lips of Ezekiel calls the nations, the church, and the family to unity, for God is glorified in a coherent unified community. Perhaps this is what drove Jesus to pray for the unity of the church:

> I pray also for those who will believe in me through their message, that all of them may be one, Father, just as you are in me and I am in you. May they also be in us so that the world may believe that you have sent me. (John 17:20–21)

We are also commanded to pursue "the unity of the spirit through the bond of peace" (Eph 4:3) in the same spirit with which Ezekiel in the Old Testament called for vigilance in achieving unity.

But we also need to consider what Ezekiel says about the nature of our unity.

> This is what the Sovereign LORD says: "I will take the Israelites out of the nations where they have gone. I will gather them from all around and bring them back into their own land. I will make them one nation in the land, on the mountains of Israel. There will be one king over all of them and they will never again be two nations or be divided into two kingdoms." (Ezek 37:21–22)

Here Ezekiel speaks about gathering the people and their return to their land and unifying them under the banner of one king. The question that we must answer is whether we are to interpret these words literally or spiritually. Some advocate that we take them literally. Should we be calling for the unity of the Jewish people, their return to their land, and the building of the temple in place of the Al-Aqsa Mosque to prepare for the return of the Lord Jesus and the establishment of the blessed millennial kingdom on earth?

In response to these questions, we say that all or most of the prophecies in the Bible have a double fulfillment; one historical and one in the future. This applies also to the subject of our study. The Jews returned historically from the exile to their land, as recorded in the books of Haggai, Zechariah, Nehemiah, and Ezra.

The future fulfillment, however, has also already happened, for Ezekiel was looking forward to the age of the Messiah. In these last days, the new nation is the church and the new leader is the Lord Jesus Christ. The prophet takes the historical model of David in the past; then he calls for a second David, a spiritual one who will reign forever (Ezek 37:24–25). Can these words apply to anyone other than Jesus Christ? Jesus came amidst us as an eternal king whose glory "we have seen" (John 1:14). He raised his tent among us, unified his people, and destroyed the wall of enmity between peoples, making the two one, thus establishing peace (Eph 2:14). Ezekiel gives an extended explanation of what this means in chapters 40 to 48.

So the prophecy has been fulfilled historically in Israel and spiritually in the church, the new Israel, in which all races, nations, and tongues are united in a new spiritual kingdom of the Messiah. The unity of the people of God that the prophet speaks about is a spiritual unity in Christ, who is the center and basis of this unity (compare Gen 17 with Rev 4:9–11). Ezekiel speaks about the new Israel and the new temple—the person of the Lord Jesus. We are one body in Christ, in whom we feed and are made strong. We may differ in our attitudes, personalities, and thoughts, yet we are one body for one King, and the love of Christ surrounds us and directs our lives. Let us listen to what the apostle has to say concerning the people of God:

> Therefore if you have any encouragement from being united with Christ, if any comfort from his love, if any common sharing in the Spirit, if any tenderness and compassion, then make my joy complete by being like-minded, having the same love, being one in spirit and of one mind. Do nothing out of selfish ambition or vain conceit. Rather, in humility value others above yourselves, not looking to your own interests but each of you to the interests of the others. In your relationships with one another, have the same mindset as Christ Jesus. (Phil 2:1–5)

Maintaining Unity

> They will no longer defile themselves with their idols and vile images or with any of their offenses, for I will save them from all their sinful backsliding, and I will cleanse them. They will be my people, and I will be their God.
>
> My servant David will be king over them, and they will all have one shepherd. They will follow my laws and be careful to keep my decrees. (Ezek 37:23–24)

The real problem we face is not to achieve unity but to maintain unity. As Paul says, it is something we have to "make every effort to keep." His words imply that we already have this unity, but need to work hard to preserve it. All of us work well as individuals, but problems start to appear when we work as a team, since we are not used to doing that. Ezekiel offers us some effective and practical ways to maintain unity.

Purification

The prophet had spoken before about the influence of their surroundings on the people, insisting that they were defiled by the idols of the surrounding nations and by their own sins. Yet God declared that this would no longer be a problem. How is that possible? Is he going to change their circumstances? No, he will change the people themselves. He promised to purify them and heal them from within, so that they will have immunity against pagan worship and will be different from those around them through the new values and morals given to them in Christ. Thus in 36:25–26 Ezekiel is speaking of the purification and change that Jesus makes in our lives. Our new life in Christ maintains the unity of the body as we work together as children of the Lord in purity of thought and heart:

> Create in me a pure heart, O God,
>> and renew a steadfast spirit within me. (Ps 51:10)

Practical Obedience

A life of constant obedience and conduct that is in keeping with the Spirit are the strongest factors promoting the unity of the body, whether at the family level or at the level of ministry in a church. Not submitting to the Lord leads to not submitting to one another, but a heart that is oriented to fulfilling the will of God, to practicing his presence, and walking in fear of him to please him is a heart that makes true peace. We know from experience that divisions appear when peoples' spiritual growth has stopped, so that they walk according to the flesh.

The Blessing of Unity

They will live in the land I gave to my servant Jacob, the land where your ancestors lived. They and their children and their children's children will live there forever, and David my servant will be their prince forever. I will make a covenant of peace with them; it will be an everlasting covenant. I will establish them and increase their numbers, and I will put my sanctuary among them forever. My dwelling place will be with them; I will be their God, and they will be my people. (Ezek 37:25–27)

Ezekiel mentions three blessings of unity in the verses above:

- *Stability and peace.* There will be no divisions or wars when God's covenant of peace is in place; consequently, there will be no lost time or effort.
- *Increase.* God promises to increase his people. All their efforts and capacities will be directed toward development and positive growth. The church will not be inert and will not shrink or withdraw; instead, it will extend and rise and possess new lands as new believers join it every day (Acts 2:47 with Isa 54). Although it is true that numeric increase is not the only measure of success, it is a clear biblical sign that God is at work. This is the reason the Lord tells the church:

> Enlarge the place of your tent,
>> stretch your tent curtains wide,
>> do not hold back;
> lengthen your cords,
>> strengthen your stakes.
> For you will spread out to the right and to the left;
>> your descendants will dispossess nations
>> and settle in their desolate cities. (Isa 54:2–3)

- *God's ongoing presence.* God refers to his choice of the people and to his continual presence among them. His presence is the greatest and most precious reward (Exod 33:12–17). It is what distinguishes God's people from other nations. By promising to be with his people, the Lord declares himself to be their protector, preserver, and shepherd. He frees them from the guilt of the past and its effects, builds his people up through the hardships of the present with its tests and pressures, and protects them from the fears and challenges of the future.

These three blessings of stability, increase, and God's presence among his people are also mentioned in Leviticus 26:6–13. Therefore, we conclude that Ezekiel takes all the promises that were made to the people in the old covenant and puts them into effect through the spiritual reality of the church in Christ.

The Message of Unity

Then the nations will know that I the LORD make Israel holy, when my sanctuary is among them forever. (Ezek 37:28)

Is not this what Jesus prayed for in John 17:23?

I in them and you in me—so that they may be brought to complete unity. Then the world will know that you sent me and have loved them even as you have loved me.

Is not this what Ezekiel emphasized in 36:23, 36, that "the nations will know"? The Lord Jesus who prayed "that all of them may be one, . . . so that the world may believe that you have sent me" (John 17:21) knows very well that the unity of the church is the way to the world's acceptance of it and of its message. The world does not accept or respect a weak and divided community; it accepts and respects and listens to the message of a united, strong community that has an effective presence in society.

Chapter Five

THE CHRISTIAN WOMAN

Mary Mikhael

Dr. Mary Mikhael is president of the Near East School of Theology, the first woman to hold such a position in the Levant. Her areas of specialization are theological education and issues concerning Christian women. She holds a master's degree in Christian Education from the Presbyterian School of Christian Education in Richmond, Virginia, and a doctorate in education from Union Theological Seminary in New York (1987). Her doctoral thesis was entitled, "Toward a Critical Theory of Teaching the Bible in the Context of Lebanon." Dr. Mikhail served for seven years as head of the women's program of the Middle East Council of Churches and has been a leading advocate for the World Day of Prayer on both the local and international levels. She has been an ordained elder in the Evangelical Presbyterian Church in Beirut since 1987.

SINCE THE START of the twentieth century, the world has witnessed many uprisings against various realities. There have been uprisings against political injustices and social marginalization and uprisings calling for equal rights and responsibilities for all. How much talk there has been about human rights and the fact that most people lack them!

An observer monitoring the United Nations' resolutions that have tried to spread the culture of human rights might be surprised by the great emphasis that has been placed on equality and justice between men and women. According to numerous international conventions, women's rights are inseparable from human rights. Thus the Universal Declaration of Human Rights (1948) includes the following statement:

> Men and women of full age, without any limitation due to race, nationality, or religion, have the right to marry and to found a family. They are entitled to equal rights as to marriage, during marriage, and at its dissolution. (Paragraph 16/1)

297

Similarly the International Covenant on Economic, Social, and Cultural Rights (1966) refers to "women being guaranteed conditions of work not inferior to those enjoyed by men, with equal pay for equal work," and the third article of the International Covenant on Political and Civil Rights (1966) reads:

> The States Parties to the present Covenant undertake to ensure the equal right of men and women to the enjoyment of all civil and political rights set forth in the present Covenant.

The United Nation's General Assembly added to these documents by producing the Convention on the Elimination of All Forms of Discrimination against Women, which it adopted on 19 December 1979, and implemented on 3 September 1981. By August 1992 some 116 countries had signed on to this agreement, which deals with a range of issues. It urges all countries to eliminate all kinds of discrimination against women, and to pursue by all appropriate means—without delay—the policy of eliminating such discrimination. Countries were required to do this by embedding the principle of equality in national constitutions and other regulations, inhibiting all forms of discrimination against women, approving legal protections for women, repealing all provisions of national penal laws that constituted discrimination against women, encouraging the participation of women in all areas of life and decision-making, and upholding women's right to work and freedom to choose their own profession, etc.[1]

There are two main reasons for this international concern and the extensive discussions about human rights and the necessity of justice and equality between men and women. First, throughout recorded history, women have been deprived of many of their human rights and have been socially marginalized with their roles greatly restricted so that society has been impoverished by the lack of their contribution. Second, in the current age of globalization, any self-respecting society has to ensure equality for all its members. Thus historical deprivations and current necessities are two reasons for the extensive debate and lobbying for the right of women to have a role in building an integrated society in which all people enjoy equal opportunities and responsibilities.

THE REALITY OF THE MIDDLE EASTERN CHRISTIAN WOMAN

It is now time to look at the status of women in the church. What is the reality that they have endured for more than 2,000 years, and what should it be, so that the Christian church is able to embody the will of its Lord in its life and witness?

---

[1] As reported in Omar Alaqrai, Ahmed Subhy Mansour, Ghanem Jawad, Muhammad Abdul-Jabbar, Nada Mustafa, Al Bagir Afif, Mohammed Abdul-Malik al-Mutawakkil, Heba Raouf Ezzat, *Women's Rights among the International Conventions and Political Islam*—6, Human Rights Debates (Cairo: Cairo Center for Human Rights' Studies, 1999).

For several decades, the church and the world in general have been going through a period of dialogue—even at times confrontation—about women in leadership and their participation in official services of the church. Anyone who has looked at the history of the World Council of Churches knows of the deep disagreements between the Orthodox Church and churches from the Reformed Protestant tradition. We heard many threats to withdraw from the World Council of Churches if it approved the ordination of women as priests. At times the dialogue has turned into painful confrontation.

For close to twenty centuries men have "sung solos" before the curtains of the temple. Men spoke and women maintained a long silence. This situation was always justified on the basis of what was said in the Bible—particularly by the apostle Paul in some of his letters. Throughout this time of men's talk and women's silence, no official dialogue took place within the church regarding the supremacy of men and the inferiority of women with respect to the gifts of the Holy Spirit and abilities in leadership and service. The situation was more of a social contract than anything else.

Why then has the issue of the participation of women in church leadership emerged now? Why not continue to live peacefully in the church and accept historical practices without considering them marginalizing for women or a violation of their human rights? Why should women knock on a door that men have kept closed for two thousand years, while they honed the practice of authoritarian leadership unchallenged and learned the principles of rhetoric?

An even more serious question concerns whether it is not contrary to the spirit of the Bible and to the will of God for women to participate in church leadership. Is it not clear that women ought not to teach in the church?

We hear these questions many times. They are asked as if to shock the conscience of women who think that they are called to leadership and seek an equal opportunity with men to share and to give. In open evangelical churches, we are often told that there is no theological or biblical reason that prevents women from participating in church leadership. The absence of women leaders is blamed on cultural and social necessity. Churches surrounded by an Islamic culture feel the need to comply with other Eastern churches in their leadership structures. If women were to participate in their leadership, these evangelical churches would be even more isolated in their society. This is just one example of the psychological, spiritual, and social pressures that face Christian women who are called to service in the Christian East.

It is axiomatic that the church exists in a world in which social and political ideologies are intertwined. It is a world in which the logic of power dominates; a world in which the strong have all the rights and the weak all the duties. Naturally the church is affected by the society around it. However, it is the church, not the society, that should have the stronger effect.

But social attitudes and the power struggle between the weak and the strong in church communities are not the only reasons women have been denied the privilege of decision-making roles in the church; it has also been claimed that the Bible declares that it is God's will that women not participate in church leadership, especially in a priestly capacity. Throughout history, all attempts by women to use their leadership capacities in the church have been suppressed on the basis of what the apostle Paul said in places like 1 Timothy 2:12.

Throughout its history, the Christian church has embraced doctrines that have become rooted in our consciousness and our expressions of faith without checking their validity or studying their origins. In both the East and the West, we have inherited traditional interpretations of the sayings of the apostle Paul that are planted deep within our stony hearts, and we have passed these on as an inheritance to those who came after us or who are affected by our teachings. We have all heard them: according to the apostle Paul, women are quicker than men to fall into temptation. Just look at Genesis to see the example of Eve. Paul stressed that women have to obey their husbands and submit to a man's authority and leadership. A wife's promise to obey her husband is a part of the marriage vows.

But the church, and the society, also has a double standard in regard to women. For example, in patriarchal societies, where men are the supreme leaders, it is frequently said that women or mothers are the supreme authority in raising men. In spite of this, every time women claim the right to equal opportunities with men, the church rises to remind them of what the apostle Paul said. We have inherited a traditional interpretation of the writings of the apostle Paul and act accordingly.

But what if we were wrong in our understanding of what Paul meant and the circumstances he was addressing? More than twenty-five years ago, I asked Bishop Kenneth Cragg what we should do with Paul's attitudes toward women. He replied, "We have to correct Paul with Paul." In other words, we have to understand the whole of Paul's teaching. We must not take one aspect of his teaching and present this unique philosopher as a man with a split personality when it comes to attitudes and concepts, leading him to hold contradictory positions. This great Christian thinker who skillfully outlined the elements of the Christian faith was not a muddled thinker. We need to learn how to read Paul and understand his intentions by studying the historical, social, and ecclesiastical context in which he wrote to various churches.

HISTORICAL PROFILES ILLUMINATE REALITY

Throughout the history of Christianity, and especially in the second half of the twentieth century, many Bible scholars have debated the apostle Paul's attitude to women. Some claim that women were given great dignity in the gospels and that Paul was the one who reduced their status. Bristow quotes Herbert J. Muller's *Freedom in the Ancient World* as saying that Paul took the story of Eve in Genesis very literally and that his words about men and women being equal in Christ were merely uttered "in passing."[2] Others insist that in Galatians Paul reveals his central convictions, and claim that

> he was not a believer in the inferiority of women. He did not advocate a secondary role for women in the Church. He did not teach some notion of a divine hierarchy with husbands ruling over their wives.[3]

Yet, can it be correct to say that the church throughout history has been wrong in interpreting what the apostle Paul said regarding women, especially since the church fathers paid great attention to his words? They interpreted them and explained their meaning, arriving at a view that was similar to that of Jewish religious leaders. They held that Eve was the source of sin and evil because it was she who was deceived and ate the forbidden fruit and gave it to her husband. According to Tertullian, even though the disobedience of Eve was paralleled by the obedience of the Virgin Mary, women still bear the shame of the original sin and have to atone for it.[4] Many other church fathers showed similarly unjust attitudes toward women as human beings when they discussed the story of the fall in Genesis 3.

Women are an essential part of the church. They have offered practical service and participated in the life of the church since before the day of Pentecost. They were part of Jesus' life and ministry and some accompanied him during the three years of his public ministry and continued permanently in the community of faith. None deny this. What does need to be discussed is the role of women when it comes to leadership in the priestly ministry of the church; that is, women being called to positions of leadership and ordained for pastoral service and ministry of the sacraments. Women have been excluded from these roles throughout the centuries, and their exclusion has been presented as if it were the will of God. In other words, it is said that it was God who planned to exclude women from priestly ministry and so set guards to prevent them from entering the holy of holies.

The topic of women's participation in church leadership or their prevention from doing so has evoked varying reactions for more than half a century. The sometimes-heated debate has generated extreme attitudes that have blurred the issue, for the subject was often not studied objectively, nor was there examination of the real source or authority—the life and practice of the Lord of the church, Jesus Christ.

The question that must be answered is this: Was the divine plan really to prevent

---

[2] John Temple Bristow, *What Paul Really Said About Women* (San Francisco: Harper Collins, 1988), 1.

[3] Ibid., 2.

[4] Myrtle Langley, *Equal Woman* (Southampton: Marshalls, 1983), 65.

women from entering the holy of holies, or is women's exclusion due to social circumstances that have existed since the dawn of the church? This is the question we will try to answer in this chapter. But before doing so, we will consider the social position of Middle Eastern Christian women or Arab Christian women.

It goes without saying that it is not easy to speak theologically about the leadership role of Christian women and their equal responsibility to men in a church that has risen and exists in a rigidly patriarchal society, a church in which civilizations have overlapped, a church that has been affected by majority cultures that have historically restricted women and defined their roles as being either a daughter, a wife, or a mother. This framework is difficult to escape.

WHAT IS THE SOCIAL REALITY?

Men and women are the two cornerstones of human society and the two poles of human society. They are equal in importance and indispensability. Men and women differ in their profiles and in some biological functions, and it is natural to preserve this distinction.

The social customs that distinguish what men do from what women do vary from one community to another. However, throughout history most societies have assumed that women work inside the home while men work outside it (although for every rule there is an exception). Biology and tradition probably account for this distinction in roles.

Biologically, women's bodies dictate that they are the ones who get pregnant, give birth, and breastfeed their children. These activities inevitably restrict their freedom of movement. Such restriction may be a healthy social necessity as women participate in the making and sustaining of life.

While women were constrained by childbearing, men historically provided the economic necessities of food, clothing, and housing. To obtain these things, they had to move around freely outside the home. We should appreciate what they have provided.

But we may want to consider whether men's freedom of movement has tempted them to guard that freedom and to keep women at home, even when there was no health-related or human necessity for the woman to be there. This type of power struggle is an old human sin. What starts as a healthy way to meet social and human needs solidifies into a rigid social structure.

Arab Christian women experience yet another stronger and deeper cultural pressure, namely their existence within first Jewish and then Islamic cultures in the Middle East.

Three major religions—Judaism, Christianity, and Islam—arose in the Middle East. These religions all speak to the supposed roles of women. Thus before embarking on our analysis of what the Old and the New Testaments have to say about the role of women, we need to consider the role and status of women in the other two religions.

This is particularly important for Arab women, for since the seventh century the Middle Eastern church has existed in a culture where the teaching of Islam has played a powerful role in women's lives and service.

WOMEN IN ISLAM

Here we cannot deal with the position of women in Islam at any length, but will have to restrict our focus to the effect Islam has had on the church's practices. Moreover, before beginning we must also note that it is wrong to generalize about even Arab societies. The position of women in Lebanon, for example, is very different from their position in Syria, Egypt, Tunisia, Saudi Arabia, or the Gulf states.

Ever since the publication of a pamphlet entitled *Our Women in the Shari 'a and Society* by Tahar Haddad in Tunisia in 1929, the winds of change have been blowing. Dr. Kamal El Saghiri had this to say:

> El Haddad laid the foundations for social reform by confronting two social scourges: discrimination against workers and discrimination against women. Tunisian society grew to achieve its ambition of independence. The first sign of this growth was Tunisian women obtaining a system of laws that is unique in the Arab and Islamic world. A code of personal status system was enacted that limited the number of wives a man might have and made divorce subject to a judicial process. It promoted real equality between men and women in all spheres (education, work, entertainment, making decisions in difficult life situations . . .), and in enjoying all civil and political rights.[5]

El Saghiri added that general associations of women to promote development "aimed at stressing the role of women and confirming their special focus on establishing the bases of the three main elements for sustainable development: the human element, the economic element, and the environmental element." While the situation in Tunisia is unique, it would be very good if it could be generalized to all Arab countries.

By contrast, in Saudi Arabia, women are denied active participation in public life; they do not vote in elections and very few of them work in public jobs or participate in any way in nation building. Women may not appear outside the house unless accompanied by a man, whether a husband, father, or brother, even in cases of emergency. A book entitled *Girls of Riyadh* describes police being called to a university cafeteria, where a female medical student is drinking coffee with a male classmate. The male student is beaten and humiliated, and the father of the girl is summoned to accompany her. The two students are prevented from talking to each other again.[6] This novel reveals the

---

[5] This comes from a paper delivered by Kamal El Saghiri to the Conference on Arab Reform Issues: Vision and Implementation, in Alexandria, 2004.

[6] Rajaa al-Sanea, *Girls of Riyadh* (New York: Penguin, 2007). Translation of *Banat El Riyadh* (Beirut: Dar El Saky, 2006).

reality of the struggle that women face. Their biggest fear is not finding a husband, for marriage is their only legitimate way to gain access to society. This is just one example that shows the deep need for change and development in the circumstances of Arab women—what is available to them and what is forbidden.

In Syria and Egypt, women play a variety of roles and have long participated in political life. They are involved in elections, vote, and have stood for office. Women have been appointed to cabinet positions where they are in charge of higher education and social affairs, and other women have been given prestigious appointments as ambassadors. In Lebanon the situation is quite different. Though Lebanese women are highly educated, they have only recently been able to participate in political life.

At this point I want to make brief mention of women's rights in Islam. In the introduction to *Women's Rights among the International Conventions and Political Islam*, Omar Alaqrai writes:

> This study is an outcome of an essential problem in regard to the principles of human rights in the Arab and Islamic world and the degree of compatibility of women's rights as stated in the international conventions with those upheld by contemporary Islamic movements in the Arab world. . . . Within this framework, religious currents in the Arab and Islamic world try to establish the idea of inequality in the field of religion and customs. Men and women in these societies are convinced about and content with these customs, and on this level they are enjoying the human rights they deserve. International laws and conventions were established on the basis of ideas about human rights in Western societies where equality is the norm, and they seek to impose these on other peoples on the grounds of natural and human law. Islamic thinkers regard this as a kind of cultural invasion that follows intellectual colonialism directed by the political and economic ambitions of Western countries.[7]

This book from which that quotation comes reflects Sunni Islamic thought. Omar Alaqrai compiled it because he recognized that there was some controversy among Islamic groups regarding women's rights. While he does not underestimate the seriousness of the controversy, he insists that it is not enough to cause division because these differences do not represent essential disagreements.

At this point I would like to remind readers that there is an important reason for discussing the status of women in Islam here, for the Middle Eastern church is a minority group and as such it has chosen to conform to the surrounding culture in many aspects of its social life. A minority that wants to live peacefully, securely, and freely must align itself and its general practices to general social norms. Obviously, the Middle Eastern

---

[7] Omar Alaqrai et al., *Women's Rights among the International Conventions and Political Islam*—6, Human Rights Debates (Cairo: Cairo Institute for Human Rights Studies, 1999). This book is part six of a compilation of human rights debates published by the Cairo Institute for Human Rights Studies.

church has maintained a lot of the distinctives of its faith. At the same time, there is still a real clash when it comes to societal norms.

In what follows, I will deal with women's rights in traditional Salafi Islamic thought, in modern Islamic movements, and in the thought of the pioneers of revival and reformation.

Though Islamic thinkers, both men and women, constantly reiterate that Islam gave women a dignity they had previously lacked, there are some essential issues in which Islamic teaching undermines women's rights. These include issues of guardianship, marriage and social rights, polygamy, and women's political, legal, and economic rights.

Traditional Salafi Thought

Salafi thinking on the principle of guardianship is based on verse 34 of Surat an-Nisa (Qu'rān ch. 4; Ar., *Sūrat an-Nisā'* ["the Women"]) in the Qu'ran, which states that "men are the protectors and maintainers of women." According to Ibn Kathir this means that a man rules over a woman and is to discipline her if she strays, because men are superior to women. Thus both prophethood and rulership are restricted to men, in accordance with the saying that those who appoint a woman as their ruler will not prosper. As a consequence of this, women are not allowed to move, travel, or leave the house without their husband's permission, for their status is like that of a slave or captive. Ibn Kathir adds that it is permissible to beat a woman who disobeys her husband.[8]

This traditional interpretation of verse 34 leaves the door wide open for men to treat women as slaves, who are despised and seen as less than fully human, thus denying the precious gift of humanity that God gives to every person, both male and female.

When it comes to marriage and social rights, most Salafi scholars agree on a woman's right to get married according to her choice. However, women are not given the same right as men when it comes to quitting a marriage by divorce. The reasons the right to divorce was given only to men are, first, because Sharia (Ar. *sharī'ah*) law requires the husband to support his wife and children and give his wife a dowry, and second because women are supposedly inherently vulnerable, despite whatever wisdom they may seem to have. If the power to divorce were in their hands, they would use it poorly.

Women are also commanded to wear a veil and not to mix with men or leave the house. Mohammed is reported to have said, "The woman is Awrah, so when she goes out, the Shaitan seeks to tempt her."

Regarding the veil, Omar Alaqrai says that a writer who was a contemporary of the Prophet "increased the separation of women from men. He prohibited even shaking hands with women." Muhammed's wife Aisha is said to have declared that the prophet

---

[8] Ibn Kathir as summarized by Al Bukhari.

accepted women's oaths of allegiance verbally and did not touch the hand of any women who did not belong to him.[9]

Whatever our attitude toward modest clothing for both women and men, it seems extreme to treat women as if they are a commodity that is so attractive that it must be handled with care. There are many pious Muslim women who do not wear the veil, and whose loyalty to Islam is not in doubt.

As for polygamy, based on verse 129 of Surat an-Nisa, both ancient Islamic scholars and contemporary Salafi scholars accept that polygamy has been a feature in Islam from its beginning. There are differences regarding the interpretation of this verse, but it is generally agreed that the key issue is being just to all wives. Some say that the impossible standard set in this verse is absolute justice in love, materially and morally. Thus, although it is permissible to marry four women, "if you are afraid that you cannot be just, marry only one wife." The focus here is on the material justice that an ordinary Muslim can accomplish if he treats all his wives equally in regard to food, clothing, housing, and spending the night with them.[10]

Polygamy is unacceptable in Christianity. It deeply affects human value in marriage and makes a woman an unequal partner. Moreover, while Muslims continue to accept the right of polygamy, the right to equal treatment has been reduced to a purely material level, and true equality is the exception. This is always the case when two sets of rights clash: one is upheld and the other is dismissed.

As regards political rights, all Salafi thinkers hold that women are not allowed to govern in the political sphere or to hold any position that gives them authority over men. These views are based on a saying attributed to the prophet Muhammed, "Those who appoint a woman as their ruler will not prosper."[11] It is common knowledge that women have been denied the right to participate in politics in most Islamic and Christian cultures. However, historically more than one Muslim woman has had a leading role in Islamic and non-Islamic countries, and those countries have prospered. This raises the question of whether this particular saying reflects a particular social context.

When it comes to legal rights, Salafi scholars and thinkers refer to verse 282 of Sura al-Baqara (Qu'rān ch. 2; Ar., *Sūrat al-Baqarah* ["the Cow"]) in giving women fewer rights than men before the law. It seems that one of the few legal rights women enjoy as citizens is the right to complain when they are hurt. These reduced rights are attributed to the prophet's saying that women are incomplete in mind and religion.[12]

Both early and recent scholars agree that women have many financial rights in Islam. They have the right to dispose of their dowry and the money they earn from their inheritance. They have the right to trade and the right of financial disclosure

---

9 Alaqrai et al., *Women's Rights*, 19.
10 Ibid., 20.

11 Ibid., 21.
12 Ibid.

independent of their husbands, fathers, or brothers.[13] On the basis of verse 11 in Surat an-Nisa, Islamic scholars unanimously agree that women receive half of the inheritance men receive. This allocation is justified by the argument that men have to spend money on a woman, but nevertheless this division of an inheritance represents inequality in the economic rights of men and women.

We can summarize women's rights in Salafi thought as follows: a woman is a valuable human being in herself, but she is not equal to a man when it comes to social, political, legal, and economic rights.

Salafi scholars tend to base their interpretations of texts on the opinions of early interpreters without further consideration. Their understanding of the status of women is derived from the verses dealing with guardianship and the Prophet's statement that women are incomplete in mind and religion. The opinions that are cited were influenced by women's isolation from the society at that time, and the absence of any urgent need to give women rights commensurate with their role in society.[14]

Such thinking is in complete contradiction with women's rights as set out in the Universal Declaration of Human Rights and also ignores women's achievements in contemporary life.

Modern Islamic Movements

Although modern Islamic movements like the Muslim Brotherhood in Egypt, the Islamic Group in Tunisia, and some leaders in Sudan are in broad general agreement, their thinking does diverge on some issues. While avoiding the opinions of extremists in these groups, it is possible to identify the following four trends:

- Modern Islamic movements are in line with traditional Salafi thought as regards the inequality between men and women. However, they offer new justifications for this inequality, confirming the urgent need for diligence in addressing this issue.
- Modern Islamic thought does not support polygamy and prefers monogamy; however, it does not dare advocate an end to polygamy, limit it openly, or issue laws to prevent it.
- Modern Islamic thought has devoted much attention to the issue of working women, women's economic role, and their participation in various fields. This change in emphasis may be due to economic realities and social developments. However, these views have had little impact on traditional thinking.
- Some modern Islamic thinkers resort to generalizations in an attempt to evade facing these issues directly.[15]

---

[13] Ibid., 22.
[14] Ibid., 23.

[15] Ibid., 34.

Pioneers of the Islamic Renaissance and Reformation

Some of the pioneers of the Islamic Renaissance and Reformation between the middle of the nineteenth century and the end of the twentieth century had strong views on women's issues.

Jamal al-Afghani

Jamal al-Afghani was one of the nineteenth-century leaders of religious reformation. From an early age, he called for intellectual freedom and the pursuit of science. He also called for women's education so that they too would be enlightened by the sciences and arts. He saw that teaching women amends their piety. It is reported that he once said that women are equal to men in mental capacity, so it is not true that a man has a full opinion and a woman has a half opinion. He attributed the disparities between men and women to the different levels of education afforded them. However, in spite of al-Afghani's openness toward women, he did not favor full equality and resisted those who advocated it.[16]

Rif'a al-Tahtawi

Rif'a al-Tahtawi believed that women can be as qualified as men and are fully equal to men in carrying out duties, if they are given the opportunity. He fiercely advocated for women's right to education, despite much opposition from those who believed that women were incomplete in mind. He regarded the lack of education for women as a custom that must change. In spite of the widespread polygamy of his time, he believed that religion called for monogamy—another position that set him apart from Salafi scholars. Tahtawi also supported the idea of women working, relating it directly to their education. In his opinion, educating women so that they could be usefully occupied was of great economic importance.[17]

Muhammad Abduh

Muhammad Abduh was a friend of science and called for research into the mysteries of the universe, respect for established facts, and reliance on them when it came to self-education and the reform of work. He believed in complete equality between men and women in all rights and duties. He made the customs of society and what people were accustomed to his point of reference as regards rights and duties. Believing that the principle of guardianship was rooted in strength and money, he argued that it would be eliminated once women had the opportunity to work and earn an income. He also called for the abolition of polygamy, saying that the prerequisite for polygamy is justice, which is lacking in polygamous households. He argued that men's mistreatment of their

---

[16] Ibid., 27–36.

[17] Ibid., 38–39.

wives in such households gave the authorities good grounds to prohibit it; and so do the jealousy and hatred that arise among the children of different mothers.[18]

Tahar Haddad

Tahar Haddad's views have already been mentioned. He said that "Islam has not issued a final judgment regarding women's rights" and so encouraged keeping pace with the evolution of society and human needs.

Haddad argued that the Qu'ranic verse permitting marriage to four wives is simultaneously the verse that prohibits polygamy, for it is not possible to treat several women with perfect justice. If it were not for the fact that polygamy was an established custom and that change needed to be gradual, this verse would have been interpreted as favoring prohibition, rather than granting permission.

Regarding women's testimony, Haddad questioned the validity of the saying that the testimony of women is worth only half the testimony of men.

Haddad considered that a veil not only limited women's physical freedom but was also psychologically harmful. He saw the statement that "the veil was commanded to avoid immorality" as a serious slur on women, implying that women are inherently immoral and that the veil is what prevents them from acting on their desires. He dismissed this idea as ridiculous and declared his respect for unveiling that is accompanied by decent dress and morals.

Haddad stressed the importance of women's education, even if they were to stay at home, since they need education in order to raise their children well. According to him, education is more than just learning and involves impressing principles into a person's character until they are firmly lodged there. This process starts when the person is a child, when his or her parents are good examples in word and deed.[19]

All the pioneers of the Islamic Renaissance and Reformation saw educating women as a move toward equality, which they all favored despite accepting the arguments supporting practices like guardianship that upheld inequality. Haddad surpassed all the others in his acceptance of the idea of full equality between men and women. However, even though he identified and rejected the provisions that harm women and hinder equality, he could offer no alternative within the bounds of Islam.

The opinions of these pioneers were all presented in the form of general speeches. There were no detailed discussions about what they would mean in practice, which meant that they remained little more than words on the page.[20]

Mahmoud Mohammad Taha

Mahmoud Mohammad Taha was active in Sudan, where he founded the Republican Party in 1945. As a republican he supported full equality between men and women,

---

[18] Ibid., 40–41.
[19] Ibid., 41–46.

[20] Ibid., 48.

which is consistent with all the conventions of human rights and women's rights. He endeavored to reach the root of the problem of inequality, which lies in the text of the Qu'ran, and suggested an approach that was consistent with the spirit of religion and the needs of the times. However, the receding of republican thought in Sudan reduced the spread of his ideas to other countries.

Mahmoud Taha argued that women have a responsibility to act in order to achieve equality. Equality is not something to be granted; it is a right that must be seized. So he advocated that women should qualify themselves with the understanding that supports their rights and reject attempts to impose guardianship in the name of religion.[21]

Prominent Women

In her book *Behind the Veil*, Sanaa al-Masri points out that it is not easy for women to seize the right of equality. She explores the suffering of Egyptian women since the rise of the Muslim Brotherhood in Egypt, showing how since 1928 (the year in which the Brotherhood was founded) members of the group have confined women and enforced absolute obedience to the ideas of Hassan al-Banna, the founder and intellectual leader of the Brotherhood and its first General Guide. The year in which the Brotherhood was founded was the same year in which women began to attend Egyptian universities in the faculties of medicine, science, and arts, after which they also began to move into the faculties of law, commerce, engineering, agriculture, and the like. Al-Banna strongly disapproved of the women's liberation movement and its claim of equality. He opposed calls for women's independence, freedom of movement, and participation in public life.

Al-Banna called the women who participated in demonstrations for women's rights "the unveiled" and accused those who advocated women's right to vote of wanting to imitate the West. He fought against the right of girls to equal education with boys and called for different curricula for girls and boys in early education.[22]

In the same book, Sanaa al-Masri tells of the bravery of Egyptian women like Doria Shafik, who was among the first generation of female Egyptian university students. She traveled to France to study for a PhD and lived there alone without a *mahram* (or guardian),[23] thus breaking a historical taboo. She also tells of Hoda Shaarawy, who formed the Egyptian Feminist Union in 1932 and entered politics. Doria Shafik, Hoda Shaarawy, Saphia Zaghlul, Esther Wisa, and others in the upper classes fought fiercely, despite the hostility of the Muslim Brotherhood, until women achieved some political rights.

To sum up, we can say that despite the work of the pioneers who advocated women's equality, there is still a need for radical change in women's position in Islam. Though

[21] Ibid., 49–59.
[22] Ibid., 7–8.

[23] Ibid., 10.

history testifies to the fact that some Muslim women have sought for and achieved education and knowledge, with some of them reaching high positions in society, their number is too small. Most women's lives are closer to the situation described in the popular saying: "women are subject to their fathers at birth, to their husband in marriage, and to their sons in old age." Women are seen as created to be subject to men.

Although the Muslim Brotherhood does not dominate Arab society in general, the patriarchal culture has set the foundations of life and behavior and has drawn the lines determining what women can and cannot do.

Dr. Hisham Sharabi has defined the mentality of the patriarchal system as involving an overall authoritarian trend to reject criticism and refuse dialogue in order to impose its own authority. He continues:

> The cornerstone of the patrilineal system is the enslavement of women. Thus this community manifests deep and continual enmity toward women, neglects their social presence as human beings, and resists any attempts to liberate them, even when raising the banner of women's emancipation. A patriarchal community does not know how to define itself as anything other than male. It is a male-dominated community in which there is no function for females but to stress the supremacy and dominance of the male.[24]

Dr. Buthaina Shaaban, a well-known Syrian writer who has held many ministerial positions, devoted a whole chapter in her book on Arab women in the twentieth century to "The Syrian Woman: Reality and Achievement." In this chapter she sets out the constitutional achievements of Syrian women, who now have laws that assist their development and ensure their right to an education that opens the way to employment in various sectors. She notes that the number of female teachers has increased rapidly, reaching 64 percent in some grades. However, the number of female university professors did not exceed 20.75 percent of the total staff in 1990. Then she adds these words:

> Yet this quantitative rise in the number of women in the field of education was not accompanied by a qualitative change in society as a whole. Although getting a better education means that more women are joining the work force and achieving greater financial independence, social attitudes are still underdeveloped. . . . Women have occupied new positions in all fields without a crucial change in their social status in the family.[25]

This leads her to ask whether our focus should be on changing the laws that govern society or on the conditions within the society within which these laws are promulgated. Sometimes even when laws are passed, social opposition leads to their being ignored or repudiated because of a lack of cooperation when it comes to implementing them.

---

[24] Hisham Sharabi, *Al-Nitham Al-Abawi wa Ishkaliyat Takhaluf Al-Mojtama' Al-Arabi* [*The Patriarchal System and the Complications of the Decline of Arab Society*] (Beirut, 2000), 26–27.

[25] Buthaina Shaaban, *Al-Mar'a Al-Arabia fi Al-qarn Al-'ishreen* [*The Arab Woman in the Twentieth Century*] (Damascus: House of Culture & Publication, 2000), 127–29.

In a very important observation that applies to the position of women in all Arab countries, even the most developed, Shaaban says that though we recognize the importance of women's presence in high political positions like the Ministry of Culture and the Ministry of Education in Syria,

> one cannot hope that this small percentage of women will have effective power in the decision-making process. Moreover, when it comes to issues that concern women, the few women in positions where they have some authority are even less effective due to the overt or covert pressure on them to behave like men in order to prove that they are qualified for these positions. Any woman who tries to insert a feminine view into her work is accused of antagonizing men or of trying to sabotage the institution in which she works.[26]

It is worth noting that Dr. Shaaban took a strong stand against Islamic fundamentalists, whom she called "fake Muslims," since the true "fundamentalists" in her opinion are those who adhere to the authentic principles of Islam. This is not done by the fake Muslims, "for killing, mutilating, terrorizing, practicing violence, and accusing others of being infidels are anti-Islam practices."[27] She also accuses them of mixing theology with jurisprudence as the Qu'ran is the source of theology, whereas jurists are human beings who may be right or wrong.

> The fake Muslims proclaim their monopoly when it comes to interpreting the Qu'ran, and wage campaigns of terror against those who disagree with their opinions. . . . They are ready to kill and terrorize in order to impose their own interpretation of the Qu'ran, . . . and these differences increase . . . when it comes to issues related to the rights and duties of Muslim women.[28]

The Arab Islamic culture in which the Eastern church has existed since the seventh century is male-dominated—even if Islam maintains that it has changed the status of women and has given them dignity and rights that have not been available to them before the Islamic era. Thus women generally remain far from equal with men in terms of being recognized as human beings with the same value as men and equal rights and responsibilities. The social customs and legacies of ancient times continue to affect the customs of society, whatever its religious basis.

The proverbs that have been handed down over the years give profound insight into the lowly status of women in society, as Ghassan Khalil and Walid Adbo point out.[29] For example, having an unmarried adult daughter is seen as a calamity, and she herself

---

[26] Ibid., 130–31.
[27] Ibid., 132.
[28] Ibid., 133, 135.
[29] Ghassan Khalil and Walid Abdo, *Huqouq Al-Mar'a—Al-iti-* *faqat Al-duwaliya walthaqafa Al-sha'abiya* [*Women's Rights—International Conventions and Popular Culture*] (Beirut: Shamali and Shamali, 1999), 9.

is not regarded as a full human being, as if marriage is the sign of entrance into full humanity. It is said that "a girl is weak," "when a daughter is born, the threshold weeps for forty days," and "the hiss of a snake is better than the voice of a girl." These and many other proverbs are rooted in the minds of Arab communities. They are repeated without hesitation as if they are divine wisdom from above. Think what such sayings do in the mind of the woman who hears them and what they reflect about the minds of those who quote them.

Discrimination against women and against their rights is a serious social scourge that undermines the humanity of both men and women. Women's rights are trampled and distorted as communities marginalize half their human resources.

The Arab world has, of course, witnessed pioneer women in many periods of time. In his book, *The Arab Women*, Karam al-Bustani says:

> In the period prior to Islam, many women's names emerge as writers and poets who loved to write and discuss poetry. There were female musicians and singers who participated in wars, encouraging, healing, and acting as messengers of peace among the tribes. Also, many women were queens. In the Islamic age, many women emerged who were comparable to men in their courage, religious commitment, and social wisdom.[30]

However great the number of women pioneers is, historians have recorded only a few of their names. For one thing, publishing the work of women writers was prohibited, and so much was lost. Dr. Buthaina Shaaban is quoted as saying,

> Dr. Samy al-Ani and Dr. Helal Nagi explained that a collection of poems by thirty-eight Arab poetesses in three volumes and totaling six hundred pages, edited by el-Merzebani, was lost except for the last fifty-nine pages of the third volume in the eleventh century. This is just one example of the lack of interest in collecting and preserving women's writing.[31]

Women's Constitutional Status

Nassif Nassar's study of the constitutional position of women in Arab state has led him to the following categorization of Arab constitutions.[32]

- *Traditional constitutions* in countries such as Kuwait, the United Arab Emirates, Bahrain, Qatar, Yemen, and Sudan link the rights of women with those of a family. Women are seen primarily as wives and mothers. In all these

---

[30] Karam Al-Bustani, *Al-nisa' Al-Arabiyat* [*Arab Women*] (Beirut: Dar Maron Abbud, 1979).

[31] Ibid., 232.

[32] The information summarized here was first presented as a lecture in June 1985 and then published in *Alwehda* (Unity) magazine. The article was later republished as a chapter in the book *Al-Takfir wal Hijra* [Excommunication and Emigration: From the Heritage to the Second Arab Revival] (Beirut: Dar El Nahar, 1997). Since that time, a number of the constitutions quoted have been amended and Yemen has been unified.

constitutions, the family is the foundation of the society, which is based on religion, morality, and patriotism.[33]

- *Progressive constitutions* in countries such as Algeria, Syria, and South Yemen have a broader perspective. They recognize the existence of educated, cultured, working, and political women as well as the existence of wives and mothers. Women's equal rights as citizens are outlined before there is any mention of family, motherhood, and children. Thus article 31 of the Algerian constitution states that all citizens enjoy equal rights in regard to participation in political, economic, social, and cultural life and article 32 specifies that these rights are also to be enjoyed by Algerian women. The Syrian constitution speaks of the role of the family, and then in article 45 it states:

> The state guarantees women all opportunities enabling them to fully and effectively participate in the political, social, cultural, and economic life. The state removes the restrictions that prevent women's development and participation in building the socialist Arab society.[34]

Article 36 of the proposed constitution for the short-lived People's Democratic Republic of Yemen stated:

> The State shall ensure equal rights for men and women in all fields of life, the political, economical, and social, and shall provide the necessary conditions for the realization of that equality.

- *Compromising constitutions* like those of Egypt and Morocco. Article 11 of the Egyptian constitution reads:

> The State shall guarantee the proper coordination between the duties of woman towards the family and her work in the society, considering her equal with man in the fields of political, social, cultural, and economic life without violation of the rules of Islamic jurisprudence.

Article 8 of the constitution of Morocco has a similar compromise when it says:

> Men and women shall enjoy equal political rights.[35]

Nassif Nassar concludes that Arab constitutions do not agree on one specific view of women's position in society. If these legal documents have such differing views, how much greater is the diversity of opinions among Arabs themselves.

Nassif Nassar did not include Lebanon in any of the categories mentioned above, but he does mention that article 9 of the Lebanese constitution issued in 1926

---

[33] Nassar, *Al-Takfir wal Hijra,* 208.
[34] Ibid., 210, 211.

[35] Ibid., 115.

guarantees that the personal status and religious interests of the population, to whatever religious sect they belong, is respected.

However, article 7 of the Lebanese constitution states:

All Lebanese are equal before the law. They equally enjoy civil and political rights and equally are bound by public obligations and duties without any distinction.[36]

According to Dr. Buthaina Shaaban, Lebanese women have been calling for liberation and opportunities for a free and dignified life since the start of the twentieth century. The Society of the Awakening of the Arab Girl was established in 1914 by famous women such as Ebtehag Kaddora, Amina Hamza, Adela Bihem, Anbara Salam, and others. In the 1920s, the Lebanese scholar Nazira Zain al-Din published her book *Unveiling and Veiling*, which caused an uproar and drew attention at the highest levels since she had undertaken a thorough study of the Qu'ran and declared that the problem lay in the laws issued in the name of Islam, some of which contradicted the spirit of Islam.[37]

Laure Moghaizel, a female attorney, has written about what Lebanese women have achieved since 1949 in the field of legislation. Their gains include recognition of their political rights, equality in inheritance, the right of a married woman to choose her nationality, freedom of movement, and the canceling of punishment for the use of contraception. All this progress was made in the early 1980s. In the 1990s, Lebanese women received legal recognition of their right to own land and be qualified to practice a trade, if their husbands agree. However, all these rights are still less than those required for the Lebanese constitution to be void of all unfair articles regarding women's rights.[38]

Egypt, Syria, and Lebanon were the first Arab countries in which women's movements formed. These movements set out to liberate women from ignorance and illiteracy by gaining the right to education, and then worked for liberty and equality in work, inheritance, marriage, divorce, and the like. The women's movement is still following a difficult path even in the most advanced countries in the region. Arab women who are married to foreigners have been struggling to gain the right to convey their nationality to their children. Arab women are also still subject to laws that deny them the right to custody of their children in the event of divorce. Women endure domestic violence that is accepted by the society and still need their husband's permission to travel, especially if a child is accompanying them. In only a few countries, and that very recently, have women been allowed to run a business on their own. Christian women, of course, suffer the same injustices as every other woman in the society.

This brief survey has outlined the position of women in the society in which the Middle Eastern church has existed since the seventh century. It is a male-dominated

---

[36] Ibid., 8.

[37] Shaaban, *The Arab Woman*, 183.

[38] Laure Moghaizel, *Halat Huqouq Al-Insan fi Lubnan* [*The Status of Human Rights in Lebanon*] (1995), 9–16.

society in which women occupy a subordinate position and rarely share in decision-making. This attitude has, of course, impoverished Arab communities since it has deprived them of the contributions of half their members.

THE POSITION OF JEWISH WOMEN

The church was planted within a Jewish culture in which women did not enjoy equality with men, and so we also need to look briefly at Jewish culture. Only after discussing the Old Testament concept of women will I turn to the New Testament writings.

The *Theological Dictionary of the New Testament* provides the following description of the status of women:

> In spite of traces of an older matriarchate, women in the Old Testament had few rights. They passed from the protection of one male to another. In Levirate marriage they had no legal choice as the males did (Deut 25:5ff.). Wives could not claim the sabbath rest (Exod 20:8ff., though cf. 2 Kgs 4:22ff). They depended heavily on their husband's decisions (cf. 1 Sam 1:5). Polygamy was a heavy burden for them (1 Sam 1:5ff). Stricter fidelity was demanded from them. Yet woman could appear in public life (Gen 24:13ff.). Daughters could inherit property (Num 27:8). Their wishes were to be consulted in marriage (Gen 24:39, 58). They could have enormous influence for good or bad (cf. Sarah, Rebekah, Abigail, and Jezebel), and in a few instances played public roles as prophetesses or national leaders (Deborah). . . .
>
> The rabbinic writings give an unflattering picture of women, portraying them as greedy, inquisitive, vain, and frivolous. Their rights and religious duties were restricted and they were assigned a special place in the synagogues. . . . Yet notes of praise are heard too. Women are said to be an adornment to their husbands and to have equal promise with them before God. Some women could be extolled for their learning or piety.[39]

The entry points out that women also had to deal with polygamy and divorce, which were always in the hands of men.

The *Jewish Encyclopedia* includes an article on the rights of women that discusses these rights under five headings:

- *Paternal power.* The power of the father over his daughter seems to have been almost complete. Though a daughter should not be forced to marry someone, if she was sold as a servant it was expected that she would be married to the person who bought her or to his son. She would have no choice in the matter. This interpretation is supported by Exodus 21:7: "If a man sells his

---

[39] Kittel, Gerhard, ed., *Theological Dictionary of the New Testament, Abridged in One Volume* (Grand Rapids: Eerdmans, 1974), 134–35.

daughter as a servant, she is not to go free as male servants do." If a daughter was employed, her father had the right to her earnings while she was under-age. According to Numbers 30, a father could also cancel a daughter's vows when he learned of them.

- *The right of inheritance.* As in all major civilizations in the past, a daughter had no right to inherit from her father unless there was no male heir.
- *Powers and duties.* A husband had to work for his wife, preserve her dignity, provide for her needs, and look after her. A wife who did not bring a dowry with her was expected to do the work of cleaning, washing, cooking, feeding babies, making beds, knitting or weaving, and so on. If she came with a slave woman, her housework would be lighter. The more slaves she brought with her, the less she would have to work. Yet a husband might still insist that she occupy herself with knitting and weaving. A wife who gave birth to sons had greater status.
- *Opportunities available to a wife.* According to the Mishnah (m. Ned. 4:3), girls could be taught to read the Torah, although they were not given instruction in the oral law.
- *The status of a mother.* The Mosaic law gave mothers more dignity than any other ancient civilization. Honoring both a father and a mother was the first commandment with a promise. The book of Proverbs is full of teachings about honoring and obeying one's mother.[40]

In the 1905 edition of the Hasting's *Dictionary of the Bible,* J. C. Lambert wrote that though a Jewish woman was a companion and helper of a man, she was of lower status and subject to him. Yet the Bible presents Sarah, Rebekah, and Rachel as standing side by side with their husbands, and at the time of the deliverance from slavery in Egypt, Miriam is ranked with Moses and Aaron (Mic 6:4). In the period of the judges, Deborah was prominent not only as a prophetess but also as a judge. The same happened in the days of the kings, where it seemed that Jezebel in the Northern Kingdom had a political role, as had Athaliah in the Southern Kingdom. Lambert also points out that in the days of Samuel, women attended religious feasts and participated in offering sacrifices (1 Sam 1–4; see also Judg 13:20) and praise in the temple (Ezra 2:65).

Thus in spite of the fact that the book of Deuteronomy puts women in a position of complete subordination to men, the rights of Jewish women were recognized and safeguarded. Thus we also find Malachi's statement about God's hatred for divorce (Mal 2:16) and the description of a good wife in the book of the Proverbs.[41]

---

[40] Lewis Naphtali Dembitz, "Woman, Rights of," *JE* 12:556–57.

[41] J. C. Lambert, *Dictionary of the Bible Revised* (New York: Charles Scribner's Sons, 1963), 1041.

Writing in the *Anchor Bible Dictionary*, Phyllis A. Bird describes the Old Testament as

the product of a patriarchal world, and more specifically of a literate, urban elite of male religious specialists. . . . The present form of the Hebrew Bible is the work of male authors and editors, whose views created or reflect the dominant theological perspectives. Women in the biblical texts are presented through male eyes, for purposes determined by male authors. This does not mean that women are necessarily suppressed in the account or portrayed unsympathetically. It does mean, however, that women are not heard directly in the biblical text, in their own voices.

She goes on to say:

The Israelite family was in all periods a male headed household . . . in which descent and transmission of property . . . were reckoned through males. . . . One consequence of patrilineal organization is that women are to some extent either aliens or transients within their family of residence. Married women are outsiders in the household of their husband and sons, while daughters are prepared from birth to leave their father's household and transfer loyalty to a husband's house and lineage.

Bird also points to the great hostility toward foreign women marrying Israelite men. This hostility was rooted in the influence a mother wields. She can affect the attitudes of her husband and, given that she is the main provider of religious education, her beliefs will be passed on to her children.

Another consequence of patrilineal family organization is that women do not normally inherit land. Exceptions treat daughters as placeholders in the absence of sons. (Num 27:1–11)

A daughter did not continue the family name and could not represent her family in the public sphere, as a man could. For this reason, men were given legal authority over the affairs of the family.

A woman worked mainly as a wife and a mother who stayed at home to provide for the welfare of her husband and children while also helping with agricultural production and weaving and sewing clothing for the family. Bird claims that a woman who worked as a midwife (Exod 1:15–21) was regarded as "a religious specialist as well as a medical technician" in ancient Near Eastern cultures. Of course, women were partners with men in worship of God.[42]

Scholars agree that there is no legal record or document setting out in detail the rights of a Jewish woman; thus we cannot say that we have documentary evidence of the experience of women in Judaism. Even those who have studied women's issues in

---

[42] Phyllis A. Bird, "Women (OT)," *ABD* 6:951–957.

Judaism and refer to sources such as the Talmud, the Mishnah, and the like are not sure of how accurate and historical these records actually are.

In the chapter "Jewish Women and Christian Origins" in the book *Women and Christian Origins*, Ross Kraemer refers to Ben Witherington writing in the *Anchor Bible Dictionary* and Monique Alexander, author of *The History of Women in the West*:

> Both sketch a monolithic Jewish society . . . that was highly "patriarchal," confining women primarily to the domestic realm, with little access to any public life. . . . One specifies that Jewish women in Palestine wore veils when they ventured out in public. They agree that menstrual impurity excluded women from synagogue participation and/ or from society for lengthy periods of time, that women could not inherit or initiate divorce proceedings and were married off by their fathers at puberty, with little regard for their own wishes. Jewish men, [Monique Alexander] claims, "maintained a prudent silence with women."

The purpose of this silence was to avoid problems and not waste time that could be better used.

> In the realm of communal religious life, women are similarly envisioned as largely absent. They . . . were exempt from morning and evening prayers, . . . and from pilgrimage to Jerusalem for the three annual festivals. . . . [They were] not obliged to attend synagogue. . . . While in theory, Jewish Law permitted women to read the Torah . . . in communal assembly, in practice they did not, out of "respect for the congregation."

Quoting Witherington, Kraemer says that

> there is no evidence that prior to Jesus' ministry it was possible for women to be disciples to a great teacher, much less travel with such a teacher, or instruct anyone other than children. In such a restrictive context, Jesus' relationship to women must have seemed radical indeed.[43]

This is a short description of how some see the culture into which Jesus of Nazareth, the head of the Christian church, was born. We will talk about the change brought about by his life and mission when we study the New Testament.

We can see many similarities between the lives of women in Arab Islamic cultures and in Judaism. Both cultures were patriarchal; in both, the roles of women were circumscribed and women lived in the shadow of men, with limited freedom. They were economically, socially, politically, and religiously marginalized—despite the great honor accorded to mothers.

---

[43] Ross Kraemer, "Jewish Women and Christian Origins," in Ross Shepard Kraemer and Mary Rose D'Angelo, eds., *Women and Christian Origins* (Oxford: Oxford University Press, 1999), 35–46.

THE POSITION OF WOMEN IN THE ARAB CHURCH

What about women in the Arab Christian church? Does their status and role differ from those of other women? Do Middle Eastern Christian women share the struggle and gains of women's liberation?

Throughout history, Middle Eastern Christian women have suffered because of general attitudes toward women, and they have joined with other women in requesting changes to laws that discriminate against them. Middle Eastern Christian women have joined in national demonstrations; they have been teachers, nurses, and founders of charitable institutions; they have cared for orphans, people with disabilities, and the marginalized; they have been writers, poets, historians, novelists, artists, and media pioneers.

The most difficult challenges they have faced come from within the church, especially in regard to anything that has to do with positions of leadership and decision-making. This was a minefield that women could not enter.

In the church, women learned submission to the church authorities, who taught that women had no right to be partners in leadership. They were taught that this system was commanded by God and was clearly set down in the Bible. Men had been given the leadership of the church and have monopolized it throughout history. We have no official records of women's objection to this monopoly on leadership because they accepted this as the will of God.

In May of 1974, the Middle East Council of Churches was formed. It was the main ecumenical movement and the forum for dialogue between churches. In 1976, the council established a program for women as part of its human rights department. Through this program, it organized studies on the position of women in the church and society. The primary goal was to shed light on what opportunities were and were not available to women to serve in the church and obtain their legal rights.

In the first two years, the program struggled to get on its feet, for many in various churches considered it an "illegitimate" Western import. So in order to avoid misunderstanding of the goals of the program, it was transferred from the department of human rights to the department of education and renewal. Officials then understood that there could be no change or renewal in regard to issues concerning women except through education, or, perhaps, reeducation. Education is the primary tool for renewal.

Since the early eighties the program has held many symposia and conducted many workshops that have included pioneering women from various churches of the Middle East. It has also conducted many courses that qualify women leaders to work in religious education and lead women's groups in the churches. Christian women from all ecclesiastical cultures and from most of the Arab countries (specifically Lebanon, Syria, Egypt, Jordan, and Palestine) have participated in these programs, which have included in-depth courses and presentations by specialists in the history of the church, theology, the Bible, the social sciences, and the like. These symposia have led to the publishing of many books and articles in various journals, as well as annual reports, etc. Here are some examples of publications:[44]

- *Women in the Church and Society of the Middle East* (1979)
- *Women in Church Theology* (1980)
- *Deaconesses in the Church* (1983)
- *Women in Theology: Their Position and Hope* (1994)
- *Women: Their Development, the Harvest of the Years* (1998). Published by the committee of the women's program in Egypt, this book tells the stories of the contributions and activities of women.

The activities of women in local churches increased and many meetings and presentations were held with women from various countries of the world during the Ecumenical Decade of Churches in Solidarity with Women proclaimed by the World Council of Churches from 1988 to 1998.

This decade provided a good opportunity to reach out to the heads of churches in the Middle East to explain the purpose of this decade and to ask for assistance and real solidarity with women in each church. It was an opportunity for Christian women from various countries and cultures to exchange experiences. It also encouraged women to raise their voices and express their desire to serve and their sense of marginalization. The goals of the decade were set out as follows in a pamphlet translated into Arabic through the women's program of the Middle East Council of Churches in 1988:[45]

- Encouraging and facilitating responses to women in their efforts to meet the challenges they face both in their countries and in the churches with which they are affiliated.
- Promoting effective participation of women in leadership and decision-making.
- Giving visibility to women's perspectives and actions in struggles for justice, peace, and unity.
- Helping churches to free themselves from racism, sexism, classism, and all teachings and practices that discriminate against women.
- Encouraging churches to stand in solidarity with women.

The decade gave Christian women a long time to become acquainted with the problems they face, and they showed matchless courage in expressing their feelings

[44] All the works cited are publications of the Middle East Council of Churches.

[45] Special Publications for the Ecumenical Decade—World Council of Churches, 1988.

regarding the injustices inflicted on them within the church. It is, however, very difficult to evaluate the impact of this decade on the thinking of church leaders in the Middle East, as I can illustrate with a personal example.

From 1988 until 1995 I reported on this program. Each year when I presented my report to the education committee, I mentioned the Ecumenical Decade of Churches in Solidarity with Women. Each year some church leaders would react as if this was the first time they were hearing about this decade. There was also some unofficial discussion among the executive committee of the Council about the ordination of women, and it was made clear that this issue should not be mentioned in the women's program. These discussions may have taken place because of global developments at the time, for many churches worldwide, including the Reformed churches in America and the Anglican Church in Britain, approved the ordination of women as priests and a woman even became a bishop. The issue of women's ordination is still controversial among member churches of the World Council of Churches.

However, to be fair, the decade was beneficial to Middle Eastern women—though the issue of ordination was avoided. Regular meetings built close relationships among women from various churches, local and regional. Women prepared many reports that were presented to their churches. Even though few of the suggestions have been implemented, some changes have started to appear in the life of women within the church. Women now serve on most church committees and have represented their churches at global conferences. They have been admitted to theological institutions as students and as lecturers, and they have written on many theological, biblical, and pastoral subjects.

DEVELOPMENTS IN THE PROTESTANT CHURCH

It is now time to look more deeply at the concept of service and women's participation in leadership in Protestant churches in the Middle East.

There are various Protestant groups in Lebanon and Syria. Some of these groups are fundamentalist and conservative, while others are more open in regard to civic matters and religious issues. In conservative churches, women's ordination is out of the question. Women cannot assume any leading role in these churches, and may not even pray aloud during public worship.

We will thus focus our attention on what are known as the Reformed churches, which grew out of missionary work done by the Reformed churches in North America and Europe. In these churches, women enjoy freedom of movement and speech.

The library of the Near East Faculty of Theology in Beirut contains a booklet reporting on the first conference of Protestant women, which was held in Dhour El Choueir from 28 June to 2 July 1939. The introduction of this booklet reads as follows:

The Protestant church still has a mission to accomplish in our East. We cannot ignore the apathy and weakness we sense due to the corruption, temptations, and lack of faith that have seeped in from the world to paralyze our spiritual growth and weaken the power of principles. Thus some zealous women have sought to hold a conference that gathers all the women of Protestant denominations in order to study the church's current state, the reasons for its weakness, and the means of reviving and developing it by acquiring the spirit of simplicity and strong faith. Women need to revive the church spiritually and socially.[46]

In the Near East School of Theology in Beirut, for example, women have the same right as men to engage in theological studies and be qualified for service in the church. There is open biblical discussion about women's participation in decision-making and leadership. Although the majority of the female students specialize in Christian education, a few study theology and are able to respond to a call to ministry at any time. It is also worth mentioning that in the Presbyterian churches of the Synod of Syria and Lebanon, women have been ordained as elders for the past fifty years. Women elders are now found in all the larger churches in the cities of Syria and Lebanon. Moreover, within the last decade the synod has authorized one woman to preach and other requests are being processed.

In Egypt, however, Protestant women are experiencing difficulties. The Egyptian church is one of the largest Arab churches in terms of numbers. Women have long been active in the church there, and many respected women have served diligently and sacrificially. Egyptian women were in fact pioneers in demanding opportunities for service and leadership in the church.

However, Egyptian society is patriarchal, and its spirituality is still very conservative, far more so than that of Syria and Lebanon. More than thirty years ago, two women were ordained as elders in the Synod of the Nile, but were eventually prevented from serving in this capacity. Those who are familiar with the activities of the Evangelical Women's Association in Egypt salute the Egyptian women for their achievements in the field of social services and their commitment to serving the evangelical faith. In recent years there has been some progress, with women once again being allowed to be appointed as elders and be involved in service and decision-making.

Those who take note of what is coming out of the Dar Al Thaqafa publishing house know that the Synod of the Nile has maintained the traditions of the early church fathers in Alexandria, who worked diligently to systematize the Christian faith. Rev. Dr. Samuel Habib has written on women in the church and in society and explored historical developments with regard to women from cultural and biblical perspectives. In the conclusion to his book, he has this to say:

---

[46] *A'mal Al-Mu'tamar Al-Nisaa'i Al-Ingeeli Al-Awal* [*Activities of the First Evangelical Women's Conference*, original translation].

Since the curtain of the temple was divided, no one has remained in the outer court. Men and women alike have had the boldness to enter into the Holy of Holies and to come before the throne of grace without any distinction.[47]

Habib called on men to understand women better and on women to live out their role biblically, being accountable to God and society for carrying out their roles to the best of their abilities.[48]

It is worth mentioning that for roughly a decade Presbyterian women in the United States of America have given money to the Evangelical Women's Association in Egypt to assist a program for the theological education of women in Egypt. This money has been used to provide training for many women. There are thus a number of theologically trained women in both Lebanon and Egypt who are capable of responding to a call to church leadership at any time.

These developments have also contributed to awakening a sense of responsibility in Arab Christian women who had felt that they would never be able to contribute to church leadership.

On a worldwide scale, many women have been ordained in many Reformed and Anglican churches. In the Lutheran and Anglican churches, there are already a few female bishops. Today there are female priests in North America, most European countries, Australia, and Africa. We have never heard that they are any less effective than men serving in the same capacity.

In July 2006, Presbyterian women in the United States celebrated the centenary of the office of deaconess, the seventy-fifth anniversary of the ordination of women as elders, and the fiftieth anniversary of the ordination of women to full pastoral service. Yet the Presbyterian Church in the United States was not the first church to accept women in pastoral service. Will the Middle Eastern church follow the example of the Presbyterian Church in the United States and of others around the world?

It is not surprising that the Presbyterian Church in the United States, which exists in a culture with deep democratic roots, has given American women the opportunity to work and struggle for the position they have today, in which they are able to participate fully in the life and service of the church. However, I must point out that for both men and women, obedience to God's call to serve must take precedence over all cultural, geographic, or other obstacles. If God calls someone to his service, who are we to refuse that service?

In the past, we used to divide theology into systematic theology, biblical theology, and practical theology. During the second half of the twentieth century, liberation theology and feminist theology were added to that list. Liberation theology stresses

---

[47] Samuel Habib, *Al-Mar'a fi Al-Kaneesah al-Mujatam* [*Women in the Church and Society*] (Cairo: Dar Al Thaqafa), 129. [48] Ibid., 131.

the idea of human freedom and insists that the freedom Jesus Christ offers is a spiritual, intellectual, and political freedom that confronts injustice, marginalization, and poverty. Feminist theology explores the issues of women's liberation as independent, complete human beings equal to men. However, for many years feminist theology has been misunderstood and equated with international movements for women's liberation, which has led to it being referred to in negative and sometimes humiliating terms.

I have selected some ideas from a study presented by Dr. Isabel Rogers to the Presbyterian Women's Association of the United States.[49] She begins by citing a definition published by Catholic theologian Leonard Swidler in his article, "Jesus Was a Feminist," published in the magazine *Catholic World* (1971):

> By a feminist is meant a person who is in favor of, and who promotes, the equality of women with men, a person who advocates and practices treating women primarily as human persons (as men are so treated) and willingly contravenes social customs in so acting.

This is a perfectly good definition that can be applied in feminist theology. But why do we need a feminist theology? Isabel Rogers answers that question as follows:

> The answer lies in our history in the Church. Throughout most of the previous two millennia our theologians have indeed excluded and denigrated women to such an extent that not too long ago Sarah Bentley and Claire Randall could write that "theology was the (often) silent partner in the oppression of women by organized religion." For the teachings of the great theologians of the past on the subject of women—mostly negative—inevitably seeped into the thinking of the Church's leadership, and they subliminally shaped attitudes toward women that linger even today. . . .
>
> The Christian theological tradition begins, of course, with the Bible. Both Hebrew and Graeco-Roman societies were male-centered and male-dominated; women most often did not count as persons to be taken seriously. Most of the Biblical documents reflect this male focus.[50]

Rogers then turns her attention to the attitudes toward women of those she calls "the giants of our theological history" who "shaped our thinking about God and humanity—great doctrines like the Trinity and the Incarnation, Original Sin and Atonement." She identifies two recurring themes in their writings:

- Women are not quite as human as men—they do not directly reflect the image of God.
- The woman is the source of sin in human life.

---

[49] Isabel Rogers, *Toward a Liberating Faith: A Primer on Feminist Theology* (Louisville: Women's Ministries Program Area, Presbyterian Church [USA], 1999), 1.

[50] Ibid, 3.

Augustine, the great fifth-century theologian who inspired Luther and Calvin, believed,

> A woman does not possess the image of God in herself but only when taken together with the male who is her head, so that the whole substance is one image. But when she is assigned the role as helpmate, a function that pertains to her alone, then she is not the image of God. But as far as the man is concerned, he is by himself alone the image of God just as fully and completely as when he and the woman are joined together into one.[51]

When Augustine said that a man and a woman together are the image of God, I agree with him, since this is consistent with Genesis 1:26–28. Yet I find it difficult to understand the distinction he makes between men and women, and thus I dare to respectfully disagree with the great St. Augustine!

Thomas Aquinas, whom Rogers describes as the "greatest theologian in the Medieval church (and much influenced by Aristotle)" believed that

> woman is a sort of misfit, a freak of nature. There is in her "something deficient or accidental. For the active power of the male seed intends to produce a perfect likeness of itself with male sex. If a female is conceived, this is due to lack of strength in the active power, to a defect in the mother, or to some external influence like that of a humid wind from the south."[52]

I cannot understand the logic behind this. If the only perfect form is male, where do mothers come from? Or are mothers not needed?

Martin Luther believed that women were created for childbearing. John Calvin, however, acknowledged one other possible purpose for women's existence—to make men's lives more comfortable.

As for Tertullian, in the early third century he addressed women in these terms:

> And do you not know that you are Eve?" . . . You are the gate of the devil, the traitor of the tree, the first deserter of divine Law: you are she who enticed the one whom the devil dare not approach; you broke so easily the image of God, man; on account of the death you deserved, even the Son of God had to die.

Many others had the same attitude. Luther, for example, believed that the fall would never have happened had the serpent first approached the man, rather than the woman.[53]

None of these great men were fair to women. It seems that their theology was shaped by the patriarchal culture around them, which they could not shake off.

But in spite of the social circumstances that marginalized women, and even though

---

[51] Ibid.
[52] Ibid., 3, 4.

[53] Ibid., 4.

men were the leaders in most world cultures, and even though the great theologians in history were not fair to women, women have not been silent regarding this injustice. They were not content to be marginalized, but did not know how to resist marginalization given that they were kept in the shadows and deprived of learning and education. Yet throughout history women have cried out for justice, even if they were lone voices crying in the wilderness. We have already spoken of the many Arab and Muslim women who rose up against the reality of prejudice and segregation. Other parts of the world stage offered more fertile ground for women to rise up against discrimination in society and the church.

There are few records of the voices of women in Europe long centuries ago. However, in the eighteenth century, the situation began to change. In 1793, Mary Wollstonecraft published a book in England entitled, *Vindication of the Rights of Woman: With Strictures on Political and Moral Subjects.* And in the nineteenth century the women of the United States rose up and in 1848 held a conference demanding women's rights. They issued a Declaration of Sentiments and Resolutions calling for an end to the "tyranny" of men and for women's right to vote. This document was considered extreme at the time and the women's movement was vilified and mocked. Because those who did this quoted the Bible as the basis of their opinion, Elizabeth Stanton and her colleagues decided to issue a new version of the Bible called *The Women's Bible*, which was finally published in 1895. All these women's movements and the like were preliminaries to the women's liberation movement of the 1970s.

> A 1961 study of the status of women sponsored by the Kennedy Administration, and Betty Friedan's 1963 volume, The Feminine Mystique, helped to open eyes and raise consciousness. The movement for liberation developed rapidly and spread across our nation, with women claiming more and more freedoms and opportunities . . . [and] a total restructuring of the relationship between women and men, moving from domination and submission toward reciprocity and partnership. As Patricia Budd Kepler put it in 1972: "Women in our struggle for freedom do not want to stand against men; we want for the first time since creation to stand beside them and with them."[54]

The idea of liberation has now extended well beyond American borders, crossed the oceans, and met many women who are engaged in the same struggle for equality and dignity. Women are now knocking on all the doors of society and entering the fields of science and work.

In the Levant today, we are still at the beginning of the path to women's liberation, though many women have shown great effectiveness in many spheres. Why then have women not attained similar goals in the church? Does the responsibility for this lie with theologians, the church, or the Bible?

---

[54] Ibid., 5.

THE BIBLICAL REALITY

When exploring the biblical reality, we will look first at the Old Testament and the story of creation and the fall. Then we will turn to some examples that show that, despite their apparent absence from much of the Old Testament, when women do appear they are clearly capable of making a difference and so should not be underestimated.

We will then move on to the New Testament, which is the church's guide to life and conduct. We will discuss the teachings of the apostle Paul regarding women's participation in the church and how his writings have affected the historical practices of the church. This section concludes with an examination of the attitude of Jesus Christ, in whom a Christian woman finds her true identity. His attitude should be the church's guide in its life, attitudes, and practices.

We believe that the message of the Bible liberates women as well as everybody else. We know, too, that the Bible has many times been used to market negative cultural principles that force women into a mold and depict them in a simplistic way that distorts their human value. Often this cultural mold has been used to oppose women's right to demand equality with men and to diminish their participation in the service and leadership of the church. This is because the content of the Holy Scriptures was formulated in a masculine culture and society in which the language used did not surpass the prevailing values—the values that made men alone the standard of real humanity and put women in a secondary, unequal position.

The Old Testament
Creation

We begin in the book of Genesis with the story of God's creation of heaven and earth. All creation came into existence by a word from God: "let there be . . . and there was . . ." The creation process was crowned by the creation of human beings, who were formed in a unique way, quite different from all the rest of creation:

> Then God said, "Let us make mankind in our image, in our likeness, so that they may rule over the fish in the sea and the birds in the sky, over the livestock and all the wild animals, and over all the creatures that move along the ground." (Gen 1:26)

It seems that God had a holy plan to crown creation by creating beings in his image and after his likeness who would bear responsibility for and "have dominion" over the whole creation. Thus God appointed a steward over all creation. Stewardship here is a blessing that should never be forgotten.

> So God created mankind in his own image, in the image of God he created them; male and female he created them. God blessed them and said to them, "Be fruitful and increase in number; fill the earth and subdue it. Rule over the fish in the sea and

the birds in the sky and over every living creature that moves on the ground." (Gen 1:27–28)

God gave human beings the authority to act according to his will in his creation, which means that this authority involves caring for and preserving creation, not exploiting it and oppressing others. After that the Bible says, "God saw all that he had made, and it was very good. And there was evening, and there was morning—the sixth day" (Gen 1:31).

This account ends with the words,

Thus the heavens and the earth were completed in all their vast array. By the seventh day God had finished the work he had been doing; so on the seventh day he rested from all his work. (Gen 2:1–2)

But then in Genesis 2:4 we start again from the beginning:

Then the Lord God formed a man from the dust of the ground and breathed into his nostrils the breath of life, and the man became a living being. (Gen 2:7)

God continued his creation, planting the garden of Eden and putting Adam in it and planting all kinds of trees, with the tree of life in the middle of the garden, as well as the tree of the knowledge of good and evil.

The story of creation continues in chapter 2, where it says that God put Adam in the garden of Eden in order to till it and keep it, and he commanded the man not to eat from the tree of the knowledge of good and evil, for if he did, he would die. Then God speaks again:

The Lord God said, "It is not good for the man to be alone. I will make a helper suitable for him." Now the Lord God had formed out of the ground all the wild animals and all the birds in the sky. He brought them to the man to see what he would name them; and whatever the man called each living creature, that was its name. . . . But for Adam no suitable helper was found. (Gen 2:18–20)

What is going on here? Do we have two different stories of creation? For example, in Genesis 1, God said "Let there be . . . And there was." This process took less time and effort than the account of creation in chapter 2, where God brought all the creatures to Adam for him to name. Yet Adam did not find a helper like him. Were all the animals and birds that Adam named in pairs, while he was alone? This is a good question.

After creating man, God saw that everything was "very good"; however, God adds that "it is not good" for Adam to be alone:

So the Lord God caused the man to fall into a deep sleep; and while he was sleeping, he took one of the man's ribs and then closed up the place with flesh. Then the Lord God made a woman from the rib he had taken out of the man, and he brought her to the man.

The man said,

"This is now bone of my bones
    and flesh of my flesh;
she shall be called 'woman,'
    for she was taken out of man." (Gen 2:21–23)

In his commentary on the book of Genesis, Terence E. Fretheim points out that many scholars believe that the first two chapters of Genesis tell two stories of the creation, one by a priestly writer and the other by a Yahwistic writer.[55] Other scholars consider that the story in chapter 2 was taken from a much longer story than the one recorded in Genesis. What is important is that both stories agree in stressing the principle that God is the creator who deserves all creation to be subject to him.

In his commentary on Genesis, Gordon J. Wenham argues that the first two chapters of Genesis constitute an introduction to the whole book. From the outset, they offer a framework to know who God is and what his relationship to the universe is. Thus these chapters are a key to interpreting not only the book of Genesis, but the whole Bible as well. However, these chapters are more than just a theological statement, they are also a hymn to the Creator in whom and for whom the universe was created.[56]

In discussing the sixth day of creation, Wenham notes that the biblical text identifies the purpose of human existence and our position in God's plan. Genesis affirms that every human being is made in the image of God, and thus the calling of both men and women is to represent God on earth. Secondly, our position in God's plan is to be responsible for all other creatures, caring for them rather than exploiting them.[57]

I do not plan to enter into a discussion of the theories that attribute the content of the book of Genesis to various sources—that is a matter for experts. I cannot but wonder about the apparent differences between the two stories, especially since the second story contains one of the biblical references that is cited to show that women are secondary to men. It is said that because the woman was formed from one of the man's ribs, women are not equal to men in being or in value. Matthew Henry had this to say about God's choice to create Eve from Adam's rib:

The woman was made of a rib out of the side of Adam; not made out of his head to rule over him, nor out of his feet to be trampled upon by him, but out of his side to be equal with him, under his arm to be protected, and near his heart to be beloved.[58]

---

[55] Terence E. Fretheim, "Book of Genesis," in *The New Interpreter's Bible: Old Testament Survey* (Nashville: Abingdon Press, 2006).

[56] G. J. Wenham, "Genesis," in *New Bible Commentary*, ed. G. J. Wenham et al. (Downers Grove, IL: InterVarsity, 1994), 59–61.

[57] Ibid., 62.

[58] Matthew Henry, *Matthew Henry's Commentary on the Whole Bible* (Grand Rapids: Zondervan; HarperSanFrancisco, 1964).

This may well be an over-the-top interpretation of the details of the creation of Eve; however, perhaps the reality of her creation from his side explains God's referring to her as "a helper fit for him."

In his introduction to the Mosaic books in *Peake's Commentary on the Bible*, S. H. Hooke comments on the second story in Genesis 2:4–25:

> The priestly writer had shown man as he is in the purpose of God, what God meant him to be. The Yahwist now proceeds to show in significant symbols the other side of the coin, the constituents of man's nature. . . . [T]he Priestly writer had depicted God as taking counsel with his heavenly court about the creation of man, "Let us make man," . . . but the Yahwist represents man as shaped by Yahweh as the potter shapes his vessel out of clay. Man is formed out of the dust of the earth and informed with the breath of life, breathed into him by Yahweh so that he becomes "a living soul." . . .
>
> The Priestly writer presents male and female as created together in one act . . . but the Yahwist represents man as at first "alone," a state which Yahweh says is not good; he is incomplete without his counterpart; so in one of the profoundest images in the OT, Yahweh builds woman of man's essential stuff. The most intimate human relationship is established, with all its potentialities for good and ill. . . . In the Yahwist's narrative the man gives two significant names to the woman; . . . the first indicates her essential relationship to himself; she is Ishshah [woman] because she has been taken out of Ish [man]; . . . but he gives her a second name, Eve, after the Fall. . . . It is a name of hope; the woman who had been a contributory cause to man's disobedience contains the seeds of life; she is to be "the mother of all living."[59]

I cannot but stand amazed at the great mystery of the story of the creation of human beings. And I cannot see in these stories any grounds for discrimination between man and woman, or any evidence that one of them is given a higher status than the other. In the first brief story, there is complete equality between the man and the woman. God created them both and both received the command to "be fruitful . . . and increase . . . and dominate." There was no functional separation, and God declared that this was very good.

Myrtle Langley states that in the two stories of creation, "man" is the crown of God's creative process. In the first story, "man," both male and female, is in the image of God and after his likeness in that human beings have intellectual and spiritual faculties and powers of communication and self-expression. In this respect they are different from all the other creatures, for they were created to be in a relationship with their creator. They were given authority over other creatures, in that they were to represent God in caring

---

[59] S. H. Hooke, "Introduction to the Pentateuch," in *Peake's Commentary on the Bible* (London, UK: Van Nostrand Reinhold, 1982), 179.

for them and preserving them. Men and women are equal here; neither is superior or inferior. To drive this point home, it is repeated in Genesis 5:1–2.

According to Langley, the second story is traditionally used to interpret human relationships within marriage, perhaps because both Jesus and Paul referred to it in that context. Since in this account the woman was created from the man and for the man, the story has been used to claim that women are inferior to men, as if she were an afterthought, a mere helper or assistant to the man.

Langley refutes those who claim man's priority because he was created before the woman. She points out that in the first story, man was created last of all creation, as its crowning glory. If we follow the same logic, in the second story, Eve is created last and is the crowning glory of all creation, including the man! To those who argue that women are inferior because Eve was taken from Adam's rib, she points out that Adam was made from the mere dust of the ground. To those who dismiss women as mere "helpers," she responds that Adam was incomplete without Eve, and that God himself said that it was not good for Adam to be alone. A helper is not inferior to the one helped, nor does the word imply submission to the one helped. On the contrary, the Old Testament often refers to God as the one who helps his people, the one who saves and rescues them. Thus being described as a "helper" gives the woman the privilege of being a helper and a source of blessing to the man. Men and women are of the same kind, equal and complementary to each other. They were created to be equal partners in an "I-Thou" relationship.[60]

For this reason, Adam's amazement and happiness knew no bounds when he saw Eve. As he said,

> This is now bone of my bones
> and flesh of my flesh;
> she shall be called "woman,"
> for she was taken out of man.

(A natural question here is, Who spoke in the verse that follows, "That is why a man leaves his father and mother and is united to his wife, and they become one flesh"? [Gen 2:24])

In my opinion, neither of the two writers (the Priestly or the Yahwistic) denigrates Eve or sees her as unequal to Adam in terms of human value or social importance—the two are to cleave to one another, and one is not subject to the other. They shared the same nature and were both created by the act of divine will; they were both made by God and both are in his image and likeness.

---

[60] Myrtle Langley, *Equal Woman* (Basingstoke, Hants, UK: Marshall, Morgan & Scott), 26–30.

Therefore I see no evidence that men are superior to women, neither in terms of their being in the image and likeness of God, nor in the responsibilities given to them, nor in terms of their value as a helper. In principle, there is no discrimination in their roles, for any work that does not concern the physical attributes of men or women is a work that either of them can perform. The issue of leadership, however, is not important. Allowing for some slight exaggeration, we might even say that perhaps it is the "helper" who has to take the initiative. This is what we understand from the story of creation.

But why have societies over the ages prevented women from doing many things that they are perfectly capable of doing? Why did communities decide that women belong in the home, and that leaving it is tantamount to disobedience? This decision has left half of society dependent and has deprived the community of the contributions women could make. The answer to this question emerges as we look at the story of the fall and human disobedience to God's commandment.

The Fall

Genesis 1, which tells us that both men and women were created in the image of God in one act, and Genesis 2, which tells of the creation of the woman from the man's rib when God saw that it was not good for Adam to be alone, are followed by Genesis 3, which tells the story of the fall and disobedience. The serpent tempted Eve, persuading her to eat the fruit of the tree from which God had commanded them not to eat and give some of the fruit to her husband to eat. As a result, God expelled Adam and Eve from the garden of Eden into a life of pain and suffering. The way this story has been told, both now and in the past, makes the woman responsible for Adam's disobedience and for humanity's exclusion from happiness in the garden of Eden.

However, Genesis clearly states that after putting Adam in the garden, God commanded him not to eat from the tree of the knowledge of good and evil, on pain of death. Eve, according to the story, had not yet been created. Then, the serpent came to have a conversation with the woman about God's command, speaking to both the woman and the man. The woman took the initiative:

> When the woman saw that the fruit of the tree was good for food and pleasing to the eye, and also desirable for gaining wisdom, she took some and ate it. She also gave some to her husband, who was with her, and he ate it. Then the eyes of both of them were opened, and they realized they were naked; so they sewed fig leaves together and made coverings for themselves. (Gen 3:6–7)

I will not attempt to justify the woman's action since her answer to the serpent shows that she was fully aware of God's command, though she was not present when Adam had heard it from God, according to the first story.

We cannot but wonder about the attitude of Adam, the silent bystander. Earlier, we referred to Martin Luther's belief that if the serpent had talked to Adam, he would have resisted the temptation. Why did Adam stand silent, listening to the dialogue between his companion and the serpent that was "more crafty than any of the wild animals the LORD God had made" without taking the initiative and the lead? Adam knew that this was a matter of life or death, yet it seems that Eve did not have to persuade him to eat the fruit—as he admitted when God asked him, "Have you eaten from the tree that I commanded you not to eat from?"

My understanding of the story is that both the man and the woman, Adam and Eve together, shared responsible for the disobedience. They were both tempted and they both fell into sin. That is why God assigned responsibility for the fall to both of them. Thus I am astonished when I read of a saint like Tertullian describing the woman as the gate of the devil who destroyed the life of man and brought him death.

Even scholars who regard the story of the fall as mythological recognize its importance:

> The myth has in fact affected doctrines and laws that concern women's status in society, and it has contributed to the mindset of those who continue to grind out biased, male-centered ethical theories.
>
> The story of the Fall was an attempt to cope with the confusion experienced by human beings trying to make sense out of the tragedy and absurdity of the human condition. Unfortunately, as an exclusively male effort in a male-dominated society, . . . its greatest achievement was to reinforce the problem of sexual oppression in society, so that women's inferior place in the universe became doubly justified. . . . In a real sense the projection of guilt upon women is patriarchy's Fall, the primordial lie.[61]

The original sin lay in the desire of both the man and the woman to have their eyes opened so that they could be like God, knowing good and evil. I sometimes wonder: Was the sin their desire to be equal with God, or was it their rejection of the reality that human beings are less than God? Perhaps the story of the tower of Babel shows us the reality of human beings' desire to make a name for themselves by building a tower that touched the sky; perhaps this was a real desire to be equal to God (Gen 11).

It is true that the woman seems to be the one who took the initiative (an attribute of a helper) in disobeying God's command; however, she does not seem more enthusiastic than the silent bystander who did not hesitate to participate in breaking a command given to him directly by God.

We must therefore stop regarding Eve as the only one responsible for the fall. The Adam who was with Eve and the Eve who was with Adam chose to test God, as we do today in spite of God's full revelation to us in Jesus Christ. So often our choices flow from desires that are not consistent with the commands of our loving God.

---

[61] Mary Daly, *Beyond God the Father: Toward a Philosophy of Women's Liberation* (Boston: Beacon Press, 1973), 45–47.

In Mary Daly's analysis, I see an attempt to understand the experience of pain in human life. It has been easy to blame all the pain in the world over the centuries on Eve's actions, which brought God's wrath and his curse. This unjust accusation has clung to women, marginalizing their human value and giving them an inferior status to men, while absolving Adam of any responsibility.

God, who knows human nature and who intended us to be free from the cares of life so that we could care for other creatures, needed to teach the first couple a new lesson. Human beings needed to learn that they are responsible for their behavior and that they bear the consequences of the decisions they make. So God did not abandon Eve, Adam, or the serpent without telling them about the kind of punishment they would each have to endure from then on. Where they had once enjoyed fellowship and life in God's presence, they would now suffer the misery of another kind of life; yet that life would not be without hope or new opportunities.

The first natural result of breaking God's command was that Adam and Eve knew that they were naked. They felt shame not only before one another but also before God. So when they heard his voice in the garden, they hid from him. Sin confuses all kinds of relationships.

Adam blamed Eve, saying "The woman you put here with me—she gave me some fruit from the tree, and I ate it." But where were you, Adam, when the serpent talked to Eve who was with you? Were you in agreement with what was said? Did you also want to taste the fruit?

Eve said: "The serpent deceived me, and I ate." This too is a specious argument, for anyone hearing the dialogue between the serpent and the woman would know that the woman was fully aware of God's command and the consequences of breaking it. But her longing for knowledge and the experience of tasting the fruit was stronger than the logic of obedience. Thus she took the fruit, ate it, and gave some to her husband who ate with her. They both did what they wanted to do.

The Punishment for Rebellion

Chapter 3 introduces the serpent simply by describing it as "more crafty than any of the wild animals." Its conversation with Eve is presented as perfectly normal, for the woman was not afraid; what happens seems to be like a chat between two neighbors. The punishment of the serpent is also not important, though one does wonder how the serpent knew about God's command and how the serpent walked. But what is important is that human beings of their own free will chose to disobey a command given to them by God.

Though God had created Adam and Eve and they had always been naked before him, now they hid themselves from him. Neither could deny what they had done, and so each tried to blame the other: "The woman you put here with me—she gave me some fruit from the tree, and I ate it"; "The serpent deceived me, and I ate." We may notice here that if the woman was deceived, Adam was not. And where Adam put the blame on God, the woman put the blame on the serpent. So they hid because of their fear, guilt, and shame.

They were right to feel ashamed, since it was because of their disobedience that their descendants would have to work hard in order to eat, that the ground would be cursed, that thorns and thistles would grow, and that women would suffer the pains of childbirth. Thus the punishment for sin included both human beings and all creation. There was a great need for the glimpse of hope in the promise that the seed of the woman would bruise the head of the serpent (Gen 3:15).

The punishment for sin was universal. However, one of the consequences that fell on the woman, who was originally created to be a helper for Adam, was that Adam the husband would rule over Eve the wife. This is the result of sin and a departure from God's intent as set out in Genesis 2:18–23. Therefore, Adam's ruling over Eve is not a heavenly right given to him from above, nor is abject submission inevitable for women. Building a patriarchal society on the basis of this incident is not in accordance with God's original plan. Its continuation over history is a continuation of the state of rebellion and separation from God.

However, I also wonder about the message of Genesis 3:15–16. Is the promise that the seed of the woman will bruise the head of the serpent intended to eliminate any ambiguity and to make it clear that the consequences of sin will disappear in the fullness of time when the seed of the woman will bruise the devil? I do not doubt it.

At the start of this section, I said that I would give some examples showing women's ability to make a difference, in spite of their general absence from the Old Testament record. Of course, there are stories of women who contributed negatively to life in Old Testament society. Like men, women are human beings who are subject to selfishness, a thirst for power, and sinful inclinations—even if they know that these inclinations are far from God's will. Yet, there are far more male examples of these defects than female ones. Though the Old Testament speaks at length about great men, it still includes occasional references to great and distinguished women.

Miriam, Sister of Moses (Exod 2:2–9)

As a young girl, Miriam stood near the basket among the reeds at the river's brink, watching to see what would happen to her three-month-old brother. When she saw that the daughter of Pharaoh had found the baby and had taken pity on him, Miriam showed wisdom and intelligence as she asked: "Shall I go and get one of the Hebrew women to nurse the baby for you?" Then Miriam went and called his mother. Thus Moses grew up in the house of his family in spite of the law that ordered the death of Hebrew male children. Later, in chapter 15, Miriam is referred to as a "prophet," a title given to very few women in the Bible.

Miriam was a musician, a singer, and a leader whom women followed praising God and celebrating him for rescuing them from slavery in Egypt. Both Miriam and Aaron spoke against Moses after he married a Cushite woman (Num 12), saying, "Has the Lord spoken only through Moses? . . . Hasn't he also spoken through us?" Then the Lord asked Miriam and Aaron to come out to the tent of meeting, and he rebuked them because of their abuse of Moses, saying: "When there is a prophet among you, I, the LORD, reveal myself to them in visions, I speak to them in dreams." Miriam became a leper, and was excluded from the camp for seven days as punishment.

Miriam was a prophet because God made himself known to her as well as to Aaron. So the role of a prophet was associated with a special relationship with God. God, not man, is the one who appoints prophets, and no one can prevent what God wants of a person, male or female. A prophet bears a message from God to the people.

The book of Numbers mentions that Miriam died in Kadesh and was buried there. This is the first time the death of a woman who is not the wife of one of the patriarchs is recorded. It is worth mentioning that we do not have a record that Miriam was married, though in rabbinic tradition she is sometimes said to be the wife of Caleb and mother of Hur.

Miriam is mentioned only a few times in the Old Testament. In addition to her mention in Exodus and in Numbers, there is another mention of her in the book of Micah (Mic 6:4), where she is named with Moses and Aaron as someone sent by God to help his people.

The biblical material gives us few details of Miriam's activities and leadership, but we can make some deductions from what is said about her:

- She was wise and skillful in times of crisis. For example, she knew how to protect her brother and arranged for him to be raised in the bosom of his family.
- She knew how to lead; she sang for the Lord and women followed her.
- She was a prophet, similar to all the other Old Testament prophets except Moses.
- She was obedient in her mission, as were Moses and Aaron.
- Even her brief death record is a sign of her importance in the life of the people.

Given the attitude to women reflected in later rabbinic writings, it is possible that these brief references to Miriam, the prophetess and leader sent from God, were retained because it was not possible to delete them from the Holy Scriptures.

In response to the question of why Miriam alone was punished for an offense that both she and her brother Aaron committed, some argue that because Aaron was the high priest, he could not receive a punishment that involved impurity and isolation.

While this argument may have been understood by the people at the time, it does raise questions about God's justice for modern readers. The most we can say is that for Aaron's contemporaries and the writer of the book of Numbers, the most important issue would have been Aaron's purity as a priest, and so this was the focus of what was eventually recorded.

Other Women Mentioned in Exodus

The book of Exodus refers briefly to a number of women who made a difference in the life of society:

- The two Egyptian midwives who courageously disobeyed the law of the Pharaoh and let the male Hebrew children live because they feared God (Exod 1:15–21).
- Moses' mother (Exod 2), who made a plan to save the life of her son by putting him in a basket in the river. While raising her son, she taught him about the history of his people and established his real identity.
- The daughter of Pharaoh (Exod 2), who acted against the command of her father and raised a Hebrew boy in her father's house. She taught him the wisdom of the Egyptians so he could distinguish between what was fair and what was not.
- The daughters of Midian's priest (Exod 2:16–22), who drew water and filled the troughs to water their father's flock. One of them, Zipporah, became the wife of Moses.

> [She] herself may have been endowed with priestly status. Most suggestive is the passage relaying the events that take place during the journey that Zipporah and Moses make back to Egypt with their son (4:24–26).[62]

These are just a few examples from what was perhaps a longer historical record that the writer of the book of Exodus saw would not serve his purpose, leading him to discard some sections. He could not omit all mention of women who had made a difference, even though, as a man raised in a male-dominated society, he did not see any point in giving more details about these women. But even the brief references to these women and the roles they played are a clear indication of their ability to make serious decisions and their willingness to break any law they considered unjust because they feared God. Such a stance requires more than a little courage and great wisdom. Even in a male-dominated society that marginalized women and kept them in a subordinate

---

[62] Drorah O'Donnell Setel, *The Women's Bible Commentary* (Louisville: Westminster John Knox, 1998), 30–31.

position, there are models of women who were not inferior to men when it comes to bearing responsibility for the family and for society.

With the women of Exodus in mind, I find myself questioning common sayings like "women are incomplete in mind and religion"; "women cannot keep a secret"; and "a nation with a woman as its leader will not prosper." Did any of the women mentioned in the book of Exodus lack wisdom, courage, leadership, fear of God, and the ability to make decisions in hard circumstances?

Of course, the Old Testament includes examples both of great women and evil women. We are all united in our distaste for Jezebel, the bitter enemy of Elijah, the man of God. She promoted Baal worship, honored false prophets and greed, and was a bad influence on her husband. On the other hand, there is also Deborah, the judge and leader of the army, the one who motivated her people to victory. We have also the prophet Huldah who knew how to understand and interpret the law of God and how to rebuke kings for their disobedience to the Word of God. She was unique in offering guidance and advice for renewing the religious community.

Abigail

Another woman we meet in the Old Testament is Abigail, the wife of Nabal, a very rich and foolish man (1 Sam 25). When David and his young men asked for a gift from Nabal in return for their good treatment of his shepherds, Nabal arrogantly refused them anything. David and his four hundred young men set out to take revenge on him. But Abigail had heard what had happened, and so she set out with an escort and gifts to intercept David before he could kill Nabal. When we read about the meeting between Abigail and David, and the way she spoke to him (1 Sam 25:23–35) as if in the spirit of prophecy, we cannot help but bow our heads in respect for her wisdom and understanding in preventing David from avenging himself. How did this meeting affect David? And did this woman give him a new understanding of how to deal with difficult circumstances? Her wisdom surely played a part in developing the character of David, who was considered a man after God's heart.

Abigail planned and spoke in the spirit of prophecy with wisdom, intelligence, and modesty. She knew that people ought to forgive because revenge is for God alone. She put herself in the place of the guilty, though she was not guilty in this matter, saying "On me alone, my Lord, be the guilt" (1 Sam 25:24 ESV). Abigail knew how to discern the will of God as a prophet who bore a message to prevent sin in the life of a man whom God had chosen to lead his people.

Ruth and Esther

Of the thirty-nine books of the Old Testament, only two bear the name of women—Ruth and Esther. The book of Ruth comes after the book of Judges and before the books of Samuel. It has a literary plot of the highest quality.

In her book, *God and the Rhetoric of Sexuality*, Phyllis Trible speaks of it as "a human comedy" in which

> a man's world tells a woman's story. With consummate artistry, the book of Ruth presents the aged Naomi and the youthful Ruth as they struggle for survival in a patriarchal environment. These women bear their own burdens. They know hardship, danger, insecurity, and death. No God promises them blessing; no man rushes to their rescue. They themselves risk bold decisions and shocking acts to work out their own salvation in the midst of the alien, the hostile, and the unknown.[63]

The book of Ruth is one of what are known as the "historical books" of the Old Testament. It is a family story. It tells how three women rearranged their lives after the deaths of their husbands, who had been the sources of their livelihood and identity. Each of them took her own stand, and each made her own decision, although the three of them had a very close relationship. Naomi decided to return to her people and advised her daughters-in-law that each should return to her mother's house and to her people. Orpah decided to do so, but Ruth chose not to return to her mother's house. She would leave her people and go with Naomi to a foreign country and a foreign people. Though the three women shared the same calamity, Ruth is the hero of the book that bears her name.

> Ruth stands alone by the force of circumstances. Her choice makes no sense. It forsakes the security of a mother's house for insecurity abroad. It forfeits possible fullness in Moab for certain emptiness in Judah. It relinquishes the familiar for the strange. Naomi rejects this radical decision.[64]

When Naomi rejected her decision, Ruth responded with the famous words:

> Don't urge me to leave you or to turn back from you. Where you go I will go, and where you stay I will stay. Your people will be my people and your God my God. Where you die I will die, and there I will be buried. May the LORD deal with me, be it ever so severely, if even death separates you and me. (Ruth 1:16–17)

Commenting on these words, Phyllis Trible says:

> From a cultural perspective, Ruth has chosen death over life. She has disavowed the solidarity of family, she has abandoned national identity; and she has renounced religious affiliation. In the entire epic of Israel, only Abraham matches this radicality, but then he had a call from God (Gen 12:1–5).[65]

---

[63] Phyllis Trible, *God and the Rhetoric of Sexuality* (Philadelphia: Fortress, 1973), 172.

[64] Ibid., 173.
[65] Ibid.

Some scholars wonder why the book of Ruth is included in the Scriptures.[66] I too am eager to know the answer to that question. What is its value in terms of biblical teaching? I cannot answer this question in technical terms, but I can say that I am amazed by the love, self-giving, loyalty, and faithfulness shown in the relationships in this story. As the writer Carolyn Pressler says,

> For many biblical theologians, Ruth is a book about hesed, that is, "loving faithfulness." Ruth, Naomi, and Boaz extend loyalty and care toward one another that goes beyond what is socially expected or legally required. . . . [It shows God] working through faithful human beings to bring about blessing. . . .
>
> The relationships are between particular individuals: It matters that Ruth is a Moabite, an ethnic group the Israelites despised. It matters that she is a woman and that her fierce loyalty is to another woman. And it matters that Naomi and Ruth, though without material resources, strategize not only for their own individual welfare but also for each other's.[67]

Ruth was a woman who had the capacity to make hard decisions, without caring about the social customs at that time. Did she have a special and deep knowledge of the God of Naomi whom she trusted? The book is silent on this point. Yet, the mention of Ruth as being in the lineage of Christ as the great-grandmother of King David supports the idea that she believed in this God and surrendered her future to him. Ruth was a bold and courageous woman. She was loyal, faithful, self-giving, and generous to a very high degree. After she married Boaz and God gave her a son, she gave him to Naomi to restore her life and to nourish her old age. The women of the village said, "Naomi has a son." (Ruth 4:17). The book adds that this child, named Obed, became the father of Jesse, the father of David. Thus Ruth as a believer entered the lineage of kings (Matt 1:5).

She is another example of the elusive women in the Old Testament whose characters are marked by courage and faith.

As for Esther, she was a beautiful young woman who took a great risk in order to save her people from a terrible fate. I will not say more about Ruth and Esther, except to mention that the book of Ruth was traditionally read during the harvest festival and the book of Esther during the festival of Purim. Thus these two books had an important place in the religious life of the Jews.

The story of women in the Old Testament is a mix of joy and misery, violence and compassion. Injustice and abuse are paralleled with love and protection. But there are stories of abuse, in which it seems that terrorizing women was a pleasure; raping them

---

[66] See Murray D. Gow, *The Book of Ruth* (Leicester: Apollos, 1992), 9.

[67] Carolyn Pressler, *Joshua, Judges, and Ruth* (Louisville: Westminster John Knox, 2002), 262, 264.

a sign of love; and cutting off their limbs an appropriate form of redress. A woman was offered in sacrifice as a vow to secure her father's victory over his enemies. A woman's body was abused by someone who was not her husband to secure an heir. Another woman was pushed into the bed of her master as if she were just a vessel or house utensil. The Old Testament does not tell these stories as models to be followed, but to show human weakness, sinfulness, and violence.

The New Testament

It is now time to delve into the New Testament material to see if there is something new regarding the status of women as human beings, their leadership role, and the opportunities offered to them. Was the New Testament really new in achieving human equality? Was the church, the community of faith in Jesus Christ, a renewing factor in the society? Or did it accommodate and cooperate with the established social contract regarding the role of women in leadership?

As previously mentioned, the Christian church was born in a Jewish environment that had been erecting walls around itself to enforce religious and cultural exclusivity for some two thousand years before Jesus was born. In spite of the real dignity given to women in Jewish culture, they were not equal to men religiously or socially. Rabbinic literature portrays women as greedy, unintelligent, and limited and views them with suspicion and arrogance. In addition, Jewish culture was mingled with Hellenic culture and other cultures around the Mediterranean Sea. None of these cultures regarded men and women as equals in terms of human value, opportunities, or human rights as we think of them today.

In every age the voices of women rose in rejection of both the injustices against them and the claims of their lack of equality with men, but their voices were not sufficiently strong and were easily suppressed. But the longing for liberty is ancient. Ever since God's promise to the woman that her seed would bruise the head of the serpent, human beings have longed for that promise to be fulfilled. It was a promise of freedom. But the patriarchal system that had existed since the dawn of time gave men absolute authority over their families or clans and confined women in the shadows. Men were strong; women were weak. Women were treated as men's possessions even though they had originally been intended to be their helpers. Throughout the ages, women themselves have believed this and have derived their human value and social identity from men.

This was the society into which Jesus came to in the fullness of time, born of a woman. With his blood he laid the cornerstone of the New Testament church. In Jesus Christ we witness the fulfillment of the promise that the seed of the woman would bruise the head of the serpent, exchanging a history of slavery to sin for a history of salvation and freedom. As Paul says, the creation itself will be liberated from its bondage to decay and brought into the freedom and glory of the children of God. (Rom 8:21)

Jesus Christ renewed history and "in this hope we were saved" (Rom 8:24). Thus in Jesus Christ we are a new creation; the old has passed away, the new has come. Through Jesus Christ creation was renewed; the sin of rebellion in the story of creation and its punishment was eliminated by his death and resurrection for all who believe in him as their Lord and Savior. "Therefore, if anyone is in Christ, the new creation has come: The old has gone, the new is here!" (2 Cor 5:17).

Rosemary Radford Ruether maintains that according to some early Christians, the inferior view of women was changed through the redemption of Jesus Christ with the result that

some women exercised leadership and prophetic teaching in some early Christian churches, and this was supported by some men in these Christian communities as an expression of their faith in a "new humanity" that overcomes gender hierarchy.[68]

However, there were others at that time who wanted to continue stressing the belief that

women were created second, sinned first, are to keep silence in church, to be saved by subordination and childbearing; but alternative views and practices on women's roles continued.

Some interpreted the reference to "male and female" in Genesis 1:27b as referring to

a second stage of creation, one that expressed a fall into sin and death. . . . Redemption reversed this last fallen stage of creation, returning the original unity in which there is "no more male or female." Some early Christians defined a theology of baptism in which this restoration to pregendered unity happens when the baptized are incorporated into a redeemed humanity "in Christ." . . .

Saint Paul rejected this theology . . . and insisted that marriage and traditional gender relations are to continue in the Christian community even after baptism.[69]

It is now time to try to understand the attitude of the apostle Paul and his teachings, which have been the foundation of much church doctrine throughout the ages, and which have been interpreted as denying women the right to participate in pastoral ministry alongside men. After that we will look at the attitude of Jesus toward women as portrayed in the four gospels. He depicts the fundamental attitude that the church

---

[68] Rosemary Radford Ruether, *Women and Redemption: A Theological History* (London: SCM, 1998), 2.

[69] Ibid., 2.

has to adopt to achieve justice, on the human and religious levels, so that the church may be enriched with the gifts and talents of women.

Paul's Attitude toward Women

The Christian church owes a great deal to the apostle Paul, the great philosopher who used his power of logic to explain Christian beliefs. As the young man Saul, he was zealously committed to Jewish teachings and knew the Scriptures well, having been taught by the great teacher Gamaliel. He saw it as his duty to oppose Christians who, according to him, had strayed from the teachings of the Torah to follow the way of Jesus of Nazareth. In his zeal, Saul did not hesitate to approve the stoning of one of those Christians. The first time we meet him, those who stoned Stephen, the first Christian martyr, were laying their garments at his feet (Acts 7:58–8:1). But, Acts 9 tells the story of Saul's encounter with Christ, his conversion (when he was named Paul), and the beginning of his Christian life.

It seems that Paul was not one to compromise. In his Jewish faith, he was conservative to the extreme. When he became a Christian, he gave himself unstintingly to this faith until the end of his life.

When we read Paul's sermons in the book of Acts, and his letters, it is clear that his unique mind, deep knowledge, and study of the old philosophies all helped him to organize the logic of the Christian faith, the mystery of mysteries, in splendid style. Paul himself was amazed at the work that God had done in Jesus for the salvation of the world. He said to Timothy,

> Beyond all question, the mystery from which true godliness springs is great:
>
> > He appeared in the flesh,
> > > was vindicated by the Spirit,
> > was seen by angels,
> > > was preached among the nations,
> > was believed on in the world,
> > > was taken up in glory. (1 Tim 3:16)

One cannot but hear this as a cry of wonder and amazement, for what God has done for the salvation of the world surpasses all understanding.

The same philosopher of Christianity who uttered this cry had earlier told Timothy:

> a woman should learn in quietness and full submission. I do not permit a woman to teach or to assume authority over a man; she must be quiet. For Adam was formed first, then Eve. And Adam was not the one deceived; it was the woman who was deceived and became a sinner. But women will be saved through childbearing—if they continue in faith, love and holiness with propriety. (1 Tim 2:11–15)

344

It is important to note that Paul's two letters to Timothy were personal, pastoral letters. They were sent to the minister of a church, not to the church as a whole, as was the case with the letters to the church in Corinth. These letters contain very valuable teachings and important principles for the Christian faith in general. Yet, what Paul wrote about women in the above paragraph is surprising! How can the same Paul who praises Timothy because his mother and grandmother raised him in the true faith say, "I do not permit a woman to teach or to assume authority over a man" (1 Tim 2:12)? How can the same Paul who advised men to love their wives as themselves, just as Christ loved the church, insist that men must dominate women or advocate such harsh treatment of young widows as he does in chapter 5? Can one person unite two extremes within himself? The only possible explanation seems to be that Paul was writing to Timothy about specific problems that Timothy had encountered.

Why did Paul, that great philosopher and wonderful believer, seem so unjust to Christian women? Why did he not go beyond the second creation narrative and the account of the fall? Why did he treat a woman as if she were created just to meet the needs of a man, as if she were the only one who sinned, as if she has inferior intellectual powers and so has only to listen and to be taught silently? That person who believed that God has renewed the creation in Jesus Christ and removed the charges against us, the one who struggled to present everyone complete in Jesus Christ—why did he speak that way about women?

It seems that Paul's writings were quite specific about the roles of women and their service in the church, forbidding women from speaking in church and asking them to learn in silence. Words like "I do not permit a woman to teach or to assume authority over a man; she must be quiet" and "the head of the woman is man" have been used by the church over the ages to assert male leadership and force women to accept an unpalatable reality. This has resulted in many doubting the credibility of the apostle Paul, which is the issue I will now address.

The words quoted above from 1 Timothy 2:11–15 have prevented women over the ages from participating in pastoral service and deprived the church of the leadership talents of women. This saying, along with Paul's words in 1 Corinthians 14:34–35, was interpreted as being a Christian law that silences women in the church forever, regardless of the kind of talk. Is all speech, of any kind, by women forbidden in the church?

In 1 Timothy 2:8, Paul says:

Therefore I want the men everywhere to pray, lifting up holy hands without anger or disputing.

Paul is here speaking about a way or type of prayer. In the next verse, he speaks about the way women should behave when they pray:

I also want the women to dress modestly, with decency and propriety.

345

His words imply that all pray, but that it should be done decently and humbly before God. Yet in many Christian churches today women are prohibited from praying aloud. In 1 Corinthians 14:34-35 Paul has this to say:

Women should remain silent in the churches. They are not allowed to speak, but must be in submission, as the law says. If they want to inquire about something, they should ask their own husbands at home; for it is disgraceful for a woman to speak in the church.

In 1 Timothy 2:11 he adds to this, saying,

A woman should learn in quietness and full submission.

I will discuss the expression "full submission" later. But in regard to the issue of women's talk, it is clear that in Corinthians and Timothy, Paul was advising women not to talk in church, even in terms of inquiring from their husbands about new teachings. We know that at that time men had more opportunities for learning and education than women. For this reason, women needed simpler explanation of what was being taught, and they used to ask their husbands for explanations during worship time, which caused a disturbance in the church. We can identify this as the problem because in the previous verse Paul spoke about order and discipline during the times of worship in the church:

For God is not a God of disorder but of peace—as in all the congregations of the Lord's people. (1 Cor 14:33)

It is apparent that what Paul meant was that "if they want to inquire about something, they should ask their own husbands at home." This, then, is the kind of speech that was forbidden for women in the church—the type of speech that disrupts worship. The same principle applies to men's speech, "for God is not a God of disorder but of peace."

Paul's words to Timothy, "I do not permit a woman to teach or to assume authority over a man" (1 Tim 2:12), have created great confusion regarding women's right to teach in the church, especially with regard to the first part of the verse. Yet, we all remember that Priscilla taught alongside Paul and her husband Aquila (Acts 18:26). This was not a problem for Paul, for he mentions Priscilla and Aquila as "my co-workers in Jesus Christ." He does not say "Aquila my fellow worker and his wife Priscilla." Bristow quotes John Chrysostom as having written, "Priscilla was the teacher of Apollos the pastor of the church in Corinth after Paul had left the church there."[70]

Paul himself mentioned Phoebe, a deaconess of the church at Cenchreae:

I commend to you our sister Phoebe, a deacon of the church in Cenchreae. I ask you to receive her in the Lord in a way worthy of his people and to give her any help she may need from you, for she has been the benefactor of many people, including me. (Rom 16:1, 2)

---

[70] Bristow, *What Paul Really Said*, 56.

In the list of those to whom Paul sent his greetings in Romans 16, we find at least four women: Mary (v. 6) and Tryphena, Tryphosa and Persis (v. 12), whom he described as working hard in the Lord. Did those women work hard at washing dishes and ironing clothes, or were they teachers like Paul? Could Paul deny that those women were teachers? Of course not, since it was not in his character to deny truth but to stand by it and defend it. Euodia and Syntyche, who worked hard with Paul in the gospel and whose names are in the book of life (Phil 4:2, 3), were no doubt also teachers.

In addition, we have Paul's words in chapter 11 of his first letter to the Corinthians. There the issue Paul was dealing with was related to leading in worship and prayer in the church community. Women already participated in the service and leadership of the Corinthian church; they were praying, prophesying, and teaching:

> Every man who prays or prophesies with his head covered dishonors his head. But every woman who prays or prophesies with her head uncovered dishonors her head—it is the same as having her head shaved. (1 Cor 11:4–5)

Here the problem that the apostle Paul was addressing was a social one. It seems that some women were leading public prayer without covering their heads, which was contrary to the social norms for decent women at that time. Thus the apostle Paul said that this was unacceptable. Why then are we arguing about this? What Paul prohibited was a practice that was socially unacceptable; it is not related to the issue of whether women should or should not teach in the church.

Paul's words in 1 Corinthians 11:3 are another source of confusion:

> But I want you to realize that the head of every man is Christ, and the head of the woman is man, and the head of Christ is God.

Earlier, he spoke of a head covering for women during prayer as if it were a social norm, but here he appears to regard it as a religious necessity. Moreover, his statement that "the head of the woman is man" seems to make women's submission to men an article of faith. What did Paul mean? We will treat the two matters separately.

The head covering, it seems, was a social norm:

> For Jews, worshiping without one's head covered was regarded with stern disapproval. . . . It was regarded as an act of reverence and humility for a person to wear a head covering during worship. . . . Jewish women were required to wear their hair bound up whenever they left their homes, [because] if a woman let her hair down in public she was seen as tempting men to sin. Therefore the Mishnah declared that a husband might divorce his wife . . . in the event that she goes out with her hair unbound.[71]

---

[71] Ibid., 79.

In talking about women's habits concerning covering their heads or loosening their hair, Bristow says that in Corinth there were pagan temples in which women with short hair served as prostitutes.[72] Thus the Greeks were familiar with the idea of women worshiping in temples with their heads uncovered, whereas the Jews did not accept women uncovering their hair during worship.

In a church that included both Jews and Greeks as brothers and sisters in Christ, combining various habits and cultures cannot have been easy. Perhaps due to the new teaching about freedom in Christ, some women began to ignore social customs. Some of them may have been praying, prophesying, teaching, and exercising leadership in the church with their heads uncovered, which created some embarrassment and difficulty in a church where things were supposed to be organized and disciplined. Confused church members may have asked the apostle Paul for his advice about how to handle these controversial matters. Paul, who wanted to be all things to all people, responded with instructions that were also not very clear, saying that "a man ought not to cover his head, since he is the image and glory of God; but woman is the glory of man" (1 Cor 11:7). Paul must have been aware that what he had written in 1 Corinthians 11:7 could be misinterpreted, and so he added verses 8–16.

Bristow says:

> Traditionally, this paragraph has been interpreted to mean that men are required to wear their hair short . . . and keep their heads uncovered during worship; while women are to cover their heads during worship.

In addition, the paragraph was interpreted to

> justify the notion that women, while they have souls, are by nature between men and animals in terms of powers of reason, ethical understanding and theological insights. . . . (After all, man is the glory of God, while woman is the glory of man.) This led in turn to a denial of education to women during the Middle Ages.[73]

However, this was not the message the apostle Paul intended to convey. Thus he added the words:

> Nevertheless, in the Lord woman is not independent of man, nor is man independent of woman. For as woman came from man, so also man is born of woman. But everything comes from God (1 Cor 11:11–12).

It seems that the second story of creation was always present in Paul's mind; yet through Christ, concepts are renewed and values are equalized. What does it matter if the woman was created from the man's rib, since a man is born from a woman, and all

---

[72] Ibid., 81. [73] Ibid., 82–83.

things are from God? As for social customs and traditions, every Christian, male and female, has to show respect.

Bristow says that the Jewish custom of wearing head coverings during worship was linked to the idea of God's radiance shining from the face of Moses. To cover this, "Moses wore a veil after descending Mount Sinai to hide the radiance of his face after being near God" (Exod 34:29–35). Thus in Jewish custom both men and women wore a veil during worship. It was still a symbol of the glory of Moses even in the time of the apostle Paul. But Paul gives a theological reason why men should not wear the veil. He reminds them that their head now is Christ, not Moses; therefore, they do not have to cover their heads. It is as if Paul was saying that

> what one does with one's head makes a theological statement about Christ. To cover one's head, Paul seems to be saying, is to act as if one were ashamed of Christ, our head, who is the image and glory of God.

As for women, what they did with their heads had a different social value. Wearing their hair up was a sign that they were married, much like a wedding ring is a sign today. Women's hair was their glory, but they were the glory of their husbands, and they should not bring shame to their husbands by dressing as if they were not married. While the specific customs many have changed,

> the principle behind these instructions, of being sensitive to the message our dress codes and styles convey to others, still holds.[74]

Still more perplexing is another statement Paul made in this passage:

> It is for this reason that a woman ought to have authority over her own head, because of the angels. (1 Cor 11:10)

Tertullian offered one suggestion on how to interpret this: "He believed that if angels looked down and saw women without veils, they might fall in love with them."[75] Yet, an angel spoke to the Virgin Mary, announcing to her that she would bear a son, and two angels spoke to Mary Magdalene and Salome and Mary the mother of James, and there is no hint of any problem regarding possible love affairs. Thus I agree with Bristow who affirms that what Paul is saying is that women are given spiritual authority in the church as teachers and as prophets, just like men.

Some thirty years ago, I heard someone teaching that women who serve in the church should have to wear the specific robe of pastors, which distinguishes them as ministers and teachers and shows their authority in teaching. This may be a good perspective on 1 Corinthians 11:10.

---

[74] Ibid., 85–86.   [75] Ibid., 87.

Male headship. In his teaching about public worship Paul says,

> But I want you to realize that the head of every man is Christ, and the head of the woman is man, and the head of Christ is God." (1 Cor 11:3)

Does Paul mean that men have a direct relationship with Christ, but women's relationship with Christ is mediated through men? Or is he referring to the hierarchical order of creation as displayed in the second story of creation, in which the woman is created after the man, so that the hierarchical order is God, Christ, men, women, so that God is all and in all? For Paul says that the head of Christ is God.

Paul was writing to a church in which he had taught, and to which he had given instructions (1 Cor 11:1). We do not know what these instructions and teachings were, but it seems that they were related to discipline and order during worship, which is similar to the order set out in the story of an orderly creation. In Colossians 1:13–18, Paul says,

> For he has rescued us from the dominion of darkness and brought us into the kingdom of the Son he loves, in whom we have redemption, the forgiveness of sins. The Son is the image of the invisible God, the firstborn over all creation. For in him all things were created: things in heaven and on earth, visible and invisible, whether thrones or powers or rulers or authorities; all things have been created through him and for him. He is before all things, and in him all things hold together. And he is the head of the body.

Does the word "head" here mean origin, beginning, or source? Christ is, of course, the head of the church since he has full authority over it, for he redeemed it with his blood.

As for the statement "the head of a wife is her husband" (1 Cor 11:3 ESV), it cannot mean that a husband has authority over his wife as Christ has authority over his church, for a husband does not redeem his wife. Bristow says that he found this statement very confusing. Many Bible scholars say that here Paul is being incoherent and is contradicting himself. So Bristow wondered whether Paul really intended us to understand what the church has understood throughout the ages, namely that a husband must have authority over his wife, and that women, instead of enjoying the liberty given to them in Christ, must live as second-class creatures.

Bristow studied Paul's words and began to think,

> If I took our English translation of his words and translated them back into Greek, my words should be similar to Paul's original words. But when I tried doing this, such was not the case, not at all! . . . In fact, our English words imply ideas that Paul deliberately avoided! If Paul had wanted to say what we think he said, then he would have chosen quite different words when he wrote . . . .
>
> Far from being an advocate of the notion that men are superior to women, Paul was in fact the first great champion of sexual equality. . . . Paul carefully chose his words, deliberately avoiding those Greek terms that, if he had used them, would have communicated

to his readers precisely what our English translations imply for us today. . . . I found that Paul stood squarely opposed to [the attitudes of Greek and Jewish societies], proclaiming instead a new order of sexual equality within the Church and within the home. This apostle championed the value of women. . . .

It was as if the veil . . . had been lifted from my own eyes, and now I could read afresh the urgent cry from Paul for churches to have women learn, to let them be leaders, to let them have the authority due to them, to realize in practice the great truth that "there is neither male nor female . . . you are all one in Christ Jesus" (Gal 3:28).[76]

Although Paul was a man of his time, he was bold enough to declare that social ideas have to be renewed in Christ.

I want to conclude my comments on 1 Corinthians 11:2–16 by referring to what Jerome Murphy O'Connor (as quoted by Francis J. Moloney) has to say on this passage. He says, first, that Paul distinguished between men and women on the basis of Genesis 1:26, 27; 2:18–22; 1 Corinthians 11:7–9. Second, he says that the renewed woman has an authority equal to that of a man (1 Cor 11:10–12). The two points are related:

New status is accorded to women, not to an ambiguous being whose "unfeminine" hair-do was an affront to generally accepted conventions. Hence, in so far as her way of doing her hair clearly defines her sex, it becomes a symbol of the authority she enjoys.[77]

Writing about the relationship between a man and a woman in a Christian family, Paul says,

Wives, submit yourselves to your own husbands as you do to the Lord. For the husband is the head of the wife as Christ is the head of the church, his body, of which he is the Savior. Now as the church submits to Christ, so also wives should submit to their husbands in everything. Husbands, love your wives, just as Christ loved the church and gave himself up for her. (Eph 5:22–25)

In Colossians 3:18–19, he says,

Wives, submit to your husbands, as is fitting in the Lord. Husbands, love your wives, and do not be harsh with them.

The dictionary meaning of the word "submission" involves subordination, as when a boss gives someone orders. If the submissiveness required from women here is obedience and carrying out orders, where is the freedom Christ brought to all? Does Christ free women only to make them slaves to their husbands? And why did Paul tell children to obey their parents and slaves to obey their masters, rather than telling them to submit to them? It is obvious that submission it not identical with obedience in Paul's thinking.

---

[76] Ibid., x–xii

[77] Francis J. Moloney, *Woman: First Among the Faithful* (London: Darton, Longman and Todd, 1984), 31.

This point is borne out by his instruction to church members to "submit to one another out of reverence for Christ" (Eph 5:21). Do church members obey each other? Who obeys whom? Who orders whom?

Bristow says that Paul uses the Greek verb translated "be subject to" in what is called "the middle voice" to indicate that women are to be loyal to their husbands. Paul was thus not imposing obedience as an obligation; rather, he was urging women to voluntarily give allegiance to their husbands as an expression of their commitment and support and of complete fellowship between a man and his wife. What applies to the Christian family also applies to the church, as when Paul told the believers in Galatia to "carry each other's burdens, and in this way you will fulfill the law of Christ" (Gal 6:2).[78] When a husband loves his wife as himself, loves her as Christ loved the church and sacrificed himself for its sake, a woman's submission or loyalty comes naturally—even more than a man deserves.

Thus both a husband and a wife are equal in their giving and in constituting a Christian family. This reminds us of Paul's words in 1 Corinthians 7:14:

> For the unbelieving husband has been sanctified through his wife, and the unbelieving wife has been sanctified through her believing husband. Otherwise your children would be unclean, but as it is, they are holy.

A man is not less than a woman; nor is a woman less than a man in the Lord. The relationship between a husband and his wife in Christian marriage is like the relationship between Christ and God: "I am in the Father, and that the Father is in me" (John 14:10).

Salvation and childbearing. In 1 Timothy 2:13–15, Paul writes,

> For Adam was formed first, then Eve. And Adam was not the one deceived; it was the woman who was deceived and became a sinner. But women will be saved through childbearing—if they continue in faith, love and holiness with propriety.

In the first part of this chapter, I spoke about the two accounts of creation and the fall. We noticed that in all his references to the story of creation Paul refers to the second story, which says that Eve was created later and that she was deceived and fell into disobedience. Traditionally, because Eve was created after Adam, she was considered less than he. But those who take this position forget that God said, "It is not good that the man should be alone; I will make him a helper fit for him." In other words, Eve's existence was a necessity for Adam to become a whole man. Only after creating Eve did God declare everything very good. How then would a woman be less important if through her existence the creation became very good?

We also noticed that the serpent, which was craftier than all the other creatures and which deceived Eve and made her break God's commandment, spoke to Eve in the

---

[78] Bristow, *What Paul Really Said*, 40–41.

presence of Adam. Adam remained silent and Eve did not have to make any effort to convince him to eat of the forbidden fruit. Thus the punishment fell on both of them. Paul himself says in 1 Corinthians 15:22, "For as in Adam all die, so in Christ all will be made alive." Here I humbly hear Paul condemning Adam as being the cause of the fall; yet I do not thereby justify Eve.

So the statement, "Yet woman will be saved through childbearing," surprises and confuses me. I cannot help but ask: Why does Paul contradict himself? In 1 Corinthians 7 he advised virgins not to be married, as time is too short:

> An unmarried woman or virgin is concerned about the Lord's affairs: Her aim is to be devoted to the Lord in both body and spirit. But a married woman is concerned about the affairs of this world—how she can please her husband. (1 Cor 7:34)

Didn't Paul spell out the doctrine of salvation through faith? Is he saying that men will be saved through faith and women through bearing children? What if the children of a woman believer do not abide in the faith? Will she be condemned with no hope of salvation? This is very strange! What about barren women? Would you solve this dilemma for us, Paul? You told the people in Galatia,

> Even if we or an angel from heaven should preach a gospel other than what we have preached to you, let them be under God's curse! (Gal 1:8)

Did you change your mind?

But Paul was not contradicting himself; nor was he being unjust to women. In his letter to the Corinthians, Paul was responding to a special situation in the church there. He also wrote to Timothy personally, addressing a young minister who was experiencing problems with his flock. But then what Paul had written was read from a philosophical perspective and interpreted in a very patrilineal culture.

In a booklet entitled *Did I Betray the Gospel? The Letters of Paul and the Place of Women*, S. Wesley Ariarajah suggests that if Paul were rewriting his letters for this present age, interpreting the circumstances and issues that were present in the churches to which he wrote, he would have corrected all the misunderstandings caused by his wording.[79] How complicated those circumstances were and how difficult to manage! Yet Paul stood against all the established practices that reduced the value of women. Paul tried to correct misunderstanding of his intentions in many of his writings regarding women, and announced that his intention was the opposite of what has been understood. This book reminded me of the words of Bishop Kenneth Cragg that I referred to earlier in this paper—"let us complain about Paul to Paul, and correct Paul with Paul."

---

[79] S. Wesley Ariarajah, *Did I Betray the Gospel? The Letters of Paul and the Place of Women* (Geneva: WCC, 1996).

Jesus' Attitude toward Women

When Jesus set out the general principles for his kingdom in the Sermon on the Mount (Matt 5–7), he did not indicate that some applied to men and others to women. They were general human values and principles by which every believer in Jesus Christ and everyone who fears God should live.

Similarly, through his works, parables, and teachings, Jesus taught general principles and did not deal with the issues of men and women separately; consequently, he himself was an example to all who believe in him. It is worth mentioning that it is through Jesus' teachings and dealings with women that we discover customs and traditions regarding women that were not recorded anywhere else.

Though we do not find specific teaching about women in the four gospels, they do offer us portraits of women who were pioneers in the faith. These were women with whom Jesus interacted and to whom he gave real human dignity.

Jesus Christ was neither a social revolutionary nor a political leader who wanted to change systems and ideologies. His mission was to raise the value of humankind, saving human beings and reconciling them to God the Father. His message offered a better life to all, men and women alike. In spite of this, the leaders of the people considered Jesus an extremist and responded to him with anger, not least because of his relation to women. Women were part of Jesus' life from his birth, through his ministry, at the cross, in his burial, and at the empty tomb. They were the first to receive the news of his resurrection and the first to see the risen Christ.

In the gospels, Jesus is shown dealing with women naturally, as human beings. He spoke with them and discussed ethical matters with them, even though his disciples considered this disgraceful. He praised women's love of knowledge and he accepted their service to him. He healed them with a touch, challenging the laws of purity and impurity. He broke the Sabbath to heal a woman's back, even though others considered this action a crime for which he deserved stoning.

It is worth noting that while Jesus argued with and challenged leaders in their groups, he is only once shown as engaged in theological discussion with an individual man. But there are four occasions in which we see him discussing theology with a woman. He was speaking to a Samaritan woman when he set out the principles regarding the type of worship that is acceptable to God. Such worship is not linked to any specific place and must be offered in spirit and truth. He told her that he is the one who gives the water of life and that he is greater than Jacob. He specifically told this Samaritan woman that he is the Christ. In talking to a Syrian-Phoenician woman, he extended the limits of his mission geographically and humanly. He came with healing in his wings for all who believe in him.

He also spoke with Martha and Mary, Lazarus' sisters, and revealed to them the deep theological truth that he is the resurrection and the life. And his dialogue with his mother at the beginning of his ministry led to the revelation of his glory through supernatural acts.

We will be looking at the portraits of women in the four gospels to see what Jesus brought that was new. But before doing that, I wish to make some general observations.

The first point I want to raise concerns why the Gospel of Matthew opens with a genealogy of Jesus that includes five women, even though genealogies generally listed only the male line. This genealogy, which is the opening chapter in the New Testament, specifically mentions Tamar, Rahab, Ruth, the wife of Uriah, and Mary. Each of these women had a story to tell.

Rahab was a prostitute who hid the men whom Joshua had sent to spy out the land around Jericho. Those two men entered her house and made a covenant with her before they left. She kept them safe from the anger of the king and they, in turn, promised to save her and her family when the Israelites invaded the city. However, the most important point in this covenant was that Rahab acknowledged that the Lord would give this land to the Israelites. She proved her faith by helping the men to escape.

We spoke about Ruth earlier in this chapter, and so will not discuss her here. But what about the wife of Uriah, she who gave birth to Solomon, the son of David? I do not know why Matthew refrained from mentioning her name. I hope he did so to remind us of what David had done when he sinned against God by killing her husband in order to marry her.

Was the mention of these women merely a coincidence? I don't think so. One of them was a prostitute, another resorted to trickery to obtain what was due to her, and the third was abused sexually. Yet each of them had such value that Matthew did not hesitate to mention them in the genealogy of Jesus.

The second point I want to make concerns Jesus' words in the Sermon on the Mount, which lays the foundation for Christian behavior:

> You have heard that it was said, "You shall not commit adultery." But I tell you that anyone who looks at a woman lustfully has already committed adultery with her in his heart. (Matt 5:27–28)

These words turned ancient customs upside down. The Old Testament was more tolerant of men having sexual relationships outside marriage than of women doing so. A man could easily enter the house of a prostitute, but the prostitute was socially and religiously despised. Women were blamed when they were raped. Moreover, rape was considered a transgression against the woman's father, and adultery was considered a transgression against the husband—it was as if the woman herself had no emotions and no independent worth. So when Jesus said, "he who looks at a woman lustfully has already committed adultery with her in his heart," he transformed a woman from "something" into "someone"—a human being.

The same thing happened when the scribes and the Pharisees caught a woman in the act of committing adultery. They reminded Jesus that Moses had commanded that such a woman should be stoned, and then they asked him, "What do you say?" They wanted to trap Jesus so that they could accuse him of going against the Law of Moses. But Jesus recognized their evil intentions and knew that the woman was being used as a pawn in the conflict between him and the Jewish leaders. So he challenged them, saying, "Let any one of you who is without sin be the first to throw a stone at her" (see John 8:2–11). He turned attention away from the woman, who was the "target," to her accusers, who became aware of their own sins. When all of them had left, and only the woman remained, Jesus restored her dignity as a human being who could enter into fellowship with him and who was able to refrain from sinning. Jesus was willing to confront the traditional values that made women worthless. What was the value of the teachings of Moses if they deprived women of the humanity God had given them?

One final observation: in Mark and Matthew we read that while Jesus was talking to the crowd, his mother and brothers stood outside asking to talk with him. When Jesus was told that they were there, he said,

> "Who is my mother, and who are my brothers?" Pointing to his disciples, he said, "Here are my mother and my brothers. For whoever does the will of my Father in heaven is my brother and sister and mother." (Matt 12:48–50; Mark 3:31–35)

The same incident is recorded in Luke 8:19–21, with the slight difference that it omits the word "sister" used in the verses above. What is striking is that none of the accounts include the words "my father." Elisabeth Schüssler Fiorenza argues that the absence of any reference to an earthly father undermines the familiar pattern of the patriarchal family, for the new family in Christ has no relation to fatherhood or motherhood. The members of the new family are those who hear the Word of God and obey his will. The disciples of Jesus are his true family, and thus everyone who fulfills the will of God is a brother, a sister, and a mother to Jesus. Similarly, when a woman cried out while Jesus was talking, "Blessed is the mother who gave you birth and nursed you," he replied, "Blessed rather are those who hear the word of God and obey it" (Luke 11:27, 28).

Fiorenza insists that one cannot attribute the absence of any mention of a father in relation to the true family of Jesus to the fact that God is the real father of Jesus Christ. Nonetheless, it is noteworthy that a mother and a sister are within this family.

This incident shows that those who fulfill the will of God are the true disciples who form the new family of Christ, and Christ is with this family in this new house. Thus the disciples, his brothers and sisters, demolish the patriarchal system of the family and establish a new family that is opposed to that system. The new family of Christ is the family of those who are "equal in discipleship."[80]

This gives rise to another question: Why did the church preserve the old system and not adopt the new system of Jesus that makes all people equal through believing in him, hearing his word, and fulfilling his will? The answer is rooted in power issues in a patriarchal society where men enjoy being in command and in control.

In his parables about the kingdom, Jesus mentioned women. For example, there is the parable of the yeast that a woman "took and mixed into about sixty pounds of flour until it worked all through the dough" (Matt 13:33). He also compared the kingdom of heaven to ten virgins who went out to meet the bridegroom. Five of them were wise and five were foolish (Matt 25:1–13).

In the Gospel of Mark, the second miracle Jesus did was to heal Peter's mother-in-law. She was the first sick woman whom Jesus is said to have touched. When he did so, "the fever left her and she began to wait on them" (Mark 1:30–31).

Jesus noticed the poor widow who put two small copper coins into the treasury and praised her by saying that her gift exceeded the large amounts others were contributing to the treasury because "she, out of her poverty, put in everything—all she had to live on" (Mark 12:42–44; Luke 20:47; 21:4).

Earlier he had warned his disciples against "the teachers of the law . . . [who] devour widows' houses" (Mark 12:38–40). This poor widow was an example of faith, for she gave all that she had, believing that God would not forsake her.

There are many accounts of Jesus dealing with women in the four gospels. In every incident in which women's characters are revealed, they show the depth of their religious and social insight and their rejection of unjust customs.

The Bleeding Woman

Consider the case of the woman who touched Jesus while he was on his way to the house of Jairus, a ruler of the synagogue, to heal his little daughter. This incident is mentioned by Matthew, Mark, and Luke. This woman

> had been subject to bleeding for twelve years. She had suffered a great deal under the care of many doctors and had spent all she had, yet instead of getting better she grew worse. (Mark 5:25–26)

She heard about Jesus, and both Matthew and Mark record her belief that, "If I just touch his clothes, I will be healed." So the woman came up behind him in the crowd that thronged around him and touched his garment. And "immediately her bleeding stopped" (Mark 5:27–29).

---

[80] Elisabeth Schüssler Fiorenza, *In Memory of Her*, 10th ed. (New York: Crossroad, 1994), 146–47.

This incident could have passed unnoticed: the woman could have stayed unknown and the secret of her disease would have not been revealed to anyone. Jesus, too, would have saved himself from the embarrassment of having been touched by a bleeding woman who, in terms of the law, was unclean. For twelve years this woman had been isolated from society, not only because she herself was unclean but also because everything she touched became unclean (Lev 15:19–31). This isolation made her life worthless. No wonder she was willing to spend all that she had in an attempt to become "clean" and be able to return to society. She had remained sick, poor, hopeless, and isolated for twelve years. She could not even join in public worship. She could not bear children because of her disease, which made her socially useless. For all these reasons, when she heard about Jesus she went out to find him. She may have approached him from behind because she would not have been allowed to approach him directly. She knew all about the rules in Leviticus.

Fiorenza suggests that this story is linked to the story of Jairus, both by the number of years the woman had suffered, which matches the age of his daughter, and by the concepts of wholeness and holiness. Touching a bleeding woman and touching a dead girl were both actions that would make Jesus unclean according to the laws in Leviticus. Jesus knew these laws, but he broke them so that both women could live in peace and wholeness. The woman was returned to her community, and Jairus' daughter grew to womanhood in that same community. The woman remains anonymous, but Jesus called her "daughter" and gave her peace.

Frances Taylor Gench goes even further when comparing these two interwoven stories. She argues that the number "twelve" is more than just a catch-word used to link the stories and suggests that it implies that the two women are restored to life so that they can fulfill their life-giving capacity as women. She also links the number with the number of Christ's disciples, and suggests that it is a "clue to the identity of Jesus' true family."[81]

I do not go as far as Gench in associating the number twelve with the disciples and the twelve tribes of Israel. However, I agree with her insight that faith is a fundamental element in these two stories. When Jesus wanted to praise the woman and her faith, he announced that her faith had saved her, and in so doing gave Jairus a lesson in faith. We learn that while Jesus was speaking to her, someone told Jairus that his daughter had died. But Jesus looked at Jairus and said, "Do not be afraid; just believe," encouraging him to follow the example of the woman who had just been healed.

Gench points out that those two stories are presented in a section of the Gospel of

---

[81] Frances Taylor Gench, *Back to the Well: Women's Encounters with Jesus in the Gospels* (Louisville: Westminster John Knox, 2004), 29.

Mark (Mark 4:35–6:6) that records four of Jesus' miracles. In the first one, he calmed the stormy sea (establishing his authority over nature). In the second, he healed a man who had been possessed by unclean spirits (establishing his authority over the evil spirits), then he healed a woman who had been diseased for twelve years, and finally he raised a dead daughter. By these miracles, Mark showed that no natural power, no satanic power, no human illness, and not even death can withstand God's power and the authority of his kingdom as manifested in Jesus' ministry. Gench quotes the words of Mary Ann Talbert regarding these striking stories:

> If faith is the response to hearing the word, the kingdom of God is revealed in transforming power that provides incredible results.[82]

Jesus insisted on acknowledging this woman by asking, "Who touched my clothes?" His disciples, especially Peter, were surprised by this question and responded, "You see the people crowding against you . . . and yet you can ask, 'Who touched me?'" (Mark 5:30–31). But Jesus had felt power go from him and knew that the woman was healed and liberated and must be acknowledged. It is as if he was asking, "Who received the power that went out from me?" Jesus wanted to proclaim the faith of this woman, praise her, and send her away in peace. Faith in Jesus gives healing and peace. Even though the law had isolated her, making her worthless, this woman was able to have great faith in Jesus, enabling her to participate in her own healing. Jesus' goal was not to embarrass her but to liberate her and make her an example of bold faith. "Daughter, your faith has healed you; go in peace and be freed from your suffering."

The woman believed that she would be healed if she touched Jesus; the disciples were surprised that Jesus asked who had touched him. I do not want to make a comparison here, but I want to stress how Jesus freed this woman, honored her faith, and restored her to society as a whole human being. He also corrected the attitude of the disciples, who reacted to his question in a tone that suggests they were blaming him for asking it. Yes, this woman was a model of faith. She had to break social prohibitions in order to be physically and spiritually liberated. This is the freedom of life in Christ.

The Canaanite Woman

Jesus' encounter with the Syrophoenician woman is mentioned only in Matthew and Mark (Matt 15:21–28; Mark 7:24–30). Gench's view is that Mark was the first to record this story, which Matthew then reformulated as he retold it to his own community. She comments,

> Jesus' unexpected encounter with the Canaanite woman proved to be a defining moment in his ministry. . . . She was an outsider with a demon-possessed daughter, and the story

---

[82] Gench, *Back to the Well*, 31.

of her encounter with Jesus is . . . extraordinary among all the Gospel stories in that it is one of the few in which a woman character is granted a significant voice. In Matthew's narrative, this account offers only the second time that the voice of a woman is heard speaking out loud.[83]

The story in Matthew is about a healing miracle, but it is also a dialogue between Jesus and the Canaanite woman. She begins the dialogue by crying out, "Lord, Son of David, have mercy on me! My daughter is demon-possessed." But Jesus did not answer her, acting as if he did not hear her. The disciples begged him to respond, saying, "Send her away, for she keeps crying out after us." This was the first time that Jesus did not respond to a cry for help. More than that, he also said, "It is not right to take the children's bread and toss it to the dogs." Mary Rose D'Angelo says,

> The callousness of Jesus' comment violates Christian perceptions about how Jesus ought to have behaved; discomfort with this picture has caused many commentators to deflect attention from the calculated insult by castigating "Jewish exclusivity."[84]

Both Gench and D'Angelo agree that Matthew stressed the great faith this woman had; but it does appear that Jesus' attitude to her contradicts all his known attitudes.

The woman speaks three times. First, she cries out, "Lord, Son of David, have mercy on me"; then she kneels before him, saying, "Lord, help me!"; and finally she answers his harsh response by saying, "Yes it is, Lord, . . . even the dogs eat the crumbs that fall from their master's table."

Matthew alone describes this woman as a "Canaanite," a term that suggests that he wanted to remind his readers that she was a foreigner and one of their ancient enemies. Yet she calls out to Jesus using Jewish messianic language, referring to him as "Lord" and "Son of David," and appealing to him to have mercy on her. According to Gench, her words echo the language of the Psalms.[85] I am reminded of Rahab, who had heard about the God of Israel and his marvelous acts and believed that he would continue to act; thus she made an agreement with the two spies to preserve her family. The Canaanite woman here shows that she had great faith even before she encountered Jesus. Did she know about the coming Messiah? Who knows? But her language is clearly that of faith and prayer. She crossed the border from Tyre and Sidon when she heard about Jesus' presence and she hurried after him as if she knew of his power and authority to heal diseases and expel evil spirits. She knew that she might not have a legal right to benefit from Jesus' power, yet she persisted in believing that Jesus did not come for just one people.

Mary Rose D'Angelo says that the woman's calling out to Jesus as the "Son of David"

---

83 Ibid., 1.

84 Kraemer and D'Angelo, *Women and Christian Origins*, 140.

85 Gench, *Back to the Well*, 6.

shows that her faith, which brought her the answer to her appeal, was not only a persistent faith but also faith that Jesus is the Messiah.[86] She was the first foreign woman to receive a healing miracle from Jesus. The dialogue between her and Jesus, in spite of his apparently callous attitude, would have taught the disciples an important lesson. This foreign woman who knew about God the creator and his goodness and his kingdom that includes all creation had a faith greater than that of many Israelites. When Jesus said to her, "Woman, you have great faith! Your request is granted" it was as if he were telling her, "you have met the challenge—you deserve to be a model of faith."

This was a foreign woman, not part of the flock of Israel to whom Jesus came. She was desperate due to her daughter's disease. Her only hope of healing lay with a miracle, and she knew that one who performs miracles is surely more than a man. Thus the woman spoke with unexpected confidence and wisdom. She was not afraid to talk to Jesus because she had great faith in him. She did her best to acquire the knowledge of the Messiah for whom the Jews were waiting. She knew that she belonged to God's creation and that God cares for all people, so she claimed her right to God's free grace. The words "Woman, you have great faith! Your request is granted" bear witness to a woman worthy of mention in the gospels.

In this chapter we cannot avoid discussing women in Jesus' teachings and ministry. If we look at each incident separately, we will discover his positive attitudes toward women as human beings. We will also discover that the writers of the New Testament wanted to stress the attributes of women that make them examples and models of faith, just like men. Women deserve to be examples of courage and boldness. They have the capacity to act independently in difficult situations and to stand against injustice. In the four gospels we see Jesus dealing with women freely and without reservation. Women were around him as disciples, servants, and followers, and some traveled with him. Some even provided for him out of their own means.

Women are found in the healing stories, where Jesus touched them and renewed their humanity, abolishing slavery to the rules of cleanness and uncleanness that chained women and made them second-class beings.

In some of Jesus' parables, a woman was the main character. He also sometimes referred to women indirectly. Women were a constant presence in his life, from the announcement of the good news of his coming to his birth, childhood, travels, death on the cross, and burial. A woman was the first to receive the news of his resurrection, to see the risen Lord, and to inform his disciples.

I find it difficult to leave this passage and go on to the last part of this chapter without mentioning some of the women who were with Jesus, according to the Gospel of John, the last of the four gospels. We are told by New Testament scholars that the

---

[86] Kraemer and D'Angelo, *Women and Christian Origins*, 175.

Gospel of John is the fruit of years of meditation on the mystery of Jesus of Nazareth. It has been compared to a pool in which small children can paddle and an elephant can swim. In the Gospel of John we get glimpses of the stories of women from John's perspective. Here we will only glance briefly at what he says, remembering that John wrote in order to proclaim who Jesus is, and that his teaching about women is given within this context.

The Samaritan Woman

John tells the story of Jesus' encounter with a Samaritan woman in a way that urges readers to meditate upon it (John 4). This is the longest recorded dialogue between Jesus and an individual in the gospels.

The woman came to draw water from Jacob's well in the middle of the day. Suddenly she found herself talking with a foreigner. She knew from his clothing that he was a Jewish rabbi, and so she was surprised when this Jewish man and teacher asked her, a Samaritan woman, to give him a drink. She knew full well that the Jews did not talk to the Samaritans, and that, according to the law, a man would not accept anything from the hand of a woman; especially if she was a stranger. So she asked him, "How can you ask me for a drink?" It is as if she were saying, "I can't believe what I am hearing!"

Jesus then told the woman that if she knew who he was, she would have asked him to give her a drink. Even more surprised, she asked him how he could give her a drink when he had no way of drawing water. Jesus responded that the water he offers is not like the water she draws; he gives living water. At this, she became so curious that she asked, "Are you greater than our father Jacob?" Jesus answered, "Whoever drinks the water I give them will never thirst." The woman then said to him, "Sir, give me this water so that I won't get thirsty and have to keep coming here to draw water." Jesus had awakened in this woman a longing for knowledge.

At this moment of amazement, Jesus revealed to the woman that he knew more about her life than she imagined. Jesus said to her, "Go, call your husband and come back." The woman answered, "I have no husband." But Jesus shocked her by saying that she had had five husbands, and the man she was now with was not her husband.

Here the woman reached the point of thinking he was a prophet. She started discussing worship, either to show him that she had some knowledge or to draw his attention away from her personal life to something she thought might be more interesting to him as a prophet. Once again, Jesus revealed something new to her—the place of worship is not important, for the worship that God demands has to be in spirit and in truth. "God is spirit, and those who worship him must worship in the Spirit and in truth." The woman drew on her religious memory and said, "I know that Messiah . . . is coming. When he comes, he will explain everything to us." It seems that she wanted to end a dialogue that had embarrassed her and depleted her religious inventory.

Yet Jesus without hesitation declared to her that he was the Messiah! How could this woman help but be amazed after hearing all these declarations and finally realizing that the one who was speaking to her was the Messiah? Anyone can see that this woman had just been born again. I often wonder whether her face was shining like that of Moses.

She left her water jar and went into the city, telling people about the man who told her all that she had done. Could this be the Christ? In the beginning of the dialogue, the woman said to Jesus, "Are you greater than our father Jacob?" But now she asks, "Can this be the Messiah?" She was sure he was, and many others believed in Christ because of her words, and even more believed in him because of his words. They asked him to stay with them for two days.

Strikingly, at the beginning of chapter 4 John told us that Jesus had left Judea on route to Galilee, and that "he had to go through Samaria." Though this is correct geographically, pious Jews often took another route so as not to pass through Samaria and be defiled by the Samaritans. Yet, Jesus intended to pass through Samaria for some purpose.

One Bible interpreter has noted a similarity between the account of what happened at Jacob's well and what happened at Calvary. Both include references to its being the sixth hour, and in both Jesus says that he is thirsty, but does not drink.[87]

Did Jesus pass through Samaria to give us a preview of Calvary? I don't think so. He passed through Samaria to complete his mission before going to the cross. Part of his mission in Samaria was meeting with a sinful woman who was thirsty. His dialogue with her shows how he broke down the wall between men and women, as well as the wall between the chosen people and other peoples. He wanted to show that God's grace is for all people, and that this grace is offered as freely as Jesus offered the Samaritan woman living water.

Jesus led this woman to believe in him and made her a missionary carrying the good news to her people. In going to Samaria and through his dialogue with the woman, Jesus made unexpected changes. There had been wrong concepts, and he wanted to correct them. There had been national and racial pride, and he wanted to abolish these. There had been artificial borders that he wanted to destroy, and a way of worship he wanted to renew. Also there had been a limited concept about God that he wanted to correct once and for all. In Jesus, we can now call God the Father of all people.

Jesus had never previously taught with such richness, clarity, and openness as he did with this woman to whom he went. The story of the Samaritan woman is the story of a troubled soul struggling in a damaged world surrounded by darkness and walls that separated individuals, peoples, and men from women. Jesus came to this soul,

---

[87] I first read and noted this in 1988, but cannot recall the reference.

challenging social and religious traditions and customs in order to offer the living water which springs up to eternal life. He wanted to declare to her that he is the Messiah who had come in the fullness of time to renew history. If this woman had been a man, Jesus would have gone to him too.

Mary and Martha

It is well known that the Gospel of John takes a different tack from the other three gospels. It contains fewer healing stories, for John's goal was to highlight the character of Jesus. One of the stories that he does record to show that Jesus is the Lord and giver of life is the account of Jesus raising Lazarus from the dead. Since our focus in this chapter is on understanding the position of women in the New Testament church, we will meditate on Lazarus' two sisters, Martha and Mary.

John tells the story in chapter 11, where he says that Lazarus was ill. So the sisters sent word to Jesus that Lazarus, whom he loved, was ill. But when Jesus heard the news, he delayed and only went to them four days after Lazarus' death. Each of the sisters met Jesus separately; then both together. Jesus had important conversations with each of them.

Mary, Martha, and Lazarus lived in the village of Bethany, where Jesus would sometimes visit them. We read about one of these visits in Luke 10:38–42. Luke records that Martha received Jesus in her house and wanted to prepare a feast for him. Meanwhile, Mary sat at Jesus' feet, listening to his teaching. Martha, who "was distracted by all the preparations," complained to Jesus that Mary was not helping her. But Jesus answered her,

> Martha, Martha, . . . you are worried and upset about many things, but few things are needed—or indeed only one. Mary has chosen what is better, and it will not be taken away from her.

Is it not strange that though Jesus seems to have rebuked Martha for being too busy with many things and praised Mary who chose to learn at his feet, the church over the ages has deliberately tried to keep women busy with household matters and disapproved of their desire to study? In other words, the church has wanted women to be more like Martha than like Mary.

Gench says that this story tends to divide readers into two groups. The first group read it as a story of women's liberation, for it reflects women's involvement as disciples of Jesus, challenging the customs that limited their role. The other group, however, read it as a story of injustice and oppression, for it pits two sisters against each other and accepts the idea of duality, with a good sister contrasted with a bad one. They claim that the story also shows that Jesus does not value hospitality and the hard work women do to honor their guests.

Gench cannot agree with the second view. She points out that Luke begins chapter

10 with an account of Jesus sending seventy people out to serve and telling them not to take food for the journey but to enter houses and stay in them, eating what is served to them. Thus hospitality is very important in his ministry. Yet, in the paragraph that preceded Jesus' visit to Martha and Mary, when "an expert in the law" tested him by asking, "What must I do to inherit eternal life," Jesus stressed that what was most important was to love the Lord with all one's heart and soul and mind. What Mary did was an expression of her love for the Lord and for his teachings. Thus she chose the good portion. Such wisdom transcended the distraction of being busy with many other things.[88]

When we turn to the account of the raising of Lazarus, we find that John shows that both sisters loved Jesus and were his disciples, each in their own way. Martha's hospitable nature is evident in the fact that when she heard that Jesus was approaching, she left her sister with the mourners in the house and went out to meet him. In her grief, and perhaps feeling that their friendship had been betrayed, she said to Jesus,

> Lord, if you had been here, my brother would not have died. But I know that even now God will give you whatever you ask. (John 11:21–22)

If her first words express the loving reproach of friendship and love, the words that follow in part say something different: "I know that even now . . ."

Did Martha expect a miracle from Jesus? She believed in Jesus' power to heal diseases, but did she believe that he could raise people from the dead? Jesus said to her, "Your brother will rise again." She answered, "I know that he will rise again in the resurrection at the last day." Here it seems as if Martha was saying to Jesus, "I know that; you are not telling me anything new." But Jesus continues,

> I am the resurrection and the life; the one who believes in me will live, even though they die, and whoever lives by believing in me will never die. Do you believe this?

We can imagine what went through Martha's mind at that moment. We are reminded of a similar moment for the Samaritan woman when Jesus told her that he was the Messiah—it was a moment of great amazement, and a moment of completion of faith. Whereas the Samaritan woman left her water jar and went to the town and told her people that she had met "the Messiah," we find Martha saying, "Yes, Lord, . . . I believe that you are the Messiah, the Son of God, who is to come into the world."

When Jesus asked his disciples: "Who do you say I am?" Peter replied, "You are the Messiah, the Son of the living God." Then Jesus told him, "Blessed are you, . . . for this was not revealed to you by flesh and blood, but by my Father in heaven" (Matt

---

[88] Gench, *Back to the Well*, 56–57.

16:15–17). Did Martha have a revelation like that here? I do not doubt that Martha spoke by the spirit of prophecy.

Why did Jesus reveal himself to Martha with such clarity and openness? It was because Martha was willing to hear and her heart was filled with faith in Jesus and in his authority. Martha's faith grew just as the faith and knowledge of the Samaritan woman grew. In both cases, Jesus honored the openness of their hearts to hear his words, and he revealed to both of them the mystery of his nature.

Mary, the sister of Martha and Lazarus, was different. Luke tells us that she enjoyed listening to Jesus and sitting at his feet, a pattern of behavior that shows that Jesus made disciples of both men and women alike, contrary to the customs at that time.[89]

When Martha told Mary that Jesus had arrived and wished to speak with her, Mary quickly went out to him. Then she fell at his feet, saying to him, "Lord, if you had been here, my brother would not have died." Jesus saw her tears and "he was deeply moved in spirit and troubled" and he wept with her. Then Jesus exerted his authority over death and life and summoned Lazarus out of the tomb. This was a moment of awe and amazement for all those present, for Jesus is the king of death and the giver of life.

Before his final Passover meal, Jesus returned to Bethany. Martha again served him and made him dinner. But whereas on the previous occasion Mary had sat at Jesus' feet, this time she poured precious oil on his feet and dried them with her hair, in complete faith and with great love. When Judas complained about this waste of precious oil, Jesus said, "Leave her alone. . . . It was intended that she should save this perfume for the day of my burial" (John 12:7).

Did Mary understand the relationship between the raising of Lazarus and the death of Jesus? She acted in the spirit of prophecy, just as Martha spoke in the spirit of prophecy.

Mary and Martha were two women believers, each of whom served Jesus in her own way. Jesus accepted both and honored their faith and revealed himself to them, also in his own special way. Surely these two women are also among Jesus' disciples.

Time is too short to speak about every woman mentioned in the New Testament and every woman Jesus dealt with, rescuing her humanity, restoring her dignity, and renewing her life. I apologize to Mary Magdalene, whose witness I would have liked to examine, and to those who carried the anointing oils on the morning of the resurrection, and to the weeping Mary who was the first to see the risen Lord through her tears. She was even the first to bear the news of the resurrection to the disciples. However, I cannot apologize to the best of all, Mary, the mother of Jesus, for she was the first who knew Jesus. She is the last one I will mention here.

---

[89] Ibid., 59.

Mary, the Mother of Jesus

Mary, the mother of Jesus, is largely a silent presence, for the New Testament is the story of Jesus Christ—his birth, ministry, and salvation—not the story of the Virgin Mary's life. Luke is the only evangelist who mentions her experience when the angel told her the good news that she would be the mother of the Savior. Luke recorded her splendid song when she was greeted by Elizabeth, her relative who was carrying John the Baptist in her womb. The apostle Paul refers to her a few times, but never mentions her name. Even in John's Gospel, which we will be looking at here, her name is never mentioned.

Mary, the mother of Jesus, was not a woman like other women, even though we often say that in the face of Mary, the mother of Jesus, we find the face of every woman in history, and that in every woman in history we find the face of Mary. Whereas Eve was tempted and fell, Mary stood straight, head bowed before God, who was pleased to use her as his instrument to achieve the dream of freedom from death that human beings had cherished ever since they had received the promise that the seed of the woman would bruise the head of the ancient serpent. Who would not want to repeat the words of Mary, "My soul glorifies the Lord and my spirit rejoices in God my Savior" (Luke 1:46)? Who would not learn a lesson about obeying God and surrendering to his will when they read Mary's words in the Gospel of Luke? Mary as a woman restored the status of women as human beings after Eve had distorted it. She well deserves to be called the second Eve.

Fr. Bertrand Ruby uses artistic terms to summarize the way Mary is represented in the Bible. He claims that in Mark's Gospel she appears as a silhouette, while Matthew draws her as a pencil sketch, with clearer lines showing her discipleship. Luke, the creative artist, gives us a portrait of Mary the disciple, and in the Gospel of John she is presented as a splendid sculpture in the marriage at Cana and at Calvary. In the book of Revelation, she appears as a woman clothed with the sun, and is a symbol of the church and believers in Jesus Christ. Mary, according to Father Ruby, was the first believer and disciple. He argues that her discipleship and her faith must have preceded her becoming the mother of Jesus Christ, because otherwise she could not have been chosen to be his mother. He quotes St. Augustine (fourth century) as saying that "she first conceived Christ through faith before conceiving him in the flesh."[90]

The discipleship of Mary is an example to all of discipleship and faith. John refers to her presence at the wedding at Cana in Galilee (John 2:1–11). There she noticed the approaching crisis as the family began to run out of wine. She went to Jesus and told him, "They have no more wine." She knew in her heart that Jesus had power and authority. She did not ask him anything; she only told him that the wine had run out. Yet Jesus' response to her was, "Woman, why do you involve me? . . . My hour has not yet come."

---

[90] S. M. Bertrand Ruby, *Mary the Faithful Disciple* (New York: Paulist, 1985), 12–13.

If we had heard this exchange, we might have been surprised at such apparent disrespect. Why does he address her as "woman" rather than as "mother"? Mary, however, simply told the servants, "Do whatever he tells you." What did she understand from Jesus' answer? Did she feel the struggle inside him as he was preparing himself to fulfill his great commission? Was she not taking a risk, after this answer, by telling the servants to do whatever he told them? At the end of chapter 1, John tells us that Jesus told Nathanael, "You believe because I told you I saw you under the fig tree. You shall see greater things than that." Mary expected greater things because her faith in Jesus was real and great. Mary was the first disciple and believer, and she was the woman whose soul was pierced by a sword. Though he called her "woman" rather than "mother," Jesus performed his first miracle and showed his glory to his disciples, of whom she was one.

John again mentions Mary in chapter 19, where Mary and other women gather at the cross of Jesus.

> When Jesus saw his mother there, and the disciple whom he loved standing nearby, he said to her, "Woman, here is your son," and to the disciple, "Here is your mother."

It is as if Jesus in these awesome moments wanted to honor Mary. In her motherhood of the disciple whom Jesus loved, we see a new family born in the womb of suffering from the cross of Jesus of Nazareth. Thus Mary became the believing disciple, the mother of the church over the ages.

The book of Acts tells us that Mary was present among the praying disciples in the upper room (Acts 1:14). No doubt she was present when the Holy Spirit was poured out on the disciples. Mary believed in Jesus and bore the message of the gospel just like all those who believed in Jesus and were around him. In the fullness of time, God sent his Son born of a woman. How great is God and how deep is his love that he was willing to be born of a woman.

Fiorenza argues that John presents discipleship and leadership as including both men and women. The women mentioned in John are examples of discipleship for both men and women alike, and he accords them a high status. The Gospel of John starts and concludes the ministry of Jesus of Nazareth with stories about a woman—at the start there is Mary the mother of Jesus and at the end there is Mary of Bethany. He parallels Nicodemus the Pharisee with the Samaritan woman, and he parallels Peter's confession that Jesus is the Christ the Son of God with Martha's confession, "You are the Messiah, the Son of God who is to come into the world." John shows us four women standing at the cross with the disciple whom Jesus loved. Mary Magdalene was not only the first to see the empty tomb, she was also the first to see the risen Lord. Thus a woman is presented as a faithful disciple and a witnessing missionary.[91]

---

[91] Fiorenza, *In Memory of Her*, 326.

Women Disciples?

As I said before, time is too short to mention every woman mentioned in the Gospel of John alone. But there is still one question that we have to address: Why were there no women among the twelve disciples of Jesus? This fact has been used to deprive women throughout history of the opportunity to participate in the pastoral ministry of the church, though it did not prevent them from participating in the same ministry in the early church. Women like Lydia and John's mother and many others led churches in their houses.

Why do we ignore the names of the women who are mentioned on the pages of the New Testament? Francine Cardman says,

> Recognized by Paul as co-workers, women were apostles, missionaries, and leaders of house churches in the early decades after the death and resurrection of Jesus. But as Christianity made its way through the Greco-Roman world, women's leadership and ministry were increasingly pushed to the margins of evolving church structures. The process of institutionalization of the churches was already under way by the end of the first century CE; by the end of the fourth, it was essentially complete. As Christian churches assumed their place among the social, political, and religious institutions of late antiquity, they began to take on the values of their culture, particularly in regard to gender roles. . . . Although excluded from the established structures of ministry by the beginning of the fifth century, women continued to exercise some form of leadership in the churches and to engage from time to time in ministries forbidden to them. As a result, bishops and councils continued to issue protests and formal prohibitions of women's ministries well into the sixth century and beyond.[92]

The history of female leaders in the early Christian centuries is the subject of serious study by many women today. Fiorenza affirms that women were effective participants in the missionary movement of the early church, though this fact was never highlighted.

Fiorenza reminds us of Peter's reference to the fulfillment of the prophecy of Joel on the day of Pentecost:

> In the last days, God says, I will pour out my Spirit on all people. Your sons and daughters will prophesy, your young men will see visions, your old men will dream dreams. (Acts 2:17)

She insists that since Pentecost, service in the Christian church has become the service equally of men and women through the power of the Holy Spirit.[93] She adds that when Paul spoke of women as co-workers, he was not implying that they merely

---

[92] Francine Cardman, "Women, Ministry and Church Order in Early Christianity," in *Women and Christian Origins*, ed. Kraemer and D'Angelo, 300.

[93] Fiorenza, *In Memory of Her*, 160.

served and helped him but saw them as equal companions in his ministry. Those who served and helped him are specifically identified as five men, namely Erastus, Mark, Timothy, Titus, and Tychicus. As for Priscilla, Phoebe, Joanna, and other women, they were ministers of the word just as he was. Paul asked the Thessalonian church to respect and esteem such women very highly in love for their labor. And he asked the church at Corinth to be subject to those who work and toil with them. Thus Paul had no problem in mentioning the names of his women co-workers in 1 Corinthians and Philippians.[94]

Fiorenza states that the Pauline community included women prophets among its leaders and points out that Luke refers to Mary, Elizabeth, and Anna as prophets, as well as the four daughters of Philip.[95] Fiorenza says,

> the second and third centuries are characterized by the struggle of the prophetic and local ministry for authority in the church. It is not the canon—as Adolf Harnack believed—but the episcopal hierarchy which replaced early Christian prophecy.

The teachings of bishops became normative by the middle of the third century.

There are indications that the male leadership of the church created what were known as women's churches, where single and independent women believers gathered in some kind of Christian female society similar to those that existed in some cults. With the rise of the episcopal system, bishops gradually came to rule over these groups of women in the church. In time, there was a growing separation between the teaching ministry of bishops and the diaconal service permitted to women.[96]

Thus as the church grew, it accommodated to society and became engaged in social and political issues. Over time, it adopted the values, traditions, and habits of the societies in which it existed. Most of these societies were strongly patriarchal, and thus Christian women lost their rights and their opportunities for leadership. Meanwhile the church lost the leadership capacities of women and their gifts of giving and instruction. Instead of the church changing society, with all its traditions that limit people's humanity and deny their natural human rights, the church allowed the society to change it and to import its barriers and customs into the church.

Where are we today regarding the concept of women in pastoral service, since they have participated in the new creation with Jesus? Do we have the courage to return to the springs of life that Jesus created to satisfy everyone? Or do we still live like those whom Paul described as still wearing the veil when they read the Old Testament? In the New Testament Jesus of Nazareth renews everything and restores the image of God to every Christian human being,

---

[94] Ibid., 169.
[95] Ibid., 299.

[96] Ibid., 302–3.

having canceled the charge of our legal indebtedness, which stood against us and condemned us; he has taken it away, nailing it to the cross. (Col 2:14)

Paul says that the veil is removed in Christ, and that when we return to the Lord, the old veil that concealed God's glory will be removed. We have to read the New Testament beholding the glory of Jesus Christ.

The church today is called to read the New Testament with an uncovered face. When we acknowledge the Christian principle that we are all kings and priests to God the Father, then all the objections that prohibit women from participating in the service of the church at all levels will be nailed to the cross.

Like all other ministries, pastoral ministry in the church is a gift and calling of the Holy Spirit. So, if God calls a woman for his service, who dares to prevent her fulfilling this calling?

To him who loves us and has freed us from our sins by his blood, and has made us to be a kingdom and priests to serve his God and Father—to him be glory and power for ever and ever! Amen. (Rev 1:5–6)

المراجع العربية (ARABIC SOURCES)

1. حاضرة "إعلان دومينس إياسوس : حول وحدانية وشموليّة الخلاص يسوع المسيح و الكنيس." الفاتيكان: مجمع للعقيدة الإيمان, 2000. منشورات اللجنة الأسقفية لوسائل الإعلام. جل الديب, لبنان.

[*Declaration* Dominus Iesus: *On the Unicity and Salvific Universality of Jesus Christ and the Church.* Congregation for the Doctrine of the Faith. The Vatican, 2000.]

2. البلاغ المسيحي, وهو احد القرارات التي اصدرها مؤتمر التبشير المسكوني المنعقد في القدس 1928. بيروت: المطبعة الأمريكانية, 1932.

[Christian Declaration Issued by the Conference of Ecumenical Preaching in Jerusalem, 1928, Beirut: al-Maṭbaʾt al-ʾAmrīkānīa 1932.]

3. القس تقرير الرابطة الكنائس الإنجيلية في الشرق الأوسط, الجمعية العامة الرابعة. إعداد القس اديب عوض. لارنكا, 1997.

[Awad, Rev. Adeeb. "Report of the Association of Evangelical Churches in the Middle East, Fourth General Assembly." Larnaca, 1997.]

4. سلامه, اديب نجيب, تاريخ الكنيسة الإنجيلية في مصر 1854–1980. القاهرة: دار الثقافة 1982.

[Salameh, Adib Najib. *The History of the Evangelical Church in Egypt from 1854 to 1980.* Cairo: House of Culture, 1982.]

5. صبرا, جورج, في سبيل الحوار المسكوني. مقالات لاهوتيّة إنجيلية. بيروت: منشورات دار النفير, 2001.

[Sabra, George. *For the Sake of Ecumenical Dialogue. Evangelical Theological Articles* Beirut: Dar Al-Nafir Publications, 2001.]

6. صهيوني, سليم, "اختبارات في المسيرة المسكونية" محاضرة غير منشورألقيت في لقاء "التحديّات النابعة من واقع وعمل الحركة المسكونية" لرابطة الكنائس الإنجيلية في الشرق الأوسط. لارنكا, قبرص 1–5 تشرين الثاني 1998. (غير منشورة).

[Sahiouny, Salim. "Experiences in the Ecumenical Journey." Unpublished lecture presented at the session, "The Challenges Arising from the Reality and Labor of the Ecumenical Movement," for the Fellowship of Middle East Evangelical Churches, Larnaca, Cyprus, 1–5 November 1998.]

7. العمل الإنجيلي في الشرق العربي. الكتاب الخامس لرابطة الكتّاب المسيحيين في الشرق الأدنى. بيروت: مكتبة المشعل, 1960.

[*Evangelical Work in the Arab East*. Book V of the Association of Christian Writers in the Near East. Beirut: Torch Library, 1960.]

8. عوده, فريد ومطر, ابراهيم, التراث الإنجيلي. بيروت: مكتبة المشعل, 1955.

[Odeh, Farīd and Ibrahim Matar. *Evangelical Heritage*. Beirut: Torch library, 1955.]

9. كوربون, جان, "الحركة المسكونية وتاريخها في الشرق" في المسيحية عبر تاريخها في المشرق. تحرير ح. بدر, س. سليم, ج. ابو نهرا. بيروت: منشورات مجلس كنائس الشرق الأوسط, 2001 ص 873–887.

[Cōrpūn, Jean. "The Ecumenical Movement and Its History in the East." Pages 873–87 in *Christianity: Through Its History in the East*. Edited by Badr H., S. Salim and J. Abou Nohrā. Beirut: MECC, 2001.]

10. /مجلس كنائس الشرق الأوسط. الجمعية العامة الخامسة-نيقوسيا, قبرص 22–28 كانون الثاني/ يناير 1990. بيروت, 1994.

[Fifth General Assembly of the Middle East Council of Churches. Nīqūsīa, Cyprus, 22–28 January 1990. Beirut, 1994.]

11. مجلس كنائس الشرق الأوسط. الجمعية العامة السابعة-دار سيّدة الجبل, فتقا, لبنان 26–30 نيسان/ابريل 1999. بيروت, 2001.

[Seventh General Assembly of the Middle East Council of Churches. Dār Sayyedat el-Jabal, Fatqā, Lebanon, 26–30 April 1999. Beirut, 2001.]

12. /مجلس كنائس الشرق الأوسط. الجمعية العامة الثامنة-ليماسول, قبرص 2–5 كانون الأول ديسمبر 2003. بيروت, 2004.

[Eighth General Assembly of the Middle East Council of Churches. Līmāssōl, Cyprus, 2–5 December 2003. Beirut, 2004.]

13. الوحدة الإنجيلية التي دعا إليها مؤتمر قادة الكنائس الإنجيلية في البلاد العربية المنعقد في بيروت من 28–30 نيسان سنة 1955. بيروت, 1955.

[The Unity of Evangelicals convened by the Conference of the Leaders of Evangelical Churches in Arab Countries, Held in Beirut. 28–30 April 1955. Beirut, 1955.]

المراجع الاجنبية (NON-ARABIC SOURCES)

Aharonian, Hovhannes P. Selected speeches in *The Armenian Evangelical Church on the Crossroads*. Edited by Yervant H. Kassouny. Beirut: MECC, 1988.

Badr, Habib. "Mission To 'Nominal Christians': The Policy and Practice of the American Board of Commissioners for Foreign Missions and Its Missionaries Concerning Eastern Churches which led to the Organization of a Protestant Church in Beirut (1819–1848)." PhD Diss., Princeton Theological Seminary, 1992.

Bassous, Michel. "Why Some Local Evangelical Churches Are Against Ecumenism." Research paper for "Contemporary Eastern Churches" (H1354), Near East School of Theology, Spring 2002.

Brown, Robert McAfee. *The Spirit of Protestantism*. Oxford: Oxford University Press, 1965.

Pacini, Andrea, ed. *Christian Communities in the Arab Middle East*. Oxford: Clarendon Press, 1998.

The Constitutions of the Near East Council of Churches. April 1964.

Constitution and By-laws of the Near East Council of Churches. 1967.

Kinnamon, M., and B. E. Cape, eds. *The Ecumenical Movement. An Anthology of Key Texts and Voices*. Geneva: WCC Publications; Grand Rapids: Eerdmans, 1997.

Gounelle, André. *Protestantisme, les grands principes*. Paris: Les Bergers et les Mages, 1994.

Rouse, R., and S. C. Neill, eds. *A History of the Ecumenical Movement 1517–1948*. London: S.P.C.K., 1954.

Al-Montada. MECC Information and Documentation Service.

Pannenberg, Wolfhart. *Ethik und Ekklesiologie. Gesammelte Aufsätze*. Göttingen: Vandenhoeck and Ruprecht, 1977.

Proche Orient Chrétien. St. Ann, Jerusalem, 1951.

Sahiouny, Salim. "The Unity of the Church in the Middle East." DMin Thesis, McCormick Theological Seminary, 1981.

Vorländer, Dorothea. *Libanon: Land der Gegensätze*. Erlangen: Verlag der Evangelischen Lutherischen Mission, 1980.

Chapter Six

THE CROSS AND THE POWER ISSUE

A MIDDLE EASTERN VIEW

Youssef Samir

Rev. Youssef Samir is senior pastor of Heliopolis Evangelical Church. He holds a BA from Ain Shams University, a B.Th. from Evangelical Theological Seminary at Cairo. Samir teaches Christian worship history and Biblical preaching part-time at the Evangelical Theological Seminary in Cairo. He is the author of *Fellowship that Changes Life* and *Philosophy of Worship History* and has translated more than fifteen books from both English and French in theology and biblical studies.

———————⟪⟫———————

THE RELATION BETWEEN the church and the elements and tools of society has not always been a harmonious one; it has not remained warm, nor will it do so in the future. Rather it has faced weakness, lack of harmony, and indifference in many situations throughout its history. The tension we here refer to lies in the distance or crisis that emerges between "terms" of divine history, such as the divine revelation, the church's ecclesiastical views, or the Christian morals, and the societal, political, economic, cultural inclinations, and other trends of the age. Biblical history is full of such examples in which we see divine revelation reject a political or economic position that clashes with the principles of the holy kingdom or the moral principles that God has called for through his holy Word.

In this article, we will address the issue of power, which is surely a societal phenomena

374

deeply linked and rooted in all levels of society and all degrees of human relations. Sociologist Anthony Cambolo describes it as follows:

> Most humans play the power game. There are husbands who want to dominate their wives, and wives who wish to possess equal power as that of their husbands. There are children who struggle to free themselves from the dominance of their parents, and parents who violently control their children. There are priests who seek to control the congregations of their churches, and church members who enjoy supremacy over their employees, who in turn form ties to impose certain policies on their work superiors.
>
> There are whites who fear to lose their power over blacks, and blacks whose cries for freedom turn into acts of extreme violence. There are politicians who might resort to every possible means to keep them in power, and the rebels who will devise any deception to seize power out of the grip of those who hold on to it. There are nations that threaten the human existence by building war machines that enable them to stay on the lists of world powers.[1]

The German philosopher Friedrich Nietzsche goes even further when he affirms that the desire for power is the basic human motivation among other human motives.[2] Christian psychologist Paul Tournier emphasizes the same view as Nietzsche, pointing out that the desire for power and domination drives many people without them realizing it.[3] Following the same line of thought, it is said that what explains history more precisely is only the realization that the passion for power is what stands behind all important activity in human societies.[4] Then we reach the tradition, narrated by political writer Imam Abdel Fattah, demonstrating the importance given by human societies to the idea of power and the image of the powerful ruler. The tradition here is taken from Persia, as Abdel Fattah states:

> It has been the custom that in ancient times, when a Persian king dies, the people are left for 5 days without a king and without law so that chaos and turmoil prevail throughout the country. The purpose was that by the end of these five days—after that looting and rape have reached their peak, whoever has managed to survive after all the wreaking havoc would have genuine loyalty for the new king. The ordeal would teach them how frightful the state of society would be in the absence of political power.[5]

One can be certain that the issue of power represents one of the most important critical contemporary issues that imposed itself upon both the world reality and the

---

[1] John Nicholas Grenfell III, "Pastoral Theology and Use of Power" (DMin diss., Asbury Theological Seminary, May 1997), 17–18.
[2] Ibid.
[3] Ibid., 19.
[4] Ibid.

[5] Imam Abdel Fattah, "The Tyrant: A Philosophical Study of Forms of Political Despotism," *Alam Al-Maarifah journal* 183 (Kuwait: National Council for Culture, Arts, and Literature; March 1994): 15–16.

Arab reality. This is particularly true after the revolutions that sparked in many of the region's countries since 2011. These revolutions have changed the intellectual and psychological composition of its citizens, specially its youth. It is clear that the revolutions of the Arab spring gave forth to an overwhelming rejection of power in most, if not all, its aspects. The normal and acceptable tendency is to revolt against patriarchal authority in all its forms whether familial, political, social, and, above all, religious. One cannot miss the sweeping resentment against anything religious or related to religious authority in many Arab youth circles, especially against the type of authority that prohibits serious questioning and the earnest search for truth, seeking to muffle mouths, eliminate logic, and dismiss thought. Author Suad Fahd Almojel describes this, saying:

> In addition to the obvious rigidity in contemporary religious thought, and the refusal of its peers of any renovation that could enable to embrace youths rather than terrorize them, it is also one of the main reasons for the youth's aversion to the thought of "preachers" and their projects, especially in the light of the reluctance or rejection of many preachers to answer some of the controversial questions about life and religion, that are usually raised by young people. They find no answer other than being accused of infidelity, and being influenced by intrusive western thought that is dangerous to Muslim societies![6]

No wonder we witness these overwhelming waves of adoption of nonreligious, atheistic inclinations that have afflicted quite a few young Arabs of all backgrounds and cultural, religious, and social circles. Tunisian researcher and writer Fathi Al-Maskini hits the nail on the head when he links the phenomenon of atheism—which strikes not a small proportion of Arab youth—and rebellion against all kinds of authority:

> The claim of atheism by young people, while it may not be the result of metaphysical contemplation of the truth of God or the meaning of transcendence or of the dismal human entity and its existential fragility, it conceals within its folds a firm rebellion against a symbolic network of power, where the paternal influence is merely the apparent halo. What the atheist teenager revolts against is a long-standing network of spiritual pillars that have so far shaped not only the techniques of deep hope for ourselves, but specifically the general forms of personification and personalizing upon which we have built the meaning of our "self" and the meaning of human "identity" and the individual "person" in general. Specifically, the network of authority consisting of the trilogy of the father/ruler/deity, as the secret code of every kind of authority; i.e., the vertical relationship with humans or the world in which they live.[7]

---

[6] Suad Fahd Almojel, "Atheism in the Arab World," *Al Qabs Al Kuweytia* 15789, 15 May 2017.

[7] Fathi Al-Maskini, "The Phenomenon of Atheist Adolescence . . . A Moral Rebellion against Parental Authority," *Al-Magala*, 16 June 2014.

Al-Maskini adds his philosophical/psychological view on this phenomenon in what seems to be a justification:

What an atheist adolescent aspires is not "infidelity "or "idolatry" in the religious sense—as the vision of the world that justifies this kind of biography in life has evaporated a long time ago—but what she aspires for is freedom from a prevailing pattern of deep authority. Emancipation through "atheism"; i.e., the deliberate concealment, obscurantism, blacking out of the screen of the power consisting of the father/ruler/deity. Atheism here only means a wide range moral concealment of the face of the father/ruler/deity that stares straight into the eye of the adolescent and conspires against him from within. It is a visual rebellion on an ethical screen that is no longer tolerated by a new kind of soul. The atheist adolescent wants to resort to the unseen part of his life, so that atheism is a rebellion against the authority of the visible, and the extension of the invisible in the view of the authority, as it is also worth considering.[8]

The researcher continues to explain the reason for this rip in the relationship between authority and adolescents in many authoritarian patriarchal loci in our Arab world, as depicted in an "empty" freedom from traditional submission, which has become a feature of youth in postmodernism. The author explains this freedom, saying that digital and virtual media have enabled young people to have more areas of liberation than ever before: liberation of the senses, liberation of the imagination, liberation of image and language, and thus liberating the living body from the moral body ready for habitation.[9]

Subsequently, the problem facing the Arab societies today is a complex one. First, there is a general revolt against power. Second, the religious establishment that was supposed to provide a moderate contemporary expression of power did not fulfill its role. On the contrary, the religious establishment abused its power for hidden targets, holding a frantic desire to control the existential thought of its followers, keep a grip on all the strings it pulls, and secure its place and status. Political writer Ammar Ali Hassan describes this conspicuous relation between the two powers, the religious and the political, saying that the bonding between these two poles has had a huge negative impact on the concept of religion. That bond has transformed religion into a mere ideology that advocates for power and paves the way ahead of it, mobilizing supporters and apostates on its behalf in order to strengthen its stature and make agendas socially acceptable because they are supported by religious text and divine authority. Therefore, abandonment of their political concepts is sacrilegious, and those who oppose them

---

[8] Ibid. The writer presents in the same article an unfamiliar concept about atheism. He says, "Therefore, the atheist is one who wants to 'deny' a dead object; i.e. to bury it. This method of concealment is a process of concealing the visible with the intention to erect the invisible on grounds that it is more appropriate for humans. Atheism is an aversion to what is seen which is appointed by the authority, and broadcasts it as a unique moral or standard screen to stare at our deep selves."

[9] Ibid.

receive only accusations of paganism and ignorance (*tagheel*; from "*gahilia*" or "the era of ignorance" prior to the acknowledgment of God).[10] The writer reaches the conclusion that many experience the bitter taste of grief and regret over the current state of the religious institution in the Arab East:

> Experience derived from history shows us that the pursuit of political power was the poisoned dagger that stabbed all religions without exception; therefore, the best interest of religion [needs] to distinguish between religion and politics before the interests of politicians. And whoever proposes religion as a project for power, or invokes that access to power is necessary to guard religion and spread it, is in fact manipulating religion, hence, employs it without piety or regard, but only for worldly benefit. So often this is associated with deception and falsehood, deceit and circumvention.[11]

Along the same line of thought, Dr. Rev. Samuel Habib, in *The Art of Leading Groups*, comments on the danger of linking power to religion:

> A dictator becomes a target for the group. Revering him becomes the primary motive for most events. If the autocratic system is linked to a religious belief, the dictator becomes a ruler in the name of God, and becomes a commander or a theocrat. And this is quite dangerous. He acts as if he worked in God's name, and with the authority of God.
>
> If the dictator applies "inhibition," depriving people of the freedom of speaking about mistakes, and drawing attention to them, the result would be a spread of corruption in all aspects of work, hence the work is impeded.[12]

Tunisian university professor Abdul-Latif Al-Hanashi goes even further when he points to the often-existing relation between religious authority and violence. He says, "Violence in a country enveloped by religion may be more intense and severe than in other countries that are not set on a religious mind frame. It is easy for the former to find sufficient religious justification for such practices through the use of religious texts and employing such texts to exercise violence and control."[13] In the rest of the study, Hanashi presents the different forms of violence that the Umayyad state resorted to during many of its kings' reigns in order to impose authority and control over all its mandates and states. The list includes physical torture, such as beating, flogging, cutting off limbs, killing, assassination, burying victims alive, and mutilation of bodies, as well as moral torture, such as curfew, alienation, exile, house arrest, and other violent measures that violate human dignity and freedom.[14]

---

[10] Ammar Ali Hassan, *Deep Society: Social and Financial Networks of Fundamentalist Groups in Egypt* (Cairo: General Egyptian Book Organization, 2016), 305–6.

[11] Ibid., 306.

[12] Samuel Habib, *The Art of Leading Groups* (Doha, Qatar: Dar al-Thaqafa, 2005), 40.

[13] Abdul-Latif Al-Hanashi, "Power and Violence in Islamic History: The Umayyad State as a Model," *Foundation of Faithfuls Without Borders*, November 2013, 3.

[14] Ibid., 9–14.

This was the same authoritative quality as represented by the Jewish priesthood in the era of Lord Jesus Christ, which was proficiently and professionally practiced by the evil pair, Caiaphas and Hanan, who, because of their power practices, were behind the verdict of crucifixion of Christ. Jewish history testifies to the corruption of this priestly family in terms of its use of authority. In one of the Jewish holy writings, we read a series of woes addressed directly to some priestly families in that era, one of which concerns the family of Hanan and Caiaphas: "Woe to me because of the house of the two Hanans. Woe unto me because of their conspiring."[15] It is clear that a main trait of this family's members was their despicable abuse of power in abominable conspiracies that did not pertain to their religious or moral role in the Jewish community. These two leaders' passion for power was deeply rooted in their creeds, which they derived from their religious heritage. In those times, the religious community was in the grip of two Jewish groups, divided by many beliefs but brought together by their lust for power and a passion for controlling the destinies of others. On the one hand, the Sadducees, to whom Caiaphas and Hanan belonged, believed that God had bestowed upon Aaron and his descendants absolute authority in terms of the implementation of the divine law, while the Pharisees and the scribes believed that God entrusted Moses, then Joshua, then the elders of Israel, then the prophets, and then they themselves with absolute authority in order to apply God's written and verbal law.[16] Hence, we can discover a strong tendency in these two groups toward the violent practice of power. This tendency was linked to an authentic religious doctrine in the thought of those who, in many cases and especially in the story of the cross, turned into a path of violence, spitefulness, and revenge—an image that remains intensely repeated in contemporary Arab societies. It is the image expressed by Rev. Samuel Habib in his important book *The Gospel and Civilization*, where he speaks of "societies that used religion for brute power, oppression and injustice."[17] And in the important book *God and Politicians*, the great theologian Ghassan Khalaf does not miss to pause in front of this blatant characteristic trait in Caiaphas' personality, when, in his analysis of him as head of the religious establishment at the time, he says:

> The stories in the Gospels reveal to us something about the layers within Caiaphas' personality sufficient to evaluate his stands. The challenge that reveals his true nature and worth more than any other test, the venue of power. Power is a force that can be used by its owner to get him through any direction. Power can be used to settle a right, or to acquit crime. The trial of Jesus before Caiaphas, at his own initiative, was the best proof of the ability of a ruler or guardian to make his influence serve his purposes.[18]

---

[15] James C. Vanderkam, *From Joshua to Caiaphas: High Priests after the Exile* (Minneapolis: Fortress, 2004), 422–23.

[16] Ellis Rivkin, *What Crucified Jesus?* (London: SCM, 1984), 21.

[17] Samuel Habib, *The Bible and Civilization: An Invitation to Renew Civilizations* (Doha, Qatar: Dar al-Thaqafa, 1997), 118.

[18] Ghassan Khalaf, *God and Politicians* (Campus Crusade for Christ Organization, 2015), 112.

We can see the irony in the combination of power, violence, and religion in the gloomy image described by Geoffrey of Villehardouin, a French eyewitness contemporary to the Crusader attack on the city of Constantinople, the capital of Eastern Christianity in 1202. He says:

> Since the beginning of creation there has been no such looting and robbery in any city. Looting and vandalism have become so common. Barons and rulers of the Latin churches who follow holy doctrines equally participated in this robbery. All of them looting whatever they could carry. In this chaos, great works of art and valuable manuscripts were destroyed or stolen; scrolls and manuscripts of Aristotle and Demosthenes were sold at the cheapest prices. Precious treasures were stolen from the palaces, as also were any items that showed evidence of relating to religious rituals of the churches such as gold and silver cups, chalices and crucifixes. . . . Finally, the soldiers of the cross publicly violated women, committed adultery; even virgin nuns did not escape their violence.[19]

In a more tragic narration, Dr. Talal Al-Jassar tells us an inspiring story in the context of what historians call "The Children's Crusade,"[20] that is, the French campaign led by the French boy Stephen, who grew up in the village of Cloyes, about 150 kilometers south of Paris. He became known in History as Stephen of Cloyes. This is the story as told by its narrator:

> On one calm day of spring, while Stephen all alone flocked his herd around the nearby hills of his village, a stranger passed by and told him that he had just returned from a journey of pilgrimage in the holy land. He was on his way home, and asked for food. Stephen would not refuse the man his request, as he was returning from a place which Stephen's heart yearned. So, Stephen asked the man to tell him some news from that land. As the stranger told him of the wonders of the East, and the legends of the heroes of the Crusades, Stephen was so touched and was eager to set foot there and participate in expelling the Muslims from the land where Christ was entombed. At the end of the story, the stranger told him that He was Christ, and that He had chosen him for his virtue, honesty and loyalty to evangelize for a crusade for those of his age to free Jerusalem. He then promised Stephen certain victory, and that he will achieve what the nobles, the knights and the soldiers were unable to achieve because of their corruption, disloyalty and weak faith. He then ordered Stephen to lead this crusade with the title of "Messenger of God", hence, he gave him a message to deliver to the king of France

---

[19] Aziz Sorial Attia, *The Crusades and Their Effect on Relations Between East and West*, trans. Philip Saber (Doha, Qatar: Dar al-Thaqafa, 1990), 71.

[20] Historians believe that this happened after the Fourth Crusade (1202) and before the fifth campaign (2013) to try to achieve what the previous campaigns failed to do: to liberate Jerusalem, which includes the tomb of Christ; but oddly, this campaign did not consist of knights or soldiers such as previous & following campaigns. Primarily it included adolescents and children, boys and girls between the ages of 10 and 17 years old. Its main purpose was to preach to the Muslims by love rather than by military means. The campaign failed due to the spread of transmittable diseases among its participants, children and adolescents, because of the hardships of the road, the cold and extreme hunger.

Philip II telling him to provide any help to this new campaign led by Stephen. He also told him that the sea will be parted open as it had for Moses—peace be upon him—to pass through and reach the Holy Land with his followers![21]

The writer then goes on to clarify and explain the background of this story. He refers to the scientist George Gray, who says, "This man is probably a disguised priest. He was watching Stephen and knew the extent of his religious hysteria and enthusiasm; hence he wanted to use that to stir up the people. Thus, he disappeared as mysteriously as he had appeared."[22] It is clear in this story how the religious authority, represented by the priest Stephen met as well as the power of religion that dominated the minds of ordinary people in those lean years of the history of the Christian church, has played a shameful role in politicizing religion in such a way that it smeared the face of the church and of Christian thought and theology until this present day with the crime of the crusades.

Therefore, in this article we attempt to reach a real starting point from which it is possible to practice power in all community circles, especially regarding the circle of the religious institution—namely, the church. When it comes to the church, the concept of authority is inseparably linked to the concept of ecclesiastical leadership, a concept that is receiving increasing attention in our present era in which the people of God yearn for a role model of rational leadership that inspires the church as a religious and social institution on how to perform its role and fulfill its mission. To reach this goal, we analyze and study some important biblical examples in order to review the various images of authority being exercised and clarify these experiences. In the second part of the study, we shall give room to study the example given in the story of the cross, which demonstrates the mature, responsible practice of power.

BIBLICAL EXAMPLES OF PRACTICING POWER
Rehoboam son of Solomon

In chapter 12 of the first book of Kings, we encounter a striking example of bad behavior in implementing judgment and the misuse of power represented by Rehoboam son of Solomon:

> And Rehoboam went to Shechem: for all Israel were come to Shechem to make him king. And it came to pass, when Jeroboam the son of Nebat, who was yet in Egypt, heard of it, (for he was fled from the presence of king Solomon, and Jeroboam dwelt in Egypt;) That they sent and called him. And Jeroboam and all the congregation of Israel came, and spake unto Rehoboam, saying, Thy father made our yoke grievous: now therefore

---

[21] Talal Abdul-Latif Al-Jassar, "The Children's Crusade," *Al Doha magazine*, no. 118 (August 2017): 151.　　[22] Ibid., 151.

make thou the grievous service of thy father, and his heavy yoke which he put upon us, lighter, and we will serve thee. And he said unto them, Depart yet for three days, then come again to me. And the people departed. And king Rehoboam consulted with the old men, that stood before Solomon his father while he yet lived, and said, How do ye advise that I may answer this people? And they spoke unto him, saying, If thou wilt be a servant unto this people this day, and wilt serve them, and answer them, and speak good words to them, then they will be thy servants forever.

But he forsook the counsel of the old men, which they had given him, and consulted with the young men that were grown up with him, and which stood before him: And he said unto them, what counsel give ye that we may answer this people, who have spoken to me, saying, Make the yoke which thy father did put upon us lighter? And the young men that were grown up with him spoke unto him, saying, Thus shalt thou speak unto this people that spoke unto thee, saying, Thy father made our yoke heavy, but make thou it lighter unto us; thus shalt thou say unto them, My little finger shall be thicker than my father's loins. And now whereas my father did lade you with a heavy yoke, I will add to your yoke: my father hath chastised you with whips, but I will chastise you with scorpions.

So Jeroboam and all the people came to Rehoboam the third day, as the king had appointed, saying, Come to me again the third day. And the king answered the people roughly, and forsook the old men's counsel that they gave him; And spoke to them after the counsel of the young men, saying, My father made your yoke heavy, and I will add to your yoke: my father also chastised you with whips, but I will chastise you with scorpions. Wherefore the king hearkened not unto the people; for the cause was from the Lord, that he might perform his saying, which the Lord spoke by Ahijah the Shilonite unto Jeroboam the son of Nebat. So when all Israel saw that the king hearkened not unto them, the people answered the king, saying, What portion have we in David? Neither have we inheritance in the son of Jesse: to your tents, O Israel: now see to thine own house, David. So Israel departed unto their tents. But as for the children of Israel which dwelt in the cities of Judah, Rehoboam reigned over them. Then king Rehoboam sent Adoram, who was over the tribute; and all Israel stoned him with stones, that he died. Therefore king Rehoboam made speed to get him up to his chariot, to flee to Jerusalem." (1 Kgs 12:1–18)[23]

The events of this story take place at a very sensitive time in the history of the people of God, when Solomon the great and wise king had just died after reigning for forty years, leaving the kingdom in a frightening political and spiritual vacuum that forecasted an unhappy future, especially with the presence of rebellious lurking elements like Jeroboam ibn Nabat, who fled from Solomon's face to Egypt. It should also not be ignored that Solomon's last years in leadership and political wisdom faced many difficulties and

---

[23] Unless otherwise indicated, all Scripture quotations in this chapter come from the KJV.

people's discontentment due to the numerous arbitrary measures which had burdened his people, such as a big increase in taxes and the implementation of forced labor to accomplish huge construction projects (1 Kgs 5:13–16), the vast majority of which, if not all, were directly serving the best interests of Solomon personally or his household, not the interest of the common people (1 Kgs 9:10–22). We may need to pause briefly here to make a quick summary of a comparison, made by Rev. Elias Maqar, between Solomon and his father David in terms of their political style:

> Perhaps the elders who lived at the time of David and Solomon realized the difference between the two men. David was the servant of the people, struggling and risking his life for them, and ruled with patience, lenience, wisdom, and gentleness. Therefore, the people loved him and served him and embraced him, unlike Solomon, who filled his stomach with food, and scorched his back with whips. He planted the seeds of hostility, hatred, and division between Judah and Ephraim. He was stupidly ignorant of the fact that the tribe of Benjamin could never forget that the throne was theirs, and usurped by another tribe.[24]

Walter Brueggemann comments on the exploitative style of Solomon's rule: his program of governance clearly sought to achieve personal goals, mainly to empower and secure himself and his family.[25] He concludes that Solomon, as his rule advanced in years, managed to put everything into his grip and succeeded in creating a reality that could not be criticized or developed.[26] It is important to note that this kind of behavior on Solomon's part is one of the most fundamental traits of a tyrannical rule. As the "difference between a king and a tyrant is that the former places the law as a limit to his power, and the best interest of the masses as the principal purpose of his rule. While for the latter, the tyrant, there is no limit for his power, and subjugates everything to his will and desires."[27] Additionally, Brueggemann notes that the transition of reign from father to son is often considered a fearsome prelude to the establishment of an undemocratic system. He testifies to this by citing the qualitative shift in the style of governance of the king of Egypt, from Pharaoh who gave shelter to Joseph and his family from Canaan, to his descendant who was unaware of the history and so led Joseph's descendants into hard labor.[28] But according to this theory, the people of Israel, after a long period of Solomon's rule, could not adapt to the suffering under the new yoke of an unjust and brutal rule. Indeed, true was the warning of the "Dean of Arabic Literature," Taha Hussein, as he often gave remarks from within the folds of many of his writings, hinting to every tyrant who rides power only to detestably control

---

[24] Elias Maqar, *Men of the Bible*, pt. 1 (Doha, Qatar: Dar al-Thaqafa, 1984), 402.

[25] Walter Brueggemann, *The Prophetic Imagination* (Minneapolis: Fortress, 2001), 23.

[26] Ibid., 25.

[27] Fattah, "The Tyrant," 117.

[28] Walter Brueggemann, *1 & 2 Kings*, Smyth & Helwys Bible Commentary (Macon, GA: Smyth & Helwys, 2000), 153.

others: "They are commanding without knowing the extent to which the parish can withstand."[29]

It is clear from the biblical story that Rehoboam was confronted with two choices: lift the exorbitant taxes as well as the forced labor exacted by his father, Solomon, or maintain the unjust system. The people's demand to alleviate their yoke would have brought on many difficult economic measures, such as rationalizing expenditure and reducing lavish extravagance in some projects.[30] Yet the second choice—to maintain this unjust system—represented a heavy load and injustice on the shoulders of the desolate people. The young king chose to follow the same path as his predecessor. Furthermore, he makes things worse by promising harsher, crueler, and tighter control over the reins of his rule. He expressed his decision by saying: "My father made your yoke heavy, and I will add to your yoke: my father also chastised you with whips, but I will chastise you with scorpions" (1 Kgs 12:14 KJV).

This situation presents a sick political principle that is behind many forms of power at every level, including the church today. It characterizes its practices and dictates its orientation. We mean the principle of dictatorship or brute power.

A simple definition of dictatorship is that it is a form of rule where an individual or a group of individuals hold absolute power.[31] And here we see this foolish king falling into the trap, as he fails to listen intently to the voice of reason, wisdom, and experience.[32]

One of the presiding ideas in the order of intellectual dictatorship is that the one with power has such high self-esteem that he refuses to listen to any advice, guidance, or criticism that would correct his course, and he rationalizes all his decisions and choices. Simultaneously, he demands from others complete submission and blind obedience. This unhealthy principal is what Fouad Zacharia observes in the orientations of dictatorial regimes everywhere. Zacharia explains, "Authoritarian dictatorships want the citizen only to be 'obedient' to the ruler's commands; a complying tool in his hand."[33] Fathi Al-Maskini goes farther on this idea in describing authoritarian dictatorship and says, "Every deep authority is keen on keeping every corner of the personality of its subject in its appropriate appearance; i.e., that is, under the absolute microscope—the eye of the father, the eye of the ruler, the eye of God. The most desired thing by the 'deep power' is to keep all the daily details of a human person under the vertical microscope of the

---

[29] Moustafa Abdel-Ghani, *The Thinker and Prince: Taha Hussein and Authority in Egypt 1919–1973* (Cairo: Egyptian Book Authority, 2005), 216.

[30] Brueggemann, *1 & 2 Kings*, 155.

[31] *The World Book Encyclopedia*, vol. 5 (Chicago: World Book, 1992), 163.

[32] Lissa M. Wray Beal points out that Rehoboam in this situation recalls the position of the stubborn Pharaoh of Egypt, who in continuous foolishness refused to listen to Moses, who repeatedly urged him to release his people from Egypt to serve the Lord. The same thing happened with Rehoboam, who caused the division of the kingdom and fulfilled the word of the Lord, which he spoke time after time. Beal, *1 & 2 Kings*, ed. David W. Baker, Apollos Old Testament Commentary (Downers Grover, IL: IVP Academic, 2014), 182.

[33] Fouad Zacharia, *Letter to the Arab Mind* (Cairo: Al-Arabi, 1987), 80.

collective eye."[34] It is an attempt to keep everything and every person in a spiral of vile control and siege that the dictator can manage at each and every moment. Hans Finzel sums up the definition of dictatorship with a phrase that every dictator believes in the depth of his heart:

> Another description of the dictatorial style in leadership is what I call the "apostolic" view of decision-making: "I know the answers because I have been given special insight, knowledge and a distinguished position; therefore, I will define the direction that we will take, because I am the leader and I know better than everyone else."[35]

At first glance, the researcher will find it no secret that the biblical text condemns this extreme autocratic position taken up by Rehoboam. As we analyze the decision taken by the young king after adopting the opinion of his peers and putting aside the wisdom of the elders, we immediately discover the real reason and hidden motive behind every autocratic tyrannical system of government: the "overwhelming desire for domination." This was expressed by Gene Rice in his interpretation of this chapter of 1 Kings: "Rehoboam's behavior is the best expression of arrogant power. He and his young advisors did not give any consideration to the rights of the governed because they believed that the power of government lies in full submission to the will of the king."[36]

Moustafa Hegazy explains this idea more clearly as he uses the El-Kawakby's definition in his book titled *Characteristics of Tyranny*: tyranny is the arrogance of one with regards to his own opinion, and his aversion to accept advice, or independence of opinion and shared rights.[37] These words emphasize the idea of the desire to dominate, which leads to establish dictatorship as a general principle and as a legitimate means to rule. We also cannot overlook a more cruel and bitter dimension in any dictatorship system, which is the violence used by the vast majority of dictators so as to strengthen the foundations of their power and secure their positions, the tenure of their thrones, their detestable control without competition or change, and their prevention of the hope to attain rights or even a breath of freedom.

Rehoboam—in great ignorance and indescribable foolishness—would not have minded to resort to any means of oppression and violence in order to guarantee the people's submission, kneeling, and even laying prostrate to his policies and decisions. Stefan Zweig, in his book titled *The Violence of the Dictatorship*, brilliantly described this link between dictatorship and violence:

> Authoritarians are tempted to turn the majority into a general consensus and to try to impose their faith on those who do not belong to any of the parties. They are not satisfied

[34] Al-Maskini, "The Phenomenon of Atheist Adolescence."

[35] Hans Finzel, *The Top Ten Mistakes Made by Leaders*, trans. Edward Wadie (Doha, Qatar: Dar al-Thaqafa, 2002), 90.

[36] Gene Rice, *1 Kings: Nations under God*, International Theo-logical Commentary (Grand Rapids: Eerdmans, 1990), 101.

[37] Moustafa Hegazy, *The Compromised Man: An Analytical and Social Psychological Study* (Casablanca: Arab Cultural Center, 2005), 76.

with their gendarmes, hypocrites, craftsmen, and the eternal followers of any authority, but they also want the free, the rare independent mentalities to turn into followers and adulators. In support of their only recognized faith, they would accuse anyone of opposing views of having committed a crime against the state. In different times, this curse associated with religious and political ideologies has always been restored—as once dictatorship is implemented, it is swamped with tyranny.

Once one loses confidence in the inherent power of his truth and resorts to brutal violence, in so doing he declares war against human freedom no matter what the idea he presents may be. When resorting to violence as a means to control and unify the hue of those with different opinions, the idea loses its idealism, rather it becomes brutal.

Even the purest truths, if imposed through violence, turn into a sin against intellect.[38]

In another section of his book, Zweig very decisively and clearly states: "One cannot imagine a dictatorship without violence; it cannot last without it. He who wants to retain power must have the tools of power in his hands. And he who wants to command must have the right to retaliate as well.[39] Moustafa Hegazy discusses this same phenomenon:

It is emphasized here that cruelty, rigor, oppression, and injustice are practiced by an individual or collective government with the seizure of power by force. Of course, these specifications must produce waste in its most severe form; making the waste of blood a matter of vulgarity, passing on to the waste of dignity and the value of existence, waste of minds all the way up to the waste of consciousness. Here is where power dominates consciousness and attempts to acquire it from within, as it exercises this through the mechanisms of total and absolute control by force and oppression.[40]

Bruce Malina explores the phenomenon of violence in the context of dictatorships, linking it to many convictions that are adopted by an authoritarian mind, such as forced submission to authority, the tendency to exercise force for the sake of practicing it, admiration for the practice of corporal violence, extreme tendency toward traditionalism, extreme sensitivity towards peer pressure, the tendency to classify (either/or; white/black), and the preference for stereotypical thought.[41]

In a similar Oriental context, Gaber Asfour presents the example of Sheikh Ali Abdel Raziq, the great Azhari thinker, who stands guard facing the attempt to link religion, politics, and violence—that offensive mix sought by the weak souls and semileaders. In opposition to this terrible triad, he says, "That which is called a throne does not rise except on the heads of humanity, and does not settle except on their necks. That which is called a crown has no life except in what it takes from the lives of humans, and it has no power except whatever power it kills in them. It holds no greatness or dignity except

---

[38] Stefan Zweig, *The Violence of Dictatorship*, trans. Faris Joakim (Beruit: Al-Furat, 2013), 18–19.

[39] Ibid., 37.

[40] Hegazy, *The Compromised Man*, 77–78.

[41] Bruce Malina, "Authoritarianism," in *Handbook of Biblical Social Values*, ed. John J. Pilch & Bruce J. Malina (Peabody, MA: Hendrickson, 1993), 12.

the greatness and dignity of which it deprives them. As when the night grows longer, the day becomes shorter—its shimmer is only that of swords and the flames of war."[42]

Robert Case makes a crucial observation when he points out that the dictatorship of the ruler, the leader, the husband, the father, or the priest, each in his position, is not derived from one's personality or their personal charisma, but is derived from the position in which he exists, and which allows him to take control and dominate. In 2 Chronicles 13:7 the spirit says about Rehoboam, "And there are gathered unto him vain men, the children of Belial, and have strengthened themselves against Rehoboam the son of Solomon, when Rehoboam was young and tenderhearted, and could not withstand them." In the sense that Rehoboam did not derive his strength from his character because he was a "weak boy." But he derived his power, authority, and domination from the place he reached and the status that descended to him from Solomon, his father.[43] The report, issued by the United Nations, from the scientific committee studying the authoritarian character confirms the validity of this psychological phenomenon:

> Despotism, or autocracy, is a compensatory phenomenon, and the despotic personality is generally present in people who lack self-confidence. Their awareness of their deficiency motivates them to compensate for it when dealing with the outer world. They use violence against any attempt to change the social order under the pretext of defending the stability of the existing system, while, in fact they are actually defending their own ego that lacks psychological stability.[44]

Naturally, a person of such weak character would derive his strength from his position. He would, lacking sound judgment or wisdom in handling various situations, defend his position using extreme violence. As in the case of Rehoboam, it is easy for them to be led to deviant perverted opinions that lack wisdom and good judgment to reach better and more successful choices.

There is no doubt that the repercussions of the story in 1 Kings 12 condemns the approach taken to achieve governance, and there are at least three clear implications.

First, the kingdom disintegrated at the hands of Rehoboam because of his rash decision, and the theological truth that we cannot overlook is that this disintegration was predestined by God because of Solomon's moral deviations (1 Kgs 11:9–13, 31–36). God is the God of history who holds all things together; he is the just judge who does not condone the spreading of evil in his kingdom when the pagan wives of Solomon lead him to worship the gods of Canaan and spread that worship all over the kingdom. But this does not by any means exempt Rehoboam from bearing the consequences of

---

[42] Gaber Asfour, *Margins on the Notebook of Illumination* (Kuwait: Dar Souad Al Sabbah, 1994), 240.

[43] Robert Case, "Rehoboam: A Study of Failed Leadership," *Presbyterion* 14 (Spring 1988): 63.

[44] Refaat El Saeed, *Democracy and Pluralism: A Study in the Distance between Theory and Practice* (Cairo: General Organization of Books, 2005), 15.

his stern stand and his foolish decision that led the whole kingdom to its disintegration and its doom. Simon J. Devries talks about this truth, saying: "It is obvious that the most important lesson to learn from this text is that it is so much easier to destroy what is solid than to build what is destroyed."[45] The dictatorship here was associated with disruption and disintegration. It was possible for this young man, who thought so highly of his own opinion and that of his foolish peers, to avoid the political collapse of the kingdom if he had only listened in humility to the experience and wisdom expressed through the mouths of the elders. These elders simply wanted to guide him to the wise use of power through which he could have avoided disintegration and collapse and would have secured him the love and trust of his people.

Nadine Sika, professor of political sciences at the American University in Cairo, discusses this fact in a research paper titled "The Dynamics of Stagnant Religious Speech and the Rise of New Secular Movements in Egypt." She says in her introduction that when the authoritarian regime takes a hostile stance in the public circles, it results in the emergence of new social movements that resist social trends and seek to impose new values that the existing regime failed to implement and manage.[46] The researcher emphases that leadership in this case does not find enough options to maintain a coherent society, hence it disintegrates in the absence of new factors or models to maintain its coherence.[47] This was the exact same experience the Egyptian society went through when the ruling regime failed before the January 2011 revolution, when it failed to exhibit that it was flexible enough to provide the needs of society, such as respect for human rights, decent living conditions, and freedom. This eventually led to an explosive situation, the collapse of the regime, and the beginning of a harsh new chapter of confusion and social disintegration.

This was what happened many centuries ago with Rehoboam, who stubbornly froze in his stance and thus forfeited his community and his people. Reverend Ghassan Khalaf expresses this so eloquently: "Society does not survive on 'consuming the blood' of its individuals. And if it does so, all of 'its blood will be shed.'"[48]

The second point is represented by the popular revolution, which manifested in the stoning of Adoram, Rehoboam's envoy (1 Kgs 12:18). The story of dictatorship has been largely linked to oppression, which leads to explosion. Christianity, in its biblical principles, excludes dictatorship in government or leadership in all its forms, as dictatorship leads those governed to live as if they were over a "hot pot" that might burst into flames at any time.

In spite of the abundance of biblical text that directs a Christian or the Christian community to submit to authority/leadership in all its forms, even if violent, revelation

---

[45] Simon J. Devries, *1 Kings*, Word Biblical Commentary 12 (Dallas: Word, 1985), 159.

[46] Nadine Sika, "Dynamics of a Stagnant Religious Discourse and the Rise of New Secular Movements in Egypt," in *Arab Spring in Egypt: Revolution and Beyond* (Cairo: American University in Cairo Press, 2014), 63–82.

[47] Ibid.

[48] Khalaf, *God and Politicians*, 122.

did not hesitate to direct superiors and leaders to lead with kindness and charity towards the people who God has placed under their command.

In Ephesians 6:4 it was the commandment of the fathers: "And, ye fathers, provoke not your children to wrath: but bring them up in the nurture and admonition of the Lord." And in the ninth verse, the apostle presents his advice to the masters saying, "And, ye masters, do the same things unto them, forbearing threatening: knowing that your Master also is in heaven; neither is there respect of persons with him."

In the third and fourth chapters of Colossians are similar texts, as the apostle thus advises: "Children, obey your parents in all things: for this is well pleasing unto the Lord. . . . Masters, give unto your servants that which is just and equal; knowing that ye also have a Master in heaven" (3:20; 4:1 KJV).

We see the same inclination when Paul the apostle speaks of the traits needed in a bishop: "patient, not a brawler . . . not lifted in pride" (see 1 Tim 3:3, 6). And the apostle Peter directs his advice to the elders, who were probably the leaders of the church at the time, encouraging them not to be tempted to misuse the power within their authority in their leadership of the congregation of God:

> The elders which are among you I exhort, who am also an elder, and a witness of the sufferings of Christ, and also a partaker of the glory that shall be revealed: Feed the flock of God which is among you, taking the oversight thereof, not by constraint, but willingly; not for filthy lucre, but of a ready mind; Neither as being lords over God's heritage, but being ensamples to the flock. (1 Pet 5:1–3 KJV)

Perhaps the following paragraph, presented by the writer Abdel Nasser Herez about political terrorism, will shed light on the parallel relationship between dictatorship and the popular revolution:

> As rulers go out of boundaries exceeding their limits with regards to the constitutional powers conferred upon them, their tyranny is a pivotal motive for many terrorist movements across the various time periods and in various countries around the world. Perhaps the most prominent example of this is the terrorism of the chaotic movements and nihilism. These movements were born as the people groaned under the injustice of the Tsar and his followers in Russia. This state of injustice and tyranny was the first motor of terrorism in that period. With the growing injustice the intensity of the terroristic attacks against the Tsar and his followers grew as well, until anarchy targeted the state as a whole, and it became its main activity as it saw it as a symbol of injustice, cruelty, brutality and tyranny. Hence, injustice and tyranny were the pivotal motives for the emergence and growth of terrorist movements in Russia and in other countries. This fact has been valid on successive historical periods and in various countries around the world.[49]

---

[49] Abdel Nasser Herez, *Political Terrorism* (Cairo: Madboly Library, 1996), 196.

So we see Christianity rejecting the dictatorship of government because it represents a prelude to popular revolution that may take some form of terrorism.

Thirdly, there is the loss of belonging and loss of identity. Here we stand before the people's words to the king: "What portion have we in David? neither have we inheritance in the son of Jesse: to your tents, O Israel: now see to thine own house, David" (1 Kgs 12:16). Perhaps the main reason behind this feeling of those who suffer under any dictatorial rule is that they sense they do not belong to the country, the institution, or the family in which they live; rather, they are exposed to strong and injuring humiliation, underappreciation, and absence of equality, which all entail the denial of community belonging.

This is because man, any human being, cannot innovate, move forward, or make a change for the better except in a climate of freedom, which unleashes his capabilities and talents. The disappearance of the sense of belonging does not necessarily materialize into the difficult decision of emigrating, leaving the country, resigning, abandoning work, or separating from and destroying a marriage; mostly it means living under these regimes without any spirit, vision, or the desire for work, or, say, for life itself. At which point, one says to himself "What portion have we in David? neither have we inheritance in the son of Jesse."

The Israelites treated Rehoboam likewise. He overlooked listening to them, embracing them as their king, and they in turn decided to ignore him and wash their hands of supporting him or glorifying his crown as loyal subjects. He chose to be the cold-hearted master, so they chose to be indifferent slaves.

What happened in this situation is exactly what modern sociologists have described as alienation. The modern dialectical meaning of this word, says Professor Sami Khashaba, has become linked to a person's sense of alienation in society, his sense of inability to influence social change, and the disintegration of an individual's personality in a bureaucratic and inflated society.[50] It is the sense that one lacks value, has lost the ability to give and fear for the public interest, and no longer has desire to innovate and develop oneself and others. It is the feeling that the issues of existence and belonging are no longer worth the trouble of defending. The picture becomes clearer when we pause and look at the careful analysis of one of the most prominent theologians of the twentieth century, Rev. Dr. John Stott, about the phenomenon of political tyranny. Stott believes that tyranny arises from a completely pessimistic view of humans: the oppressor looks at the people around him and sees them as very dull to a point that they do not know what is good for themselves or good for the community; if they do know, then they are either unable or unwilling to come to an agreement.[51]

Practically, and realistically, emigration is the palpable, visible expression of the

---

[50] Sami Khashaba, *Terms of Modern Thought*, pt. 1 (Cairo: Egyptian Book Authority, 2006), 74–75.

[51] John Stott, *Christianity and Contemporary Issues*, trans. Najib Jarjour (Cairo: Dar Al Thaqafa, 1993), 68.

alienation people feel. It is the result of a misuse of authority, which becomes a tool of pressure, intimidation, alienation, and marginalization. By observing the waves of emigration that happened in the Middle East for many decades, one can realize the striking organic link between the two phenomena. For example, when Rev. Riad Jarjour, former secretary general of the Middle East Council of Churches, presents his vision for the future of Christians in the Arab world,[52] he refers to a "demographic hemorrhage," meaning the growing decline in the number of Christians of the Middle East, where the current number is between ten and twenty million compared to the much higher rates of forty years ago. The writer attributed this decrease to the continuous, rapid, and increasing emigration of Arab Christians to non-Arab countries.

Jarjour does not omit a dangerous phenomenon that represents one of the most important motivating factors for the migration of minorities from the Middle East, namely, the fierce politicization of religion following the Arab Spring revolutions, which presented a fertile soil for the emergence of a monstrous religious extremism, represented by the groups of death and destruction such as *Da'esh* (ISIS). As a result, there is an ever-growing number of cases of political and religious asylum in the West. Additionally, racist laws called the laws of "contempt of religions" are trying to silence mouths, provide extremism legal legitimate immunity, and corner all moderate thinkers who work their minds on examining religious texts. These "contempt of religions" laws have helped cause a serious increase in atheism and hostility against religion because, for many, especially young people, religion is considered to be the worst type of power as it monopolizes speaking in the name of God and uses God to confiscate the opinion of others, infringing on their rights. And let's not forget to mention the forced evictions of Copts, who are kicked out of their homes, as it happened and is still happening in Egypt's Delta and in Upper Egypt.

Dr. Shak Bernard Hanish also analyzes this same phenomenon, saying that many political regimes in the Middle East lack democracy and consideration for human rights (the contemporary description of what Rehoboam committed in the past). Thus, many feel alienated in their home countries and a lack of freedom, especially religious freedom, which leads them to leave their homes and go to other countries where they can get what they were missing.[53]

---

[52] Riad Jarjour, "The Future of Christians in the Arab World," in *Who Are the Christians in the Middle East?*, ed. Betty Jane Bailey and J. Martin Bailey (Grand Rapids: Eerdmans, 2003), 12–21.

[53] Shak Bernard Hanish, "Why the Eastern Christians Are Fleeing the Middle East?," *International Journal of Humanities and Social Science* 4, no. 10 (August 2014): 62–71. For further study on this phenomenon and its causes and repercussions, see Habib C. Malik, *How Christians and Other Native Minorities are Faring in the Unfolding Arab Turmoil of 2011* (Vatican City: Pontifical Academy of Social Sciences, 2012), 212–32; Brian Katulis, Rudy deLeon, and John B. Craig, "The Plight of Christianism the Middle East: Supporting Religious Freedom, Pluralism, and Tolerance During a Time of Turmoil," *Center for American Progress*, March 2015, https://www.americanprogress.org/issues/security/reports/2015/03/12/108473/the-plight-of-christians-in-the-middle-east/; Todd M. Johnson and Gina A. Zurlo, "Ongoing Exodus: Tracking the Emigration of Christians from the Middle East," *Harvard Journal of Middle Eastern Politics and Policy* 3 (2013–2014): 39–49.

Thus, we reached that Christianity rejects the principle of dictatorship because it leads to the collapse of the institution, whether political, religious or social. Also, because it leads to the human disturbance, which undoubtedly creates chaos and insecurity. And finally, because it ignores the principle of respect for human rights, which leads people to lose their sense of belonging.

Abimelech and Jotham

And Abimelech the son of Jerubbaal went to Shechem unto his mother's brethren, and communed with them, and with all the family of the house of his mother's father, saying, Speak, I pray you, in the ears of all the men of Shechem, Whether is better for you, either that all the sons of Jerubbaal, which are threescore and ten persons, reign over you, or that one reign over you? remember also that I am your bone and your flesh. And his mother's brethren spake of him in the ears of all the men of Shechem all these words: and their hearts inclined to follow Abimelech; for they said, He is our brother. And they gave him threescore and ten pieces of silver out of the house of Baalberith, wherewith Abimelech hired vain and light persons, which followed him. And he went unto his father's house at Ophrah, and slew his brethren the sons of Jerubbaal, being threescore and ten persons, upon one stone: notwithstanding yet Jotham the youngest son of Jerubbaal was left; for he hid himself. And all the men of Shechem gathered together, and all the house of Millo, and went, and made Abimelech king, by the plain of the pillar that was in Shechem.

And when they told it to Jotham, he went and stood in the top of mount Gerizim, and lifted up his voice, and cried, and said unto them, Hearken unto me, ye men of Shechem, that God may hearken unto you. The trees went forth on a time to anoint a king over them; and they said unto the olive tree, Reign thou over us. But the olive tree said unto them, Should I leave my fatness, wherewith by me they honor God and man, and go to be promoted over the trees? And the trees said to the fig tree, Come thou, and reign over us. But the fig tree said unto them, Should I forsake my sweetness, and my good fruit, and go to be promoted over the trees? Then said the trees unto the vine, Come thou, and reign over us. And the vine said unto them, Should I leave my wine, which cheereth God and man, and go to be promoted over the trees? Then said all the trees unto the bramble, Come thou, and reign over us. And the bramble said unto the trees, If in truth ye anoint me king over you, then come and put your trust in my shadow: and if not, let fire come out of the bramble, and devour the cedars of Lebanon. Now therefore, if ye have done truly and sincerely, in that ye have made Abimelech king, and if ye have dealt well with Jerubbaal and his house, and have done unto him according to the deserving of his hands; (For my father fought for you, and adventured his life far, and delivered you out of the hand of Midian: And ye are risen up against my father's house this day, and have slain his sons, threescore and ten persons, upon one stone, and have made Abimelech, the son of his maidservant, king over the men of Shechem, because he is your brother;) If ye then have dealt truly and sincerely with Jerubbaal and with his house this day, then rejoice ye in Abimelech, and let him also rejoice in you: But if not, let fire come out from Abimelech, and devour the men of Shechem, and the house of Millo; and let fire come out from the men of Shechem, and from the house of Millo, and devour Abimelech. And Jotham ran away, and fled, and went to Beer, and dwelt there, for fear of Abimelech his brother. (Judg 9:1–21)

Abimelech and the Mania of Power

In Judges 9:1–6, the writer tells us the story of how Abimelech the son of Jerubbaal (Gideon) overtook the reins of power among the people of Shechem. The road he followed to acquire the king's position was a crooked path in which Abimelech resorted to twisted and thorny methods. Arthur Cundall goes to the heart of truth when he hints that what Abimelech did here was not because of his political shrewdness, his managerial abilities, his bargaining skills, or any other kind of proper dealings with people, rather it was on account of his greed. This was what pushed him to plant fear in the hearts of the people of Shechem and hence accept him as their king without dispute or objection.[54] Sarah Locke draws our attention to another factor that contributed to the formation of this sick mentality, thirsty for power: a compelling sense of inferiority that consumed Abimelech because he was the son of a gentile woman from Shechem, a slave to his father Gideon. These feelings put pressure on him that affected his decision making and how he implemented those decisions to attain his ambitions.[55] Once again, we find a relation between the lust for power and the use of violence. Abimelech, who found himself enslaved to his feverish desire to reign, saw no alternative other than to kill his seventy brothers in a horrific bloodbath. And it was on account of fear, not conviction, that the people of Shechem made this tyrant their king.

Abimelech set down three ploys to attain power, and examining each one will prove insightful for understanding tyrants. Each is described below.

Use of Tribalism

In Judges 9:2, Abimelech speaks to his family, the people of Shechem: "Speak, now, in the hearing of all the leaders of Shechem, 'Which is better for you, that seventy men, all the sons of Jerubbaal, rule over you, or that one man rule over you?' Also, remember that I am your bone and your flesh" (NASB). So Abimelech resorts to the trick of striking the tribal chord—the ethnic tension between the people of Shechem, to whom he is related on his mother's side, and the people of Ephraim, to whom he is related on his father's side.[56] The language here is in perfect harmony with

---

[54] Arthur Cundall, *Judges and Ruth*, trans. Bahij Youssef, Modern Interpretation Series of the Bible (Cairo: Dar Al Thaqafa, 1991), 125.

[55] Sara L. Locke, "'Reign over Us!': The Theme of Kingship in Judges 8–9" (MACS diss., McMaster Divinity College, Hamilton, Ontario, 2009), 111.

[56] Silviu Tatu, "Jotham's Fable and the 'Crux Interpretum' in Judges IX," *Vetus Testamentum* 56, no. 1 (2006): 105–24.

authoritarian transcendent (despotic) mentality, which often imposes the equation of thought and choice in the form of: "I or others." There is no room or place for any other than the person who imposes his authority. To this day, this element remains a large element in totalitarian control, as in placing people who lack competence, experience, or integrity in leading positions. Till now, the principle of "those who are trusted" continues to outweigh the principle of "those with experience." Or as Dr. Ahmed Zaki says, "favoritism places the wrong man in a rank where he renders the work corrupt, whether it be in production or public service."[57] Egyptian historians do not forget the difficult period in which the Muslim Brotherhood came to power, and how they adopted the policy of "family and clan." They planted their elements in all sections of the Egyptian state with no regard for experience or skill. The only criterion that mattered for selection was total loyalty to the brotherhood. No doubt this method of running the country was one of the most important factors that hurried the fall of this regime and put an end of its rule over Egypt in less than one year. Similarly, in many Middle Eastern societies, both in the civil and ecclesiastical spheres, the judgment and selection of people in leadership positions is still based on purely subjective criteria, not on any objective sense or logical principle. The satisfaction of the person becomes much more important than the quality of the work, service, or performance.

Misuse of Money

In the fourth verse, the writer of this revelation says: "They gave him seventy pieces of silver from the house of Baal-berith with which Abimelech hired worthless and reckless fellows, and they followed him" (Judg 9:4 NASB). Money in itself is a double-edged sword; either it is a tool for service, construction, achievement, and production, or it is used to be a means of pressure, of earning and profit, to buy peoples' conscience and souls, taint facts and make them invisible, obstruct work, dictate policies, and impose opinions. Abimelech strayed in his use of money when he allowed the money under his disposal to be contaminated with the worship of idols in the temple of Baal-berith, which led the people astray. Abimelech went even further when he exploited the influence over his tribe and began to handle the money in his possession irresponsibly. He hired a handful of bandits to form what resembled a gang of outlaws. The text reports something even worse: Abimelek used the money to get help killing his brothers, clearing the path to grasp all the power for himself without competition.

Throughout history, the misuse of wealth, wanton extravagance in spending it, the

[57] Ahmed Zaki, "Equality . . . Yes, But in What," *Freedom* (Cairo: El Arabi Books, 1984), 60.

attempt to seize control, even usurpation, have been the trait of those who held brute power. This happened with dictators Ferdinand Marcos of the Philippines,[58] Nicolai Ceausescu of Romania, and Saddam Hussein of Iraq. This also happened with the medieval church, which invented the so-called "instruments of forgiveness" to seize the earnings of the poor. The same happened with the Muslim Brotherhood's fall in their rule of Egypt, which was signified by the rule through the power of the "family and the tribe" who lacked all experience or skill.

The fall of the regime of former president Mubarak was evident in the conspicuous pairing of power and money. It was only normal that it would drive many sectors of the population to object and revolt, to be determined to put an end to these practices, which formed a huge gap between a minority that controlled the economy, and the majority who could barely earn enough to meet their needs.

Following a Policy of Annihilation (Extermination)

In the fifth verse we read: "And he went unto his father's house at Ophrah, and slew his brethren the sons of Jerubbaal, being threescore and ten persons, upon one stone." Here, Abimelech resorts to the most famous procedure used by every ruler or dictatorial leader to extend his authority and tighten his grip—getting rid of all competitors. It is important to note here that such action is closely linked to a point previously referred to, that those who exercise this type of authority are intrinsically weak. This vulnerability is therefore a threat to them. Thus, in order to achieve the security they lack, they eliminate all external threats, such as competitors, so that the arena is always free for them to practice their influence.

Along these lines, we can only recall one of the most obvious examples that combined power and violence: Herod the Great. Throughout his headship of Judea from 37 to 4 BC, the language of violence and blood prevailed over his logic in every step he took and every decision he made. As one traces the history of this man, one can easily observe the line of physical liquidation he exercised against anyone whom he suspected was trying to overtake the throne, to the point of killing his wives and children to protect his office. It is clear that the deep fear over the pillars of his rule is what drowned Herod in the sea of paranoid suspicion, which drove him to eliminate anyone who gave him the slightest hint of competition or the possibility of battling him over his power. Father Matthew the Poor quotes the famous Jewish historian Flavius

---

[58] Journalist writer Salah Montasser tells a segment of the story of the organized looting carried out by Ferdinand and Emilda Marcos in the Philippines during their rule. He writes, "In early 1983, Emilda made a trip to New York, Rome and Copenhagen. Her purchases exceeded bills for five million dollars during that trip." She bought several famed New York apartments, and when she fled with her husband to Hawaii in February 1986, after their fall from power, what was found was a collection of dresses from the finest fashion brands, and 1060 pairs of shoes. Montasser, "August 21, 1982, Assassination of the Leader of the Opposition on Stairs of Plane," *Tales of Days*, Family Library (2008): 110–11.

Josephus saying that at the beginning of his reign Herod killed forty-five Jewish elders who were among his enemies.[59]

Eduard Lohse reviews other horrors, such as the murder of Herod's dear wife Mariamne; because of her lineage from the Hasmonean family who preceded him in the reign, he felt fiercely threatened by its members. Thus, it was easy for him to kill his beloved wife when he doubted her loyalty to him. He killed his son Alexander Aristopoulos for the same reason. And despite his strong love for his eldest son, Antipater, Herod still sentenced him to death on charges of treason and conspiracy shortly before Herod's own death.[60] Lohse briefly analyzes the personality of that tyrant:

> Doubt shrouded all Herod's actions: the biblical story of the massacre of Bethlehem perfectly corresponded to his personal image (Matthew 2:16). Herod was cautious all along of the threats against his rule from any direction. He never hesitated to take violent, harsh and decisive measures to eliminate them. Nor did he hesitate to kill anyone who might pose a threat as a rival to his power.[61]

Sometimes, when opposition would grow in his kingdom, Herod would not hesitate to stifle it using the most horrendous and brutal methods. Giovanni Papini describes his weak character and his panic at the risk of losing the throne: "He quivered before the new princes, the aging villains, even a passing breeze nymph, or the rustling of leaves. He would panic in face of the slightest hint of someone claiming his throne. When he learned from the Wise Kings [The Magi], that a 'King of the Jews' has come to be, his barbaric heart pounded in horror."[62]

Jesuit Father Sami Halaq gives a detailed report on the massacres Herod committed when he felt his authority was threatened. He says,

> His assaults became more violent when he uncovered several conspiracies against him, especially by his family. History tells that he ordered the slaughter of all the children of the Hashmouny family; i.e. the legitimate descendants of the king's family.
>
> And when he suspected that his wife, Miriam Al-Hashmoniya, was plotting to assassinate him, he handed her over to be tortured, although she was the only wife among his ten wives whom he loved. When she died under torture, he buried all her sons with her. He also killed five of his sons born to him by his other wives for the same reason. One day prior his death, he had his son Antipater beheaded. That is why Augustus Caesar commented on this saying: "In Palestine, it is better to be a pig than to be a son of Herod" as Augustus was aware that Jews would not slaughter a pig as they do not eat its meat.[63]

---

[59] Father Matta El Meskeen (aka Matthew the Poor), *History of Israel* (Cairo: St. Maqar Convent, 2007), 276.

[60] Eduard Lohse, *The New Testament Environment* (London: SCM, 1976), 39.

[61] Ibid.

[62] Giovanni Papini, *The Biography of Christ*, trans. Adib Mosleh, Series of the Twists 8 (Police Library Publications, 2003), 20.

[63] Jesuit Sami Halaq, *Society of Jesus: Traditions and Customs* (Beirut: Dar Al Mashreq, 1999), 37.

Returning to Judges, we should not miss the double ending: the death of the people of the Tower of Shechem, who were burned by the leader who commanded them (Judg 9:46–49), and the end of Abimelech, who was killed by a stone thrown by a woman from above (Judg 9:50–57). First, does this stone remind us of the one used by Abimelech to kill all his seventy brothers? The scribe of the revelation presents this observation in clear words at the end of the story, where he analyzes the events from a celestial point of view:

> And when the men of Israel saw that Abimelech was dead, they departed every man unto his place. Thus God rendered the wickedness of Abimelech, which he did unto his father, in slaying his seventy brethren: And all the evil of the men of Shechem did God render upon their heads: and upon them came the curse of Jotham the son of Jerubbaal. (Judg 9:55–57 KJV)

Jotham and the Revealing Example

Now we come to the example uttered by Jotham, Gideon's youngest son, through which he analyzes the corrupt power practiced by his half-brother, Abimelech, announcing at its end the inevitable result of this sick form of absolute power, which stands on the pillars of violent policy, and a logic of alienation. Jotham formulated this result in a suggestive speech:

> If ye then have dealt truly and sincerely with Jerubbaal and with his house this day, then rejoice ye in Abimelech, and let him also rejoice in you: But if not, let fire come out from Abimelech, and devour the men of Shechem, and the house of Millo; and let fire come out from the men of Shechem, and from the house of Millo, and devour Abimelech. And Jotham ran away, and fled, and went to Beer, and dwelt there, for fear of Abimelech his brother. (Judg 9:19–21 KJV)

In this speech, Jotham brings us back to what we said at the end of our earlier passage, about the end of Abimelech and the people of Shechem, where we see that brute power turned against all its partakers. The loss includes everyone: Abimelech, who exercises power, and those on whom the injustice falls, who will not tolerate his policy for long. Fire will come forth from the people of Shechem and consume him. The loss will also include the people of Shechem; they gave legitimacy to brute power, and thus the fire breaks forth from Abimelech to consume the people of Shechem.

The people of Shechem found themselves in a fatal predicament, as they had nothing but loss from all sides because of their miserable pact with Abimelech. At the time of his rule and control over them, they would receive all harm under his leadership; and at the end of his rule, they would be adversely affected by his dark fate. Furthermore, they would face the same fate as he does, as we discover at the end of the story.[64]

---

[64] Tatu, "Jotham's Fable and the 'Crux Interpretum' in Judges IX," 124.

Many interpreters, such as Martin Popper and Gerhard von Rad, have argued that the sheer strength and eloquence of this example makes it the strongest poetic ballad written against the dictatorship of power in all the history of human literature.[65] J. Lyle Story believes that this example is perhaps the defining point in Judges in terms of the order of life that the people of Israel will live in the future. In previous times, the people were led by leaders chosen by Jehovah, as it was the case with Moses, Aaron, and Joshua. These leaders were able to bring the people out of the land of Egypt and lead them on the journey of the wilderness into the promised land. When the people settled in the new land, the pressing question emerged as to how things would be managed from then on: would leadership be in the spirit of authority or service? That's what Jotham puts forth in his famous example.[66]

Clearly, Jotham, who draws a very sharp-toned, sarcastic, ridiculous image of the leadership and power crisis in the era of Abimelech, also presents many important lessons and vital principles in the world of leadership and exercise of power in our modern world. These can be summarized in the following three points.

First, the story asserts that the seeker of absolute power is in fact lacking in achievement and self-realization in his practical life. In Jotham's parable, the olive tree, which is one of the most expensive and valuable trees, did not accept authority over the trees because it could not neglect the production of its oil, which is useful in worship and in anointing kings and priests ("my fatness, wherewith by me they honor God and man," v. 9). The fig tree which produces one of the most delicious fruits, and whose thick leaves give shade (see 1 Sam 25:18), in turn refused to leave its basic role for another that would not make it a better tree by any means (Judg 9:11). The vine as well, which production of grapes was considered one of the most important sources of wealth in Palestine at the time, under which sitting was a significant indication in those days of God's happy rule over his people, would not relinquish directing all its energy to give fruit in order to become queen of the other trees and exercise trivial authority over them (v. 13). The three trees did not have the time or the desire for something they considered small. How could they leave their fruitful role to adopt a comic status devoid of fruit simply to rule over the other trees! Especially when we learn that many translations present "the king of the trees" as no more than the tree whose branches go higher than the rest yet without bearing any useful fruit[67] and without benefiting the trees over which it reigns. The only tree that accepted this authority was the bramble, a strong tree that can grow in any soil but does not produce fruit. Bramble has many thorns, and some scientists believe that it belongs to a certain species of trees that accumulate toxins, preventing

---

[65] Jeremy Schipper, *Parables and conflict in the Hebrew Bible* (Cambridge: Cambridge University Press, 2009), 26.

[66] J. Lyle Story, "Jotham's Fable: A People and Leadership Called

to Serve (Judges 8:22–9:57)," *Journal of Biblical Perspectives in Leadership* 2, no. 2 (Summer 2009): 29–50.

[67] Ibid., 42.

them from producing useful fruit. This tree's only benefit is to use its wood as firewood. It is no surprise at all that such a tree, which had no value, would have found its worth in controlling others. The bramble tree here symbolizes Abimelech. And on a broader scale, it symbolizes every leader or holder of power whose only vision is to seize power and practice it unjustly on all who fall under his atrocious control without possessing any qualifications for this function.

A quick glance at our Eastern societies, especially in regard to the family, gives a lot of weight to this point. In many families in these societies, the husband, who is supposed to represent kind leadership and responsible command, may deviate from this route to exercise an authoritarian leadership that tightens its grip on all members of the family. Then relations exist in violence, control, physical and psychological abuse, stubbornness, and the absence of dialogue. Orders that should be followed without understanding or conviction are given in a loud tone. Only the father possesses—and no one else—full management as he is the head of the family. When we ask why, the answer is often that this husband and father is failing in other areas, so he has no other area to prove himself except within the family. In such a case, we have someone who feels he has no voice outside the walls of his own house. And once he is inside these walls, he turns into a vicious monster; no one can stand up to him or disobey him. It is a case of "psychological and social schizophrenia" due to an internal emptiness and weakness.

Second, on the other hand, many interpreters see that Jotham uttered this example addressing the people of Shechem, who failed to take command among themselves, opening the way for an unqualified person like Abimelech. In an article discussing whether the purpose of such an example is to attack monarchy in general, Eugene Maly says, "The biblical application of this parable does not hold criticism of the king's function. It mainly criticizes those who were so foolish as to anoint a man who was not suited to be a king. And indirectly, it criticizes the self-anointed king."[68]

This idea takes us to the other side of the picture: the arrival of an unsuitable leader to a position of leadership is quite often a result of the weak disposition of the group, or their failure to function efficiently, and the spread of a culture of indifference and nonresponse to the challenges of reality and requirements of the present moment; the weak group has given preference to personal interest rather than public interest. In such a lax climate and empty space, semileaders appear.

Third, it is important to notice the outcome of the relationship between the bramble and the cedar trees at the end of Jotham's example. In verse 15 we read, "And the bramble said unto the trees, If in truth ye anoint me king over you, then come and put your trust in my shadow: and if not, let fire come out of the bramble, and devour

---

[68] Eugene H. Maly, "The Jotham Fable—Anti-Monarchical," *Catholic Biblical Quarterly* 22, no. 3 (July 1960): 304.

the cedars of Lebanon." These words lead us to the personality and the inclination of the person who misuses authority. For him, authority is not a means by which he reaches a nobler and higher end. Rather authority is the goal in itself. To summarize the bramble's view of power: either it rules or it destroys everyone else. The bramble among other plants is nothing but a useless short tree. But once the chance to seize power is presented to it on a silver platter, it holds on to it and ruthlessly fights. It is seen as an irreplaceable opportunity to feel a false value and false high esteem. In reality, this was the case with Abimelech, who upon finding the chance to take control was ready to annihilate everyone around to keep the power, even if it destroyed the people of Shechem who chose him as ruler in a moment of foolishness and ignorance. Such a ruler can be a threat to every good and beautiful aspect in the community, symbolized in this example by the expression, "Cedar of Lebanon."[69]

Perhaps the best expression of this attitude is what Barnabas Lindars said: "Abimelech was a cynic, skeptical, and cruel, and always ready to bite the hand that fed him."[70]

We can summarize the morality of this example in the convergence of two types of the practice of power. The first is represented in the three trees: the olive tree, the fig tree, and the vine, which may have represented the rule of Gideon, Abimelech's father, who followed the path of fruitfulness and sought the best interest of the community, relying on altruism to deal with matters. The second is represented by Abimelech, who adopted the path of selfishness, the search for personal interest, desperately and violently defending the throne of power as he led the people of Shechem towards annihilation and destruction. Zvi Adar points out the generality of this idea and emphasizes that the purpose of this chapter in Judges concerns "not the rise and fall of Abimelech alone, but the rise and fall of every tyrant of all generations."[71]

THE CROSS AND POWER

The question that imposes itself on the course of this discussion is the following: What is the best image that the Bible and Christian theology offer us to exercise authority at any level? More precisely, considering the purpose of this article: What model does the cross of Christ offer to the relationship between the ruler and the governed, the shepherd and the parish, the father and the family, the leader and the led, the authority and the people? In practical terms, what is the model presented by the church contrasting a dictatorship of power or brute power? Is there an alternative? To answer this, we visit the attic during the Last Supper between Christ and his disciples, where Luke tells this story:

---

[69] Story, "Jotham's Fable," 42.

[70] Barnabas Lindars, "Jotham's Fable—A New Form—Critical Analysis," *Journal of Theological Studies* 24, no. 2 (October 1973): 359.

[71] Story, "Jotham's Fable," 46, quoting Zvi Adar, *The Biblical Narrative* (Jerusalem: Department of Education and Culture of the World Zionist Organization, 1959), 11.

And there was also a strife among them, which of them should be accounted the great-est. And he said unto them, The kings of the Gentiles exercise lordship over them; and they that exercise authority upon them are called benefactors. But ye shall not be so: but he that is greatest among you, let him be as the younger; and he that is chief, as he that doth serve. For whether is greater, he that sitteth at meat, or he that serveth? is not he that sitteth at meat? but I am among you as he that serveth. Ye are they which have continued with me in my temptations. And I appoint unto you a kingdom, as my Father hath appointed unto me; That ye may eat and drink at my table in my kingdom, and sit on thrones judging the twelve tribes of Israel. (Luke 22:24–30 KJV)

The "strife" among the disciples that night was not a simple misunderstanding, an ordinary discussion between a group of friends. Rather it was, as seen by the majority of interpreters of the Holy Bible, a real dispute with loud voices and heated arguments. In fact, Lord Jesus spoke with such strength, firmness, and decisiveness, which does not make it a merely ordinary discussion. But he intended to show the rebellious disciples, discussing things with a calm mind and serene dialogue, a new, unfamiliar model for leadership: the "serving authority." Therefore, the image that the Lord Jesus placed before his disciples, who fought about the entitlement of authority and advancement, was the image of the servant.

Christ repeatedly mentioned to his disciples the purpose for which he came to the world. He told them on more than one occasion that "the Son of Man did not come to be served, but to serve" (Matt 20:28; Mark 10:45; Luke 22:27). We should pause once again at John Stott's comment on this phrase: "The emphasis of Jesus that the 'Son of Man did not come to be served but to serve' was an innovative assertion, because the Son of Man in the vision of Daniel was given authority to be served by all people and nations (Dan 7:13–14). Jesus claimed the title, but He switched the role."[72] Jesus' life, as pointed out in one of the specialized studies, bares both opposing poles: authority and service. In the pages of the Gospels, especially Mark, we encounter Jesus Christ, who carries all the strings of power, and at the same time we see in him the traits of the pained servant. He simultaneously gives power to his disciples, while resolutely and unequivocally ordering them to serve the people apart from power and sovereignty. John Stott explains this paradox in Jesus' thought and method of service and his influence on those around him:

Service means lowly humble work, so it is farthest from being an excuse for boasting and pride. Jesus especially distinguished between "sovereignty" and "slavery", or "power" and "service". He added that, although the former was a commended trait in pagans, the second was a characteristic of His followers. Therefore, the Christian servant should

---

[72] John Stott, *The Cross of Jesus*, trans. Najib Jarjour (Cairo: Dar Al Thaqafa, 1995), 333.

not follow the role model of the gentiles (or the Pharisees) who favored sovereignty and domination, but rather follow the role model of Christ who came to serve.[73]

Stott tries to examine the fine line that separates—or perhaps connects—power and service:

> This does not mean any denial for our part of the presence of some authority in service. All there is to the matter is that we define it and draw its limits. The power is that one that is accompanied by proper teaching and a role model who is harmony with itself. It is not authoritarian so that one man monopolizes and controls another's thoughts, conscience or will. Sovereignty is exactly what the Pharisees practiced in an attempt to keep people under their control. The same was with the priests before the reform. They fortified their despotic authority by convincing people that they held the keys to Heaven.[74]

Jesus emphasized numerous times to his disciples that he did not come to be served but to serve as a "servant of God," which is mentioned in the songs of the pained servant (the Man of Sorrows of Isaiah), who is about to be glorified through pain only. And here, again, Jesus tells us to follow Him. This invitation and path of leadership is an unfamiliar matter in the times of Christ. It remains unfamiliar in the twenty-first century. In the world order of today, rulers are intent on imposing their control over those around them, influencing them by dubious means, exploiting them, and imposing tyranny upon them. As Jesus asserted, "But it shall not be so among you" (Matt 20:26 KJV). His new group must be organized according to a different principle and according to a different model—the principle of modest service rather than unjust power.[75]

Washing the Disciples' Feet

We cannot overlook, as we pause before the words of the Lord Jesus in the attic in Luke 22:24–27, that Jesus' words come in the context of another situation: washing the disciples' feet. The Lord Jesus' comments during this episode are close to the content of his speech in Luke 24:22–27.

In John 13:12–15, Jesus says, "Know ye what I have done to you? Ye call me Master and Lord: and ye say well; for so I am. If I then, your Lord and Master, have washed your feet; ye also ought to wash one another's feet. For I have given you an example, that ye should do as I have done to you." The emphasis also in this position is on the principle of serving power (ministering). The teacher and master is the one who took the initiative to wash the feet of the disciples. This should be the image of that who assumes greatness or who holds the keys of power. The spiritual and practical authority

---

[73] John Stott, *Christ the Controversialist* (Downers Grove, IL: InterVarsity, 1978), 195.

[74] Ibid., 195–96.

[75] Peter K. Nelson, "The Flow of Thought in Luke 22:24–27," *Journal for the Study of the New Testament* 43 (1991): 121.

in the incident of washing the feet relies in the real challenge that the Master has put before the disciples in such a palpable and vital form, in order to ignite in them the spark of serving love which they must follow and adopt in their lives.[76]

Hugo Zorrilla suggests that the center of the theological content of this episode is in the desire of the Lord Jesus to show the disciples how a minister's love should be. In other words, understanding this incident and applying its concept in practical life is a partnership with Christ in challenging the cross.[77]

The direct message Christ wanted to give his disciples on that last night with them before the cross is the message of the "humble servant," or humble minister: the servant who goes out to the people, wherever they may be, to minister to them, even to the point of bowing down to wash their feet. The minister would not be too proud, nor would the minister retract from performing the humblest service if it is in the best interest of the one being served. The minister/servant should not regard himself, his status, or esteem highly. Instead, he puts first the success of the service, the advancement of the mission, and the benefit of others; this servant honors—as the basic principle in his path of ministry—the slogan "imparting love."

The Lord wanted to leave his disciples an image that would never leave their minds about real leadership in the kingdom of God. A leader, or a holder of power in the kingdom of heaven, or on any other level, moves among the people not with the authority of his power, severity, or endorsement but with the authority of his love and understanding of the people's conditions, by embracing their weaknesses, encouraging them, and endorsing their capabilities. Leading by this approach is what creates a healthy environment of understanding, innovation, and security in the family, church, and society. Leading by this method is an art in which a leader should excel in using its tools.

In *Leadership Is an Art*, Max Depree says, "The first responsibility of the leader is to clarify the way, and his last responsibility is to thank those who work with him, and between these two, the leader should become a servant. In short, this is the art of leadership."[78] This is exactly what John C. Hutchison expresses when he refers to Robert Greenleaf's book on serving leadership, published in 1977. Here Greenleaf presented a new theory on leadership. At the time this theory earned him vast recognition in the field of management. The theory illustrates what Jesus Christ called for two thousand years ago when he emphasized that service and the spirit of the servant should be the general nature of the leaders in any institution.

Greenleaf noticed that whenever leaders start seeing themselves as servers they become more capable of establishing stronger institutions, more capable of performance and of

---

[76] Hugo Zorrilla, "A Service of Sacrificial Love: Foot Washing (John 13:1–11)," *Direction* 24, no.1 (Spring, 1995): 75.

[77] Ibid., 84.

[78] David L. Tiede, "The Kings of The Gentiles and The Leader Who Serves," *Word and World* 12, no. 1 (Winter 1992): 23–24.

satisfying the needs of the benefactors. Moreover, they find more personal gratification in practicing their leadership roles.[79]

In Jesus' heart, this spirit of servitude is not simply linked to being a model of service, a social hero who plays an exceptional role, a reformer, or one who illuminates others in his circle, nor would he portray a religious image that favors oneself. Rather, the spirit of servitude is linked in principal to the core of his personality and his being the Son of God.

This is the assertion that the Gospel of John is keen to point out. John does not want us merely to put Christ in the traditional context as a model of the servant leader without returning to the theological idea that establishes this idea and gives it weight. The theological background that supports the image of Jesus the Servant is undoubtedly the fact that he is the Son of God sent to the world. It is worth noting that the verb "send" is repeated forty-one times in the Gospel of John. And this repetition emphasizes that the writer clearly means to leave this theological impression: that the Father sends his Son because he loves the world (see John 3:16, 17; 4:34; 5:23–24; 6:37–40; 7:16–18; 8:16–18; 9:4; 10:36; 11:42; 12:44–45; 13:20; 14:24; 15:21; 16:5; 17:3, 21–25; 20:21).

The service of the Son cannot be separated from his being or his mission, which is different in concept and application from any earthly leadership or authority. Truls Åkerlund believes that the episode of the washing of the feet we are studying here best translates Lord Jesus' response towards God sending him.[80] This incident, exclusively told in the Gospel of John, transported the idea of power and authority from the scope of "power that prevails" to "the power that serves and advances"—that is, the power that chooses to relinquish sovereignty over people in order to serve and give to them.[81]

In the ministry of Jesus to which he calls us, the principle of washing the feet is what transported him from being the one of whom the Baptist was not deserving to bend down to unlace his shoes to being the servant who bows in front of those he serves to teach them and us how to live the mission in its true essence.

In the book *Men against Humanity*, French existentialist philosopher Gabriel Marcel says that in the age we live in, the image of the servant has become a meager image. The servant in our imagination is the person who is forced to obey, who was brought up and raised to be negatively, who works out of fear, and who would not obey if there was a way to do so without getting punished.[82]

What Jesus did when he washed the feet of his disciples was that he presented a new image of the servant who obeys, works, offers, blesses, and gives, not because he

---

[79] John C. Hutchison, "Servanthood: Jesus' Countercultural Call to Christian Leaders," *Bibliotheca Sacra* 166 (January–March 2009): 53–69.

[80] Truls Åkerlund, "Son, Sent, and Servant: Johannine Perspectives on Servant Leadership Theory," *Scandinavian Journal for Leadership and Theology* 2 (2015): 1–12.

[81] Ibid.

[82] John A. Mackay, "The Form of a Servant," *Theology Today* 15, no. 3 (October 1958): 304–14.

is forced but because he loves and cares for those he serves. There is a vast difference between Jesus and the examples presented by Rehoboam and Abimelech, who, on the contrary, embody "unjust power" that attempts to fortify its pillars by silencing tongues and marginalizing people, their role, and their rights to make choices, to have freedom, or even life.

The example set by Lord Jesus, the example of "giving love," the "leader servant," or rather the "Son of God who washes feet," shows that the real path to successful leadership is the power of love that washes feet. Or in more contemporary terms, the love that feels the people's concerns, interacts with them, and tries by any means to wash away the dangers in their paths, the heart-aches of life, and the struggling to make a living. Hans Kung expresses it well in a chapter titled "The Meaning of the Cross" in his important book *The Identity of the Christian*. There he says,

> It is apparent—more than anything else—from the life, pain, and death of Jesus that God is for people, defending them without limit. He is not a God that resembles any ruler who horrifies "from above". Rather He is a God who feels for the people and loves them. . . . God, who manifested in Jesus, is not a harsh God; a God of control and law; instead, He is a God who came to meet man in the form of redeeming love; a God of solidarity with the suffering man in the person of Jesus. Where can this manifestation be evident except in the cross?[83]

There is no doubt that the model of washing the feet was not just a liturgical commemoration in our celebration of Holy Thursday (Maundy Thursday) but a daily model of humility, self-denial, and honor, with which all Christians who call themselves children of God interact.

I believe that this model is of great importance in "masculine" societies, such as our Eastern societies in general and the Egyptian society to which I belong in particular. The discussion here focuses on the coercive relationship that widely prevails in the relation between husband and wife in the family. Perhaps the stereotype imprinted in the minds of Egyptians, and perhaps in all Arab countries, is the image of Si-el-Sayyed (Master), created by the talented Nobel laureate Naguib Mahfouz in his famous trilogy. This image brilliantly summarizes the family situation in Egyptian society over the course of so many years during which the role of the man has been glorified. His status, rights, and gains have grown at the expense of the continued marginalization of the role of women, in addition to a flagrant violation of her rights and her dignity, along with the deliberate limitation of her personality, freedom, and effectiveness in society as a whole.

With the crystallization of this state, on one hand, man senses his superiority, while,

---

[83] Hans Kung, *The Identity of the Christian*, trans. Jesuit Father Subhi Al-Hamawi (Beirut: Dar Al-Mashrek, 2006), 177.

on the other, he senses the inferiority of women. As a result, men wash their hands of any family responsibility thinking that his image as a man will be compromised before himself and others if he helps his wife and shares the burden of raising the children and of household chores and errands. Ultimately, the relation resembles that of the slave and the master instead of that of wife and husband in a matrimonial partnership, enjoying warmth, love, and equality. We see a live portrait of this tragedy drawn by the words of Maxim Gorky, the Russian author, in his novel *Creatures That Once Were Men*. There is a scene where a group of desolate men sit together in a filthy bar sharing a conversation about their personal suffering, and about mistreating their wives to the point of beating them. The baker, Mukay Anisimov, tries to explain a man's relationship with his wife in suggestive words that only make things worse. He says, "The wife . . . is a friend . . . so if we look at the matter from this side, we see that she is like a restraint, chained to you for life. You are like two slaves on one of those old ships sailed by slaves . . . so try to keep up with her step by step or you will feel the pull of the chains."[84] The conversation continues between the men about the legitimacy of beating their wives, and one of them tries to dissuade one of his comrades from doing so, not out of empathy for the wife, or her status, or out of respect for marriage or family warmth, but only so that the wife or her pregnancy would not be injured. Then her husband would have to spend his money treating her and would have to care for her:

> "Do you know Kof why I did not like it?
>
> "Let's deal with this from a general point of view, and see what you are really doing, and what comes out of it. Your wife is pregnant. You hit her last night on her sides and chest. That means you not only hit her, but the baby too. You could have killed it. Your wife could die, or get seriously ill. You won't be happy taking care of a sick woman. That's too tiresome and costs a lot of money, because sickness needs medicine, medicine is money. If you haven't killed the baby, you might have crippled it, so he is born deformed. Not even on either sides, or a hunchback. That means he will not be able to work, while it's very important to you that he will be a strong worker. Even if he is born ill, that would be very bad, because it would prevent his mother from working. . . . I only want to tell you that if you cannot help hitting her, do it carefully so you don't compromise her health or the health of the baby. Besides, it is not helpful to hit a pregnant woman . . . not on her stomach or her sides or chest. Hit her on the neck . . . or grab a rope and hit her on a soft spot of her body."[85]

The great Lebanese theologian Costi Bendali explains this unfortunate and obnoxious phenomenon:

---

[84] Maxim Gorky, *Creatures That Once Were Men*, trans. Saad Tawfiq (Cairo: American University in Cairo Press, 1953), 38.

[85] Ibid., 36–38.

The prevalent idea in our society—and to a certain extent in all current human societies, even if they claim to have achieved "women's liberation"—is the belief that a woman is "weak" by nature . . . [that] she has limited perception, is superficial, has unstable opinions, her decisions are emotional, she is very weak in terms of commitment, confrontation, bearing responsibility, etc. These perceptions originally emerged from men who have ruled all human societies since ancient times—and still do (specially our eastern societies). Therefore, they direct their thoughts and perceptions according to their own interests and inclinations, and ingrain an ideology that supports their dominance and justifies their privileges (that is, "ideology" in the true sense of the term: "speech organizing a rule").[86]

The incident of washing the feet addresses this situation at its core, and penetrates this issue in depth. Man, because of social factors and much cultural and intellectual heritage, has a distorted position towards women, especially towards his partner. That results in him treating her with arrogance, thinking that he is thereby achieving his authority over her. He needs to clash with the model of Christ, which is the manifestation of God in the body, who has all the power and authority over humans. He bends to wash the feet of his disciples as a symbol and emphasizes the spirit that should merge with the exercise of power, that is the spirit of service, humility, giving, and sacrifice.

Bendali quotes the great Syrian poet Nizar Qabbani, whose inspiring phrase throbs with longing to achieve this image in Eastern societies. He says, "I demand the 'humanization' of the relationship between the Arab man and the Arab woman and to make it more transparent and compassionate."[87] Jesus Christ effectuates this great dream when he teaches us and invites us to a new horizon and a level we are not familiar with, which we can call "the bowing power."

It is not to be believed that service in this way is merely a utilitarian means of dominating and controlling others. The Lord Jesus never taught this his entire life. The leader, the head of the family, the shepherd, or the ruler does not deserve this title if, for a moment, he serves those around him because he wishes to control them. After washing the disciples' feet, Christ did not gather them around him to become one team that demolishes the Romans and establishes a new kingdom for himself.

Instead, a few hours later, he was crucified for those whose feet he washed in the attic. He never washed the feet of his disciples to rule over them but because he saw them as worthy people to serve. Then the service becomes as Christ wanted it to be. Or as expressed by T. W. Manson, "Serving in the kingdom of God is not an expression of nobility: it is nobility itself."[88] The same idea is emphasized by Max Warren: "The

---

[86] Costi Bendali, *Woman in Her Place and Her Hope*, Middle East Council of Churches (Dar Al-Alam: Al-Arabi, 1994), 15.

[87] Ibid., 37.
[88] Stott, *Christianity and Contemporary Issues*, 341.

Christian leadership has nothing to do with self-assertion, but it has everything to do with encouraging others to assert themselves."[89]

The Suffering Servant

One of the most important models of service and servant is provided by the prophet Isaiah in the pages of his travel chronicles in what scholars believe to be called "Poems of the Suffering Servant." In these four poems, Isaiah presents an image of that servant or slave whom God uses and leads through suffering and severe difficulty to find redemption for lost sinners. These four poems are in Isaiah 42:1–6; 49:1–6; 50:4–9; and 52:13–53:12.

Theological opinions and biblical interpretations have varied about the personality of that slave. Perhaps we should revert at this point to the brief presentation given by Rev. Makram Naguib of those different views. He presents three interpretations of the personality of that slave.[90]

The Slave of God "Israel"

The Jewish interpretation of the texts of the suffering slave is that this slave represents the Israeli nation that was subjected to captivity. Then God allowed them by his love and grace to return to their homeland in Jerusalem. Hence, they saw the image of the Lord's redemption and salvation. Those who call for this interpretation build their views on certain verses that link the term "servant of the Lord" to Israel, as we see in Isaiah 49:3 (NKJV),

> You are My servant, O Israel,
> In whom I will be glorified.[91]

The Slave of God: Individual

Opinions have varied about who may be that person whom Isaiah calls "the slave of God." Some say Jeremiah, while others see him as Josiah, Ezekiel, or a contemporary of Isaiah the prophet. The biblical scholar Haller goes with the view that the slave is someone in the inner circle of the prophet Isaiah. The prophet placed in him all his spiritual aspirations after the end of the role of Cyrus, who did what he had to according to God's plan for his people.[92] Volz also sees that the person in question is the prophet Isaiah himself, who, through the words of his prophecy and his service in the midst of Judah, God will grant salvation for his own and establish his kingdom on earth.[93] Some

---

[89] Stott, *Christianity and Contemporary Issues*, 342.

[90] Makram Naguib, *Poems of Isaiah and the Mission of Christ: Reading the Prophecies* (Cairo: Dar Al Thaqafa, 1998), 7–9.

[91] Samuel Youssef, *Introduction to the Old Testament* (Cairo: Dar Al Thaqafa, 1993), 272.

[92] Otto Eissfeldt, "The Ebed Jahwe in Isaiah XL–LV in the Light of the Israelite Conceptions of the Community and the Individual, the Ideal and the Real," *The Expository Times* 44, no. 6 (March 1933): 261–68.

[93] Ibid., 263.

assumed that these poems could perhaps be related to the prophet Moses, the mediator of the covenant, who mediated for his people and died bearing their grievances.[94]

The Slave of God: The Messiah

This interpretation is the most famous and the closest to biblical interpretations. The image drawn by Isaiah indicates a person more than a people. But this person is not an ordinary man, as he is portrayed in a special image: "He is immaculate. . . . He has committed no sin" (Isa 53:9). Moreover, his role and mission demand a unique person to get them done (Isa 42:4; 49:5; 53:4–6). When we look to the New Testament, we find that method and direction followed by the writers of the New Testament in handling all the texts of the Suffering Slave focused on its application of the life, mission, and the act of atonement of Lord Jesus. In his huge reference work *The Entrance to the Old Testament*, Reverend Samuel Youssef tells some of the examples of these applications, which can be summarized as follows:[95]

In the story of the Ethiopian eunuch (Acts 8:26–39), who read the fourth poem of the suffering servant (Isa 53) and was unable to understand it, when Philip wanted to explain to him the truth and meaning of what he was reading, he applied the words of this poem to the Lord Jesus, who is the real suffering slave.

In parts of his gospel, Matthew interprets life situations of Lord Jesus by referring to some segments of the poems of the suffering slave. Matthew 12:14–21 speaks of the qualities of Christ, God's chosen child referring to what is in Isaiah 42:1–4, where the prophet says:

> Behold my servant, whom I uphold; mine elect, in whom my soul delighteth; I have put my spirit upon him: he shall bring forth judgment to the Gentiles. He shall not cry, nor lift up, nor cause his voice to be heard in the street. A bruised reed shall he not break, and the smoking flax shall he not quench: he shall bring forth judgment unto truth. He shall not fail nor be discouraged, till he have set judgment in the earth: and the isles shall wait for his law. (KJV)

Along the same lines, Christopher Wright points out how Jesus viewed himself, then how the early church viewed him, through this perspective of Suffering Slave of God, and says:

> There are strong bases that Jesus viewed Himself as being a slave. He interpreted His ministry, especially His sufferings and death as per the phrases expressed in Isaiah 53. A sure matter here is that the First Church also made this correlation. Most probably they took this concept from Jesus, and did not invent it themselves. One of the oldest terms that refer to Jesus among his followers in the Book of Acts is: "Holy Child" (Acts

---

[94] Youssef, *Introduction to the Old Testament*, 273.   [95] Ibid., 274–75.

3:13–26; 4:27–30). Peter, one of those who closely shared Jesus' thoughts, found his mind also turning to Isaiah 53 when he was thinking how Jesus had set an example for us of enduring pain without retribution (1 Peter 2: 21–25).[96]

Traits of the Servant

When we stop before the four poems to contemplate on the image of the servant as presented to us by the slave of God, which is our main concern here, we find that the example of the servant here embodies the following traits—as opposed to the authoritarian example which shortcomings we have previously seen.

Nonrelenting Perseverance

It is clear through careful reading of the poems of the Suffering Slave that his ministry would not be easy, nor will its anticipated results be achieved effortlessly or smoothly. On the contrary, his ministry faced all kinds of rejection, resistance, and defamation. The slave appointed by God for an important mission and huge responsibility, "to produce truth into safety." Safety here means governance and justice—justice not in its conventional sense, related to worldly courts, but divine justice, the justice of God, or the law of God.[97] We say that this slave came for this vital assignment to restore the law of God and obedience to the heart of Israel. His mission was not a pleasant or peaceful journey. It was a war. It was turbulent, harsh, and full of strife. The slave in the midst of struggle did not resort to the easiest solution, which is to escape. Rather, in strenuous perseverance, and positive patience strode through the path of service, such that these divine words were fitting: "He shall not fail nor be discouraged, till he have set judgment in the earth: and the isles shall wait for his law" (Isa 42:4). Then the servant in his third poem, following the same idea and direction, says, "For the Lord GOD will help me; therefore shall I not be confounded: therefore have I set my face like a flint, and I know that I shall not be ashamed" (Isa 50:7 KJV). Once more we see the perseverance of the slave to achieve the service and complete the mission. Notice that perseverance and determination were not inclined to violence that would oust others so that the mission would succeed. It took a peaceful, humble path. For this slave, who "made his face like the stone," says about himself in the same context, "The Lord God hath given me the tongue of the learned, that I should know how to speak a word in season to him that is weary" (Isa 50:4 KJV).

This is the point at which we should pause to discuss the idea of authority. For the slave of God embodies the model of the servant, the leader, the shepherd, the head of the family, or the ruler who is patient with his flock and his servants. He is not harsh and does not pressure them till he obtains what he wants, but he believes that they are

---

[96] Christopher Wright, *Knowing Jesus Through the Old Testament*, trans. Hoda Bahig (Cairo: Dar AL Thaqafa, 2010), 193.

[97] H. H. Rowley, "The Servant Mission, the Servant Songs and Evangelism," *Interpretation* 8 (1954): 259–72.

much more important than his dreams and ambitions. In reality, they are his dream and ambition. This is one of the important elements missing in a dictatorial rule and leadership. A man who is a dictator by nature does not see but himself, his success, and achieving his own ambitions. He does not see beyond himself, and does not want to. Therefore, to him, human value diminishes greatly. This is what happened in the communist experiment, which did not relate to the human being, respect him, or consider his limitations; so it trampled him and crushed his dreams, underestimated his pain and hopes with enviable cruelty. And this is what happens with every disfigured model that practices power without any consideration to man as a human being.

The human being of the modern age has become exposed to the threat of being trampled and crushed by fierce enemies. The first enemy is represented by the West, meaning extreme materialism, technological advancement, the tyranny of speed, and the fevered desire for accomplishment that converts man into a mere cog in the wheel of progress and development of civilization. Antoine Nouis, who lives in the Western culture, which is immersed in severe materialism, says:

> Our society gives more importance to place than time! We know a person for how much he owns and the extent of his possessions; the width of his house, and the amount of his trips. Never by the quality of his comfort, his heed to history, and his capability to invest his experience in those younger than himself. The short term, what is now, and instant consumption are the preferred matters with regards to time, more than other matters like commitment, loyalty and long-term investment.[98]

The second enemy is in the East, meaning the violent power, crushing dictatorship, the sick aspiration to control, along with everything that accompanies these elements—corruption at all levels. Here, a human becomes a mere gear in a huge wheel of conflicting interests seeking to win the biggest piece of the cake of power and control. The two enemies, West and East, have no concern except the success of their endeavors, both disregarding man under the weight of their cruelty.

When we contemplate the life of the Lord Jesus, we find that he has presented in the finest form the model of the servant who is patient with others' weaknesses and persists in an unrelenting challenge until he takes them out of the tunnels of failure and confusion and delivers them to the safe shores of strength and accomplishment. We see him act patiently with Nathanael the fanatic, violent John and James, impulsive and reckless Peter, troubled-with-skepticism Thomas, unsettled John the Baptist in prison, and the disciples, who, until the night of the cross, were still quarrelling about

---

[98] Antoine Nouis, *The Law Today: Contemporary Reading of the Ten Commandments and the Sermon on the Mount*, trans. Youssef Samir (Doha, Qatar: Dar al-Thaqafa, 2015), 64.

who was the greatest among them. We see Jesus, in the midst of all of these, with the roof of his patience reaching higher, his mind broader, and his heart bigger for these "human trivialities."

Here, we come to another indispensable trait in all those who rightly claim authority, namely patience and tolerance. Patience is an attribute that cannot be overlooked in the leadership of the human community, which is full of weaknesses, imperfections, sins, and diseases of all kinds. The true, effective power in such a climate is acutely aware of the human nature—fallen, weak, and distorted—and, therefore, interacts with human nature and the circumstances surrounding it, tolerates the people, and patiently withstands the challenges encountered. In the book of Isaiah, the slave of God is linked to the city of God, Jerusalem. This is a sign that the holder of power is integrated, not isolated, from those he leads, or rather carries.

The patience and tolerance of the true servant of God, Jesus Christ, was not limited to his position. It transcended that to include patience to bear the pains he was subjected to. The servant is a suffering slave, who surrendered his back to the assailants, his cheek to the hunters. He did not hide his face from shaming and spitting. Christ knew that if he did not have patience towards those who inflicted pain and crucifixion upon him, it would inevitably represent a significant stumbling block in the path of the plan of salvation.

Therefore, we notice a remarkable intensification in the story of the cross. The forces of darkness unleash a sequence of situations that target Jesus' psyche in an attempt to overcome his magnificent patience. In all of this, we find the Master exerting outstanding self-control as he embraces the ordeal with an unrelenting psychological and spiritual perseverance.

- In the beginning, in the garden of Gethsemane, the Lord confronted Judas, the traitor, who delivered him with a kiss, and in a remarkable patience he called him "friend" (Matt 26:50). Then Jesus dealt with the rush of Peter, who cut off the ear of the priest's servant. Jesus stopped the acceleration of violence, reminding Peter that violence only breeds violence.
- In the same situation, the Lord indicated that he could declare his discontent and wrath upon those who came to arrest him like a thief; he could ask the Father for twelve armies of angels (Matt 26:53), but we meet again with the divine patience shown by the blessed suffering servant of the Lord.
- During the religious trial before Hanan and Caiaphas, one of the soldiers slapped the Savior (John 18:22). What if a person with dictatorial tendencies were exposed to such a situation? However, the Lord Jesus, the perseverant and patient servant of suffering, contained the foolishness of that soldier and extended the cover of tolerance also to this situation, and so he answered:

"If I have spoken evil, bear witness of the evil: but if well, why smitest thou me?" (John 18:23 KJV).

- The peak of his patience and tolerance was at the base of the cross with the hammering sarcasm and screaming of curses on the head of the crucified. This was crueler than the nails in his hands and feet. Yet his patience and perseverance rose above as he prayed for those who were cursing and killing him, saying: "Father, forgive them; for they know not what they do" (Luke 23:34 KJV).

The principal key to the success of God's servant was his perseverance, his tolerance of the weaknesses of others, and the pains he suffered. In all this, Jesus presents a model and path of success for the leader, servant, ruler, head of family, and the minister in any place or time. It is the key contemplated by the Egyptian Christian author Habib Said, who compares Jesus' example with the human inclinations and tendencies against patience and perseverance:

> An English writer named Carlyle had a passion for writing the history of the French Revolution. When the people of London were indifferent to his political views, he looked out of his window down on the city and said, "In this city there are three million people, most of them idiots and fools." When we think of these words, we recall another man looking out over his great city from the top of the mountain, and from His lips come words of tenderness and caring. We hear him say, "O Jerusalem, Jerusalem, thou that killest the prophets, and stonest them which are sent unto thee, how often would I have gathered thy children together . . . and ye would not?"[99]

Unceasing Sacrifice

In the third and fourth poems of the Suffering Slave, it is clear that the suffering man is about to sacrifice himself for the good of the mission and its success. In Isaiah 50:6, the servant of Jehovah says: "I gave my back to the smiters, and my cheeks to them that plucked off the hair: I hid not my face from shame and spitting."

In the fourth poem, the theme of the sacrifice of the servant is the one that dominates the entire poem, the verses accumulate towards this concept as shown:

> Surely he hath borne our griefs, and carried our sorrows: yet we did esteem him stricken, smitten of God, and afflicted. But he was wounded for our transgressions; he was bruised for our iniquities: the chastisement of our peace was upon him; and with his stripes we are healed. . . . He was oppressed, and he was afflicted, yet he opened not his mouth: he is brought as a lamb to the slaughter, and as a sheep before her shearers

---

[99] Habib Said, *Scattered Papers: Studies in Religion, Ethics and Conference* (House of Authorship and Publication of the Episcopal Church, n.d.), 81–82.

is dumb, so he openeth not his mouth. He was taken from prison and from judgment: and who shall declare his generation? for he was cut off out of the land of the living: for the transgression of my people was he stricken. And he made his grave with the wicked, and with the rich in his death; because he had done no violence, neither was any deceit in his mouth. Yet it pleased the LORD to bruise him; he hath put him to grief: when thou shalt make his soul an offering for sin, he shall see his seed, he shall prolong his days, and the pleasure of the LORD shall prosper in his hand. He shall see of the travail of his soul, and shall be satisfied: by his knowledge shall my righteous servant justify many; for he shall bear their iniquities. Therefore will I divide him a portion with the great, and he shall divide the spoil with the strong; because he hath poured out his soul unto death: and he was numbered with the transgressors; and he bare the sin of many, and made intercession for the transgressors. (Isa 53:4–5, 7–12 KJV)

We notice that expressions and phrases such as bore, carried, stricken by God, humiliated, wounded, bruised, stripes, dumb, being led to slaughter, silent sheep before its captors, hit, sacrifice sin, casted to death itself. These are words and phrases that clearly express the idea of sacrifice and offering that were experienced and exercised by that old servant.

Jesus' Ministry in the Gospels

When we review the mission of the Lord Jesus, the great slave of God, as presented by the many writers of the revelation of the New Testament, we discover that the Lord summed up his "missionary role" or "service philosophy," saying, "for even the Son of man came not to be ministered unto, but to minister, and to give his life a ransom for many" (Mark 10:45; Matt 20:28). This motto indicates the concept of sacrifice (offering and paying ransom in the terms used by the Gospel writers) and is deeply rooted in Jesus' vision of dwelling among humans.

Many interpreters connect the words of Jesus in Mark 10:45 (and Matt 20:28) and those of Isaiah about the slave of God: "Therefore will I divide him a portion with the great, and he shall divide the spoil with the strong; because he hath poured out his soul unto death: and he was numbered with the transgressors; and he bare the sin of many, and made intercession for the transgressors" (Isa 53:12 KJV). Many see Isaiah's words as the biblical and divine foundation upon which the New Testament is able to understand the meaning and the depth of the mission of Christ. The biblical scholar F. F. Bruce sees that these words of Jesus in Mark 10:45 summarize better than any other script in the Gospels the spirit of service/ministry that flows from the fourth poem of the suffering slave.[100] For example, on the night of the Last Supper, the Lord Jesus says as he presents the cup, which is also an indication of sacrifice: "This is my

---

[100] F. F. Bruce, *This Is That* (London, Paternoster, 1982), 98.

blood of the new testament, which is shed for many" (Mark 14:24). The apostle Paul emphasizes this same view to his disciple Timothy in his pastoral speech: "For there is one God, and one mediator between God and men, the man Christ Jesus; Who gave himself a ransom for all, to be testified in due time" (1Tim 2:5, 6). The apostle uses the same expression in his epistle to the church of Philippi: "Yea, and if I be offered upon the sacrifice and service of your faith, I joy, and rejoice with you all" (Phil 2:17).

The biblical scholar Wellhausen refers to the relation between the two parts of Mark 10:45, saying that Christ's path was one of offering and sacrifice in all circumstances. It was a sacrifice in his life (Mark 10:45a) and in his death (Mark 10:45b), or the sacrifice of Jesus in his life led him to sacrifice for mankind through his death. Roloff expresses the same conclusion in different terms: "The death of Jesus is the ultimate result of His path of offering and sacrifice during His life."[101] We follow this thread to point out that the sacrifice we read about in the poems of the slave of God, or in the mission of Christ in the New Testament, or the different notes of the scripture, was never a momentary sacrifice or a "sacrifice out of circumstance." Rather, it was a genuine and deep direction that affects all choices of life and ministry.

Note that Jesus, speaking in Mark 10:45 of his self-offering as a ransom for many, comes very close to echoing his speech in the attic (Luke 22). In Mark 10:35–40, John and James, along with their mother, issue a plea to be seated on the right and left of Christ in his kingdom. Mark points to the disciples' reaction to this plea in verse 41: "And when the ten heard it, they began to be much displeased with James and John." Here, Jesus repeats what he said in Luke 22:24–27. Then, he adds words that merit our pause in verse 45. Jesus responds to the disciples' quest for glory, authority, and mastery with the example of sacrificial service, which is the truest example of a great life that practices its authority with the power of love, sacrifice, and giving, not by the power of the sword, fire, violence, and tyranny.

An additional observation given by Joachim Jeremias on the word "offer/give," orig-inated from the Greek term *dounai* (δουναι), when he points out that it means to "give willingly."[102] The disciples of Christ who follow his example in ministry and service face the temptation of falling into the brutal use of power, which overtakes many leaders, officials, ministers, priests, and parents. One has to choose with a conscious will and responsible openness to adopt a different approach, and a different method, namely that of giving and sacrifice—willful giving and loving sacrifice.

Here I quote the words of Charles W. Colson from his article "The Illusion of Power," in which he presents the conflict between the frantic use of the power of authority—or more precisely the authority of power—and the serving leadership:

---

[101] G. R. Beasely-Murray, *Jesus and the Kingdom of God* (Grand Rapids: Eerdmans, 1986), 280.

[102] Joachim Jeremias, *New Testament Theology*, vol. 1, *The Proclamation of Jesus* (New York: Scriber's, 1971), 292.

The lure of power can distance Christians who are most adhering to their principles away from the true nature of Christian leadership, which is to serve others. It is difficult to sit in an ivory tower and wash the feet of those who sit beneath you. This same temptation was the first that led to commit the first sin. Eve experienced to eat from the tree of knowledge—distinction of good and evil—to become like God, and to gain the power that was for God alone . . . for the sake of proclaiming the Kingdom of God, and give His sacrifice against the fall; Jesus threw out all traditional concepts of power.

When the disciples quarreled over who was the greatest among them, Jesus rebuked them: "But ye shall not be so: but he that is greatest among you, let him be as the younger; and he that is chief, as he that doth serve" (Luke 22:26). Imagine the effect of this phrase in a context of politicians, in the chambers of members of boardrooms, or alas, in some religious empires.[103]

Jesus' Concept of Ministry and That of Jews and Gentiles

When comparing Christ's concept of service to that of his Jewish counterparts, we discover that, despite some similarities, a fundamental difference divides them at the practical level. This divide grows wider and deeper when it comes to giving and sacrifice in service. Christianity and Judaism agree on the possibility of self-sacrifice for God; however, they totally differ when it comes to sacrifice and self-sacrifice on behalf of another human being. David Litwa indicates that Judaism forbids self-sacrifice for another human being based on two theological justifications: first, God is the only one who possesses the human entity, and second, man is created in the image of God. The greatest good according to Jewish morality lies in human life, which is considered sacred and should not be compromised because it is good (i.e., sacred) in itself.

Holding human life as sacred reaches a point where it is permitted to breach the provisions of holy law to preserve life. According to the Jewish scholar Nahmanides, saving human life is a "great commandment." The Jewish view of human life demands that preservation of human life is a "great moral priority" because, according to Jewish tradition, God possesses the human soul since he created and breathed his soul into it (Gen 2:7; Jer 38:16). God alone has the right to retrieve the soul at any time he deems appropriate (Deut 32:39), and God does not allow any being to take this right from him. Therefore, Jewish thought affirms that God does not give a person the right to die in order to save another person's life. This concept is confirmed by Rabbi Akiva in the second century when he clearly rejects the idea of replacing one person's life with another. He states that in the event of a conflict between the life of a human being and another human being, "your own life has priority." He builds his view on Leviticus

---

[103] Charles W. Colson, "The Illusion of Power," in *The Religion of Power*, ed. Michael Scott Horton (Dar Al Thaqfa, 2008), 27, 28.

25:36: "Take thou no usury of him, or increase: but fear thy God; that thy brother may live with thee." According to Akiva's account of this verse, one must live so that his brother may live also; this commandment cannot be attained if he dies. Therefore, it is forbidden that a person would offer his life to save another from death.

Christianity is in full agreement, heart and soul, with Judaism concerning the sanctity of human life, which has been created by God who reigns over it. This is what is expressed in the words of Pope Jean Paul II when he says, "God alone is the Master of life from its start till its end." But Christianity does not see the issue from this angle alone. Christianity holds an additional factor that cannot be overlooked, namely, the life of Christ as a giving sacrifice. It is love in its highest form (*agape*) that ties the human self-righteousness with benevolence towards others, to the point of dying to attain this higher good.

The first church comprehended this radical difference, which transcends the value of this giving love, and sang of it in one of its most profound and most famous hymns, which was quoted by the apostle Paul to speak of Christ's humility: "Who, being in the form of God, thought it not robbery to be equal with God: But made himself of no reputation, and took upon him the form of a servant, and was made in the likeness of men: And being found in fashion as a man, he humbled himself, and became obedient unto death, even the death of the cross" (Phil 2:6–8).[104]

The narrow Jewish view greatly distorts the idea of sacrificing for the other by restricting it in the act of doing good for a small and limited specific group of human beings, namely the Jews. Furthermore, this applies only to a particular group of Jews and excludes some sects (e.g., Samaritans). History books and biblical studies are full of indications as to how Jews viewed others, whether other nations in general, or other Jews belonging to different Jewish denominations. It is sufficient here to refer to a small passage where John Stott describes this image about how Jews regard those from other nations:

> Jews hold a big grudge against the (other) nations. Jews said about the gentiles that God created them to be fuel for the fires of hell. And that God loved the children of Israel out of all the peoples He created. . . . Jews considered it wrong to help—even—a gentile woman in labor so that she may not give birth to another gentile into the world. That deep hatred Jews had toward the gentiles continued until Christ came. There was an absolute barrier standing between Jews and the gentiles. If a Jew married a gentile woman, or if a Jewish woman married a gentile man, a funeral ceremony would be held for the Jewish party, because this marriage was considered to be like a death."[105]

---

[104] M. David Litwa, "Self-Sacrifice to Save the Life of Another Person in Jewish and Christian Traditions," *Heythrop Journal* 50 (2009): 912–22.

[105] John Stott, *Ephesians*, The Bible Speaks (Episcopal Publications House, 2003), 74, 75.

What a huge difference in this aspect between this intransigent, fanatical view, closed towards sacrifice and charity to others, and the view of Christ, which embraced everyone in the circle of giving and self-sacrifice.

The Arab Christian church of our day direly needs to return to the word of Christ and to the principal of service as ordained and indicated in Mark 10:45. One of the dangerous and difficult ailments afflicting this side of the world is the disease of "fanaticism," which has been transmitted from the larger society into the society of the church to the point that Egyptian philosopher Mourad Wahba refers to the term "fanatic" as being taken from the origin "Fanaticus," which in turn is from the word "Fanum," the Latin word meaning "House of Worship"—a direct reference to the concept of intolerance historically linked to religion.[106]

So far we have examined only Jewish thought. As for the gentiles—the other nations of the world—we find that in an important article titled "Power and Service in Mark 10:41–45" by David Seeley, a professor at the University of Claremont, California.[107] Seeley gives an extensive account of Greek literature on power and service, which includes the idea that a person in power should have a sense of service toward those he serves.

In this study, we pause before a historical survey of the concept of "domineering ruler/good ruler." This text clearly combines these two ideas, which stand on the opposite ends of the spectrum, in a vivid picture whose background depicts many thoughts and texts propagated in classic literature, especially in the Greek classics. In Seeley's point of view, the principle advocated by these words is that the ruler must be a servant to those he serves. This is derived, even if only in theory, from what E. R. Goodenough calls "The Political Philosophy of the Hellenic Rule."[108] Goodenough believes that the best representative of this principle in the ancient world is the Greek orator Dio Chrysostom, who wrote, for example, that a good king obtains his post from the king of the gods, Zeus, provided that he plans and studies for the welfare of his subjects.[109]

Chrysostom summarizes this philosophy, adding phrases such as: "He (the good king) appreciates and loves righteousness, and at the same time extends his care for all," that "no one practices compassion and empathy φιλανθροπια better than a good king," and that he "shows a kind gentle spirit towards all."[110] Chrysostom adds that the king experiences a kind of equivalence and equality with his servants, saying that the king should not rejoice in the title of "master" even in his relationship with his slaves because he regards himself as king not only for himself but for everyone.[111]

In his third article about the king, Chrysostom says that the best metaphor for a good king is the sun, for the king of God does not stop, just like the sun, serving us as

---

[106] Mourad Wahba, *The Angel of Absolute Truth* (Dar Qibaa, 1999), 248.

[107] David Seeley, "Rulership and Service in Mark 10:41–45," *Novum Testamentum* 35, no. 3 (1993): 234–50.

[108] Ibid., 235–36.

[109] Ibid., 236.

[110] Ibid.

[111] Ibid.

his servants and doing whatever is necessary for our good. This view does not belong only to Dio Chrysostom, but it is preceded by one of his teachers, the Greek stoic philosopher Musonius Rufus (AD 25–95), who emphasized that the first mission of the king is to be able to protect and benefit his people. He should strongly resemble Zeus and, like him, be a father to his people. In the same sense, the Greek stoic philosopher Archytas (428–347 BC) points out that the best ruler is one who does nothing for his own interest and everything for the good of his subjects.[112]

In a manuscript by the Pythagorean writer Diotogenes, he says that the king is occupied in doing what is good for his people and brings them benefit, has to think with a graceful refined spirit with regard to his leadership, and for him the greatest of pleasures must be derived from acts that include good deeds and great accomplishments rather than personal pleasure. He would also provide aid, not in one way, but by every possible means. The writer of the article then takes us back to sources that are stronger and more widespread when he mentions that Plato, the great Greek philosopher, states in his *Republic* that the real ruler by nature does not search for his personal interest but searches for the best interest of those he rules. Yet rulers should be labeled saviors and helpers. They perform their duties diligently to serve the state and carry out their role for the welfare of the city.[113]

Despite the existence and spread of such political, social, and philosophical contexts, the ancient Hellenistic culture lacked the elements of giving, benevolence, and sacrifice that revelation states in Mark 10:45. The model of service in the New Testament is not merely the resounding slogans and brilliant principles. It goes much further, as the servant—as Jesus presented in his words and life—is the one who is ready to offer sacrifices and is giving to those he serves. For, in the mindset of Jesus Christ, the path to greatness inevitably passes through the path of service, and there is no way to satisfy the desire to excel except through self-denial for the sake of others. Jesus Christ, who said these words and recommended them to his disciples, lived by them and ultimately died following the same principle. In that way, the cross was the strongest manifestation of those words.

We can go further by saying that many historical biblical studies focusing on studying the cultural backgrounds of the Bible point out that the sacrificial system, followed in the ancient Roman world in which the beginnings of the New Testament took place, was not entirely religious. It carried many hidden political aims.

In an extensive study of the sacrificial practices in the Christian and Roman worlds, the author, George Heyman, says that, at the time of Jesus' crucifixion at the beginning of the first century AD, sacrifices already had a set system in the Greco-Roman world, especially when it came to the political/religious aspect. The sacrifice in its ritual form

---

[112] Ibid., 236–37.

[113] Ibid., 238.

had a dual function: to guarantee the appeasement of the gods and to symbolize the political authority of the emperor. Heyman's conclusion draws on the fact that the sacrifices that were made in that civilized environment of the gods (being the protectors of the state) were also presented to the emperor as the representative of the deity on earth. Historical rhetoric tells the story that when Caesar died, a man called Amatius built an altar in the same spot where he was buried, and made a sacrificial offering for Caesar as a God. A marble tombstone was erected in that position, and since then they started making sacrificial offerings in the name of Caesar.[114] That was how sacrificial offerings created a new reality that people had to accept, that is, that the dominance of the emperor over his entire empire is a necessity, not only a matter of politics but religion also, a matter that has to be recognized and to be lived by.

Here we confirm again that there is a vast uncrossable gap between the sacrifice within that exploitative logic, which seeks to secure power, impose control, and hold the reins of matters, and that of Christ, a sacrifice of love and self-denial, looking out for the other, for his good and for his salvation. Christ translated what he pronounced in Mark 10:45 in the scope of his ministry on earth, where he drew close to others, felt their pain, and touched their needs. This rendered his authority over them an authority of love, not an authority of oppression, and brute force.

J. T. Holland, an academic expert in the field of pastoral theology, brilliantly summarizes the attributes of Christ's service in concise points, which all refer to that concept of "the authority of love."[115] These points can be summarized as follows:

1. Jesus' service was distinguished primarily by caring for man as a human being. He focused his attention on individuals. Throughout his life, the Lord was able to give his attention to the person before him. In his encounter with the leper we see that he "moved with compassion" and "put forth his hand, and touched him" telling him, "I will; be thou clean" (Mark 1:41). We can easily put our hand on the remarkable encounter between Jesus, who descended with amazing love from the heights of his glory to embrace all those in need.

2. Another feature of the service of Jesus was evident in the warmth of his relations with others. Everywhere he went, huge masses followed him and found him to be compassionate and pleasant in all his interactions with them. He had the capacity to build bridges with human beings, whichever their needs or state. Therefore, many could approach him fearlessly to share with him their needs, pains, doubts, and inquiries. Perhaps one of the best examples of this was the amazing closeness he practiced with children whose parents brought them to

---

[114] George Heyman, *The Power of Sacrifice: Roman & Christian Discourses in Conflict* (Washington, DC: Catholic University of America Press, 2007), 78, 79, 95.

[115] J. T. Holland, "Jesus, A Model of Ministry," *Journal of Pastoral Care* 36, no. 4 (1982): 260–64.

THE CROSS AND THE POWER ISSUE

receive his blessing. This was one of the most honest gestures that demonstrated this Galilean teacher to be a person with overflowing compassion and a warm heart. Approachable and easy to interact with, he broke down barriers to get closer to them. Christ, in all his dealings with people, never regarded them as meaningless numbers, without an inner sense, feelings, or value. Instead, he embodied love, service, and giving: the foundation on which to build all desire for true spiritual leadership. This is transcribed by the great theologian Nicholas Berdyaev: "In some sense, every human soul possesses meaning and value more than all history with all its empires and wars and revolutions, and the rise and fall of its civilizations."[116]

3. Jesus' ministry was also characterized by being completely removed from the spirit of judgment of others, which contradicted the prevailing religious tendency of that time. This made the common people moan under the yoke of religion whose sword was upon their necks. Religious leaders used (or rather misused) their official status to apprehend people. Expulsion from the temple, which was coupled with accusations of atheism and misconduct, became the closest and easiest means of terrorizing society in those times. Then here comes Jesus to change the despicable concept people had about religion. Jesus became famous for his "love for publicans and sinners" (see Matt 11:19; Luke 15:2). Sinners here are "the people of earth," who were preoccupied with earning their living to the extent that they neglected being committed to the commandments. And in their ignorance, society counted them as sinners and rogues. But Jesus saw them differently. He did not pour curses of damnation upon them; instead, he gave them the chance to repent, them and many other stray groups in society, with loving patience.

The master's words to the disciples in the attic on the night of the cross, or in the face of the plea of James and John and their mother, were a real shock to that community who had absorbed since childhood the Jewish traditional image of the Messiah and the nature of his work. We cannot dismiss that the fall of the people of God into the Babylonian captivity for more than seventy years, as well as their falling under the fires of Roman colonization for decades, had contributed to the formation of a certain image of the victorious Messiah. This image in its larger frame was tied to victory and triumph, without a hint of weakness. The thought of the Messiah was related, in the common people's minds, to the political and military role of the Son of David. Therefore, Jesus' words about "giving and sacrificing service" did not line up with the

---

[116] Nicholas Berdayaev, *The Fate of Man in the Modern World*, quoted in "Working the Angles," by Eugene Peterson (Grand Rapids: Eerdmans, 1987), 159.

messianic concept. The Messiah to them was a victorious leader, not a man of suffering. He should live as a king of Israel and could not be denied.[117]

CONCLUSION

In conclusion to this chapter, once more we say that the Bible proposes the model of giving service to correct the desire for power and its misuse. In contrast to the arrogant Rehoboam and the cruel tyrant Abimelech, the suffering servant appears. This servant picks up a towel, pours water to wash the feet of those who are far less than himself. Lord Jesus turns our traditional vision of greatness upside down. The approach of Jesus, as Donald Crabil says, is looking up from the base, not down from the top.[118] Such a position shakes the value of modern individualism, which seeks to satisfy its desire to control and dominate.

There is nothing better or more beautiful than what Juan Arias wrote, as he paused before the personality of Pope John XXIII. Despite ascending the Papacy in Rome in a transitional period, John XXIII was said to have caused many troubles to the institution of the church. Yet, he took the Catholic Church—along with history itself—around a new turn. Juan Arias paused before this character in his famous book *The God I Don't Believe In*, and said these words:

> The day we dare place people like the Apostle Peter, or Pope John to lead our Christian groups; people whose only law is love; their only style of ministry is evangelical simplicity; people whose doors are wide open to every risk, and every adventure, and every heroism; who are led by the revelation of the Spirit of the Living God; people whose flaming love devours all human obstacles such that there is the light of hope, food for each hungry person. . . . That day, the crisis of power will disappear, and with it will the crisis of obedience.[119]

---

[117] C. H. Dodd, *Founder of Christianity*, trans. Rafiq and Najwa Farah (Al-Meshaal, 1975), 97–98.

[118] Donald Crabil, *The Kingdom: Does the Church Today Express the Kingdom of God?*, trans. Wagdy Wahba (Doha, Qatar: Dar Al-Thaqafa, 2004), 228–29.

[119] Juan Arias, *The God I Don't Believe In*, 3rd ed., trans. Jesuit Father Kamil Heshema (Beirut: Dar Al Mashrek, 1992), 125.

Chapter Seven

CULTURE AND IDENTITY

Andrea Zaki Stephanous

Rev. Dr. Andrea Zaki Stephanous is the general director of the Coptic Evangelical Organization for Social Services, vice-president of the Protestant Churches of Egypt, and president of the Fellowship of Middle East Evangelical Churches. He also lectures in politics and social change at the Evangelical Theological Seminary in Cairo. Dr. Zaki has studied in Egypt, Canada, the USA, and the UK. He earned his PhD from the University of Manchester in 2003. He is the author of *Jesus and Historical Criticism* and *Social Change and Political Islam, Citizenship and Minorities*, as well as numerous articles that have appeared in the news media and Christian magazines.

ARAB CHRISTIANS LIVE in a political context where religion colors personality and determines identity. Religion has also become the portal to individual political activity, a portal at which national and intellectual currents count for less than fundamental religious currents. There has also been an escalation of the supposed confrontation between Islam and the West. All these circumstances leave Arab Christians in an increasingly complicated and unsettled situation in which the quest for a religious frame of reference for thinking about current reality is not a luxury but an urgent need. The future of Arab Christians in the Middle East will be determined by their ability to cope with the social, economic, and political changes at the threshold of the third millennium.

Issues of culture and identity assume a prominent role in how we handle the current, tense reality in the Middle East. Arab Christians are once again subject to the old temptation to withdraw into isolated enclaves in an attempt to avoid their faith melting into the Muslim majority. At the same time other Arab Christians advocate appeasement and adoption of the premises and ideas of political Islam as an alternative to Arabism or nationalism.

In this chapter, I will endeavor to offer a vision for asserting the distinctive plural identity of Arab Christians without either dissolution or alienation.

I will begin by focusing on Arab nationalism as an ideological basis for cultural and political participation, although I acknowledge that the emergence of political Islam has contributed to nationalism's being replaced by Islam as the basis for social, political, and cultural inclusion. It is thus imperative that we study the relation between Islam and Arabism and consider whether it is possible for Arabism to be a reference point as well as a cultural framework for Arab Christians. I will try to present a new concept of Arabism, one that goes beyond religious uniformity and is capable of embracing religious plurality, taking into account the eras that preceded the rise of Islam in the political thinking of various groups in the Middle East.

Within this framework, I will discuss the process of modernization and its influence on identity through the concept of an Arabism that accepts a plurality of identities and repurposes language as a tool for the renewal of an Arab theological discourse that is committed to various readings of the text and is capable of presenting prophetic examples founded upon the Scriptures and rooted in our contemporary Arab culture.

I will then move on to study the attributes of minorities as manifested within the Christian minority in the Arab region, and will outline key aspects affecting the way the Arab Christian minority deals with daily life.

In the course of this chapter, I will also examine the understanding of key terms such as *identity*, *belief*, *nationalism*, and *citizenship* in light of contemporary Arab reality. I will also be inquiring into the attitude of some groups—both Islamic and Christian—to issues of identity and nationalism and their relationship to religion. I will also deal with the concepts of universality of belief and natal citizenship and discuss the difference between religion—with its global or universal attributes—and nationalism, with its exclusive and exclusionary spatial orientation. Thereafter, I will present a new vision for formulating a different type of Arab theological thinking that supports the principle of citizenship and acknowledges the effectual and dynamic existence of Arab Christians on the basis of positive values that are established for the general good of society as a whole, rather than for the benefit of a specific category or group.

Finally, I will look at the transforming role of Jesus Christ, highlighting his acute insight as well as his ability to respond creatively to the conditions around him. He did not simply surrender and accept the limitations imposed by his circumstances. I will also attempt to shed light on the way in which the early church formulated its faith in language that suited its own age, how it dealt with what is constant and what is mutable in its beliefs, and how this can be applied in our time, so as to arrive at a theological understanding appropriate to the Middle Eastern Arab context in which we live.

DEFINITIONS: CULTURE AND IDENTITY

At the outset, it is important to define two key terms related to the issue under study, namely *culture* and *identity*.

As an epistemological term, "culture" has a depth of meaning and many connotations that cannot be grasped without reference to the field of anthropology, especially cultural anthropology or ethnology, which is the science that compares cultures. However, it can be said that there are two main definitions of the concept of culture: the first sees culture as composed of values, convictions, norms, intellectual constructs, symbols, ideologies, and all their intellectual consequences. The second defines culture in terms of a people's entire lifestyle and the personal relationships and trends among the members of that culture.

Still others see culture as a living reservoir, a holistic composite and an accumulative growth, rooted in the residue of knowledge, learning, thoughts, beliefs, arts, literature, morals and manners, laws, customs and traditions, as well as in the mental and sensory perceptions and linguistic, ecological, and historical heritages that shape one's thought and produce the moral and social values that shape one's conduct.

As for the concept of identity, I agree with those who state that identity is not immutable but is born of contrast and exists in relation to another. Thus others are a prominent element in the specification of identity and the determination of one's own self.

The more an entity is exposed to external factors that target its existence, the more closely it clings to the components of its identity, the clearest of which is place, which becomes a protective cocoon and the realm of complete privacy and clarity about identity. At the same time, it will cleave to the past and some of its values or symbols, or at least the bright elements that are able to respond to whatever is targeting the entity.

The Lebanese philosopher Ali Harb insists that identity is not equivalent to a closed culture that withdraws into its past and its popular, religious, and dogmatic heritage. Rather, identity is the product of the constant struggle between modernization and this heritage. It is born of the struggle of individuals to resolve this struggle in relationship to themselves and to others, whether this resolution takes the form of conflict or harmonization or an attempt to understand the situation.

The concept of identity has been left undefined by anthropologists, who recognize that besides cultural identity with all the factors that play into it there is also a political identity with national or racial dimensions, rooted in cultural or political or ideological structures.

The Arab world has witnessed the rise of political Islam, which asserts that religious identity is the sole key to political and cultural participation and which has thus contributed to the diminution and reduction of the rich variety of forms of identity. By focusing on religious identity, it reduces pluralism and insists on a single allegiance. This approach also increases the scope for religious manipulation.

In an age where globalization has become a reality and where some have responded by embracing rigidity, isolation, and extremism, we need to reexamine ourselves and sift the basic principles that mold our identity to be able to formulate a theology that deepens our loyalty to our homelands and our Arab region and helps us be active and influential citizens.

DYNAMIC ARABISM

We also need to understand the cultural framework that forms the theological reference point for Arab Christians. This chapter is part of a combined work by a number of Arab theologians, and what I have to say may not represent the views of all the contributors. However, it is an attempt to determine the relationship between the dominant culture in the Arab world and the new theological development represented by this book.

We will start by discussing the development of Arab nationalism as an ideological basis for political and cultural engagement, while acknowledging that the emergence of political Islam has contributed to a retreat from nationalism and the enshrinement of the principles of Islam as the foundation for political, cultural, and social participation. So we need to study the relationship between Islam and Arabism and see whether some new form of Arabism may offer a reference point and a cultural framework for Arab Christians.

The Rise of Arab Nationalism

Arab nationalism is a modern phenomenon and an outcome of new circumstances.[1] However, its exact origins are a matter of debate in the Arab world. What cannot be denied is that the concepts of patriotism (identity and loyalty defined by country) and nationalism[2] (language and presumed ethnic origin as the basis of identity) were brought

---

[1] The roots of Arab nationalism can be traced back to Rifa'a al-Tahtawi who promoted the concepts of fatherland and patriotism. Jamal ad-Din al-Afghani and Muhammad Adbuh took up the idea of the love of country and citizenship. It is not only al-Afghani's concept of an Islamic league that is important; so were his ideas about language. One can thus argue that the birth of Arab nationalism goes back to the end of the nineteenth and beginning of the twentieth centuries. For more details see C. Ernest Dawn, *Al-Haraka al-Qawmiyya al-'Arabiyya fi-Mi'at 'Am 1875–1982* [*One Hundred Years of the Arab Nationalism Movement, 1875–1982*], ed. Nāgī 'Alūsh (Amman: Dar El Shorouk, 1997), 16 and Beverley Milton-Edwards, *Contemporary Politics in the Middle East* (Cambridge: Polity Press, 2000), 45–46.

[2] Nationalism is the demand for political autonomy by members of a specific nation, a demand that usually has as its goal the establishment of an independent nation. However, it is very

difficult to define what constitutes a "nation." It may suffice to say that a nation is a body that includes a group of people who are related by race, language, culture, or religion. Many nationalist movements have emerged in the modern world and have contributed to major political changes. Early nationalist movements, like those in Germany and Italy in the nineteenth century, aimed to build strong nations by combining many small states into one. In the twentieth century, nationalist movements focused on opposing imperial and colonial rule. Many developing countries have been born of nationalist movements or have witnessed attempts by provinces to separate from the mother country. In Europe, nationalist movements like those in Scotland and the Basque region are dominated by separatists. Separatism is also evident in the emergence of many minorities and nationalities in the former Soviet Union, which has led to serious conflicts in Georgia, Armenia, Azerbaijan, Moldavia, and Yugoslavia, where different groups

to the Middle East from Europe in the nineteenth century.[3] Bernard Lewis indicates that, although these two imported concepts often clashed, they had an enormous impact in the Middle East,[4] leading to the development of Arab nationalism with its reaffirmation of the role of language and emphasis on Arabism as a cultural framework and to the rise of independent movements seeking national independence based on patriotism.

Patriotism cannot be divorced from issues of identity with and loyalty to a country. However, it may conflict with nationalism in Arab countries that share one written language but have different ethnic roots. This problem arises because many countries in the Middle East include a number of different ethnic groups, for country boundaries were drawn by colonial powers without regard to the ethnic map of the Middle East.

As a result a definition of "country" based on geographical boundaries and a political elite contradicts the second element of nationalism, which assumes ethnic homogeneity. Both patriotism and nationalism are in contradiction with political Islam, which links identity and loyalty to religion and country to the Islamic *umma*, which has no fixed boundaries. However, the two terms did represent a new line of thought in the Middle East.

Nationalism was more suited to the Middle Eastern context than patriotism, for it regarded Arabic and Arabism as unifying elements and a cornerstone of the new ideology of Arab nationalism. As a result, an understanding of nationalism is crucial to our understanding of Arab nationalism.

Nationalism has many definitions. Calhoun describes it as the product of political, social, economic, constitutional and religious differences. It manifests itself in the social phenomenon of people working collectively to increase their participation in an existing state or to achieve independence, national autonomy, and self-determination. However, nationalism is sometimes perceived as a threat by those who are culturally different from the majority.[5] Khalfallah sees nationalism as the group of cultural bonds emerging from the existence of a human group living in one place and sharing one history and common interests.[6] Zubaida believes that there are two kinds of nationalism. The first is the nationalism of citizenship by which all the inhabitants of a certain region are citizens, regardless of their ethnic roots and language. This model is represented

---

have sought to establish independent countries. Both Liberals and Communists have tended to underestimate nationalism, describing it as an illogical phenomenon that appeals to the most primitive elements in the human nature. However, few are able to deny the massive power of emotions and national prejudices. The dissolution of the USSR constitutes the clearest testimony that nationalism is more in line with human nature than other political ideologies.

[3] Bernard Lewis, *The Multiple Identities of the Middle East* (London: Phoenix, 1998), 20–21.

[4] Ibid., 21.

[5] Craig Calhoun, *Nationalism* (Buckingham: Open University Press, 1997), 6.

[6] Muhammad Ahmad Khalfallah, "Al-Takwīn al-Tarīkhī li-Mafāhīm al-Umma, al-Qawmiyya, al-Wataniyya, al-Dawla wa-al-'Ilāqa fīmā baynhā" ["The Historical Construction of the Concepts of *al-Umma*, Nationalism, Citizenship, State and the Relationship between Them"], in *Al-Qawmiyya al-'Arabiyya wa-al-Islām* [*Arab Nationalism and Islam*], 3rd. ed. (Beirut: Centre for Arab Unity Studies, 1988), 20.

by France. The second model is the nationalism of unification, in which small states come together, as in the case of Italy and Germany. This second model is closer to the Arabic one; here nationalism is a unifying factor.[7]

There are four main views concerning the development of Arab nationalism in the Middle East. These views are not wholly distinct from each other and reflect the political context of the early twentieth century.

First, there are those who see Arab nationalism as an opposition movement that started during the Ottoman Empire and continued to grow in the nineteenth and the first half of the twentieth centuries, during the period of decline of the Ottoman Empire and growth in the power of the West. The establishment of the state of Israel in 1948 was a shocking and significant event for Arabs. Surprised by the rapid modernization of the West, Arabs started to reevaluate their own situation, especially since most of them believed that the development of the West was a consequence of Islamic civilization.

Arab nationalism then emerged as a response to Arab political decline and a sense of cultural inferiority. Thus Ernest Dawn states that the origins of Arab nationalism go back to the failure of Islamic Ottomanism and to Islamist feelings of inferiority to the West,[8] even though Arab civilization was felt to have fostered Western progress. This sense of inferiority caused a return to the central strength of reformed Islam to counter Western power. Muslims believed that the problem lay in them, not in their religion. Islamic reformism emerged to accommodate Western modernization and from there the roots of both modern political Islam and the secular trend developed in the Arab world.

The second view associates Arab nationalism with state building, socialism, religion, and self-determination:

> Nationalism in the Middle East has taken many forms and guises including state nationalism, patriotism, pan-Arabism, pan-Islamism, Zionism, Islamic nationalism, Arab nationalism, Ba'thism, Nasserism, Maronite nationalism, Kurdish ethno-nationalism and so on.[9]

"Nationalism" has two distinct meanings. The first is related to the Western notion of the *nation-state*, as established in the second decade of the twentieth century; the second is more indigenous and related to the concept of community (*al-umma*).[10]

It is important to note that Islam and the Arabic language were unifying elements in the political process for nations that accepted Islam, but that this unifying power did not eradicate the ethnic and national characters of these nations after Islamization.

---

[7] Sami Zubaida, "Al-Naz'a al-Qawmiyya wa-al-Islām al-Siyāsī" ["Propensity toward Nationalism and Political Islam"] in *Al-Qawmiyya: Mard al-'Asr am Khalāsuh?* [*Nationalism: Is it the Disease of the Age or Its Salvation?*], ed. Falh Abd Al-Jabar (Beirut: Al-Sāqī, 1995), 84–85.

[8] C. Ernest Dawn, "The Origin of Arab Nationalism," in *The Origins of Arab Nationalism*, ed. Rashid Khalidi et al. (New York: Columbia University Press, 1991), 23.

[9] Milton-Edwards, *Contemporary Politics*, 41.

[10] Ibid., 44.

Their ethnic and national commitments reemerged with the colonial division of the Arab world. For example in the period after the First World War, the Arabic East was divided into different nations with different forms of nationalism. In the case of Lebanon, nationalism became a tool for state building; in the case of Egypt and Palestine it became a tool for liberation from a colonial power.

The new borders of Arab states drawn by colonial powers came to affirm state nationalism in different forms.[11] New borders were in fact a crucial element in the promotion of state nationalism. In that context, Arabism was used to support state nationalism or it was kept at a theoretical level to give political legitimacy to regimes' regional aims. However, because not all regimes regarded Arabism as a political reference, state nationalism reestablished itself.[12]

The third view links Arab nationalism with movements towards independence. The similarities between the Ottoman feudal system and the feudal system in the Arab world resulted in common interests between the political elites in the Arab world and in the Ottoman Empire. In reaction to Ottoman reform and the promotion of Ottomanism, Arabic political and social elites promoted Arabism as their cultural framework to distinguish themselves from Ottomanism. In that context, Arabism became a tool for independence and liberation. The collapse of the Ottoman Empire and the spread of colonialism in the Arab World affirmed Arab nationalism as a tool for political independence.[13] However, once independence had been achieved, the unifying function of Arab nationalism declined because its main objective had been achieved with the creation of nation states. The defeat of 1967 marked the end of the Arab dream of unification; it became clear that each Arab state has its own agenda. The role of the Arab League[14] was limited to financial assistance and political support in international meetings.

The fourth view holds that Arab Christians initiated Arab nationalism in order to introduce a modern political concept that was distinct from religion. It offered a new basis for identity which, in principle at least, would make Arab Christians full and equal participants in the polity—something they could never hope to attain in a religiously

---

[11] Hasan Kh. Gharib, *Fi-Sabīl ʿIlaqa Salima bayn al-ʾUrūba wa-al-Islām* [*Toward a Correct Relationship between Arabism and Islam*] (Beirut: Dar Al-Talia, 2000), 279–80.

[12] Ibid., 281.

[13] Ibid., 274–75.

[14] The idea of forming an Arab League first arose during the Second World War as a result of the Western, regional, and international changes of that time. In 1943 the British government declared that it was sympathetic to an Arab economic and cultural union. In 1944 Mustafa el-Nahhas, the prime minister of Egypt, initiated a conference with Arab presidents and kings regarding the idea of establishing such a league. Some of the participants wanted the union to cover Greater Syria (the Fertile Crescent). Others wanted a general union of Arabic countries. Some of the latter recommended a federal union between countries, while others recommended some mode of collaboration that would retain the freedom and dominion of each of the countries involved. The structure of the Arab League was decided in 1944, and in 1945 the official document establishing the Arab League was signed. For more details see Al-Sayyid Yasin, ed., *Al-Taqrīr al-Istrātīji al-ʾArabi* [*The Arabic Strategic Report*] (Cairo: Al-Ahram for Political and Strategic Studies, 1998), Shiʾūn ʿArabiyya 1982 and www.arableagueonline.org

defined society.[15] In support of this idea of an emerging new political ideology as a basis for political participation, Cragg wrote,

> Arab nationalism necessarily implied an end to dhimmī status, inasmuch as all Arabs within independent statehood(s) would share identity and citizenship. Contrariwise, continuing in the Turkish-led Ummah meant perpetuation of the inferior status in al-dhimmī tradition. It is not, therefore, surprising to find Christians—Syrians in particular—taking up nationalist aspirations, despite the fact that nationhood(s) dominated by Arab Muslims constitute an unknown risk.[16]

Christians thought they had discovered an ideology that they could share with Muslims without *being* Muslims. Christians of the Levant were the major contributors to Arabism, thereby affirming that Arabism, and not Islam, was the basis of identity. Christians spearheaded this new development. In doing so, they were able to confront the Turkish Muslims who were in power at that time.[17] El-Bishry too reflects the suspicion of Muslim thinkers about the fact that the Christians of Syria and Lebanon were advocates of Arab nationalism. He is convinced that the promotion of Arab nationalism by Christians reflected the ambitions of Christian minorities to share political power with Muslims.[18] Among Christians in Lebanon, there are those who think that Arab Christians favored the concept of Arab culture based on the Arabic language, the greatest single tie binding Christians and Muslims in the Arab world.[19]

I see Arab nationalism as a relatively modern political concept. It arose because various social and political factors created a need for it. Many groups contributed to its development; some were nationalists offended by Turkish efforts to promote the Turkish language and culture, and others were Arab Christians who preferred a political base not defined solely by religion. Leaders of independent political movements saw Arabism as a way to separate themselves from Turkey.[20] Thus Arab nationalism emerged from the social and political developments of the early twentieth century.

The Decline of Arab Nationalism

There are a number of explanations for the decline of Arab nationalism. Did the death of Egyptian President Gamal Abdel Nasser in 1970, and the resulting vacuum of leadership in the Pan-Arab movement, put an end to the idea of Arab nationalism once and

---

[15] Bernard Lewis, *The Shaping of the Modern Middle East* (Oxford: Oxford University Press, 1994), 21.

[16] Kenneth Cragg, *The Arab Christian: A History in the Middle East* (London: Mowbray, 1992), 25.

[17] Mustafa al-Fiqi, *Tajdīd al-Fikr al-Qawmī* [*The Renewal of National Thought*] (Cairo: Dar El-Shorouk, 1994), 17.

[18] Tarek El-Bishry, *Fī-al-Masʾāla al-Islāmiyya al-Muʿāsira, bayn al-Islām wa-al-ʾUrūba* [*In the Modern Islamic Issue, between Islam*

and Arabism] (Cairo: Dar El-Shorouk, 1998), 48.

[19] Girum Shahin, *Al-Masīhiyya ʿAbr Tārīkhiha fī-al-Mashriq, al-Masīhiyūn wa-al-Nahda al-ʾArabiyya* [*Christianity Through Its History in the East, Christians and the Arab Renaissance*] (Beirut: MECC, 2001), 797–807.

[20] It is important to note that the leaders of independent political movements promoted Arabism as a tool against Turkey, and Islam as a tool against Europe.

for all?[21] Certainly the internal conflict between Arab states, competing leadership, and regional conflict contributed to the decline of Arab nationalism. Haykal describes the issues in terms of a conflict between what he calls "the desert" and "the valley." In the desert there was a conflict between the monarchies in Jordan and Saudi Arabia, and in the valley there was conflict between Egypt and the rest. Nasser's charismatic personality had enabled him to stimulate the imagination of the masses with the concept of Arab nationalism. But the Arab *umma* was involved in an internal conflict that hindered the development of Arab nationalism.[22]

Many regimes encouraged the competing ideology of Islamist politics, which had goals distinct from those of Arab nationalism. The reality is that Arab nationalism was being used to call into question the legitimacy of existing regimes. Thus most leaders viewed it as a threat to their political authority, even though there was vast support for nationalism among the Arab masses.[23]

Haykal suggests that the Yemen War between 1962 and 1963 added a military dimension to Arab nationalism that contributed to its decline. So did the three Gulf Wars (1990, 1991, and 2003). The West saw Arab nationalism as being against its own interests.[24]

Was it the secularization of Arab nationalism that led to its decline? Did Arab nationalists attempt to reduce Islam to the status of merely a cultural factor? Arab Christians and Muslims are united within one language group that constitutes a nation; Turks, who share Islam with the Arabs, are foreigners.[25]

Gabriel Habib admonished some Christian nationalists for attempting to ignore religion and base their social philosophies on the objective of a completely secular society. Christian nationalists forgot that the Muslims were not willing to cast off Islam for any nationalist ideology and saw the Prophet Muhammad as "a purely political figure, one to whom all Arabs owed primary allegiance as the founder of a united Arab nation."[26] He recognized that

> the process of transforming the religious society by way of nationalist movement into a secular society where religion and state are separated, is now being reversed and political power is being withdrawn from the state in favor of the religious community.[27]

[21] Asad Abukhalil, "A New Arab Ideology? The Rejuvenation of Arab Nationalism," *Middle East Journal* 46 (1992): 26

[22] Muhammad Husayn Haykal, *Harb al-Thalāthīn sana 1967, al-Infijār* [*The Thirty Years War 1967, the Explosion*] (Cairo: Al-Ahrām, 1990), 796–803.

[23] Elie Podeh, "The Struggle over Arab Hegemony after the Suez Crisis," *Middle Eastern Studies* 29 (1993): 93.

[24] Muhammad Husayn Haykal, *Harb al-Thalāthīn sana 1967, sanawāt al-Ghalyān* [*The Thirty Years War 1967, the Years of Boiling*] (Cairo: Al-Ahrām, 1988), 624–45, 720–22.

[25] Bassam Tibi, "Islam and Arab Nationalism," in *The Islamic Impulse*, ed. Barbara Freyer Stowasser (Washington: Croom Helm and Centre for Contemporary Arab Studies, Georgetown University, 1978), 67.

[26] Gabriel Habib, "Aspects of Political Ethics in the Middle East," in *Perspectives on Political Ethics—An Ecumenical Inquiry*, ed. Koson Srisang (Geneva and Washington, D.C.: WCC Publications and Georgetown University Press, 1983), 118.

[27] Ibid., 123.

Is it possible to regard nationalism as a form of racism? Islamic scholar Yusuf al-Qaradawi does not reject nationalism if it is defined in terms of love of one's country, but does reject it if it is defined as Muslim loyalty to a specific piece of land or race. Islamic society is based on doctrine—not on nation, region, or race. It sees all believers as brothers.[28]

Any attempt to create an ideology that ignores cultural and political differences and marginalizes Islam is doomed. Arabism is not an alternative to religion. Abu Al-Majd is right in saying that Arabism cannot exist separate from Islam because it would involve defining Arabs as a race. There is no Arabic culture that is independent of Islam. Islam has a cultural dimension that can accommodate both Muslims and non-Muslims.[29]

Abu Al-Majd's analysis was based on the concept of nationalism as linked to race and on the universality of Islam. (He saw Islam as inclusive religion and culture contributing to a new Arabism that transcended a limited concept of simple nationalism.)

It seems that the conditions that led to nationalism in Europe did not occur in the Arab world. In Europe the separation of religion and politics led to the decline of universal Catholicism and encouraged nationalism; in the Arab world the universality of Islam accommodated all nationalities. But one cannot ascribe the decline of Arab nationalism solely to the efforts of Christian and Muslim nationalists who tried to lessen the importance of religion or regarded Islam as a cultural phenomenon; there were a number of other socio-economic and political factors at play.

Arab Christians had a longing for political equality, and they supported Arab nationalism to get political status. However, Arab nationalism was not wholly political; it was both political and cultural. As Calhoun reminds us, "nationalism is not only a matter of politics, but of culture and personal identity."[30] For Gellner, nationalism "is a political principle which maintains that similarity of culture is the basic social bond."[31]

What did Arab nationalism mean for Arab Christians? It was a political ideology that Arab Christians espoused because Arabism, in its wider form, could open the door to political participation on grounds other than religion. However, with the decline of Arab nationalism, a new political ideology was needed.

Islam, Arabism, and the Concept of Identity

It is now time to deal with the relationship between Islam and Arabism, a relationship that is hotly debated in the Arab world. Each of these ideologies has a different approach

[28] Cited in Tarek El-Bishry, *Fī-al-Mas'ala al-Islāmiyya al-Mu'āsira: Bayn al-Jammā'a al-Dīniyya wa-al-Jammā'a al-Wataniyya fi-al-Fikr al-Siyāsī* [*In the Modern Islamic Issue: Between Religious Community and National Community in Political Thought*] (Cairo: Dar El Shorouk, 1998), 7–8.

[29] Ahmad Kamal Abu Al-Majd, "Nahwa Siyāgha Jadīda li-al-'llāqa bayn al-Qawmiyya al-'Arabiyya wa-al-Islām" ["Towards a New Formula for the Relationship between Arab Nationalism and Islam"], in *Al-Qawmiyya*.

[30] Calhoun, *Nationalism*, 3.

[31] Ernest Gellner, *Nationalism* (London: Phoenix, 1997), 3.

to issues of ethnicity and identity. The Islamist approach is based on the political bond of culture, society, and religion. Non-Muslims are excluded from high office because all such positions involve religious duties. All Muslims, however, are treated as equals—regardless of their race, culture, or national origin—because citizenship is based only on religion. By contrast, Arab nationalists see culture and language as the pillars of the political state, society, and citizenship. On this view, all native speakers of Arabic and bearers of Arabic culture are full members of the Arab nation, enjoying all rights of citizenship, regardless of race, religion, and sect.

Both visions fail to take into account subidentities within their broad frames of reference. For example, in the Lebanese war (1975–1989) Shia Muslims and Sunni Muslims killed each other more often than they killed Christians; Maronites killed Maronites. In addition, the advocates of Arab nationalism in the two Ba'athist regimes in Iraq and Syria have taken actions that have discredited each other.[32]

The concept of identity is at the heart of each philosophy. Acceptance of religion as nationality produces an Islamic state that excludes non-Muslims from power. Accepting nationalism as the core of state formation implies a secular state in which religion is separate from politics—a position that is unacceptable to the majority of ordinary Muslims who see Islam as an all-embracing religion.

The statement that "Arabism is Islam" marginalizes Arab Christians, as religion becomes the only basis for identity. Thus they seek to go beyond Arabism to either Pharoahism or Phoenicianism to find a basis for their identity in these ancient cultures. This dilemma creates a context where the majority religion tends to exclude other faiths. Arabism was the political framework on which Arab Christians based their hope for political participation, but the decline of Arab nationalism and the emergence of Islamism led Arab Christians to seek a political alternative.

In the second half of the twentieth century, the process of modernization and secularization was greatly disrupted by the emergence of political Islam, which resulted in a radically changed concept of nationalism. The relationship between Arabism and Islam was reevaluated and Islam was promoted as the basis of Arabism.

Is Arabism wider than Islam? Any idea of an Arabism that transcends Islam is rejected by some Muslims. The nationalization of Arabism and efforts at sidelining Islam led many Islamic ideologists to condemn Arabism and to reaffirm Islam as the basis of Arabism. They insist that Arabism is a product of Islam, and in some cases they argue that it is a synonym for Islam. The concept of Western nationalism is alien.

Al-Jabri recognizes that the cognitive environment has made Arabism a concept

---

[32] Saad Eddin Ibrahim, *Al-Ta'adudiyya al-Isniyya fi-al-Watan al-'Arabi* [Ethnic Diversity in the Arab World] (Cairo: Al-Ahram Center for Political and Strategic Studies, 1995), 4–11.

that belongs more to the past than to the present. As soon as Islam spread and became entrenched, it became the dominant ideology for both Arabs and non-Arabs. Thus the concept of Arab and Arabism became too narrow compared to the breadth of Islam. In most cases, the concept was determined not in relation to Islam as a religion, nor in relation to a civilization, but in relation to the ruling Turks.[33]

Qutb regards nationalism and doctrine as of equal importance, and claims that Islamic society is the only society that considers doctrine—not nationality or race—as the basis for defining a people. He insists that Islamic culture was never Arab; it was never nationalistic and was always doctrinal. He sees Arabs as having had no independent identity before the coming of Islam. It was Islam, not Arabism, that gave Arabs

the sweeping force that destroys thrones, conquers empires, and brings down the false, deviating and incorrect leaderships in order to take over the leadership of mankind.[34]

Al-Qaradawi believes that Islam is the basis of the Arab nation and that Islam is the maker of Arab history, pride, and culture. Imam Al-Ghazali supports the view that Islam is the religion that builds the spirit and the flesh of the Arab nation.[35] El-Bishry suggests that Arabism is very close to Islam when it distances itself from secularism; it is far from Islam when it approaches secularism. Islam and secularism never meet; the Islamic call is based on implementation of the Islamic Law and what is needed is to present Islamic thought in a way appropriate to the current age and context.[36]

The clash between Islam and Arabism is artificial; al-Fiqi insists that they are two sides of the same coin. Islam is the basis of the continuity and spread of Arabism; Islam was the motivation that enabled Arabs to gain control over other nations and to dominate other well-established cultures. He claims that the real distinction between Arabism and Islam came from those who advocated Islam as religion and correspondingly as nationalism.[37] He offers the following main ideas necessary for the renewal of national thought:

- Arab reconciliation must be viewed as the gateway for renewal and development of Arab national thought;
- There must be a balance between what is fixed and what is changeable to maintain tradition while dealing with new developments;

---

[33] Mohammed Abed al-Jabri, *A Viewpoint: Towards Reconstruction of the Issue of the Contemporary Arab Thought* (Beirut: Center for Arab Unity Studies, 1994) 23–26.

[34] Sayyid Qutb, "What are the Arabs Without Islam?" *Islamic Future* 39 (1994). Available online at sunnahonline.com/library/contemporary-issues/767-what-are-the-arabs-without-islam.

[35] Cited in Tarek El-Bishry, *Fī-al-Masʾala al-Islāmiyya al-Muʿāsi-ra: Bayn al-Jammāʿa al-Dīniyya wa-al-Jammāʿa al-Wataniyya fī-al-Fikr al-Siyāsī* [*The Modern Islamic Issue: Between Religious Community and National Community in Political Thought*] (Cairo: Dar El Shorouk, 1998), 9–10.

[36] Ibid., 91.

[37] Mustafa al-Fiqi, *Tajdīd al-Fikr al-Qawmī* [*The Renewal of National Thought*] (Cairo: Dar El Shorouk, 1994), 14–15.

- National commitment and commitment to the entire Arab nation must be respected, and commitment to Egypt or to Lebanon must not imply lack of commitment to the Arab world;
- Arabism is to be seen as the basis of economic integration;
- Minorities must be viewed as contributors to the life of the Arab world since they contribute to Arab Islamic culture and political pluralism is the character of the age;
- The trend towards Islam playing an effective role in political life must be accepted, and support must be given to the relationship between Islam and Arabism that includes non-Muslims as partners; equality between the different peoples and groups that comprise the national Arab community must be adhered to.[38]

Clearly Al-Fiqi is trying to reconcile Islam and Arabism through a political project that uses a wider definition of Arabic political community.

Al-Jabri believes that both Arabism and Islam are reactions to colonialism in the Arab world. Arabism is not defined by its relationship to Islam but rather by its relationship to Turkish rulers and the European colonial powers that swept through the Arab world. In both cases Islam and Arabism fought together against the Turkish and European influence on the Arabs. Arabism and Islam were not in conflict but worked together to protect their identity. Al-Jabri concludes that it is inappropriate to ask Arabs to be either Arabs or Muslims; they are both at the same time. Both Arabism and Islam contributed to independence and to the development of Arab unity.[39]

While Al-Jabri's analysis is important, it is, perhaps, only partly correct. Opposition to colonial rule did contribute to the emergence of Islam and Arabism as protectors of identity, but this is not the whole story. Although they did work together to oppose colonialism, they clashed when it came to the formation of nation states. At the beginning of the twentieth century, these states were based more on Arabism than on Islam.

Along with al-Jabri, we ask whether the Arab culture is something of the past. Is it possible to plan for it as part of the culture of the future? Al-Jabri states,

> The current Arab cultural history is a mere rumination, repetition, and poor reproduction of the same cultural history laid out by our ancestors under the pressure of the conflicts in their era, within the limits of the scientific and methodological potential available in their time. So, we are still captivated by ancient concepts and the visions that directed our forefathers and thus dominated their outcome. Such concepts push us too—without

---

[38] Mustafa al-Fiqi, *Ru'ya al-Ghā'iba* [*The Vision of the Absent*] (Cairo: Dar El Shorouk, 1996), 49–52.

[39] Mohammed Abed al-Jabri, *Mas'ālt al-Hawiyya, al-'Urūba wa-al-Islām wa-al-Gharb* [*The Issue of Identity: Arabism, Islam, . . . and the West*], 2nd ed. (Beirut: Centre for Arabic Unity Studies, 1997), 42–55.

our being aware of them—to engage with bygone discords and problems that keep our present preoccupied with our past so that we see the future through the lens of the problems and hardships of the past. Accordingly, we are in need of a re-writing of Arab cultural history in a critical spirit.[40]

Al-Jabri believes that Arab Islamic culture actually began with the era of codification, rather than in the era of ignorance (*jāhiliyyah*), because in the era of codification Arab culture witnessed its first, comprehensive planned system in which the Arabic language was standardized and taught using scholarly methods.

In the time of codification, the time of ignorance was reconstructed and, through translation, the ancient heritage of civilizations like those of Babylonia, Phoenicia, Syria, Egypt, Alexandria, and Greece was fused together within one Arab Islamic culture. In other words, all these cultures contributed to the creation of Arab culture. The result was a diversity of creeds and perspectives within Arab Islamic culture. Such fusion and variety invalidates the claim that Islamic culture developed in isolation.[41]

A further step is needed to find a new understanding of the relationship between Islam and Arabism and to question the Islamist view that Arabs and Muslims have one combined history. Al-Qimni noted that many countries in the Arab world had their own history before Islam. The Egyptians had a Pharaonic and Coptic history, the Iraqis had a Kurdish one, and so on; one must distinguish between heritage and history. The Islamic heritage is the history of conquered Arab tribes that dates from the first Islamic state established in Medina.[42] This Islamic heritage became the doctrine and heritage of the conquered countries, but these countries also had a history *before* Islam. The Islamic heritage became part, but not all, of the heritage of these conquered countries. Al-Qimni believes that the first step towards resolving the identity crisis is to recognize the pluralistic history, and the pluralistic society, of each country. History is not wholly Islamic; pre-Islamic history can enrich citizenship.[43]

Islam and Arabism are directly connected and complement each other. This reconciled relationship between Islam and Arabism developed and widened with Al-Qimni to a pluralistic concept where other religions beside Islam as well as other histories contribute to the current status of Arabism.

I argue that the concept of a pluralistic history is crucial, for it introduces a new element to the concept of Arabism. Arabism is not limited only to Islam; it includes other religions and cultures in the Middle East, each of which contributed to Arabism as we know it today. Pluralism in terms of history, culture, and religion could lead to new concepts for identity formation in the Arab world.

---

[40] Ibid., 174.

[41] Ibid., 176.

[42] Here Al-Qimni is referring to nomadic Arab tribes who did not produce civilizations like those of the Canaanites or the Pharaohs.

[43] Sayyed Al-Qimni, *Al-Fāshiyūn wa-al-Watan* [*The Fascist and the Country*] (Cairo: The Egyptian Institute for Cultural Research, 1999), 149–56.

The term "modernity" is crucial to our understanding of the relationship between Islam and democracy. Were the Islamic reformists modernists? Modernization is a political project associated with the establishment of the nation-state in the first half of the twentieth-century. Since it was introduced to the region, the debate between modernization and Islam has not ceased. Perhaps it would be helpful at this stage to look at the differences between modernization and modernity. Hopwood draws the following distinction between them:

> Modernization is the introduction into society of the artifacts of contemporary life— railways, communications, industry (less often nowadays), technology, and household equipment. Modernity (modernism) is a general term for the political and cultural processes set in motion by integrating new ideas, an economic system, or education into society. It is a way of thought, of living in the contemporary world and of accepting change.[44]

Modernization began in Europe through the economic processes by which people adopted new methods of production and distribution and abandoned the traditional modes of economic relations. They began to make individual economic choices and decisions that led them to leave the traditional way of life and "become more mobile, and capable of conceiving and absorbing change."[45]

> Modernization is the process normally leading to modernity, which begins when a society assumes an attitude of enquiry into how people make choices, be they moral, personal, economic, or political.[46]

In this chapter the terms "modernization" and "modernity" (modernism) are used to indicate the Western concept of modernization that led to modernity. In other words, I will consider modernization as one side of a coin, with modernity as the other.

Western modernization developed between the sixteenth and eighteenth centuries, during the Renaissance and Enlightenment, but it only became an international model in the nineteenth and twentieth centuries. Ali has this to say about it:

> The West conceives of modernization in several ways: as a process of change in the social structure and social system through an increased knowledge in science and technology; as a movement of transition from a traditional society of religion, magic, and superstition to a modern and postmodern society that is free from religious matrix and traditional norms; as a process for change in the set of relationships between the individual and society; as a process of mobilization, differentiation, industrialization, and secularization;

---

[44] Derek Hopwood, "The Culture of Modernity in Islam and the Middle East," in *Islam and Modernity: Muslim Intellectuals Respond*, ed. John Cooper et al. (New York: I. B. Tauris, 1998), 2.

[45] Ibid., 2.
[46] Ibid.

as a process toward high economic growth, stable democracy, and a capitalist economy; as a process to overcome nature and become independent of its control; as a movement toward the construction of a healthy, peaceful, content, and prosperous society; and as Europeanization, Americanization, and Westernization.[47]

He also adds that these forces put reason above revelation.

Another definition comes from Abdel-Qader Yassine:

> Modernism . . . is what characterizes the new way of thinking that has occurred in the West as a result of, or at least alongside, the industrial and scientific revolutions. It is marked by a strong belief in the powers of science and reason, and by a basic skepticism towards any substantial, absolute truth.[48]

It is important to note that the distinction between modernization and modernity is also present among Islamic reformists who seek to benefit from the advancements of modernization rather than of modernity, in the sense of culture and values. It is also clear that some Islamic groups accept modernization as a technological development that is needed by the Islamic world but reject modernity, which they see as the values and principles of Western culture.

There are thus two major trends in the Middle East's response to modernization. The first rejects the idea that Islam and modernity are compatible and affirms the sufficiency of Islam as the basis for a comprehensive political project. The second sees Islam and modernity as compatible, with the conditional redefinition of basic principles of both. On the basis that Islam is not external to modernity, Sayyid questions the kind of relationship that exists between the two. He also questions whether there is only one modernity, or different modernities. If there were an Islamic modernity, what would it look like? Sayyid believes that the problem of the party advocating Islamic modernization is that they understand modernization to be identical to Westernization.[49]

The Islamist methodology is based on the idea that the literal word of God as revealed in the Qur'an, buttressed by the Sunna and Hadith,[50] and exemplified in Sharia law (Ar. *shari'ah*) is relevant to the temporal order. This relevance to the temporal order is based on the

> principles of tawhīd (unity), the unity of God, and the interpretation of the divine law, possible through the institutions of ijmā' (consensus), qiyās, by analogy or in theory by

---

[47] Mohammad Mumtaz Ali, "The Concept of Modernization: An Analysis of Contemporary Islamic Thought," *The American Journal of Islamic Social Sciences* 14 (1997): 14–15.

[48] Abdel-Qader Yassine, "Understanding Modernity on One's Own Terms," *The American Journal of Islamic Social Sciences* 15 (1998): 47.

[49] Bobby S. Sayyid, *A Fundamental Fear: Eurocentrism and the Emergence of Islamism* (London and New York: Zed Books Ltd, 1997), 103.

[50] The Sunna and the Hadith are the practice and sayings of the Prophet Muhammad.

ijtihād (innovative reasoning) but in accordance with the principles of al-Sharī'ah and thus ultimately on the basis of revelation as the underlying epistemological principle.[51]

Given this context, Joffe argues that the concept of divine truth cannot deal effectively with the concept of Western modernism. This incompatibility results from the contradiction between the principles of scientific analysis, innovation, and unfettered rational speculation—the basis of modernism—and those of the Islamic world, which seeks solutions to temporal problems by referring back to the eternal verities of Islamic doctrine.[52]

Arab Christians sought to steer Arabism toward a path of equality and reciprocity, for they perceived that Arabism is broader than Islam. So they participated in developing an ideology that could open the way to their inclusion as equal, loyal citizens.

Arabism as a pluralistic concept presents new opportunities for cultural and political participation in the Arab world by making religion just one of the various grounds for formulating identity. Such a concept of an inclusive and dynamic identity is sorely needed. There is also a need for further attempts to redefine the identity and stance of Arab Christians.

With the impact of political Islam, the nature of nationalism in the Arab world creates problems. Nationalism is assumed to be based on language and culture, but in the Arab world there is a strong bond between religion and language. Arabic is the language of the Qur'an and the spiritual strength of the Qur'an is enhanced by the Arabic language. There is a direct relationship between language and religion. The Arabic language is the basis of the Qur'an and a contributor to its concepts. Language is not simply a matter of words; it implies concepts and a framework of thoughts.

Culture is the second component of nationalism, and here the relationship between Islam and Arabism is evident. The effort to secularize Arabism failed because Islam is central to the concept of Arabism.

In the West, the context is different. Although Christianity has made many significant contributions to European cultures, there is not the same direct relationship between language and religion. Christianity is not the basis of British or German cultures in the same way that Islam contributes to Arabism. The bond between religion and culture is of a quite different order.

Consequently one can argue that while nationalism in the West is an outcome of economic and social circumstances, nationalism in the Arab world is based on a language and culture with close ties to religion. This is clear in the Islamization of Arab nationalism. Nationalism in the Arab world is entirely bound up with religion.

---

[51] George Joffe, "Democracy, Islam and the Culture of Modernism," *Democratization* 4 (1997): 142.

[52] Ibid., 140–41.

Nationalism with strong ties to religion limits pluralism. Promoting language and culture as the sole legitimate basis of identity while failing to acknowledge the importance of religion causes problems. It cannot be denied that nationalism contributes to the process of state building and asserts a collective identity, but in the Arab world its close connection with the Muslim religion and nonpluralistic nature have led to the exclusion of those of different faiths. In the case of political Islam, religion became the defining element of nationalism; in the words of Qutb, "Nationalism *is* Islam."

The restriction of nationalism to Muslims allowed little room for pluralism; and Arab nationalism became suspect as a cultural framework for Arab Christians because of the close ties between nationalism, identity, and religion. Thus Arab Christians need to rethink the idea of Arabism as a cultural framework and as one of the constituents of their identity. However, in its broad and pluralistic sense, Arabism may still be an appropriate cultural portal for an Arab theology.

Arabism as a Dynamic Concept

Pluralism does not imply the absence of a unique culture, to which many factors may contribute. These factors include the following:

- *Identity.* Individuals endeavor to define themselves through language, religion, and the like.
- *Heritage.* A culture's heritage includes the most prominent historical symbols in which its people take pride. Is there debate about the significance of heritage as a constituent of identity, or is it discarded as a cumbersome burden?
- *Reality.* Nations question their current reality; are they falling behind other nations or are they outstripping them, and if so, by how much?
- *Alternative opportunities.* What options are available? Do some of them preclude others? Which option is the most successful?
- *Future.* What effect do other cultures have on identity?

Factors like these shape unique cultures and determine the principal orientations of identity.[53]

To mitigate these challenges, we propose the introduction of Arabism as a cultural reference. Arabism, which draws on religions, histories, and cultures, is inherently dynamic rather than static. So too is identity.

Thus we here have to deal with the metaphysical concept of nationalism, which sees it as determining a nation's character and its culture through some constant, intellectual and

[53] Amr Hosein, "Cultural Privacy: Problematic in the Way of Communication," islamonline.net.

psychological essence unaffected by social, economic, historical, or intellectual circumstances, which are ignored when dealing with issues relating to lifestyle and the future.[54] On this view, nationalism is immutable, the essence of identity, and is not affected by external factors.

This metaphysical concept of national identity has been criticized and an alternative sociological perspective presented. In sociological terms, national identity is regarded as more or less equivalent to the dominant patterns of thinking, feeling, and acting that change with the tides of history and radical changes. Nationalistic identity is thus historical and relative; in other words, it is shaped by history and not inherited; it is not inherent or intrinsic.[55]

This brings us back to the concept of Arabism as a sociological construct that is not limited to one religion, one history, or one culture, as stated above. Arabism can be seen as the product of the interactions of history, religions, geography, and cultures. These interactions are ongoing and variable. Thus the characteristics of any people are the product of the variable forces of history. Cultural contact, wars, migrations, inventions, crises, political and social conflicts, ideological progressions—none of these factors are fixed national characteristics like geography, human nature, instinct, and race.[56] In line with this, Nasr Abu Zayd asserted that identity cannot be constrained within unchangeable sayings or found solely in religion. Defining it in those terms makes identity something that is fully manufactured and immutable.[57]

At this juncture, we inquire whether nationalism has been immutable throughout history. In other words, if we adopt Arabism as a cultural frame of reference for Arab Christians, what is the Arabism we adopt today? In this regard, Nadim Al-Bitar discusses the concept of Arabism as something that has developed. He questions whether today's Arabs are the same as those of the era of ignorance. Such questioning requires us to distinguish between the metaphysical concept of nationalism—which claims that the essence of nationality cannot change—and the sociological historical one that holds that identity is a product of history and is thus subject to alteration.[58] National identity is not blind and rigid but reflects a socially constructed tradition, produced by dealing with a context, particularly a cultural and historical context. This means that a national identity may vary.[59]

Regarding the issue at hand, Seif Abdel Fattah affirms that identity is always under construction, for there is no specific stage when it is fully achieved. It is not even possible to achieve it perfectly, for perfection is something we cannot attain but can only approach. Therefore identity requires continual renewal.[60]

---

[54] Nadim al-Bitar, *The Boundaries of National Identity: Universal Criticism* (Beirut: Bisan, 2002), 113.

[55] Ibid., 13.

[56] Ibid., 13–14.

[57] Mustafa Ashour, "Who Are We? The Question of Passion and Identity," islamonline.net.

[58] Bitar, *The Boundaries*, 23–24.

[59] Ibid., 36.

[60] Ashour, "Who Are We?"

From this standpoint, we can see that it is possible for Arab Christians to participate in forging nationalism, for Arabism is not a rigid, unalterable legacy but a concept related to culture that all can participate in developing and molding. National identity is the result of two factors: the internal or domestic factor—represented by traditions assembled over the years—and the external factor that reflects how a nation handles a changing global environment. In light of these interactions, the community strives to work within its domestic traditions or to amend them. Thus, the community grasps that its past is not inevitably its present and its future.[61]

It is important to recognize these internal and external factors when formulating Arabism as a cultural reference for the Arab world in general and for Arab Christians in particular. The internal factors include the religious awakening, the resurrection of a social heritage through tradition, a reliance on partisanship and tribalism, a retreat from the idea of modernization, a sense of isolation, and the risk of assimilation. These internal factors cannot be separated from the external factors that include successive waves of globalization, the rise of the theory of a clash of civilizations, the war against terrorism, and the contradictory Western stance toward Islam. These internal and external factors are at the core of national identity as it is formulated at the present time.

Hassan Hanafi sees an overlap between the external and internal factors. As Westernization is increasing and Western values are spreading, especially among the elite who hold the reins of power, the masses shun these values and cling to their culture and traditions. Fundamentalism then emerges as a way of defending authenticity and upholding identity. Nasr Hamid Abu Zayd agrees that the emphasis on religion as a key definer of identity is a response to successive Western attacks on the Islamic world and the attempt to link decline to religion.[62]

This raises the question of the role of internal factors in the construction of national identity in the Arab world. Is this due to what some orientalists call "the decline of the Arab world"? Are the reasons for decline linked to a specific race or culture? We must again insist on the importance of avoiding making such linkages. All human groups share the same genetic potential; the differences between groups are related to the way they deal with and adapt to external factors.

Scientific research confirms that the genetic differences between peoples are very small. So we cannot attribute major differences between peoples to genetic factors. Such factors have a very limited role to play in the rise or decline of nations. A far more important factor is the way people deal with external challenges. This is what largely determines the shape of their national identity. Thus we affirm that national identity springs from a dual source: human nature with its common potentials and possibilities,

[61] Bitar, *The Boundaries*, 37.

[62] Ashour, "Who Are We?"

and a social and historical reality that determine what possibilities and potentials will be realized and the form they will take. We must consider both of these as we reflect on the concept of national identity.[63]

It should now be clear why it is so important to grasp that the concept of national identity is changeable or dynamic. A rigid concept of national identity requires an ahistorical, achronic approach with people locked into earlier identities that cannot even be shown to have existed. But the dynamic concept of an identity that is affected internally by the struggle with its heritage and externally by international circumstances allows for a new vision of self and others. Within this framework, Arab Christians want to share with Arab Muslims in the shaping of their ancient identity with a new concept of Arabism as the cultural frame of reference, moving from a mono-affiliation to pluralism in every sense of the word.

Arab Christians, the Challenge of Identity, and the Clash of Civilizations

Arab Christians generally, and evangelicals in particular, face challenges as regards their relationship with the West. Many aspects of this complicated relationship overlap with the subject of this chapter. So I will discuss the theory of the clash of civilizations and its effect on the concept of identity in the framework of the relationship between the Arab world and the West and its influence on Arab Christians.

In *The Clash of Civilizations and the Remaking of World Order*, Huntington states that the future of the world will be determined by civilizations, and that future conflicts will spring from clashes between civilizations. Because cultural identity is our most important value, what divides people will not be ideology, politics, or economy but their civilization. Thus coming conflicts will not be between the rich and the poor or between different social classes but will be between civilizations and cultures. To stress the seriousness of this matter, Huntington notes that in the future, people will define themselves through alliances and cultural similarities.[64] He sees religion as an important feature in defining civilizations since it is the central force that motivates and organizes human beings.[65] Huntington then discusses the assumption that economic and social modernization will reduce the influence and role of religion. In his opinion, the factors that contribute to modernization are the same ones that contribute to a religious revival. He affirms:

> The most obvious, most salient, and most powerful cause of the global religious resurgence is precisely what was supposed to cause the death of religion: the processes of

---

[63] Bitar, *The Boundaries*, 156.
[64] Samuel Huntington, *The Clash of Civilizations and the Remak-* *ing of World Order* (New York: Simon and Schuster, 1996), 20–37.
[65] Ibid., 64–70.

social, economic, and cultural modernization that swept across the world in the second half of the twentieth century. Longstanding sources of identity and systems of authority are disrupted. People move from the countryside into the city, become separated from their roots, and take new jobs or no job. They interact with large numbers of strangers and are exposed to new sets of relationships. They need new sources of identity, new forms of stable community, and new sets of moral precepts to provide them with a sense of meaning and purpose. Religion, both mainstream and fundamentalist, meets these needs.[66]

When it comes to identity, Huntington sees religion as providing solutions and religious groups as offering a social context that replaces what people lose during the process of urbanization. Religion offers people a source of identity by distinguishing between believers and nonbelievers. In the absence of Communism and with the dwindling of ideologies, religious nationalism has become the basis of identity and self-definition.[67] With the emergence of civilization as a source of identity, we can say that civilization will redefine identity.

Huntington also discusses the idea of a universal civilization arising from

the cultural coming together of humanity and the increasing acceptance of common values, beliefs, orientations, practices and institutions by people throughout the world.

But he dismisses this idea as unrealistic, for global acceptance of some values such as the rejection of murder and shared belief in the importance of stable families does not necessarily imply a global civilization. These common values can explain human behavior but they cannot explain history, which shapes human behavior.[68]

He also dismisses the notion that the spread of consumer culture and Western culture will establish a global civilization. There is no sign yet of a universal language and a universal religion, which are prerequisites for a universal civilization.[69]

Huntington gives a number of reasons why the conflict between the West and Islam will assume great importance. He notes the unemployment and dissatisfaction among Muslim youth, which will push them to embrace Islamic extremism. Fundamentalist trends will also encourage the idea that Islamic civilization and Islam as a religion are superior to Western civilization. At the same time, the cultural and political supremacy of the West will contribute to the mobilization of Muslims. Factoring in the attempt by both the Islamic world and the West to affirm their unique identities, as well as other factors, Huntington foresees growing intolerance between the Islamic world and the West, which will feed into public rejection of the West in the Islamic world.[70]

---

[66] Ibid., 97.
[67] Ibid., 97–100.
[68] Ibid., 56.

[69] Ibid., 55–76.
[70] Ibid., 213–14.

Huntington developed his theory of the clash of civilizations more than twenty years ago, and since then the attacks of September 11 and the subsequent conflicts between the Arab world and the West have confirmed the importance of discussing this theory earnestly and deeply.

Yet there are also many objections to this theory. Some argue that Huntington has said nothing new and that the idea of a clash of civilizations is simply a racist reframing of conflict. The Egyptian philosopher Fouad Zakariyya goes so far as to suggest that the theory of the clash of civilizations was propagated by the CIA in an attempt to ignite global conflict in the era after the fall of Communism in order to stabilize the American weapons market.[71] In his preface to the Arabic translation of Huntington's book, Salah Qunswah sharply criticizes Huntington. He argues that global conflicts should not be oversimplified or reduced to a mere clash of civilizations and points to the Second World War, which witnessed a profound struggle between Italy and France, both of which were Catholic countries.

Qunswah distinguishes between civilization and culture. "Culture" refers to the spiritual or moral aspects of life including traditions, customs, and a system of values and beliefs, whereas "civilization" represents physical matters such as trade, the means of production, and other physical aspects that contrast with the spiritual and moral aspects. Qunswah dismisses Huntington's theory as unrealistic and reflective of a narrow and limited view of civilization.[72]

Huntington raised many important issues concerning the relationship between religion and identity, including noting that religious revival can redefine identity; that the global conflict will be greatly affected by the clash of civilizations and identities; and the key role of Islam.

The theory of the clash of civilizations casts a heavy shadow on the Arab world and its relationship to the West. It brings new pressures to bear on Arab Christians since it resurrects the old conflict between Islam and Christianity, bringing to mind the medieval Crusades, and suggests a future based on the clash between Islam and the West. Thus, I find it necessary to distinguish between Eastern and Western Christians, emphasizing the close relationship between Eastern Christians and the Arab world.

Another important idea put forward by Huntington concerns the role religion plays in shaping civilization and identity. At this point, we have to discuss the theoretical framework for political Islam's view that religious identity is the sole identity. We may even find some convergence between the theory of the clash of civilizations and the thesis of political Islam concerning the role of religion in formulating identity. Though

---

[71] Fouad Zakariyya, "The Culture of the CIA and the Concept of the Clash of Civilizations," *Al-Musawer* (June 1998): 22. Also, "Our Civilization and the Concept of the Clash," *Al-Musawer* (July 1998): 26.

[72] See pages 16–21 of Salah Qunswah's introduction to Tal'at Al-Shayib's translation of Huntington's *Clash of Civilizations* into Arabic (Cairo, 1998).

religion is one of the important factors in formulating identity, defining identity solely in religious terms is severely problematic in the Arab world today.

One part of the theory of the clash of civilizations is what may be called the clash of religions. It describes the close ties between religion, civilization, and identity; so close, in fact, that civilization and identity can become synonymous with religion. Here the situation becomes increasingly complex and ambiguous.

Recent global incidents—the cartoons that offended Islam; Pope Benedict's remarks on a historical matter that were interpreted as offensive to Islam; the increase in suicide bombings; the escalating rejection of the West through armed resistance in Iraq and Afghanistan; the political, military, and religious attacks by the West on Islam and the Islamic world; and many other such incidents—may be seen as confirming in one way or another the theory of the clash of civilizations. Yet an important question remains: Is the global conflict merely a religious conflict or a clash of civilizations and identities? Of course, the global conflict is ongoing and religion plays an important part in it; yet religion alone does not constitute civilization and identity. There are many civilizations, and identity is multifaceted (as mentioned above). Introducing the concept of pluralism at the local and global level may contribute to reducing the risks of the clash of civilizations.

In this context, Arab Christians seek a new concept for cultural reference. This concept springs from internal developments, but also recognizes the regional and global challenges. This internal interaction in the context of multiple waves of globalization will expose the dynamic nature of Arabism that develops and flourishes positively among religions, cultures, histories, and races. This Arabism has no fixed identity but is dynamic and developing, since it is the product of domestic and worldwide cooperation. Such an Arabism may be an important cultural reference for Arab Christians.

THEOLOGICAL THINKING AND A MINORITY MINDSET

The development of civil society through the practices of democracy can contribute to the formation of flexible relationships between majorities and minorities. In the case of Arab Christians, the dynamic concept of minority must be supported by a theological stance that promotes citizenship and coexistence. However, the theology of minorities in the Arab world is characterized by either passive resistance or sectarian violence. Bebawi notes that the dreams and the visions of the Christian minority focus on the second coming of Jesus Christ and his millennial reign. This focus reflects the desire to overcome current problems. However, insistence on a literal interpretation of the Bible makes criticism difficult and reduces the possibility of developing a theology that can meet the needs of the community.[73]

---

[73] George Habib Bebawi, "The Mentality of the Minority" (unpublished).

Despite the importance of the debate in Egypt and the Arab world in the 1990s regarding the concept of a minority, and whether the Christians of Egypt and the region can rightly be called a "minority," I will not deal with that debate here. I will simply use the term "minority" to refer to those who are a religious minority in terms of numbers.

Minorities tend to share a certain mentality. In the case of Arab Christians, the key features of this mentality can be summarized as follows:

A Focus on Divine Intervention and the Millennial Kingdom

There is great interest in the apocalyptic hopes represented by the return of Christ to establish his millennial kingdom. This event will end the pressure the minority faces and will result in the creation of a new society in which the very idea of being a religious minority will vanish. Christ's thousand-year reign on earth will provide an ideal model of a government based on divine truth that is free from discrimination and brings equality.

Here I will not deal with disputes regarding the theology of millennialism but with the political, social, and cultural implications of this doctrine.[74] It can easily become an opportunity to escape from the pressures of the present into an ideal future. But when a minority transfers its attention from the present world to the next world and focuses on heavenly matters, they lose interest in historical events and their thinking is restricted to matters that are not open to analysis and study.

A Focus on Miracles

The increasing pressure on a minority leads to miracles being seen as a confirmation that God is with their community and that he intervenes on their behalf. In the face of forces that question their faith and beliefs and threaten their very existence, minorities cling to miracles that give them assurance of divine protection. It is possible that the frequent references in the second half of the twentieth century to individual and collective experiences of apparitions and miracles by the saints of old are examples of this kind of mentality.

Identity Issues

Political Islam makes religious identity the sole condition for political and cultural participation. This attitude has resulted in a restructuring of identity that has led to cultural upheaval. National affiliation and loyalty have been replaced by religious affiliation and loyalty. This change in what constitutes identity has created a new

---

[74] The concept of the millennial kingdom is rooted in the belief that Christ will return to earth again to rule for a thousand years. Christians hold varying views on this topic, with some advocating a literal interpretation of the verses referring to this, some offering a more symbolic interpretation, and others totally rejecting the notion of a millennium.

situation for Christians as their national and cultural affiliation and loyalty have been called into question. This is the context of dialogue about the relationship between Arab Christians and the West.

While it is impossible to deny the importance of a religious framework, reducing all forms of identity to religious identity contributes to a reduction in pluralism and the creation of a single allegiance. It encourages hiding behind religion.

The issue of religious identity brings out some of the contradictions within the mentality of a minority. At a time when it needs to push the society towards a national identity, it retreats into its religious identity. This contradiction creates paradoxical thought and affects the consistency of national affiliation. At the same time, a minority is always aware of the danger of assimilation, and so clings to its religious identity.

This complex situation makes for confusion and may sometimes encourage extreme religious affiliation, in which the religious identity serves political goals and personal ambitions. This is another reason why it is important to have more than one basis of identity, as discussed earlier.

Linguistic Isolation

As a subculture, minorities can become linguistically isolated by using a private language, which it views as setting itself apart. Yet, this separation often leads to isolation and misunderstanding. To see this, consider the way in which the church presents the doctrine of the Trinity in an Islamic society. This doctrine was clearly formulated theologically in the fourth century using words like *homoousios* and *hypostasis* when speaking of the oneness of God who is himself plural. Though this sort of terminology was clearly understood in the historical context in which it arose, changes in the cultural environment and the rise of Arab Islamic civilization require the church to reformulate the same theological idea in new vocabulary.

Language plays an important role in communication. Thus the church needs to use language that the public can understand. Creating a closed, private culture leads to isolation, relegation, and marginalization. Therefore, the church needs to rethink the language it uses so as to be capable of building bridges, facilitating cooperation, and promoting creative coexistence.

Cultural and Social Alienation

A sense of alienation is one of the important features of a minority mentality. It is the product of a long period of exclusion and marginalization. Though the constitutions of Arab states do not in general distinguish between citizens on the basis of religion or race, there are those in positions of power who do practice such discrimination individually and sometimes institutionally. Such attitudes play an important role in fostering a sense of alienation, and a creation of a negative collective self-image that is confirmed through various situations and circumstances.

Social alienation is dangerous, but cultural alienation represents an even greater danger and contributes significantly to sectarian tension. The absence of any representation of Arab Christians in the Arab media in general, the absence of Christian history from most history curricula, and the perception of the Arab world as solely Islamic all contribute to the cultural and social alienation of minorities.

Selectivity in Dealing with Their Heritage

The Arab Christian minority also shows selectivity in dealing with its heritage. When tolerance is being advocated, historical situations and texts that call for love, respect, and coexistence are quoted; but in times of tension and crisis, texts that condemn and accuse others of disbelief are quoted. This selectivity in regard to history and heritage contributes to instability and ambivalence when it comes to coexistence. It is seen as dependent on initiatives by the majority. Thus tolerance is a superior attitude that depends on the desire of the majority and the luck of the minority.

An Absence of Freedom of Belief

Freedom of belief is a thorny subject in the Arab world today. Converting from Christianity to Islam is encouraged, but converting from Islam to Christianity is not only harshly discouraged but even illegal in most Arab countries. This type of oppression entrenches discrimination and inequality. It also creates a pervasive sense of depression and contributes to building the mentality of a frightened minority, threatened by dissolution.

The absence of freedom of belief has contributed to the creation of a climate of tension for minorities. They are caught between the desire to proclaim their faith and the necessity of coexistence. They are treated with skepticism by all, including the Arab media, which contributes to the creation of tension and fear and further encourages isolation and insularity.

This concludes the brief presentation of some of the factors that shape the mentality of the Arab Christian minority. Arab Christians must accept the reality that they live in an Arab Islamic civilization and are numerically a minority. Acknowledging both aspects of this situation is important when formulating contemporary Arab theology. Thus within the framework of the kingdom of God, we need to think long and deeply about how we express our theology. We may need to think about what message we communicate when we contrast "our heavenly home" with "our earthly home," or stress that our religious identity trumps our national loyalty. These and other expressions that may communicate the wrong message need to be reformulated.

IDENTITY, DOCTRINE, NATIONALISM, AND CITIZENSHIP

Political Islam uses belief as a substitute for nationalism and citizenship. Though political Islam as a new phenomenon stems from the second half of the twentieth century, the linkage of identity, belief, and nationalism began with the Islamic reformers of the early twentieth century. Al-Afghani, for example, believed that historic Islam does not recognize national alliances or ethnic groupings. It recognizes only a single Islamic religious community. Thus, Muslims in different countries reject any concept of ethnicity and are fully committed to their beliefs and the religious unity established by their common use of the Arabic language.[75] Thus, for Al-Afghani the source of identity is not ethnic but moral.[76]

In the same vein, Mohammed Abduh totally rejected the concept of nationalism. He argued that Muslims do not recognize nationalism and its conditions do not apply to them. He saw nationalism among Europeans as similar to tribalism among Arabs.[77]

Hassan al-Banna took a different approach to Islamic nationalism. He argued that if nationalism involves honoring ancestors, being proud of one's family roots, and taking pride in work and *al-jihād* in order to achieve group objectives, then it does not run counter to Islam. Nationalism clashes with Islam only when it is used to restore traditions from the age of ignorance and to promote cultures that undermine and marginalize Islam. He rejected any form of nationalism that favored one nation over another and encouraged hostility between them. He maintained that the Muslim Brotherhood did not believe in any narrow nationalism based on Pharaohism, Phoenicianism, and Arabism. The borders of Islamic citizenship are defined by doctrine, whereas the borders of other communities' citizenship are geographical.[78]

Abul A'la-Maududi believed nationalism to be the source of evil and corruption. He argued that the principles of nationalism contradict the principles of Islam and that when nationalism enters, Islam departs.[79]

Sayyid Qutb too rejected all forms of nationalism. He believed that the nationality required by Islam is the nationality of doctrine, since all nations "are equal under the banner of God."[80] Thus he stated that Islamic society is the only society that is based on belief, not nationality or race, for all Muslims are united in one nation under one God.[81] He wrote that Islamic civilization

---

[75] Jamal al-Din al-Afghani, *Complete Works*, ed. Muhammed Imara (Cairo, 1968), 349–350. See also *Khatirat Jamal al-Din al-Afghani* (Beirut, 1931), 416.

[76] *Khatirat Jamal al-Din al-Afghani*, 139.

[77] Mohammed Abduh, *Complete Works*, ed. Muhammed Imara, 2 vols. (Cairo: Dar El Shorouk, 1993), 2:506–508.

[78] Hassan al-Banna, *The letters of Imam Hassan al-Banna, the Martyr* (Alexandria: Dar El Daawa, 1990), 24–27.

[79] Abul A'la Maududi, *The Muslim Nation and the National Issue*, trans. Samir Abd El Hamid Ibraheem (Cairo: 1981), 153–69; Abul A'la Maududi, *Islamic Governance*, trans. Ahmad Idris (Cairo: 1977), 140.

[80] Sayyid Qutb, *Milestones* (Cairo: Dar El Shorouk, 1987), 26–29.

[81] Ibid., 120.

was not an "Arabic civilization," . . . it was purely an "Islamic civilization". It was never a nationality but always a community of belief.[82]

Abbud al-Zumar also considers nationalism incompatible with Islam.[83] Kamal el-Sayed says that the relationship between Muslims is beyond space and time; it is a religious bond.[84]

The general orientation of political Islam is clear. It completely rejects the concept of nationalism and asserts that the Islamic faith is the basis of relationships among Muslims. Nationalism as a concept is regarded as contradicting Islamic notions of the universality of Islam.

Christians, too, tend to reject nationalism and regard it as an evil to be confronted. Some believe that as Christians we should not regard any geopolitical area as our "home" or country but should be concerned for the whole world. Our "nationalism," in biblical terms, is focused on heaven, which is the source of our true identity, rather than the finite country in which we happened to be born.[85] Since the coming of Christ to earth, the people of God do not belong to a specific racial group or have a specific home, for the worldwide fellowship of believers includes people of various nationalities and racial backgrounds.[86]

This view is very similar to that of political Islam. Both focus on the universality of the message and the irrelevance of geographical and ethnic boundaries in the community of believers who are related to each other within the bonds of faith and admit no kind of discrimination.

The Christian trend that rejects nationalism tends to consider our earthly home as temporary and believes that the main goal of our existence is to reach our heavenly home. One theologian supporting this view states that Christians believe that their home is in heaven, not on earth. We are commanded to obey our earthly governors but our loyalty is elsewhere.[87]

Some of the hymns sung in Egypt and elsewhere in the Arab world reflect this theological vision.

Hymns and songs are an effective way of conveying a theological, social, and political vision. It is said that the key to the success of the Arians in early church history was that Arius set out his theology and vision in a group of hymns that were widely sung. Hymns, through their words and melody, reflect the relation between theological thinking and the dominant culture. In addition, they are greatly affected by the dominant

[82] Ibid., 59.

[83] Abbud al-Zumar, "The Curriculum of Islamic *Al-Jihād*," in *The Militant Prophet–1: The Rejectionist*, ed. Sayed Rifaat Ahmed (London: Riad El Rayyes, 1991), 116.

[84] Kamal el-Sayed (1991), 227.

[85] Christopher Catherwood, *Whose Side is God On? Nationalism and Christianity* (London: SPCK, 2003), xiv.

[86] Ibid., xiv.

[87] Ibid., 6.

political, economic, and social climate and reflect a particular human experience. The hymns in the Bible can help us grasp this point. Take the hymn of Moses and Miriam in Exodus 15:1–19:

> I will sing to the Lord,
>> for he is highly exalted.
> Both horse and driver
>> he has hurled into the sea.
> The Lord is my strength and my defense;
>> he has become my salvation.
> He is my God, and I will praise him,
>> my father's God, and I will exalt him.
> The Lord is a warrior;
>> the Lord is his name.
> Pharaoh's chariots and his army
>> he has hurled into the sea.
> The best of Pharaoh's officers
>> are drowned in the Red Sea.
> The deep waters have covered them;
>> they sank to the depths like a stone.
> Your right hand, Lord,
>> was majestic in power.
> Your right hand, Lord,
>> shattered the enemy.
> In the greatness of your majesty
>> you threw down those who opposed you.
> You unleashed your burning anger;
>> it consumed them like stubble.
> By the blast of your nostrils
>> the waters piled up.
> The surging waters stood up like a wall;
>> the deep waters congealed in the heart of the sea.
> The enemy boasted,
>> "I will pursue, I will overtake them.
> I will divide the spoils;
>> I will gorge myself on them.
> I will draw my sword
>> and my hand will destroy them."
> But you blew with your breath,
>> and the sea covered them.
> They sank like lead
>> in the mighty waters.

Who among the gods
　　is like you, LORD?
Who is like you—
　　majestic in holiness,
awesome in glory,
　　working wonders?
You stretch out your right hand,
　　and the earth swallows your enemies.
In your unfailing love you will lead
　　the people you have redeemed.
In your strength you will guide them
　　to your holy dwelling.
The nations will hear and tremble;
　　anguish will grip the people of Philistia.
The chiefs of Edom will be terrified,
　　the leaders of Moab will be seized with
　　　　trembling,
the people of Canaan will melt away;
　　terror and dread will fall on them.
By the power of your arm
　　they will be as still as a stone—
until your people pass by, LORD,
　　until the people you bought pass by.
You will bring them in and plant them
　　on the mountain of your inheritance—
the place, LORD, you made for your dwelling,
　　the sanctuary, Lord, your hands established.
"The LORD reigns
　　for ever and ever."

When Pharaoh's horses, chariots and horsemen went into the sea, the LORD brought the waters of the sea back over them, but the Israelites walked through the sea on dry ground.

The background to this song is a political situation of slavery and oppression by Pharaoh of a scattered people who had lost their identity and their land. The dominant theme was scattering and fear resulting from the long absence of effective leadership. They had a culture of surrender and submission to circumstances.

The hymn confronts these attitudes and the dominant culture and highlights the God who is fighting beside his people. This God has dominion over nature and is capable of confronting other gods. In this context their experience of victory is presented as Yahweh's conquering of other gods and Israel's victory over the nations.

Let us look also at the song of the Virgin Mary (Luke 1:46–55):

> My soul glorifies the Lord
>> and my spirit rejoices in God my Savior,
> for he has been mindful
>> of the humble state of his servant.
> From now on all generations will call me blessed,
>> for the Mighty One has done great things for me—
>> holy is his name.
> His mercy extends to those who fear him,
>> from generation to generation.
> He has performed mighty deeds with his arm;
>> he has scattered those who are proud in their inmost thoughts.
> He has brought down rulers from their thrones
>> but has lifted up the humble.
> He has filled the hungry with good things
>> but has sent the rich away empty.
> He has helped his servant Israel,
>> remembering to be merciful
> to Abraham and his descendants forever,
>> just as he promised our ancestors.

These words were spoken in a context of colonization and humiliation. We can see evidence of a crushing economic crisis and a long absence of prophecy and divine revelation. The dominant mood is a desire to be free from Roman tyranny ("He has brought down rulers from their thrones"). This song praises God for his marvelous deeds in the context of his absolute authority. It also offers a prophetic vision of the future victory of the church through humility and meekness.

These songs and others in the Bible reflect their political, social, and economic setting, and reveal the dominant culture of their time. Similarly, all hymns and songs express in one way or another the personal or communal state of people in a specific time and reflect their theological response to their societal position.

Today common hymns in the Arab world include words such as these:

> I am not from here;
>> this is a dying world.
> No matter money, wealth, or prestige,
>> I have another home.
> As long as I live here I am waiting,
>> as every minute passes I wish
> that Jesus comes again
>> to take us to the joys of glory.

> By faith we live waiting,
>> by faith you will come and take us.
> By faith we will reach our home.

Critical analysis of a number of widely used songs reveals theological beliefs that reject nationalism and embrace a heavenly affiliation that transcends racial and geographical borders. But at the same time, these words reflect the mentality of a minority facing assimilation and dominated by a culture of alienation, enduring current pressures for the sake of eventual freedom and victory.

The theological trend to reject nationalism draws its vision from the covenant that God made with Abraham in which he said that "In you all the nations of the world will be blessed." The blessing is not for a specific people but is part of God's plan for the whole humanity. It is impossible to read the covenant with Abraham and the blessing as glorifying a single nation or exalting one nation over another. Rather, God is using one community as a vehicle to bless the others. The covenant with Abraham also confirms the equality of all people. Yet despite the importance of this interpretation, the group that rejects the idea of nationalism interprets the blessing from the narrow perspective of denouncing national differentiation. A wider interpretation of this covenant is that it frees faith from the fanaticism of national affiliation, but does not thereby reject nationalism and political citizenship.

There are many situations in the Bible that indicate that national affiliation does not guarantee God's blessing. For example, it is not enough to merely be a Jew. Thus the Bible contradicts nationalist movements that emphasize a person's birthplace and thus his or her nationality. The choosing of Jacob over Esau is the best example to show that blessing is not granted merely on the basis of national affiliation.

There are also stories in the Bible that affirm that religious affiliation can transcend geographical borders. For example, there is the story of Naaman the Syrian. In the book of Esther, too, we see that God could be with his people in the land of exile just as he had been with them in the land of the promise, for the people of God are not bound to a specific geographic location. We even see the prophet Ezekiel longing for the day when foreigners living within the borders of Israel would enjoy the same rights as the people of God.[88]

It is clear that such beliefs are not in harmony with nationalism and can lead to it being seen as a source of evil. Narrow national affiliation can even be seen as opposed to faith, which is universal in nature and transcends race and geography. Thus at this point we need to consider some important questions: Is belief the same as nationalism, as political Islam claims? Or does belief contradict nationalism, as the Christian view outlined above claims?

---

[88] Ibid., 53.

In answering these questions, I introduce another theological concept that offers a somewhat different view of the relation between belief and national orientation. In other words, is dynamic Arabism a possible cultural frame of reference for Arab theology or does this conflict with our faith? Or is there some other theological concept that can serve to link faith and nationalism?

Universality of Belief and Natal Citizenship

It is important to distinguish between nationalism as a basis for the civic and political structure of a country and faith as a relationship with God. A faith is a way of understanding a holy text combined with a way of worship, convictions, and practices. Confounding nationalism as a political approach with faith as a universal pattern for the relationship between human beings and God, leads to confusion.

This confusion is due to Christians' basic orientation to witness to the gospel and affirm the universality of the message of Christ, which transcends racial and geographical boundaries. In the early stages of his mission, Christ's message was directed to the Jewish nation, but in a later stage he declared that his message was universal, transcending the limits of the Jewish religion and nationality. In so doing, he broke with tradition. The universality of the message did away with concepts such as the unique status of the people of Israel as God's chosen people and broke the link between religion, nationalism, and genealogy. The universality of his message precluded any notion of destroying others and exposed and removed the boundaries erected by discrimination and egotism.

The parable of the Good Samaritan offers a clear model to illustrate this point. There was intense racial and religious conflict between the Samaritans and the Jews. To understand the racial dimension of this conflict, we can look at the contemporary clashes between Arabs and Jews. Their relationship is characterized by hatred, malice, fear, and a desire to destroy the other party and wipe out its identity. To understand the religious dimension of this conflict, we can compare it to the struggle between Muslims and Serbs in Bosnia, where the goal is not to evangelize the other side but to destroy them. These conflicts give us some insight into the struggle between the Jews and the Samaritans.

In this complex religious and nationalist context, Jesus tells the parable of the Good Samaritan, which declares that faith transcends belief and nationalism. The man who was injured and abandoned on the road was a Jew. Two clergymen who shared his faith and nationality saw him but ignored him. The one person who did come to help him was different from him in his nationality and faith. However, he helped the man and cared for him with love and kindness, expressing his belief in the one God and in a human brotherhood that transcends faith and nationalism.

Christ started his mission in the context of Judaism and nationalism, but he surpassed it, teaching instead universality or, in contemporary language, global thinking: "For God so loved the world that he gave his one and only Son, that whoever believes in him shall not perish." Thus we conclude that one of the main features of the message of the Lord Jesus is the call to approach the other, even if it necessitates transcending nationalism and belief.

One of the other social results of a theological orientation that was prominent in the early church is the absence of racism based on nationalism. Christianity clearly declared that Christ offers a new way of salvation. All who believe in him receive new life and become children of God. Thus, they taught that religion transcended nationalism and was no longer associated with a specific people, for Christianity presented a new concept of the people of God, transcending racism with the idea of the one body of Christ embracing all. This was one reason it clashed with the society of the day, for racism and discrimination were prominent features of Judaism at that time.

This new theological thinking rejects racism and unifies human beings while calling for the destruction of all racial fetters and supporting integration and honest communication among peoples. The other is no longer unclean and forbidden; all have become one, and all are pure in Jesus Christ. Therefore, the prohibition against eating with the Gentiles fell away, for there was no longer any reason for it.

The confrontation between Paul and Peter illustrates this change. Peter backed away when he saw how some Jews disapproved of his eating with Gentiles. But Paul confronted him, affirming the need to reject the old social values removed by Christ, and support the new social values of integration and communication.

The universality of the message of Christ introduces a divide between a government, which is based on nationalism and citizenship, and faith, which reflects a personal relationship with God. Mixing religion with politics leads to serious conflict between national affiliation and faith. Separating religion from politics allows the political system related to geographical borders, national affiliation, and religious pluralism to be a dynamic and developing as domestic and international circumstances change. The role of religion is to offer the moral system that can ignite the conscience of the nation that judges whether the political system is valid or not. When this happens, the relationship between a faith and citizenship is positive.

Toward an Arab Theology of Citizenship

Arab Christians need to develop an Arabic political theology that can contribute to the emergence of civil society, encourage democracy, and promote dynamic citizenship. Such a task is crucial in developing the role of Arab Christians and can replace religious boundaries with social and political ones. A political theology that transcends the barriers of the past and contributes to the development of dynamic citizenship will enhance coexistence and affirm pluralism. Some ideas for such a theology are suggested below.

Loyalty

Arab theology must take a broader view of loyalty and replace commitment to a single religious concept with pluralistic affiliations, for loyalty in its broader sense accepts the views of others and sees the kingdom of God as a model of pluralism and diversity.

The theological approach that produces this concept of loyalty will open the way for interaction between faith and the society in a way that establishes citizenship. For while citizenship is not the same as religion, religion is a partner in constructing citizenship. We need to work for political and theological recognition that religious obligations are only one of the components of identity. However, recognition that identity is relative and flexible also requires a theology that believes that no one owns the absolute truth. Only then can pluralism become rooted in a religious context that tends to believe that there is only one truth. This notion of absolute truth is one of the root causes of theological problems in the Arab world. To encourage a theology that recognizes multiple loyalties, pluralistic identity, and transcends a single legitimate truth requires various interpretations of the religious texts.

The Pluralistic Interpretation of Religious Text

The pluralistic interpretation of religious texts is a key concept in developing a political theology that promotes pluralism, which is the basis of dynamic citizenship. Tazini, Abu Zayd, and Bibawi all advocate pluralistic reading and interpretation of religious texts. Arabic political theology also needs this tool to promote pluralism at different levels of the church and society. Such pluralism will enhance the practice of the concept at the theological level as well as at the social and political levels. The church will then accept the need for openness and involvement with other religious communities.

Solidarity

Arabic political theology considers solidarity the basis of coexistence. But pluralism does not mean fragmentation. A theology that sees solidarity as a tool for common struggle and coexistence can contribute to the realization of dynamic citizenship. Solidarity must be based on the doctrine of creation, which gives all humans an equal right to exist and to thrive. Equality and justice must thus come before solidarity. Religious doctrines are selective by nature and tend to exclude those who are different. A political theology that can establish a concept of solidarity and go beyond the limitations imposed by doctrine will contribute to the notion of unity and diversity that is essential for civil society and democracy. Solidarity as a theological concept will also contribute to the socialization of the church and encourage religious institutions to become an active part of civil society.

Jesus' parable of the Good Samaritan may be the best argument for the kind of solidarity that transcends belief.

Institutionalization

Institutionalization is a necessary component of a political theology that contributes to dynamic citizenship. The absence of the concept of social sin characterizes an individualistic approach to society. This notion is clear in the current Coptic political theology that separates the kingdom of God from life on earth. However, a political theology that promotes institutionalization as a theological concept will encourage the church to have an institutional role that is independent of the state and will contribute to building bridges between the church and society. Institutionalization will bring the church to the heart of civil society and help it to overcome the isolation and alienation that it faces in Arabic society. It will also establish the role of the church as an institution, limit the role of individuals to some extent, and encourage democracy. Institutionalization will affirm the role of God's people as a community committed to equality, justice, and full involvement—issues that are the essence of dynamic citizenship. These ideas are needed to develop a political theology that can respond to the social and political development of the Arab world. They can act as catalysts to meet the needs of Arab Christians as they strive to achieve dynamic citizenship.

Partnership

As used here, the word "partnership" has a meaning that goes beyond its traditional narrow sense. Partnership means equality—another word that has many meanings. Here, however, I will focus on it in relationship to partnership.

Christianity has a special understanding of partnership. Christians believe that human beings were created in the image of God (Gen 1:27) and that sin spoiled this divine image. However, through the death and resurrection of Christ, this image was restored. The apostles Peter and Paul expressed this idea by saying that we human beings participate in or share the divine nature (2 Pet 1:4) and are children of God (Rom 8:14, 16, 19, 21; 9:8, 26; Gal 3:26). This means that we have been restored to the image in which we were first created.

We can thus see the deep meaning of partnership as giving from the depth of the soul. In this kind of giving, the giver and the receiver become one. I think this is the essence of the Christian faith. God descended and expressed himself in the incarnation in order to bestow goodness and divine love on human beings, so that they could be restored to the image of God, which they had borne at creation.

The partnership between God and human beings is a genuine partnership that reflects practical love. Christ's words in Matthew 25 reflect this vision clearly:

> When the Son of Man comes in his glory, and all the angels with him, he will sit on his
> glorious throne. All the nations will be gathered before him, and he will separate the

people one from another as a shepherd separates the sheep from the goats. He will put the sheep on his right and the goats on his left.

Then the King will say to those on his right, "Come, you who are blessed by my Father; take your inheritance, the kingdom prepared for you since the creation of the world. For I was hungry and you gave me something to eat, I was thirsty and you gave me something to drink, I was a stranger and you invited me in, I needed clothes and you clothed me, I was sick and you looked after me, I was in prison and you came to visit me."

Then the righteous will answer him, "Lord, when did we see you hungry and feed you, or thirsty and give you something to drink? When did we see you a stranger and invite you in, or needing clothes and clothe you? When did we see you sick or in prison and go to visit you?"

The King will reply, "Truly I tell you, whatever you did for one of the least of these brothers and sisters of mine, you did for me."

Then he will say to those on his left, "Depart from me, you who are cursed, into the eternal fire prepared for the devil and his angels." (Matt 25:31–41)

Partnership is of the essence, since all people are made equal by Christ's death and resurrection.

Teamwork

A close look at the New Testament clearly shows the collective vision of the Christian faith. Christ opted for teamwork when he trained his disciples. When he called for repentance, he emphasized repentance for sin against others. Perhaps the Sermon on the Mount best reflects this vision. In it, he talked about the poor, mourners, those who hunger and thirst for righteousness, the merciful, and the peacemakers. He also spoke out against adultery, murder, anger, and revenge, and called for loving our enemies. All the things he condemned are related to life in a community.

The teachings of Christ also make it clear that it is impossible to have a relationship with God without having a relationship with the community. John makes the same point in his letter to the early church in which he insists that fellowship with God requires fellowship with others.

This is the message we have heard from him and declare to you: God is light; in him there is no darkness at all. If we claim to have fellowship with him and yet walk in the darkness, we lie and do not live out the truth. But if we walk in the light, as he is in the light, we have fellowship with one another, and the blood of Jesus, his Son, purifies us from all sin. (1 John 1:5–7)

Thus we affirm that sin has two dimensions, individual and collective. Each leads to the other, and genuine repentance involves repentance of both individual and societal sin. Moreover, if our relationship with God cannot be separated from our relationship with society, then teamwork is necessary to effect change. This is the role of the church as a community that Christ describes as being salt and light because it has the capacity to influence and change society. So the only way to fully express Christianity is through a relationship with both God and the community. This necessitates a collective vision and working together, which is the essence of citizenship.

Creative Work

The New Testament attests to the importance of the work of the Holy Spirit in an individual and a community. The spiritual gifts mentioned in the New Testament, including healing, speaking in tongues, teaching, and so on are some of the clear manifestations of the Holy Spirit in the church. Here I will not discuss the issue of spiritual gifts because what I want to highlight is the unique relationship between God and the community through the work of the Holy Spirit. A look at the early church clearly shows the need among the communities at that time for a divine touch to confirm God's divine presence with his people. In fact, this need was not restricted to the early church; the history of the church reveals that the absence of the work of the Holy Spirit in the community has led to dark periods in the history of Christianity and to rigidity and isolation.

The interaction between the Holy Spirit and the community of faith has led to the emergence of creative gifts that have contributed to the spread of the message of faith and support for Christianity. The gifts mentioned in the New Testament are all related to supporting the community, the spread of the message, and the growth of the church through each member serving other members with their spiritual gifts.

Spiritual gifts are not something to boast about but are to be used to build the body of Christ (1 Cor 12:7). However, the critical question we need to address here is whether these gifts are limited only to the contexts found in the New Testament. Or is the Holy Spirit creative, working in each community in various ways according to the needs of that community and its historical circumstances? Answering this question requires much research. However, what I have seen is that the Spirit of God has not stopped working, and that the interaction between the Holy Spirit and the community is what leads to the ongoing effectiveness of the church in the world.

Thus the relationship between God and the community is reflected in creative works that have the effect of improving the mission of the community and supporting its vision. Looking beyond the debate over spiritual gifts, I see that the uniqueness of Christianity is its matchless experience of the divine presence in the life of the community, which is reflected in new creative works. In this respect I agree with Gutierrez who has said that theology is not something with which we are indoctrinated but something we practice.

THEOLOGICAL THINKING AND PRESENT CHALLENGES

Since the earliest days of Christianity, theology has been related to reality. Its message addressed the reality of the community and was authentically related to the culture of the time. Theology was the tool of expression and the culture of the society was the model and framework that shaped that thought. The church was not isolated from society and did not use a special language of its own; rather, it presented its vision of the faith in language that was understood and in a way that was culturally relevant. Its message was thus strong and effective.

A quick look at the renewing role of Christ the Lord and New Testament models will help us to come closer to this positive attitude, for they offer us a rich example of the interaction between faith and reality.

The Renewing Role of the Lord Jesus Christ

Christ responded to the religious system in his age and thus he regularly visited the synagogue and participated in religious debates. His early message was very responsive to the environment in which he lived, as we can see from the following examples.

Careful Use of Language and Significant Actions

Christ the Lord took great care in how he expressed himself verbally and in his actions. For example, he avoided using the term "Messiah" because this was a loaded term in a region colonized by Rome and because of its religious implications for the Jews. His ability to bypass that term in its usual significance and to use alternatives that had the same meaning played a decisive role in the continuation of his mission until he had fulfilled its purpose. He used words that had messianic connotations in Jewish religious thought in order to refer to the issue without using the term "Messiah." One of these terms was "Shepherd," since one of the main characteristics of the Messiah was that he would be a shepherd of his people. Christ also used practical situations to confirm the same meaning. For example, his triumphal entry to Jerusalem and his cleansing of the temple confirmed his messianic nature and his authority.

Alternatives and the Value of Change

Christ presented alternatives that overrode traditional models. In regard to faith, he offered a model that surpassed the rigidity of the laws and was based instead on the effectiveness of the person of God and his power. In the area of religious rituals, he announced a radical change that acknowledged the old but did not continue it, since it is not fitting to put new wine into old wineskins. Here we can see the value of change: the Jewish system was based on the law and its rituals. That law had played a historic role in protecting humanity; however, the new system was based on the effectiveness of the person of God and his divine work. The Lord offered many alternatives including authentic repentance, caring for one's neighbors, showing mercy, and acceptance of others, which were all alternatives that transcended the traditionalism and ritualism of the Law, reflecting instead a free, regenerated mind that interacts with God and others.

Religion Involves Realism and Moral Commitment

The Lord Jesus criticized the scribes and Pharisees for many things. However, his criticism was not a complete rejection of them. The scribes and Pharisees had played an important role in preserving the faith over the centuries; they had been able to develop theological approaches, a system of worship, and ways of dealing with situations. Not all of them were wicked or corrupt. What Jesus criticized was that they had turned religion into something difficult and complex. They put new burdens on people that were hard to bear. Consequently, religion had been transformed from its natural simplicity into a complex system of rituals and obligations that made commitment to it very difficult, even impossible. So people donned masks and became hypocrites as they attempted to convince others of their piety. This was because of the gulf between the complicated moral requirements associated with religion and humanity's ability to live up to these standards.

By contrast, Jesus proclaimed a simple message: "Repent and believe in the gospel." A real relationship with God starts with repentance and continues through authentic and effective faith. A close reading of the sayings of the Lord Jesus in the New Testament clearly shows his pragmatism and the way he makes religion a positive element in human life. He said of himself: "I am the way and the truth and the life. No one comes to the Father except through me" (John 14:6). The role played by the clergy in his time led Jesus to call for the simplifying of religious life and affirm moral commitment.

Faith Is a Call for the Activation of the Coming Age in Our Own Age

Christ the Lord called for the coming of the kingdom of heaven, yet he did not explain what this kingdom meant. Many scholars have suggested that he did not need to do so because the Jews in his time were familiar with this expression. The kingdom that he proclaimed was the same kingdom the teachers of the Law proclaimed. But the Lord Jesus taught about life in this kingdom.

We can clarify this by looking at the words of the Lord's Prayer, "your kingdom come, your will be done, on earth as it is in heaven." The kingdom is a reality that we can live here on earth and therefore the coming age is present now in our world.

The eschatological call presented by the Lord Jesus was unique in its kind. He came to a world that was waiting for the Messiah and dreaming of the divine power that would free them from colonization, enrich the earth, and give economic, political, and even spiritual victory. These eschatological expectations made the Israelites passive and careless, since the Messiah was the one who would free them, satisfy them, and make them lords of this world. Within this eschatological context of passivism, the Lord Jesus proclaimed that the kingdom is present and effective, and that eternity and the reality we live in are linked so that we cannot separate our life here from the life to come.

The principles of the kingdom can be practiced and believers are called to relate the coming age to the one in which we live at present. In other words, we are called to taste the coming age in the present age. The call for the kingdom is a call to turn a future dream into a reality and to relate what is to come to the context we live in.

Speaking about Faith in Jesus in Contemporary Language

Careful reading of the Gospels shows that the church used contemporary language when talking about its faith. There are many situations in which we see the depth of the Christian message expressed in a manner that was comprehensible to the people in that time.

For example, the word "logos" (word, discourse, reason) was not a new term in the age of Christ; it was a Greek word referring to the mediator between the divine and the human (and/or to that which was the ordering principle of the universe). John recognized that this term had overtones that resembled Christian teaching. Thus he introduced Christ as being "the Word," namely, the mediator between God and man (and the one who ordered/created the universe). He did not stop at the limited Greek concept attached to the word "logos" but extended its meaning to express Christian truth. He added that the incarnate Jesus who lived and died among us and was raised from the dead was the Word (the mediator). In his life, death, and resurrection, Jesus made a bridge we could cross to God and approach him as children.

The meaning with which John infused the Greek term "logos" went well beyond the Greeks' limited use of the word to refer to a created mediator between the divine and humanity. John introduced the idea that the Word is God incarnated in Jesus Christ who became a mediator so that people could approach God through him. Thus, the Word is a divine expression and the incarnation of divine love. The mediator here is not a creature; he is God himself:

> In the beginning was the Word, and the Word was with God, and the Word was God. He was with God in the beginning. Through him all things were made; without him nothing was made that has been made. (John 1:1–3)

The prologue of John reveals the courage of the early church and its ability to express a theological concept within a specific cultural reality. The church did not hesitate when it came to expressing its theology in contemporary language.

Being Responsive to Social Norms

The struggle experienced by the church in Corinth was both theological and social. The theological struggle manifested itself in intellectual divisions and various teachings, whereas the social struggle manifested itself in relation to the issue of equality between men and women.

The issue of equality dominated the thinking of the early church as Christianity broke down the racial barriers between Jews and Gentiles and then the barriers between men and women. This equality led to new freedom, and so the early Christians felt that they had been released from social fetters and women felt that they were free to express themselves. The concept of equality in Christianity is authentic. In Christ there is no Greek or Jew, no slave or free, no male or female, for all are equal. This realization pushed the early church to adopt social values that clashed with the dominant values in the society of the time.

At that time, social norms dictated that a pious woman covered her head when she appeared in public or at social gatherings, whereas prostitutes' heads were uncovered. People saw the head covering as distinguishing a pious woman from a prostitute. That was the norm of that time. But Christian women, in light of the teachings of the church, felt free of all the restrictions imposed by the pagan society. They wanted to ignore the cultural values of their society and demonstrate the new values and social customs flowing from the theology that proclaimed equality between men and women. The result was a clash with the wider society. The church realized that this conflict would have wide social repercussions, and thus it called on women to cover their heads. This call was not a sign of theological regression but of a move to fit into society in its present form.

The early church was characterized by prophetic ability, so as it taught a new theology it was also sensitive to the society in which it was located and chose various ways of engaging with it, starting with appeasement and ending with clashing. In all these situations, the church was working to move society toward change and renewal.

Communicating with Sensitivity

In writing their gospels, both Matthew and Luke set out to glorify Christ. Both presented him as omnipotent and victorious, for they rightly declared his authority and lordship. However, comparison of the Gospels shows that each Gospel writer expressed himself in a way that reflected his theology, his culture, and his religious sensitivity. For example, Mark wrote:

> He could not do any miracles there, except lay his hands on a few sick people and heal them. He was amazed at their lack of faith. (Mark 6:5–6)

Matthew, on the other hand, put it like this:

> But Jesus said to them, "A prophet is not without honor except in his own town and in his own home." And he did not do many miracles there because of their lack of faith. (Matt 13:57–58)

Matthew has omitted the words "could not," which might be read as implying that Jesus' ability was limited, and "amazed," which might be read as implying that his knowledge was limited. Though the core idea in both texts is the same—that Jesus did not do many miracles in his home town due to their lack of faith—the way this idea is expressed varies in line with the theological sensitivity of each writer.

Similarly, in Mark 4:40, Jesus asked his disciples, "Why are you afraid? Do you still have no faith?" Whereas, in Luke 8:25, all he says is, "Where is your faith?" In both situations the reality is the same—the disciples showed a lack of faith. Yet the wording of Luke is diplomatic and shows the disciples in a more positive light than the stronger wording in Mark.

In Mark 8:29, Peter says, "You are the Messiah," whereas in Matthew 16:16, he is recorded as saying, "You are the Messiah, the Son of the Living God." Comparing the two texts shows that Matthew wants to give more details about the truth, explaining that Christ is the Son of the living God and so confirming his divinity and authority.

There are many places in the New Testament that reveal similar shades of theological emphasis. In each case, the fundamental reality and truth are the same, but the wording varies because the writers were sensitive to the community to which they were writing and to the general circumstances surrounding their message.

SUMMARY

Commitment to a theological frame of reference and relating to a cultural context are important if we are to raise the level of contemporary Arab theology. Though Christians have made great contributions to the advancement of Arab culture, most of our theology, especially that of evangelicals, is still based on Western models. I do not want to repudiate this link with Western theology, for the European Reformation contributed greatly to the reformulation of the Christian role on the domestic and international levels. Western theological scholars have contributed greatly to our understanding of holy texts and how to relate them to contemporary reality. Their critical and historical studies have helped to advance the Christian vision and have yielded creative prophetic insights. However, for many years the Arab church has longed to develop an Arab theology, one that is shaped by our own cultural context. We as Arab Christians have historical roots in this area and represent a range of ethnicities including the Christians of South Sudan, Armenians, Syrians, Berbers, Egyptians, and Lebanese. Most of us speak the Arabic language and we are generally referred to as Arab Christians. Thus in this context we need to adopt Arabism as our basic cultural reference. But in doing so we face many challenges, the most important of which is the question of whether Arabism is the same as Islam. Or is it broader than one religion? Does it imply a fixed religious identity? Or is it a product of internal and external interaction?

Our answers to these questions help us to offer an initial suggestion regarding how Arab Christians should understand their cultural milieu. We suggest that Arabism is a historical and sociological concept, thus indicating that national identity is not immutable but is the product of local and international interaction. Arabism involves religions, cultures, and histories. It develops through internal interactions or, to be more specific, through critical interaction with our heritage and a critical openness to regional and international changes. Arabism is something we construct and improve, and it cannot be reduced to a single religion or a specific ethnicity.

From this perspective Arabism can be seen afresh as an open construct to which Arab Christians contribute, one that is an integral part of their cultural frame of reference. Arab Christians can then build bridges between the Arab world and the West. This relationship with the West then becomes free and open, divorced from conspiracy theories and notions of a clash of civilizations; instead, it will exist in the context of a creative exchange through which it influences and is influenced. This type of dynamic and developed Arabism is the cornerstone of the cultural framework for Arab Christians. Active Arabism will contribute to overcoming a minority mentality and will break new ground for cultural theological interaction. Arab Christians will then be able to make an effective contribution to the development of identity and the support of the common good in the Arab world.

This cultural context will help Arab Christians adopt a fuller concept of identity, one that is rooted in pluralism and which distinguishes between the universality of the message and national affiliation. In so doing, Arab Christians can offer a crucial alternative to political Islam, which holds that national identity is the same as faith. This linkage actually contradicts the universality of the message, for it advocates the building of a single religious country worldwide, based on one religion. The universality of the message of both Islam and Christianity strongly contradicts territorial affiliation. Therefore, it is vital that we separate the universality of the message from nationality, citizenship, and affiliation if we are to be effective in constructing a multifaceted identity.

Perhaps our reading of the words of Christ our Lord concerning separating faith from nationalism is helpful. The Jewish faith was inextricably linked to nationalism and this led to the rejection of others, wars, and bloodshed. But Christ came to distinguish the message from national affiliation. His message does not reject nationalism or citizenship or override territorial affiliation, but what it does do is separate out two areas: the first is doctrinal and directs its message to the whole world, whereas, the second is political, and is the arena in which nationalism and citizenship play an important role. This kind of distinction is very important when formulating our mission of going into "all the world," and is necessary for understanding national and territorial affiliation.

A close reading of the life of Christ our Lord affirms this prophetic vision. He criticized the dominant systems in his time and freed the faith from national boundaries.

However, this close reading also affirms the importance of national identity. Christ was not separated from the culture of his time; instead, he interacted with it in a constructively critical way. In the same way, the early church showed great sensitivity in its interactions with the dominant culture and formulated its thoughts in a manner that was comprehensible to the masses and penetrated the society of its time. Thus close examination of the life of Christ and the bold, dynamic attitudes of the early church can inspire us today as we work to develop a contemporary Arab theology in the context of an Arab culture and a multifaceted identity.

SCRIPTURE INDEX

Genesis

1 . . . . 20, 22, 329, 333
1–2 . . . . 48, 330
1–11 . . . . 15–18, 22, 52
1:1–2:4 22
1:1 20
1:26 . . . . 20, 328
1:26–27 351
1:26–28 . . . . 48, 326
1:27 . . . . 20, 459
1:27–28 329
1:27b 343
1:28 20
1:31 . . . . 25, 329
2 . . . . 20, 36, 329, 330, 333
2:1–2 329
2:1–22 22
2:4 329
2:4–25 331
2:7 . . . . 289, 329
2:16–17 . . . . 20, 26
2:18–20 329
2:18–22 351
2:18–23 336
2:19 22
2:21–23 330
2:24 . . . . 164, 332
3 . . . . 37, 301, 333
3–6 37
3:6–7 333
3:10 37
3:14–19 26
3:15 . . . . 243, 336
3:15–16 336
3:19 37
3:21 37
3:22 37
4:7 37
5:1–2 332
6 38
6:5 37
6:5–6 26
6:11–13 37
6:18 48
8–9 26
9:1–7 . . . . 20, 48
9:1–9 38

9:5–7 48
9:8–11 48
9:8–17 36
9:9 59
10 198
10–11 . . . . 18, 20
11 . . . . 18, 334
12 . . . . 18, 74
12–50 . . . . 23, 26, 33
12:1–3 49
12:1–5 340
12:1–7 222
12:3–4 51
12:10–12 23
12:20 23
12:1 20
13 74
13:14–17 222
13:15 77
13:16 50
14 33
14:9 20
14:18–20 23
15 . . . . 38, 74
15:1–6 19
15:1–21 222
15:2 143
15:3 82
15:5 . . . . 27, 50
15:7 19
15:7–21 19
15:16 27
15:18 . . . . 49, 222
15:18–19 33
15:18–21 27
16:7–14 38
16:8–21 23
16:15 82
17 . . . . 60, 74, 294
17:1–2 60
17:1–8 49
17:1–22 222
17:6 54
17:7 46
17:8 77
17:9–14 60
17:19 82
18:16–19:29 . . . . 23, 38

18:19 60
19:15 29
20 23
20:3–7 . . . . 22, 27
20:17–18 38
21:13 82
21:15–21 38
21:21 82
21:22–32 47
21:20 38
22:1 50
22:3 143
22:15–18 222
22:17 50
22:18 60
24:2 143
24:4 101
24:7 77
24:10 102
24:13ff 316
24:16 175
24:35–36 51
24:39, 58 316
25:20 102
25:23 82
26:2–5 52
26:3 74
26:4 . . . . 50, 74
26:5 60
26:12 51
26:13 74
26:24 51
26:28 38
28:3 50
28:13 19
28:14 27
31:43–54 47
35:11–12 50
35:11–48 51
35:19 108
37–50 23
37:2 143
41:57 38
48:4 50
48:7 108
49:8–12 55
49:10 249
50:24 74

Exodus

1:7 . . . . 23, 27
1:15–21 . . . . 318, 338
2. 338
2:2–9 336
2:16–22 338
2:24 54
3:1–5 259
3:7, 9 28
3:15–16 54
4:22 173
4:24–26 338
5:1 21
5:2 19
6:2–8 54
6:6 36
6:7 . . . . 46, 82
8:22 . . . . 23, 27, 38
9:14 . . . . 23, 27, 38
9:16 . . . . 23, 27, 38
9:29 27
11:5 28
11:6 28
12. 23
12:29 28
13:11–15 36
13:17 33
14:31 143
15. . . . . 23, 336
15:1–2 20
15:1–19 452–53
15:3 33
15:11 19
15:13 36
15:18 . . . . 19, 23
15:30 28
17:30 28
18:8–12 23
18:13–27 198
19. 223
19:1–4 25
19:3–6 60
19:4–6 . . . . 23, 46, 52
19:5 . . . . 27, 267
19:5–6 38
19:6 . . . . 82, 199, 240
20 . . . . 23, 223
20:1–17 64–65
20:2 66
20:2–3 72
20:3 . . . . 66, 252
20:4 25
20:4–6 . . . . 66, 72
20:7 . . . . 66, 72
20:8ff. 316
20:8–11 . . . . 66, 72
20:12 . . . . 66, 72, 77
20:13 . . . . 66, 73

20:14 . . . . 66, 73
20:15 . . . . 66, 73
20:16 . . . . 66, 73
20:17 . . . . 66, 73
21–23 63
21:7 316–17
21:28–32 63
22:16 175
23:14–17 64
24:1 198
24:3–8 60
24:8 57
25–32 287
28:41 124
29:45 46
33:12–17 296
34:6–7 . . . . 27, 32
34:6–10 56
34:10 43
34:29–35 349

Leviticus

11. 171
11:45 46
15:19–31 358
19–26. . . . . 63, 66
19:18 32
20:7–8 66
22:33 46
25:23 . . . . 74, 255
25:25–34 36
25:38 46
25:48–52 36
26 258
26:3–12 82
26:6–13 296
26:12 46
26:45 46

Numbers

10:9 33
11:16–17 198
12. 337
12:6 258
14:8 32
14:17–20 56
14:28–30 75
14:45 33
20:18 33
21:1, 23, 33 33
24:17–19 . . . . 243, 249
25:12 46
27:1–11 318
27:8 316
30 317
31:4–7 33

Deuteronomy

1:1–6 47
1:7—4:49. 47
4:6 38
4:20 46
4:21 75
4:25–27 74–75
4:31 32
5–11 . . . . 47, 71
5:1–21 64
5:2–3 61
5:6 66
5:7 66
5:8–10 66
5:11 66
5:12–15 66
5:16 66
5:17 66
5:18 66
5:19 66
5:20 66
5:21 . . . . 65, 66
5:33 173
6:4 176
7:1–6 32
7:6 . . . . 46, 82
7:6–8 52
7:7 32
7:12 46
7:25 32
8:18 61
8:19–20 33
9:4–6 33
9:5 46
9:7 32
10:14 . . . . 52, 74
10:15 52
10:16 . . . . 56, 82
10:17–18 66–67
10:19 67
10:22 50
11:18 56
12–26 63
12:1–31 71
12:10 76
13:1–14:27 71
14:2 46
14:28–16:17 71
16:11, 14 67
16:18–18:22. 71
18:15 . . . . 110, 176, 243
18:18, 19 243
19:1–22:8. 71
21:22–23 172
22:9–23:18. 71
23:1 56
23:1–7 53
23:3 56

23:19–24:7 71
24:8–25:4 71
24:18–22 38
24:19–21 67
25:5ff. 316
25:5–16 71
26:5 102
26:17–19 46
27–28. 47
27:9 46
27:19 67
28 258
28:1–14 . . . . 56, 61
28:9 46
28:15–68 61
29:1 61
29:12–13 . . . . 46, 54
30:6 . . . . 56, 82
30:14 56
30:19 47
32. 47
32:1 47
32:18 20
32:39 416
34:5 143

Joshua

1:4 192
2:9–11 51
6. 31
6:20–21 17
8. 17, 31
8:33 199
9. 48
11. 31
19:15 108
21:43–44 76
21:43–45 240
24. 47
24:12 31
24:24–27 61
24:29 143

Judges

5:31 33
9:1–6 393
9:1–21 392–93
9:2 393
9:4 394
9:9 398
9:11 398
9:13 398
9:19–21 397
9:46–49 397
9:50–57 397
9:55–57 397
13:20 317

Ruth

1:16–17 340
4:17 341

1 Samuel

1–4 317
1:5 316
1:5ff. 316
2:10 124
12:3 124
12:22 46
15:28 192
17:12 108
17:33 143
18:1–4 47
24:20 . . . . 192, 199
25. 339
25:18 398
25:23–35 339
25:24 339
26:3 124
26:19 236

2 Samuel

5:3 124
7. . . . . 54, 59, 223
7:5, 8 . . . . 144, 160
7:8–16 54
7:13 243
7:13–16 61
7:16 . . . . 124, 243
7:24 46
7:26 124
7:29 . . . . 124, 243
12:1–7 259
14–16. 61
19:21–22 124
22:51 124
23:1 124
23:5 59

1 Kings

4:21 240
5:13–16 383
8:23 43
8:39–43 53
8:46–50 174
9:10–22 383
11:9–13 387
11:29, 30 259
11:31–36 387
12. . . . . 381, 387
12:1–18 382
12:14 384
12:16 390
12:18 388

15:19 48
17–2 Kgs 2. 254
19:16 124
19:17ff. 82
19:18 196
21 . . . . 254, 256, 257
21:2 255
21:7 255
21:17–29 256
21:27–29 258
22 258

2 Kings

4:22ff. 316
5. 51
10:10 144
11:17 . . . . 46, 61
13:14 259
23:3 61

1 Chronicles

16:22 124

2 Chronicles

6:42 124
7:14 258
13:7 387
36:1–20 264

Ezra

2:65 317

Nehemiah

8:1–8 120
8:1–12 61
9:7–8 240–41
9:36 76

Job

1:8 144
2:3 144
5:20 37
6:23 37
11:7–9 219
17:15, 16. 288
23:3 219
31:1 175
33:6 22
38:33 25
42:7–8 144

Psalms

2. 173
2:2 124

2:5 30
2:7 124
2:12 30
3:7 31
8. 25
8:3–6 134
8:5 26
8:6 25
19. 25
19:7–10 175
19:14 37
24. 33
24:1 . . . . 25, 255, 266
24:2 25
24:8 30
25:22 37
26:1 28
26:11 37
27:16–20 26
31:5 37
33. 20
33:5 22
33:12 46
33:28 37
37:11 76
44:26 37
46 33
49:7–8, 15 37
51:10 . . . . 22, 295
56:7 30
69:19 37
72. . . . . 33, 61
73. 271
73:23–26 26
76:9 28
78:35 37
79:5–7 30
80:8 199
81:11–12 30
82:8 28
86:5 32
89. 33
89:3 59
89:3–4 54
89:11 25
89:28–36 61
90:2 20
93:1 20
94:2 28
95. 25
95:5 25
95:7 46
100:3 46
102:18 22
103:4 37
103:14 22
104. . . . . 20, 25, 33
104:9 25
104:15 25

104:24 25
104:27–30 17
104:30 20
105:6 173
105:15 124
105:42 143
105:42–45 241
107:2 37
108:4 32
110:1 109
110:4 185
110:5 30
118:22 130
119:14–16 68
119:35, 44–48, 97–105 68
119:134 37
132:10 124
137. 266
137:1–4 266
137:4 236
137:9 31
139:19–22 238
145:8–9 32
145:9 22
148:4 25

Proverbs

3:19–20 25
6:23 194
8:23–30 245
16:4 20
23:11 37

Isaiah

1:1 259
1:9 196
1:19–20 53
1:24, 25 34
2. 39
2:1 259
2:1–5 51
2:2–4 128
2:2–5, 25–27, 40–66. 223
4:19 21
5:1–7 259
6:13 197
7:14 . . . . 175, 285
7:14–16 260
8:23–9:6 61
9:1–2 102
9:2–7 128
9:6 . . . . 34, 245, 260
9:6–7 . . . . 125, 244, 249
9:7 244
10:5 28
10:5–14 34
10:12 30
10:22 . . . . 56, 196

10:23 56
11. 39
11:1 55
11:1–5 125
11:1–9 . . . . 61, 245
11:1–10 125
11:6–8 261
11:11 56
11:13 292
11:21 244
12. 39
13–23 30
13:5 28
13:6–8 128
13:20–21 260–61
17:7 22
19. 39
20:3 . . . . 144, 149
24:14–23 128
25. 30
26:2 274
27:1 34
27:11 22
28:16 230
32:15–18 277
34:2 30
34:4 . . . . 247, 282
37:4 274
37:31 56
38:6 21
40–55 . . . . 24, 26, 38, 39, 144,
                     154, 155, 156, 160
40:1 39
40:2 154
40:12, 22, 26 25
40:27 38
40:27–31 25
40:28 . . . . 25, 39
40:29–31 . . . . 24, 39
41:8–13 . . . . 144–45, 155
41:10, 13–14 24
41:14 24
41:20 . . . . 21, 22
41:21–29 23
42–53 172
42:1 . . . . 39, 143, 159
42:1–3 160
42:1–4 . . . . 146, 409
42:1–6 . . . . 145, 408
42:1–7 . . . . 151, 154, 155
42:4 . . . . 39, 409, 410
42:5 39
42:9 21
42:13 31
42:14 . . . . 21, 24, 39
42:18–19 24
42:18–24 . . . . 146, 155
42:24–25 154
42:19 142

43:1 . . . . 20, 24, 26
43:3 39
43:4 . . . . 24, 39
43:5 24
43:7 . . . . 24, 39
43:10 173
43:10–12 . . . . 147, 155
43:10–13 23
43:11 173
43:15 24
43:18 24
43:18–19 39
43:20 . . . . 173, 199
43:21 24
43:22–44:3 . . . . 148, 155
43:24–25 39
43:24–28 154
43:28 30
44:1 . . . . 24, 143, 159
44:1–2 24
44:2 24
44:2–3 39
44:6 17
44:6–8 23
44:8 24
44:21 . . . . 39, 143, 159
44:21–23 . . . . 148, 155
44:22 154
44:22–28 25
44:24–28 . . . . 149, 155
45:1–4 . . . . 149–50, 155
45:4 173
45:5 39
45:5–6 23
45:9 . . . . 22, 24
45:11 24
45:11–12 25
45:11–17 25
45:14 . . . . 23, 31
45:18 26
45:18–21 23
45:22–23 . . . . 31, 39
46:3–4 . . . . 24, 39
46:9 23
46:22 173
47:6 30
47:8–10 23
48:16 39
48:20 . . . . 150, 155
49. 199
49:1–6 . . . . 39, 408
49:1–7 . .146, 150–51, 152, 154, 155
49:3 . . . . 143, 408
49:5 . . . . 24, 143, 409
49:6 . . . . .39, 51, 143, 159, 160, 263
49:7 157
49:13 39
49:14 38
49:14–15 24

49:19–21 . . . . 21, 24, 39
50:1 154
50:1–3 25
50:4 410
50:4–9 . . . . 146, 151, 408
50:4–10 . . . . 152, 155
50:6 . . . . .152, 157, 413
50:7 410
51:2 50
51:3 39
51:5–6, 8 39
51:9–11 26
51:12–16 25
51:13 . . . . 20, 24
51:16 24
52:9 39
52:10 39
52:12–12 128
52:13 . . . . 143, 159
52:13–53:12 . . . . .146, 151, 152,
                   153–54, 155, 245, 408
52:15 147
53. . . . . 129, 147, 156, 158, 160,
           172, 199, 220, 409, 410
53:3 157
53:4 160
53:4–5 . . . . 154, 155, 414
53:4–6 409
53:5 . . . . 158, 160
53:5–6 39
53:6 . . . . 158, 160
53:7–12 414
53:8 . . . . .39, 147, 157, 158
53:9 . . . . 154, 160, 409
53:11 . . . . 158, 159
53:11–12 39
53:12 . . . . .157, 158, 160, 414
54 . . . . 220, 295
54:2–3 295
54:4 24
54:4–10 25
54:5 25
54:5–10 39
54:6 24
54:8 24
54:9–10 . . . . 39, 56
54:10 . . . . 46, 57
54:11 39
55–66 24
55:3–5 . . . . 56, 156
55:8–9 219
56–66 38
56:1–8 . . . . 24, 39
56:3–7 51
56:3–8 . . . . 31, 56
57:16 22
57:18 39
59:20–21 83
59:21 56

60:10–16 . . . . 24, 39
61:1–3 . . . . .224, 229
61:21 39
63:16 173
64:6–7 30
64:8 . . . . 22, 173
65–66 39
65:17 . . . . 24, 39, 277
65:18 22
66:6–13 . . . . 24, 39
66:13 39
66:18–19 31
66:18–20 24
66:18–22 39
66:22 . . . . 24, 39, 277
66:23 31

Jeremiah

1:5, 10 31
1:11, 12 259
1:24–27 61
3:17 31
5:12–17 28
5:24 25
6:13–15 28
6:19 29
7:4–11 236–37
7:23 46
10:25 30
11:4 46
11:11, 23 29
12:14–16 31
13:11 46
13:14 29
16:14–16 39
16:19–21 31
18. 259
18:1–6 22
18:7–10 . . . . 31, 257–58
18:8, 11 29
21:7 29
23:5 244
23:5–6 61
23:25 258
24:1–8 237
24:5 237
24:7 46
25:9 28
25:31 31
27:5–6 28
27:6 28
27:8 28
29:5–7 266
29:21 30
30:8–9 61
30:9 244
30:22 46
31:1 46

31:22 21
31:31 55
31:31–34 . . . . . . .58, 223, 231, 241,
249, 252, 285
31:33 56
31:34 . . . . 56, 57, 83
31:34–37 177
31:35–36 25
31:35–37 39
32:7–8 36
32:27 31
32:40 56
32:38 46
33:14–26 61
33:20 59
38:16 416
43:10 28
45:5 31
46–51 30
46:8, 15, 17, 25 30
48:26, 29, 30, 35, 42 30
50:5 56
50:24–27 30
50:25 . . . . 28, 30
50:29 30
50:31–32 30
50:44 28
51:6, 11, 25, 26, 56 30
51:45 30

Lamentations

4:20 130

Ezekiel

1. 237
2:1 134
3:22–23 287
3:26 56
4. 291
4:1–3 259
5. 291
7:27 29
10:1–22 22
10:15 237
11. 263
11:3 264
11:1–13 263
11:6 22
11:13 267
11:14–21 262–63
11:16 . . . . 264, 266
11:17–20 267
11:18 268
11:19 . . . . 56, 231, 265, 268
11:20 . . . . 46, 56
11:21 . . . . 264, 268
11:22 237
11:22–25 263
14:11 46

16. 259
16:44–45 102
16:63 56
17:12–19 47
20:33–44 249
22 22
22:31 30
23. 259
24:1 269
25:14, 17 30
29–32 269
29:1, 2 270
29:1–16 268
29:3–9 270
29:10–16 270
29:16–32 269
29:12 270
34:11–31 292
34:24 46
34:24–25 57
34:25–31 56
36:1–7 30
36:22–30 292
36:23 296
36:24–28 267
36:25–26 294
36:26 231
36:26–28 . . . . 56, 223
36:28 46
36:36 296
37. . . . . 287, 291
37:1 . . . . 287, 288
37:1–14 . . . . 199, 286–87
37:2 288
37:3 289
37:4–8 289
37:9, 10 289
37:11 291
37:12–14 56
37:15–20 292
37:15–28 . . . . 287, 290–91
37:21–22 293
37:21–23 292
37:21–28 292
37:23 46
37:23–24 294
37:24–25 293
37:24–27 292
37:24–28 244
37:25–27 295
37:26 57
37:27 46
37:28 . . . . 292, 296
40–48 293
47:21–23 75

Daniel

2. . . . . 247, 280, 282
4:17 272
7. . . . . 135, 140, 247, 280

7:13 . . . . 135, 139, 224
7:13–14 . . . . . . 130, 134–35, 136,
140, 199, 220, 224,
245, 401
7:14 135
7:15–27 220
7:18–27 224
7:26–27 135
7:27 . . . . 197, 199
8. . . . . 247, 280
8:9–11 . . . . 247, 280, 282
8:17 245
8:19 280
8:23–25 . . . . 247, 280
9:24–27 280
9:25 124
11. . . . . 247, 280
11:5 280
11:21–45 . . . . 247, 280, 282
11:31 . . . . 247, 282
11:36–12:4. 280
12:1–3 . . . . 261, 280
12:7 280
12:11–12 280

Hosea

1. 259
1:9 46
1:10 50
1:10–11 56
1:11 292
2. 259
2:14–23 56
2:16 199
2:18 59
3:4–5 125
4:1–3 75
8:7 29
9:1–3 75
10:13 29
11:1 285
11:4, 9 32
12:1 48

Joel

2:13 32
2:28–29 253
2:31 . . . . 247, 282
3:9–10 35
3:18 292
3:18–20 260

Amos

1. 30
1–2. 30
1:1 259
3:2 28

3:7 144
4:12 259
5:21–24 84
7:1, 7 259
8:1 259
8:1–3 259
9:6 20
9:7 . . . . 22, 32, 223
9:7–8 31
9:11 61
9:11–12 263

Jonah

1:3 22
1:9 22
3. 258
3:10 223
4. 259
4:2 . . . . 28, 223
4:10–11 223

Micah

1:1 259
4:1–5 51
4:3–4 34–35
4:3–5 253
5:2 . . . . 108, 244
5:2–5 61
5:4–5 125
6:4 . . . . 317, 337

Habakkuk

1:2, 3 271
1:13 271
2:1–4 271
2:4 271

Zephaniah

3:17 31

Haggai

1. 258
1:12, 14 56

Zechariah

1:4–6 257
1:14–15 30
2:10–13 51
2:11 46
8–14. 75
8:8 46
8:11, 12 56
8:21–23 53
8:22, 23 31

9:9 . . . . 165, 259–60
9:9–10 . . . . 125–26, 129
9:13 259
11:7–14 292
11:10, 14 292

Malachi

1:2–4 82
1:11 223
2:16 317
3:17 56
4:5 128

Matthew

1. . . . . 109, 113, 355
1:1 . . . . 100, 198
1:1–17 51
1:5 . . . . 209, 341
1:6 100
1:17 . . . . 57, 100
1:21 123
1:23 285
2. 198
2:1 170
2:2 113
2:15 285
2:16 396
3. 198
3:8–9 50
3:9 240
3:17 131
4. 198
4:12–17 102
5. . . . . . . 180, 181, 182, 183, 198
5–7 354
5:5 76
5:17 . . . . 182, 191, 224, 241
5:17–20 . . . . 121, 179
5:20 . . . . 169, 181, 224
5:21 169
5:21–48 . . . . 121, 171
5:22 180
5:23, 24 58
5:27 . . . . 169, 180
5:27–28 355
5:31 169
5:32 180
5:33 169
5:34 180
5:37 180
5:38 169
5:38–39 181
5:43 169
5:44 32
5:44–45 181
6:1–7:5 122
6:9–13 . . . . 122, 229
8:10 173

8:16–17 160
8:29 131
9:11 224
9:16–17 182
10. 198
10:6 197
10:40–41 224
11:11 229
11:19 421
11:25 224
11:25–30 220
11:27 . . . . 130, 131
12:1–14 121
12:14–21 409
12:15–21 160
12:17–21 146
12:22–24 109
12:28 229
12:48–50 356
13:1–52 229
13:33 357
13:57–58 465
15:1–20 122
15:21–28 359
16:13–16 137
16:14 128
16:15–17 365–66
16:16 . . . . . 129, 131, 133, 173, 466
16:17 . . . . 129, 130
16:18 224
16:21 138
17:5 131
17:22–32 138
18. 122
19:1–12 122
19:3–9 180
19:28 . . . . 140, 198
20:17–19 138
20:26 402
20:28 . . . . 401, 414
21:10 165
21:33–43 199
21:39–41 179
21:41 178
21:43 . . . . 169, 178, 224, 230
22:7 179
22:34–39 122
22:41–46 114
22:46 115
23. 171
23:3 181
23:37 281
23:37–38 246–47
23:38 178
24. . . . . 246, 247, 250, 273,
281, 282
24:1–2 247
24:2 281
24:15 247

24:15–16 281
24:29–31 139
24:34 282
24:42 224
25. . . . . 122, 459
25:1–13 357
25:31 . . . . 136, 248
25:31–33 139
25:31–41 459–60
26:28 . . . . 57, 158
26:29 131
26:39 131
26:42 131
26:50 412
26:53 412
26:63 172
27:18 181
27:51 195
27:63 183
28:11–13 167
28:19 178

Mark

1:11 131
1:14–15 227
1:15 . . . . 199, 224
1:16 163
1:21 162
1:29–34 162
1:30–31 357
1:39 162
1:41 420
1:45 162
2:1 162
2:7 . . . . 137, 170
2:10 137
2:16 170
2:21–22 184
2:22 164
2:24 171
2:27–28 137
3:1–6 . . . . 162, 171
3:7 163
3:11, 15 171
3:19 162
3:22 171
3:28 134
3:30 171
3:31–35 356
4. 229
4:1 163
4:35–6:6 359
4:40 466
5:21 163
5:25–26 357
5:27–29 357
5:30–31 359
5:39 163

6:1–6 163
6:3 163
6:5–6 465
6:7 171
6:56 163
7:1 163
7:2 171
7:2–3 163
7:6–9 163
7:14–15 164
7:15, 18–19 171
7:19 . . . . 137, 164
7:24–30 359
8:11–12 164
8:15 164
8:27–29 137
8:29 . . . . 123, 129, 466
8:30–31 137
8:31 . . . . 138, 164
8:38 . . . . 131, 137, 139, 141
9:1 246
9:1–12 137–38
9:12 156
9:30 164
9:30–31 138
9:31 164
9:41 224
10:1–12 164
10:2–9 171
10:9 164
10:32–34 138
10:33–34 164
10:35–40 415
10:41–45 418
10:42–45 158
10:45 . . . . 194, 401, 414, 415,
                                418, 419, 420
10:45a 415
10:45b 415
11:7–10 165
11:12–14 165
11:13 165
11:15–18 166
11:18 . . . . 166, 172
11:28–33 166
12:2–8 166
12:8 179
12:9 . . . . 178, 179
12:35–37 114
12:37 . . . . 109, 115
12:38–40 357
12:42–44 357
13. . . . . 250, 273, 282–83
13:7–27 260
13:24–27 139
14:11 167
14:18, 21 167
14:24 . . . . 57, 158, 415
14:36 . . . . 130, 131

14:53 129
14:61 173
14:61–62 . . . . . . 123, 130, 140, 169
14:62 224
14:64 130
15:10 181
15:26 167
15:37–39 195
15:38 195
15:39 131
16:15 53

Luke

1–3. 188
1:32–33 114
1:46 367
1:46–55 454
1:55 50
1:69 126
1:71 126
2:1–7 170
2:4 114
2:11 126
2:21 119
2:21–23 114
2:26 126
2:29–32 114
2:30–32 191
2:40. 120
2:46–47 . . . . 120, 162
2:49 130
3. . . . . 109, 113
3:22 131
3:31 100
4:1–13 229
4:14–30 229
4:16 170
4:16–21 . . . . 120, 121, 224
7:1–10 143
7:2 159
8:19–21 356
8:25 466
9:20 129
9:21 137
9:22 . . . . 137, 138
9:35 . . . . 128, 131
9:44 138
10. . . . . 122, 266, 364–65
10:1 198
10:1–24 224
10:21 224
10:22 . . . . 130, 131
10:38–42 364
11:2–4 229
11:20 224
11:25–27 224
11:27, 28 356
12. 122

12:8 141
12:32 . . . . 183, 224, 273
12:42–43 143
13:10–17 171
13:29 230
13:35 178
14. 122
14:24 179
15. 122
15:2 421
16:16 229
17:7–10 142–43
18. 122
18:31–33 . . . . 138, 157
19:44 165
20:35–36 132
20:41 100
20:41–44 114
20:47 357
21:4 357
21:25–27 139
22 415
22:20 57
22:24–27 . . . . 402, 415
22:24–30 401
22:26 416
22:27 . . . . 158, 401
22:37 157
23:34 413
23:45 195
23:46 131
24:21 130
24:22–27 402
24:44 . . . . 123, 180
24:49 131

John

1. 368
1:1 132
1:11–12 115
1:14 . . . . 132, 195, 293
1:14–18 . . . . 194, 220
1:18 132
1:20 128
1:29 194
1:34, 36 129
1:40 129
1:41 . . . . 124, 129
1:49 131
2. 107
2:1–11 . . . . 108, 367
2:16 . . . . 131, 172
2:21 107
3:3–5 228
3:16, 17 404
4. . . . . 362, 363
4:9 115
4:10 196

4:20–24 196
4:22 115
4:22–26 115
4:34 404
4:42 196
5:16–17 133
5:18 . . . . 133, 173
5:23–24 404
5:26–29 140
5:27 136
5:39 . . . . 115, 121
6:15 129
6:37–40 404
6:41–42 115
6:51, 63 193
7:12 183
7:16–18 404
7:40–52 170
8:2–11 356
8:12 194
8:16–18 404
8:26–28 193
8:30–31 109
8:31–36 69
8:33 50
8:36 131
8:41 173
8:44 109
8:48 109
9:4 404
9:35 142
10:10 290
10:16 208
10:36 404
11. 364
11:21–22 365
11:42 404
11:45–50 169
12:7 366
12:20–24 173
12:44–45 404
12:49–50 193
13:12–15 402
13:20 404
13:34 193
14:3 224
14:6 . . . . 194, 463
14:10 352
14:13 131
14:18 246
14:24 . . . . 193, 404
15:1–2 199
15:21 404
16:2 204
16:5 404
17:1 . . . . 131, 132
17:3 404
17:5 131
17:20–21 293

17:21 . . . . 131, 296
17:21–25 404
17:23 296
17:24 131
18:22 412
18:23 413
18:36 . . . . 129, 228
19. 368
19:20 121
20:17 131
20:21 404

Acts

1:3 192
1:6 192
1:6–7 129
1:14 368
2:17 369
2:23 178
2:24–36 116
2:36 123
2:39 173
2:47 295
3:1 181
3:13 . . . . 116, 143
3:13–14 159
3:13–15, 17 178
3:13–26 409–10
3:22 116
3:25 116
3:25–26 . . . . 50, 159, 173
3:26 . . . . 116, 143
4:1–3 167
4:7 167
4:8–10 178
4:11 167
4:12 173
4:18 168
4:24–30 159
4:25 143
4:27 143
4:27–30 410
4:30 143
5:12 181
5:17–18 168
5:17–40 168
5:30 178
5:38, 39 169
6:11–14 184
6:15 178
7:1 178
7:5–6 50
7:52 178
7:54–8:1 168
7:56 . . . . 134, 140
7:58–8:1. 344
8:1–3 168
8:26–39. 409

8:27 173
8:32–35 160
8:34 155
9. 344
9:1–2 168
9:3–5 168
9:13 197
9:20–22 133
10:38 124
10:43 123
12:1–10 168
13:14 238
13:22–23 116
13:32–33 132
13:44–46 187
13:46–47 263
13:47 . . . . 151, 160
14:1 238
15:14–17 263
15:17 174
17. 205
17:1 238
18:5 130
18:26 346
20:32 77
21:20–26 182
21:27–32 . . . . 168, 174
21:40 121
22:2 121
22:17 182
22:22 174

Romans

1:3 55
1:3–4 . . . . 116, 118, 132
1:17 92
2:6–11 231
2:28–29 230
3:9 231
3:20, 28 .92
3:29–30 231
4. 230
4:13 77
4:13–18 .50
5:2 232
5:8 66
5:12–21 226
5:14 226
7:12 191
8:14 459
8:15 130
8:16, 19 459
8:21 . . . . .232, 342–43, 459
8:24 343
8:27 197
8:28 272
9. 82
9–11. . . . . 81, 83, 196, 201, 202, 232
9:3 187

9:3–5 . . . . 116, 209
9:5 208
9:6 . . . . 50, 82
9:6–8 . . . . 82, 234
9:7–9 82
9:8 459
9:10–13 . . . . 82, 232
9:14–21 232
9:22–25 232
9:23–24 197
9:25–26 . . . . 231, 232
9:26 459
9:26–29 .82
9:27 196
9:27–29 232
9:29 196
9:30–31 .81
9:30–10:21 232
9:33 231
10. 82
10:2 241
10:4 . . . . 193, 201
10:12–13 234
11. . . . . 82, 94
11:1 . . . . 50, 232
11:1–2 81
11:1–14 232
11:4 196
11:12 81
11:14–24 233
11:16–24 . . . . 82, 192
11:18, 21 81
11:18–22 82
11:23 82
11:25 81
11:25–32 233
11:26a 83
11:26b 83
11:27 83
11:28–29 . . . . 189, 202
11:28–34 81
11:30–31 81
11:33–36 233
13:1–8 226
13:11–14 226
13:12 225
14:17 . . . . 199, 229
15:8–12 117
16. 347
16:1, 2 346
16:6 347
16:12 347

1 Corinthians

2:8 140
7. 353
7:14 352
7:34 353
9:6 77

10:1–2 198
10:1–11 227
11. 347
11:1 350
11:2 193
11:2–16 351
11:3 . . . . 347, 350
11:4–5 347
11:7 348
11:7–9 351
11:10 349
11:10–12 351
11:11–12 348
11:23–25 57
11:25 . . . . 57, 231
12:7 461
13:10 202
14:33 . . . . 197, 346
14:34–35 . . . . 345, 346
15:22 353
15:45–50 226

2 Corinthians

3:1:1 197
2–3 58
3. 210
3:3 58
3:6 . . . . 57, 58
3:7–8 232
3:14–15 .58
5:12 . . . . 117, 209
5:14 117
5:14–21 194
5:14–15 210
5:15 117
5:15–17 117
5:16 117
5:16–17 210
5:17 . . . . 118, 343
5:19 220
6:8 183
6:16 231
10:3–4 246
11:2 78
11:5 117
11:18–23 117
11:22 50
13:8 90

Galatians

1:8 353
1:9 187
1:13 168
2:14 187
2:16 187
2:21 187
3:7 50
3:8 53

3:9 . . . . 51, 53
3:13 172
3:14 . . . . 51, 53
3:14–16 118
3:16 . . . . 50, 77
3:17 231
3:19 226
3:19–22 187
3:23–29 250
3:24–25 187
3:26 459
3:26–28 190
3:26–29 50
3:27–28 208
3:27–29 234
3:28 . . . . 230, 241, 250, 351
3:29 . . . . 77, 230
4:6 130
4:21–31 61
5:6 187
5:15 92
5:21 77
6:2 352
6:9 289
6:10 226
6:15 187
6:15–16 210
6:16 . . . . 192, 199, 267

Ephesians

1:9–10 226
1:15 197
2:4–6 248
2:4–10 66
2:11–22 234
2:14 293
2:14–3:11 227
2:18–19 267
3:1–11 233
4:3 293
4:10 208
5:15–17 226
5:21 352
5:22 256
5:22–25 351
5:32 . . . . 193, 199
6:2–3 77
6:4 389

Philippians

1:6 87
2:1–5 294
2:6–8 417
2:8 161
2:13 87
2:17 415
3:2–3 230
3:3 210

3:4–8 206
4:2, 3 347
4:21 197

Colossians

1:4 197
1:13–18 350
1:20–22 194
2:14 371
3. 389
3:5–6 209
3:11 230
3:18–19 351
3:20 389
4. 389
4:1 389
4:5 226

1 Thessalonians

2:14–16 . . . . 81, 187
5:2 225
5:4 225
5:5–6 225

2 Thessalonians

1:7–8 136
2:3–12 260

1 Timothy

2:4–6 231
2:5 . . . . 194, 415
2:6 415
2:8 345
2:11 346
2:11–15 . . . . 344, 345
2:12 . . . . 300, 345, 346
2:13–14 226
2:13–15 352
3:3, 6 389
3:16 344
5. 345
5:10 197

2 Timothy

2:8 118
3:16–17 15

Titus

2:11–13 281

Hebrews

1. 222
1:1–2 193
1:1–3 220

1:4 221
2:5–9 134
2:6 134
2:16 110
2:16–17 118
2:17 . . . . 110, 194
3:1 194
3:3 185
3:5–6 185
4:14–15 194
5:5 194
5:6 185
5:10 194
6:20 . . . . 186, 194
7:11 185
7:12 . . . . 185, 194
7:14 . . . . 110, 118, 194
7:17 194
7:18 191
7:18–19 185
7:25 194
7:26 194
7:27–28 185
8. 182
8:1 194
8:4–5 186
8:5 186
8:8 57
8:8–12 . . . . 58, 285
8:13 . . . . 57, 92, 185, 186
9:8 186
9:10 186
9:11 186
9:12 194
9:14 174
9:15 57
9:20 57
9:22 174
9:23–24 186
9:26 194
9:28 174
10:1 185
10:10 . . . . 185, 194
10:11–23 234
11:13–16 249
11:18 50
11:39–40 192
12:1–3 192
12:22 78
12:24 57
12:25–29 234
12:28 234
13:10 . . . . 92, 186, 200
13:12 179
13:24 197

James

2:8, 12–13 69

1 Peter

1:4 77
1:4–5 249
2:7 130
2:9 . . . . 194, 199, 240, 267
2:10 267
2:21–24 160
2:21–25 410
5:1–3 389

2 Peter

1:4 459
3:13 78

1 John

1:1–4 249
1:5–7 460
2:1 194
3:10 266
3:17 266
5:5 133
5:18 133

2 John

3. 133

Revelation

1. . . . . .286c
1:1 . . . . 250, 273, 284, 285

1:2 284
1:3 284
1:4 276
1:5–6 371
1:6 . . . . 194, 199
1:9 276
1:12–18 141
1:13 134
1:14 136
2–3 . . . . .286c
2:5 284
2:9 186
2:11 248
2:16, 21, 22 284
3:3 284
3:12 78
3:19 284
4. 273
4–8 . . . . .286c
4–22 250
4:1 284
4:9–11 .294
5:5 . . . . 115, 246
5:8 197
5:9–10 194–95
7:1 281
7:1–8 116
7:9 53
8–11. . . . . .286c
11:8 186
12–14. .286c
12:1–5 .115

12:3–5 .243
12:11 284
13:9, 10 284
14:1–6 .116
14:13 284
14:14 134
15–16. .286c
16:15 284
17–19. .286c
17:3 284
19:9 284
19:15 246
20–22 .286c
20:6. 284
21:1 78
21:1–5 88
21:2 . . . . 78, 191, 193
21:9 . . . . 78, 193
21:9–14 192
21:10 284
21:22 . . . . 193, 196
21:24 78
22:7 284
22:8 . . . . 276, 284
22:10 284
22:16 115
22:17 78
22:18 284
22:19 284

SUBJECT INDEX

Aaron (priest), 19, 23, 33, 38, 109, 118, 185, 186, 317, 337–38, 379, 398
"abba," 120, 130, 131
Abdel Fattah, Seif, 441
Abduh, Muhammad, 308–9, 450
Abigail (wife of Nabal), 316, 339
Abimelech (Philistine king), 47
Abimelech (son of Jerubbaal, or Gideon), 392–95, 397–400, 405, 422
"abomination that causes desolation," 247, 281–82
Abraham, 18–19, 21, 27, 33, 38, 44, 47, 49–56, 58–61, 69, 74, 76, 77–79, 81, 82, 88, 95, 101–2, 104, 110, 111, 113, 115, 116, 118, 143–45, 159, 173, 178, 183, 187, 189, 196–98, 202, 208, 219, 222–23, 226, 230, 231, 240–41, 250, 278, 340, 454, 455
Abrahamic covenant ("covenant with Abraham" in text), 47, 49–54, 55, 58, 59–60, 61, 74, 219, 222–23, 231, 240, 241, 455
    elements of the, 49
    the promises of the, 50–54
Adam, 22, 26, 35, 37, 48, 78, 101, 111, 118, 134, 164, 196, 208, 226, 245, 275, 289, 329–30, 332–36, 344, 352–53
Adar, Zvi, 400
Adbo, Walid, 312
Adonis (god), 103, 109, 111
Afghani, Jamal al-(Jamāl al-Dīn al-Afghānī), 308, 426n1, 450
Afghanistan, 446
Ahab (king), 196, 254–56, 258
Aisha (wife of Muhammad), 305–6
Åkerlund, Truls, 404
Akiva, Rabbi, 416–17
al-Ani, Samy, 313
Alaqrai, Omar, 304, 305
A'la-Maududi, Abul, 450
Al-Aqsa Mosque, 213, 293
al-Banna, Hassan, 310, 450
Al-Bitar, Nadim, 441
al-Bustani, Karam, 313
al-Din, Nazira Zain, 315
Alexander, Monique, 319
Alexander Aristopoulus, 396
Alexander the Great, 121, 235, 241, 247, 280, 282
Alexandria, 237–38, 323, 436
al-Fiqi, Mustafa, 434–35
Algeria, 31
Al-Ghazali (imam), 434
al-Hajj, Kamal Youssef (philosopher), 103–4, 105
Al-Jabri, Mohammed, 433–36
Al-Majd, Abu, 432

Al-Maskini, Fathi, 376–77, 384
al-Masri, Sanaa, 310
Almojel, Suad Fahd, 376
al-Qaradawi, Yusuf, 432, 434
Al-Qimni, Sayyed, 436
al-Sammak, Muhammad, 216
alternatives (presented by Christ), 462–63
al-Zumar, Abbud, 451
Amatius (Pseudo-Marius), 420
Anchor Bible Dictionary, 318, 319
ancient Near Eastern laws and the Old Testament, 62–64
angels, 110, 118, 132, 136, 137, 139, 141, 221, 229, 248, 276, 344, 349, 412, 459, 460
Anglican Church, 94, 322
Anna (prophetess), 128, 370
Annas (high priest; aka Hanan in text), 167, 379, 412
annihilation (of competitors), 395, 400
Antiochus Epiphanes, 241, 247, 260, 280, 281, 282
Antipater II, 396
anti-Semitism, 86, 91, 92, 95, 203, 204, 205
"apocalyptic," meaning of the word, 273
apocalyptic style: why it emerged, 273–75
apocalyptic texts (or, apocalyptic literature)
    in the Bible, 280–85
    why it is dangerous to interpret them literally, 251
    and eschatological thinking, 279
    features of, 276–77
    how to interpret, 275–76
    practical applications of, 286–96
    and prophecies, 278
    three reasons it is important to know something about, 273
Apocrypha, 128, 275
apokalypsis, 250, 273
apostle. *See individual apostles by name*
Arab Christians
    the challenge of identity and the clash of civilizations for, 443–46
    the cornerstone of the cultural framework for, 467
    the key features of the shared mentality of, 447–50
    and the Old Testament. *See chapter 1* (11–40)
    what Arab nationalism meant for, 432
Arab church, the position of women in the, 320–22
Arab defeat of 1967, 214, 291, 429
Arabic language, 428, 430, 436, 439, 450, 466
Arabism, 204, 424, 426–30, 432–36, 439–43, 446, 450, 456, 466–67
Arab-Israeli conflict, 84, 212. *See* Palestinian question
Arab League, 429
Arab nationalism
    the decline of, 430–32

four views concerning the development of, 428–30
the rise of, 426–30
the roots of, 426n1
Arab Spring, 376, 391
Aramaic language, 107, 120–21
Arameans, 31, 48, 101
Archytas (philosopher), 419
Arians, 97, 451
Ariarajah, S. Wesley, 353
Arias, Juan, 422
Aristotle, 326, 380
Armenia, 119, 426n2
Armenians, 466
A Rocha Lebanon, 48n11
ascension, 57, 65, 131, 208, 226
Asfour, Gaber, 386–87
Assyria, 223, 235, 241, 274
Assyrian Empire, 235
Assyrian exile, 74, 75, 223, 235, 241
Assyrian laws, 63
Assyrians, 33, 47, 48, 175, 235
Ateek, Naim, 86, 216
Athaliah (queen), 317
atheism, 72, 376, 377, 391, 421
atonement, 118, 174, 325, 409
Augustine, Saint, 36, 200, 326, 367
Augustus, 114, 396
Auschwitz, 204
autocracy, 387
awareness, 287–90
Azerbaijan, 426n2
Aziz, Faheem, 250–51, 273–74, 278, 283
Baal (god), 101, 102, 104, 105, 109, 196, 237, 339
Babylon, 25, 28, 29, 30, 51, 100, 107, 145, 150, 172, 197, 198, 223, 235, 237, 260–61, 263, 264, 266, 269, 280, 286, 288, 291
Babylonia, 436
Babylonian Empire, 120, 280
Babylonian exile, 24–25, 51, 55, 56–57, 61, 74, 75, 76, 100, 107, 120, 145, 147, 149, 150, 172, 174, 175, 197, 198, 219, 223, 235, 237, 238, 239, 240–41, 244, 263, 264, 265, 266, 269, 272, 274, 280, 288, 291, 293, 421
three phases of the, 264
Babylonians, 33, 150, 237, 269, 288
Bahrain, 313
Bakker, Jim, 215
baptism, 131, 166, 198, 198n119, 343
Bar Kokhba revolt, 92
Barr, James, 130
Barth, Karl, 80, 91, 92, 206
Barth, Markus, 80
Bathsheba (wife of Uriah), 51, 355
Baur, F. C., 184
Bebawi, George Habib, 446
Beelzebul, 171
Bell, Daniel (prof.), 213
Bendali, Costi, 406–7
Benedict (pope), 446
Berbers, 466

Berkovits, Eliezer, 88
Berlin Wall, 292
Bibawi, Nabil Luqa, 458
Bible
apocalyptic texts in the, 280–85
the Christian faith is rooted in the, 42
covenants in the. *See under* covenant/s
biblical theology, 42, 242, 324
big government, 255
Bihem, Adela, 315
Bird, Phyllis A., 318
bishops, the rise of, 370
book of Enoch, 127–28, 136, 275
book of Jubilees, 275
book of Revelation. *See* Revelation (book)
Bristow, John Temple, 301, 346, 348, 349, 350–51, 352
Bruce, F. F., 414
Brueggemann, Walter, 42, 62, 383
Buddha, 112
Burge, Gary M., 86
Bultmann, Rudolf, 12, 282
Cain, 38, 298
Caiaphas (high priest), 167, 379, 412
Calhoun, Craig, 427, 432
Calvin, John, 67, 75, 326
Calvinism, 91
Cambolo, Anthony, 375
Canaanite-Phoenicians, 103, 106
Canaanites, 32, 51, 101, 104, 106, 118, 241, 436n42
Cardman, Francine, 369
Carlyle, Thomas, 413
Carter, Brandon, 218
Case, Robert, 387
Catholic Church, 91, 95–96, 97, 184, 281, 422
Catholic World, 325
Ceausescu, Nicolai, 395
Central Conference for American Rabbis, 94
Chafer, L. S., 190
Chagall, Marc, 204
change, the value of, 462–63
Chapman, Colin, 79, 86
childbearing, 302, 326, 343, 344, 352–53
"Children's Crusade," 380–81
chosen people, 12, 16, 18, 28, 30, 33, 34, 39, 45, 53, 79, 80, 102, 173, 189, 199, 222, 223, 234–35, 240, 363, 456
Christ. *See* Jesus
Christian Coalition, 215
Christian East, 299
Christianity, 83, 85, 86, 90–98, 99, 103, 105–7, 112, 123, 130, 175n85, 176n89, 177, 179, 181, 184, 186, 188, 191, 192, 199, 200, 202–5, 207, 209, 222, 300, 302, 306, 344, 369, 380, 388, 390, 392, 416, 417, 439, 445, 449, 457, 459, 461–62, 465, 467. *See also* Zionist Christianity
as a Jewish denomination, 181–83
the relationship between Judaism and, 181–202
Christian woman, the. *See chapter 7* (297–373)
the reality of the Middle Eastern Christian woman, 298–300
Christian Zionism (or, Zionist Christianity), 85–86, 214, 216, 217, 242

Chrysostom, Dio, 418–19
Chrysostom, John, 346
church. *See also* Anglican Church; Roman Catholic Church; Presbyterian Church
    divisions, 292–93
    the early. *See* early church
    Middle Eastern church, 303, 304, 315, 324
    not all the West (or the East) is the, 203
    the position of women in the Arab, 320–22
    relationship between the society and the, 266–67
church fathers, 43, 73, 188, 190, 200, 301, 323
CIA, 445
citizenship
    the basis of dynamic, 458
    ideas for an Arab theology of, 457–61
City on a Mountain, A (217)
civilization, universal, 444
civil rights movement, 214
clash of civilizations, 213, 442, 443–46, 467
classical Dispensationalism, 67, 78–80
    the covenant in, 78–80
    the main tenets of, 80
Code of Hammurabi, 63, 64
Code of Ur-Nammu; Codex of Lipit-Ishtar, 63
codification, 436
Colson, Charles W., 315–16
Communism, 444, 445
Communists, 427
Confucius, 112
contemporary typological approach to interpretation, 254
context, 14–15
Convention on the Elimination of All Forms of Discrimination against Women, 298
Copeland, Kenneth, 215
Council of Jerusalem, 174
covenant/s
    in the Bible
        with Abraham. *See* Abrahamic covenant
        with David. *See* Davidic covenant
        new. *See* new covenant
        with Noah, 16, 21, 48–49, 56, 59
        at Sinai, 54, 60–61, 74
    a biblical and theological study of the, 45–62
    in classical Dispensationalism, 78–80
    common elements between the new covenant and other, 56
    definition of the word, 46
    differences between the new covenant and other, 56
    of grace, 43–44, 78, 80, 87
    "of grant," 47
    the importance of the concept of the, 43–45
    the land and the, 74–78
    and the law, 62–71
    "of law," 43–44
    and the Palestinian question, 71–84
    of redemption, 78
    in Reformed thinking, 78
    the Ten Commandments in the context of the, 65–66
    theological views on the relationship between the promised land and the, 78–83
    and treaties in the ancient Near East, 46–47

Covenant Code, 63
coveting, 65, 73n56
Cragg, Kenneth (bishop), 86, 300, 353, 430
Cranfield, C. E. B., 282–83
Crawley, Dale, 215
creation
    the divine presence in, 21–22
    Israel's identity and its relation to, 24–25
    as it relates to women, 328–33
    the language used to describe the act of, 20–21
    the relationship between the Creator and His, 21
crucifixion, 95, 111, 130, 165, 167, 169, 177, 181, 234, 379, 412, 419
Crusades, 380, 381, 445
cultural and social alienation, 448–49
culture. *See in general chapter 7, "Culture and Identity"* (423–68)
    meaning of the word, 425, 445
Cyrus the Persian (aka Cyrus the Babylonian), 149, 150, 223, 235, 237, 241, 267, 408
Da'esh (ISIS), 391
Dallas Seminary, 190
D'Angelo, Mary Rose, 360–61
Daniel, book of, 124, 134–35, 140, 141, 245, 280–81
Dar Al Thaqafa publishing house, 323
Darby, John, 190, 214, 279
David (king), 21, 44, 47, 53, 54–55, 58, 59–60, 61, 83, 99–100, 108, 109, 111, 113–15, 116, 118, 124–26, 129, 132, 134, 143–44, 155–56, 159–60, 165, 170, 176, 197, 205, 223, 235, 236, 243, 244, 263, 290–91, 293, 294, 295, 339, 341, 355, 360, 382, 383, 390, 421
Davidic covenant ("covenant with David" in text), 21, 54–55, 58, 59–60, 61, 223
    five main elements of the, 55
Daw, Botros, Father, 106–7
day of Pentecost, 116, 123, 167, 189–90, 199, 200, 301, 369
Dawn, Ernest, 428
dead, the, the difference between the living and, 288
Dead Sea Scrolls, 112
Deborah (judge), 316, 317, 339
Declaration of Sentiments and Resolutions (on women's rights), 327
De Haan, Richard, 215
"demographic hemorrhage" in the Middle East, 391
demons, 109, 131, 162, 171
Depree, Max, 403
despotism, 387
Deuteronomic Code, 63
devil, the, 109, 124, 228–29, 266, 271, 277, 278, 286, 326, 334, 336, 460
Devries, Simon J., 388
diaspora, 241
dictatorship, 384–90, 392, 398, 400, 411
Diotogenes (Pythagorean writer), 419
discernment, 206, 216
disciples
    strife among the, 401
    women, 369–71
discrimination
    against women, 298, 303, 313
    religious, 448

dispensationalism, 43, 67, 78–80, 81, 83, 188–90, 214, 218–19
  the main tenets of, 80n70
  seven dispensations through which God relates to humankind, 189
divine intervention, 447
divorce, 122, 164, 171, 180, 303, 305, 315, 316, 317, 319, 347
doctrine
  of the Trinity, 96, 103, 176–77, 329, 448
  should not be based on a single word or text in isolation, 246
Doomsday argument, 218
dowry, 305, 306, 317
dry bones, the vision of the, 286–88, 291
dualism, 227
Dutch Reformed school, 80
early church, 12, 122, 133, 146, 151, 155, 156, 159, 160, 167, 168, 170, 178–83, 187, 323, 369, 409, 424, 451, 457, 460, 461, 464, 465, 468
Eastern Christianity, 98, 203, 380. *See next*
Eastern Christians, 84–85, 98, 445
Ecumenical Decade of Churches in Solidarity with Women, 321–22
Edwards, Johnathan, 190
Eichrodt, Walter, 21
Egypt, 13, 19, 23, 25, 27, 31, 33, 36, 47, 50, 55, 60, 64, 65, 67, 72, 74, 75, 101, 102, 104, 186, 198, 215, 216, 219, 235, 240, 260, 268–70, 272, 280, 303, 304, 307, 310, 314, 315, 317, 320, 321, 323, 324, 337, 338, 381, 382, 383, 384n32, 388, 391, 394, 395, 398, 405, 429, 431, 435, 436, 447, 451
Egyptian church, 323
Egyptian Empire, 27
Egyptian Feminist Union, 310
Egyptian midwives, 338
Egyptians, 19, 27–28, 31, 242, 270, 338, 405, 436, 466
ekklēsia (church), 200
El (God/god), 18, 101, 104, 105
El-Bishry, Tarek, 430, 434
election (divine), 21, 81, 86, 189, 202
Elijah (prophet), 124, 128, 137, 138, 144, 229, 254, 255, 256, 258, 339
Elizabeth (mother of John the Baptist), 367, 370
Ellis, Marc, 87
El Saghiri, Kamir, 303
Esau, 82, 232, 455
el-Sayed, Kamal, 451
emigration, 119, 390–91
end of the world, 80, 212–14, 242, 252, 260, 277
End of the World, The (Leslie), 218
England, 93, 94, 327
Enlightenment, 437
Enuma Elish, 103
environment, the (nature), 48, 58, 218
Episcopal Church, 86
Epistle of Barnabas, 93, 200
equality, secular philosophies that affirm human, 97–98
eschatology
  the development of, 222–27
  meaning, 218

and the message of the prophets, 223
in the Old Testament, 222–23
and the teaching of Jesus, 224–25
in the thought of the apostle Paul, 225–27
two broad schools of thought concerning, 218–19
Essenes, 112
Esther (queen of Persia), 339, 341, 455
Ethiopian eunuch, 155, 160, 173n84, 409
Eucharist, 57. *See* Last Supper
European Reformation, 466. *See* Protestant Reformation
Evangelical Lutheran Church in America, 86
evangelicals, 45, 85, 214, 216, 217, 251, 267, 443, 466
evangelism, 45, 93, 94, 225
Eve, 22, 26, 37, 48, 101, 164, 300, 301, 326, 330–36, 344, 352–53, 367, 416
evil, the temporary prevailing of, 271
exile, 13, 176, 235, 378. *See* Assyrian exile; Babylonian exile
extermination, 91, 95, 204, 395
Ezekiel (prophet), 57, 75, 102, 134, 155, 237, 244, 250, 262, 264, 266, 267, 269, 273, 288, 289, 291–96, 408, 455
faith in Jesus, speaking about, 464
fake Muslims, 312
fall, the (of man), 78, 177, 226, 301, 326, 328, 331, 333–34, 345, 352, 353, 416
Falwell, Jerry, 215
Fares, Fayez, 213
Fattah, Abdel (imam), 375
Fee, Gordon, 275
Feminine Mystique, The (Friedan), 327
feminist theology, 325
Fertile Crescent, 98, 100, 101, 102, 120, 429n14
figs, prophecy of the, 237, 265
Finzel, Hans, 385
Fiorenza, Elizabeth Schüssler, 356–57, 358, 368, 369–70
First Zionist Congress (Basel, Switzerland), 214, 241
food (clean), 164, 171
Former Prophets, 254
foundation, the image of Judaism as a, 191–92
France, 91, 93, 217, 310, 380, 428, 445
France, R. T., 195
freedom of belief, 449
French Revolution, 97, 213, 413
Fretheim, Terence E., 21, 330
Friedan, Betty, 327
Fukuyama, Francis, 213
Gager, John, 80
Galilee of the nations, 102, 110
Garaudy, Roger, 217
Gellner, Ernest, 432
Gench, Frances Taylor, 358–60, 364–65
General Assembly of the Presbyterian Church in America, 216
genetic differences between peoples, 442
Gentiles, 51, 52, 61, 80, 82, 83, 95, 106, 113, 114, 116–17, 118, 124, 126, 138, 145, 146, 147, 151, 154–55, 156, 157, 158, 159, 160, 164, 168, 173–74, 178, 182, 187, 189–90, 197, 198, 201–2, 206, 207, 208–9, 210, 228, 230, 231,

232–33, 242, 263, 267, 401, 402, 409, 416, 417, 418, 457, 465
Georgia (nation), 426n2
Germany, 89, 91–92, 93, 95, 292, 426n2, 428
"ghettos," 93
Gideon (also, Jerubbaal in text), 392–93, 395, 397, 400
gifts of the Spirit, 299
Girls of Riyadh (al-Sanea), 303
globalization, 298, 426, 442, 446
God
    the Creator, 20–26
        and maker, 22–23
        in the prophetic books, 23–25
        in the Torah, 20–23
        in the Writings, 25–26
    and the gods, 18–20
    the kingdom of God, 227–30
    the Old Testament introduction to, 18
    the people of, 230–42
    the Redeemer, 35–39
        in the Prophets, 38–39
        in the Torah, 37–38
    the righteous Judge, 26–35
    self-description, 66–67
    sovereignty of, 16, 21, 25, 34, 160, 197, 272
    the Ten Commandments a gift of, 67–68
    ultimate goal of, 23
    and war, 31–35
Goodenough, E. R., 418
good Samaritan, parable of the, 456, 458
good works, 43, 65, 82, 122, 171
Gorky, Maxim, 406
gospel, the relationship between life, the message of Ezekiel 11, and the, 267–68
Gospels, Jesus' ministry in the, 414–16
Gray, George (scientist), 381
Greeks, 173, 174, 348, 464
Greenleaf, Robert, 403–4
guardianship, principle of (in Islam), 305, 308
Gush Shalom (Israeli peace group), 87
Gutierrez, Gustavo, 461
Habib, Gabriel, 431
Habib, Samuel, 323–24, 378, 379
Haddad, Tahar, 303, 309
Hadith, 438
Halaq, Sami (Jesuit father), 396
Haller, M., 408
Hamza, Amina, 315
Hanafi, Hassan, 442
Hanan (or Annas), 167, 379, 412
Harnack, Adolf, 182, 370
Harrelson, Walter (prof.), 70
Harrop, Gerald G., 254
Hanashi, Abdul-Latif, Al-, 378
Hanish, Shak Bernard, 391
Harb, Ali, 425
Hastings' Dictionary of the Bible, 317
Haykal, Muhammad Husayn, 431
head covering, 347–49, 465

Hegazy, Moustafa, 385, 386
Hegel, Georg Wilhelm Friedrich, 213
Helal, Reda, 214
Helmke, Ann E., 86
Henry, Matthew, 330
heresy (Marcion's), 12. *See also* 88
Herez, Abdel Nasser, 389
hermeneutics. *See* interpretation, principles of
Herod Antipas, 159, 164, 168
Herod the Great, 198, 395–96
Herodians, 162, 171
Herzl, Theodor, 241
Heyman, George, 419–20
Hezekiah, 155, 175
history
    apocalyptic writers' view of, 278
    of Israel, 235–36
Hitler, Adolf, 91, 92
Hittites, 32, 47, 241
Hodel, Don, 215
Holiness Code, 63, 66
Holland, 91, 93
Holland, J. T., 420
Holocaust, 89, 91–92, 95, 98, 172, 203, 204
Holy Communion, 199–200
Holy Spirit, 14, 51, 56n25, 57, 59, 69, 78, 103, 107, 114, 124, 126, 127, 159, 167, 199, 200, 206, 209, 221, 226, 228, 229, 246, 249, 265, 279, 289, 290, 229, 299, 368, 369, 371, 461
homiletics, 257
Hooke, S. H., 331
Hourany, Youssef, 104–6
human beings
    the dual nature of, 35–36
    the gulf between God and, 219, 220
    risks facing, 218, 411
    two fierce enemies of, 411
    were made in God's image, 177
Humbard, Rex, 215
Huntington, Samuel P., 213, 443–45
Hutchison, John C., 403
hymns, 105, 417, 451–55
Ibn Kathir, 305
identity. *See in general* chapter 7, "Culture and Identity" (423–68)
    Islam, Arabism, and the concept of, 432–40
    of Jesus
        cultural, 119–22
        dual, 197–99
        ethnic, 113–19
    meaning of the word, 425
    of the true Israel, 232
idolatry, 96, 377
idols, 96, 231, 262, 263, 264, 268, 274, 290, 294, 394
incarnation, 57, 96, 103, 104, 105, 106, 107, 193, 208, 228, 279, 280, 325, 459, 464
Independence Day (film), 214
India, 112
Indonesia–East Timor conflict, 85

inheritance
   of believers, 77
   and replacement, 199–200. *See* replacement theology
   right of (for women), 306, 307, 315, 317
injustice, 16, 30, 33, 98, 99, 127, 203, 204, 253, 254, 258,
   271, 297, 315, 322, 325, 327, 341, 342, 361, 364, 379,
   384, 386, 389, 397
institutionalization, 369, 459
International Covenant on Economic, Social, and Cultural
   Rights (1966), 398
interpretation
   pluralistic, 458
   principles of, 242–51
   prophetic motto approach to, 255–56
   prophetic parable approach to, 256–57
   prophetic typological approach to, 255
intertestamental period, 57, 124, 126, 135–36, 139, 245,
   273
Iraq, 85, 101, 120, 222, 395, 433, 446
Irenaeus, 188, 200
Isaac (patriarch), 19, 27, 33, 38, 50, 51, 52, 60, 74, 82, 101,
   113, 116, 159, 189, 202, 232
Ishmael, 23, 82, 232
ISIS, 391
Israel
   "according to the flesh," 210, 232
   comparison of the events of Jesus' life with the
      successive events in the history of, 198–99
   dividing of the kingdoms of, 235
   the history of, 235–36
   identity of the true, 232
   the main sin of, 232
   1948 establishment of the state of, 11, 89, 98, 428
   what our attitude should be to the modern state of,
      240–42
Israeli–Palestinian conflict. *See* Palestinian question
"Israelis" versus "Israelites," 44n4
Islam, 98, 99, 204, 302–16, 423–28, 430–40, 442, 444–
   46, 449–51, 455, 466, 467
   women in, 303–16
   modern movements, 307
Islamic Group, 307
Islamic Renaissance and Reformation, pioneers of the,
   308–10
Islamist methodology, the basis of the, 438–39
Islamization, 428, 439
Italy, 93, 426n2, 428, 445
Jacob (patriarch), 19, 27, 33, 47, 51, 60, 74, 82, 101, 113,
   114, 116, 119, 159, 189, 198, 202, 232, 244, 290, 295,
   354, 362, 363, 455
Jacob (as a name for the Israelites), 145
Jarjour, Rev. Riad, 391
Jaspers, Karl, 182–83
Jeremiah (prophet), 29, 30–31, 33, 42, 46, 57, 79, 128, 155,
   236–37, 259, 264, 265, 266, 269, 271, 408
Jeremias, Joachim, 113, 282–83, 415
Jerubbaal (aka Gideon in text), 392–93, 395, 397, 400
Jerusalem, fall/destruction of, 92, 174, 179n93, 235, 239,
   241

Jesus
   ascension, 57, 65, 131, 208, 226
   attempts to separate Jesus from His Jewish background,
      98–113
         the claim that Jesus was of Syrian-Syriac-
            Aramean origin, 99–102
         the claim that Jesus' identity was Galilean-
            Phoenician-Lebanese, 102–113
   attributes of his service, 420–21
   baptism of, 131
   birthplace of, 170
   the Christian attitude to the Jewish, 203–10
   and the church as the completion of Judaism, 191–202
   cleansing of the temple, 165–66, 172
   concept of ministry (versus that of Jews and Gentiles),
      416–22
   crucifixion, 95, 111, 130, 165, 167, 169, 177, 181, 234,
      379, 412, 419
   cultural identity of, 119–22
         his language, 120–21
         his religious upbringing, 120
         his teaching, 121–22
         his upbringing and home life, 119–20
         his use of the Old Testament, 121
   derivation of the name, 123
   dual identity of, 197–99
   eschatology and the teaching of, 224–25
   ethnic identity of (in the New Testament), 113–19
         his ethnicity in Acts, 116
         his ethnicity in Hebrews, 118
         his ethnicity in the letters of the apostle Paul,
            116–18
         his ethnicity in the Synoptic Gospels, 113–115
         his ethnicity in the writings of John, 115–16
   and Judaism. *See chapter 3* (89–209), esp. 161–69
   the Old Testament messianic concepts and images were
      fulfilled in, 243
   progress in acknowledging the Jewishness of, 91–98
   reasons for Judaism's rejection of, 169–77
   the renewing role of, 462–64
   resurrection of, 111, 116, 118, 132, 167, 176, 192n112,
      199, 208, 246, 354, 361, 369, 459
   return of. *See* second coming of Christ
   titles for
         four titles he used for himself, and their
            implications, 122–61
         Messiah or Christ, 123–30
         servant of the Lord, 142–61, esp. 156–58
         Son of God, 130–33
         Son of Man, 133–42
         other titles for, 161
   virgin birth of, 100, 175, 176
   washing the disciples' feet, 402–5, 407
"Jewish Christianity," 113
Jewish Encyclopedia (article on women's rights), 316
Jews, 15, 45, 67, 69, 79, 80, 82–84, 86, 89–104, 106, 107,
   109, 110, 113, 115–18, 120–21, 123, 126, 128, 129, 130,
   133, 135, 161, 167–78, 180, 182, 183, 186, 187, 188n106,
   189, 190, 191, 196–210, 214, 223, 224, 228, 230–39,

241–42, 245, 246, 250, 252, 264, 266, 274, 279, 280, 281, 293, 341, 347, 348, 361, 362, 363, 396, 416, 417, 456, 457, 462, 463, 465
    the early church's attitude to Jews, 187
    growing dialogue between Christians and, 92–97
    Western Christianity's attitude toward the, 204–7
Jews for Jesus, 96
Jezebel (queen), 254, 255–56, 316, 317, 339
Joffe, George, 439
John the Baptist, 112, 128, 129, 194, 367, 411
John XXIII (pope), 95, 422
Jordan, 101, 320, 431
Joseph (husband of Mary), 100, 107–8, 110, 112, 114, 115, 119, 161, 198, 205, 229
Joseph (son of Jacob), 23, 38, 74, 383
Josephus, Flavius, 395–96
Jotham, son of Jerubbaal, 392–93, 397–99
Judaism
    the argument for a radical separation of Christianity from, 184–88
    the attitude of Jesus and the early church to, 178–202
    the Catholic Church's statement regarding, 95
    the core passage that reveals Jesus' relationship to, 179–81
    holistic attitude of historical Christianity re: the Jewishness of Jesus and, 207–10
    Jesus and. *See chapter 3* (89–209), esp. 193–94
    Jesus and the church as the completion of, 191–202
    Jesus' relationship to, 161–69
    the methodology for unifying the Christian view of, 179
    the relationship between Christianity and, 181–202
    why it rejects Jesus, 169–77
judgment
    of God a natural consequence of human sin, 28
    of God upon gentile nations, 30–31
Julius Caesar, 420
Justin Martyr, 93, 175, 188, 200
Kaddora, Ebtehag, 315
Kaiser, Walter, 182, 252, 254
Kanawaty, Father George, 222
Kepler, Patricia Budd, 327
Khalaf, Ghassan, 379, 388
Khaldun, Ibn, 218
Khalfallah, Muhammad Ahmad, 427
Khalil, Ghassan, 312
Khashaba, Sami (prof.), 390
Khedr (Khodr), George (bishop), 84–85, 110–13, 130n74, 203–4, 208
kingdom of God, 227–30
kings, God cuts off and appoints, 272
Kittel, G., 183
Kraemer, Ross, 319
Krishna, 112
Küng, Hans, 202, 405
Kuwait, 85, 313
Ladd, George, 200, 273
La Grange Declaration Against Christian Zionism, 85–86
Lambert, J. C., 317

land, the
    and the covenant in the Old Testament, 74–76
        and the concept of rest, 76
        as the gift of God, 74–75
        the promise of the, 74
    and the covenant in the New Testament, 76–78
Langley, Myrtle, 331–32
language
    Jesus' careful use of, 462
    speaking about faith in Jesus in contemporary, 464
    spoken by Jesus, 107, 120–21
Last Supper, 57, 158, 400–401, 414–15
Latter Prophets, 254
law
    ancient Near Eastern laws and Old Testament, 62–63
    Assyrian, 63
    the covenant and the, 62–71
    of Moses, 55, 67, 92, 114, 121, 126, 171, 181, 184, 189, 356
    what Jesus meant in saying he came to fulfill the, 180–81
laws
    ancient Near Eastern, 62–64
    unique elements in Old Testament, 63–64
Lebanese (people), 107, 315, 466
Lebanese war, 433
Lebanon, 85, 101, 103, 104–8, 110, 111, 303, 304, 314, 315, 320, 322, 323, 324, 392, 400, 429, 430, 435
Leeser, Isaac, 94
Lenin, Vladimir, 213
Leslie, John, 218
Levi, 185
Levites, 195
Lewis, Bernard, 427
liberation theology, 324–25
Lindars, Barnabas, 399
Lindsey, Hal, 214
linguistic isolation, 448
"Little Apocalypse" (Mark 13), 282–83
little horn, 247, 281, 282
liturgy, 58, 92
Litwa, David, 416
Lohfink, Norbert, 57n26, 80
Lohse, Eduard, 396
Lord's Prayer, 122, 463
loyalty (as a means to develop an Arab theology of citizenship), 458
Luther, Martin, 91, 184, 326, 333–34
Lutheran Church, 324
Lutheran Church–Missouri Synod, 86
Lutheranism, 91
Maccabean revolt, 238, 241
Maccabees, 106, 110, 235, 236, 274
Magi, 112, 113, 396
Mahfouz, Naguib, 405
male headship, 350
Malina, Bruce, 386
Maly, Eugene, 399
Mann, Thomas W., 24

Manson, T. W., 407
Maqar, Elias, Rev., 383
Marcel, Gabriel, 404
Marcion, 12, 31, 188
Marcos, Ferdinand and Emilda, 395
marginalization, 12, 297, 321, 325, 327, 391, 404, 448
Mariamne, wife of Herod the Great, 396
marriage, 87, 122, 132, 164, 256, 266, 297, 300, 304, 305, 306, 309, 311, 313, 315, 316, 332, 343, 352, 355, 390, 406, 417
Marx, Karl, 213
Mary, mother of Jesus, 50, 100, 107, 108, 110, 119, 198, 204–5, 206, 207, 208, 301, 349, 355, 366–68, 370, 454
Mary Magdalene, 349, 366, 368
Mary and Martha of Bethany, 354, 364–66
materialism, 411
Matthew the Poor, Father, 395–96
Medo-Persian Empire, 280. See Persian Empire
Melchizedek, 23, 104, 109, 118, 185–86
Mennonite Church USA, 86
"Messiah," or "Christ," 123–30
messianic Jews, 96
Middle East
    current number of Christians in the, 391
    the three major religions in the, 302
Middle East Council of Churches, 85, 216, 320, 321, 391
Middle Eastern church, 303, 304, 315, 324
millenarianism, 217–18
millennial kingdom, 79, 214, 222, 261, 270, 293, 447
Millennium, 190, 447n74
ministry, Jesus', the Jews', and the Gentiles' concept of (compared), 416–22
minorities, 254, 271, 272–73, 391, 424, 426n2, 430, 435, 446–47, 448–49
minority mentality, 446–49
miracles, 106, 108, 162, 163, 359, 361, 447, 465–66
Miriam (sister of Moses), 19–20, 23, 33, 38, 317, 336–37, 452
Mishnah, 317, 319, 347
Mitri, Tarek, 217, 242–43
modernism, defined, 438
modernity (modernism), 437, 438
modernization
    and modernity, the distinction between, 437–38
    two major trends in the Middle East's response to, 438
Moghaizel, Laure, 315
Moldavia, 426n2
money, misuse of, 394–95
Montasser, Salah, 395n58
Montefiore, Claude J. G., 94–95, 183
Moors, 93
moral commitment, 463
Morris, Amos Benny, 87
Morris, Leon, 275
Morocco, 314
Moses (patriarch), 15, 19, 21, 23, 32–33, 43, 44, 54, 55, 60, 67, 74–75, 76, 90, 92, 110n60, 114, 116, 118, 119, 121, 126, 137, 138, 143, 164, 168, 171, 180, 181, 182, 183–85, 186, 188n106, 189, 191, 194, 198, 226, 232,

234, 239, 259, 275, 278, 317, 336, 337, 338, 349, 356, 363, 379, 381, 384n32, 398, 409, 452
Moses' mother, 338
Moucarry, Chawkat, 85
Moule, C. F. D., 169
mother, the status of a (Jewish), 317
Mubarak, Hosni, 395
Muhammad, 305–6, 431, 438n50
Muhammad cartoons controversy, 446
Muller, Herbert J., 301
Muslim Brotherhood, 307, 310, 311, 394, 395, 450
Muslims, 11, 93, 98, 99, 203, 306, 312, 380, 428, 430, 431, 432, 433, 435, 436, 440, 443, 444, 450, 451, 456
Musonius Rufus, 419
Naboth (OT character), 254–56
Nagi, Helal, 313
Naguib, Rev. Makram, 408
Nahmanides, 416
Naimy, Mikhail, 112, 188n106
Nassar, Nassif, 313–14
Nasser, Gamal Abdel, 430–31
Nathanael (NT), 107, 131, 368, 411
National Council of Churches (of Christ), 216
national identity, the dual source of, 442–43
nationalism
    Arab. See Arab nationalism
    defined, 426n2, 427–48
National Middle Eastern Presbyterian Caucus in America, 216
Nazareth, 107, 110, 111, 112, 114, 119, 120, 121, 161, 163, 170, 229
Near East School of Theology (Beirut), 323
Nebuchadnezzar, 28, 29, 47, 197, 269, 270, 272
Neturei Karta (ultra-Orthodox Jewish group), 87
new covenant, 42, 45, 46, 54, 55–59, 78, 79, 80, 81, 95, 192, 184, 185, 186, 199, 210, 222, 231
    characteristics of the, 59
    in the New Testament, 57
New Testament
    Jesus' ethnic identity in the, 113–19
    the land and the covenant in the, 76–78
    the new covenant in the, 57
    use of "Son of Man" in the, 137–42
Nicene Creed, 106, 207
Nietzsche, Friedrich, 375
1967 Arab-Israeli War, 98, 214, 242, 291, 429
Noah, 16, 19, 21, 26, 36, 48–49, 54n18, 56, 59, 197
Noahic covenant, 16, 21, 48–49, 56, 59
North, Christopher, 160n80
Northern Kingdom (Israel), 223, 235, 241, 317
Nostradamus, 217–18
Nouis, Antoine, 411
obedience, practical, 295
obscure texts, clear passages should not be interpreted by, 245
Old Testament
    Arab Christians and the. See chapter 1 (11–40)
    eschatology in the, 222–23
    God is the central character in the, 13

the most important collections of laws in the, 63

must be interpreted in the light of the New Testament, 243

must be read with an understanding of its context, 14–15

number of texts Jesus quoted from the, 121

presents a relationship, not a systematic theology, 13–14

the product of a particular culture, 17–18

prophecies and their New Testament fulfillments, 165, 260, 263, 369

sections of the, 15

the "servant of the Lord" in the, 143–56

oppression, 33, 88, 89, 90, 97, 153, 157, 253, 325, 334, 364, 379, 385, 386, 388, 420, 449, 453

original sin, 177, 301, 325, 334

Ottoman Empire, 241, 428, 429

paganism, 378

Palestine, 43, 44–45, 71, 77, 79–81, 83, 84, 86, 94, 98, 100, 101, 106, 107, 120, 176, 207, 235–39, 241, 265, 280, 319, 320, 396, 398, 429

Palestinian question (the Arab-Israeli conflict), 45, 71–87

Pan-Arab movement. See Arabism

Papini, Giovanni, 396

parable

of the banquet, 179n93

of the good Samaritan, 456, 458

of the tenants, 179n93, 199

of the yeast, 357

partnership (to develop an Arab theology of citizenship), 459–60

paternal power (over women), 316–17

patriarchal system, 311, 342, 356

patriotism, 99, 314, 426–27, 428

Passover, 57, 119, 199, 200, 366

Paul (apostle; formerly Saul), 50, 51, 53, 57, 58, 61, 76–77, 81–83, 87, 92, 94, 95, 104, 111, 113, 116–18, 130, 132, 133, 151, 160, 168, 172, 174, 178, 181–82, 184, 186–88, 190, 191–92, 193, 194, 196, 197, 198n119, 201–2, 205, 206, 208, 209–10, 222, 225–27, 229, 230–33, 238, 246, 248, 250, 263, 267, 289, 294, 299, 300–301, 328, 332, 342–53, 367, 369–71, 389, 415, 417, 457, 459. See also Saul of Tarsus

attitude toward women, 344–53

eschatology in the thought of, 225–27

Jesus' ethnicity in the letters of, 116–18

PC(USA), 86, 324. See also Presbyterian Church

Pelikan, Jaroslav, 204–5

Persia, 112, 150, 270, 375

Persian Empire, 223, 235, 237, 280

people of God, the, 230–42

People's Democratic Republic of Yemen (or, South Yemen), 314

persecution, 88, 93, 95, 96, 98, 135, 136, 159, 167, 168, 172, 181, 203, 207, 238, 241, 245, 274, 280, 284, 285

Peter (apostle), 50, 77, 116, 123, 124, 129, 131, 133, 137–38, 159, 160, 167, 168, 173, 181, 187, 200, 224, 240, 357, 359, 365, 368, 369, 389, 410, 411, 412, 422, 457, 459, 466

Pharaohism, 450

Pharisees, 109, 121, 122, 162, 163, 165, 170–71, 179, 181, 183, 206, 224, 274, 356, 379, 402, 463

"Philistines" versus "Palestinians," 44n4

Phoebe (early church deaconess), 346, 370

Phoenicia, 436

Phoenicianism, 433, 450

Pierre, Abbé, 217

Pius XII (pope), 91

plagues (of Egypt), 27–28

pluralistic interpretation of religious texts, 458

pluralism, 425, 435, 440, 443, 446, 448, 457–58, 467

poetry, 14, 260, 313

Poiret, Pierre, 190

Poland, 91, 204n130

political Islam, 424, 425, 426, 427, 428, 433, 439, 440, 445, 450, 451, 455, 467

politics

definition of the word, 211

religion and. See chapter 4 (211–96)

polygamy, 305, 306, 307, 308, 309, 316

Popper, Martin, 398

popular revolution, 388, 389–90

postmodernism, 212, 377

power. See in general chapter 6, "The Cross and the Power Issue" (374–422)

Abimelech and the mania of, 393–97

biblical examples of practicing, 381–400

the cross and, 400–422

preachers, 205, 242, 251, 376

Preisinger, Arthur, 86

Presbyterian Church, 216, 219, 242. See also PC(USA)

Presbyterian Women's Association of the United States, 325

Pressler, Carolyn, 341

priests, female, 324

principle of guardianship (in Islam), 305, 308

principles of interpretation, 242–51

Priscilla (wife of Aquila), 346, 370

progressive revelation, 32, 222, 227, 248, 252

promises of God

to Abraham, 49–54

to David, 55

prophecy

the ceasing of, 274

literal interpretation of, 213, 215, 447n

prophetic books (the Prophets). See prophetic texts

God the Creator in the, 23–25

God the Redeemer in the, 38–39

prophetic motto approach to interpretation, 255–56

prophetic parable approach to interpretation, 256–57

prophetic style, 258–59

prophetic texts, 251–73. See also prophetic books

interpreting, 253–62

a better approach to, 257–62

four inadequate approaches to, 254–57

steps to, 259–62

practical applications of, 262–73

prophetic typological approach to interpretation, 255

prophets

the essence of their message, 257–58

who they were, 251–52

Protestant Reformation (aka European Reformation), 43, 73, 184, 215, 466
Pseudepigrapha, 126, 128, 135
Ptolemies, 235, 280
Ptolemy I Soter, 280
punishment for rebellion (in Eden), 335–36
purification, 182, 220, 265, 268, 292, 294
Qabbani, Nizar, 307
Qatar, 313
Qumran, 57, 112
Qunswah, Salah, 445
Qur'an, 99, 438, 439
Qutb, Sayyid, 434, 440, 450–51
Rabbi Akiva, 416–17
Rachel (wife of Jacob), 51, 317
racism, 204, 209, 321, 432, 457
radicalism, 203
Rahab the Canaanite, 51, 209, 355, 360
Ramses II, 47
rapture, 189, 190, 234
Raziq, Sheikh Ali Abdel, 386
Reagan, Ronald, 214, 215
realism (as a need for religion), 463
reason, 384, 438, 464
reasoning, 15, 439
rebellion, the punishment for (in Eden), 335–36
Rebekah (wife of Isaac), 51, 102, 316, 317
redemption, 16, 23, 26, 31, 35, 36–38, 58, 78, 103–4, 105–6, 194, 221, 234, 249, 278, 284, 343, 350, 408
    the covenant of, 78, 234
    defined, 36
Reed, Ralph, 215
Reformation. See Protestant Reformation
Reformed Church in America, 86
Reformed churches, 322, 324
Reformed school, 43, 73, 80, 83
Reformed theology
    covenant theology one of the most important features of, 42
    the essential disagreement between classical Dispensationalism and, 79
    three kinds of covenants in, 78
Rehoboam son of Solomon, 380–82, 384, 385, 387, 388, 390, 391, 405, 422
Reimarus, Hermann Samuel, 182
religion
    the danger of linking power to, 378
    an example of the irony in the combination of power, violence, and, 380
    involves realism and moral commitment, 463
    and politics. See chapter 4 (211–96)
    the relationship between life and, 264–66
    the rise of, 214–15
religious extremism, 391
remnant, 56–57, 82, 142, 155, 191, 196–97, 224, 232, 263, 264, 267, 274
Renaissance, 215, 437
repentance, 51, 65, 83, 116, 128, 174, 252, 257, 258, 265, 268, 284, 285, 460, 463

replacement theology, 80, 199–200
rest, the (promised) land and the concept of, 76
return of Christ. See second coming of Christ
resurrection
    of Christ, 111, 116, 118, 132, 167, 176, 192n112, 199, 208, 246, 354, 361, 369, 459
    the first, 248
    of a nation. See dry bones, the vision of the
Revelation (book), 115, 140, 186, 192, 194–95, 245–46, 250, 280–81, 283–86, 367
    chapter breakdown of the, 286 (see chart)
    differences between other apocalyptic writings and the, 284–85
    main purpose of the book, 88
    origin of the name, 283
revelations, 276–77
Rice, Gene, 385
right-wing religious groups, 213–14
Roberts, Oral, 215
Robertson, A. Willis, 215
Robertson, Pat, 215
Robison, James, 215
Roloff, J., 415
Roman Catholic Church, 91, 95–96, 97, 184, 281, 422
Roman Empire, 188n103, 280, 281
Rogers, Isabel, 325–26
Ruby, Fr. Bertrand, 367
Ruth (the Moabitess), 51, 209, 339–41, 355
Saadeh, Antoun, 99–101
Sabeel Ecumenical Liberation Theology Center, 216
Sabra, George, 217, 242–43
Sabbath, 64, 72, 111, 121, 133, 137, 162, 170, 171, 173, 181, 187, 199, 205, 229, 354
Saddam Hussein, 395
Sadducees, 183, 379
Said, Habib, 413
Salafi thinking on women's rights, 305–7
Salam, Anbara, 315
Salama, Salama Ahmed, 212
Saleel Center, 86
salvation, 22, 23, 36–37, 39, 43–44, 45, 51, 54, 65, 78, 80, 82, 83, 86, 94, 114, 115, 126, 142, 151, 154, 156, 160, 173, 174, 177, 188, 189, 191, 192, 196, 197, 199, 201, 202, 204, 205, 207, 209, 221, 222, 223, 224, 225, 227, 232, 233, 234, 249–50, 263, 269, 277, 278, 283, 284, 340, 342, 344, 352, 353, 367, 408, 412, 420, 452, 457
    meaning of the word, 36
    summary of the Torah's way of, 177
Samaria, 168, 235, 363
Samaritans, 115, 362, 363, 417, 456
Sanders, E. P., 183
Sanders, James A., 256
Sanhedrin, 168
Sarah (wife of Abraham), 50, 51, 316, 317
Satmar (Hasidic group), 87
Saudi Arabia, 303, 431
Saul (king), 197, 235
Saul of Tarsus, 131, 168, 344. See Paul (apostle)
savior, Old Testament images of a, 243–45

Scofield, Cyrus I., 214, 279
Scofield Reference Bible, 190, 214
second coming of Christ (or, return of Christ), 79, 80, 83, 212–13, 215, 222, 224, 225–26, 229, 242, 245, 246–47, 262, 270, 279, 280, 282, 446, 447
Second Gulf War, 213
second death, 248
Second Vatican Council, 95, 96
Second World War, 95, 204n130, 213, 429n14, 445
secularism, 434
Seeley, David, 418
self-control, examples of Jesus exerting, 412–13
sensitivity, communicating with, 465–66
separatism, 426n2
service
    attributes of Jesus', 420–21
    the fine line that separates (and connects) power and, 402
    the meaning of, 401
Septuagint, 143, 159, 175, 200
Serbia–Kosovo conflict, 85
Sermon on the Mount, 180, 184, 193, 198, 354, 355, 460
servant, meaning of the word, 142–43
"servant of the Lord," 142–61
    the early church and the, 159–60
    identity of the, 155–56
    in Isaiah, 144–56
    Jesus and the title, 156–58
    in the Old Testament, 143–56
Servant Songs, 39, 144–54, 156–58, 245
700 Club, 215
Shaaban, Buthaina, 311–12, 313, 315
Shaarawy, Hoda, 310
Shafik, Doria, 310
Shahak, Israel, 96
Sharabi, Hisham, 311
Sharia, 305, 438
Shia Muslims, 433
Sika, Nadine, 388
Simeon (Gospel of Luke), 114, 126, 128
sin
    natural consequence of human, 28
    two dimensions of, 460
Sinai covenant, 54, 60–61, 74
Six-Day War. *See* 1967 Arab-Israeli War
Sizer, Stephen, 86
slavery, 16, 23, 36, 61, 64, 65, 72, 74, 317, 337, 342, 361, 401, 453
"small horn," 247, 281, 282
social alienation, 448–49
socialism, 255, 428
social norms, 304, 347, 464–65
society, relationship between the church and the, 266–67
Society of the Awakening of the Arab Girl, 315
Sodom and Gomorrah, 23, 28, 31, 38
solidarity (as a means to develop an Arab theology of citizenship), 458
Solomon (king), 53, 55, 126, 174, 235–36, 240, 241, 291, 355, 381, 382–84, 387

Solomon's Colonnade, 181
Solomon's Temple. *See* temple: first
"Son of God," 130–33
Songs of the Suffering Servant (aka Servant Songs), 39, 144–54, 156–58, 245
songs (as a way to convey theological, social, and political ideas), 451–55
"Son of Man," 133–42
    interpretation of the name in Daniel, 135
    interpretation of the name in the intertestamental period, 135–37
    meanings of the title, 134–35
    use in the New Testament, 137–42
Southern Kingdom (Judah), 223, 235, 241, 317
South Yemen (the People's Democratic Republic of Yemen), 314
sovereignty of God, 16, 21, 25, 34, 160, 197, 272
Soviet Union, 213, 426n2
Spain, 93
Spath, L. Michael, 86
spiritual authority (for women), 349
spiritual death, 248, 288
spiritual gifts, 461
Stanton, Elizabeth, 367
state building, 428, 429, 440
Stephen of Cloyes, 380–81
Stevens, Marty, 68
Stott, John, 86, 390, 401–2, 417
Strauss, David, 182
submission, 16, 256, 320, 327, 332, 336, 344, 346, 347, 351–52, 377, 384, 385, 386, 453
submissiveness, 351
subordination (of women to men), 317, 343, 351
Sudan, 307, 309, 310, 313, 466
Suffering Servant, 39, 51, 144, 245, 408–9
    three interpretations of the personality of the, 408–9
    traits of the, 410–14
    the perseverance of the, 410–13
    the unceasing sacrifice of the, 413–14
suicide bombings, 446
sun-clothed woman, 115, 367
Sunna, 438
Sunni Muslims, 433
Supersessionism, 80n71. *See* replacement theology
Swaggart, Jimmy, 215
Swidler, Leonard, 325
symbolism, 195, 250, 276, 285, 291
Synod of the Nile, 323
Syria, 101, 188n103, 235, 238, 247, 280, 282, 303, 304, 312, 314, 315, 320, 322, 323, 429n14, 430, 433, 436
Syrians, 101, 430, 466
systematic theology, 13, 324
Taha, Mahmoud Mohammad, 309–10
Taha Hussein, 383–84
Tahtawi, Rif'a al-, 308, 426n1
Talbert, Mary Ann, 359
Tazini, Tayyeb, 458
teamwork, 460–61
temple
    the body of Christ, 209, 231

first (Solomon's, in Jerusalem), 53, 55, 61, 101, 148, 149, 174, 197, 213, 223, 236, 237, 241, 264, 265, 280, 317
heavenly, 186
Jesus as the new, eternal, 196, 294
second (in Jerusalem), 22, 114, 116, 119, 120, 159, 162, 165–66, 167, 168, 170, 172, 174, 175n85, 178, 181–82, 186, 191, 195–96, 205, 228, 239, 241, 247, 281–82, 283, 324, 421, 462
rebuilding of a (third), 80, 242, 293
Ten Commandments, 64–71
contain principles applicable in multiple circumstances, 70–71
a contemporary formulation of the, 70
in the context of the covenant, 65–66
an expression of God's love for us, 67–68
a gift from God, 67–68
list of, 64–65
the order and number of the, 65
practical applications for today, 71
reflect God's character, 66–67
the social dimension of the, 69–70
a source of freedom, 69
a source of joy and pleasure, 68–69
tent of meeting, 195, 337
Tertullian, 188, 200, 301, 326, 334, 349
theocracy, 249
theological concepts, 13, 218–42
Theological Dictionary of the New Testament (on the status of women), 316
theology
biblical, 42, 242, 324
feminist, 325
liberation, 324–25
Reformed. *See* Reformed theology
replacement, 80, 199–200
systematic, 13, 324
theonomy, 67
theory of the clash of civilizations, 443, 445–46
Thomas Aquinas, 326
time, the value of, 226
Times (Brit.), 213
titles Jesus used for himself (and their implications), 122–61
conclusion concerning all four, 160–61
Messiah or Christ, 123–30
servant of the Lord, 142–61
Son of God, 130–33
Son of Man, 133–42
Torah, God the creator in the, 20–23
Torrey, Charles C., 277
Tournier, Paul, 375
traditionalism, 386, 463
tree and branches (as an image of Judaism and Christianity), 192–93
tribalism, 209, 393–94, 442, 450
Trible, Phyllis, 340
Trinity, 78, 96, 103, 104, 105, 176, 329, 448
true Israel, identity of the, 232

Tunisia, 303, 307
Turkey, 93, 104, 188n103, 430
Turks, 93, 431, 434
tyranny, defined, 385
Umayyad state, 378
United Arab Emirates, 313
United Church of Christ, 86
United Methodist Church, 86
United Nations, 70, 85, 297, 387
United Nations General Assembly, 298
Universal Declaration of Human Rights (1948), 70, 297, 307
unity
the blessing of, 295–96
the call for (in Ezekiel), 290–94
maintaining, 294–95
the message of, 296
universal civilization, 444
universality of belief and natal citizenship, 456–57
urbanization, 444
van Wijk-Bos, J. W. H., 62
veil (head covering), 305, 306, 309, 319, 349
Vietnam War, 214
violence
the link between dictatorship and violence, 385–86
the relation between religious authority and, 378
virgin birth, 100, 175, 176
Volz, P., 408
von Rad, Gerhard, 398
Wagner, Donald E., 86
Wahbe, Mourad, 418
Walker, P., 86
Walvoord, John, 215
war
God and, 31–35
the 1967 Arab-Israeli, 98, 214, 242, 291, 429
the three Gulf wars, 431
Lebanese, 433
in Vietnam, 214
the Yemen, 431
Ware, Bruce, 80–81
Warren, Max, 407–8
Watts, Isaac, 190
welfare state, 255
Weinstock, Harris, 94
Wellhausen, Julius, 415
Wenham, Gordon J., 330
West, the, 89, 91, 98, 99, 203, 207, 212, 214, 215–16, 235, 242, 300, 310, 391, 411, 423, 428, 438, 439, 443, 444–45, 446, 448, 467
Western church(es), 204, 205
Western Christianity's attitude toward the Jews, 204–7
Western Christians, 90, 445
Westernization, 438, 442
Western modernization, 428, 437–38
Wisa, Esther, 310
Witherington, Ben, 319
Wollstonecraft, Mary, 327
women. *See individual biblical women by name*

in the Arab church, 320–22
are given spiritual authority in the church, 349
the biblical reality concerning, 328–71
the Canaanite (Syrophoenician) woman, 354, 359–62
the Christian woman. *See chapter 7* (297–373)
the daughter of Pharaoh; the daughters of Midian's priest, 338
discrimination against, 298, 303, 313
disciples, 369–71
first conference of Protestant, 322–23
in Islam, 303–16
    constitutional status of, 313–16
    modern Islamic movements and, 307
    prominent, 310–13
    Salafi thought on the rights of, 305–7
Jesus' attitude toward, 354–68
Jesus' genealogy lists five, 355
Lebanese, 304, 315
mentioned in Exodus, 336–38
in the Old Testament, 328–42
participation in the Protestant church, 322–27
Paul's attitude toward, 344–53
the position of Jewish, 316–19
prophets in the Pauline community, 370
the Samaritan woman, 115, 196, 354, 362–63, 365, 366, 368
the Syrophoenician woman, 354, 359–62
the woman clothed with the sun, 115, 367
the woman with the issue of blood, 357–59
whom Paul mentioned in Romans and Philippians, 347
Women's Bible, 327
women's liberation, 256, 310, 320, 325, 327, 364, 407
women's rights, 297, 304, 305, 307, 309, 310, 313, 315, 316, 318, 327
Women's Rights among the International Conventions and Political Islam (Alaqrai), 304
World Council of Churches, 95, 216, 299, 321, 322
World War II (aka Second World War), 95, 204n130, 213, 429n14, 445
Wright, Christopher (Old Testament scholar), 84, 409–10
Writings, God the Creator in the, 25–26
Yahweh Elohim, 19
Yammine, Youssef (Maronite priest), 107–10, 111n62
Yancey, Philip, 206–7
Yemen, 313, 314, 431
Youssef, Samuel, 409
youth (Arab), 376–77, 444
Yugoslavia, 426n2
Zacharia, Fouad, 384
Zaghlul, Saphia, 310
Zakariyya, Fouad, 445
Zayd, Nasr Abu, 441, 442, 458
Zechariah (priest), 126, 128
Zechariah (prophet), 53, 125, 165, 223, 250, 257, 273
Zedekiah (king of Judah), 29, 47, 264, 269, 272
Zionism, 84–85, 86, 87, 99, 203, 214, 215, 216, 223, 235, 241, 428. *See also next*
Zionist Christianity (or, Christian Zionism), 85–86, 214, 216, 217, 242
Zionists, 89, 99, 205, 217. *See* Zionism
Zionist trends and radical evangelicals, 214
Zipporah, 338
Zophar the Naamathite, 219
Zorilla, Hugo, 403
Zubaida, Sami, 427–28
Zweig, Stefan, 385–86